*Courtesans, Concubines,*
*and the Cult of Female Fidelity*

Harvard-Yenching Institute Monograph Series 83

*Courtesans, Concubines,
and the Cult of Female Fidelity*

Gender and Social Change in
China, 1000–1400

BEVERLY BOSSLER

Published by the Harvard University Asia Center
Distributed by Harvard University Press
Cambridge (Massachusetts) and London 2013

Cover Illustration: Detail of (twelfth-thirteenth century) Anonymous, *Palace Orchestra Rehearsal Ge yue tu juan* 歌樂圖卷, from *Qian nian dan qing: Riben, Zhongguo cang Tang Song Yuan hui hua zhen pin* 千年丹青：日本中國藏唐宋元繪畫珍品 [Masterpieces of Ancient Chinese Paintings: From the Tang to Yuan Dynasty in Japanese and Chinese Collections], vol. 1, 46. Courtesy of Shanghai Museum.

© 2013, 2016 by the President and Fellows of Harvard College

Printed in the United States of America

The Harvard-Yenching Institute, founded in 1928 and headquartered at Harvard University, is a foundation dedicated to the advancement of higher education in the humanities and social sciences in East and Southeast Asia. The Institute supports advanced research at Harvard by faculty members of certain Asian universities and doctoral studies at Harvard and other universities by junior faculty at the same universities. It also supports East Asian studies at Harvard through contributions to the Harvard-Yenching Library and publication of the *Harvard Journal of Asiatic Studies* and books on premodern East Asian history and literature.

Library of Congress Cataloging-in-Publication Data

Bossler, Beverly J.
Courtesans, concubines, and the cult of female fidelity / Beverly J. Bossler.
  p. cm. — (Harvard-Yenching Institute monograph series ; 83)
Includes bibliographical references and index.
ISBN 978-0-674-06669-4 (hardcover : alk. paper)
ISBN 978-0-674-97064-9 (pbk : alk. paper)
 1. Concubinage—China—History—To 1500. 2. Courtesans—China—History—To 1500. 3. Wives—China—History—To 1500. 4. Sex role—China—History—To 1500. 5. Man-woman relationships—China—History—To 1500. 6. Women—China—Social conditions. I. Title.
HQ684.B67 2012
305.40951--dc23
            2012031807

Index by the author

∞  Printed on acid-free paper

First paperback edition 2016

Last figure below indicates year of this printing

25 24 23 22 21 20 19 18 17 16

To James

# *Acknowledgments*

In the more than fifteen years I have been working on this book, I have incurred innumerable debts to people and institutions. It gives me great pleasure at last to be able to express my gratitude to them publicly, though the list is long indeed.

The very earliest incarnation of the research that was to become this book was supported by an American Council of Learned Societies-Chiang Ching-kuo Fellowship and by a University of California President's Fellowship in the Humanities; as the project evolved I received support from a National Endowment for the Humanities Fellowship for University Teachers and from a second University of California President's Fellowship. A series of Faculty Research Grants from the U.C. Davis Committee on Research helped to fund travel and other expenses over the years of research and writing. My research was also greatly facilitated by the support of a number of libraries and research centers. An early visit to the rare book room at Peking University alerted me to the possibility of studying courtesans. Further development of that research was possible only because I had access to numerous electronic databases of Chinese materials that began to become available in the mid-1990s. I am grateful to Phyllis Wang of the U.C. Davis library for negotiating early access to the electronic *Si ku quan shu* database, and to Jim Cheng (then of the U.C. San Diego International Relations and Pacific Studies library) and the staff of the San Diego supercomputer center for keeping that database up and running in its rocky early days. I also thank Annie Lin and Myra Appel of the U.C. Davis library for their more recent efforts to provide the critical continued access to the web-based version. I would like to express my appreciation to the scholars and staff of the Institute of History and Philology at Academia Sinica in Taiwan for generously permitting access to the electronic *Song hui yao*.

One of the joys of academic life is the opportunity it affords to meet and interact with colleagues around the world. Many of the ideas set out in the chapters below were worked out in the context of scholarly presentations in Japan and China. I am grateful to Professors Hirata Shigeki, Kojima Tsuyoshi, Kondo Kasunari, and Shiba Yoshinobu for giving me opportunities to present my research in Japan, to Professor Liu Ching-cheng for inviting me to Taiwan, and to Professors Zhang Guogang and Deng Xiaonan for multiple invitations to China. On one of those visits, Professor Zhang Fan of Peking University generously let me make use of his personal electronic version of the *Yuan dian zhang*. I would also like to thank Professor Ge Zhaoguang for his gracious hospitality during my time at the National Institute for Advanced Humanistic Studies at Fudan University in Shanghai. For translation help with work I have presented or published in Chinese and Japanese, I am indebted to Li Gutong, Wu Yating, Wu Yulian, Lin Shan, and Asahi Naya; Wu Yulian also helped me locate the illustrations with which the book is graced. In the United States, I have benefited from attending stimulating conferences organized by Susan Mann and Dorothy Ko, Paul Smith and Richard von Glahn, Joan Judge and Hu Ying, Tony DeBlasi and Charles Hartman, Anne Walthall, Peter Bol, and Joseph Lam. Patricia Ebrey and Ellen Cong Zhang generously welcomed me to their respective campuses, where I learned much from my interactions with them and their colleagues.

Many of those just mentioned should also be recognized for providing ongoing encouragement, inspiring conversation, and scholarly assistance over the years. Peter Bol, Deng Xiaonan, Pat Ebrey, Charles Hartman, Hirata Shigeki, Liu Ching-cheng, and Paul Smith all deserve to be mentioned again in this context, along with Bao Weimin, Hugh Clark, Ron Egan, Ben Elman, Huang Kuan-chong, Lau Napyin, Joe McDermott, Frieda Murck, Oshima Ritsuko, and Takatsu Takashi. Steve West graciously allowed me to sit in on his class in Chinese drama and, more recently, has been unstinting with advice on poetry translation. I have also been blessed with wonderful colleagues on my own campus: Bob Borgen, Katharine Burnett, Chen Xiaomei, Mark Halperin, Kyu Kim, Don Price, Michelle Ye, and Li Zhang have kept our East Asian scholarly circles lively and enjoyable. I would also like to acknowledge the late G. William Skinner, whose brilliant mind and warm friendship are sorely missed. Among my colleagues in the History department, Joan Cadden, Cathy Kudlick, and Lorena Oropeza deserve special mention for hours of camaraderie and emotional sustenance: I

# Acknowledgments

am especially grateful to Joan for her extraordinarily helpful comments on the manuscript at a critical juncture. To Susan Mann, who has been the best senior colleague, mentor, and friend that anyone could hope for, I owe scholarly and other debts far too great to requite here.

The book as it appears benefited from the useful suggestions of two anonymous readers for the Harvard University Asia Center, as well as from the assiduous efforts of Kristen Wanner, who has been an unfailingly helpful and encouraging editor. Many details of the final version of the manuscript were improved by the thoughtful and meticulous readings of Mark Halperin and Judith Zeitlin. For the all too many flaws that remain, I alone am responsible.

When I first began research on this book, my beloved daughters Alyson and Mia were respectively two and six years old: they are now young women on the cusp of adulthood. My work on the book was a constant backdrop to their childhood and teen-age years, so it somehow seems fitting that, as they begin to make their way in the world, the book, too, is finally leaving my hands. Through those long years of work and childrearing, my husband James has been an unflagging source of support and companionship. To him this book is lovingly dedicated.

—BJB

# Contents

*List of Figures* xiii

Introduction 1

PART ONE: *Culture, Politics, and Gender in the Northern Song* 11
  1 Courtesans and the Northern Song Elite 13
  2 The Courtesan as Concubine 52
  3 Prose, Politics, and Prodigies 129

PART TWO: *Markets, Mayhem, and Morality in the Southern Song* 161
  4 Performance Anxiety 163
  5 Entertainers to Ancestors 208
  6 Loss, Loyalty, and Local Leverage 250

PART THREE: *Conquerors and Culture in the Yuan* 291
  7 Exemplary Entertainers 293
  8 Performers, Paramours, and Parents 327
  9 Entertaining Exemplars 363

Conclusion 411

*Reference Matter*
  Bibliography 433
  Index 457

# List of Figures

1. A tenth-century winehouse    17
2. The Six Dynasties entertainer Green Pearl of the Liang    87
3. Wang Zhaoyun, beloved concubine of Su Shi    95
4. The filial son Zhu Shouchang    125
5. The heroic wife of Wang Ning    140
6. The filial son Xu Ji, shown worshipping at the tomb of his parents    153
7. The courtesan Yan Rui of Tiantai    192
8. Exiling a crafty tenant    219
9. The Maiden of Huyin    256
10. Principled Woman Cui, daughter-in-law of Bao Zheng    262
11. Principled Woman Liao, wife of Ou Xiwen    269
12. The Yuan courtesan Liu Poxi    310
13. The loyal courtesan-concubine Li Cui'e    329
14. Pure Wife Wang of Linhai    374
15. Faithful Widow Yu, wife of Yu Xin    404

*Courtesans, Concubines, and the Cult of Female Fidelity*

*Introduction*

This book traces changing gender relations in China between the tenth and the fourteenth centuries by examining how writings about courtesans, concubines, and exemplary women developed and changed over that period. This particular framework, as is so often the case in historical research, came into being through a series of nagging questions, false starts, and serendipitous discoveries. The project began as an inquiry into women's literacy in the Song dynasty (960–1270); but when preliminary research demonstrated the importance of courtesans in the production of poetry in the period, my interests began to shift. In general understandings of Chinese history, courtesans are most commonly associated with the late Tang dynasty (618–907), when they first became a notable phenomenon in urban settings, and the late Ming dynasty (1368–1644), when their relationships with eminent men helped spur a celebration of romantic "emotion" (*qing* 情). The Song dynasty, by contrast, tends to be best known as the era that developed Neo-Confucianism, the conservative moral philosophy that advocated strict personal moral cultivation and warned against the dangers of human desire. I was startled, therefore, when I began to investigate the presence of courtesans in Song social life, to discover how prevalent they were. I was curious about their social roles and began to wonder how the ubiquitous presence of such women could be reconciled with—or whether it was somehow related to—the development of Neo-Confucian morality.

These questions became more complicated—and more interesting—when I realized that some of the entertainers described in my sources, although sometimes called courtesans (*ji* 妓), were actually more like what we think of as concubines: rather than living in brothels, they belonged to the household of their master and entertained for him and his guests. Patricia Ebrey, in her early work on Song concubines, had mentioned such women, but she did not attempt to explore how they differed, on the one hand, from courtesans in the marketplace, or, on the other, from concubines who were not entertainers.[1] Meanwhile, an important study of laws on concubinage from the Tang to the Ming had emphasized the impact of Neo-Confucian thinking on concubines' place in the family, and argued that during this period concubines had become "domesticated," that is, they had come to be treated increasingly like family members, especially in ritual and law.[2] Again, the juxtaposition intrigued me: what was the role of entertainer-concubines in Song households, and to what extent were they associated with changing Neo-Confucian ideas about what a proper concubine should be?

Finally, probably the most obvious and widely acknowledged change in gender relations between the Tang and the Ming dynasties was the development of the "cult of widow fidelity."[3] The ideal of women being loyal to their husbands, and not remarrying after their husbands' deaths, had been articulated in classical times in China, but prior to and even during the Song most women had not been expected to adhere to that ideal. Moreover, even when they did so, they were admired but not particularly celebrated. By Ming times, however, women in the thousands were publically extolled for remaining faithful—sometimes even to the point of committing suicide—after their husbands' deaths. Shrines and other monuments were built in their honor, and volumes devoted to the recording of their biographies.[4] Since at least the early twentieth century, historical scholarship had attributed the origins of the fidelity cult to the influence of Neo-Confucianism, but the precise mechanisms of that influence remained unexplored.[5] Recent studies by Bettine Birge

---

1. Ebrey, "Concubines in Song China," 7–8.
2. Katkov, "The Domestication of Concubinage."
3. This is sometimes called the "chaste widow cult" or "chastity cult." On early twentieth-century views of the cult, see Mann, "Widows," 37–40.
4. There is an extensive literature on the fidelity cult in later imperial China. Important studies in English include Elvin, "Female Virtue and the State"; T'ien, *Male Anxiety and Female Chastity*; and Carlitz, "Desire, Danger, and the Body" and "Shrines." Paul Ropp provides an excellent critical survey of the majority of English language literature on the subject in "Passionate Women."
5. On twentieth-century views, see Ropp, "Passionate Women," 4–6.

and Zheng Guiying demonstrated that new laws promulgated by the Mongol Yuan dynasty (1271–1368) encouraged widow fidelity by making remarriage more difficult economically. Birge in particular argued that those laws, which restricted widows' right to take property into a new marriage, grew out of a confluence of Neo-Confucian ideology and Mongol property regimes.[6] But neither Birge nor Zheng addressed the development of the fidelity cult per se. What specific factors, I wondered, had led to the widespread and public honoring of faithful women, and to what extent was Neo-Confucianism implicated in that development?

In addressing these questions, this book has benefited from the considerable knowledge that scholars of Chinese gender relations have produced over the last few decades.[7] In English, Patricia Ebrey's numerous studies have drawn a general picture of women's lives and kinship ideology under the Song, and my numerous debts to her pioneering work will be obvious.[8] Likewise, although my findings challenge some of her conclusions, Bettine Birge's research on women's property rights in the Song and Yuan has raised important questions and drawn attention to the centrality of women and their property in household strategizing.[9] Paul Smith's studies of Han elite families under the Yuan have profoundly influenced my own understanding of Yuan society.[10] More broadly, scholarship on gender in both earlier and later periods of Chinese history has also helped to illuminate many aspects of male-female relations in these "middle period" centuries.[11] All of this work has provided an important foundation for the explorations I have undertaken here.

The period examined in this book encompasses nearly five centuries: this *longue durée* allows me to trace subtle changes in gender ideology that would be invisible in a shorter time frame. These centuries saw the

---

6. Birge, "Women and Confucianism"; Zheng Guiying, "Yuan chao fu nü."
7. In Chinese, in addition to the scholarship cited in the chapters below, I have learned much from works by Deng Xiaonan, Liu Ching-cheng, Jen-der Lee, and Angela Chi Ke Leung.
8. See the various works by Ebrey cited in the bibliography.
9. Birge, *Women, Property, and Confucian Reaction* and "Women and Confucianism."
10. See especially Smith, "Family" and "Fear of Gynarchy."
11. The bibliography on gender relations in Early Imperial, Late Imperial, and twentieth-century China is now (thankfully) too extensive to cite exhaustively. Important studies for this book are cited individually in the chapters below.

rise and fall of several dynasties and a major reconfiguration of Chinese political and social systems. Although the general contours of these changes are well established, they form the backdrop to this study and so are worth reviewing here.

The period known to historians of China as the "Tang-Song transition" began with political decline and growth in population and the economy during the late eighth and ninth centuries. Over the next few centuries, Chinese society was marked by a southward shift of population, rapid improvement in agricultural output, growing commercialization and urbanization, and the emergence of markets. These developments were associated with political decentralization that lasted from the mid-eighth to the late tenth centuries, and were accompanied as well by the precipitous demise of a quasi-aristocratic ruling class that had dominated Chinese political life for centuries. In the late tenth century, the early Song emperors expanded the merit-based examination system, turning it into the main route to political success. By relying on the examinations for the majority of official recruitment, the Song government substantially undermined hereditary access to office-holding, while also making it possible for descendants of newly wealthy families to enter the bureaucracy. In combination with continued economic expansion and the spread of printing technology and education, this contributed to the dramatic growth of a literate elite class. Over the course of the Song, the expansion of this class outstripped the ability of the government to employ it, with the result that the elite—and the definition of elite status—became increasingly independent of the government. No longer defined by office-holding, the so-called local elite of the Southern Song and later dynasties derived wealth and power from landholding (often supplemented with wealth from trade or other commercial enterprises) and dominance in local affairs, while reaffirming its membership in an empire-wide elite group through participation in classical learning and the examination system.

The development of the local elite was also marked by changes in kinship relations. For centuries, Chinese families had practiced partible inheritance, with property in theory divided equally among all sons. As family status came to depend on the continuing accomplishments of its members, and society in general became more competitive, partible inheritance meant that downward mobility became a serious threat to elite families. Those families responded by creating new kinship institutions designed to keep patrilineal kin groups together in the interests of prosperity for all. Annual ceremonies at ancestral graves were held to enhance kin-group solidarity. A few families established charitable estates (*yi zhuang* 義莊), corporate property-holding entities the income from which (at least theoretically) benefited all members of the group. Those members were identified in newly-compiled genealogies that encompassed all male descendants from a specified apical ancestor (often one who had made the family prosperous in the early Song).[12] These developments also had implications for women, who were exhorted to devote themselves to the support and perpetuation of their husbands' family lines.

All of these changes also coincided with the articulation and development of Neo-Confucian philosophy. That philosophy, usually credited to the Northern Song brothers Cheng Yi 程頤 (1033–1107) and Cheng Hao 程顥 (1032–85), reasserted classical Confucian ideals but gave them a new cosmological grounding. The classical gender ideology that the Cheng brothers and their followers taught frequently (though, as we shall see, not always) supported contemporary family practices associated with an increasingly patrilineal orientation of society.

By the turn of the eleventh century, the Song dynasty had unified most of China into a centralized polity, but the Song was never able to take complete control of northern territories that had been under Chinese rule in the Tang. Instead, the Song lived under constant threat from hostile northern neighbors, and was ultimately demolished by them in two stages: in 1126, the capital and roughly the northern half of erstwhile Song territory was conquered by the Jin dynasty, leaving a reconstituted Song regime in charge of a much-diminished empire in southern China.[13] A century and a half later, in 1279, the Southern Song was annihilated by the Mongols, who ruled China for a little less than a century before their own dynasty, the Yuan, was brought down by internal rebellion in 1368.[14]

---

12. Ebrey, "Early Stages."

13. Historians thus refer to the period from 960–1126 as the Northern Song, and the period from 1127–1279 as the Southern Song.

14. The Mongols had conquered the Jin and taken control of erstwhile Song territory

Long before these conquests, the Song government had been weakened by virulent factional politics. Factional infighting began as early as the 1040s, but intensified greatly in the period between 1068 and the end of the Northern Song, when the policies of the reformer Wang Anshi 王安石 (1021–86) polarized the bureaucracy. Factional infighting continued through the next several decades as the throne supported first one group, then another, until the capital was overrun in 1126. Once the new emperor Gaozong (r. 1127–62) had been declared in the south, new factions crystallized around the issue of foreign policy, with one side determined to retake the north at all costs, and the other, more pragmatic, willing to make peace with the Jin. Over the succeeding century, the pacifists generally prevailed, but the government continued to be riven by factional conflict until the Mongol conquest.

In general, the Mongol Yuan dynasty has been less well studied than others, and there is still much we do not (and, given the poor state of the sources, may never) know about politics and life under the Yuan regime.[15] We do know that the Mongols brought with them radically foreign ideas about society and government, which they attempted, not always successfully, to impose on their Chinese subjects. In particular, they abolished the examination system, preferring to rely on recommendation to staff their bureaucracy. They were largely dubious of Confucian scholarship and were especially hostile to Han Chinese in the south, who had resisted their rule so resolutely. Even after the court was persuaded to resume examinations in 1313, standards were more difficult for southern Chinese. As a result, the majority of southern Chinese elites found themselves disenfranchised under the Yuan, which furthered the process of elite separation from government. More generally, misrule and lawlessness rendered the Yuan a time of social instability and frequent violence, forcing the elite to adopt new strategies of survival.[16]

---

in the north in 1234, but the dynasty was not declared until 1271. The Mongols' conquest of the Song was effectively complete by 1276, when they took the Southern Song capital, but a rump resistance held out until 1279.

15. Von Glahn, "Imagining Pre-Modern China," 36. The studies in the volume in which this essay appears represent some of the best recent work in English on the Yuan and surrounding dynasties.

16. See Smith, "Fear of Gynarchy," 3–27.

All of these factors conditioned the developments I trace in this book, and also how those developments can be traced. Any historical inquiry is shaped by the available sources, and the changes between Northern Song, Southern Song, and Yuan significantly affected the nature of the sources that survive from those periods. Generally speaking, the sources for the Song are much more numerous and varied than those for earlier periods in Chinese history, as the development of printing in the late Tang helped insure that many more texts survived from subsequent periods. But, as I have described elsewhere, the surviving record of the Song shifts systematically between the first and second halves of the dynasty, with more information on the capital and its denizens available for the earlier period, and more information about local elites in the countryside from the latter.[17] The inquiry here necessarily reflects those biases. Similarly, both Southern Song sources and surviving Chinese sources from the Yuan are dominated by works of southerners, so we cannot be sure how well the picture they provide applies to northern China.

In addition to these historical shifts in the sources, any study of gender relations in the Song and Yuan is also constrained by the fact that the surviving record is virtually all from the hands of men: with very few exceptions, almost no writings by women from the Song and Yuan are extant. Our understanding is also hampered by the formality and formulaic nature of a significant part of the historical record. Longstanding generic conventions restricted both what could be said and how it could be said, and this left many important aspects of life—including much of the interaction between men and women—unrecorded.[18] Finally, the highly conservative nature of the Chinese written language itself also conspires to disguise historical change: the persistence of specific words over centuries has hidden the extent to which the meanings of those words changed over time. Indeed, one central argument of this book is that common understandings of the critical terms *ji* (妓, courtesan), *qie*

---

17. Bossler, *Powerful Relations*, 24–34.
18. One important silence in available sources relates to footbinding: we know from archaeological evidence and a few textual references that the practice of footbinding was spreading during the period under study here. This practice was certainly implicated in gender relations, but the sources are too sparse to allow me to address the topic in any meaningful way.

(妾, concubine), and *jie fu* (節婦, principled or faithful wife or widow) were transformed over the course of the Song and Yuan.

In order to elucidate the sometimes subtle processes of transformation, this book is structured by time period and topic: I examine the categories of courtesan, concubine, and exemplary woman through each of the Northern Song, Southern Song, and Yuan dynasties. This frankly schematic organization highlights political disruptions that, perhaps surprisingly, often had a significant impact on gender norms. At the same time, it allows us to consider each time period from multiple perspectives, juxtaposing the image of the period that we get from writings on courtesans and concubines with the very different images that appear in writings on exemplary women. This juxtaposition in turn helps reveal coincidences and correlations that would be obscured or rendered invisible by a single point of view.

Accordingly, chapters 1 through 3 explore how the growth of commerce and the broadening of the elite contributed to the commercialization of women's bodies for entertainment and reproduction. The development of entertainment culture in the Northern Song created new concerns about familial roles and social stability. These concerns erupted in late Northern Song political debates that focused heightened attention on the roles of concubines in families, as well as on the faithfulness of upper-class widows. Entertainment culture played into the latter development as well, as popular genres of writing about courtesans and their romantic fidelity to their lovers began to be deployed to describe other types of faithful women.

Chapters 4 through 6 demonstrate that the popularity of both courtesans and concubines spread throughout society in the Southern Song. The proliferation of female entertainers caused disruption to families and government alike, precipitating a conspicuous cultural reaction. Moralists railed against the pernicious influence of courtesans on local government offices, while both funerary inscription writers and judges in law cases increasingly emphasized the familial rights of concubines as mothers of literati descendants. Over the same period, faced with the trauma of the Northern Song conquest and continued political instability, literati authors began to commemorate the loyal martyrdom of upper-class women as a means to encourage political loyalty in men. By the end of the Southern Song, concerns for family stability and concerns for dynastic survival came together in funerary inscriptions insisting that, like those martyrs, upper-class widows who did not remarry should also be seen as exemplars and models for male loyalty.

Chapters 7 through 9 reveal that, under the Yuan, the talents and humanity of courtesans came increasingly to be appreciated by literati men, while the entertainment functions of concubines were even further downplayed. As the idealized role of concubines became ever closer to that of wives, an explosion of text production celebrated the fidelity of upper-class widows, depicting them now not only as models for the behavior of others, but as central to the expression and survival of Confucian culture.

When I began researching the three categories of courtesan, concubine, and exemplary woman, I did not know how or even whether their stories would intersect; but the chapters below reveal that transformations in the roles of courtesans, concubines, and exemplary women were intimately related not only to each other, but to the social and political upheaval that marked Chinese society from the tenth to the fourteenth centuries. In particular, although this is not a book about Neo-Confucianism, its findings force us to reassess the putative role of Neo-Confucian thought in determining the trajectory of gender relations in China, and, more generally, its leading role in the social developments of the Song and Yuan. More broadly, the investigations in this book help us see both how the Song and Yuan periods set the foundation for the gender order of Late Imperial China, and also what distinguished the Song and Yuan from the Ming and Qing (1644–1911).

Inevitably, given the nature of the sources, this book is more about men's writing about women than it is about the experiences of women themselves. But looking at what men wrote about women allows us to glimpse aspects of social life that are invisible in other sources. It reveals that men were thinking about women, interacting with women, and reacting to them more often than we sometimes assume. It shows that men's relationships with other men were often conditioned by the presence of women. And it shows that men's concerns about women's place in family and society helped shape their understandings of their own social and gender roles, and vice versa: as men's social roles shifted, so did their concerns about women. By exploring the different ways that Song and Yuan men understood various categories of women in society, and by tracing the ways those understandings changed over time, we gain important new perspectives on a transformative period in Chinese history.

PART ONE

*Culture, Politics, and Gender
in the Northern Song*

# I

# *Courtesans and the Northern Song Elite*

## Wen Wan 溫琬

The courtesan of Gantang was surnamed Wen; her given name was Wan, and she was known to her friends as Zhonggui. Her original surname was Hao, and as a child she had been called Shinu. She was born into a respectable family: her father Kui was a traveling merchant. In the "Attaining Harmony" period (1054–55) he was struck with paralysis, and in the space of a year he died. He had no male descendants and the family was very poor, with barely four walls around them. Wen Wan's mother could only take Wan and entrust her to the family of her sister's husband, Guo Xiang, in Fengxiang. Wan's mother herself went alone to stay in the prefectural hostel, where she eventually became a courtesan.

Wan's disposition was delicate and refined; even when young she did not like to play games. At the age of six *sui* she was bright and clever; when they taught her the [Classics of] *Poetry and History* she [studied] all night without sleeping. Her aunt instructed her in music; her methods were intense and strict, but Wan accepted the teaching happily. When she had leisure she would recite the *Thousand Character Classic* and was able to penetrate its general meaning. She enjoyed calligraphy: when she wielded her brush her characters were not at all like those of a woman, but solid and firmly structured. She once donned boy's clothing, and her schoolmates lived with her for several years without realizing she was a girl. People of the village spoke of her, saying, "The Hao family has a promising son!" Accordingly, after some time, Guo Xiang conferred with his wife, saying, "This girl is quite intelligent; if we teach her without stopping, in the space of several years she will put things together and be able completely to understand current affairs. I'm afraid she may develop untoward ambitions and undermine my teachings." So they put away the poetry and prose she had been reading and had her concentrate on women's affairs. Wan was already enamored of the [Classics of] *Poetry and History* and deeply understood their fascination, to the point that day and night she would silently recite them to herself without stopping. She was amiable and honest, so that all the relatives took delight in her. Her aunt especially loved her, treating her as her own child.

When she was fourteen *sui*, they began to discuss her marriage. Go-betweens coming to seek her hand followed one on the heels of the next. In the end they chose a boy surnamed Zhang. The preparatory rituals were already underway when her mother came to visit. At first they did not return Wen Wan to her; she then brought suit and put an end to the betrothal. Wan at this point secretly understood her mother's plans, silently saying to herself, "When I was little I learned to read, and now I generally understand the principles of the Dao, all due to the grace of my aunt and uncle. They told me I was to live out my life in a respectable family, but that did not match my poor fate, and now it has come to this!" She cried in inconsolable grief. Then she went back east to Shaan to attend her mother, and lodged at the prefecture.[1]

In this manner, the eleventh-century biographer of the virtuous courtesan Wen Wan begins his lengthy story of her trials and tribulations. Stories like these circulated widely among the literate classes of the Song and Yuan dynasties, and their popularity suggests that Song and Yuan men found their subject matter endlessly fascinating. Refined and lovely young women, variously skilled in singing, dancing, playing music, and composing poetry, courtesans provided elegant entertainment to gentlemen of wealth and discernment.[2] They were an indispensable feature of the incessant official banquets that (then as now) were part and parcel of bureaucratic life in China. Northern Song men wrote about such women in fictionalized stories like Wen Wan's biography, but also in commentaries on poetry, in collections of pithy sayings, in discussions of political life and policy, and in moralizing essays. These writings reveal not only the centrality of female entertainers in the social life of the Northern Song, but that such entertainers played a central—if sometimes contested—role in defining the identity and character of the elite. The pages below first describe the nature and origins of Northern Song

---

1. Liu Fu, *Qing suo gao yi, hou ji*, 7.166–67, "Wen Wan." For a brief description of Wen Wan and English translations of some of the poetry attributed to her, see Idema and Grant, *The Red Brush*, 334–36.

2. I use the term "courtesan" to translate a variety of terms (principally *ji* 妓 and *chang* 娼 and their numerous cognates) that Song and Yuan authors used to describe female entertainers. As the discussion below will show, the standard modern Chinese translation of the term *ji*, "prostitute," grossly misrepresents the social roles of *ji* in the Song. This is not to deny, however, that sex was part of the repertoire of entertainments they provided. For a fuller discussion of this issue, see Bossler, "Shifting Identities," 6–7. Dorothy Ko has discussed the same issue in the context of later imperial China (*Teachers of the Inner Chambers*, 253–54).

institutions of courtesanship, demonstrating their importance in the political and social life of the Northern Song court, capital, and countryside.³ I then show how courtesans were implicated in contestations over the proper parameters of official behavior and elite identity, as the state, its officials, and the expanding literati class vied to determine how elite status was to be defined and performed. In the mid- to late Northern Song, factional politics and new ideas about Confucian morality led some to suggest that the enjoyment of courtesans was inimical to proper moral behavior; but these suggestions had little impact at the time, and with the support of the artistically inclined Emperor Huizong 徽宗 (r. 1101–26), courtesan entertainments remained an esteemed perquisite of official life until the fall of the capital.

## *The Institutionalization of Courtesans in the Northern Song*

The ubiquity of female entertainers in Song social life was very much a legacy of Tang and Five Dynasties (907–60) practices. Although for centuries well-to-do men had enjoyed keeping troupes of female entertainers to provide musical and other sorts of diversions, the Tang, and especially the late Tang, saw significant developments in the role of these entertainers in elite social life. These developments were consonant with other important shifts in late Tang society, yet much of the change in entertainment life originally emanated from the court.⁴ Music had always been important to the ritual ceremonies of Chinese governance, but the mid-Tang Emperor Xuanzong (r. 712–56) departed from earlier precedents in creating a "Court Entertainment Bureau" (*jiao fang* 教坊) devoted to training court musicians in popular music and entertainment.⁵ Xuanzong's action can, in turn, be seen as a response to secular

---

3. As I have described elsewhere, Northern Song sources tend to focus on the court and higher levels of the bureaucracy, where Southern Song sources tell us more about life outside the capital. The discussion in parts 1 and 2 of this book necessarily reflects these differences.

4. The best succinct account of late Tang social change is Twitchett, "Merchants, Trade, and Government."

5. Kishibe Shigeo notes that an earlier *jiao fang* was established in the 620s by the Tang founders, but argues that this early *jiao fang* was meant to provide music for the

changes in the extremely cosmopolitan society of the Tang, especially the growing popularity of "Western" (*hu* 胡) music brought over the Silk Road.[6] Another important innovation that appears to have taken place in the late Tang was the establishment (or at least the regularization) of a system of government-courtesans: entertainers maintained by the state at higher-level government offices throughout the realm. Known variously as "government-courtesans" (*guan ji* 官妓) or "barracks courtesans" (*ying ji* 營妓), these women were responsible for providing entertainment at official banquets and other government functions.[7] Finally, a third significant development in the social role of entertainers was associated with the expansion of cities and development of an urban merchant class that began to take place in the last century or so of Tang rule. In the winehouses of the two capital cities Chang'an and Luoyang, but also in major regional cities like Yangzhou, Xiangyang, Suzhou, and Hangzhou, courtesans entertained their customers with music, dance, and clever banter.[8] By the ninth century, Tang literati were celebrating their relationships with courtesans in poetry and short stories.[9] All of these trends continued through the Five Dynasties into the Northern Song.

## THE COURT ENTERTAINMENT BUREAU

The early Song emperors Taizu (r. 960–76) and Taizong (r. 976–97) followed the lead of Tang Xuanzong and, with the establishment of their

---

women of the inner court, and thus was very different in function from that established by Xuanzong (Kishibe, "Tōdai kyōbō," 115–20).

6. Kishibe, "Tōdai kyōbō," 112.

7. The precise origin of the institution of "government" or "barracks" courtesans remains obscure (see Bossler, "Vocabularies of Pleasure"), but the two terms were used interchangeably in the Tang and Song. I translate both *guan ji* and *ying ji* as "government-courtesan."

8. Liao Meiyun, *Tang ji*, 36–51, 190–91.

9. Zheng Zhimin traces the relationship between courtesans and literati in the Tang, showing that these relationships became both more frequent and more intimate in the late eighth and ninth centuries (*Xi shuo Tang ji*, 103–88). For a discussion of the same topic in English, see Yao Ping, "The Status of Pleasure." Song Dexi observes that the term *chang* 娼 first emerges in this period ("Tang dai de ji nü," 68). See also Rouzer, *Articulated Ladies*, 201–83.

1. The building on the right is a tenth-century winehouse, distinguished by the elaborate decorative scaffolding in front of the entryway. Through the window on the top floor we see guests taking their ease, while an attendant is visible just inside the main front door. Detail of Anonymous, *A Water-Mill at Sluice Gate* (*Zha kou pan che tu juan* 閘口盤車圖卷). Five Dynasties. From *Qian nian dan qing: Riben, Zhongguo zang Tang Song Yuan hui hua zhen pin* 千年丹青：日本中國藏唐宋元繪畫珍品 [Masterpieces of ancient Chinese paintings: From the Tang to Yuan dynasty in Japanese and Chinese collections], vol 1, 38. Courtesy of Shanghai Museum.

capital in Kaifeng, created their own Court Entertainment Bureau.[10] Initially separate from the Court of Imperial Sacrifices (*tai chang si* 太常寺), which provided ritual music for court ceremonies, the Song *jiao fang* served as a training school-cum-theatrical institute designed to provide the highly skilled performers—men as well as women—required for frequent court festivities. *Jiao fang* entertainers presented music (both instrumental and vocal), dance, and a variety of theatrical arts ranging from humorous skits to acrobatics.[11] They performed at imperial birthday parties, accompanied the emperor on his seasonal perambulations around the capital, and displayed their arts at banquets convened by imperial decree to honor high officials and imperial family members.[12]

The influence of the *jiao fang* on the society of the capital was also significant because the female *jiao fang* entertainers, unlike most women attached to the court, were not cloistered. Court officials were titillated by the appearance of *jiao fang* entertainers at all-day banquets held in the palace. Celebrating the magnificence of such banquets in the late Northern Song, the official Wang Anzhong 王安仲 (1076–1133) observed:

> Several dozen female musicians were arrayed to the south of the palace court, exquisitely robed in lively colors, their ranks in perfect order. The wine went around and the singing began, the notes and rhythm clear and bright. While the music was playing the dancers entered, their voices and movements elegant and beautiful: all were drawn from the best of the [Court Entertainment Bureau]. At the time the midwinter snows had just fallen, but the atmosphere was elegant and warm, already creating spring feelings.[13]

But the *jiao fang* entertainers were not only visible to members of the court bureaucracy. Many of their performances took place in semi-public

---

10. Kishibe, "Sōdai kyōbō," 317–18; Gong Yanming, *Song dai guan zhi ci dian*, 279–81.
11. Tuotuo, *Song shi* (hereafter *SS*) 142.3350–51; Gong Yanming, *Song dai guan zhi ci dian*, 279–81. For a translation of the detailed account of an imperial banquet provided by Meng Yuanlao 孟元老 in his *Dongjing meng hua lu* 東京夢華錄, see Idema and West, *Chinese Theater*, 48–55. (Cf. Meng, *Dongjing meng hua lu zhu* [hereafter DJM] 9.219–23.)
12. Gong Yanming, *Song dai guan zhi ci dian*, 279. For further detail, see Bossler, "Gender and Entertainment," 265–67.
13. Wang Anzhong, *Chu liao ji* 1.6a–b. "Spring feelings" is a common euphemism for erotic sensations. Wang uses the term *fa bu* 法部, an archaic reference to a division of the Tang Pear Garden, to refer to the Court Entertainment Bureau.

venues, such as on imperial boats floating down the river, or on outdoor platforms erected to celebrate seasonal festivals.[14] Still more striking, the *jiao fang* performers were evidently free to leave the palace precincts at will. After imperial banquets were over,

> All the [members] of the Girls' Troupe exited through the right side gate. Swashbuckling youths competed to present them with precious gifts and welcome them with food and wine. Each mounted an elegant steed and returned [home], some in flowered caps, some dressed up like men. Along the Imperial Way they galloped, competing to show off their brilliant beauty. The [throng of] onlookers was like a wall.[15]

In other words, the *jiao fang* entertainers became the popular celebrities of their day: Meng Yuanlao 孟元老 (fl. 1126–47), author of the passage just quoted, is able to list the top performers by name. The gorgeous costumes of the Entertainment Bureau's Girls' Troupe helped set fashion for the court, and thereby for the entire capital.[16] Meng remarks that "their clothing was out of the ordinary—there wasn't one who was not in the latest style of the day."[17]

The high visibility of the *jiao fang* performers in the Song capital ensured that courtesan entertainments would signify status, elegance, and political power. Moreover, the *jiao fang* entertainments at court set the tone for similar entertainments throughout the government bureaucracy. For just as the Northern Song court provided *jiao fang* entertainers to enliven banquets at the capital, so too did it continue the practice of maintaining government-courtesans at every prefectural yamen to serve at official banquets there.

---

14. For a description of a boat performance observed by "10,000 people of the capital," see *SS* 113.2696–97; for performances on public platforms, see *SS* 113.2697–98.

15. *DJM* 9.223; I have slightly emended the translation provided in Idema and West, *Chinese Theater*, 55. Cf. also Bossler, "Gender and Entertainment," 266.

16. According to his contemporary Jiang Xiufu 江休復, Sima Guang once complained that literati women were following the fashion of courtesans (Jiang Xiufu, *Jiang lin ji za zhi* 5.150). Complaints about courtesans and other performers violating sumptuary regulations were common; see e.g., *SS* 153.3577.

17. *DJM* 9.222.

## GOVERNMENT AND INDEPENDENT COURTESANS

Like the *jiao fang*, the Song institution of government-courtesans in the prefectures appears to have been based on Tang and Five Dynasties precedents, though little is known of its bureaucratic structure.[18] The "Treatise on Music" in the *Song History* (*Song shi* 宋史) merely remarks that, in addition to the various troupes of court musicians and the emperor's private musicians, "There are also. . .the yamen musicians (*ya qian yue* 衙前樂) of Kaifeng prefecture. . . [and] the various prefectures all have yamen musicians."[19] The designation *ya qian* (a term used more generally in Song times to describe corvée labor associated with providing services to prefectural and county offices[20]) suggests that the labor of courtesan entertainers was seen as a type of corvée duty that musician households owed to the state. Other sources intimate that government-courtesans evolved out of the institution of yamen slaves. Thus one account of mid-Song date observes,

> Songstresses (*chang fu* 娼婦) in the prefectures are subordinate to the prison officials and are akin to female prisoners. In recent eras they select those of good looks and have them practice singing and dancing to welcome and send off functionaries and guests and serve at banquets. They call them "disciples" (*di zi* 弟子), and the leaders are called "head of the guild" (*hang shou* 行首).[21]

This passage recalls the age-old Chinese practice whereby criminal offenders and prisoners of war were registered as dependents of

---

18. Interestingly, the institutional sources, which are quite detailed on the subject of the *jiao fang*, say almost nothing about the bureaucratic structures that oversaw courtesans in the prefectures. Most of what is known about this aspect of government-courtesans comes from snippets of information in legal and anecdotal sources. See the information provided by Zhu Xi 朱熹 (1130–1200) in his indictment of Tang Zhongyou 唐仲友 (1136–88), discussed in chap. 4. On pre-Song precedents, see Bossler, "Vocabularies of Pleasure."

19. *SS* 142.3361.

20. For an extended discussion of the onerousness of this and other corvée duties, see *SS* 177.4295–346.

21. Zhu Yu, *Pingzhou ke tan* 3.169; cf. Wang Shunu, *Zhongguo chang ji shi*, 109. The term *di zi* is a reference to the special group of courtesan-musicians that the Tang emperor Xuanzong set up in a palace precinct known as the "Pear Garden" and who received the emperor's personal instruction; thus they were called "Disciples of the Pear Garden." As Zhu notes here, by Song times *di zi* had become a general term for courtesans; Yuan drama shows that by that period the term had become an insulting epithet.

government offices, where they served as slave labor. But by the Song, courtesans and other entertainers had come to be classified as belonging to "miscellaneous households" (*za hu* 雜戶), not fully "dishonorable" or base (*jian* 賤) as slaves, though still outside the boundaries of the "four classes" (scholar-officials, farmers, artisans, and merchants) of people who composed respectable society.[22] Moreover, if some government-courtesans entered service as government slaves, anecdotal sources show that by the Song not all (and perhaps not even most) government-courtesans were recruited this way.[23] In one Northern Song story, the eight-year-old orphan Tan Yige 譚意歌 is adopted into the home of a carpenter, whence she happens to catch the eye of the government-courtesan Ding Wanqing 丁婉卿. Ding convinces the carpenter to sell the girl to her, and under her tutelage, Tan Yige becomes a popular government-courtesan, her "doorway [crowded] like a market." Tan impresses a succession of prefectural officials with her ability to compose clever lines of poetry, until, at her request, one of those officials signs the documents that will finally "release

---

22. Liang, "Song dai ji yi ren," 2:102. The issue of the status of various grades of unfree households in the Song is complex, and it is not clear precisely where government-courtesans fell on the spectrum. Some scholars argue that government-courtesans were officially registered as belonging to musician households, and thus that their status was somewhat higher than that of slaves per se (Kishibe, *Jukkyō shakai*; Zhu Gansheng, *Nubi shi*, 2). In his work on the history of social status in the Song, Takahashi Yoshirō argues that permanent slave status did not really exist in the Song; although individuals might enter economic servitude temporarily, they were not seen as inherently "slaves." At the same time, however, the concept of "honorable" and "dishonorable" *occupations* continued to exist, and in that respect all entertainers were regarded as *jian*. Takahashi suggests that the Ming government built on the concept of occupational dishonor to (re)create hereditarily dishonorable classes. See Takahashi, *Sō-Sei mibunhō no kenkyū*, especially chaps. 1 and 4. Dai Jianguo argues that the category of *jian* was still juridically significant in the Northern Song, though it gradually fell out of use over the succeeding centuries. See Dai Jianguo, "'Zhu pu zhi fen.'"

23. A Southern Song law stipulated that women who committed adultery with more than three people were to be relegated to *za hu* status and registered as government-courtesans as a form of penal servitude. See *Ming gong shu pan qing ming ji* (hereafter *QMJ*) 12.448 and 12.449–50. In their translation of the latter case, Brian McKnight and James T. C. Liu understand the punishment as two years of penal servitude followed by government prostitution (*Enlightened Judgments*, 425–26), but the text implies penal servitude as a government-courtesan, and the latter interpretation is confirmed by information in both the previous case and a Yuan anecdote (see Fang Hui, *Gu jin kao xu* 36.10a–11a).

her from the registers" (*tuo ji* 脫籍).²⁴ The "respectable commoner" (*liang min* 良民, *liang ren* 良人) origins of the many Song courtesans, combined with their frequent and often intimate interaction with officials, helped further undermine the idea of fixed social categories.²⁵ In other words, the widespread popularity of courtesans was an important contributing factor in the breakdown of boundaries between "respectable" (*liang* 良) and "dishonorable" (*jian* 賤) groups in late Tang and Song society.

Many scholars have assumed that all Song courtesans, whatever their origins, were registered with the government, but Wen Wan's biography and other Song short stories indicate otherwise. In fact, independent (or "private" *si* 私) courtesans also appear to have existed since at least the late Tang.²⁶ In the Tang and nominally even in the Song, the services of government-courtesans seem to have been intended as the exclusive prerogative of mid- to high-ranking officials, but the expansion of the economy and the growth of urban centers in the late Tang and Five Dynasties periods meant that other men were increasingly able to afford—and anxious to sample—the entertainments that courtesans provided.²⁷ To serve this market, privately run courtesan houses proliferated: their presence in the Northern Song capital is well documented in both the anecdotal literature and in memoirs of the capital like the *Dongjing meng hua lu*.²⁸

---

24. Liu Fu, *Qing suo gao yi, bie ji*, 2.212–14.

25. Writing in the late twelfth century, Fei Gun declared that distinctions between *guan hu* (official slave households), *za hu* (miscellaneous households), and *liang ren* (respectable commoners) were no longer used by judges in his own day (*Liangxi man zhi* 9.113).

26. Liao Meiyun argues that private courtesan houses first arose after the An Lushan rebellion (755–63), when, partly because of the decline in opportunities for musicians at court, the music of court and aristocrats gradually became available to the developing urban populace. She indicates that by the late Tang courtesan houses and entertainment districts were well established (*Tang ji*, 175). Kishibe agrees that such courtesans existed in large cities like Chang'an during the Tang, but argues that they became far more numerous and flourishing in the Song (*Jukkyō shakai*, 215). However, Kishibe's conclusion that, because of the proliferation of these private courtesans, government-courtesans and household-courtesans were no longer necessary in the Song, is clearly not sustainable. The phenomenon of household-courtesans is addressed in detail in chap. 2.

27. Liao Meiyun, *Tang ji*, 190–91.

28. See, for example, the descriptions translated by Stephen H. West in "The

The relationship between independent courtesans and their sisters on the government registers, and for that matter the relationship of private courtesan houses to the government more generally, is not well documented. Song authors for the most part do not use special terminology to distinguish "independent" courtesans, referring simply to "courtesan" (*ji* 妓) rather than the more specific "government-courtesan" (*guan ji* 官妓).[29] Yet they show clearly that many practicing courtesans were not on the government registers. Wen Wan, for example, having joined her mother, soon realizes that her only means of making a living to repay her mother for the gift of life is to become a courtesan herself. Even then, however, she prefers reading books to playing music. Still, she becomes well known enough that ultimately,

> The prefect heard of her, and wanted to have Wan enter the government registers (*guan ji* 官籍). She demurred on the grounds that she didn't play music or sing and thus would not be any fun at banquets. Instead, the prefect put a younger "sister" on the registers, and so excused Wan. This happened several times.[30]

But even though Wan was not officially on the registers, "when a famous official or virtuous gentleman visited, [the prefect] would send for her." One day he summoned her to serve at a welcoming banquet in honor of the eminent Grand Councilor Sima Guang 司馬光 (1019–86), who had returned home from the capital. When she succeeded in impressing Sima Guang (with her knowledge of the *Mencius*, no less), "the prefect was absolutely delighted; he treated her with even greater generosity than before, and ultimately had her listed on the government registry."[31]

---

Interpretation of a Dream," 86–87. As West notes elsewhere, the *DJM* attests to a "plethora of brothels" in Kaifeng: see West, "Playing with Food," 71.

29. To my knowledge, the only Song source that uses a distinct term for independent courtesans is the late Southern Song text *Meng liang lu*, which distinguishes between *guan ji* and *si ming ji* 私名妓 (independent famous courtesans) (Wu Zimu, *Meng liang lu* 20.310), sometimes indicating both with the phrase "official and private courtesans" (*guan si ji* 官私妓, e.g., 2.149). Anecdotal sources occasionally use the term *ming ji* (conventionally understood as "famous courtesan") that would become the standard way of referring to a high-class courtesan in the Ming and thereafter, but that term was not yet widely used in the Song. Modern scholars like Kishibe Shigeo (*Jukkyō shakai*, 214) use the term "commoner's courtesan" (*min ji* 民妓), but this is a neologism that does not appear in Song sources.

30. Liu Fu, *Qing suo gao yi, hou ji*, 7.168.
31. Liu Fu, *Qing suo gao yi, hou ji*, 7.169.

If we can trust short-story writers, then, young girls could be reared to "enter the registers" of government-courtesans, and adult courtesans could move from independent status onto the government registers. Independent courtesans could be called upon to attend at government banquets. And, although government regulations assumed that the services of government-courtesans were restricted to officials of specified ranks, the "crowds" at Tan Yige's doorway hint that government-courtesans could also see private clients. Both on and off the registers, the structures of Northern Song courtesan life exhibit features familiar from the fully developed (and better-documented) courtesan cultures of other times and places. In the story of Tan Yige we see the practice, common elsewhere, of courtesans adopting young girls to rear into the profession and provide for the "mother's" support.[32] In the biography of Wen Wan we see that women who belonged to a particular courtesan establishment generally regarded each other as fictive kin. In the common figure of the "little chignon" (xiao huan 小鬟)—very young (and presumably virginal) courtesans distinguished by their distinctive hairstyle of chignons on either side of the head—we seem to have a precursor of the system of apprentice courtesans well known from later Japan.[33]

These details provide further evidence that courtesan culture in the Northern Song was well established and highly sophisticated. But if the structures of courtesan life were common to both independent and government-courtesans, what was the distinction between them?

Some scholars have suggested that government officials were prohibited from consorting with independent courtesans,[34] and there is some

---

32. This practice is documented even for the late Tang: see Sun Ch'i and des Rotours, *Courtisanes Chinoises*, 25.

33. Known as *maiko*, apprentices in the geisha houses of twentieth-century Japan underwent intensive training prior to making a formal debut as a geisha. See Dalby, *Geisha*, 5–6, 18–20, 44–46. A *maiko* was always presumed to be a virgin: when an apprentice courtesan took her first patron as a geisha, she changed her hairstyle. Similarly, the term "*huan*" designates a hairstyle worn by young girls, perhaps especially servants, before they were of betrothal age. See Zhou Xibao, *Zhongguo gu dai fu shi shi*, 294. As later chapters will show, the virginal *xiao huan* had erotic appeal for many Song men.

34. West, "Playing with Food," 98.

evidence to support such a conclusion. Shortly after the founding of the dynasty, one Wang Zhu 王著 was demoted for getting drunk and staying overnight at the house of a songstress (*chang jia* 娼家)—though he was punished for this crime only after he angered Taizu by coming to an audience drunk.[35] A century or so later, another official was indicted for (among other crimes) selling a gold belt belonging to his deceased father and using the proceeds to visit courtesans.[36] More dramatically, in one of the most controversial law cases of the Northern Song, the renowned literary figure Su Shunqin 蘇舜欽 (1008–48) was stripped of office and reduced to the status of commoner for selling off old government paper money in order to hire courtesans for a banquet. Su himself was convicted of theft of government property in this incident, but a number of the other participants were tried for "consorting with courtesans" (*yu ji nü za zuo* 與妓女雜坐).[37] Ultimately, however, these examples are ambiguous, for officials could also be indicted for improper interactions even with government-courtesans. Although the Song government clearly regarded courtesan entertainments as necessary to the proper performance of official life, it disapproved of officials developing personal relationships with the women provided for this purpose. In particular, "privatizing" (*si* 私, in this case implying a sexual relationship with) a government-courtesan was an indictable offense, and men who were too blatant about their fondness for courtesans were subject to charges of debauchery.[38] In 1044 the prefect Jiang Tang 蔣堂 (980–1054) was dismissed in part for "repeatedly privatizing government-courtesans" (反私官妓),[39]

---

35. Li Tao, *Xu zi zhi tong jian chang bian* (hereafter *Chang bian*) 4.83.
36. Zhao Bian, *Qing xian ji* 7.27b, in a memorial indicting Zhou Yongzheng 周永正.
37. *Chang bian* 153.3715–16. See also Xu Song, *Song hui yao ji gao* (hereafter *SHY*) *zhiguan*, 64.48b; *SHY*, *zhiguan*, 64.49b–50; *SS* 442.13079.
38. Tang policies seem to have been more relaxed in this regard. Kishibe (*Jukkyō shakai*, 215) describes *guan ji* as essentially the private courtesans of officials, because officials were able to take them along on official assignments or exchange them as presents. Liao Meiyun (*Tang ji*, 151) stresses that in particular the military commissioners (*jie du shi* 節度使) of the late Tang period seem to have been able to use government-courtesans as they pleased, and she also provides anecdotal evidence of other Tang officials "privatizing" government-courtesans, apparently without penalty (153–61). I have discussed the Song government's concern and some of the examples given below in a slightly different context in Bossler, "Shifting Identities," 17–19.
39. *Chang bian* 153.3725; *SS* 298.9913.

and a friend of Zhang Fangping 張方平 (1007–91) purportedly saved him from the same fate by persuading Zhang's lover, the government-courtesan Chen Fengyi 陳鳳儀, to hand over his love letters so they would not end up misused by an enemy.[40] The censor Liu Huan 劉渙 (1000–1080) was not so lucky: he was demoted because a letter he wrote to a government-courtesan fell into the wrong hands.[41] Here it is also telling that the authors of fictional sources presume that officials would be among the customers—indeed, were the preferred customers—of independent courtesans. Thus, of the Hengzhou (Hunan) entertainer Wang Youyu 王幼玉 we learn, "Those with whom she associated were all ranking officials and ministers; beyond these, even the wealthiest merchants and rich traders could not pique her interest."[42] Such stories imply that officials could be expected to interact with independent as well as government-courtesans.

For the entertainers themselves, being on the government registers seems to have offered both advantages and disadvantages. Serving as a government-courtesan meant that a woman was under the protection of the prefecture, and she may well have received some basic support from the government, as did entertainers at the court.[43] At the very least, she could count on receiving tips when she served at official functions, and these tips could sometimes be very generous. At a courtesan banquet attended by Fan Zhongyan 范仲淹 (989–1052), the officials held an archery contest, and at each bull's-eye the attending courtesans received silver coins.[44] Government courtesans also had more frequent

---

40. Zhang Bangji, *Mo zhuang man lu* 1.31. Cf. Ebrey, "Women, Money, and Class," 628.

41. *Chang bian* 114.2672; *SS* 324.10493. The *SHY*, in reporting the case of Liu Huan, does not mention the courtesan directly but indicates that Liu was cashiered in part for debauchery (*yu lan* 瑜 瀾) (*SHY, zhiguan*, 64.33). The term *yu lan* (also written 逾瀾) is used frequently in Song documents to refer to sexual excess. Liu's letter was particularly damning because, as noted below, censorial officials were forbidden from even attending courtesan banquets.

42. Liu Fu, *Qing suo gao yi, qian ji*, 10.95.

43. Liao Meiyun, *Tang ji*, 153, cites Tang regulations stipulating that government slaves (which she takes to include courtesan-musicians) receive food and clothing from the government. Yan Ming, *Zhongguo ming ji yi shu shi*, 58, says this was still the case in the Five Dynasties. Whether independent courtesans were required to pay taxes is unclear.

44. *Chang bian* 143.3457.

opportunities to interact with—and perhaps develop closer relationships with—men of official status, as we have seen above. At the same time, however, being attached to the government registers might also constrain a courtesan's actions. Bound to service, she had to perform when summoned by the prefect.[45] She was also highly vulnerable to the depredations of corrupt or cruel officials.[46] More importantly, she could not leave government service without the documented permission of the presiding prefectural official. Tan Yige used her clever poetry to persuade the local prefect to release her from service; Wen Wan, having joined the registers, pleaded for years to be released, and even once attempted to run away, before her request was finally granted. Even so, service as a government-courtesan was not a lifetime occupation: the expectation was that government-courtesans would be released from the registers after a set term of service, or on reaching a certain age.[47]

Ultimately, the clearest distinction between government and independent courtesans seems to be simply that some women were officially registered and others were not, a distinction that appears primarily to reflect the government's inability to maintain control over the rapidly increasing and highly mobile entertainer population. Expanding markets in goods, services, and people meant that the government was unable to keep track of all persons who took up entertaining as a means of eking out a living. It was forced to tolerate the existence of unregistered entertainers, even while insisting on its prerogative to commandeer the services of others.[48] Still, the conspicuous presence of independent courtesans reveals that courtesan entertainments, with all their associations of power and prestige, were becoming widely available to those outside the political elite,

---

45. Liang, "Song dai ji yi ren," 2:104.
46. That officials might beat or otherwise abuse government-courtesans under their jurisdictions is widely attested in the sources. For one example, see Wei Tai, "Lin Han yin ju shi hua," 332–33.
47. See further discussion in Bossler, "Shifting Identities," 13. What government-courtesans did upon release from the registers is not clear. Some may have married; others presumably entered the market for domestic service; others may have moved into the management of private brothels.
48. Wu Zimu, after listing the names of both government and independent courtesans, states that the singing of the latter did not equal that of the former. This would seem to suggest that the state made an effort to keep the best or most talented entertainers under its own purview (*Meng liang lu* 20.310).

who could thereby emulate the trappings of official privilege. Meanwhile, the government itself struggled to control the relationships of its officials with both the entertainers it provided to them and those it did not. In this fluid context, it is hardly surprising that interactions with courtesans became an important mechanism through which elite male status was asserted and negotiated.

## Courtesans and Elite Status in the Northern Song

As is evident in the very existence of government-courtesans, courtesan entertainments in the Northern Song were an expected perquisite of achieving a certain level of political status. Indeed, newly minted *jin shi* degree-holders were introduced into official life with a courtesan banquet held by the emperor.[49] The connection between courtesan entertainment and political success is amusingly expressed in an anecdote concerning the Grand Councilor Song Xiang 宋庠 (996–1066), who, having spent New Year's Eve reading the *Book of Changes* in the imperial library, discovered that his younger brother Song Qi 宋祁 (998–1061) (also a high official) had rung in the New Year by lighting decorated lanterns and drinking with courtesans (*ge ji* 歌妓) until dawn. The next day Xiang sent a message to his brother, reproaching him for his inordinate extravagance and asking, "I don't know if you remember the New Year we spent together in that prefectural school, eating minced pickles and boiled rice?" In response Qi merely laughed, saying, "He needs to remind me? Doesn't the Grand Councilor know *why* we were at that prefectural school eating minced pickles and boiled rice?"[50] For Song Qi, banqueting with courtesans was an emblem of official privilege, the just reward for years of diligent study and deprivation.

Courtesans were a sign of official privilege as well because they afforded men the opportunity to demonstrate characteristics associated with official success, such as refinement and aesthetic judgment. Thus one anecdotalist describes how Grand Councilor Yan Shu 晏殊 (991–1055) and two of his retainers took a pleasure-boat ride without even a servant to man the tiller, but with "several courtesans" (*zhu ji* 諸妓)

---

49. Wei Tai, *Dong xuan bi lu* 6.68–69.
50. Qian Shizhao, *Qian shi si zhi*, 71.

along for the ride.⁵¹ Servants were dispensable to elegant outings; courtesans were not. The image of the courtesan as a requisite accoutrement of cultivated and sophisticated social life appears in numerous Northern Song poems. Though many, many examples could be cited, Han Wei's 韓維 (1017–98) "Matching Registrar Zhu's 'Roaming the Garden'" (和朱主簿遊園) is typical:

| | |
|---|---|
| 白首昏昏度歲年 | White-headed, I pass the years in muddled confusion, |
| 忽聞春至便開顏 | But suddenly hearing that spring has arrived, my face brightens. |
| 溪頭凍水晴初漲 | Snowmelt at creek's head gushes forth as the weather clears. |
| 竹下名園畫不關 | Beneath the bamboo the famous garden stays open all day. |
| 旋得歌辭教妓唱 | Quickly coming up with a song lyric, I instruct the courtesan to sing it; |
| 遠尋梅艷喚人攀 | Seeking a gorgeous plum branch in the distance, I call someone to pluck it. |
| 如今尚有官拘束 | Today you are still bound by official duties, |
| 解組歸來始是閒 | True leisure begins only when you give up the seal of office.⁵² |

The courtesan here is essentially background, but like the rushing water and the garden scenery, her presence is central to the atmosphere of refinement that the poem simultaneously creates and commemorates.

Other poetry in this category goes further, deploying the figure of the courtesan to highlight the aesthetic sensibility of the men described: it asserts that the ability to appreciate the clear notes of the courtesan's voice or the precision of her dance is akin to an ability to appreciate the luminescence of the moon over the mountains or the multicolored aura of the setting sun. Indeed, admiration of courtesans and their artistic talents may have helped inspire the growing interest in aesthetic appreciation that, as Ronald Egan has shown, came to characterize Northern Song intellectual life.⁵³ By the same token, judgments of courtesans could be a means of asserting sophistication and savoir-faire. An author of humorous aphorisms

---

51. Kong Pingzhong (fl. 11th c.), *Tan yuan* 3.319. The presence of the courtesans is incidental to the point of the anecdote, which involves a joke about Yan as helmsman (of both the government and the boat) "not steering straight."

52. Han Wei, *Nanyang ji* 9.12a–b. I am grateful to Stephen West for advice on translation of this and other poems; he should not, however, be held accountable for the results.

53. See Egan, *The Problem of Beauty*.

(*za zuan* 雜纂) displayed his cultivated, urban aesthetic by including among his definitions of "depressing" (*lang dang* 郎璫) "a village courtesan singing a long lyric" (村妓娼長詞), and by describing as "laughable" (*ke xiao* 可笑) "a village courtesan at her toilette" (村妓妝梳).[54]

Precisely because courtesan entertainments were so central to elite and especially official social life, courtesan banquets became a central—if not *the* central—venue for elite male socialization in the Northern Song.[55] Courtesan banquets were the setting in which ambitious young men of the Northern Song established reputations and friendships, and where they demonstrated their command of the ritual courtesies that distinguished the sort of men who, if not already officials, were worthy of becoming so. A gracious host honored his guests by inviting them to feast, but also by providing entertainers to enhance their enjoyment of the occasion. The guests honored the host by eating and drinking without restraint, but also by exhibiting proper appreciation for the occasion. A thoughtful guest, for example, advertised his host's generosity in poetry. When Su Shi's 蘇軾 (1036–1101) friend Zhao Chengbo 趙成伯 (n.d.) brought out the Sichuan courtesan Yang Jie 楊姐 at his banquet, Su Shi composed a poem playing on her surname and Sichuan origins to compare her to the famous *femme fatale* Yang Guifei. In doing so, he not only enhanced the courtesan's status, but advertised the largesse and sophistication of the friend who had invited Yang Jie to the party.[56] By the same token, a considerate host might order the entertainers to solicit poetry from the notable writers among his guests, giving the latter a chance to display *their* talents. Thus Li Xin 李新 (1090 *jin shi*) explained in the title of one of his poems, "The Brocade Pavilion Lament: Commissioner Li of Jiazhou prefecture ordered the government-courtesan Duan Qian to request a poem, and I composed this there at the banquet."[57]

---

54. Wang Junyu, *Za zuan xu*, 67, 73.

55. Paul Rouzer has described the ninth-century Tang courtesan quarters as a place where educated young men began to feel that "they must acquire a certain 'cultural capital' or prestige in order to define themselves as a class" (*Articulated Ladies*, 257–68). The social dynamics Rouzer describes were even more salient in the Northern Song, when the society was more fluid and signifiers of status even less well defined.

56. *Su Shi shi ji* 47.2538. Although the identification of this "Chengbo" as Zhao Chengbo is not definitive, other references in Su's collected works to his friendship with Zhao Chengbo suggest that he is the most likely candidate.

57. Li Xin, *Kua ao ji* 3.7a. For other examples see Shen Kuo, *Meng xi bi tan* 16.123–24, and Chen Shidao, *Hou shan shi hua*, 314.

As these examples suggest, the requesting and receiving of poetry was central to the social exchanges that took place at banquets; this in turn was a direct reflection of the importance of poetry in Northern Song political life. Although the Northern Song saw new debates about whether poetic skill should be the central standard for examination success, the ability to compose poetry remained a critical means of establishing one's credentials as a gentleman/literatus (*shi* 士).[58] The importance of poetic performance at banquets, and the significant roles courtesans played in such performance, is evident first of all in the attention paid to the poetic skills of courtesans themselves. Northern Song men remarked that certain courtesans were "good at poetry" (*shan wei shi ci* 善爲詩詞),[59] and that others had earned a reputation for poetic composition (*you shi ming* 有詩名).[60] Northern Song romantic fiction likewise celebrated courtesans for their literary talents. A substantial portion of the story of the courtesan Tan Yige is devoted to quotation of the clever verses she composed in response to the demands of eminent officials who insisted she "match lines" with them, and an appendix to the biography of the erudite Wen Wan contains a set of about thirty poems purportedly by her hand.[61] Some anecdotes even depict courtesans displaying poetic virtuosity at the expense of their male clientele, as when Qin Cao 琴操 corrected the rhyme of a patron, or Su Qiong 蘇瓊 worked into her poem the fact that Cai Jing 蔡京 (1047–1126) was ranked ninth in the *jin shi* examinations.[62]

Courtesans' skills (or putative skills) at composing poetry were critical in qualifying them for their far more socially significant social role as *consumers* thereof. At courtesan banquets female entertainers sought

---

58. John Chaffee describes the repeated efforts of reformers to make the civil service examinations more substantive by eliminating poetic skill as a criterion for selection. Chaffee observes that although efforts to remove poetry questions from the examinations were successful for intermittent periods in the Northern Song, poetry tended to be the candidates' preferred examination option whenever it was available. He suggests that in part this was because "literary skills were the mark of a gentleman" (*The Thorny Gates of Learning*, 67–73).
59. Chen Shidao, *Hou shan shi hua*, 308.
60. Ibid., 314.
61. Liu Fu, *Qing suo gao yi, bie ji*, 2.212–14, 8.175–80. For English translations of a few of Wen Wan's poems, see Idema and Grant, *The Red Brush*, 334–36.
62. E.g., Wu Zeng, *Neng gai zhai man lu* 17.483, 17.476–77. These anecdotes were recorded in the Southern Song but describe Northern Song incidents.

the poetic largesse of literati writers, who composed song lyrics that the women could add to their repertoire. The surviving poetry of Northern Song writers includes many examples of poems presented to courtesans, often in the context of banqueting. At a party held at the home of an official, Xu Xuan 徐鉉 (916–91) heard a courtesan sing a lyric written by a colleague; he was thereby moved to offer her a poem of his own.[63] In a poem entitled "At a Banquet, Presented to Xiao Ying" (筵上贈小英), the eminent official Zhang Yong 張詠 (946–1015) suggested that the courtesan Xiao Ying must be an incarnation of the constellation Charming Girl (*wu nü* 婺女), or else an immortal attendant of the Queen Mother of the West who had been sent to earth as punishment for a minor transgression. Courtesans may have welcomed such poetry as a form of advertisement: the impression that Zhang Yong's poem was intended as publicity is heightened by the fact that he took care to indicate the location of the entertainer's residence.[64] But anecdotal sources also tout the popularity of song lyrics composed by well-known officials, suggesting that literati earned prestige by having their poetry in demand in the courtesan quarters. One author asserts that when the poet Wei Ye 魏野 (960–1019) wrote a poem praising the Chang'an courtesan Tiansu 添蘇, she "was as delighted as if she had received a treasure; and in the course of one night all of Chang'an was singing it."[65] Another describes how an anxious host despaired of getting the government-courtesans to write new lyrics for

---

63. Xu Xuan, "At a banquet at Drafter Jian's home, there was a courtesan who sang a lyric by Drafter Han of Hezhou, so I proffered this" 江舍人宅筵上有妓唱和州韓舍人歌辭, 因以寄 (*Qi sheng ji* 2.6a). See also 3.12b, "Offered to the Western Zhe Courtesan Yaxian (composed at a banquet)" 贈浙西妓亞仙 (筵上作). In a poem written to see off "Inspector Chao," Wang Yucheng has the line "Drunk, the government-courtesan requests a song-poem; on expensive Shan-creek paper I transcribe a new lyric" 醉中官妓乞歌詩, 剡谿紙貴抄新詞 (Wang Yucheng, *Xiao xu ji* 12.8a–b).

64. Zhang Yong, *Guai ya ji* 2.13. The editors of the *Si ku quan shu* collectanea suggest that this poem is not Zhang's work (Yong Rong, *Qin ding Si ku quan shu zong mu* 152.7a–b), although the poem is included in the *Si ku* version of his collected works. James Hightower suggests that several songs by the poet Liu Yong were likewise "plugs" for the women named therein ("The Songwriter Liu Yung: Part 1," 373).

65. Wenying, *Xiangshan ye lu*, *xu lu*, 81. This elaborate anecdote purports to explain the origins of a line of poetry written by Wei Ye, but see also Wu Chuhou, *Qing xiang za ji* 6.60–61, where a completely different anecdote explains what is essentially the same line of poetry.

a party honoring Ouyang Xiu 歐陽修 (1007–72). He was relieved but puzzled when at the banquet Ouyang listened intently to their songs, drinking a full cup in acknowledgment of each: the courtesans, the host later discovered, had honored his guest by singing lyrics Ouyang himself had composed.[66] The same phenomenon is reflected from a different angle in Chen Shidao's 陳師道 (1053–1102) forlorn complaint that when he was stationed out in the countryside only one of the village courtesans was interested in his lyrics.[67]

The epitome of poetic brilliance was the ability to compose extempore, and banquets were the venue par excellence for showcasing such ability.[68] A classic example here is an anecdote involving Ouyang Xiu, who, along with his courtesan lover, had annoyed the senior statesman Qian Weiyan 錢惟演 (962–1034) by arriving late to his banquet; they then compounded the affront by continuing to make eyes at each other across the room. When the irate Qian reprimanded the courtesan for her tardiness, she explained that they had been trying to find a lost hair ornament, which was still missing. Qian responded that if Ouyang Xiu could come up with a verse, he would make up her loss. On the spot, Ouyang devised a brilliant lyric; Qian accordingly ordered the courtesan to drink a toast to him and had her hairpin replaced from the public coffers.[69] An early Southern Song source credits Su Shi with an even more ostentatious display of creative genius: he is depicted composing a lengthy song lyric even as the tune for it was being played.[70] Not incidentally, in repeating such stories, anecdotalists asserted their own ability to appreciate poetry and thereby their membership in the elite circles defined by such appreciation.[71]

---

66. Chen Shidao, *Hou shan tan cong* 3.44.

67. Chen Shidao, *Hou shan ju shi wen ji* 9.10a–b.

68. Egan notes that "a person's level of learning, his intelligence, character, and taste were often assessed by the poetic lines he produced on demand" (*The Problem of Beauty*, 73).

69. Qian Shizhao, *Qian shi si zhi*, 65. This anecdote is repeated in Tang Guizhang, *Song ci ji shi*, 31.

70. Wu Zeng, *Neng gai zhai man lu* 17.500.

71. In the early Southern Song, such anecdotes also became part of a literature of nostalgia for the glories of the Northern Song court, a topic explored further in chap. 4.

## Romance and Its Limits

Anecdotes and poetry celebrating the glories of courtesan banquets suggest that the ideal Northern Song gentleman was not only sophisticated and skilled at poetry, but was a man of profound emotional sensitivity with a predilection for romance. This masculine ideal can be traced back to late Tang times, when romantic literature emerged in the form of "talented man, beautiful woman" (*cai zi jia ren* 才子佳人) stories that featured brilliant, politically promising young men paired almost exclusively with lovely, intelligent, and sensitive courtesans.[72] To be sure, there were significant changes in the ways that courtesans figured in Tang literature and the ways they appeared in the Song. Although Song *chuan qi* (傳奇) romances continue the Tang tradition of depicting beautiful and talented courtesans becoming the paramours of clever scholars, Song stories acknowledge that scholars now compete with merchants and other wealthy parvenus for courtesans' attentions. Tang stories rarely concern themselves with the courtesan-heroine's origins, and in one notable case that does so, she is described as the daughter of a prince and his maidservant; by contrast, the heroines of Song stories are frequently acknowledged as girls of modest but respectable family who have fallen into courtesan status.[73] Such changes indicate tacit acknowledgement that the society in which young men of the Northern Song were trying to make their way had become far more fluid than that of the late Tang. Another important shift in romantic writing from Tang to Song was the development of the genre of

---

72. See Owen, *The Chinese "Middle Ages,"* 130–73; Rouzer, *Articulated Ladies*, 216–83. Although both Owen and Rouzer confine their arguments to the literary realm, the centrality of courtesans in late Tang literature was almost certainly a reflection of their increasing importance in the social life of the period.

73. The Tang example is the eponymous heroine of *Huo Xiaoyu zhuan*: the daughter of a nobleman and a serving maid, she is essentially illegitimate in the status-conscious society of the Tang. With no hope of a proper marriage, she becomes a courtesan, but given her refined background, she seeks a patron of similarly refined status. In contrast, we can see Wen Wan as the quintessential Song courtesan: the legitimate daughter of a petty merchant, she is of respectable but not noble family. A family crisis leads to her fall into marginal status, and although she at first resists, in the end she accepts her bitter fate out of filial duty to support her mother. The late Tang *Beili zhi* indicates that even at that point, some girls of *liang min* background were reared to be courtesans, but Tang stories do not highlight this fact (Sun Qi, *Beili zhi*, 25).

*ci* or song lyric poetry. Although Northern Song authors did write *shi* poems for and about courtesans, in general the expression of romantic sentiments was associated with the genre of *ci* poetry.[74] As others have argued, the increasing legitimacy of *ci* poetry as an artistic form seems to have made the expression of male romantic and aesthetic sentiment more acceptable in literati writing; we might add that the ubiquity of courtesan banquets in themselves is likely to have helped foster that acceptability.[75] Still, the persistent association of romance with the *ci* genre also suggests a compartmentalization of romance away from other aspects of life, as something that could not quite legitimately be admitted as the subject of more classical literary forms. These changes hint at a certain ambivalence about the role of romance in literati life, an ambivalence that would eventually be expressed more explicitly.

These changes notwithstanding, however, the poetic record is consistent with the notion that the Tang ideal of literatus as romantic hero persisted through most of the Northern Song. As the Song was being established, for example, Xu Xuan wrote a "Song for Yuezhen" (月真歌), in which he described a love affair between his friend, a Hanlin drafter surnamed Yin, and a Yangzhou courtesan named Yuezhen (月真 "Moon-pure"). This poem tells us that "Yuezhen at fourteen or fifteen could play the pipa and was skilled at singing and dancing," while Yin was a rising star at court. The moment he saw her, "it was as if he'd always known her," but cozy scenes of "Yuezhen playing the pipa while he keeps the beat" were interrupted by his official duties. Xu Xuan ends the song by exhorting the couple to enjoy their love while it lasts:

| | |
|---|---|
| 殷郎月真聽我語 | Master Yin, Yuezhen, listen to what I say |
| 少壯光陰能幾許 | How long can youth and vigor last? |

---

74. The close association between courtesans and the development of the *ci* genre has long been understood by scholars of Chinese literature. See, for example, Kang-i Sun Chang, *The Evolution of Chinese Tz'u Poetry*; Fusek and Chao, *Among the Flowers*; Lin Shuen-fu, *The Chinese Lyrical Tradition*, 1–61. Anna Shields has argued that *ci* poetry first became a respectable genre for literati authors at the court of the Five Dynasties kingdom of Shu (*Crafting a Collection*, 7–8). In contrast, Egan (*The Problem of Beauty*, chap. 5) maintains that *ci* remained a suspect form in the early Northern Song, becoming truly respectable only with Su Shi's innovations in the genre after the 1070s.

75. See Egan, *The Problem of Beauty*, 347–49.

| 良辰美景數追隨 | Special moments and lovely scenes pass quickly |
| 莫教長說相思苦 | Don't make me go on about the bitterness of mutual longing.[76] |

Poetry in this vein was also used to express publicly men's feelings—especially sadness on parting—for courtesans they had loved or admired. Xu Xuan also wrote a poem to be appended to a letter he was sending to the courtesan Yuebin (越賓, "Guest from Yue"), suggesting his unhappiness at their long separation: "Don't say the young men seldom laugh or smile/After years of separation they still think of her absence."[77] In the same mode the famous upright official Fan Zhongyan composed a *shi* poem to commend a favorite but very young government-courtesan (whom he compared to an "unopened flower") to the care of his successor; and the poet Zhang Lei 張耒 (1054–1114) wrote two verses for the government-courtesan Liu Shunu 劉淑奴.[78] He Zhu 賀鑄 (1052–1125), on receiving a *shi* poem from a courtesan from whom he had been long separated, reworked her words into a song describing the scene of their parting.[79] Still other writers were also moved to depict sad stories of their contemporaries' love affairs. Thus Yang Yi 楊億 (974–1020) explained, "At a gathering, Registrar Zhu said that the current Remonstrator Zhang of Jingnan, when he was in charge in Xiangyang, was once in love with a courtesan. He was rather afraid of his wife, so in the end was unable to have her near him. When he was transferred to Jingzhu, they parted in tears at the post station, and a song about it became popular in the Ba region. I was moved by this affair, and so wrote a continuing song."[80] Yang's poem invokes the standard romantic topoi of tearful parting and insurmountable melancholy—while his preface hints that jealous wives could spoil romantic adventures. In a variation on this theme, men used poetry to demonstrate their sympathy for the sad fates that befell beautiful young women. Shen Liao 沈遼 (1032–85) and Huang Xiaoxian 黃孝先 (n.d.) wrote mourning poems for Shen's erstwhile lover, the government-

---

76. Xu Xuan, *Qi sheng ji* 2.4a–5a. Xu Xuan's friendship with Yin is evident in the numerous other poems he dedicates to him.
77. Xu Xuan, *Qi sheng ji* 3.5a–b.
78. Wu Zeng, *Neng gai zhai man lu* 11.307, 17.496.
79. Ibid., 16.484.
80. Yang Yi, *Wuyi xin ji* 2.8b.

courtesan Zhang Yujie 張玉姐, dead (several years after her affiliation with Shen) at the age of nineteen *sui*.[81] Liu Cizhuang 劉次莊 (1074 *jin shi*) wrote a ballad, an "explication" (*yi* 譯) in the subject's voice, and a commentary (*jian* 箋), all depicting the story of a courtesan who had angered the local prefect and been exiled from the area.[82]

Finally, poetry for courtesans could also be a site for expressing erotic appreciation. In such poetry Northern Song literati recorded their delight in the spectacle of exquisite young girls arrayed for their enjoyment, and described their appreciation of "scallion-like fingers," of "vermilion lips" and "white-jade skin."[83] In verse Chao Buzhi 晁補之 (1053–1110) could give vent to the emotions stirred by observing his friend's courtesan lover at her toilette, and a military man could tell his superior that as a reward for victory he did not want noble titles, but only the lovely government-courtesan who had waited on them.[84]

In short, in poetry such as this Northern Song men valorized a literati identity that embraced erotic and emotional sensitivity. A true literatus, we are told, is not only a creative genius who can compose a brilliant poem on a moment's notice; he is also a man who enjoys an aesthetic appreciation for women (or perhaps girls) as objects of erotic desire, and a man of high sensibility who feels profoundly the sorrow of parting from his lover. He is also a man who deplores deeply—and describes in heartrending verse—the pathetic fates of courtesans he and his friends have known.[85]

Yet, although Northern Song poetry like this perpetuated the late Tang model of the dashing, emotional, romantic man of letters, by the turn of the twelfth century we begin to see some retreat from this ideal. The limits to the acceptability of romantic involvement with courtesans are clearly evident in the famous case of the young scholar Liu Yong 柳永 (1034 *jin shi*), who thrilled and scandalized his contemporaries (and

---

81. Wu Zeng, *Neng gai zhai man lu* 17.496, 17.497–98.

82. Ibid., 16.481–82.

83. Wu Zeng, *Neng gai zhai man lu* 17.489; Ge Lifang, *Yun yu yang qiu* 15.606. On the close association of entertainers and eroticism in the Ming dynasty, see Joseph Lam, "Reading Music."

84. Zhou Hui, *Qing bo za zhi jiao zhu* 9.414–15 (item 25); Chen Shidao, *Hou shan shi hua*, 314.

85. See Wu Zeng, *Neng gai zhai man lu* 11.316–17 and 11.321–22 for poetry, even sets of linked poems, inspired by the sad stories of courtesans the authors have known.

later generations) by writing unabashedly passionate and often erotic *ci* poetry depicting life and love in the courtesan quarters.[86] Liu Yong's poetry is particularly unusual in expressing romantic sentiments from a male perspective: that is, he expresses first-person sentiments of love and longing without adopting the masquerade of a female persona, as had been conventional in earlier poetry.[87] In this respect, his work reveals the extent to which romance had become an accepted aspect of elite male identity and self-expression. Yet, although Liu Yong's poetry has survived, and as nearly as can be determined he himself went on to have a perfectly adequate political career, even before the end of the eleventh century his persona was under attack, as anecdotalists circulated tales of how his poetry had offended his superiors and derailed his career.[88] Meanwhile, by the same period, the focus of literati writings on romance—or at least those preserved in the collected works of famous men—had largely shifted from courtesans outside the home to concubine-entertainers maintained within the inner quarters: after the very early Northern Song, the record of poetry for public courtesans is largely preserved not in literati collected works but in gossipy miscellanea from the early Southern Song.[89] In short, even as some men continued to celebrate courtesans as figures of artistry and romance, another strain of opinion had come to see courtesans as at best vulgar and crude, and at worst dangerous to the discipline and character of both elite men and the wider society.

### Courtesans, Dissipation, and Danger

Negative images of courtesans appear occasionally in Northern Song poetry after the early eleventh century, as when the sensual pleasures of wine and women are contrasted with the more austere (and presumably

---

86. Liu Yong is widely regarded as a major innovator of the *ci* form, and there is a voluminous literature on the man and his poetry. See e.g., Hightower, "The Songwriter Liu Yung: Part I" and "The Songwriter Liu Yung: Part II," which provide both a careful review of what is known about Liu Yong's life and a translation of more than half of his surviving corpus. Lap Lam has translated other lyrics and considered the reasons for later scholars' disapproval of Liu's work. See Lam, Lap, "A Reconsideration of Liu Yong."
87. Hightower, "The Songwriter Liu Yung: Part I," 351.
88. For example, see Zhang Shunmin, *Hua man lu*, 218. Cf. Lap Lam passim.
89. This point is discussed further in chap. 2.

spiritually superior) delights of communing with nature or perusing fine art. Han Qi 韓琦 (1008–75), in describing the lakeside pavilion he has built for enjoying his retirement, notes that it lacks many of the appurtenances of its Tang model (a pavilion built by Bai Juyi 白居易 [772–846]), including the troupe of exquisite child-courtesans who had played for Bai there. In Han's garden, instead of admiring seductive serving maids, guests will survey the luxurious greenery; rather than hearing the sounds of the "strings and pipes" they will listen to a flowing spring (妖妍姬侍目嘉卉, 咿啞絲竹聽流泉).[90] A more emphatic rejection of courtesan entertainments was articulated by Wen Tong 文同 (1018–79) in a poem sending off a departing colleague. After extolling the refined pleasures of tea drinking and art appreciation, the poem insists:

| 清歡雅興自無厭 | Simple pleasures and elegant amusements naturally do not fatigue, |
| 妓樂喧煩誰願進 | Courtesan music, raucous and irritating—who is willing to present it?[91] |

Here—in contrast to what we have seen above—the sensuous enjoyment of courtesan entertainment is depicted as coarse and even slightly uncouth, especially in comparison with appreciation of the beauties of nature or the connoisseurship of tea and fine art.

Much more commonly, however, negative images of courtesans in the early Northern Song appear outside of poetry and were associated with concerns about government malfeasance or dereliction of duty. As early as 969 Xiang Gong 向拱 (912–86) was demoted when his penchant for courtesans led him so to neglect his responsibilities that bandits were robbing people in the marketplace.[92] We have seen above that in the mid-eleventh century, Su Shunqin was cashiered for using government funds to throw a courtesan banquet. In about the same period, Cai Xiang 蔡襄 (1012–67) requested the demotion of the official Wei Jian 魏兼 (n.d.), on the grounds that during a recent posting as military commissioner in the drought-stricken Liangzhe region Wei had ignored the plight of the people and spent his days and nights banqueting with courtesans. Cai added that when Wei's proclivities became known, neighboring

---

90. Han Qi, *Anyang ji bian nian jian zhu* 3.119–20.
91. Wen Tong, *Dan yuan ji* 16.1.
92. *Chang bian* 10.231.

prefectures sent courtesans and musicians to welcome and attend him, to the point that in one case musicians even drowned en route. So infamous was Wei's behavior, Cai claimed, that Suzhou people chanted a ditty containing the lines "Reverberating are the songs of the courtesans; earthshaking are the cries of the starving" while Hangzhou artists sold in the marketplace a picture entitled "Illustration of the Military Commissioner's nighttime drinking."[93]

Concern that courtesan entertainments might lead to government malfeasance was reflected in the promulgation, over the course of the Northern Song, of a number of edicts regulating officials' use of such entertainments. In the early eleventh century the prefect of Huzhou had led his fellow officials out to the suburbs to pray for rain, taking advantage of the excursion to banquet with courtesans. Returning at dusk their boat had overturned, resulting in the deaths of one of the officials and two musician-courtesans (*sheng ji* 聲妓). In response to this incident, the emperor decreed that officials could not abandon their work for drinking parties except on official holidays.[94] A few decades later, in the 1040s, the emperor approved a memorial prohibiting the use of courtesans by officials in the sensitive border areas, evidently for fear that said officials would be distracted from their critical defense responsibilities.[95]

Even so, throughout most of the Northern Song, concerns about the vulgarity or corrupting influence of courtesans remained a minor theme in an otherwise largely positive discourse. Enforcement of government restrictions tended to be halfhearted: involvement with courtesans was seldom prosecuted unless it was part of a pattern of serious malfeasance, and punishments tended to be mild and temporary.[96] A regulation promulgated in 1040 stipulated that even low-level officials who had been penalized for debauchery in the context of courtesan banquets could be reconsidered for office if for ten years they had not committed

---

93. *Cai Xiang ji* 18.331–32.
94. *Chang bian* 71.1603.
95. *SHY, xing fa*, 2.26.
96. Thus Jiang Tang's privatization of a government-courtesan was merely the last straw after he had alienated the populace in his district by raiding a local temple for materials to build a fancy pavilion, and his "punishment" was to be transferred from one prefecture to another (*Chang bian* 153.3725).

another personal crime.⁹⁷ Over the last fifty years of the era, however, this generally sanguine view of courtesans was increasingly challenged. Although there is no evidence that courtesan entertainments decreased in popularity (indeed, perhaps because they had *increased* in popularity), they became the focus of intensified criticism. This development was associated in part with the increasingly bitter factional politics of the era.

## Courtesans in the Politics of the Late Northern Song

As others have amply documented, from the reign of Shenzong 神宗 (r. 1068–85) through the fall of the Northern Song government in 1126, politics became virulently factionalized, and factional conflicts became increasingly lethal.⁹⁸ The factionalism was engendered in large part by the radical government reforms initiated by Shenzong's minister Wang Anshi (1021–86). Wang's policies were highly controversial, but he had the emperor's support, and his critics were ruthlessly silenced.⁹⁹ At Shenzong's death, however, his heir Zhezong 哲宗 (r. 1086–1100) was only a boy of nine; during the first eight years of his reign the government was controlled largely by his grandmother the Empress Dowager Xuanren 宣仁 (1021–93, r. 1086–93). The Empress Dowager was an enemy of Wang Anshi's "New Policies": under her authority, the reforms were rapidly and systematically undone, and the men who had enacted them now found themselves demoted and even exiled in turn. The conservative triumph was short-lived, however, for when Zhezong attained his majority and took over the reins of power, he brought the reformers back to court.

Critical to the rapidly shifting factional politics of this period was that each side was convinced that it had the moral right, that only their policies had the support of Heaven and would bring peace and prosperity to the realm. This attitude led to the extreme moralization of political rhetoric, with factional enemies castigating each other not only as

---

97. *Chang bian* 128.3045.
98. Ari Levine demonstrates the increasingly brutal tactics employed by political factions from the 1070s through the 1090s. See Levine, *Divided by a Common Language*. On factional conflict in Wang Anshi's time in office, see also Smith, "Shen-tsung's Reign."
99. There is a large literature on the politics of this period. For synthetic discussions in English, see Smith, "Shen-tsung's Reign" and Levine, "Che-tsung's Reign."

wrongheaded or incompetent, but as deceitful, corrupt, and depraved.[100] In this context, officials' relationships with courtesans became the focus of intensified scrutiny.

Even in earlier periods, charges of improper relations with courtesans had been a convenient mode of attacking a factional enemy. Popular opinion held that back in 1044, the unfortunate Su Shunqin and his companions had been the victims of a factional attack directed in part at his father-in-law Du Yan 杜衍 (978–1057).[101] Given that revelry with courtesans was so much a part of regular bureaucratic life, and given the ambiguity about the permissible limits of official involvement with courtesans, almost any official could be vulnerable to accusations of inappropriate behavior. Accordingly, during the period of intense factional infighting that marked the reigns of Shenzong and Zhezong, officials accused each other of misbehavior with courtesans with great regularity.[102] Often these charges involved men prominent on one side or the other of the factional conflict. In 1071 an intendant was ordered secretly to investigate charges that Fan Chunren 范純仁 (1027–1101) and others were "repeatedly getting together for banquets and using courtesans until very late at night." In 1076 a whole group of officials was indicted for traveling to Hangzhou and calling in courtesans for a banquet, "as if it were an imperial birthday," and in 1081 another group of officials was similarly charged.[103] In 1084 the attendant censor Zhang Ruxian 張汝賢 (1073 jin shi) accused the Vice Grand Councilor Wang Anli 王安禮 (1034–95)

---

100. Levine, *Divided by a Common Language*, chaps. 5 and 6. As I shall show in later chapters, the other side of this moralizing rhetoric was the depiction of the court as the center of all that was virtuous and auspicious.

101. See *Chang bian* 153.3715–16, where Su Shunqin's political demise is depicted as a factional attack against the Qingli reformers, including Du Yan. Wei Tai offers an alternative explanation, suggesting that Su was exposed by a disgruntled colleague who had been excluded from the party (*Dongxuan bi lu* 4.41).

102. The *Chang bian* records nearly twice as many indictments (nineteen in all) for misbehavior with courtesans during the roughly thirty years of these two reigns than for the preceding one hundred years combined, though admittedly the *Chang bian* provides a much more detailed record of these two reigns than for the first century of the dynasty. A number of other indictments are preserved in the surviving collected works of men who lived through this era, though often those indictments cannot be precisely dated.

103. *Chang bian* 220.5357, 275.6732, 311.7538.

(brother of Wang Anshi) of visiting courtesan houses on a daily basis while he was in office, and of having allowed courtesans to participate in local government when he had served in prefectural posts.[104]

With men on both sides of the factional infighting casting their agenda in terms of moral transformation, inappropriate indulgence with courtesans was no longer merely a social or even a political *faux pas*: it was a personal moral failing that rendered the individual completely unfit to serve in government. As Yao Mian 姚勔 (1059 *jin shi*) exclaimed in his 1093 indictment of Sun Fen 孫賁 (n.d.), "his reputation for debauched behavior reaches the four quarters! How can he take on the responsibility of furthering moral transformation, regulating the people, and correcting customs?"[105]

Not surprisingly, then, this period also saw stricter government regulation of courtesan entertainments. From early in the dynasty, certain types of supervisory officials (most notably judicial commissioners [*ti dian xing yu* 提點刑獄]) had been forbidden to take part in courtesan entertainments except when celebrating imperial birthdays, apparently out of concern that courtesan banquets might provide occasions for bribery or graft. In the 1070s this prohibition was extended to regional inspectors (*jian si shuai* 監司率) and other officials with similar surveillance functions,[106] and in 1078 the restriction was extended to education officials (*xue guan* 學官) as well.[107] In 1089, the penalty for surveillance officials caught breaking these rules was increased: henceforth, such officials were to receive the rather draconian punishment of two years' exile.[108] In 1098, a brand-new rule forbade officials from requisitioning needed items from the local populace, and from overseeing the clothing of courtesans and musicians.[109] Although the indictments leading to these edicts may have been motivated by factional politics, they also

---

104. *Chang bian* 347.8329. Concerns about courtesans' involvement in government were to become a major theme in the Southern Song, as discussed in chap. 4.
105. *Chang bian* 480.11427. On the tendency of both sides of Northern Song factional conflicts to castigate their enemies as morally bankrupt, see Levine, *Divided by a Common Language*.
106. Zhang Shunmin, *Hua man lu*, 216–17.
107. *Chang bian* 287.7015.
108. *Chang bian* 435.10491.
109. *Chang bian* 501.11937.

betray mounting concern about the effects on government administration of the spread of courtesan entertainments.

The stricter government rules also coincided with the appearance of more virulent criticism of courtesan entertainments by officials in and out of court, and increasingly explicit insistence that courtesan banquets were incompatible with moral cultivation. These views are clearly explicated in two rather obscure but striking essays from the period. The earlier of the two was composed in 1071 by one Huang Chang 黄裳 (1044–1130). Huang Chang was later to become a prominent official, but he wrote this essay while still a student, more than a decade before he took top honors in the *jin shi* examination of 1082. The essay commemorates the author's visit to a Reviewing the Ancients Hall (*yue gu tang* 閲古堂).[110] In it, Huang identifies two possible uses for the hall. On the one hand, he says, the hall's solitude can help to purify people's hearts, its loftiness can influence people's substance (*qi* 氣). Thus the hall could be used to help officials make proper judgments, such that they would inspire awe and respect in onlookers. Alternatively, he suggests, one could

> invite elegant guests, line up servants, and have musical instruments playing in the front of the hall and actors' comedies and skits arrayed below the hall. The songs and sounds of instruments would rise and fall, the serving and toasting go back and forth, the talk and laughter be alternately stilled and erupting. One could practice numberless rounds of shooting, pass numberless rounds of drinks. The sober would sing, the drunk would dance—wouldn't it be delightful?

Huang then goes on to complain that, in his day, scholars are unable to make the proper choice between these two, because "what is esteemed is not lofty, thus external things can overcome it; what is cultivated is not firm, thus external things can disrupt it." Elaborating on these points, Huang cites passages from Mencius showing that a true sage has no interest in luxurious feasts and female attendants (because what he esteems is the principles of the ancients), and demonstrating the moral failure of those who do unrighteous things for the sake of owning beautiful houses

---

110. Huang Chang, *Yan shan* ji 17.1–2b. Huang Chang is one of the high-ranking officials (he ultimately held the post of vice grand councilor) of the late Northern Song about whom the surviving historical record says almost nothing. Several Northern Song authors had written on the Reviewing the Ancients Hall, but this essay does not refer to its predecessors in any way.

and supporting large numbers of wives and concubines. After arguing for the urgency of moral study, Huang concludes,

> How, then, should we use this hall? We ought to select the bequeathed books of the sages and the commentaries of the hundred scholars from across the ages, surround ourselves with them and sit among them, investigating the way the ancients did things. If I can do this for one day, this can be extended as a technique of helping the age and aiding the people. A scholar [who can do this] will be able to respond to the changes of the world, a military man will be able to overcome chaos. I am delighted that gentlemen have been able to name this hall; since no one has yet been able to express its ambitions, I have tried to articulate them.

For Huang, wild parties and courtesan entertainments are no longer harmless or even inappropriately crude diversion; rather they are a threat to a man's ability to devote himself to moral cultivation, and men of true moral ambition should eschew them altogether.

Huang's attitude was echoed some decades later by the minor prefectural official Li Xin, in an extraordinary "Discourse on Sun Wu."[111] Li's essay is a reinterpretation of the famous episode recorded in the *Shi ji* (*Records of the Historian*) in which the military tactician Sun Wu 孫武 (Sunzi 孫子) was asked to prove the effectiveness of his methods by demonstrating that he could turn even the king's women into disciplined soldiers. As the story is told in the *Shi ji*, Sun formed a company out of the king's serving maids, with two of the king's favorite concubines as drill commanders. When the women responded to his orders with giggles, Sun summarily executed the two favorites, after which the remaining women became ideal, disciplined troops. In its original context, the Sun Wu story is about the effectiveness of rigorous and impartial military discipline, but Li Xin reinterprets the story to very different effect. Li argues that Sun Wu's real intent was to free the king of his attachment to women, which was clouding the king's ambition:

---

111. *Quan Song wen* (hereafter *QSW*) 134: 2892.103–5. Li Xin's reinterpretation of Sun Wu cannot be precisely dated: he was in and out of office between the 1090s and 1125. I suspect it was written in the 1120s, in response to Emperor Huizong's love of entertainment and refusal to take seriously the military threat at his borders. The fact that Li Xin also memorialized the court during Huizong's reign to request that the use of courtesans in the "Exhorting Agriculture" ceremonies be forbidden (*QSW* 133: 2881.330–31) adds further weight to this possibility.

> Alas, the dangers of women are extreme! If a ruler is somewhat befuddled by them, he will look at his opportunities to carry out affairs and make contributions and decide that today he has no spare time to do so; and when it comes to tomorrow, he will have no time then either. He will say things like, "I labor bitterly and worry anxiously in concern for the people; wouldn't it be better to preserve the old ancient policies of non-action and enjoy my pleasures?" If he is greatly befuddled by them, he will no longer think about [preserving] his body or his responsibilities to his office or the dynasty. If he is slightly befuddled his will (*zhi* 志) will become lazy; if he is greatly befuddled, his will will become disordered. If his will is disordered, defeat and annihilation will follow.

Li points out that Sun was not in a position to say to the king directly, "If you want to use me to help you make a name among the princes, you must first eliminate music and women. I request to execute your two favored concubines and present their heads; only then can you and I accomplish things in the world." Instead, Li argues, Sun pretended to turn the women into soldiers as a means of ridding the king of them. Li Xin goes on to explain why Sun's method was far more effective than mere remonstrance, and then concludes

> Alas, of the petty people at the sides of the ruler, who brings greater disaster than women? If there are men of ambition who want to get rid of the evil of petty people for their sage emperor, I hope you will tell them about Sun Wu's technique of "trying soldiers."[112]

For Li Xin as for Huang Chang, female entertainments threaten not merely to distract men from their duties, but to undermine their moral will and thereby engender "disaster."

There is no reason to think that either of these essays circulated particularly widely in their day: they are interesting not because they were influential, but because they are framed in a conceptual vocabulary similar to that more commonly associated with the moral philosophy of the Cheng brothers (Cheng Hao 程顥 [1032–85] and Cheng Yi 程頤 [1033–1107]). The Cheng brothers are regarded as the founders of Neo-Confucianism and are famous for articulating the view that emotions (*qing* 情) and especially physical desire (*yu* 欲) could undermine the individual's true moral self. Only by "establishing the will" (*li zhi* 立志) and engaging in rigorous self-cultivation could the individual overcome the bodily desires that would otherwise undermine the innate

---

112. *QSW* 134: 2892.103–5.

moral tendencies of his heart-and-mind (*xin* 心). Over the course of the Song, such views eventually came to dominate intellectual life, redefining Confucian morality in the process.[113]

Against this background, the essays of Huang Chang and Li Xin are interesting for two reasons. First, they reveal that ideas in the mode of Cheng Learning were held by men not particularly associated with their philosophical circle.[114] In other words, the moral vocabulary we attribute specifically to the Cheng brothers may have been more widely shared than generally recognized.[115] Second, these essays are striking because they associate the moral dangers of physical desire specifically with female entertainers: in contrast, the Cheng brothers themselves had virtually nothing to say about courtesans or the entertainments they provided.[116] In short, although the Cheng brothers' philosophy was consonant with a view that saw courtesans as morally threatening, they did not originate or even articulate that view—but some of their contemporaries did.

The essays of Huang Chang and Li Xin are also important because, together with the political rhetoric castigating officials for interactions with courtesans, they introduced a newly negative attitude toward the roles of entertainment in official life. This attitude was not widely

---

113. There is an extensive literature on the development of Neo-Confucianism. For work in English on Northern Song developments, see Bol, *"This Culture of Ours"*; cf. also Egan, *Word, Image, and Deed*, 93–97.

114. Neither Huang nor Li was recognized as a Cheng disciple; Huang seems to have been known more for Daoist than for Neo-Confucian proclivities. And although Li Xin was cashiered as a member of the so-called "Yuan-you faction," as were many Cheng brothers adherents, he is more closely associated with Su Shi than with the Chengs. Still, not only these essays but the collected works of both men employ philosophical concepts and vocabulary reminiscent of the Chengs.

115. Here these essays add to the evidence, recently adduced in an important article by Li Cho-ying and Charles Hartman, that the Cheng brothers and their followers did not have a monopoly on moralistic rhetoric in the late Northern and early Southern Song periods. See Li Cho-ying and Hartman, "A Newly Discovered Inscription."

116. The only evidence of the Cheng brothers' attitudes toward courtesans that I have been able to find is a comment, attributed to Cheng Yi by the Ming writer Huang Zongxi, in which the master castigates a disciple for engaging in a relationship with a courtesan. Even then, the comment suggests that Cheng Yi's concern was not sexual desire per se but status hierarchy: Cheng Yi objected to the fact that the disciple was pairing himself with a "degraded entertainer" (Huang Zongxi, *Song Yuan xue an* 32.1131–32). Cf. Bossler, "Shifting Identities," 33–34.

shared: some men even explicitly protested against it, arguing that condemnations of courtesan entertainments were often self-righteous and hypocritical. Wei Tai 魏泰 (fl. ca. 1070–1110) described the case of a top-ranked examination graduate during the tenure of Wang Anshi who, in the name of improving customs, had sanctimoniously called for an end to the courtesan entertainments with which new degree-holders were traditionally feted. Impressed, the powers at court rewarded the graduate with a plum appointment, only to see him convicted shortly thereafter on charges of examination fraud. In their anxiety to "improve customs," Wei grumbled, the administrators of the reform period had led men to do all sorts of unprincipled things.[117] Wu Chuhou 吳處厚 (1053 *jin shi*), writing in 1087, railed against the contemporary tendency to assume that any man who wrote on romantic topics was necessarily evil, and that those who wrote of "benevolence, righteousness, and morality" were necessarily morally upright. Wu argued strenuously against this view, and to demonstrate his point he proceeded to cite romantic verses by honorable officials of earlier eras, including such paragons of virtue as Han Qi and Sima Guang.[118]

Other evidence likewise shows that the views of moralistic conservatives had little influence on actual practice in the late eleventh century. In spite of stricter government rules, punishments for improper behavior with courtesans remained mild: the court responded to Yao Mian's indictment of Sun Fen's "debauched behavior" merely by changing Sun's assignment as prefect of Xingzhou to the somewhat less desirable post as prefect of Huaiyang commandery.[119] And even the men who made the new rules were not above changing them: contemporaries complained that the reformer Lü Wenqing 呂溫卿 (fl. 1070) requested (and obtained) a special dispensation to hold a courtesan banquet when he was about to be transferred to a new post, in spite of the fact that he himself had earlier requested that such banquets be prohibited.[120]

---

117. Wei Tai, *Dong xuan bi lu* 6.68–69.
118. Wu Chuhou, *Qing xiang za ji* 8.81–83. Note that the latter part of the passage in this edition of the text incorporates material that must be a later addition, as it cites Southern Song texts like the *Tiao xi yu yin*. The *Si ku* version of the text contains only the first half of the passage.
119. *Chang bian* 480.11427.
120. *Chang bian* 498.11853.

Moreover, with the accession of Huizong courtesan entertainment flourished as never before.

## Courtesans at the End of the Northern Song

Huizong was renowned for his love of all the arts, music and theater not least among them.[121] The emperor's spectacular banquets were commemorated in poetry and his infatuations with courtesans became grist for the mill of later anecdotes and popular literature.[122] Whether or not this state of affairs was the inspiration for Li Xin's essay (which in any case Huizong almost certainly never saw), the emperor was unreceptive, even hostile, to those who suggested that courtesan entertainments should be curtailed in the name of morality. This is evident in his almost petulant response, in 1119, to a group of officials who urged him to limit participation at courtesan banquets in the prefectures to only the two most senior prefectural officials. Much to the disappointment of the petitioners, the emperor flatly refused their request, commenting,

> When prefectural and county officials are resting from their official duties, to eat and drink and have banquets with music is not a great crime. If they become tipsy beyond measure and as a consequence neglect their duties, then they will lose their employment. If harm occurs the details can be memorialized by the officials.[123]

In other words, Huizong saw nothing wrong with courtesan entertainments per se, and felt that existing bureaucratic procedures were sufficient to deal with cases in which drunken officials behaved inappropriately. Far more important, however, was that Huizong's pronouncement for the first time recognized—and explicitly legitimized—the use of courtesan banquets by *county* as well as prefectural officials. In doing so, Huizong may simply have been acknowledging an existing state of

---

121. See Idema and West, *Chinese Theater*, 29, on Huizong's fondness for entertainment.
122. Wang Anzhong wrote an extended poem describing one of Huizong's banquets, the preface to which was cited above (*Chu liao ji* 1.6–11). Huizong's putative affair with the courtesan Li Shishi was described in literati anecdotes beginning in the thirteenth century (see Zhang Duanyi, *Gui er ji, xia*, 6a, for what appears to be the earliest surviving reference) but was more widely circulated in the Yuan *hua ben* 話本 story *Xuanhe yi shi* 宣和逸事.
123. *SHY, xing fa,* 2.75b. The source does not identify the officials who made this request.

affairs; still, his edict represented not only a blunt repudiation of his officials' request, but a major departure from the government's policy up to that point.

Huizong's edict attests to the fact—and itself helped to insure—that at the end of the Northern Song the institution of courtesan entertainments remained central to bureaucratic life at all levels.[124] As late as 1126, in the face of imminent invasion, court officials accused the erstwhile Vice Grand Councilor Cai Mao 蔡懋 (n.d.) of ignoring the grave political crises of the day, instead amusing himself in daily banquets with courtesans, creating elaborate costumes for the performers, and getting drunk with actors and musicians.[125]

## *Conclusion*

Over the course of the Northern Song, courtesans became a central feature of literati life. The government underwrote their presence at court and in the prefectures, ensuring not only that officials would have frequent interaction with them, but that they would become symbols of official power and prestige. Inextricably linked with the elegance of official life, courtesans were central figures in the development of romantic poetry and helped to create a model for elite male behavior that valorized passion and sentiment. Fueled by ever-growing demand, markets in women provided independent courtesans to entertain those not eligible for the services of government-courtesans, creating flourishing urban entertainment districts.

By the late Northern Song, the influence of entertainers in society and government was profound enough to engender increased government regulation and, more importantly, occasional diatribes about the moral implications of their presence in literati lives. Yet, although administrators made minor moves to curb excesses, negative views of courtesans remained marginal. In fact, under the indulgent eyes of a bon vivant emperor, in the late Northern Song courtesan entertainments were extended to even lower levels of the bureaucracy: they remained

---

124. Anecdotal sources corroborate the presence of courtesans at the county level at the end of the Northern Song. See He Wei, *Chun zhu ji wen* 4.54.
125. *Chang bian* 352.8438.

a defining characteristic of official life until the fall of the capital. Moreover, the ubiquity and importance of female entertainment in the social life of elite males was not confined to the public sphere. For even as government rules and social disapprobation discouraged men from letting their relationships with public courtesans become too personal or intimate, in the inner quarters of literati households a new fashion for entertainer-concubines was taking hold.

# 2

## *The Courtesan as Concubine*

### Wang Zhaoyun 王朝雲

Master East Slope's attendant-concubine was called Morning Cloud (Zhaoyun); her cognomen was Zixia, her surname Wang. She was a person of Qiantang. She was clever and loved righteousness. She served the master for twenty-three years, always loyal and respectful as at the first. In the third year of Shaosheng (1096), on the *ren zhen* day of the seventh month, she died in Huizhou, at the age of thirty-three. On the *geng shen* day of the eighth month, she was interred in the southeast of the temple on Qichan Mountain. She bore a son named Dun, who died in his first year. She once studied Buddhist doctrine with the nun Yizhong, and she roughly understood the essential meaning. At her death, she recited the four-sentence gatha of the Diamond sutra as she expired. The inscription reads: "The Buddha is to be gazed upon, Sangharama is to be relied upon; as with your original mind, this is only a return to the Buddha."[1]

In this short encomium, Su Shi memorialized the young woman who had been the love of his life. His account, not untypical for the genre, tells us very little about her, beyond the already notable fact that he chose to honor her (and dignify their relationship) by composing a formal funerary inscription for her in the first place. Largely because of Su Shi's later fame as one of the preeminent writers of the Northern Song, his relationship with Morning Cloud is better documented than most concubine-master relationships, and I shall return to it below. The relationship is also significant, however, in that Morning Cloud and others like her represented a new model of entertainer-concubines in elite households of the Northern Song.

This chapter traces the proliferation of concubines, and especially entertainer-concubines, in Song society—a proliferation that paralleled

---

1. *Su Shi wen ji* 15.473–74 ("Zhaoyun mu zhi ming" 朝雲墓誌銘).

the expanding presence of courtesans outside the home. Like the spread of courtesans, the expansion of concubinage was related to the secular trends of population growth, commercialization, and urbanization that began in the late Tang and continued into the Northern Song. It was also a function of innovations in government recruitment, most notably the expansion of the examination system in the late tenth century, which, along with Northern Song economic growth, helped undermine long-standing social hierarchies. Among the elite, distinctions between families of office-holding status and those who were merely wealthy blurred, as new educational opportunities made it possible for the "newly risen" to participate in the examination system and enter office. Within the lower echelons of society, distinctions between "respectable" and "base" were becoming obscured as new labor markets drew "respectable" commoners into short-term indentured servitude, with the expectation that they would return to "respectable" status when the term of the contract was up.[2]

These shifting social contexts changed not only the extent of concubinage but the functions and social perceptions thereof. New wealth meant that increasing numbers of men could afford concubines, and sumptuary restrictions that had once limited concubinage to the households of high officials were abandoned. New labor markets meant that women were readily available to fill the increased demand for concubinage, even as the breakdown of social status distinctions helped blur, though not entirely eradicate, the boundaries among slaves, servants, and concubines. The fashion for entertainment and romance that had made the courtesan quarters a center of elite social life was imported into elite households, such that concubines became a vehicle for expression of male friendship, the objects of long-term love affairs—and sometimes the mothers of literati sons. As the spread of concubinage and the changing roles of concubines created new dynamics in elite households, concern about those dynamics ultimately made concubinage a focus of

---

2. On this phenomenon, see Guo Dongxu, *Song dai fa zhi yan jiu*, 407–9; Yanagida Setsuko, "Song dai de gu yong ren he nubi," 8–9. Guo shows that Song labor contracts began to replace the terms "bondman" and "bondmaid" (nubi 奴婢) with more neutral terms like "laborer" (*ren li* 人力) and "maidservant" (女使). Yanagida, pointing out that some laborers were not freed at the end of their contracts, argues that in practice a class of permanently indentured persons persisted into the Song.

political debate. The expansion of printing in the Song period meant the survival of sources that let us see these developments in some detail.³

## A Brief History of Concubinage in China

In order to see how concubinage was changing in the Northern Song, it will be useful briefly to review how concubinage functioned in Chinese society prior to that time. Polygyny seems to have been a feature of the Chinese family system from earliest times, though many details of the early marriage system remain obscure. In classical times, brides in the highest-ranking families were often accompanied by nieces or younger sisters, designated as *ying* 媵, who served as secondary wives and at least sometimes succeeded to the position of wife when the first wife died.⁴ This custom of "accompanying in marriage" died out long before the Han dynasty (206 BCE–220 CE), but the term "ying" continued to be used to refer to women other than the main wife who had an intimate relationship with the master. In contrast, the word *qie* 妾 in its earliest formulation had had the sense of a woman who had been enslaved for having committed a crime,⁵ but by Han times this word, too, had come to mean something approaching our conventional understanding of the word "concubine," as reflected in the compound term *ying qie* 媵妾. Still, the term's initial meaning of "servant" or "slave" was not entirely abandoned; as late as the Song, in popular usage the word *qie* often referred to serving women in general, without necessarily implying a

---

3. As will become apparent over the course of this chapter and chap. 4, the sources on concubines reflect the broader biases in surviving sources from the Northern and Southern Song periods. That is, information on the Northern Song tends to be limited to the families of the high-ranking political elite, while information on the Southern Song tends to focus on families of lesser (though still elite) status. See Bossler, *Powerful Relations*, 10–34.

4. See Kinney, *Representations of Childhood*, 121. As Kinney explains, the pre-Han marriage system was dominated by the need to establish political alliances between the rulers of petty states. Once the empire had been unified under the Qin (221–206 BCE), this system fell into disuse. My own very limited reading of classical texts has not convinced me that *ying*, as women accompanying the bride, were automatically expected to serve as secondary consorts in classical times, though the term was certainly understood that way in later eras.

5. Wang Shaoxi, *Xiao qie shi*, 1.

consort relationship with the master.⁶ This ambiguity of usage is important: it reflects the underlying social reality that the distinctions between "concubines" as consorts of the master and other servile women in the household were extremely fluid.⁷ The ambiguity was also expressed in the compound term *bi qie* 婢妾 (slaves/bondmaids and concubines), used from Han times on, and very commonly in the Song, to refer collectively to the various subordinate women in a man's household. As this discussion may already suggest, by no later than Han times, the status of the wife was recognized as distinct from, and superior to, that of all other consorts. The Han ritualist Cai Yong 蔡邕 (fl. 170) observed,

> Only one of those married can be called a wife (*qi* 妻). The rest are all concubines (*qie*). Their status is far inferior, thus they cannot be called wife.⁸

There is some evidence that in Han times concubinage was limited to men of high official rank, as, if the ritual texts can be believed, it had been in classical times. Cai Yong first describes the various ranks of women in the imperial harem and then goes on to explain that imperial marquises (*zhu hou* 諸侯) could have a total of nine consorts ("one wife and eight concubines [*qie*]"); ministers (*qing dai fu* 卿大夫) could have one wife and two concubines; and servicemen (*shi* 士) could have one wife and one concubine. (Cai does not mention commoners here, though elsewhere he suggests that commoners had one wife [*qi* 妻], period.)⁹ Anne Kinney likewise observes that recently excavated Han legal texts show that the

---

6. Examples of the more generalized use of the term *qie* in Song times include *Su Shi wen ji* 15.473, where Su Shi refers to his "mother's concubine," and in a legal text where a woman is referred to as the *qie* of the man in whose household she works, despite the fact that she is married to someone else (*QMJ* 12.441). Patricia Ebrey has noted that Song concubines seemed more like servants or slaves than did their successors in later imperial times. See Ebrey, "Concubines in Song China," 1–24.

7. Maria Jaschok and Rubie Watson both suggest that this fluidity continued to be a common feature of concubinage even into the nineteenth and twentieth centuries (Jaschok, *Concubines and Bondservants*, 76; Watson, "Wives, Concubines, and Maids" 241–46).

8. Cai Yong, *Cai zhong lang ji* 3.17b. Liu Zenggui argues that distinctions between wives and concubines were more strictly observed as the Han wore on (*Shi lun Han dai hun yin guan xi*, 12).

9. Cai Yong, *Cai zhong lang ji* 1.9.

"allowable number of concubines depended on a man's aristocratic status." Still, Kinney also cites contemporary complaints that wealthy men and officials "kept scores of women in their households," suggesting that, even in the Han, laws tying numbers of consorts to political status were honored largely in the breach.[10] And certainly by the Six Dynasties period (220–589), large numbers of serving women were a standard feature in the households of aristocrats, regardless of official rank.[11]

To be sure, not all the women in these households were what we now think of as concubines. As Kinney has shown, the Han court, especially from the reign of Han Wudi on, was filled with female slaves. These were women and girls who had been reduced to slave status as prisoners of war, through the crimes of their parents, or through outright sale. Imperial consorts were frequently drawn from the ranks of these slaves, and a few slaves even ended up as empresses.[12] In other words, Cai Yong's injunctions notwithstanding, in Han times there appears to have been no juridical or social proscription against raising a slave to the position of concubine or even wife (for empresses were the official wives of emperors), at least in the imperial family.

With the collapse of the Han dynasty and the shift to quasi-aristocratic social values under the Six Dynasties, however, the importance of maintaining distinctions between the main wife and concubines was reiterated. In an edict of 274, the first emperor of the Western Jin dynasty (265–420) decreed:

> The distinctions between principal and lesser [wives] (*di shu zhi bie* 嫡庶之別) are what separate superior and inferior and clarify noble and base. But in recent eras it has been common to raise private favorites to the position of empress and imperial consort, muddling the precedence of honorable and ignoble. From this point on, it is forbidden to raise concubines (*qie ying*) to serve as the principal legitimate [wife].[13]

---

10. Kinney, *Representations of Childhood*, 345, nn. 72, 129.
11. Liu Zenggui, "Wei, Jin, Nan bei chao shi dai di qie," 62–64.
12. To cite one of the more famous examples, Wei Zifu, a slave girl in the court of an imperial princess, caught the eye of the princess's brother, Emperor Han Wudi. The princess gave the girl to her brother, and she became an imperial concubine. Ultimately, after bearing a son, she was named empress. See Kinney, *Representations of Childhood*, 120–25.
13. Fang Xuanling, *Jin shu* 3.63; Liu Zenggui, "Wei, Jin, Nan bei chao shi dai di qie," 75–76.

This edict upheld the critical distinction between wives and concubines, but it did not address the distinction between concubines and other servile women. Some women, especially those of some family standing, were clearly brought into the household expressly to serve as secondary consorts. The *Shi shuo xin yu*, a Six Dynasties collection of anecdotes about famous people, describes how the official Zhou Jun (ca. 250–ca. 300) took refuge from the rain at the home of a wealthy man and happened to spy his host's daughter, Luoxiu, who was quite beautiful. Zhou sought her as a concubine, and although her father and brothers were initially reluctant, she convinced them that an alliance with such a noble household would be advantageous, urging them not to "begrudge a lone daughter." She accordingly became a concubine in the Zhou household, and ultimately bore three sons.[14]

Presumably, women taken in explicitly as consorts, with some sort of marriage ritual, had more status in the household than those merely raised out of slavery.[15] There is, however, some evidence of a procedure for formally recognizing a "promotion" from slave to concubine status. An oft-cited passage from the biography of Gao Cong 高聰 (452–520) remarks that Gao kept more than ten female entertainers (*ji* 妓), and adds that "whether they had borne children or not, all were registered as concubines (有子,無子,皆注籍爲妾)." Although the nature of this "registration" is not specified, it appears to imply household registration with the government, which suggests that clear (though not unbridgeable) status distinctions separated entertainers and other slave women from concubines. This passage also implies that elevation to concubine status was typically reserved to servile women who had borne children.[16] At

---

14. Liu Yiqing, *Shi shuo xin yu* 5.179 (*xian yuan* 19, no. 18). For an English translation, see Mather, *A New Account* 350, no. 18.

15. Liu Zenggui, "*Wei, Jin, Nan bei chao shi dai di qie*," 69–70. Throughout Chinese history, ritual was a critical marker of the distinction between wives and concubines. For a Six Dynasties example, see the *Shi shuo xin yu* anecdote in which, because the groom did not return the bride's bow during the wedding ceremony, his son by a previous wife refused to acknowledge the legitimacy of the marriage, constantly humiliating the new wife by referring to her as "concubine" (*qie*) (Liu Yiqing, *Shi shuo xin yu* 6.237 (*you hui* 33, no. 2; Mather, 471, no. 2).

16. See e.g., Wei Shou, *Wei shu* 68.1523. Cf. Liu Zenggui, *Wei, Jin, Nan bei chao shi dai di qie*, 67; Liao Meiyun, *Tang ji*, 32; Yao Ping, "The Status of Pleasure," 33. At the same time, a woman who had borne children did not necessarily become a concubine:

the same time, the passage also points to the fact that women brought into the household as entertainers were especially likely to attract the master's attentions. This is hardly surprising: girls trained as entertainers were often chosen for their beauty to begin with, and in their roles as singers and dancers they were both rendered highly visible and displayed to particular advantage. The custom of keeping large troupes of such entertainers in elite households seems to have become especially popular in the Six Dynasties period, with some men maintaining dozens of such women.[17] Indeed, it appears that the term *ji*—the same term that in the late Tang and the Song indicated public courtesans—in the Six Dynasties period was used exclusively for entertainers who were household dependents.[18] The slippage is evident in the work of later poets, who frequently evoked the pleasures of outings with courtesans by alluding to the Six Dynasties aristocrat Xie An 謝安 (320–85), whose "eastern mountain wanderings" with the entertainers kept in his household had become proverbial.[19]

With the restoration of long-term political stability under the Tang dynasty, the excesses of the Six Dynasties aristocrats seem to have gone out of fashion, at least temporarily. Although there is every reason to assume that men continued to take concubines both formally and informally, relatively little evidence of their relationships with their concubines

---

Ruan Xian (234–305), a nephew of the famous poet Ruan Ji (210–63), "favored" a Xianbei slave girl belonging to his aunt. The slave girl ultimately gave birth to his eldest son Ruan Fu, but Xian continued to refer to her as a slave (Liu Yiqing, *Shi shuo xin yu* 5.190–91 (*ren dan* 23, no. 15; Mather 376, no. 15). Maria Jaschok suggests that in the later imperial period the consent of the legal wife, "expressed in a ritual act of welcome," was necessary before a new woman entering the household could be recognized as a concubine. I have found no evidence that such a convention existed in the Song. See Jaschok, *Concubines and Bondservants*, 95.

17. Liu Zenggui, *Wei, Jin, Nan bei chao shi dai di qie*, 67.

18. In this period, the term *chang* 娼 was used for entertainers whose services were for public sale. See Bossler, "Vocabularies of Pleasure."

19. The locus classicus for Xie An "wandering freely hand in hand" (*yong chi you si* 攜持游肆) with entertainers is Liu Yiqing, *Shi shuo xin yu* 3.106 (*shi jian* 7, no. 21; Mather, 207, no. 21), and the related commentary. Later writers tended not to distinguish between Xie An's entertainer-concubines and the public courtesans of their own day. In Xie An's day, all entertainers known as *ji* 妓 were found in households. See Bossler, "Vocabularies of Pleasure," passim.

survives before the latter half of the eighth century.[20] The survival of the Tang legal code, however, does permit us to see for the first time some of the legal parameters of concubinage—parameters that were later incorporated wholesale into Song law.[21]

The Tang code's discussion of concubinage strongly reiterates the principle that, at any point in time, a man could have only one wife (though a man whose wife had died could take a second, successor wife). Moreover, the law decreed strict punishments for a man who raised a concubine or bondmaid to the status of wife, or who reduced a wife to the status of concubine.[22] A wife was to be "taken in with ritual" (*li qu* 禮取),[23] and her marriage created carefully specified and reciprocal mourning obligations to her husband and his family. In contrast, a concubine was purchased: her position was juridically inferior to that of the wife, and a man with a concubine but no legal wife was regarded as "unmarried."[24] Thus, although the law described concubines themselves as "married," the marriage of a concubine did not create a reciprocal relationship. Tang sumptuary regulations further specified the numbers and types of concubines that men could have in accordance with their official rank: princes and rank one officials were allowed ten high-ranking concubines (*ying*); rank two officials could have eight; rank three officials six; rank four, four; and rank five, three. Officials of rank six and below did not have *ying*, but only regular concubines (*qie*).[25] Lower-ranked officials were

---

20. On late Tang literati-concubine relationships see Wong, "Tōdai," 131–59; Yao Ping, *Tang dai fu nü*, 134–72.

21. It is quite possible that similar laws existed well before the Tang, but there are no records of them. For discussion of these laws in the Song context see Ebrey, "Concubines in Song China," 5–7; *Inner Quarters*, 218.

22. Zhangsun Wuji, *Tang lü shu yi* 13.16–18; Wong, "Tōdai," 145. Only if a wife died or was divorced could a man take a second legal (successor) wife. In earlier periods in Chinese history, it had sometimes been possible for a man to have more than one legal wife, as well as concubines (Wang Shaoxi, *Xiao qie shi*, 21). We will see in later chapters that Song Chinese were also aware that steppe societies permitted men to have more than one legal wife.

23. Wong, "Tōdai," 147, notes that late Tang funerary inscriptions use this term to distinguish between women married as wives and those taken in as concubines.

24. Zhangsun Wuji et. al., *Tang lü shu yi* 13.16b; Wong, "Tōdai," 132.

25. Liu Xu, *Jiu Tang shu* 43.1821–22; Katkov, "The Domestication of Concubinage," 178–79.

presumably expected to abide by the "one wife, one concubine" (*yi qi yi qie* 一妻一妾) standard that had been set in the classical period, though the regulations do not say this explicitly.

The code went on to clarify the distinction between concubines and slaves or bondmaids. Because concubines were in some senses regarded as married, they were expected to be of juridically respectable (*liang ren* 良人) status. Slaves and bondmaids were by definition of base (*jian*) status and thus "not of the type to be a partner" (*fei chou lei* 非儔類).[26] At the same time, however, the law acknowledged both a man's right to sexual access to the servile women in his household, and the importance of the production of descendants in the Chinese family system, by adding this critical qualification: "If the bondmaid has a child and has already been manumitted, it is permitted for her to be a concubine." The commentary on this passage goes further, explaining that "if a bondmaid is favored by the master and thus has a child, or even if there is no child but she has been manumitted to respectable (*liang ren*) status, she may be a concubine."[27] In other words, although the law was adamant that neither a bondmaid nor a concubine could be raised to the status of legal wife, and asserted a juridical distinction between bondmaids and concubines, it left the actual determination of bondmaid or concubine status up to the whim of the husband/master: if a man chose to make a bondmaid with whom he had been intimate into his concubine, and to recognize her children as legitimate, he was perfectly free (though, significantly, not obligated) to do so.

Recent work on late Tang concubines has shown that, within this legal context, a wide variety of concubinage was practiced. Women of genteel background might be taken in as concubines but accorded face-saving marriage rituals, while others were raised to the status of concubine from positions as lowly bondmaids.[28] Men who had not yet married, or who

---

26. Zhangsun Wuji et. al., *Tang lü shu yi* 13.16b. Cf. *Song xing tong*, 12.10b. The law strictly forbade intermarriage between people of respectable and base statuses (cf. Wong, "Tōdai," 145). In the rhetoric of the law, the status categories of "respectable" and "base" were primarily hereditary, although a respectable commoner could be reduced to base status as punishment for a crime.

27. Zhangsun Wuji et. al., *Tang lü shu yi* 13.17b; *Song xing tong* 13.15. See also *Song xing tong*, 12.10b.

28. Wong, "Tōdai," 141; Yao Ping, *Tang dai fu nü*, 154.

could not afford a formal marriage to a woman of their own class, could nevertheless have families, with concubines bearing numerous children for them.[29] Concubines could have very tenuous relationships with their husbands/masters, for unlike wives, they could be expelled on a whim, and the concubines of unmarried men seem to have been expected to leave when a wife entered the household. On the other hand, in the absence of a main wife, a concubine could take on virtually all the responsibilities expected of a wife, and might enjoy wife-like status. In some instances, legal niceties notwithstanding, concubines even became de facto wives.[30]

Perhaps the most striking aspect of concubinage in the late Tang, however, was the proliferation of female entertainers in literati households, and especially their assimilation as quasi-concubines. It appears that, in the early Tang, relatively few men kept female entertainers. Indeed, an edict of 706 decreed that only officials of rank three and above were permitted maintain a troupe (*bu* 部) of female musicians (*nü yue* 女樂), while officials between ranks five and three could keep no more than three individuals; men of lower ranks were presumably not allowed to keep any.[31]

This situation changed dramatically in the mid- to late Tang, beginning with the reign of Emperor Xuanzong. As noted in chapter 1, Xuanzong was famously fascinated by musical entertainments and developed new court institutions to train musicians, especially female musicians, in popular music. Ever the populist, Xuanzong also loosened the legal strictures on maintaining female musicians at home, decreeing in 751 that officials above rank five, as well as high-ranking circuit officials, could keep musicians in their households without restriction on number.[32] Xuanzong himself may have been responding to the larger

---

29. Wong, "Tōdai," 136–37; Yao Ping, *Tang dai fu nü*, 134–43. This phenomenon may have been particularly common in the Tang—I am aware of only one Song case of an unmarried man having children with a concubine.

30. Wong, "Tōdai," 146–47, 148–49.

31. Liao Meiyun, *Tang ji*, 59; Song Dexi, "Tang dai," 73. The term *bu* classically denoted a group of ten individuals. This edict seems to reflect government concern about growing interest in maintaining troupes of musicians, especially since the same edict also forbids "licentious music." See Wang Pu, *Tang hui yao* 34.9b.

32. Wang Pu, *Tang hui yao* 34.9b.

secular changes of the period, especially the spread of popular entertainments in the capital and regional cities. In any event, by the last century or so of Tang rule, the keeping of what now began to be called "household-entertainers" or "household-courtesans" (*jia ji* 家妓) had become common not only among those who occupied the very highest reaches of the bureaucracy, but among aspiring scholars and literati more generally.[33]

In practice, of course, in earlier eras virtually all entertainers who served high officials had been in effect "household-courtesans"—that is, they were entertainers maintained as dependents in the private households of the elite. They were not necessarily intimate with their master, though of course he could choose to "favor" any of them. Yet until the late Tang, such women were called simply *ji*. It was apparently only in the late Tang, when commercial entertainment had become broadly available to the public in urban teahouses, that entertainers who were kept in a man's household needed to be distinguished from those who plied their trade publicly.[34]

In the late eighth and early ninth centuries, women called household-courtesans graced the homes of men like the scholar Han Yu 韓愈 (768–824; known best for his opposition to Buddhism and advocacy of a return to Confucian government), who had two, and the famed poet Bai Juyi 白居易 (772–846), who is known to have had at least six.[35] In late Tang and Song sources, a household-courtesan was generally understood to be an entertainer kept in a man's home with whom he enjoyed a romantic and erotic attachment.[36]

The popularity of household-courtesans in late Tang culture is amply reflected in the literary works of the period. Although early Tang authors had written about watching courtesans at banquets, or taking courtesans on outings reminiscent of Xie An, in the late Tang we begin to see men writing about their own interactions with household-courtesans, and especially about relationships between their friends and the female entertainers

---

33. Song Dexi, "Tang dai," 78; Liao Meiyun, *Tang ji*, 161–62; Yao Ping, "The Status of Pleasure," 30.
34. For fuller discussion, see Bossler, "Vocabularies of Pleasure."
35. Liao Meiyun, *Tang ji*, 162.
36. The term "household-courtesan" went out of fashion in the Ming. Although the term *jia ji* occasionally appears in Ming and Qing texts, it is almost always in the contexts of discussions of Tang or Song societies.

they had acquired.³⁷ Thus Liu Zongyuan 柳宗元 (773–819) wrote a mourning poem for the niece of one of his own household-courtesans and a funerary inscription for a singer who had become an "outside wife" (*wai fu* 外婦) of one of his friends.³⁸ Shen Yazhi composed a poem about a courtesan "praying for skill" to the Weaving Maid on "Seventh Night," written at the request of the courtesan's "husband" (其夫). He also wrote an essay in praise of a woman who, taken into his friend's household as a musician, encouraged her master to give up drinking and devote himself to his studies. Finally, Shen wrote a funerary inscription for a dancer (and mother of two children) who appears to have been his own entertainer-concubine.³⁹

As these examples suggest, by the late Tang many elite men were keeping female entertainers in their households, and status distinctions that had designated such women as juridically base chattel were beginning to erode.⁴⁰ An anecdote preserved by a Northern Song compiler nicely reveals both continued awareness of the legal distinction and the way in which that distinction could be obviated in practice. The anecdote concerns the punctilious official Liu Gongchuo 柳公綽 (765–832), who once took a "charmer" (*ji* 姬) into his household. When his colleagues heard of it, someone requested that he bring out his "courtesan" (*ji* 妓) to show his friends. Liu responded by insisting, "Gentlemen may have one wife and one concubine (*qie*) to do the cooking and cleaning; I bought a concubine, not a courtesan (*ji*)."⁴¹

---

37. On this development, see Zheng Zhimin, *Xi shuo Tang ji*, 103–35.
38. Liu Zongyuan, *Liu Hedong ji* 13.19b; *wai ji, shang*, 12b.
39. Shen Yazhi, *Shen xia xian ji* 2.4b–5, 11.9b–10, 11.10b–11. For further examples of literati writing for household-courtesans, see Yao Ping, "The Status of Pleasure." Wong Yu-Hsuan argues that in the late Tang many women taken in as concubines had musical skills, as expressed in the common use of the term *ji qie* 妓妾 ("Tōdai," 145). That term had also been used in the Six Dynasties period (see Liu Zenggui, *Wei, Jin, Nan bei chao shi dai di qie*, 67), but in that earlier period the term seems to be used more to mean "entertainers and concubines" than "entertainer-concubine."
40. Wong points out that in the late Tang distinctions between *liang* and *jian* were not strictly enforced ("Tōdai," 145). Likewise, Kishibe asserts (without, however, presenting evidence) that in the late Tang household-courtesans were "neither bondmaids nor concubines" ("婢でもなく妾でもない") and were neither officially base nor officially respectable. (See *Jukkyō shakai*, 214.)
41. Wang Dang, *Tang yu lin* 3.203; cf. Yao Ping, "The Status of Pleasure," 33, and Liao Meiyun, *Tang ji*, 165. I follow Liao's reading of the anecdote.

Even before the founding of the Song dynasty, then, "concubinage" had become a complex institution that could encompass women of widely varying statuses. The complexity was to continue and even increase during the Song.

## Parameters of Concubinage in the Northern Song

In spite of the realities of economic growth and social change that continued from the late Tang into the Song, early Song law preserved Tang stipulations that only women of respectable (*liang*) status could be taken as concubines. Of course, we have seen that to a large degree such distinctions were always somewhat moot, given the legal sleight of hand that allowed "favored" bondmaids to be raised to respectable status. Long before the Song, that rule had ensured that the actual position or role of any woman, other than the legal wife, serving in the household depended primarily on the nature of her personal relationship to her master.[42] But by Northern Song times the distinctions between respectable and base status among serving women were becoming even more fluid. This was especially the case because, in the Song, women who were household chattel were increasingly not slaves but indentured servants, almost always of respectable background. Their juridically inferior status was thus temporary: it could end when their indenture was up and they left their masters' families (as many did), or when they gave birth to children or were otherwise officially recognized as concubines. In short, although the Song government recognized a juridical difference between maids and concubines, those differences did not reflect hereditary, ascriptive status as they had in earlier eras. And notably, when speaking in general terms, Song people tended to treat maids and concubines (*bi qie* 婢妾) as a single category of person, erasing the juridical differences between them altogether. As a result, even more than before, the status of non-wives in Song families was determined by their functional roles and personal relationships—relationships that could change over time.[43] Moreover, those functional roles could be exceedingly diverse,

---

42. Rubie Watson and Maria Jaschok have both made this point with respect to concubines in the nineteenth and twentieth centuries. See Watson, "Wives, Concubines, and Maids," 241–42; Jaschok, *Concubines and Bondservants*, 76.

43. Takahashi Yoshiro argues that the Song was distinct from both earlier and later

as evident, first of all, in the plethora of complex terminology used in Northern Song sources to designate non-wives.

A few common terms, such as those for high-ranking concubines (*qie ying, ying qie* 媵妾, and *qie yu* 妾御), simply reproduce the language of classical ritual texts, and thus tell us little about the nature of concubinage in the Song. But other terms reflect the continuum of statuses that concubines could occupy, ranging from servant (*bi qie* 婢妾, *pu qie* 僕妾, and *qie ni* 妾妮, all implying bondservant status); to entertainer (*ji qie* 妓妾 "entertainer-concubine"); to intimate companion (*shi qie* 侍妾 or *qie shi* 妾侍, both meaning "attendant-concubine," *ji qie* 姬妾, "charmer-concubine," and *bi qie* 嬖妾, "favored concubine").[44] Some of these terms seem deliberately designed to erase respectable/base distinctions by replacing designators of base status with more attractive homophones (for example, *bi qie* 嬖妾, "favored concubine" for *bi qie* 婢妾, "bondmaid concubine"; *jia ji* 家姬, "household-charmer" for *jia ji* 家妓, "household-courtesan").

Northern Song authors also employed a number of terms that did not contain the character *qie* but were used interchangeably with terms that did. Concubines who gave birth to children were often politely referred to by the metonymic *ce shi* 側室 (side chamber).[45] This term highlighted the fact that, in bearing children, a concubine was similar to a wife (as wives were also referred to as "chambers" [*shi* 室]). From the perspective

---

eras in not having a juridically enforced system of private slavery. Government slaves still existed (including but not limited to the women who were registered as government-courtesans), but in contrast to earlier practice such slaves were not distributed to private individuals, but rather remained attached to government offices. People who were indentured to private individuals might be treated as slaves during the period of their indenture, but were not regarded as having permanent slave status. Takahashi argues, in short, that "base" became an occupational rather than a personal status in the Song (Takahashi, *Sō-Sei mibunhō no kenkyū*, 11–12; 157–67). Dai Jianguo has argued that over the course of the Song, *liang-jian* distinctions were reconfigured into quasi-familial master-servant relationships. See Dai Jianguo, "'Zhu pu zhi fen,'" 64ff.

44. Cf. Ebrey, *Inner Quarters*, 217–34.

45. In the Southern Song, the similar term *ci shi* 次室 (second or secondary chamber) came to be used to mean *concubine* as well. In Northern Song sources, however, all uses of the term 次室 that I have found refer to second (successor) *wives*, women who replaced a first wife who died. This slippage again indicates the blurring of status lines. For further discussion, see Bossler, "Song-Yuan mu zhi," 100–101.

of those children, a concubine mother was a *shu mu* 庶母 ("concubine mother") or, more commonly, a *sheng mu* 生母 or *suo sheng mu* 所生母 (birth mother). At the other end of the spectrum, the aesthetic and erotic functions associated with concubines were highlighted in terms like *jia ji* (household-charmer), *ji shi* 姬侍 or *shi ji* 侍姬 (charmer-attendant, attendant-charmer), or, more informally, *shi'er* 侍兒 (lit. "serving-babe," hereafter rendered as "serving maid").

The individual concubines we know most about tend to be those who served as secondary consorts and came to enjoy a substantial and respected role in their master's families. Han Qi (1008–75), one of the Northern Song's most eminent grand councilors, wrote a fond funerary inscription describing his birth mother, née Hu (966–1030), a literate woman from a respectable, even upper-class family: her father had served the Latter Shu regime in Sichuan.[46] When Hu's father died she had followed her mother into a second marriage, but the new husband had gotten into trouble and left the family without support. Hu was accordingly married off (*gui* 歸) to Han Qi's father as a concubine. She bore him two sons, Qi and an older brother. At least according to Han Qi's account, the relationship between his birth mother and his legal mother was amiable, and Hu's skill at managing the women's quarters was such that Han Qi's father put her in charge of running the household. When she was nearly sixty, long after the deaths of his legal parents, Han Qi passed the examinations (she had been forty when he was born).[47] She traveled with him to his first post, where, Qi tells us, he and his wife attended her with great care. She died in 1030, and in 1045 Qi buried her with his parents at the ancestral graves, albeit, he assures us, in an inferior coffin and in a slightly separate location, in order to preserve the proper status distinctions.[48]

---

46. This inscription has also been described in Ebrey, "Concubines in Song China," 14–15. A late Song anecdote gives a different view of her heritage: it claims that her father was a soothsayer who, realizing that she was destined to be ennobled one day, brought her to the capital to find an auspicious-looking partner. After three years of searching, he encountered Han Qi's father and offered her to him. See Zhang Duanyi, *Gui er ji*, xia, 15a.

47. Han Qi's father died in 1011, only three years after Qi's birth. The date of his legal mother's death is unknown, but Qi indicates that it was "before I was grown."

48. Han Qi, *Anyang ji bian nian jian zhu* 46.1411–12.

In a similar case, about the time that Han Qi was preparing for the examinations, another young woman of a respectable capital family lost her parents and found herself "married off to serve" (*gui shi* 歸侍) the only son of the grand councilor Xia Song. As her funerary inscription explains, because her husband Xia Anqi was an only son, the family was quite concerned "that the lines of descent were not yet broad" (*si xi wei guang* 嗣裔未廣). The entire household was accordingly thrilled when this concubine, née Li, bore a son. Li is given credit for rearing the son, Xia Bosun, and for seeing him into an official career. We are told that because she liked the capital so much Bosun never sought office in the provinces. When she died in 1091, he was so grief-stricken that he did not eat for four days, and followed his mother in death. Like Han Qi's mother, Li, too, was buried slightly apart from the ancestral graves.[49]

Both Hu and Li, then, were wife-like concubines who took on familial responsibilities, reared children, and remained with their husbands' families throughout their lives and even in death. In Hu's case, at least, her position in the family may have been due in part to her relatively high-status background, and to the education or skills with which such a background had endowed her. That both she and Li bore sons was also undoubtedly critical in enhancing their standing in their masters' families (and is of course the only reason that we have evidence of their existence today). It is tempting to take Hu and Li as representatives of a particularly genteel type of Song concubinage, more akin to marriage than to servitude—and perhaps indeed they are examples thereof. But it should also be pointed out here that we do not really know in what

---

49. Yang Jie, *Wu wei ji* 14.5–6. Li's funerary inscription plays down the fact that she was a concubine rather than a wife; no other wife is mentioned (and indeed Chang Bide, *Song ren zhuan ji* [5.1181], identifies her as Xia Anqi's wife). The ambiguity is compounded by the fact that Xia Anqi is known to have married an upper-class woman surnamed Li (Xia appears as a son-in-law in a funerary inscription for one Li Yunji [李允及] [Yin Zhu, *Henan ji* 12.6b–9b]). However, Li Yunji's inscription also mentions that his three youngest daughters (including the one married to Anqi) had died by the time of Yunji's death in 1038. Moreover, the inscription for Bosun's mother says her ancestry is utterly obscure, and refers to her as Bosun's "birth mother" (*suo sheng mu*) rather than simply his mother. Finally, the funerary inscription of Xia Anqi's father, Xia Song, mentions two grandsons but not the son of this woman, suggesting that her son had not yet been born at the time of Xia Song's death in 1051. It appears, then, that Xia Anqi had both a wife and a concubine surnamed Li.

capacity these women were first taken into their masters' households: we see them only from the perspective of their sons, and in a genre designed to confer on them the maximum respectability and dignity. If they had been brought into the household as entertainers or serving maids, we would probably not learn of it here. This point is important, for our sources suggest that the great majority of women who became concubines in the Northern Song entered the household precisely as entertainers or serving maids, and often as both at once. And we shall see that it was not unheard-of for such women to become the much-revered mothers of literati sons.

Entertainer-concubines (or household-courtesans, which was simply another term for the same category of woman) were extremely popular in the Northern Song. This phenomenon undoubtedly reflects the importance of entertainers in literati life more generally, as discussed in chapter 1. Like professional entertainers, household-courtesans were associated with the trappings of political status and power. This is evident, first of all, in the famous edict in which the founding emperor, Taizu, gently suggested to his generals that they give up their military commissions and retire to a well-earned life of leisure in the countryside. To ensure that "between lord and minister there will be no suspicion," he promised to marry his children to theirs, and urged them in the meantime to "set up lots of singers and dancing girls, and live out your lives daily drinking wine and enjoying yourselves" (多置歌兒舞女, 日飲酒相歡以終其天年).⁵⁰ In fact, Northern Song men kept household entertainers skilled in a wide variety of performing arts: they not only sang and danced, but played the flute, the nomad lute (*hu qin* 胡琴), the pipa, and so forth.⁵¹

Female attendants of every variety were particularly numerous in the households of imperial clansmen and others with close ties to the court.⁵² One imperial prince, a brother of Emperor Yingzong (r. 1064–67), is said to have expelled dozens of attendant-concubines (*shi qie* 侍妾) when

---

50 *Chang bian* 2.50, as cited in Tang Daijian, "Song dai qie de mai mai," 58. The *Chang bian* reports that the next day all the generals, pleading illness, asked to be relieved of their commissions.

51. Xie Ke, *Zhu you ji* 6.7; Chen Shunyu, *Du guan ji* 12.20; Guo Xiangzheng, *Qing shan ji* 15.1.

52. John Chaffee has suggested that the fecundity of Song imperial clansmen was related to their easy access to concubines. See Chaffee, *Branches of Heaven*, 33, 58–59.

he went into mourning for his mother. The wife of Zhao Zongkai 趙宗楷, a great-grandson of the second Song emperor Taizong, was praised for not becoming jealous even though she was surrounded by concubines (*ying qie man qian* 媵妾滿前).[53] That entertainers, in particular, were expected to be among these women is reflected in references to the singularity of men who did *not* have them. Fan Zuyu found it remarkable that, despite his position, an imperial prince did not keep musicians and entertainer-concubines (*sheng yue ji qie* 聲樂妓妾) in his household. He characterized another prince's household management as "humble and simple" (*han su* 寒素) because the prince "abjured the pleasures of musician-courtesans" (*jue sheng ji zhi wan* 絕聲妓之玩).[54] And although surely not every woman serving in these households had intimate relationships with the master, that many of them did is attested in numerous edicts awarding noble titles to the birth mothers (*suo sheng mu* 所生母) of imperial clan descendants. Significantly, the regular awarding of such noble titles to concubine mothers appears to have been a Northern Song innovation, and was an early sign of changing attitudes toward the concubine's role in the family.[55]

Official families more generally seem to have kept somewhat fewer women: Su Shi admits to having had "several" concubines (*qie*), but notes that they left him when his political fortunes declined; Huang Tingjian suggests he would have liked to "purchase someone graceful and charming," but lacked the necessary funds.[56] As with the court nobility, contemporaries seem to have assumed that men of official rank would naturally keep serving women: sounding a by now familiar refrain, Su Song marveled that even after becoming an official, Zhang Yuxi 掌禹錫

---

53. Fan Zuyu, *Fan Taishi ji* 51.2b, 48.4a.
54. Fan Zuyu, *Fan Taishi ji* 46.11a, 47.7a.
55. E.g., Hu Su, *Wen gong ji* 19.245. According to the *SS* 245.8700, the custom of enfeoffing the birth mothers of imperial clansman began with Zhao Zongmin 趙宗敏, whose birth mother née Fan is awarded a title in one of the edicts drafted by Hu Su. (Cf. also Chaffee, *Branches of Heaven*, 58.) Similar edicts can be found in numerous collected works across the Northern Song. In addition, among the numerous funerary inscriptions composed by Fan Zuyu for members of the imperial family, nearly a dozen show that their subjects were sons of concubines (*Fan Taishi ji*, *juan* 45–51). Wong points out that the term *suo sheng mu* first appears in funerary inscriptions in the Northern Song ("Tō Sō boshi," 49).
56. *Huang Tingjian quan ji*, *zheng ji*, 4.89.

(d. 1066) ran his household in the same manner as when he had been a commoner, eschewing concubines (*ying qie* 媵妾) and waiting upon himself at table, refusing to change even when others made fun of him for his abstemiousness.⁵⁷ Moreover, among officials, as among the nobility, it was assumed that some such women would be entertainers. Thus Han Qi remarked on the extraordinary frugality of the minister Du Yan, who did not keep musician-courtesans in his household, and literatus-poet Mei Yaochen fantasized about buying a young serving maid and teaching her how to play the flute.⁵⁸

Although many if not most officials kept concubines and serving women, by the Northern Song the ability to purchase such women had become a factor of wealth rather than of official status. We have seen that traditionally concubinage was limited to men of the official class, and even into the late Tang the keeping of household-courtesans was subject to sumptuary regulation. There is some evidence that the early Song government also initially made a half-hearted attempt to enforce laws prohibiting ordinary commoners from taking concubines.⁵⁹ Even though such efforts seem to have been quickly abandoned, as late as 1039 the association between official rank and the privilege of keeping serving women persisted in some people's minds. In that year, the official Yin Zhu urged the court to augment its military budget by selling noble titles that would confer on the purchaser the right to keep "serving maids" (*nü shi* 女使) and use silver utensils.⁶⁰ But Yin's suggestion was hopelessly impractical, for wealthy merchants and powerful magnates had long since become accustomed to

---

57. Su Song, *Su Weigong wen ji* 57.870.
58. Han Qi, *Anyang ji bian nian jian zhu* 43.1341, "Ji Zheng xian Du gong wen" 祭正獻杜公文; Mei Yaochen, *Mei Yaochen ji bian nian jiao zhu* 27.961.
59. See the very interesting memorial by Yang Yi requesting that two commoners of Longquan county not be forced to divorce their "minor" or "secondary" wives (*xiao qi* 小妻; *ci qi* 次妻). Yang argues that an edict of 990 had exempted those who had taken in such women during the Wu-Yue period from having to divorce them, and points out that in any case the "Revised Edited Statutes" (*Shan ding bian chi* 刪定編敕) no longer included the statute that would have condemned them (*QSW* 14: 287.247–48).
60. Yin Zhu, *Henan ji* 19.7a–8a and 22.8a–9a. Yin's plan was to have two levels of ranks, purchasable by 100 *shi* or 500 *shi* of grain respectively. According to the *SS*, Yin's suggestion was never acted upon (179.4351), though a few years later another official complained that both offices and ranks were being sold, "confusing and muddling the official stream" (*yao za shi liu* 淆雜仕流 [*SS* 302.10011]).

adorning their households with household-courtesans and other serving women. The court simply ignored Yin's repeated memorials.[61]

For men who could afford them, keeping one or more entertainers in the household offered several advantages over buying the services of publicly available courtesans. Keeping household-courtesans not only allowed a man to entertain his friends at home, it helped him avoid the dangers of inappropriate or illegal relationships with professional entertainers. Because a "household-courtesan" was a member of her master's household, her position was legally very distinct from that of courtesans in government offices or in the marketplace. An official who had an intimate relationship with a public woman could be indicted for criminal behavior; but no one could fault a man for intimacy with an entertainer in his own household. Even so, in the Northern Song the household-courtesan occupied a somewhat ambiguous position between slave-like entertainer and cloistered consort. As an indentured servant, she was regarded as chattel, and men are described as "keeping" (*xu* 畜) household-courtesans, the way one keeps or raises livestock or pets.[62] And, as with pets, masters enjoyed the privilege of naming their household-courtesans, usually endowing them with poetic or romantic sobriquets.[63] Like professional courtesans, household-courtesans were often expected to serve at parties and to amuse the master's guests, "urging the wine cup" (*you zun* 侑樽, *you shang* 侑觴) with musical diversion and feminine flirtation. But although some men readily brought out their household-courtesans to entertain their guests, others treated them more like cloistered concubines, allowing them to perform for friends only from behind a screen.[64]

---

61. For evidence of wealthy commoners keeping entertainers, see both the 1030 memorial by Zhang Fangping and Shen Kuo's anecdote regarding a wealthy but boorish neighbor of Shi Yannian, discussed below.

62. The same term is sometimes used with reference to concubines as well.

63. Zhou Hui, *Qing bo za zhi* 3.101–2. Although this is a Southern Song source, the names of the concubines of Northern Song men attest to the same practice. Ebrey (*Inner Quarters*, 225) also describes this practice, but does not distinguish between household-courtesans and more consort-like concubines. My sense is that only the former were given special poetic names.

64. Liao Meiyun indicates that in the late Tang concubines were distinguished from household-courtesans in that the former could not be shown to guests, and adds that household-courtesans could even be ordered to sleep with guests (*Tang ji*, 165). In the

The role of household-courtesans was ambiguous in other ways as well, for often entertainment was only one aspect of the service they provided. Huang Tingjian, for example, indicates that his young and homely "little chignon," while "clever at fixing her hair and makeup," was also good at sweeping floors and collating books.⁶⁵ This situation was in turn associated with the fact that, as Mei Yaochen's fantasy hints, many household-courtesans in the Song were not purchased as highly skilled adult musicians, but rather as young and inexperienced girls to be trained in the households of their masters. A Northern Song short story reveals something of this process:

> Director Li—I forget his name—was a person of the capital. His family was powerful and he was frequently in charge of local government. Milord was a man of outstanding abilities, and he treated himself very well. In the Jiayou period (1056–63) he bought a female slave named Little Lotus, who had just turned twelve. He taught her music [lit., strings and reeds], but she was incapable; he instructed her in women's [needle]work, but she wasn't skillful. After several days, milord wanted to return her to the go-between, but the slave cried and implored him, "If you will shelter and train me, later I will certainly find a way to repay you." Milord was intrigued by her words. After some time, she very gradually was able to sing and dance, and her appearance daily grew more lovely and seductive.⁶⁶

The advantages of training a girl in one's own home were several. First was economy: an untrained girl undoubtedly cost less than a highly skilled young woman. In addition, as generations of Chinese mothers-in-law had discovered, a young girl could be more easily socialized into the household than a grown woman, a fact that was undoubtedly as true of concubines as it was of "little-daughters-in-law" (*tong yang xi* 童養媳).⁶⁷ Finally, a prepubescent girl was likely to be a virgin, which was

---

Song the status of the two types of women seems to be much closer, and I have seen no evidence that household-courtesans were expected to sleep with anyone but the master.

65. *Huang Tingjian quan ji, zheng ji*, 4.89. Huang uses the term *xiao huan*, the same term used to refer to apprentice professional courtesans. The poem is translated and discussed in more detail below.

66. Liu Fu, *Qing suo gao yi, hou ji*, 3.128. The story gives her age as thirteen, but since in Chinese reckoning babies were a year old at birth, I have adjusted her age to conform with Western convention. As expected, the girl ultimately becomes Li's concubine, though she later turns out to be a fox spirit.

67. On the custom of little-daughters-in-law and women's involvement therewith, see Wolf, *Women and the Family*. Note that although Wolf's data come from late

not necessarily true of concubines purchased at older ages.[68] In addition to whatever erotic appeal sexual inexperience may have had, from a very practical standpoint purchasing concubines as young girls helped insure that any children born to them would be the master's own.[69]

Whether a household-courtesan was trained in-house or purchased as an adult, the multiple roles of Song maids and concubines can be seen as a reflection of the broadening of the Song elite and the growing popularity of entertainment: while the wealthiest and most powerful households may have been able to afford the services of highly trained and skilled musicians, few literati seem to have been able to do so. The solution was to have maids who could act both as servants and as entertainers, as the occasion required.

## Markets and Mobility

The proliferation of servants and concubines in the households of the expanding elite of the Northern Song helped to fuel a flourishing market in female labor. This market not only created extraordinary opportunities for women to move both up and down the social ladder; it assured a constant interchange between elite and non-elite individuals in the intimate context of the family.

One source of concubines and maids to serve the elite class (as we have already seen in the case of Han Qi's birth mother) was elite households themselves. When well-to-do families encountered sudden reversals of fortune, the proper marriage of a daughter was not only a luxury they could ill afford; the daughter herself became an asset too valuable to ignore (perhaps especially when, like Han Qi's mother, she was only a stepdaughter). There is some evidence that in the Five Dynasties, elite families strategized by sending daughters as concubines to powerful

---

nineteenth- and early twentieth-century Taiwan, the custom was already well established in the Song.

68. See below for the frequent movements of concubines from house to house.

69. Stephen West has suggested that virgin concubines may also have been prized for their usefulness in quasi-Daoist sexual practices (personal communication, March 2012). According to popular theory, sexual intercourse with young virgins would nourish a man's vital essences, contributing to long life and virility. The erotic depictions of very young entertainers seen in some Song poetry lend credence to this theory. See the discussion of shared erotic appreciation later in this chapter.

men: thus the early Song writer Liu Kai (948–1001) unabashedly admits that one of his cousins was a concubine of the Five Dynasties minister Wang Yi.[70] Such openness on the part of an elite man about a concubine relative is extremely rare later in the Song, perhaps because concubines had come to be seen as little different from maids. On the contrary, for most of the period we learn of erstwhile upper-class women becoming concubines only through biographies composed by their successful sons or—far more often—in accounts of literati men rescuing gently bred women from potential or actual servitude. One of the earliest such accounts appears in a funerary inscription for the official Fu Qiu 傅求 (1003–73):

> [Fu] once bought a concubine and noticed that her deportment was unusual. Upon inquiry, he discovered that she was the daughter of an office-holding family and had even once been the wife of a man of the scholarly class. It turned out that Fu had known her father, and he was greatly distressed for her. He made inquiries of her family, but her mother had already remarried. Therefore he prepared the items necessary to marry her off with proper ritual, and even recommended her new husband [for office]. His devotion to righteousness was often like this.[71]

The account is sketchy: we are not told what happened to the concubine's first husband (was she widowed? divorced?) or her father, though her mother's remarriage suggests that her father had died. What is clear is that no one among her agnates or her mother's new affines was willing to take responsibility for providing her with a proper dowry.

A similar story is related by Su Che, in a funerary inscription he composed in 1088 for his uncle, the mid-ranked official Su Huan (1001–62):

> Once milord went out and saw a woman in tattered clothing carrying water. Looking at him, she said, "That is Section-head Su." Surprised, he sent someone to question her. She responded, "Alas, I am the daughter of Revenue Secretary Liao, but have declined and become someone's bondmaid (*bi* 婢)," and she began to cry. Milord was distressed, approached her master and paid to redeem her. He set her up in an empty room in the county offices and selected a trustworthy and careful woman to watch over her. Mr. Liao had formerly worked with milord on

---

70. Liu Kai, *Liu Hedong ji* 14.5b. Liu explains that because of his cousin, Wang Yi treated him as an affine.
71. Zhang Fangping, *Le quan ji* 36.41b. Cf. Ebrey, "Women, Money, and Class," 622–23.

the staff at the prefecture, so milord led his colleagues and associates to marry her off.[72]

Here again, details are lacking, but the anecdote shows that upper-class girls whose fathers died were at significant risk of ending up as concubines or worse.

The above accounts are unusual in that they are recorded in "formal" sources, but the vulnerability of upper-class women is even more strikingly reflected in anecdotal literature. One anecdote tells how a low-level functionary sought to acquire a plum post by telling a prospective patron that, failing a desirable assignment, he would be forced to sell his two daughters as maids to obtain the funds needed for travel to a more distant post (the prospective patron, disgusted, ended the interview: we never learn what happened to the girls).[73] By the early twelfth century, the plight of upper-class girls who had fallen into concubinage had become grist for the mills of romantic storytellers and poets, who recounted in poignant detail the humiliations their heroines suffered at the hands of jealous wives and feckless husbands.[74] Still other stories praised the selfless virtue of literati who saved such women from the clutches of callous and uncouth merchants.[75] Such tales had obvious parallels in the romantic stories Northern Song men wrote about the sad plight of courtesans: they exhibited the author's sympathetic nature and emotional sensitivity, or highlighted the heroism of men who came to the victim's rescue. On the one hand, then, these stories reflect the very real fact that women born into elite status could be vulnerable to falling into servitude, as the cases of Han Qi's mother and others like her show. On the other hand, these stories also reflect upper-class male anxieties about the tenuousness of status in their day. Here as elsewhere, male fears and apprehensions are displaced onto the bodies of women.

Despite elite men's fascination with the precarious fates of women of their own class, such women probably represented only a small fraction

---

72. Su Che, *Luan cheng ji* 25.520.
73. Wei Tai, *Dong xuan bi lü* 5.56–57.
74. See, e.g., the story of Wang Qiongnu and the associated poem attributed to Wang Anguo (1028–74) in Liu Fu, *Qing suo gao yi* 3.35–38. Cf. Ebrey, "Women, Money, and Class," 623–24.
75. Bossler, "Shifting Identities," 35–36, details several such stories.

of those who came to serve as concubines and maids. Some men found their household-courtesans among the ranks of professional entertainers, though this was a risky proposition. Although in the late Tang it seems to have been permissible for men, even officials, to take professional courtesans as household-courtesans or concubines, this was no longer the case in the Northern Song. We saw in chapter 1 that officials could be indicted for privatizing government-courtesans, and men who took independent courtesans as concubines were also frequently prosecuted, presumably on the basis of laws that still forbade intermarriage between people of respectable and base statuses. In the early 1080s, the censor Lai Zhishao 來之邵 was demoted explicitly for having taken a woman from an entertainer household (*chang jia nü* 倡家女) as his concubine (*qie*).[76] A decade later, the imperial clansman Zhao Shixian 趙士倪 was demoted and removed from the line of succession for the same crime.[77] Still, it appears that less prominent men—and especially men who were not officials—were unlikely to be prosecuted for finding their concubines among professional entertainers. Northern Song writers took it for granted that, when her term of service ended, a lucky courtesan might hope to *cong liang* (從良, lit. "follow the respectable"), that is, to marry a respectable commoner and thereby shed her own base status. Tales of professional courtesans being bought out of service by their literati lovers were among the most popular in the storyteller's repertoire, and anecdotal literature suggests that some did enter the households of officials.[78] Even if such cases were rare, they demonstrate awareness and acceptance of the possibility that a woman could rise from professional courtesan status to become a consort in an elite household.

Sometimes the wives or daughters of commoner families were kidnapped or coerced into concubinage: Sima Guang cites an early Song case in which the founding emperor was forced to placate a villager whose daughter had been appropriated by one of his generals.[79] Somewhat later,

---

76. *SS* 355.11181.
77. *Chang bian* 455.10904.
78. E.g. Wu Zeng, *Neng gai zhai man lu* 17.497. We shall see in chap. 5 that by Southern Song times taking a courtesan as a concubine was a fairly common, if still suspect, practice.
79. Sima Guang, *Su shui ji wen* 1.16. Note that essentially the same story is told of a different official in Ouyang Xiu's *Gui tian lu* (*Ouyang Xiu quan ji* 126.1916).

the official Lü Tao (1029–1105) memorialized that one Guo Maoxun 郭茂恂, in charge of horse pasturage in Shaanxi, had imprisoned women who had committed no crime, then sold them as serving women (*nü shi* 女使) for money.[80] These examples show first of all that commoners in general had little recourse in the face of official malfeasance: commoner women were thus exceedingly vulnerable to the depredations of local authorities. Guo Maoxun's case also reveals that the market was sufficiently developed that traffic in women could be a lucrative sideline for such authorities.

Still, by far the majority of girls who ended up as maids and concubines were undoubtedly from commoner families who decided that their daughters were either expendable or too expensive to maintain.[81] This could happen under any circumstances, especially in times of famine or other economic catastrophe, but several sources suggest that the trade in maids and concubines had a regional dimension. An eleventh-century observer noted that during the Five Dynasties taxes in the southeastern kingdom of Wu-Yue had been especially onerous, leading parents to abandon their infants or to sell their children as servants and concubines (*tong qie* 僮妾). He credits the emperor Zhenzong 眞宗 (r. 998–1022) with doing away with the taxes and thereby improving the customs of the Wu region.[82] Still, the reputation of the southeast as a place that produced many concubines persisted. In a preface to a poem entitled "My Fate Is Poor" (妾薄命), the author Xu Ji (1028–1103) remarked,

> There was a concubine who passed through a river inn and wrote a "parable poem" on the wall. Her language was exceedingly mournful, and she said herself that she was from Wu. Gentlemen told each other about it and were moved by it. I have long taken ill the fact that the custom of Wu is mostly not to marry off daughters: they prefer to give them to people as maidservants or concubines, to the point that unfortunately there are girls of respectable family who are despoiled (*shi shen* 失身) by people. It is extremely pitiable. Because I was moved I wrote "My Fate Is Poor" to implore the fathers and elders of Wu. Perhaps they will feel pity and remorse about this, and feeling remorse, rectify it.[83]

---

80. Lü Tao, *Jing de ji* 5.53.
81. Guo Dongxu, *Song dai fa zhi*, 408–9.
82. Wenying, *Xiangshan ye lu, shang*, 11
83. Xu Ji, *Jie xiao ji* 11.7–8. The title could alternatively be read "Concubines Are Ill-Fated," because the standard humble first-person pronoun for women, *qie*, is the same as the word "concubine." The phrase "my fate is poor" goes back to a biography of Empress Xu (許皇后, d. 8 BCE) of the Han, who was deposed when the emperor

Whether or not child-selling was more common in the southeast than elsewhere in the country, the demand for concubines, and especially concubine-entertainers, seems to have grown over the course of the Northern Song. Thus a very late Northern Song miscellany observes:

> When buying a concubine (*qie*) in the capital, every 5,000 cash is referred to as a "ge" (箇), and the cost of a beauty is thirty to fifty "ge" [that is, 150,000 to 250,000 cash]. In recent years, the nobility particularly pride themselves on erotic entertainment (*sheng se* 聲色). The price of concubines has jumped as high as 5,000 strings [5,000,000 cash], and they no longer count in terms of "ge." Even after the contract is signed, [the girl's] parents and relatives extort further [compensation], calling it "helping hand money."[84]

Particularly notable here is not only the inflation in the price of concubines, but the author's assumption that the role of concubines (*qie*) is to provide *sheng se* (lit., music and beauty). That elite men were personally acquainted with the process of acquiring concubines is further reflected in a collection of amusing aphorisms compiled in the late Northern Song. Here the author lists "Finding servant girls" under the category of "Things That Cannot Be Entrusted to Others." He hints at the intricacy of the process by listing "The marketplace speech of go-betweens" under the category of "Difficult to Understand." Likewise, he acknowledges the frequently ambiguous origins of concubines by designating as "Unreliable" both "The vows of the go-between," and "When buying a concubine (*qie*), asking about her background." Finally, the same author tacitly acknowledges that much of the trade in women was illegal by categorizing "Waiting for the appointed days [for reporting crimes at the yamen] to report a stolen wife or daughter" as an example of "Not Understanding Urgency."[85] The frequent reference in these aphorisms to

---

Chengdi (r. 51–7 BCE) became enamored of the notorious Zhao sisters (Ban Gu, *Han shu*, 97 xia, 3997). Cao Zhi of the Six Dynasties period wrote a set of poems entitled "My Fate Is Poor" in the persona of Empress Xu, and the theme was taken up by Li Bo and others in the Tang. By the late Tang and into the Song the phrase was no longer explicitly associated with the Han story, becoming instead a general title for poems about desolate women, as Xu Ji uses it here. For an English translation of Xu Ji's poem, see Ebrey, *Inner Quarters*, 224. Chap. 3 discusses Xu Ji's life and work in detail.

84. Zhu Yu, *Pingzhou ke tan* 1.127. In another late Northern Song anecdote, the price of a concubine is given as 900,000 cash (Shao Bowen, *Shao shi wen jian lu* 11.121).

85. Wang Junyu, *Za zuan xu*, 74, 63, 59, and 64, respectively.

markets in women once again demonstrates the ubiquity of concubines in the lives of the elite.

In sum, although the Northern Song evidence on markets in concubines is far from abundant, we should not doubt the centrality of those markets to the lives of elite and commoner families alike. At least in urban areas, there would have been few eminent families who did not at some point negotiate the purchase of a maid or concubine; similarly, it must have been a rare village that did not send at least a few girls into serving-maid or concubine status. For upper-class women, the specter of concubinage was an ever-present reminder of the fragility of social position; for poor commoners, concubinage represented at once a fall from respectable status and the opportunity for social advancement. For elite men, concubines served both as emblems of social status and as vehicles for defining and negotiating relationships with other men.

## *Household-Courtesans and Literati Social Life*

We saw in chapter 1 that courtesan banquets were a critical venue for the expression of literati sociability in the Northern Song. Part of the popularity of household-courtesans in the Northern Song was the ability they provided to entertain guests at home. Some sense of the importance of such home banquets in Northern Song social life is evident in Su Shi's decision, on New Year's Day 1076, to invite friends over in spite of the fact that he himself was too ill to drink with them. Su Shi describes how, asking his friend Zhao Chengbo to serve as the banquet's host, he leaned on a table amidst his friends, his own spirits lifted by watching their drunken revelry.[86]

### CONCUBINES, ETIQUETTE, AND CONNOISSEURSHIP

In many respects, banquets at home served social functions similar to more public courtesan banquets. They were a venue in which literati men could display to one another their poetic skills and social finesse, could celebrate friendship, compete for status, and establish their identity as literati. One aspect of this identity was mastery of the elaborate rules for proper etiquette that governed the behavior of both host and

---

86. *Su Shi shi ji* 14.663–65.

guest, as revealed in several Song anecdotes. The famous polymath Shen Kuo (1031–95), for example, described the experience of Shi Yannian 石延年 (994–1041), who attended a banquet at the home of a wealthy neighbor. The neighbor was unaccustomed to interacting with scholar-officials, but he liked to drink; hearing that Shi did too, he invited him over. When Shi arrived, he was disconcerted to find that his host was carelessly dressed and appeared to know nothing of the proper greeting ceremonies. There followed an extravagant feast, complete with exotic foods and entertainment by nearly a dozen beautiful household-courtesans; but after five rounds of wine the women retired and the host, too, suddenly got up and left without ceremony. Shi was left to see himself out. Shen Kuo relates Shi's astonishment at seeing so ignorant and stupid a man living in such luxury, concluding, "What the ancients called 'the idiot rich' (*qian chi* 錢癡) surely exist!"[87] Here Shen Kuo attempts to distinguish between wealthy men in Song society and what he sees as the true elite, the scholar-officials or *shi* 士. Both groups of men might enjoy banquets and entertainment, but only the scholars understood the proper rules for behavior that governed such occasions.

In a similar vein, Wei Tai in the early twelfth century described with disdain a disastrous banquet held by Yang Hui 楊繪, an official Wei describes as "incautious and without restraint," who "constantly interacted with petty people (*xiao ren* 小人)." One of the guests at Yang's banquet was the minor official Hu Shiwen, from a powerful commoner family. Hu had passed the examinations, but, Wei tells us, "he was quite lacking in gentlemanly restraint (*shi jian* 士檢)." As the banquet progressed, Hu became somewhat drunk and began to make passes at Yang's household-courtesan, who had been brought out to entertain the guests. Mortified at this indecent behavior, Yang's wife (who had been observing the proceedings from behind a screen) called the girl to her and began to chastise her. Hu got up from his place and approached Yang to get him to call the courtesan back out; Yang, humiliated in front of his wife, instead called an end to the party. Enraged, Hu began beating Yang ferociously. The other guests were forced to intervene, and even so Yang barely escaped with his life. Wei Tai concludes tendentiously:

---

87. Shen Kuo, *Meng xi bi tan* 9.74–75. In the original anecdote, Shi Yannian is referred to by his sobriquet, Shi Manqing (曼卿).

"When favored officials do not value themselves, to the point that they are insulted and bullied by petty people, gentlemanly discourse (*shi lun* 士論) despises them."[88] Here, although Hu had passed the examinations and thus was technically a scholar-official, his behavior did not live up to proper *shi* standards, and the reputation of his host Yang Hui likewise suffered from their association. For both Shen Kuo and Wei Tai, knowing how to behave at private banquets had become a mark of gentlemanly (*shi* 士) status in an era when wealth and even office were becoming available to men whose families did not have long traditions of government service or the concomitant elite standing. Like good manners anywhere, the proper performance of gentlemanly behavior was a way of asserting or upholding social distinctions that were challenged by social change, and by the Northern Song one important element in such behavior was knowing how to interact with one's host's household-courtesans.

Household-courtesans also served as a vehicle for the performance of literati status in being a focus for the increasingly popular pastime of connoisseurship.[89] Household-courtesans, like antiques, paintings, and fine calligraphy, were a focus for admiration and appreciation, and like those items could be collected, displayed, and commented on. Such art objects were the focus of social gatherings that allowed both host and guests to demonstrate their refined taste, and such gatherings became a central aspect of literati life in the Northern Song, as they were to be throughout later imperial China.[90] But Northern Song poetry composed at such gatherings is remarkable for the extent to which it includes household-courtesans among the objects appreciated. Numerous poems show household-courtesans being shown off for the enjoyment of the host's compatriots. In a poem entitled, "Again Matching 'Yang Zhimei's Household's Pipa Courtesan'" (又和楊之美家琵琶妓), Han Wei

---

88. Wei Tai, *Dong xuan bi lu* 7.77–78. Cf. also Ebrey, *Inner Quarters*, 225–26, where this story is cited as evidence of men using concubines to entertain their guests.

89. On the cultural implications of the new craze for collecting in the Northern Song, see Egan, *The Problem of Beauty*, and de Pee, *The Writing of Weddings*.

90. On the social uses of poetry in the Song, see Hawes, *The Social Circulation of Poetry*. There is now a considerable literature about the social functions of connoisseurship in later imperial China. See, e.g., Meyer-Fong, "Making a Place for Meaning." On literati connoisseurship of male entertainers in the seventeenth century, see Volpp, "The Literary Circulation of Actors."

teasingly describes his friend and colleague Yang Zhimei as a paramount lover of antiques, a self-described aesthete of singular tastes who collects what the world has discarded, selecting the exquisite from among the dregs. Han then catalogs the objects of Yang's connoisseurship, observing that Yang "purchases youths and teaches them music, and collects paintings and calligraphy" (買童教樂收圖書). When guests come, Yang sometimes sets out his paintings and scrolls for them to admire, and other times calls the "youth" to "attend to the strings" (呼童理弦索). Han jokes about the dilapidated state of Yang's books and paintings: the silk and paper is tattered and torn, the ink smeared and barely readable (破縑壞紙抹漆黑，筆墨僅辨絲毫餘); likewise the courtesan is a mess, "over her entire face white and red [makeup] is sloppily applied" (滿面狼籍施鈆朱). Still, Han concedes that when the girl plays "The Woodpecker" song she is able to change the mood of the entire group into joy, and he concludes the poem by affirming that Yang is interested only in ultimate skill and extraordinary relics (苟非絕藝與奇迹，楊君視之皆蔑如). Han's poem makes clear that Yang's pipa-playing courtesan is but one of the numerous artifacts in his collection.[91]

As the title of Han's poem suggests, he was not the only one of Yang's compatriots to comment on the talented pipa player. Both Mei Yaochen and Ouyang Xiu wrote of her, and even Sima Guang, well known for his seriousness and imperviousness to feminine charms, was drawn into aesthetic appreciation of her skills.[92] Sima explains in the title of his own poem: "I went with Zheng Shengmin to visit Yang Zhimei and heard his pipa slave girl play 'The Woodpecker' tune. Having seen the songs presented by the various masters, the next day I offered this as a token of gratitude" (同張聖民過楊之美聽琵琶女奴彈啄木曲，觀諸公所贈歌，明

---

91. Han Wei, *Nanyang ji* 5.8–8b. "Zhimei" appears to be Yang's sobriquet. The title of Han Wei's poem suggests the existence of a prior one on the same subject, but although Han's collected works does contain other poems addressed to Yang Zhimei, none of them relate to this topic.

92. Yang Zhimei is the same person as "Lecturer Yang Bao" (Yang *zhi jiang* Bao 楊直講襃) referred to in a poem by Ouyang Xiu that in turn responds to one by Mei Yaochen, all on the subject of Yang's pipa player. See *Ouyang Xiu quan ji* 7.109–10; Mei Yaochen, *Mei Yaochen ji bian nian jiao zhu* 27.981. The modern editors of Mei's work date this exchange, in which Mei's poem matches rhyme words with that of Ouyang, to 1057.

日投此爲謝).⁹³ The poem itself suggests that Sima Guang and his friend stopped in at Yang's place uninvited, and were thrilled to be treated to the pipa performance. Sima vows that for three days he will not wash his ears, to preserve the vestiges of the tune ringing in them. But Sima's poem is not only an appreciation of the courtesan's performance; it is an explicit bid to participate in a poetic circle created through the appreciation of Yang's talented household-courtesan. Although he does not attempt to match rhymes with the earlier poems, Sima Guang's poem plays with the themes and repeats actual phrases from poems others had written in honor of Yang's pipa player, including that of Han Wei but also those of Ouyang and Mei. It is also worth noting that the poetic circle constructed around recitals by Yang's performer transcended time and space: the title of Ouyang Xiu's poem indicates that he saw Yang's "slave girl" (*nü nu* 女奴) perform at the home of "Liu Gongcao" 劉功曹, while Sima Guang's poem, which was explicitly written after the others, suggests he saw a completely different performance at Yang's home.

Here the ongoing circulation of poetry focused on Yang's slave girl defined a community of privileged insiders, all of whom had been invited to appreciate Yang Zhimei's art "collection" (including his lovely and talented slave girl), presumably because of their highly developed artistic sensibilities. The poetry served both as public assertion of membership in this community, and as a vehicle for competition within it.⁹⁴ At the same time, these poems also begin to reveal, albeit obliquely, some aspects of the relationship between Yang and his pipa player. The girl (one of the poems suggests she was only ten years old) is clearly depicted as Yang's possession, not a partner, and some of the poetry suggests she was not particularly well cared for (she is described as thin and poorly dressed).⁹⁵ The authors admire her skill and also evince some sympathy

---

93. Sima Guang, *Sima wen zheng gong chuan jia ji* 2.13–14. Zhengmin is the sobriquet of Zhang Chu 張☐ (1015–80).

94. Elsewhere Ouyang Xiu actually disparages Yang Bao's aesthetic judgment, characterizing him as someone who "likes but does not understand" paintings and calligraphy (褒於書畫好而不知者也) (*Ouyang Xiu quan ji* 138.2195–6, "Tang Xue Ji shu" 唐薛稷書).

95. Hawes, *The Social Circulation of Poetry*, 54–55, provides a partial translation of Ouyang's poem and suggests that Mei and Ouyang were shocked to see Yang's household-courtesan poorly dressed and apparently underfed (though in fact the last line of

for her, but it is the sort of sympathy one might extend to a pet. Like a pet, she is described only in the third person: none of the authors dignifies her presence by addressing her directly. This may be in part because she was so young, but it also suggests that some household entertainers were in fact regarded as little better than chattel.

## Friends and Lovers: Concubines, Romance, and Intimacy

Like poetry for public courtesans, then, poetry about household-courtesans served as a vehicle for participating and competing in literati culture, and could serve as a vehicle for literary display.[96] But this poetry had other functions as well. Like the frequent gifts literati exchanged with one another, poetry functioned in Song culture to help forge and cement bonds of friendship. Su Shi wrote a much-celebrated poem affectionately teasing Zhang Xian for the fact that, at eighty-five years old, he was still purchasing concubines.[97] On another occasion, Su composed a poem entitled, "Zhao Chengbo's household has a beauty who, I am honored to say, is from my hometown. Unwilling to raise her wine cup, she merely chanted lovely lines about spring snow; I playfully matched her rhyme (趙成伯家有麗人, 僕忝鄉人, 不肯開樽, 徒吟春雪美句, 次韻一笑).[98] Zhao Dingchen composed what he himself describes as a "crude" poem to chide a friend who had skipped a group outing on pretext of illness, but who was later discovered to have been occupied with his beautiful new concubine.[99]

---

Ouyang's poem seems to defend Yang from Mei's critique). Sima Guang's poem refers to this obliquely, suggesting that such a beauty has no need of elaborate silk garments.

96. In one famous example, a favorite household-courtesan belonging to Han Jiang asked Su Shi to write a poem on her fan. Su responded with a brilliantly clever poem incorporating an anagram for the characters of the dancer's name in the first line, and in the second line alluding to the fact that, earlier in the banquet, she'd been stung by a bee (*Su Shi shi ji* 30.1565–66. Cf. Zhao Lingzhi, *Hou qing lu* 侯鯖錄, 4.100). Another time, Su Shi ordered his own singing and dancing concubine to seek a poem from the monk Daoqian 道潛, who responded with a playful verse proclaiming his spiritual imperviousness to her charms (Daoqian, *Canliaozi shi ji* 3.5b).

97. *Su Shi shi ji* 11.523. The poem played on the relationships with concubines of several historical figures also surnamed Zhang, and was repeated with delight in gossipy anecdotal sources from the Northern Song on: see Zhao Lingzhi, *Hou qing lu* 7.178.

98. *Su Shi shi ji* 47.2526–27. Many other examples could be cited. For a brief history of Su Shi's friendship with Zhao Chengbo see "Mizhou tong ban ting ti ming ji" 密州通判廳題名記, in *Su Shi wen ji* 11.376.

99. Zhao Dingchen, *Zhu yin ji shi ji* 6.6b–7a.

When a household-courtesan enjoyed an intimate place in her master's domestic circle, poetry about her could provide a way of expressing a particularly intimate kind of friendship. Huang Tingjian, for example, wrote several poems about a flute-playing serving maid belonging to his friend Wang Shen 王詵 (sobriquet Jinqing 晉卿). In one of these, he flatters the entertainer (and her master) by suggesting that her playing can "call up the dragons from under the water," and bring forth a "frosty day's falling-leaf wind" to dispel the summer heat. But significantly, rather than simply referring to her as "flute-playing maid" in the manner of those who wrote about Yang Zhimei's pipa player, Huang reveals his close relationship with Wang Shen by referring to the maid by name in the poem's title: "At Summer's Height, at a Water Pavilion, Listening to Radiance of Jinqing's Household Play the Flute" (大暑水閣聽晉卿家昭華吹笛).[100] Elsewhere, Huang further demonstrates his intimacy with Wang by writing a poem that teases Radiance, while also gently chiding Wang for not having the plum blossoms Huang had hoped to obtain from him. The title of the poem reads: "I Sought Thousand-petaled Plum [blossoms] from Commandant Wang; He Said They Had All Already Fallen. I Wrote This as a Joke Teasing the Flute-playing Serving Maid" (從王都尉覓千葉梅;云已落盡.戲作嘲吹笛侍兒). The poem plays with two levels of meaning:

| | |
|---|---|
| 若爲可耐照華得 | If you can stand to wait, you can get radiant flowers, |
| | *If you can stand it, you can get Radiance,* |
| 脫帽看髮已微霜 | But removing my cap you can see my hair is already lightly frosted [i.e., I'm getting too old to wait]. |
| | *But if you remove her cap you will see that her hair is already lightly frosted [i.e, she's getting old].* |
| 催盡落梅春已半 | The plum blossoms are all fallen and spring is half gone; |
| | *Her plum-like beauty is faded, her years half over;* |
| 更吹三弄乞風光 | Play again "[Plum Blossom,] Three Variations" to seek for the lovely scenery. |
| | *When she plays again "[Plum Blossom,] Three Variations" you can seek her former charm.*[101] |

---

100. *Huang Tingjian quan ji, bie ji*, 1.1472. The poem is dated 1088.
101. *Huang Tingjian quan ji, wai ji*, 11.1136. "Plum Blossom, Three Variations" was (and is) the title of a popular tune. I am indebted to Stephen West for alerting me to the double-layered meaning of this poem.

Huang took similar teasing about his own serving maid from his friend Kong Wuzhong (Changfu) 孔武仲, after sending Kong a present of fine tea. Accompanying the tea, Huang had sent a playful poem suggesting that Kong's assiduous recitation of the classics must be making him thirsty, and adding that the tea he was sending would go well with certain pastries. Kong's answering poem, Huang tells us, included the line "For fried pastries it will be necessary to trouble Green Pearl" (煎點徑須煩綠珠), Green Pearl being the name of a famously beautiful concubine during in the Six Dynasties period.[102] Huang evidently understood this as a teasing reference to his own rather homely serving maid, for he responded:

| | |
|---|---|
| 小鬟雖醜巧妝梳 | Although [my] "little chignon" is ugly, she is clever at fixing her hair and makeup; |
| 掃地如鏡能檢書 | She sweeps the floor till it is like a mirror and is able to collate books. |
| 欲買娉婷供煮茗 | I'd like to buy someone graceful and charming to serve the tea, |
| 我無一斛明月珠 | But I don't have a bushel of moon-bright pearls. |
| 知公家亦闕掃除 | I know that your household also lacks someone to sweep the floors, |
| 但有文君對相如 | But you have a Wenjun to match [your] Xiangru. |
| 政當爲公乞如願 | I really ought to seek a Ruyuan for you: |
| 作牋遠寄宮亭湖 | I'll write a note and send it afar to Gongting Lake.[103] |

The numerous allusions in this poem implicitly compare Huang's friend to the actual and would-be masters of famous entertainer-concubines of the past. The phrase "A bushel of moon-bright pearls" refers to Green Pearl, who according to one anecdote was purchased for three bushels of pearls. Zhuo Wenjun and Sima Xiangru were famous married lovers of the Han dynasty, so "Wenjun" here refers to Kong's wife. The

---

102. As recorded in the *Shi shuo xin yu*, Green Pearl was a beautiful and talented flute player belonging to the fabulously wealthy Shi Chong. The general Sun Xiu sent a messenger requesting the girl, but Shi Chong refused, emotionally explaining that he loved her. Although he offered instead a choice of any of the dozens of his other slaves and concubines (*bi qie*), the general never forgave the slight, a situation that ultimately led to Shi Chong's demise. Liu Yiqing, *Shi shuo xin yu* 6.245 (*chou liao* 36, no. 1; Mather, 489–90, no. 1). Later commentators insisted that Green Pearl remained faithful to Shi Chong, committing suicide at his death, though the *Shi shuo xin yu* does not say this.

103. *Huang Tingjian quan ji, zheng ji*, 4.89.

2. The Six Dynasties entertainer Green Pearl of the Liang (Liang Lü Zhu 梁綠珠) as featured in a Late Imperial collection of virtuous women, where she is celebrated for her loyalty to her master. Here she is shown throwing herself out a window after his death, in recompense for his refusal to give her up to a more powerful man. From Liu Xiang 劉向, *Hui tu Lie nü zhuan* 繪圖列女傳 (Illustrated biographies of exemplary women), edited by (Qing) Wang Geng 汪庚, illustrations by (Ming) Qiu Ying 仇英. Reprint of Zhi bu zu zhai cang ban (Taipei: Zheng zhong shu ju, 1971), 7.5b–6.

line hints that Kong's wife is preventing Huang from getting Kong a concubine—after a story in which Xiangru was going to take a concubine but desisted when Wenjun wrote a poem called "White-haired Lament." Ruyuan was a serving maid whom the god of Gongting Lake bestowed on a favored mortal, as recorded in a story from the *Sou shen ji*, a fourth-century collection of supernatural tales.[104]

This sort of playful teasing about courtesan-concubines was quite common in Northern Song poetry. In addition to serving as a vehicle for the expression of affection between men, such poetry is also notable for treating the entertainers themselves as something more than mere possessions. The women are included, if peripherally, in the teasing of their masters, suggesting that they also share in the intimacy that such teasing betokens.

---

104. See Ren Yuan (fl. 1145), *Shan gu ji nei ji shi zhu* 6.9a–9b. Ren also points out that several of the phrases of Huang's poem allude to earlier poetry by Du Fu.

If playful teasing about serving maids expressed one level of male friendship, another sort of intimacy was evoked in poetry that hinted at shared erotic appreciation of friends' concubines. In a poem sent to his friend Liu Chang, Ouyang Xiu reminisces about their last meeting, drinking at Liu's home on the eve of his departure to take up an official post.[105] Ouyang admits to having gotten so drunk on this occasion that later he had no memory of bidding Liu goodbye. He does remember, however—and makes a point of reminding Liu—how taken he was with the "little chignon" whom Liu had just acquired at that time, and whom Ouyang compares to a "just-blossomed flower that no hand has yet touched" (愛君小鬟初買得，如手未觸新開花). Though couched in metaphoric language, Ouyang's phrase not only expresses his appreciation for the physical charms of Liu's new playmate, it frankly acknowledges the erotic nature of those charms by emphasizing the girl's virginal appearance. Mei Yaochen employs similar rhetoric in a poem entitled "Watching Liu Yuanzhong's Little Serving Maid Dance" (觀劉元忠小鬟舞):

| | |
|---|---|
| 桃小未開春意濃 | The young peach hasn't yet blossomed, but the springtime feelings are deep. |
| 梢頭綠葉映微紅 | The green leaves on the tree-tips glint with faint pink. |
| 君家歌管相催急 | In your home the songs and pipes urge each other on: |
| 枝弱不勝花信風 | The fragile branch can't stand up to the flower-blossoming wind. |

Here the eroticism suggested by the phrase "springtime feelings" is heightened (as in Ouyang Xiu's poem) by reference to the girl's youth and evident virginity. The last two lines titillate with their suggestion that the "fragile branch" will not be able to withstand the warm spring wind that forces flowers to open, especially in this setting where songs and music "urge each other on."[106]

Although not as explicitly sexual as some Northern Song *ci* 詞 poetry, these poems are striking because they refer not to unspecified ladies of

---

105. *Ouyang Xiu quan ji* 6.93.
106. Mei Yaochen, *Mei Yaochen ji bian nian jiao zhu* 28.1005. Liu Yuanzhong was the cognomen of Liu Jin 劉瑾. The phrase *hua xin feng* 花信風, which I have translated as "flower-blossoming wind," refers to the spring wind that causes flowers to bloom. The wind arrives in twenty-four phases, each phase opening another type of flower. Significantly, the phrase *hua xin* can also imply a girl coming to maturity, and Mei seems to be playing on this double meaning here.

the night, but to women belonging to the households of other literati—women who at least theoretically might someday become mothers of other literati. At the very least, such poems bespeak a frankness about the sexuality of concubines that was to become less and less acceptable as the Song wore on (though it fascinated later anecdotalists).[107] But such poetry also clearly functioned as a vehicle for male bonding: by sharing in the appreciation of a friend's actual or potential erotic partner, the poet placed himself (or revealed his place) in the friend's intimate circle.[108] At the same time, in imagining the entertainer as the object of her master's sexual desire, these poems also invested her with somewhat more humanity than those that made her simply a decoration. She is still objectified, but she is also valorized as a worthy focus of her master's attentions, and imbued with the possibility of becoming something more to him.[109]

That household-courtesans did sometimes become more than mere playthings of their masters is evident in poetry that highlights men's romantic relationships and emotional attachments to them. For example, in a poem entitled, "To the Tune of 'The Beauty,' Presented to Grand Master Zhongli's Serving Maid" (麗人曲, 贈鍾離中散侍姬), Guo Xiangzheng describes a beautiful dancer—presumably the recipient of the poem—happily (if perhaps perilously) in love with his friend:

| | |
|---|---|
| 髮如盤鴉面如玉 | Hair coiled raven-black, a face like jade; |
| 飄飄羅袖長芬馥 | Floating, her silk-gauze sleeves waft a lovely fragrance. |

---

107. Egan, in *The Problem of Beauty*, argues that open expression of sentiment and romance became increasingly acceptable across the Northern Song, reaching its apogee in the late eleventh and early twelfth centuries in the *ci* lyrics of very late Northern Song poets like Yan Jidao (d. ca. 1106) and Zhou Bangyan (1056–1121). Yet while mid-Northern Song literati may have been hesitant to write too frankly about romantic adventures in their *ci* poetry, they seem to have been quite willing to address these issues in their *shi* poetry, as we have seen. Perhaps, paradoxically, the dubious reputation of the *ci* form made men more hesitant to write about their own romances in that form. For the present discussion, the significant point is that frank references to romance and erotic enjoyment with concubines were not unusual even in the mid-Northern Song.

108. Volpp discusses a similar phenomenon in the context of elite connoisseurship of actors in the seventeenth century in "The Literary Circulation of Actors."

109. See Rouzer, *Articulated Ladies*, chap. 6, on the Tang shift to portrayal of women as worthy partners for men.

| | |
|---|---|
| 妙年得侍碧虛鄉 | In the bloom of youth she serves in the land of the azure void. |
| 自道一生心已足 | She says herself that her heart's desire is already fulfilled. |
| 黃鶯流語春日長 | The oriole prattles, spring days are long; |
| 綠窗繡出金鴛鴦 | At the green window, she embroiders a pair of golden mandarin ducks. |
| 朝暮祝卿千萬壽 | Morning and evening, she utters, "Long life, my darling," |
| 不識相思能斷腸 | Not realizing that love-longing can break one's heart.[110] |

The poem combines images of beauty and romance (the azure void) with images of connubial bliss (mandarin ducks). It acknowledges the romantic happiness shared by the couple, while warning that such a state may not be permanent.

In a slightly different vein, Mei Yaochen wrote two poems extending his encouragement to his friend Shao Yue, whose flute-playing concubine had recently recovered from a life-threatening bout with malaria. The first poem, entitled, "On Hearing That Shao Jingchun's Serving Maid Has Recovered from Malaria (聞刁景純侍女瘧已)," opens with the lines,

| | |
|---|---|
| 前時君家飲,不見吹笛姬 | Recently when drinking at your house, I didn't see the flute-playing charmer; |
| 君言彼娉婷,病瘧久屢治 | You said that the little lovely was ill with malaria, and had been receiving treatment for a long time. |

Mei then proceeds to describe the course of her illness and the attempts at treatment, which involved calling in both doctors and Daoist priests, each with their different diagnoses. Mei's poem suggests that she survived in spite of, more than because of, those ministrations, concluding,

| | |
|---|---|
| 今雖病且已,皮骨尚尪羸 | Now, although her illness has subsided, her wasted body is still frail and feeble. |
| 豈暇理舊曲,未能畫蛾眉 | How can she have the leisure to play the old tunes, when she is still not able to paint her moth eyebrows? |
| 當期重相見,風月臨前墀 | When the time comes we'll see each other again, facing the breezes and moonlight in the front courtyard.[111] |

---

110. Guo Xiangzheng, *Qing shan ji* 13.14b.
111. Mei Yaochen, *Mei Yaochen ji bian nian jiao zhu* 23.690. The phrase "breezes and moonlight" (*feng yue* 風月) also have the sense of "romance," so the last line could be translated, "When the time comes you'll see each other again, as romance reaches the front courtyard."

Mei's poem reveals both his familiarity with his friend's paramour and the considerable effort that Shao's household has expended in taking care of her. The references to her "moth eyebrows" and "breezes and moonlight" underscore the romantic nature of her relationship with her master. Their romance is further alluded to in Mei's second poem, entitled "Jingchun, Because his Serving Maid was Ill, Agreed to Drink with [Liu]Yuanfu When the Moon is Full" (景純以侍兒病期與原甫月圓爲飲). Here we learn that Shao's "house has an excellent flute that is able to please milord" 家有善笛能娛侯, where clearly the flute is metonymic for the flute-player. Mei describes how, when Shao first brought the girl back to the capital from the south, he had her play for his friends from behind a screen. He concludes by urging Liu Yuanfu to be patient in awaiting her full recovery, for if she becomes ill again they will never catch a glimpse of her.[112]

Mei's second poem in turn inspired another member of their circle, Han Wei, to write "Matching Shengyu [Mei Yaochen]'s [Poem] on Hearing Jingchun's Flute-playing Courtesan had Recovered from Her Illness" (和聖俞聞景純吹笛妓病愈)[113] Here again, the double meaning of the lines gently teases Shao: the first two lines employ a double entendre that refers simultaneously to his reputation as a man-about-town and the "happy event" of acquiring a concubine. The last two play on poems and commentary from the *Shi jing* 詩經, in which the Zhou king is described as "frustrated" (*liu zhi*) because he is unable to return from the east, and in which a "reserved/lovely" (*yao tiao*) woman is described as an appropriate partner sought by a gentleman.

| | |
|---|---|
| 刁侯好事聞當年 | I heard years ago that Milord Shao was a man of many affairs; |
| | *I heard about Milord Shao's happy event that year;* |
| 至今風韻獨依然 | Down to today he remains as dashing as ever. |
| | *Down to today she remains as alluring as ever.* |
| 歸來不作留滯歎 | Since he returned he doesn't sigh in frustration: |
| 能出窈窕夸樽前 | He is able to bring out a beauty to grace the banquet hall.[114] |

---

112. Mei Yaochen, *Mei Yaochen ji bian nian jiao zhu* 23.690–91.
113. Han Wei, *Nanyang ji* 4.7b–8a.
114. For these allusions, see Karlgren, *The Book of Odes*, 2, and Ouyang Xiu, *Shi ben yi* 5.13b.

Han then reminisces about a spectacular performance he has heard Shao's flutist give, and concludes with evident anticipation:

| | |
|---|---|
| 氣羸曲節宜少緩 | If her energy is weak, the rhythm of the tune ought to be rather languorous; |
| 體軟舞態當益妍 | If her body is enervated, the appearance of her dancing should be even more seductive. |
| 人生行樂不可後 | In life the pursuit of enjoyment can't be postponed; |
| 幸及華月秋娟娟 | Fortunately, when the full moon comes the autumn will be lovely. |

In these poems we again see male intimacy asserted in both shared appreciation of the charms of the girl herself, and in the knowing evocation of their friend's romantic attachment to her. Mei Yaochen's second poem also reveals that the semi-cloistered nature of household-courtesans made them particularly useful as symbols of intimacy: letting others see a cloistered entertainer was a gesture of special friendship.[115]

Shao Yue's friends, knowing his affection for his serving maid, celebrated her recovery; in less happy circumstances, men also wrote poetry consoling their friends for the loss of beloved concubines. Xie Ke composed a set of two poems entitled, "Li Bu's Household Had a Serving Maid Named Miaoli Who Was Good at Singing and Dancing: Everyone Pitied her Death and Wrote Poetry, so I Too Wrote" (李簿家有侍兒妙麗善歌舞諸人惜其死爲賦詩予亦賦).[116] Sometimes bereaved men even took matters into their own hands: the imperial cousin Li Duanyi 李端懿 honored his deceased *shi'er* by taking the unusual step of obtaining formal mourning poems (*wan ci* 挽詞) for her from the celebrated poet Cai Xiang 蔡襄. Calling her "Lady Fenyang" (Fenyang *fu ren* 汾陽夫人), Cai compared her to an immortal who had returned to her Heavenly abode.[117]

---

115. For another example, see Li Peng's (11th c.) poem celebrating a purchase of a concubine by Su Shi's son Dai 迨, in which Li urges Dai not to put up the screen and hide the girl when Li visits. Li Peng, *Ri she yuan ji* 8.16b.

116. Xie Ke, *Zhu you ji* 6.7a–7b. Xie's poems juxtapose conventional images of sadness and desolation with memories of banquets and flashing smiles.

117. *Cai Xiang ji* 6.106. *Wan ci* were a formal genre of mourning poetry typically composed in honor of high-ranking officials and members of the imperial family. This is the only *wan ci* I have seen that is dedicated to a household-courtesan.

Poetry such as this also reveals that household-courtesans could be objects of affection and caring. To be sure, our sense of these relationships is indirect: Northern Song poetry rarely expresses attraction to or passion for a woman openly, and when such poems do appear (most often in *ci* form) they are virtually always addressed to an abstract and unspecified other.[118] And although we occasionally see poetry in which a man expresses affection for his wife (though this nearly always turns out to have been composed after the wife's death), the poetry men wrote for their *own* serving maids was seldom preserved. One important exception—an exception much commented upon by the romantically inclined in later eras—was Su Shi, whose collected works contains both poetry and prose dedicated to his household-courtesan Wang Zhaoyun ("Morning Cloud").

## Su Shi and Wang Zhaoyun

Much of what little is known about Morning Cloud comes from Su Shi's funerary inscription for her, seen at the opening of this chapter. In the inscription he calls her his attendant-concubine (*shi qie* 侍妾) and notes that she had borne a son and that she had studied Buddhism. The inscription presents her very much in the mode of the virtuous upper-class woman: clever, righteous, respectful, loyal. Yet her status as a concubine, rather than a wife, is evident, not least in that the inscription reveals (however indirectly) that she was a child of ten when she entered Su's household in 1073 (Su was thirty-seven at the time; his second wife, also surnamed Wang, was twenty-five, and had just given birth to their second [and last] son in the previous year).[119]

Su's intimacy with Morning Cloud is better revealed in a set of two poems Su wrote mourning the child she bore him. The title of the poems serves as an explanatory preface: "On the twenty-seventh day of the ninth month of last year [1083], in Huangzhou, my son Dun 遯, whose baby name was Gan'er 幹兒, was born. He was well built and intelligent. This year on the twenty-eighth day of the seventh month, he

---

118. The poetry of Liu Yong is the most obvious example here.
119. I am assuming that Su's middle son, Dai, was the second wife's child, but have been unable to find evidence one way or the other. He could have been borne by an unnamed concubine.

died of illness at Jinling. I wrote these two poems in mourning."[120] The first poem indicates that Su was forty-eight (forty-nine *sui*) when Gan'er died, so the baby was born when Morning Cloud was just twenty-one. It goes on to describe how like Su the child was ("truly my son" 眞吾兒, he says), the delight he took in the baby's antics, and the terrible suddenness of the baby's death. The second poem emphasizes the profound grief Su shared with the child's mother:

| | |
|---|---|
| 我淚猶可拭,日遠當日忘 | My tears can still be brushed away, days long past will be days forgotten. |
| 母哭不可聞,欲與汝俱亡 | Your mother's cries cannot be borne, she wants to join you in death. |
| 故衣尚懸架,漲乳已流床 | Your old garments still hang on the rack; milk from her swollen breasts flows on to the bed. |
| 感此欲忘生,一臥終日僵 | Faced with these feelings, I want to forget about life; I lie prostrate, numb, the entire day. |

We learn still more about Su Shi's relationship with Morning Cloud in a poem he wrote for her some ten years later, in 1094, shortly after they arrived in Huizhou (where Su had again been sent into exile). The poem first invokes the Tang poet Bai Juyi, who had written a poem honoring the loyalty of his serving maid Fan Su (she had refused to leave him when he was ill). After noting that, ultimately, Fan did leave Bai, Su remarks, "My household had several concubines (*qie*) who, in the space of four or five years, successively took their leave. Only the one called Morning Cloud followed me to the south. Because I was reading Bai Juyi's collected works, I jokingly wrote this poem." The first quatrain of the poem makes oblique reference to the death of their child and to Morning Cloud's Buddhist studies, while the last four lines invoke the couple's present, past, and future relationship:

| | |
|---|---|
| 經卷藥爐新活計 | Sutra chapters and alchemical furnaces are our new occupation, |
| 舞衫歌扇舊因緣 | The dancing garb and singing fan were our old karmic connection. |
| 丹成逐我三山去 | When the elixir is ready follow me to the Three Peaks; |
| 不作巫陽雲雨仙 | Don't become the rain and cloud immortal of Wu Mountain.[121] |

---

120. *Su Shi shi ji* 23.1239–40.
121. *Su Shi shi ji* 38.2073–74. "Three Peaks" is the legendary home of Daoist immortals.

## The Courtesan as Concubine

3. Wang Zhaoyun 王朝雲, beloved concubine of the great Song poet Su Shi. Their relationship was celebrated by romantics throughout the later imperial era. In this illustration from a late Ming collection entitled "Lotuses in the Mud," Zhaoyun is shown entertaining Su Shi with clappers, a percussion instrument commonly used to accompany vocal performance. From Mei Yujin (Dingzuo) 梅禹金 (鼎祚), comp., *Hui tu Qing ni lian hua ji* 繪圖青泥蓮花記 (Beijing, Zi qiang shu ju), 1910, *yuan*.2b. Ming dynasty. Courtesy of Hathi Trust. (http://hdl.handle.net/2027/mdp .39015070911931?urlappend=%3Bseq=327; Google-digitized, image of page n136).

These lines play on the couple's exiled state, suggesting that they were withdrawing from the world to practice both Daoist and Buddhist cultivation. (They may also refer to Su's very real interest in Buddhism and Daoism, which is amply attested to in other sources.) The final couplet begs Morning Cloud to follow Su, when they are sufficiently cultivated, to the abode of immortals on the Three Peaks. At the same time, the quatrain makes reference to the "old karmic connection" that binds them, a connection based on Morning Cloud's role as a singer and dancer.[122] This line is particularly notable, for it makes clear that Morning Cloud served in Su's household as an entertainer.

The preface to this poem reveals that Morning Cloud was not the only concubine who served Su, which raises fascinating but unanswerable questions about the status of the others and about what became of them when they left Su's employ. We can surmise that Morning Cloud's decision—and Su emphasizes that it was hers—was a difficult one: by the time Su was sent into exile Morning Cloud had been with him for more than twenty years (two thirds of her life to that point), and they had borne and mourned a child together. It is difficult to imagine that she could have left him casually, or what her alternatives would have been had she done so. On the other hand, Huizhou was understood to be a backward, uncomfortable, and malarial place: exile there was widely recognized as a death sentence, as indeed it proved to be in Morning Cloud's case. Clearly Su saw her decision to remain with him as an act of unusual loyalty, and his poem is a gesture of gratitude and love.

Su's attachment to Morning Cloud is further evident in a mourning poem and a dedicatory prayer he wrote for her ("Dao Zhaoyun" [悼朝雲], and "Huizhou jian Zhaoyun shu" [惠州薦朝雲疏]).[123] In

---

The text notes that, according to Southern Song commentators, the last line referred to a poem that Qin Guan wrote for Zhaoyun, in which he compared her to an immortal on Wu Mountain.

122 The terms Su uses hark back to a poem by the Six Dynasties poet Yu Xin 庾信 (513–81), entitled "Watching courtesans with Prince Zhao." The first line of Yu's poem evokes the "singing fan" of Green Pearl and the "dancing garb" of Zhao Feiyan (a famous entertainer-concubine at the court of a Han emperor). See Yu Xin, *Yu Zishan ji* 4.50b. The phrase was picked up by a number of poets in the Tang before Su Shi used it here.

123. *Su Shi shi ji* 40.2202–03; *Su Shi wen ji* 62.1909–10.

the preface to the poem, Su explains that Morning Cloud became ill and died in Huizhou, and was buried near a Buddhist temple there. Elaborating somewhat on the funerary inscription, Su notes Morning Cloud had originally been illiterate but had later studied and attained some ability to read and write. He also describes her as studying with the Buddhist nun Yizhong at Sishang 泗上, a piece of information that allows us tentatively to date Morning Cloud's studies to late 1084 (the date suggests that her Buddhist studies were inspired by the death of her child).[124] The dedicatory prayer indicates that Su Shi likewise took comfort in Buddhism after Morning Cloud's own death, as it describes auspicious signs that indicated her acceptance by the Buddha.

Su's writings for Morning Cloud can hardly be called emotionally effusive, but the relatively frank affection they express is quite striking when we compare them with texts Su composed (or didn't) for his two wives. Su did write a funerary inscription for his first wife upon her death in 1065, although he indicates in the inscription that he did so at the command of his mother. The text is polite and praises the deceased's virtues, but (like his funerary inscription for Morning Cloud) it betrays little emotion.[125] Su did not compose a funerary inscription for his second wife, who died shortly before he went into exile in Huizhou. Three of the four texts he did write for her are simply dedications to Buddhist iconography commissioned in her memory, two of which were initiated by Su's sons. The most personal of the texts Su wrote for his second wife is a sacrificial ode (*ji wen* 祭文), which praises her for being a good wife and mother and following him south without complaint during an earlier exile, but it certainly doesn't reveal deep emotional attachment.[126] In short, Su's surviving writings suggest that he enjoyed a more intimate relationship with Morning Cloud that he did with either of his wives. Some evidence suggests that Morning Cloud's presence may even have served as a poetic inspiration for Su. In a recent discussion of Su Shi's *ci*

---

124. Su Shi is known to have been traveling in that area in late 1084. See Wang Shuizhao, *Song ren suo zhuan san Su nian pu hui kan*, 66–67.

125. Su expressed somewhat more emotional attachment in the *ci* poem "Jiang cheng zi, yi lao zheng yue er shi ri ye ji meng" (江城子, 乙卯正月二十日夜记梦), believed by later scholars to have been written for his first wife ten years after her death. See Yu Chaogang and Zhou Hang, *Fen lei xin bian Liang Song jue miao hao ci*, 755.

126. *Su Shi wen ji* 15.472, 20.586, 21.619, 66.2086, 63.1960.

poetry, Ronald Egan observes that although Su wrote very little in the *ci* style prior to 1073, from 1074 on he began to write copiously in this form. Egan characterizes many of the poems Su wrote in the early part of this period as conventional banquet songs. The evidence is only circumstantial, but it is at least plausible that the introduction of Morning Cloud into Su's household in 1073 inspired him to devote more of his energies to the *ci* form, producing works that she (and perhaps others with her) could sing for his entertainment. As Egan points out, Su's experimentation in the *ci* form ultimately transformed the genre.[127]

Finally, it is tempting to take some of Su Shi's many wry aphorisms as providing a final covert glimpse into his relationship with Morning Cloud. Was Su Shi speaking from personal experience when, under the category of "Unhappy," he listed "Being stuck with a jealous wife into old age," or when, under the heading of "Cannot Be Reasoned With" he included "A husband and wife quarrelling about a serving maid (*bi*)"? Was he remembering the very young Morning Cloud when, in the category of "Evoking Tenderness in People" he included "A young courtesan who is good at dancing and singing"? And was he thinking of his own situation when he defined "This Time Able to Be at Ease" as "The favored concubine (*chong qie* 寵妾) alone accompanies her master to his official post"?[128]

Although his poetry reveals only tantalizing hints of Su Shi's feelings for Morning Cloud, the couple serves as an example of the relative openness with which romantic relationships with concubines were treated in the Northern Song. Many sources attest that Su Shi's friends were aware of her place in his life. Huang Tingjian wrote a poem for Su in which he made a pun on Morning Cloud's name, obliquely suggesting that for Su taking up a new post might not be as good as "ending up in obscurity, keeping the morning clouds company."[129] Su himself, in a letter to his friend Chen Jichang 陳季常, indicated that he was traveling to Huizhou accompanied by "my youngest son Guo and Old Cloud, as well as two old serving maids" (幼子過及老雲幷二老婢). In referring to Morning Cloud with the casual and familiar prefix "old,"

---

127. Egan, *The Problem of Beauty*, 359–60.
128. Su Shi, *Za zuan er xu*, 89, 97, 88, 91.
129. *Huang Tingjian quan ji, wai ji*, 3.914.

## The Courtesan as Concubine

Su reveals the shared intimacy that must have obtained between the three.[130] Similarly, in a letter to his friend Li Zhi (Fangshu) 李廌 (方叔), Su first expresses his sympathy for the illness of one "Lady Chang'an" (Chang'an *jun*) and recommends a special prescription for her illness. He then reports Morning Cloud's death, explaining that she died some time ago in Huizhou and adding that since they had last parted from Li, Morning Cloud had learned to read and had studied Buddhism. Su describes both how she died reciting a sutra and the arrangements he made for her burial. He concludes, "She was greatly beloved of milady, and so I have written in such detail."[131] Although it is no longer possible to identify Lady Chang'an, she appears to have been a member of Li Zhi's household. Clearly Su was acquainted with her, and equally clearly both Li Zhi and Lady Chang'an were acquainted with Morning Cloud (indeed, the diction of Su's letter suggests he is responding specifically to an inquiry about her). Thus Morning Cloud's status as Su's companion was widely acknowledged in his own day. By the Southern Song their romance had become a favorite topic of anecdotalists, and it remained so throughout the later imperial period.

In spite of their intimacy, Su Shi's writings for Morning Cloud never overstepped the bounds of propriety: we have no evidence that he was anything but punctilious with respect to maintaining the proper status distinctions between his wife and his concubines. Other Northern Song sources reveal that this was not always the case, and they betray a growing concern with the tensions in family life that concubinage could engender.

### Concubines in Moral Discourse

Concubines were implicated in two kinds of moral discourse in the Northern Song. One, expressed especially by moral philosophers, harked back to classical discourse and was concerned with the maintenance of proper hierarchies within the family. The other, which appeared in broader social discourse and echoed the sorts of concerns about

---

130. *Su Shi wen ji* 53.1570, sixteenth of sixteen letters for Chen Jichang. See also Egan, "Su Shih's 'Notes' as a Historical and Literary Source," 577

131. Su Shi, *Dongpo quan ji* 77.3, in the final of four letters to Li Fangshu ("Yu Li Fangshu si shou" 與李方叔四首). I have been unable to locate this letter in the modern edition of Su Shi's works.

courtesans we saw in chapter 1, depicted even concubines within the household as a potential symbol of sexual license and excess.

Confucian ideology from its inception had posited a close relationship between political and household order, insisting that good government was predicated on the maintenance of proper social distinctions within individual households. Northern Song moralists, anxious to reinvigorate the Confucian tradition, articulated this premise explicitly, and wrote extensively about proper management of the household.[132] Somewhat surprisingly, then, the Northern Song moralists had relatively little to say about the roles and management of concubines. What they did say focused almost exclusively on preservation of ritual hierarchies. Sima Guang's manual for family life, for example, cites the ritual classics to emphasize that serving women and concubines should be distinguished from the main wife in all respects, down to the clothing they wear and the food they eat.[133] He relates a Han anecdote to show that even a concubine who has borne the family heir must never take precedence over a wife, whether the wife herself has borne children or not. Only once does he acknowledge that in practice ritual hierarchies are sometimes abrogated: he describes a situation in the Latter Tang (923–36) when an emperor—whom Sima characterizes as "ignorant of ritual"—honored his own birth mother as dowager empress while treating his father's empress (that is, his "legal" or ritual mother) as a dowager concubine. Here Sima praises the two women for maintaining a congenial relationship despite the situation: "the dowager concubine did not become resentful, the dowager empress did not dare to be self-important."[134] In other words, Sima suggests, ritual precedence must be upheld, and when it is not, the women involved must behave in such a manner that domestic harmony can be preserved.[135]

---

132. See Ebrey, *Confucianism and Family Rituals*, 45–53.

133. Upholding the same principle, Sima Guang also argued vehemently that the enfeoffments awarded to honor the ancestors of imperial concubines (fei 妃) must not be equal to those awarded to the ancestors of the empress, for distinctions between concubine and mistress *(qie zhu zhi fen* 妾主之分*)* had to be maintained. Sima Guang, *Sima wen zheng gong chuan jia ji* 10.373, memorial of 1062. See also Ebrey, "Concubines in Song China," 3–5; "Women, Money, and Class," 658–59.

134. Sima Guang, *Jia fan* 10.6–8.

135. It may be relevant here that Sima Guang himself was known among his contemporaries for his disinterest in sex. Several anecdotalists repeated the story of how Sima

Writing in roughly the same period, the brothers Cheng Hao and Cheng Yi wanted to invigorate ritual distinctions with individual moral cultivation and, as seen in chapter 1, they argued strenuously that human desires (*ren yu* 人欲) posed a major obstacle to such cultivation.[136] But whereas the Cheng brothers warned against the dangers of desire in general, they did not single out sexual desire as more or less problematic than, for example, the desire for food or material comfort, and they said almost nothing about concubines as objects of desire. When they did broach the subject, the Cheng brothers (like Sima Guang) suggested that desire for concubines was morally problematic only when it disrupted the ritual hierarchy of the household. Thus Cheng Yi, citing a poem from the *Book of Odes* in which a nobleman's concubines lament their subservient status, remarked:

> When base (*jian*) concubines achieve the intimate favor of their lords, usurpation and self-indulgence can occur and proper boundaries can be breached. If instead [the concubines] can "take care when carrying the coverlet and chemise," and know that their "fate does not match [that of the main wife]," then moral transformation will be accomplished.[137]

Not only is Cheng Yi concerned above all with the preservation of status hierarchies, he (again like Sima Guang) suggests that it is the concubines' responsibility to know their place and not challenge the superior status of the main wife. Strikingly, in this formulation, the master bears no responsibility for the "moral transformation" of his household. In this instance Cheng Yi puts the onus for maintaining hierarchy (and harmony) on the concubines, but elsewhere he also

---

ignored the concubine his wife had bought for him, and chased her out when (on his wife's orders) she entered his study alone (Shao Bowen, *Shao shi wen jian lu* 11.121–22; Zhou Hui, *Qing bo za zhi* 392, n. 3).

136. Cheng Hao maintained that people knew in their hearts how to behave, but because this knowledge was obscured by human desire, they forgot Heavenly Virtue. Cheng Yi went further, suggesting that human desire and Heavenly Principle were directly opposed: any action not in accord with Heavenly Principle was ipso facto motivated by selfish desire. Conversely, any action—even those not strictly in accord with ritual—would accord with Heavenly Principle as long as it was not motivated by human desire. See Cheng Hao and Cheng Yi, *Er cheng ji* 11.123, 15.144.

137. Cheng Hao and Cheng Yi, *Er cheng ji* 21b.274. The reference is to the twenty-first song of the "Zhou nan" cycle, "Little stars" (*xiao xing* 小星). See Karlgren, *The Book of Odes*, 12–13.

acknowledges the role of wives. Citing two poems from the *Book of Odes* that celebrate the birth of many sons, and that were commonly understood as referring to wives' relations with concubines, Cheng remarks:

> The "Zhong si" poem says only that one shouldn't be jealous; [if one can be as in the poem] "Fu Yi," then things will be even more harmonious. When [the commentary] says "The women are pleased to have sons," it is saying that when the concubines are all without fear, they will be happy to have sons.[138]

Once more, the harmony, and by extension the reproductive success, of the family is regarded as solely the responsibility of women. Although the passages above implicitly recognize that concubines could be a threat to the wife's status in the household, more generally Cheng Yi and other Northern Song philosophers seem to have regarded concubines as so inferior to wives that they did not count as marital partners. For example, Cheng Yi opposed on moral grounds remarriage for either sex, saying, "When people get married, when do they ever agree that 'if one of us dies, the other will get remarried'? They only promise to end their lives as husband and wife." But he conceded that some men could not help but remarry, as they needed a woman to take care of their parents and tend to household affairs. Significantly, however, Cheng found remarriage acceptable only for men below the rank of grand master (*dai fu* 大夫). Men above that rank, he observed, could have lesser consorts (he uses the archaic term *pin fei* 嬪妃) to attend to household duties, and for them remarriage was morally unacceptable.[139] Cheng Yi's assumption that his contemporaries obeyed classical sumptuary rules about who could keep concubines was spectacularly out of touch with Northern Song realities, but the larger point here is that for Cheng, the distinctions between wives and concubines were apparently great enough that he did not consider the keeping of concubines as relevant to the issue of spousal loyalty.[140] In short, in spite of their suspicion of human desire, the Confucian moral

---

138. Cheng Hao and Cheng Yi, *Er cheng ji* 11.128. Patricia Ebrey notes that Sima Guang, too, saw the problems of concubines as best solvable by "more ritual and hierarchy" (Ebrey, "Women, Money, and Class," 658).

139. Cheng Hao and Cheng Yi, *Er cheng ji* 303.

140. Here the ambiguity between the sexual and other types of service provided by concubines obscures the question of whether Cheng Yi assumed a man would remain sexually faithful to his wife after her death.

philosophers of the Northern Song do not portray indulgence with concubines as a major moral issue for men.

The reticence of moral philosophers on this point is especially notable in that, as discussed in chapter 1, within the broader cultural milieu of the Northern Song, sexual restraint was frequently associated with morality. And, just as writers assessed their contemporaries' relations with courtesans, in biographical and anecdotal sources alike they depicted men's interactions with concubines as emblematic of their moral character.[141] We have seen that men were sometimes praised for their refusal to keep concubines, especially those of the entertainer variety. In the Northern Song this restraint with regard to sexual pleasures was often associated with a more general disinterest in luxury and extravagance: in his 1057 sacrificial ode for the deceased Grand Councilor Du Yan, Han Qi observed: "Ah! Milord's nobility was not like that of others. He did not buy land and houses, he did not keep musician-courtesans. He ate vegetables and gruel, his garments were coarse and his coverlet cotton." The Vice Grand Councilor Ding Du (990–1053) was similarly credited with having a "pure nature, and not standing on ceremony. He lived in one room for more than ten years, and did not have charmer-attendants waiting on him."[142] The same conflation of morality with lack of desire (and with concerns about status) was highlighted in the many stories, noted above, of men who refused to accept concubines of genteel background. Shao Bowen related how Wang Anshi, on questioning the concubine his wife had newly purchased for him, discovered that the woman had previously been the wife of an army commander who had sold her to pay back the government for loss of a boat transporting tax grain. Deeply distressed by this discovery, Wang determined the price paid for her and restored her to her husband without asking that any of the money be returned. Shao praises Wang for "not being interested in erotic entertainment, not coveting office, and not accumulating wealth"[143]

Conversely, if indifference to concubines was the mark of an upright

---

141. Buddhism, with its wholesale rejection of the physical body, may have been influential here.
142. *Chang bian* 174.4191.
143. Shao Bowen, *Shao shi wen jian lu* 11.121–22.

individual, excessive indulgence with concubines, like that with courtesans, appears in Northern Song sources as a conventional sign of evil or decadent character. Su Shi's father Su Xun wrote about a powerful magnate in their home district who had cheated his brother's children out of their inheritance, was obsessed with erotic entertainment, and whose "glittering carriages and horses and gorgeous serving girls" were undermining local morality by leading petty people astray.[144] In the 1030s, the young Zhang Fangping likewise warned of the dangers to proper governance of the decadent lifestyles of wealthy merchants:

> [Now] those under Heaven pursuing agriculture are few while the wandering and disorderly are many; degraded customs flourish while honest farmers are in difficulty. Those who travel about pursuing buying and selling have attendants riding behind them; those who sit in the counting houses planning for profit have huge houses, one leaning against another; good things to eat are lined up in pots, their clothing is sufficient for the four seasons, and in song-pavilions and private rooms courtesan-concubines crowd around to serve them; at a single word the latest novelties of the four directions appear.

After comparing this opulence to the bitter lives of farmers, Zhang adds:

> I have heard that the officials of Zhou used restrictions to teach restraint, and thus the people knew sufficiency. Now food and sex (*yin shi nan nü* 飲食男女) are what people most desire; to live and die in poverty and bitterness are what people most abhor. Thus desire and abhorrence are the key elements of human emotion, and regulation and restraint is the key method of ordering the people. When the people know that they cannot transgress the limits of their station, then their propensity to greed and extravagance will be stilled, and the notions of humanity, righteousness, modesty, and forbearance will arise. For this reason, the key element of the Kingly Way must begin with regulation and restraint.[145]

To Zhang Fangping, indulgence with concubines is a sign not only of individual decadence but of broader social decline. Here concubines— especially entertainer-concubines—figure as objects of luxury consumption that undermine proper hierarchies not only within the family but in

---

144. Su Xun, *Jiayou ji jian zhu* 14.391.
145. Zhang Fangping, *Le quan ji* 11.12b–15. This essay is part of a "Discourse on Rites and Music" (*li yue lun* 禮樂論) that was itself part of a lengthy set of memorials addressing virtually all aspects of governance. Although the text is not dated, Su Shi's funerary inscription for Zhang indicates that it was written in the 1030s.

society in general.¹⁴⁶ Echoes of this view appear frequently in writings on Northern Song family and political life.

## Concubines in Family Life

Although the writings of Northern Song moralists distinguished strictly between wives and concubines, they made no distinction between different types of concubines. Yet we have seen that the term "concubine" encompassed a wide variety of women in the household, from the slavey who mopped floors to the cultivated beauty who entertained at banquets, from kitchen maids to women who served as intimate companions and reared the household's children. In the context of family life, status distinctions among these women, and between them and the legal wife, became critically important. Moreover, in the context of family life such distinctions were determined more through personal interactions than by law and moral strictures.

In theory, the position of the legal wife was unassailable: both law and moral discourse were explicit that a concubine could never take the place of a wife. In at least some cases, the law was enforced. In the late 1080s the imperial clansman Zhao Zongjing 趙宗景 created a minor scandal in the capital by attempting to elevate his attendant-charmer, a woman surnamed Yang, to the position of his deceased wife.¹⁴⁷ Zhao was indicted by one Chen Cisheng 陳次升, who risked angering the emperor by arguing passionately that Zongjing's action threatened to sully the honor of the imperial clan. Fortunately for Chen, the emperor was persuaded by his rhetoric, with the result that Zongjing was demoted and his marriage to Yang dissolved.¹⁴⁸

---

146. Christian de Pee has remarked on the Northern Song court's concern, in the face of a prospering economy, to keep the circulation of goods within the construct of an ordered, hierarchical system and to stem destructive and destabilizing competition. He notes that in their penchant for luxury, the elite of Kaifeng "denied the natural inherence of this social hierarchy as well as the court's authority to determine its configuration" (de Pee, "Purchase on Power," 168, 175).

147. Contrast the case of Zhao Shixian, above, who was demoted for taking a courtesan as a concubine.

148. Chen Cisheng, *Dang lun ji* 1.20–20b. Chen stressed that Yang came from lowly (*bei wei* 卑微) background, and reminded the court that imperial clan members were not permitted to marry with performers or people from artisan, merchant, or "mixed

But even as the legal and social systems provided some protection for the legal wife, those systems undercut her position in other ways.[149] Concubinage was, after all, perfectly legal, and that legality was in turn based on the broader social imperative of producing heirs. Not only did a wife have no legal basis for objecting to the introduction of a concubine into the household, but a virtuous woman was expected to encourage her husband to take a concubine, in the interests of providing descendants for the ancestors. As Song observers well understood, however, the power of erotic attraction and the dynamics of human intimacy meant that the arrival of a concubine in the inner quarters could easily wreak havoc on the socially sanctioned power relations therein. Thus an author of humorous aphorisms noted wryly that one of the "Things That Are Hard to Cope With" in life was "A maid who presumes on [the master's] favor" (*shi chong bi* 恃寵婢). For, although authority within the inner quarters theoretically rested in the hands of the legal wife, she could maintain that authority only as long as she had her husband's unequivocal support. However much moralists might shake their heads in disapproval, wives had little recourse when their husbands became besotted with serving maids: Wang Kui's wife was humiliated by his concubine, but her complaints to her husband elicited no response. Although Su Xun railed against the local power-holder who had set his concubine above his wife, he acknowledged that others were untroubled by the man's behavior.[150]

These structural tensions between the wife's theoretical position in the household, on the one hand, and the realities of the power relations shaped by her husband's sexual and emotional attachments, on the other, made women's jealousy a central issue in Chinese family life.[151]

---

categories" families (*ji shu gong shang za lei zhi jia* 伎術工商雜類之家). On the riskiness of Chen's action, see the preface to this work by Chen Anguo (*yuan xu*, 1b). Cf. Chaffee, *Branches of Heaven*, 58–59.

149. For an extended discussion of the multiple factors conditioning the relationships between concubines and wives in later imperial China, see Bray, *Fabrics of Power*, 335–68.

150. Wang Junyu, *Za zuan xu*, 53; Chen Shidao, *Hou shan tan cong* 5.64–65; Su Xun, *Jiayou ji jian zhu* 14.391.

151. Both Cheng Yi's and Sima Guang's comments suggest this. Ebrey describes Sima Guang's concerns that wives and concubines not be jealous ("Women, Money, and

Such jealousy was not necessarily a sign of a woman's own attachment to or affections for her husband: even if a wife had no particular feelings for her husband and was not interested in his affections, she had reason to be concerned how his relationships with maids or concubines might affect her authority in the household.

Women's biographies suggest that, indeed, relations in the inner quarters of the elite were becoming increasingly fraught over the course of the Northern Song. We see this particularly in the new tendency of women's biographers to focus on their subjects' treatment of maids and concubines.[152] Such authors repeatedly insist on assuring us that their subjects treated the serving maids "graciously," "with kindness," or at least "without anger."[153] Others find virtue in the fact that their subjects treated concubines "strictly" or "correctly," thereby keeping the inner quarters "peaceful and orderly."[154] Many authors protest, perhaps too much, that their subjects were not jealous, and a few women—especially those who had no sons—are credited with selecting concubines for their husbands.[155] Occasionally, the tensions created by the presence of concubines are more explicitly acknowledged. One author admits that, when confronted with concubines, many women were simply beside themselves (迫於不得已). Another illustrates a mother's love for her only daughter by noting that she wanted her daughter to marry someone who did not have charmer-concubines.[156]

In the face of these structural and emotional complexities, the individual personalities of the denizens of the inner quarters could powerfully shape the dynamics of household life. Anecdotes and short stories

---

Class," 648). On jealousy as a literary theme in later imperial China, see Yenna Wu, *The Lioness Roars*.

152. By contrast, before the late Tang funerary inscription authors almost never mention concubines.

153. Liu Bin, *Peng cheng ji* 39.512; *Ouyang Xiu quan ji* 36.531–32, 37.549–50; Xie Yi, *Xi tang ji* 9.15; Fan Zuyu, *Fan Taishi ji* 49.3b.

154. Lu Dian, *Tao shan ji* 15.12; Murong Yanfeng, *Chi wen tang ji* 14.23; Wang Anshi, *Wang wen gong wen ji* 98.1002.

155. On the absence of jealousy see, among others, Fan Zuyu, *Fan Taishi ji* 48.4 and 45.16b; *Huang Tingjian quan ji* 22.1392; Shen Kuo, *Changxing ji* 13.9b. On selecting concubines, see Wang Anshi, *Wang wen gong wen ji* 99.1012; Huang Chang, *Yan shan ji* 33.12b and 34.2b–3.

156. Zhao Dingchen, *Zhu yin ji shi ji* 19.3b–4; Li Zhaoqi, *Le jing ji* 30.1–1b.

of the Northern Song describe strong-willed wives who prevented their husbands from taking in other women, but also wives who were driven out or even murdered by their husbands' concubines. Some wives regarded young concubines—who might well be the same age as the wives' daughters—with indulgent affection; others were unspeakably cruel. Here we should note that, if law and social custom gave a modicum of protection to wives, they gave none at all to concubines. For wives to beat concubines was perfectly legal, but for a concubine to hit a wife was a serious crime.[157] A concubine's only protection was the affection of her master, who had the authority to discipline his wife. But a master who cared about social niceties might well be reluctant or embarrassed to reprimand his wife, even if he had some fondness for his concubine.

Whatever the personal dynamics in the household, few Northern Song concubines could hope for the kind of permanent home that most wives could expect upon marriage; it seems to have been assumed that most concubines—and perhaps especially entertainer-concubines—would have only a temporary relationship with their masters' households. As status symbols and objects of connoisseurship, entertainer-concubines lost value as their looks and skills deteriorated, and could find themselves unceremoniously sold or married off to other men. In 1074, Chen Shunyu described how he and his friends discovered that a singer who had been the household-courtesan of a high-ranking military official was now a different colleague's bondmaid (*shi bi* 侍婢). Hearing that she had wept on recognizing one of their number from former days, they took wine to pay her a visit:

> The wine went around, but Zhengchen [the bondmaid's new owner] was unwilling to bring her out to urge the guests to drink. He only had her sing behind a screen, play a few tunes on the flute and barbarian lute, and that was all. All of her melodies were clear and skillful. Only Ziye [i.e., Zhang Xian 張先 (990–1078)], because of his old association with her, was able to go behind the screen and ask about [her old master] Fan's vicissitudes and how she had come to be there. Ziye said, "At one time, she was Fan's most beloved." At that, all the guests

---

157. Inscription sources, particularly in the Southern Song, often praise women for not beating concubines, suggesting that such restraint was unusual. Short stories detailing the sad fate of concubines take it for granted that concubines would be beaten and humiliated at every turn.

pitied her. They also admired the purity of her skill, and regretted that they were unable to see her.¹⁵⁸

Alternatively, sometimes being too attractive led to a woman being expelled: when the famous official Yan Shu doted too fondly on a young singer he had purchased, his wife pressured him to get rid of the girl.¹⁵⁹ Sometimes men reached a point in their lives when they were no longer interested in keeping household-courtesans: we saw above that, after his mother's death, a brother of Emperor Yingzong renounced musical entertainments and expelled his numerous serving maids.¹⁶⁰

Still other concubines left their masters by choice. A funerary inscription by Zhao Dingchen for his younger sister describes how she persuaded maidservants who sought to leave to stay on a bit longer, suggesting that a maid whose contract had expired had some say in whether she wanted to extend her term of service.¹⁶¹ Anecdotal literature indicates that an ex-concubine might remain close enough with her former master that she could deploy the connection to obtain political favors: a descendant of the grand councilor Fan Gongcheng relates how the prosecution of an evil monk in Luoyang was complicated by the fact that the monk's lover, a teahouse courtesan, had formerly been the concubine of a powerful minister.¹⁶² Finally, even a concubine who stayed with her master to the end of his life often seems to have been expected to leave the household when he died;¹⁶³ a favored concubine of the grand councilor Han Jiang

---

158. Moved by the pathos of the occasion, Chen composed a poem expressing what he imagined to be the courtesan's emotions. Chen Shunyu, *Du guan ji* 12.20, "Shuang xi xing" 雙溪行.

159. See the anecdote recorded in Tang Guizhang, *Song ci ji shi*, 23–24. I have discussed this incident and translated the anecdote in Bossler, "Shifting Identities," 24.

160. Fan Zuyu, *Fan Taishi ji* 51.2b.

161. Zhao Dingchen, *Zhu yin ji shi ji* 19.5b–7b. Southern Song evidence shows that by that time at least, maids were hired on term contracts. See Tang Daijian, "Song dai qie de mai mai," 59, and Ebrey, *Inner Quarters*, 222–24. To my knowledge, there is no explicit evidence that such contracts were used in the Northern Song, but the extant evidence does suggest practices consistent with those seen in the Southern Song.

162. Fan Gongcheng, *Guo ting lu*, 54–55. Fan explains how his grandfather handled the matter in such a way that the concubine's ex-master arrived too late to interfere, and justice was able to prevail.

163. See Ebrey, *Inner Quarters*, 226, on Su Shi's distress in seeing a deceased friend's household-courtesan entertaining at another man's house. Ebrey also points out that

was reportedly able to take a large amount of the family property with her when she remarried after his death.¹⁶⁴ Song law, which decreed severe punishment if a wife remarried while still in mourning for her husband, explicitly exempted concubines from this restriction, apparently assuming the concubines would be married out sooner rather than later.¹⁶⁵

From our current vantage point, it is difficult to know what factors affected a family's decision to keep a concubine on after her master's death. It seems likely that genteel women who were taken in with formal rituals (such as Han Qi's mother), were more apt to stay there permanently than women who entered the household as entertainers or maids. Long service in the family was probably also a factor: Su Shi's family kept on the woman he refers to as his *mother's* concubine, Golden Cicada, because she had served as his younger brother's nursemaid.¹⁶⁶ Finally, having produced a son for the family probably increased a woman's likelihood of remaining with her master. The birth mother of Zou Hao's maternal uncle died in her husband's household nineteen years after his death, having reared and educated two sons; similarly, a number of wives are described as filially serving the birth mothers of their husbands.¹⁶⁷ Still, having borne a son to the family did not secure a concubine's place in her master's household. The father of the imperial clansman Zhao Lingwan 趙令峴 (1062–89) died when Lingwan was still an infant, so his birth mother was remarried to someone else (*shi ren* 適人). Similarly, when Chen Anding's 陳安定 natural father died three days after he was born, his birth mother Zhang left that family and took him to the household of the official Chen Guan 陳瓘; there she left Anding to be reared as an adopted son.¹⁶⁸

---

since concubines were often considerably younger than their masters, they were quite likely to outlive them (*Inner Quarters*, 231). In the Southern Song, Zhou Hui noted with disgust that before a master's body was cold other men were scheming to acquire his serving maids (Zhou Hui, *Qing bo za zhi* 3.101–02; Bossler, "Shifting Identities," 30).

164. Fan Gongcheng, *Guo ting lu*, 344.

165. *Song xing tong* 1.12b.

166. *Su Shi wen ji* 15.473. As Ebrey has noted, family servants "might be kept on as a charitable act" (*Inner Quarters*, 231).

167. Zou Hao, *Dao xiang ji* 38.16b; Chen Xiang, *Gu ling ji* 20.1–4b; Huang Tingjian *quan ji, wai ji*, 22.1394; Zhao Dingchen, *Zhu yin ji shi ji* 19.5b–7b.

168. Fan Zuyu, *Fan Taishi ji* 49.9; Chen Xiang, *Gu ling ji* 20.11. The sources do not explain Zhang's relationship to Chen Guan, or indicate why she left Anding behind.

Chen Anding's circumstances also remind us that, from the perspective of children, concubine parentage also complicated family relationships.[169] Just as a serving woman's status in the family depended greatly on how her master chose to regard her, so too did the status of her children depend largely on his decision to legitimate them. Given the cultural imperative to produce heirs, Northern Song lawmakers and most other observers seem to have assumed that men would automatically wish to acknowledge any sons born to them.[170] And from the perspective of larger society, there seems to have been little prejudice against concubines' sons (as is perhaps not surprising given the propensity of eminent men in this period to produce children by concubines).[171] Many sons of concubines became successful officials in the Northern Song, and neither they nor their biographers hesitate to acknowledge the circumstances of their birth. Still, social prejudice was not entirely absent. The mother of Chao Zaizhi 晁載之, a scion of one of the Northern Song's most eminent families, reportedly commented that "As for concubines' sons who have attained reputation, nobility, and wealth, there are some like Han [Qi]; but there have never been any who were truly cultured" (*wei you wen shi ye* 未有文事也), and her remarks were circulated by a noted writer of the day.[172] And sometime in the mid-eleventh century the scion of an eminent family successfully petitioned the court to end the practice whereby sons of imperial clanswomen received noble titles "without regard to *di* and *shu*" (that is, whether they were sons of the legal wife or of concubines).[173]

---

169. See also Bray, *Technology and Gender*, 343–48.
170. Guo Dongxu, *Song dai fa zhi*, 438–39 indicates that "legally born children" (sons of wives and/or concubines) had equal property rights in Song law, and adds that even children of illegal or illicit relations (including adultery but also relations with a maidservant [*bi*]) were legitimate and were coparceners if recognized by the father. On the other hand, children not recognized by fathers during the latters' lifetimes were seldom recognized by the state. The latter category could include sons who were born when a pregnant concubine was expelled.
171. This is evident especially in funerary inscriptions for members of the imperial family, a large percentage of whom were children of concubines. See Fan Zuyu, *Fan Taishi ji* 46.11, 48.4, 51.2. See also Chaffee, *Branches of Heaven*, 33, 58.
172. Chen Shidao, *Hou shan shi hua*, 309. On the Chao family see Bol, "*This Culture of Ours*," 60–75 and 345–54.
173. Fan Zuyu, *Fan Taishi ji* 42.6b, in a funerary inscription for Lü Xidao. See also a funerary inscription for a concubine surnamed Wu, whose husband was related to

Even if general social prejudice against the sons of concubines was relatively mild, however, within the context of the family the disparities between the sons of wives and the sons of concubines could be keenly felt. The Northern Song system of inheritance for titles and enfeoffments still privileged sons of the legal wife over those of concubines. Similarly, the Northern Song interest in restoring classical models of the family, with emphasis on the descent-line heir, militated against equality for concubines' sons, as did the moralist concern to maintain hierarchy between wives and concubines.[174] And, although nominally any child recognized by the father was legitimate and an equal coparcener in his estate, Chen Anding's case reveals that if a family chose not to rear a concubine's son, they were under no compulsion to do so. Thus, unlike a son born to the legal wife, a concubine's son's place in the family was not automatically assured.[175] One suspects that the position of daughters of concubines was even more precarious—that they were more likely than their "principal" half-sisters to be quietly disposed of at birth, or to be married out as concubines themselves—but explicit evidence is lacking. Equally salient were the emotional complexities generated by the presence of children born to concubine mothers. Ritually, all children were regarded as belonging to the legal wife, and in return the legal mother was to regard all the children as her own, without distinction. But it was well understood that many wives did not feel the same way about children born to other women as they did toward their own, and in the Northern Song we begin to see writers praising women for rearing concubines' children as their own.[176] Nor was the lot of the concubine mother herself an easy one. In child-rearing, as in all else, concubine mothers were expected to

---

Grand Councilor Yan Shu and was married to a younger sister of Wang Anshi. Wu's son Yan Fang (1053–1100) entered office by privilege, but held only very low offices. Wu's epitaph stresses her son's poor and simple lifestyle, praising him for being respectful and not presuming on his relatives' status to act in a haughty manner. One wonders whether his concubine maternity might have been a factor in his lack of success (Xie Yi, *Xi tang ji* 9.11a–12b).

174. On Northern Song efforts to restore a classical family system, see Ebrey, "Early Stages," 35–39.

175. Watson suggests that concubines' children suffered in not being "legitimately mothered," that is, they did not have maternal kin able to look out for their interests ("Wives, Concubines, and Maids," 246–51).

176. *Ouyang Xiu quan ji* 37.549–50; *Huang Tingjian quan ji* 22.1395.

defer to the legal wife: Han Qi describes how, whenever his birth mother attempted to whip him or his older brother, their legal mother, furious, would run over to save them.[177] More striking is an account from Huang Tingjian that tells of how, at least in some parts of the country, once a concubine's children were grown it was customary that she continue to act as a servant, waiting upon even her own sons and daughters-in-law.[178] Evidently, in some places during the Northern Song the notion that a concubine should be entitled to the filial attentions of her sons was still novel. Finally, concubine mothers who were expelled from the family lost the opportunity even to see their own children.

From the standpoint of children, too, having two mothers complicated family relations. This was especially the case given the resurgence of interest in Confucian ideals in this period. Even ritual experts disagreed about the appropriate expressions of filial piety, especially with respect to mourning, due to legal versus concubine mothers. Within the context of the family, children had to negotiate the complicated emotional and ritual demands of being filial in different degrees to their respective birth and legal mothers. Northern Song texts say little about how children managed these relationships, although one text mentions that an imperial clan member served both his legal and birth mothers "without contravening ritual."[179] Negotiating the relationship between a man's birth mother and his legal mother was even more tricky for daughters-in-law, who had to serve two mothers-in-law of disparate status without offending either. Some sense of what this involved is conveyed in an inscription Zhao Dingchen wrote for his youngest sister:

> At the time [my sister's husband's] legal mother Lady Cui was still alive, and his birth mother Lady Huang served and supported her. Lady Cui's personality

---

177. Han Qi, *Anyang ji bian nian jian zhu* 46.1412. Cf. Ebrey, "Concubines in Song China," 14–15.

178. *Huang Tingjian quan ji, wai ji*, 22.1394. Huang Tingjian describes how his aunt (d. 1098) served her husband's birth mother with the ritual due a mother-in-law, adding, "The custom in Fenning [county, Hongzhou, Hebei] was that birth mothers always waited on their sons and their sons' wives. When people heard of Madame's deportment, they were delighted and admiring." This is a useful reminder of potential regional differences that our sources largely obscure.

179. Fan Zuyu, *Fan Taishi ji* 47.8. How girls negotiated these demands we can only guess: biographies of women seldom say much about their lives before marriage.

was strict and severe, so the daughters-in-law were all anxious and did not dare casually approach her. My youngest sister served her morning and evening with great respect. Retiring, she extended her personal consideration to Lady Huang. Respect, affection, and proper precedence she negotiated without contravening [what was proper]. Both ladies were delighted, saying "This daughter-in-law understands ritual deeply indeed."[180]

When a concubine mother had been expelled from the family, the demands of filiality became particularly difficult to fulfill. Northern Song inscriptions contain several examples of men who experienced a sort of psychological crisis when they learned as adults that their mothers were concubines. The imperial kinsman Zhao Lingwan, for example, did not learn that he was born of a concubine until he reached maturity; he then exhausted his income in seeking for her. When he finally located her, he welcomed her to the palace and attended her assiduously. Only then, his biographer tells us, was Lingwan able to be at peace with himself and regain his will to live. In similar fashion, the birth mother of imperial clansman Zhao Shicai (1040–89) had been expelled when Shicai was still a child, and the family had lost track of her. After Shicai's legal parents died, "he was grief-stricken and distressed, as if in a trance." He sought out his birth mother and had her awarded a noble title.[181] The minor official Zhou Bang (d. 1124) was less fortunate. Reared by his father's successor wife, he had no idea that his birth mother was a concubine no longer in the family. The secret was passed on to a family friend by Bang's older brother's son, who on his deathbed instructed the friend that, should Bang pass the examinations, he should be told of his birth mother's existence.[182] When Bang passed the examinations and learned the truth, he vowed that he would see his mother. Discarding his official robes and donning coarse clothing and straw sandals (that is, mourning garments), he sought his mother far and near. One night he dreamt that as the rain cleared someone pointed to a grave and said, "There is your mother." The very next day Bang met an old man who related that his mother had been dead for several years, pointing out her grave as the rain cleared, just as in the dream. The grief-stricken Bang arranged for his

---

180. Zhao Dingchen, *Zhu yin ji shi ji* 19.5b–7b.
181. Fan Zuyu, *Fan Taishi ji* 49.9, 52.15b.
182. We shall see in the following section of this chapter why this information might be particularly important to a man about to enter office.

mother's reburial and for three years wore mourning for her, while his friends contributed funds for the sacrifices.[183]

These particular accounts were created in a period when filial piety to concubine mothers had become a significant political issue. Yet there is no reason to doubt that some men were driven to exert considerable effort to locate their lost birth mothers. Moreover, that Northern Song writers celebrated such efforts contributed to the growing acceptance of concubine mothers as appropriate objects of filial sentiment.

Finally, however the presence or absence of concubine mothers complicated parent-child relationships in the family, the existence of concubines' children also complicated relationships between siblings. A Northern Song aphorism points out that "The mourning relationships of stepbrothers" are "Difficult to Comprehend," reminding us that the putative equality of all children of the family was constantly undermined by ritual strictures that underscored the differences between wives' and concubines' children.[184] And, although another aphorism suggests that young sons and daughters were "Secretly Delighted" on "Hearing that a maidservant (*nü shi*) is pregnant" (presumably at the prospect of new playmates), writers on family ethics, such as Sima Guang, recognized that strained relationships between wives and concubines could lead to animosity between their sons.[185] Such animosity frequently expressed itself in lawsuits, as when a commoner from Linchuan county in Jiangxi insisted that his stepbrother, born of a concubine, was actually "of a different surname."[186] As this admittedly laconic description of the lawsuit hints, the real issue in such conflicts was usually the disposition of property (a person of a different surname would have no right to family property). In the Southern Song, such disputes were to become of major concern to Confucian ethicists.

In sum, the nearly ubiquitous presence of concubines in elite Northern Song families profoundly affected the dynamics of family life, and in particular raised new questions about the correct ordering of the inner quarters and the proper expression of filial piety. These questions took

---

183. Ge Shengzhong, *Danyang ji* 13.17b–19b.
184. Wang Junyu, *Za zuan xu*, 56, 63.
185. Sima Guang, *Jia fan* 7.14b. Cf. Ebrey, "Women, Money, and Class," 658.
186. Li Gou, *Li Gou ji* 30.351. The commoner originally won his case by bribing a clerk, but a lecture by the magistrate (the subject of the funerary inscription in which the case is described) led him to a change of heart.

on increasing salience over the course of the eleventh century, as concubines came to be featured at the center of several major political scandals. By the last fifty years of the dynasty, concubines, especially concubine mothers, had become a central focus of the factional conflicts that dominated political life.

## Concubines and Politics

The attention paid to concubines in Northern Song politics is yet another sign of their growing importance in the social life of the period. At the top of the political hierarchy, court officials fretted over the propensity of several different emperors to let attachments to concubines interfere with their duties and ritual proprieties. Outer-court worries about imperial indulgence with palace women were nothing new, of course, but the Northern Song examples reflect the changing social context of such concerns. Very early in the eleventh century, court ministers were horrified when, after the death of his first empress, Emperor Zhenzong suggested that he promote to her position a childless woman, Liu, who had originally entered his household as an entertainer, skilled in hand drums. Most Song empresses were drawn from the families of officials, and in the ministers' eyes the entertainer's dubious origins rendered her unfit for the position. Despite their protests, however, the emperor got his way: the erstwhile hand-drum player went on become the "mother of All-under-Heaven" and ultimately de facto ruler of the empire.[187] Her experience stands as a remarkable example not only of the importance of entertainment and markets in women in Northern Song social life, but also of the shifts in social status that concubinage could engender.

Some eight decades later, a different set of ministers was even more horrified when Emperor Zhezong wanted to go so far as to set aside his reigning empress (that is, his legal wife), née Meng, and replace her with a concubine favorite, Virtuous Consort (*xian fei* 賢妃) Liu. Remonstrator Zou Hao took the emperor to task in no uncertain terms, reminding Zhezong that he

---

187. *SS* 242.8612–14. For a detailed discussion of the empress's political career, see Chaffee, "Rise and Regency." For a discussion of her place in the entertainment culture of the Song court, see Bossler, "Gender and Entertainment."

himself had been furious when the imperial kinsmen Zhao Zongjing had attempted to make a concubine into a wife. Zou asked rhetorically,

> If after this by chance a gentleman or official sets up his concubine as his wife and the officials impeach him, how will Your Majesty deal with it? If you do not deal with it, then you will endanger moral transformation and destroy customs, and there will be no principle by which to administer the country. "What those above do, those below imitate": it will be difficult for you to reprimand others.[188]

Once again, the ministers' protests were to no avail: Zou Hao was stripped of his offices and sent out of the capital under arrest, and Virtuous Consort Liu became empress.[189] But Zou's protest is notable for his insistence on the parallel between the emperor's household and those of ordinary officials. The parallel was not entirely precise: even an official who had no living wife could not legally promote a concubine to be his wife, whereas empresses could be and frequently were promoted from lower consort ranks. But the real crux of the conflict was the setting aside of a reigning empress in order to promote a favorite lesser consort. In arguing that the emperor's action would set a dangerous precedent, Zou reveals that the threat posed to wives by concubines was very much a part of late Northern Song literati consciousness.

Although imperial indiscretions with concubines were one source of concern for court officials, a more common problem was the potential for concubines to be the source or cause of political malfeasance. We saw in chapter 1 that dalliance with public entertainers was often associated with corruption or dereliction of political duty, and concubines could be the source of similar problems. In 1059 the prefectural official Sun

---

188. *Chang bian* 515.12249–52, cited passage on 12250–51. Zou acknowledged that Zhezong had some cause to set aside Empress Meng, whose fights with the favored concubine Liu had shocked the palace, but he wanted the emperor to demote both women and choose a new empress not implicated in the scandal (as Emperor Renzong 仁宗 [r. 1023–63] had done in a similar situation).

189. *SS* 243.8638; see also the biography of the deposed Empress Meng, *SS* 243.8632–38. There appears to have been a factional dimension to the conflict between these women as well; Empress Meng had been selected for the emperor by the empresses of his father and grandfather, and her *SS* biography associates her appointment as empress with the return of conservative officials to power in the Yuanyou period. Empress Liu, by contrast, was associated with the reformer Zhang Dun.

Mian 孫沔 was charged with several instances of inappropriately using his authority to obtain concubines. In the most egregious of these, Sun had sought to obtain a young woman in his district who was already betrothed to another man. When Sun's attempts to buy off the prospective mother-in-law failed, he had the older woman jailed on trumped-up charges of adultery with a monk. Meanwhile the girl herself was brought to his prefectural residence, where she became his constant companion. Sun Mian was also accused of accepting a household-courtesan who had formerly belonged to another official. Both men were demoted as a result.[190]

In this last instance, it is not clear whether the household-courtesan was understood as a bribe, but numerous sources suggest that concubines could be used that way. At the capital, the provision of women to powerful men in return for political favors caused two major scandals in the Northern Song. In 1005, Zhao Jian 趙諫 and his brother were sliced in half in the marketplace after an investigation revealed that they had a long history of bribing and blackmailing court officials and the capital nobility and interfering with government. Some seventy members of the court's top elite were implicated in the case when letters discovered in Zhao's house revealed that they had purchased goods and women through him. Only timely intervention by the censor Lü Wenzhong 呂文仲 persuaded Emperor Zhenzong not to carry out wholesale imprisonment of the implicated officials.[191] Their counterparts in a similar case in 1039 were not so lucky. In that year, a dozen officials, some of them very prominent, were demoted for various nefarious dealings with the corrupt head of the Kaifeng police office, Feng Shiyuan 馮士元. Among them, Edict Attendant Pang Ji 龐籍 was demoted to a prefectural post outside the capital, and Erudites Lü Gongchuo 呂公綽 and Lü Gongbi 呂公弼 were each fined ten *jin* of copper, because all three had purchased women through Feng.[192] Contemporaries observed that Feng sold both lodgings and entertainers to the wealthy and powerful as a means to

---

190. *Chang bian* 190.4578. This case is also recorded in the *SHY*, *zhiguan*, 65.18–19. Sun Mian was also charged with raping and/or seducing several other women under his jurisdiction.
191. *Chang bian* 60.1345–46; Wenying, *Yu hu qing hua*, 5.45.
192. *Chang bian* 125.2939–40; *SS* 292.9767, 311.10199.

ingratiate himself with them, and when his crimes were exposed, the case rocked the capital.[193]

Even officials themselves were sometimes caught brokering women to other officials: in the eighth month of 1055, Zhao Bian 趙抃 accused the minor bureaucrat Xiao Ruli 蕭汝礪 of engineering an inappropriate advancement to an influential appointment, in part by constructing tall buildings and pavilions at his home and staffing them with courtesan musicians to entertain young men of powerful families. Evidently the emperor found Zhao's accusation persuasive, for Xiao was subsequently demoted to a prefectural position. By the early twelfth century, similar problems were observed even outside the capital. An 1124 memorial warned that justice was easily subverted when local officials were entertained by the maids and concubines (*bi qie*) of elite families in their districts.[194]

Other Northern Song political scandals involving concubines centered on the failure of men to control the behavior of the women in their households. The career of Grand Councilor Chen Zhizhong was ultimately derailed after a young maid in his household died of a beating. When the case first became a subject of court discussions in the last month of 1054, there was considerable uncertainty about what exactly had transpired: some said the grand councilor himself had beaten the girl to death; others said that her death came at the hands of Chen's cruel concubine A-Zhang. But, an irate censor pointed out, either way Chen could be considered responsible for the girl's death, and he added that a man who was so patently unable to keep his own house in order could hardly be relied upon to help rule the realm.[195] The case raged for nearly six months, the investigation hampered by unexplained changes in the personnel in charge and by Chen's refusal to send his household staff to the court for questioning. But ultimately, in the face of repeated accusations and denunciations, the emperor finally demoted Chen to a purely honorary position.[196]

---

193. Zeng Gong, *Zeng Gong ji* 8.573, in inscription for Wang Kui 王逵. The impact of this event on contemporary sensibilities is evident in the numerous references to it. See Su Song, *Su Weigong wen ji* 63.963; Sima Guang, *Su shui ji wen* 8.151; Su Shi, *Dongpo zhi lin* 4.8; Hu Su, *Wen gong ji* 36.435; Wang Anshi, *Wang wen gong wen ji* 88.933.

194. Zhao Bian, *Qing xian ji* 7.25b–26; *SHY, xing fa*, 2.92.

195. *Chang bian* 177.4296.

196. *Chang bian* 180.4352; cf. Ebrey, "Women, Money, and Class," 628–29.

The attacks on Chen Zhizhong alarmed many members of the bureaucracy. Even some of those who found fault with Chen's policies were distressed at the way the case developed. The head of the Remonstrance Bureau, Fan Zhen 范鎮, argued that Chen should be judged on the basis of his performance in office, not on his family affairs; otherwise, he suggested, the emperor's officials would be too busy regulating their families to concentrate on their duties. Fan further took issue with the notion that Chen should be called to testify in the case, pointing out that from the perspective of governmental structure it was "not convenient" for a prime minister to have to testify in court on behalf of a maid (*bi zi* 婢子). Finally, and most vehemently, Fan objected to the idea that the death of a mere maid could bring down a high-ranking minister: "Ordinary people can kill a maid and not be indicted, but a prime minister is constrained and humiliated: this is the reason that I am angry and frustrated and sigh deeply." He reminded the emperor of the importance of strictly maintaining hierarchical distinctions, and urged that the case be openly debated.[197]

To Fan, the death of a maid in Chen's house was regrettable but basically irrelevant to Chen's performance in office. He saw the censors' attacks as dangerously diminishing the dignity of that office, commenting, "The court establishes the censorate to prevent malicious gossip, not to create it."[198] To the censors, on the other hand, the shocking violence in Chen's inner quarters proved that he was totally unfit for office. More broadly, the case suggests that changes in Song households were creating new attitudes toward the role of personal life in political careers. In the context of late Northern Song factionalism, the notion that a man's personal life was intensely relevant to his fitness for office would gain further sway.

---

197. *Chang bian* 178.4314–15. The assumption of all parties seems to have been that had Chen himself killed the maid in punishment for a transgression, he would not be guilty of a crime. But for his concubine (she is at one point called *bi qie* 婢妾) to kill the maid was a serious crime, and for Chen to cover up that crime would also be a criminal act.

198. *Chang bian* 180.4353.

## Concubines and the Politics of Family

Chapter 1 related how the period of factional politics ushered in during the reign of Shenzong 神宗 (r. 1068–85) was marked by desperate attempts by each side to claim moral legitimacy and the concomitant approval of Heaven. These attempts often took the form of virulent condemnation of the putative immorality of the opposition. Just as interactions with courtesans were a focus of many indictments, so, too, were inappropriate relations with concubines fodder for political attack. In 1084, in addition to accusing Wang Anli of licentious indulgence in courtesans, Zhang Ruxian claimed that when Wang served as prefect of Runzhou, he had often had drinks in the home of the elderly official Shao Yue 勺約, and ultimately had an illicit relationship with Shao's serving maid. After Shao's death, under the guise of taking charge of the funeral, Wang enticed Shao's maids Wang and Xie to return with him. "Now," continued Zhang darkly,

> The two maids are at his home, and moreover the maid Wang has already had a child. In his inner quarters there are numerous conflicts, to the point that some wanted to take his private affairs to court, but Anli used various means to prevent it. Since this is how Anli conducts himself and manages his family, how can he possibly regulate the numerous officials and manage the myriad people for Your Majesty?[199]

Like the critics of Chen Zhizhong, Zhang explicitly argues that Wang's moral turpitude—evident in his illicit relationship with and eventual appropriation of his colleague's concubines—rendered him unfit for office. The correlation between household order and fitness for office was similarly at issue when, in 1086, Sima Guang requested his own demotion for having once recommended the official Sun Zhun 孫準. Sun had recently been fined six *jin* of copper because disputes between his wife and his concubine had led the wife's brother to file a lawsuit. Even after the emperor brushed off his first mea culpa, Sima Guang argued that the disharmony in Sun's inner quarters was a clear blemish on Sun's behavior, and that, since he had been blind to these faults in Sun's character, he should be demoted along with Sun.[200]

---

199. *Chang bian* 347.8329. Wang Anli's crime was compounded by the fact that one of the concubines was surnamed Wang, thus violating the strict taboo on same-surname marriage.
200. Sima Guang, *Sima wen zheng gong chuan jia ji* 56.677–78.

The idea that a man's relationships with the women in his household revealed his moral character was expressed even more insistently in a very different kind of case involving concubines—one of the most celebrated and most culturally significant political cases of the late Northern Song. It centered on the figure of Li Ding, who was indicted for his putative failure to mourn his concubine mother.

As other authors have pointed out, Li Ding's case was inextricably tied up with the factional politics surrounding Wang Anshi's New Policies.[201] Wang and Li had long been friends, and on learning in early 1070 that Li Ding was a supporter of the Green Sprouts reforms, Wang Anshi had him meet with the emperor. Pleased with Li's assessment that the New Policies were going well, the emperor attempted to appoint Li to a substantial post. That appointment and subsequent attempts to offer Li significant offices were met with a series of objections by conservatives opposed to Wang Anshi's policies.[202] With Wang Anshi urging the emperor to stand firm, the attacks intensified. In this context, in the fifth month of 1070 the acting censor Chen Jian accused Li of having failed to leave office and take up mourning when his birth mother had died.[203] In the face of the outraged clamor of conservative officials, the emperor was forced to order an investigation.[204]

The issue of proper mourning for concubine mothers had been the focus of political discussion at least twice earlier in the dynasty. In 1016, in response to an official who requested to remain in office rather than mourn his birth mother, court ritualists had determined that there were contradictory precedents, variously calling for mourning a concubine mother for three years or for returning to work immediately after the burial. They recommended a compromise, in which the bereaved would temporarily resign from office, but return to work after his birth mother's burial while continuing to "mourn in the heart" (*xin sang* 心喪) for

---

201. The outlines of this case and its significance for understanding Song regulations for the mourning of concubine mothers are elegantly set out in Katkov, "The Domestication of Concubinage," 91–95. See also Smith, "Shen-tsung's Reign," 365 and Ebrey, "Women, Money, and Class," 629–31.
202. *Chang bian* 210.5103–07.
203. *Chang bian* 211.5121.
204. *Chang bian* 213.5173.

three years.²⁰⁵ A few decades later, a request by one Xue Shen to mourn his concubine grandmother (the birth mother of his father) gave rise to an elaborate and extended debate. In the end, the ritual experts determined that because the court had once recognized Shen's grandmother's status by permitting a special enfeoffment for her as the birth mother of Shen's father, and also because Shen had been reared by her, he should leave office and mourn her at grade 2a for three years (that is, in the same way one would mourn a legal mother).²⁰⁶ In both cases, then, the court recognized that a concubine mother had a claim on the filiality of her son and his heirs, though how that filiality should be expressed remained ambiguous. By the 1070s, however, a general consensus seems to have been reached: a son who was not his father's heir should mourn his birth mother for a full three years at grade 2a; a son who was the heir (and thus of higher status in the family) should mourn for three months at grade 5, followed by three years of mourning in the heart, during which time he could resume regular activities.²⁰⁷

When Li Ding came under attack, his defenders first claimed that he had not known that the woman was his birth mother (though she was his father's concubine and his own wet nurse); and indeed his father had denied that she was.²⁰⁸ In the face of his father's denial, Li Ding claimed, he had not dared to leave his post to mourn her. Instead he requested leave to attend his father and proceeded to carry out mourning in his heart for the deceased woman.²⁰⁹ After some time, Li Ding's supporters prevailed, and his erstwhile attackers were demoted.²¹⁰

---

205. *SHY, zhiguan*, 77.2b–3a; Katkov, "The Domestication of Concubinage," 89–90. Katkov points out that this already indicates a more extensive mourning than was customary in the Tang.

206. *SHY, li*, 36.6b.

207. Katkov, "The Domestication of Concubinage," 92. This was substantially longer than had been required in the Tang.

208. Later commentators suggested that Ding's mother had actually been (or later became?) a courtesan, which might explain the father's reluctance to acknowledge her, though the suggestion may also have been a factional attempt to denigrate Li further. See Lu You, *Lao xue an bi ji* 1.6.

209. Katkov, "The Domestication of Concubinage," 90–92.

210. *Chang bian* 211.5123; Katkov, "The Domestication of Concubinage," 93. On pp. 93–94 Katkov notes that this case reveals how sensitive mourning for concubine mothers had become, as well as the ambiguity of the status of concubine's sons like Li Ding.

But the matter did not end there. For months thereafter, Li continued to be the target of virulent denunciations.[211] The conservative Sima Guang, requesting a preemptive dismissal from his own court posts, reminded the emperor that the brilliant Su Shi had been the victim of political attack and added pointedly, "Although [Su] Shi is not perfect, how is he less virtuous than Li Ding who didn't mourn for his mother, worse even than birds and beasts!"[212] Others warned the emperor that by employing such a monster of unfilial behavior so close to the throne, he risked losing Heaven's favor.[213] Eventually, consistent demotions of the attackers succeeded in stemming the flow of outright criticism of Li Ding, but the treatment of birth mothers became a central theme in the persistent culture wars that characterized the factionalist politics of the succeeding decades.

The first salvo in these culture wars came very shortly after Chen Jian's first accusation of Li, when the court was asked to honor the minor official Zhu Shouchang 朱壽昌 for his exceptional filiality to his birth mother.[214] Zhu's mother had been a concubine, and when Shouchang was two years old, she had been married off to a commoner.[215] Some fifty years later, the filial Shouchang was driven to search for her. After demonstrating his seriousness by undertaking all sorts of Buddhist austerities (including copying a scripture in his own blood), he gave up his official post and took leave of his family, saying he would not return unless he found his mother. When he did finally locate her, she was over seventy. In the intervening decades, she had married and had had several children, all of whom Zhu welcomed back to his home in the

---

211. See *Chang bian* 214.5201–02, 216.5263–65, 219.5325–26, 219.5330–31. The timing of the events surrounding Li Ding is somewhat obscure due to the bowdlerized condition of the historical records for this period. On the problems of the Northern Song textual legacy, see Hartman, "A Textual History."
212. *Chang bian* 214.5201–02.
213. *Chang bian* 216.5263–65.
214. Chang bian 212.5143–44; cf. Ebrey, "Women, Money, and Class," 633.
215. The *SS* gives a somewhat different version of the story, claiming that his mother had been expelled from their household as soon as she had become pregnant, and that Shouchang was several years old before he was returned to his father's family (*SS* 456.13404–05). Such discrepancies expose the mythological character of these "filial son" stories.

4. The filial son Zhu Shouchang 朱壽昌 (*Qi zhi xun qin* 棄職尋親) kneeling before the concubine mother he had given up office to seek. From *Si wu ju shi* 四勿居士, *Lun tu bian lan* 倫圖便覽 (Ban cang Pei ying shu ju, 1886), 1.52a. Courtesy of the C. V. Starr East Asian Library, University of California, Berkeley.

capital.²¹⁶ Shenzong responded by granting Zhu Shouchang an audience and restoring him to office. Court records duly reported that later, after Shouchang's mother died, he cried until he was almost blind, while auspicious albino ravens gathered at her grave.²¹⁷

The surviving historical sources claim that when Zhu's case was brought to the attention of the court, Wang Anshi's sensitivity about Li Ding led him to be so suspicious that he subjected Zhu to an additional court investigation. There is some reason to doubt these sources which so emphatically cast Wang in a negative light, but contemporaries on both sides of the reforms do seem to have recognized Zhu Shouchang's case as an effective propaganda tool. The propaganda effect was enhanced by eminent scholars and others who composed and circulated poetry in honor of Zhu's filiality. Su Shi wrote both a poem and a gatha prayer for Zhu; Sima Guang honored him with a poem.²¹⁸ Even Wang Anshi himself composed a (somewhat ambiguously worded) verse in Zhu's honor.²¹⁹ Within a few years, Zhu's son had collected the poetry into a volume and secured a long biographical preface by the noted writer and painter Wen Tong.²²⁰ This format of a poetry volume with a biographical preface helped secure Zhu's place in the standard iconography of filial behavior from that point on.²²¹

Contemporaries drew an explicit connection between the celebration of Zhu's filiality and the attacks on Li Ding. Several saw a line from Su Shi's poem for Zhu ("Such [filial] affairs do not exist today, though they

---

216. *Chang bian* 212.5143–44.

217. *Chang bian* 212.5143–44. The more detailed account in Wen Tong, *Dan yuan ji* 26.4a–6a indicates that the emperor also bestowed a title of nobility on Zhu's mother. Interestingly, the *SHY* does not record any government award for Zhu Shouchang.

218. *Su Shi shi ji* 8.386–88; *Su shi wen ji* 22.643–44; Sima Guang, *Sima wen zheng gong chuan jia ji* 9.139.

219. Wang Anshi, *Linchuan xian sheng wen ji* 31.344. The poem reads 綠衣東笑上歸船,萊氏歡娛在晚年,嗟我白頭生意盡,看君今日更悽然. It is tempting, but perhaps overreaching, to see the last line ("Seeing you, today I am even more desolate") as reflecting Wang Anshi's mixed feelings about Zhu's celebrity.

220. Wen Tong, *Dan yuan ji* 26.4a–6a.

221. Later chapters will show that such poetry volumes eventually became the favored format for writing about upper-class female exemplars. Note that Zhu Shouchang is celebrated as a famous filial son even on the Internet today (e.g., http://history.culturalchina.com/en/38History5757.html, accessed 6/13/2012).

were sometimes heard of in the past" [*ci shi jin wu, gu huo wen* 此事今無古或聞]) as a satirical comment on Li Ding, and court gossip attributed Li's later indictments of Su to his anger over this poem.[222] That Su Shi did indeed have Li Ding in mind when he wrote about Zhu Shouchang is suggested by an item in Su's later miscellaneous writings. Here Su satirized the court official Cai Yanqing 蔡延慶, who had not initially mourned his birth mother but who, on seeing the uproar over Li Ding, asked permission to mourn her retroactively. Su emphatically contrasted such behavior with that of Zhu Shouchang, commenting "how vast are the differences between virtuous people and evil people."[223]

In the wake of Zhu Shouchang's case, the treatment of concubine mothers became an increasingly prominent feature of political and cultural discourse. The search for concubine mothers began to appear prominently in funerary inscriptions and other texts attempting to highlight the exemplary filiality of their subjects.[224] Such accounts emphasized the psychological crises men faced when they realized they had been unknowingly separated from their birth mothers, and detailed their desperate and painstaking attempts to find and honor the women who

---

222. Shao Bowen, *Shao shi wen jian lu* 13.147–48. Wei Tai, *Dong xuan bi lu* 10.114–15, attributes Li's enmity to a poetry preface (*shi xu*) Su wrote.

223. More specifically, alluding to a passage from the *Book of Ritual* (*Li ji* 禮記), Su commented derisively, "From this we know that [he who relies on] crab shells and cicada strings is not only the younger brother of Cheng." The passage to which Su alludes (*Li ji, Tan gong, xi*) says: "There was a man of Cheng, who did not go into mourning on the death of his elder brother. Hearing, however, that Zigao was about to become governor of the city, he forthwith did so. The people of Cheng said, 'The silkworm spins its cocoons, but the crab supplies the box for them; the bee has its cap, but the cicada supplies the strings for it. His elder brother died, but it was Zigao who made the mourning for him.'" (*Li ji*, as translated by James Legge, *The Chinese Text Project*. [http://chinese.dsturgeon.net/text.pl?node=9479&if=en] Tan Gong 檀弓 2, 210 [accessed August 25, 2011]).

224. For example, the biographer of Li Gui (d. 1076) made a point of the fact that, when Li returned home for the funeral of his birth mother, the area had been experiencing several years of drought. As he ordered the ancestral graves, a spring gushed forth, and his neighbors saw this as a supernatural response to his filial piety (Su Song, *Su Weigong wen ji* 58.909). This was not the first time in Chinese history (nor the last—consider the Cultural Revolution hero Lei Feng) when celebration of exemplars became a significant social phenomenon. On the obsession with stories of filial piety during the Six Dynasties period, see Knapp, *Selfless Offspring*.

had borne them.²²⁵ This discourse in turn began to influence attitudes and even regulations about concubines' connections to Song families. As early as 1073, the emperor had decreed that henceforth any serving women (*nü shi*) who had borne sons for the imperial clan could not be resold to anyone within imperial mourning circles; in 1104 this rule was expanded to say that such a woman could not be sold into any other position at all.²²⁶

## *Conclusion*

Over the course of the Northern Song, concubines proliferated in the households of the nobility, wealthy merchants, and the office-holding elite, giving rise to new family structures and dynamics, as well as to new social and political problems. Just as courtesan entertainment had become central to the public life of officials and literati, a fashion for entertainer-concubines took hold in literati households. Like courtesans, entertainer-concubines served as vehicles for both male competition and male bonding, and like courtesans, they could be the focus of romantic discourse. They differed critically from courtesans, however, because as legitimate members of the master's household they could, if he desired, bear his children legally. As such women became fully integrated into elite households, by the late Northern Song their widespread presence and the new social and household dynamics they created gave rise to two parallel discourses about them. One strand (similar to discourse about courtesans) emphasized the danger that concubines posed as figures of luxury consumption and sexual license. But another, more powerful strand of discourse began to emphasize the role of concubine mothers as the objects of filial attentions from their literati sons. Political factionalism helped create and intensify a new focus on family relations, especially new concerns for the exhibition of exemplary behavior within the family. These in turn were to have profound implications for the role of literati wives.

---

225. See the discussion of the filial sons Zhao Lingwan, Zhao Shicai, and Zhou Bian above.

226. *Chang bian* 247.6030; SHY, *di xi*, 4.27b, 5.19a. Chaffee, *Branches of Heaven* (324, n. 110) takes the first of these edicts as denying clan status to the children of maids.

# 3

## Prose, Politics, and Prodigies

### Madame Wu 吳夫人

Madame Wu was a person of Linchuan. Her family had been scholars for generations and were broadly learned. When young she was intelligent; when she married and was widowed, her husband's friend Wang Anshi mourned [her husband], saying, "Kangzi was a man of great talent, and had a wife who was also [talented]." This was to say she was a clever wife of a poor but virtuous man.[1] The Wangs and the Wus were both important families in Linchuan; they produced many notable personages and intermarried over generations. Therefore Anshi knew of her virtue in detail. In the third month of the seventh year of the Yuanyou reign period [1092], [the prefect of] Tangzhou reported, "I respectfully observe that in Shangma village in Biyang county of this prefecture, the daughter of the former administrative supervisor of Jiangning prefecture, Wu Fen, was married at the age of twenty-two *sui* to the commoner Wang Ling. Before a year was out, Ling died. At the time the Wang daughter-in-law was just twenty-three *sui*, and had only a posthumous daughter. Her brother wanted to flout [her intentions] and marry her off. She cried and screamed and would not permit it. She returned to the home of her elderly parents, where she lived in seclusion, farming and raising silkworms to serve her brother and sister-in-law. She wore plain clothing and did not adorn herself. She was like this for thirty-two years. Now she lives alone at Yellow Pond Slope in said county, where she manages the local affairs. Every year in the slack season she personally leads more than several thousand farmers to repair the dikes, collecting the water and irrigating the fields. The benefit extends to the entire area. The people of the area follow her direction. If among the young men there are those who do not obey, she personally takes up the cudgel and seeks to punish them. The farmers are without knowledge: without strong punishment, they cannot be unified. If it were not for someone of unusual integrity and righteousness, how could they be made to submit? I would like to request that the court specially bestow a government award." By imperial edict, ten lengths of coarse silk and ten bushels of rice were bestowed. Later, she died of old age at her residence in Biyang.[2]

---

1. Lit., "the wife of Qian Lou." A story from the *Lie nü zhuan* (Biographies of Exemplary Women) describes how, after the death of the righteous recluse Qian Lou of Lu 魯黔婁 (whose posthumous name was "Kang"), his wife debated with a disciple who was distraught at the master's poverty. The wife argued that in his righteousness her husband was not poor. See Liu Xiang, *Lie nü zhuan* 2.75.

2. Wang Ling, *Guangling ji, fu lu*, 22a–23a, "Wu fu ren zhuan."

This biography of Madame Wu (1035–93), prepared for inclusion in the "Virtuous Women" section of the *National History,* is one of a very small number of Northern Song texts celebrating wifely fidelity.[3] Readers familiar with the cult of fidelity in later imperial China will recognize Madame Wu's tearful refusal to remarry, her abstemious lifestyle, and the government award acknowledging her virtue as standard features in texts celebrating the integrity of wives and widows in the centuries that followed. Yet in Madame Wu's own day, and for more than a century thereafter, emphasis on these aspects of widow behavior, and for that matter on widows themselves, was rather novel. The focus on her role as a faithful widow represented the first stirrings of an intensified rhetoric celebrating fidelity—especially a wife's fidelity to her husband—as the paramount female virtue.

Over the course of the Song dynasty, men wrote constantly about women: they wrote about courtesans who were objects of romance, pathetic victims, or dangerous seducers; they wrote about concubines as symbols of excess and dissolution, as affectionate soul mates, or as tender mothers. They also wrote about women of their own class, describing them as effective household managers, dutiful daughters-in-law, and sometimes capable widows devoted to rearing their sons. But in the Song dynasty, elite men paid relatively little attention to the category of "faithful wives" (*jie fu* 節婦) that was to become so dominant in men's writing about women in the later imperial period. Indeed, even the central term "faithful wife" meant something different in the Song than later. Before and throughout most of the Northern Song, the term *jie fu* had rather broad implications, and is most accurately rendered as "woman of integrity" or "principled woman." Later chapters will show that by the end of the Song, the term was beginning to be understood in a much narrower sense as "faithful wife" (or "chaste wife") or even "faithful (chaste) widow." In the Yuan and after, as the rhetoric of women's fidelity exploded, a veritable industry grew up around the celebration of faithful women in biographies, monuments, and shrines, and fidelity came to be regarded as the signal female virtue.

---

3. This text was almost certainly based on a funerary inscription composed about 1117 by her husband's nephew Wang Yun 王雲. See *Guangling ji, fu lu,* 22a–23a. The *National History* was the draft version of the *SS*. Interestingly, however, Wu did not make it into the final version of the *SS*, perhaps due to her close connections with Wang Anshi.

This chapter traces the first stirrings of this heightened interest in female fidelity. The argument has two intertwined components. I shall show how, on the one hand, factionalism in Northern Song politics gave rise, almost incidentally, to increased celebration of faithful widows as exemplars of a classical form of female virtue. On the other hand, meanwhile, writings about the romantic devotion of female entertainers helped create new templates for the public celebration of female loyalty, templates that ultimately came to be used to honor the fidelity of upper-class wives. I explore this latter development first, beginning by considering the generic conventions that shaped biographical writing about women prior to the late Northern Song.

## Women's Biography in China

The biographical tradition in China is long and varied and has been the subject of considerable scholarly attention.[4] Throughout the Early Imperial period, most biographical writings in all genres were focused on men. Moreover, up until and throughout most of the Northern Song dynasty, when men did write biographies about women they employed almost exclusively one of two different forms or genres: *zhuan* (傳, lit. "transmissions," often translated simply as "biography") or funerary inscriptions. The two forms had different functions and audiences.

### The *Zhuan* Genre

Biographies called *zhuan* were established as a central mode of historical writing by Sima Qian (ca. 145–85 BCE), founder of China's historical tradition, who structured much of his *Historical Records* (*Shi ji*) in biographical form. Almost all Sima Qian's biographies were about men, and this continued to be the case in other formal historical writings. Women received individualized biographies in the early standard histories only when they were prominent palace ladies, such as empresses or other high-ranking

---

4. A number of articles on the Chinese biographical tradition are collected in Wright and Twitchett, *Confucian Personalities*. The tradition is reappraised from a gendered perspective in Ying Hu and Judge, *Beyond Exemplar Tales*. Some aspects of the discussion below are developed in greater detail in my article in that volume, "Fantasies of Fidelity."

consorts. A biographical tradition focusing on women was, however, initiated not long after Sima Qian by Liu Xiang (79–78 BCE). Liu's work, the famous *Lie nü zhuan* 列女傳 (Biographies of Exemplary Women), featured biographies of women divided into six categories of exemplary female virtue, ranging from "Matronly Deportment" to "Accomplished Disputation," supplemented by a chapter devoted to negative exemplars under the heading "Depraved Favorites."[5] Notably, although Liu's biographies featured a number of women who exhibited exemplary loyalty to living or deceased spouses, fidelity was not one of his main categories of virtue. In other words, although wifely fidelity was established early on as an admirable virtue, it was only one of many types of behavior so regarded.

Perhaps due to Liu Xiang's influence, the later standard dynastic histories, although modeled on Sima Qian's work, included chapters devoted to female exemplars that balanced the much more numerous biographies devoted to male exemplars (filial sons, righteous gentlemen, and so on). In state-sponsored historiography, the biographies of exemplars, male as well as female, fulfilled several functions. On the most direct level, it was believed that publicizing the behavior of moral exemplars would inspire others to behave morally. Second, because Chinese political theory assumed a mutual relationship between the quality of governance and the morality of the people, the presence of exemplars in a dynastic history served as evidence that the government had been doing its job correctly. Finally, as Sima Qian himself had suggested, commemoration for posterity was regarded as a just reward—and far too often the only reward—for upright and moral behavior.[6]

---

5. An excellent introduction to the *Lie nü zhuan*, as well as the entire text in Chinese, is available through a website constructed by Anne Behnke Kinney of the University of Virginia (http://etext.virginia.edu/chinese/lienu/browse/Lienu.html, last modified 1999). My translations of the chapter titles differ slightly from Kinney's. On the background to the writing of the *Lie nü zhuan* and the uses of the text over time, see Raphals, *Sharing the Light*.

6. This idea is explicitly articulated in Sima Qian's biography of Bo Yi 伯夷 and Shu Qi 叔齊, which opens the biographical chapters of his *Historical Records* (*Shi ji*). In this biography, Sima Qian questions the existence of a "Way of Heaven" according to which the virtuous are rewarded and the evil punished. Citing many obvious examples to the contrary, he suggests rather that virtue earns its just reward only when the names of virtuous are passed down to posterity (see Sima Qian, *Shi ji* 61.1–8). The

Similar assumptions about the functions of biography also motivated the literati authors of privately compiled *zhuan* biographies, which circulated outside the standard histories. But such privately compiled biographies tended to be far more eclectic and idiosyncratic than those in the standard histories. Although they sometimes focused on exemplars, privately compiled biographies could also describe historical figures who attracted an author's interest, or obscure individuals whose stories illustrated a particular argument or point that an author wanted to make. Still, like their standard history counterparts, privately compiled *zhuan* commonly focused more on men than on women, and those written about women tended to highlight women notable for exemplary or heroic (*lie* 烈) behavior. Among the few surviving examples of private *zhuan* biographies for women compiled before the Song we have Li Ao's (771–842) account of Heroic Wife Yang (Yang *lie fu* 楊烈婦), who, when her husband's district was under attack by bandits, convinced him to stay and fight, exhorted the local people with rewards, and successfully led them to fight off the invaders.[7] Du Mu (803–52) recorded the story of Heroic Girl Dou, about a woman captured by a rebel leader. Dou used her beauty and cleverness to trick the rebel into divulging all his secrets ("even those his wife and sons didn't know"), and her schemes ultimately succeeded in bringing the rebellion down, though not before she herself was murdered.[8] Another Tang woman, also surnamed Dou, earned a biography for her heroism in helping her injured husband escape from his enemies, while a young girl surnamed Zhao was recorded for her heroic efforts to save her salt-merchant father from being executed for tax evasion.[9]

In the Northern Song, the relatively small number of *zhuan* biographies composed for women became even more eclectic, although they still focused largely on moral exemplars. A very early Northern Song *zhuan* biography, preserved in a later text, sang the praises of Faithful Wife Mo, whose husband left on an official assignment without even

---

same sentiments animate Sima Qian's famous letter to his friend Ren An, in which he explains why he has chosen to undergo castration (instead of taking the more honorable path of suicide) in order to be able to survive to finish his work. For English translations of both the letter and the biographies, see Birch, *Anthology of Chinese Literature*, 95–105.

7. Li Ao, *Li Wen gong ji* 12.2b–4a.
8. Du Mu, *Fanchuan wen ji* 3.7b–9b.
9. Sikong Tu, *Sikong Biaosheng wen ji* 4.5b; Pi Rixiu, *[Pizi] wen sou* 6a–7a.

saying good-bye. Though years passed, Mo refused to remarry, instead devoting herself to serving her in-laws, enriching her family, and rearing her children. When her husband finally returned after twenty-six years in service to the court, she welcomed him home.[10] As the dynasty progressed, other authors wrote about a filial daughter who refused to accept funds from local clerks to help with her father's funeral, and a heroic wife who drowned herself to protest her husband's poor treatment of his brothers.[11]

In short, *zhuan* biographies of women in the late Tang and Northern Song depicted a wide variety of behaviors, and—in clear contrast to later eras—even those biographies that celebrated heroic women were rarely concerned with wifely fidelity, and their subjects were rarely martyrs. During the late Tang and Northern Song, moreover, the *zhuan* form was also being adapted to new narrative uses.[12] On the one hand, the developing genre of *chuan qi* romances frequently took the form of *zhuan*-style biographies of courtesans, such as that of the courtesan Wen Wan discussed in chapter 1. Although the courtesan protagonists of these stories were sometimes also exemplary figures (especially in the sense that they remained loyal to their literati lovers), these stories functioned more as entertainment than as moral exhortation. Sometimes, as in Wen Wan's case, these *zhuan* biographies also figured as prefaces to collections of poetry by or about the subject. On the other hand, during the same period, writers also began to experiment with explicitly playful or tongue-in-cheek parodies of didactic *zhuan* biographies, taking as their subjects inanimate objects like ink stones ("he kept his nose to the grindstone") and fruits.[13] These two trends sometimes even converged, as in Zhang Lei's (1054–1114) much-imitated biography of "Lady Zhu" (Zhu fu ren 朱夫人), which played on the fact that "bamboo lady" (also *zhu fu ren* 竹夫人) was the popular Song name for the bamboo mats that were placed over chairs or beds to help keep the occupant cool in hot, humid

---

10. See "Mo jie fu zhuan," originally composed by Zhu Ang (925–1007), as preserved in Wenying, *Yu hu qing hua* 5.44. Mo's biography (differing in some details) was later appended to that of her husband, Zhou Wei (*SS* 204.10056–57).
11. *Cai Xiang ji* 32.583–84; Wang Ling, *Guangling ji* 22.1–2b.
12. On this transition, see McMullen, "The Real Judge Dee," 64.
13. E.g., *Su Shi wen ji* 13.424–27. For a more extended discussion of this biography, see Bossler, "Maidens," 755–56.

weather. In Zhang's portrayal, Lady Zhu became a lovely and virtuous palace attendant hailing from the green forests of the south, who never left the emperor's side during the summer but found herself discarded when the weather turned cool in the fall.[14]

In sum, by the late Northern Song period the *zhuan* biography had become a highly versatile genre, employed to amuse and entertain as much as to edify. Both didactic and playful *zhuan* biographies circulated publicly and tended to be somewhat abstract in tone, meant more to convey a message than to describe the contours of an individual life. Finally, on the relatively rare occasions that *zhuan* biographies focused on women, their subjects tended to be women not known personally to the author, and were most often women of the lower classes. In other words, men did not write *zhuan* biographies for women of their own or their friends' families. All of these features contrasted sharply with the other major genre used for women's biography, that of funerary inscriptions.

## Funerary Inscriptions

Throughout the Song dynasty, the form literati men most often used when they wrote biographical accounts of women of their own class was the funerary inscription. Funerary inscriptions were composed at the time of the subject's death and were meant to provide a permanent record of his or her life for posterity.[15] Whereas *zhuan* were written on the author's own initiative, funerary inscriptions were generally composed

---

14. Zhang Lei, *Ke shan ji* 43.504. Some parts of this paragraph are drawn from Bossler, "Fantasies of Fidelity," 161. Many Song, Yuan, and Ming authors played with the anthropomorphized image of "Lady Bamboo" in poetry as well as prose. Zhang's contemporary Huang Tingjian was famous for insisting that "supporting a man's legs is not the proper occupation of a lady" and proposing that the mats should be called "Green Slave" (*Qingnu*) instead (*Huang Tingjian quan ji, zheng ji*, 10.246). Another contemporary, Lü Nangong, anthropomorphized what appears to be the same object in his "Biography of Lady Pingliang ('Flatcool') (Pingliang *fu ren zhuan*)" in *Guanyuan ji* 18.4a–6a.

15. The general rubric "funerary inscription" encompasses several different types of biographical accounts meant to be inscribed on stone and either buried with the deceased or set up on steles outside the tomb (such as *mu zhi ming* 墓誌銘, *shen dao bei* 神道碑, *mu biao* 墓表, *mu ji* 墓記, *kuang zhi* 壙誌, and so forth), as well as the "accounts of conduct" (*xing zhuang* 行狀), draft biographies on which most of these other types of funerary inscription were based.

at the request or commission of a relative or friend of the deceased and were based on a record of the deceased's life that was provided by the family. Sometimes the author was also personally acquainted with the deceased, and funerary inscriptions accordingly contained a level of personal detail absent from *zhuan* biographies.[16] Likewise, although funerary inscriptions were "public," in the sense that they were meant to be carved on stone and preserved (albeit in the covered tomb), and in some cases were later circulated as part of the author's collected works, they generally functioned more as private family records than as public statements by the author. Accordingly, they were not usually intended to be clever or entertaining or to serve symbolic or polemical purposes.[17] Most upper-class women could expect to have their lives recorded in funerary inscriptions, and indeed most upper-class men seem to have regarded it as a filial duty to see that their mothers were commemorated in this way.[18]

Funerary inscriptions were expected to portray their subjects in a flattering light, and tended to be formulaic. A typical woman's funerary inscription in the Northern Song stressed that she served her in-laws well and personally took care of the sacrifices to the ancestors; that she got along with her sisters-in-law and was generous to those in need; and

---

16. This was especially true in the Northern Song, when highly stylized parallel prose gave way to simpler, more naturalistic description. For a more detailed discussion of Song funerary inscriptions for women and how they differed from those of the Tang, see Bossler, *Powerful Relations*, 12–24.

17. This situation began to change in the late Southern Song and Yuan, when members of the Learning of the Way movement (and Zhu Xi in particular) began to use funerary inscriptions as a platform for their cause. See Tillman, *Confucian Discourse*, 131–32, 206–7.

18. Citing the ancient injunctions that "women do not get involved in external matters" (*fu ren wu wai shi* 婦人無外事), and that "inner words do not reach to the outside" (*nei yan bu chu* 內言不出), a few Northern Song moralists suggested that composing funerary inscriptions for women was inappropriate (see, e.g., Sima Guang, *Sima Wen zheng gong chuan jia ji* 78.969). This attitude seems to have made some men self-conscious about writing funerary inscriptions for women, such that they paid lip service to the notion that women's lives should not be publicized. However, such comments are always contravened by the author's insistence that the virtue of his particular subject must be celebrated (e.g., Chao Buzhi, *Ji lei ji* 64.21b–22; Zeng Gong, *Zeng Gong ji* 45.611; Zhao Dingchen, *Zhu yin ji shi ji* 19.14b). Ironically, even Sima Guang composed funerary inscriptions for women outside his own family.

(as we saw in chapter 2) that she was kind to servants and concubines. Some inscriptions mention that the subject was literate and intelligent, or skilled at needlework. But although funerary inscriptions always portrayed their subjects as virtuous, in this period they did not as a rule highlight dramatic exemplary behavior. Accordingly, Northern Song funerary inscriptions of widows typically portray their subjects as devotedly educating their children, living frugally, and serving their in-laws diligently, but until very late in the period they rarely make an issue of widowhood per se. For example, in writing of his widowed mother (d. 1051), Li Gou stresses their poverty and how hard she worked to support his studies, directing farm work during the day and doing needlework at night, but he says nothing at all about her decision not to remarry. Similarly, Su Shunqin describes how a friend's widowed mother pawned her clothing to provide for her sons' guests, but says nothing about her loyalty to her deceased husband.[19]

Very late in the Northern Song, however, some authors of funerary inscriptions began to put unusual emphasis on the exemplary loyalty of widows. To understand the origins of this heightened interest in female fidelity, we need to consider both the philosophical and political environments in which it developed.

## Men, Women, and Loyalty in the Northern Song

As other scholars have pointed out, several influential Northern Song thinkers responded to the chaos of political disunity that preceded the founding of the Song by asserting new and more restrictive standards for the loyal behavior of men, especially men who served in

---

19. Li Gou, *Li Gou ji* 31.358–60; Su Shunqin, *Su Shunqin ji* 15.197–98. For another example, see Chen Xiang, *Gu ling ji* 20.1–4b. Wong Yu-Hsuan surveys nearly a hundred Northern Song funerary inscriptions for widows. Wong argues that faithful widowhood was more common in the Northern Song than is generally recognized, and was becoming more important in that period than in the Tang. Yet Wong's evidence shows that a number of inscriptions emphasizing faithful widowhood came from the pens of a relatively small number of authors (the latter include Wang Gui and Wang Anshi, both of whom were active in the New Policies regime). Moreover, close inspection reveals that even these inscriptions do not highlight the subject's loyalty to their husbands. See Wong, "Tō Sō boshi," 41–58, esp. 47.

government.[20] In particular, in their historical discussions of the Five Dynasties period, eminent writers like Sima Guang and Ouyang Xiu argued that the disorder of the Five Dynasties had stemmed in part from the immoral conduct of its officials, and they excoriated those officials for switching loyalties from one regime to another.[21] The new and more stringent ideals for male loyalty had implications for women, in part because from earliest times Chinese political theory had understood a minister's loyalty to his ruler as analogous to a woman's loyalty to her husband.[22] Both Sima Guang and Ouyang Xiu made this connection explicitly. In Sima Guang's formulation,

> In the home there are husbands and wives, outside there are rulers and ministers. Wives [should] follow their husbands, and not change throughout their whole lives; ministers [should] serve their rulers and should not change their allegiance even if [it means] their deaths: these are the cardinal principles of human morality.[23]

Ouyang Xiu had expressed this idea in far more dramatic form.[24] In the preface to the "Miscellaneous Biographies" of his own historical work, the *Xin Wudai shi* (New History of the Five Dynasties), Ouyang first observed the sad state of political morality in the Five Dynasties period. After lamenting that he had been able to identify only three gentlemen of complete integrity, he added,

> I once obtained a story (*xiao shuo* 小説) from the Five Dynasties period that recorded the affair of the woman Li, the wife of Wang Ning. Now if even a woman could behave like this, we know that the age definitely once had [virtuous] people; it was only that they did not become prominent.

---

20. Jay, *A Change in Dynasties*, 94–95; Standen, *Unbounded Loyalty*, 59–62. Standen contextualizes the Song innovations in a brief historical summary of Chinese concepts of loyalty from the Warring States period on (41–63).

21. Naomi Standen argues that Ouyang Xiu and Sima Guang radically reinterpreted earlier ideas about loyalty. Where earlier concepts of loyalty were understood to be shaped by the political conditions of the age, Ouyang and Sima reversed the relationship so that loyalty or its absence were seen as creating conditions of peace or instability. In this new formulation, inadequacies of the ruler no longer excused a minister from his obligation to be loyal (*Unbounded Loyalty*, 60–61).

22. On the classical analogue, see Raphals, *Sharing the Light*, 11–14.

23. Sima Guang, *Zi zhi tong jian*, as translated in Standen, *Unbounded Loyalty*, 60.

24. I have discussed this example in Bossler, "Maidens," 751–53.

He went on,

> [Wang] Ning lived between [the districts of] Qing and Qi. He was a Revenue Manager in Guozhou, and died of illness while in office. Ning's family had always been poor, and [he left behind] one young son. [His widow] Li returned home, leading her son by the hand and carrying Ning's remains on her back. [Heading] east she passed the city of Kaifeng and stopped at an inn. The innkeeper, seeing a woman alone holding a boy, became suspicious and wouldn't let them stay. Li, seeing that the sky was already darkening, did not want to leave. The innkeeper then grabbed her arm and threw her out. Crying out to heaven, Li wailed, "I am a woman who already has been [forced to move about in public and thus] unable to retain my honor. And now this hand has been grabbed by a man! I cannot let my whole body be polluted because of one hand!" So she cut off her arm with an axe. People in the street who saw this gathered around in distress. Some wrung their hands, some were crying. The official administrator of Kaifeng heard of [her action] and reported it to the court. The officials bestowed medicine to cure her wounds and gave generous alms to Li, and the innkeeper was flogged. Alas! Those scholars who have little regard for their bodies and endure shame in order furtively to survive—when they hear of Li's heroism, they ought to feel [at least] somewhat mortified.[25]

Ouyang Xiu's point here was to castigate disloyal men, but he employed a dramatic case of *female* fidelity to make his case. In employing an example of female morality to reproach the conduct of men, Ouyang Xiu was reanimating a rhetorical device that had been used in the biographies of exemplary women in earlier eras, and was to be imitated by writers of the Southern Song and later periods. Significantly, however, this rhetoric was rare in Ouyang Xiu's own day.[26] More importantly, although Sima Guang and Ouyang Xiu both invoke the parallel between male loyalty and female fidelity, their point in these writings was to promote a new model of political loyalty for men, not to improve the moral conduct of women. Perhaps for this

---

25. Ouyang Xiu, *Xin Wudai shi* 54.611–12. Cf. the somewhat less literal translation by Richard Davis in Ouyang Xiu, *Historical Records*, 439. Wang Ning's wife, with her hacked-off hand, figured prominently in later imperial illustrations of virtuous women: for an example see Elvin, "Female Virtue and the State," 145. Carlitz discusses the impact of such illustrations in "Desire, Danger, and the Body," 110, and "Social Uses," 118.

26. This point has been made by Richard Davis, who sees the violence in Ouyang Xiu's writings on virtuous women as inconsistent with his otherwise judicious approach to historical narrative ("Chaste and Filial Women," 204–5).

5. Wang Ning's wife (Wang Ning *qi* 王凝妻). Ouyang Xiu's tale of Wang Ning's wife, who cut off her arm because an innkeeper had grabbed it, became one of the most iconic stories of loyalty in the late imperial period. Here her child clings to her and a crowd of onlookers gasps in horror as her severed hand falls to the ground. From Liu Xiang 劉向, *Hui tu Lie nü zhuan* 繪圖列女傳 (Illustrated biographies of exemplary women), edited by (Qing) Wang Geng 汪庚, illustrations by (Ming) Qiu Ying 仇英. Reprint of Zhi bu zu zhai cang ban (Taipei: Zheng zhong shu ju, 1971), 9.48b–49a.

reason, their writings had no discernable impact on contemporary attitudes about female conduct.

Somewhat surprisingly, the same can also be said of a third influential Northern Song figure, the moralist philosopher Cheng Yi. Since at least the early twentieth century, Cheng Yi has commonly been viewed as the Northern Song's strictest interpreter of female fidelity, most notably for his notorious comment that "starving to death is an extremely small matter, whereas losing integrity is an extremely large matter."[27] This comment came in response to a question about the permissibility of widow remarriage in cases of extreme poverty, and Cheng Yi has long been seen as cruelly advocating that women accept death rather than compromise their integrity by remarrying. He is thus often regarded as

---

27. Cheng Yi's comment was recorded, some decades after his death, by Zhu Xi, who collected and passed on records made by the Cheng brothers' disciples. See Cheng Hao and Cheng Yi, *Er cheng ji*, vol. 1, "Er Cheng yi shu," 22b.301.

the originator of the escalating demand for female fidelity in the Song and after.[28] But to understand Cheng Yi in this way greatly overstates both his concern for female fidelity and his influence on late Northern Song culture. First, although he was addressing a case of widow remarriage, his statement about integrity did not refer only to women: for *any* person to lose integrity was, to Cheng Yi, a "large matter." We saw in chapter 2 that he believed that both spouses should remain faithful to one another, and that neither widows nor widowers should remarry. In other words, Cheng Yi did indeed disapprove of women remarrying, for he wanted all men and women to live by a high moral standard, and he saw the lifelong fidelity of husband and wife as an important moral principle. But he was not especially concerned with female fidelity per se. Further evidence for this last point is found in the fact that these statements—recorded long after Cheng Yi's death—represent the sum total of his discussion of female fidelity.[29] He did not devote any particular effort to proselytizing the notion that women should not remarry, and indeed his surviving oeuvre does not even mention the term "faithful wife" or "principled woman." In fact, in every case in which Cheng Yi talks about the virtue of "upholding integrity" (*shou jie* 守節)—a phrase that later became synonymous with a woman's refusal to remarry—he is referring to the integrity of *men*.[30] Thus rather than see Cheng Yi as a major advocate for female fidelity in the Northern Song, we should see him as but one of several thinkers concerned with the revival of classical morality more generally.

In short, it is true that the Northern Song saw increased concern with the values of loyalty and integrity. This was both part of a broader cultural trend toward a reinvigoration of Confucianism and a reflection of the fragile political position of the Song state, which was constantly battling enemies on its borders and was therefore particularly concerned with the political loyalty of its ministers. Still, before the very late Northern Song, few authors expressed particular interest in the fidelity of women, and when they did it was to hold them up as models for men. To the extent that we can trace an enhanced interest

---

28. Cf. Ebrey, "Women, Money, and Class," 613–16.
29. Note that both of these statements were passed on to posterity by Zhu Xi, who did attempt to promote female fidelity.
30. For example see Cheng Hao and Cheng Yi, *Er cheng ji* 2.809, 3.899.

in women's fidelity to the Northern Song, it originated not with the demands of moralist philosophers, but with the political infighting of the late Northern Song court.

## Late Northern Song Factionalism and the Politics of Virtue

Chinese political theory held that good governance at court would radiate outward, influencing and improving the moral conduct of the emperor's subjects; conversely, moral conduct in the realm would be rewarded by Heavenly blessings, signs of Heaven's approval of a virtuous ruler. I have shown in earlier chapters that this theory helped to animate the notoriously bitter factional politics of the late Northern Song, with its extreme moralization of political rhetoric. Each side's need to assert its moral superiority led on the one hand to vituperative attacks on the putative moral failings of political opponents, and on the other hand to the enhanced significance of signs that might demonstrate Heaven's support for the current regime. Not the least of these signs was the presence of moral exemplars in the realm. In this setting, formal state recognition of such exemplars became a kind of political theater, not only encouraging desired behavior, but demonstrating the righteousness of the political faction that shaped the emperor's policies.

Government recognition of moral exemplars had played a significant role in Chinese politics from the Han dynasty on, when the government developed a system of bestowing awards on exemplary subjects. In the Han, the most sought-after virtues were summed up in the phrase "filial sons, obedient grandsons, pure maidens, and righteous women (*xiao zi, shun sun, zhen nü, yi fu* 孝子, 順孫, 貞女, 義婦)."[31] By the Six Dynasties period these categories had been amended to "filial sons, obedient grandsons, righteous men, and principled women (*xiao zi, shun sun, yi fu, jie fu* 義夫, 節婦)," though in practice other kinds of behavior, such as meritorious service in office and excellence in learning, also received rewards.[32]

---

31. For an extended discussion of the historical development of the awards system, see Fei Siyan, *You dian fan dao gui fan*, 69–91; in English see Elvin, "Female Virtue and the State," 115–18. Some elements of the discussion below are drawn from Bossler, "Martyrs," 512–17.

32. Shen Yue, *Song shu* 6.113; Fang Xuanling, *Jin shu* 90.2332; Yao Silian, *Liang shu* 49.694.

Awards frequently had both a material and a symbolic dimension: in addition to receiving valuable silk or rice, an exemplar's household or even the whole village sometimes received a plaque or monument (*jing biao* 旌表) announcing that a filial son or principled woman was resident there.

The process of identifying and rewarding moral exemplars was highly bureaucratic, and here biographical writing played a central role. The process began with the submission to county officials of biographical materials documenting the candidate's exemplary behavior. Having verified the accuracy of the submitted documents, the county officials were expected to send the materials up to the prefecture. The prefectural officials in turn sent the dossier up to the Board of Rites. If they approved it, the request for a reward was then sent to the Department of State Affairs, which ultimately issued the order to bestow an award. The order then made its way back down through the Board of Rites, the prefecture, and finally to the county officials, who actually issued the award.[33] In theory, exemplary behavior could be rewarded at any time, but sometimes—especially in periods of crisis or in response to ill omens—the central government also issued specific calls for cases of extraordinary virtue to be brought to its attention.

The emperors of the early Northern Song maintained the long tradition of rewarding exemplary behavior, though they made several innovations in the practice. In the reign of Taizong (r. 976–997), for example, the state issued a large number of awards in the novel category of "Righteous Households" (*yi men* 義門, families who had lived communally together for numerous generations), presumably because it was in Taizong's interest to secure the allegiance of powerful regional families.[34] The great majority of the awards bestowed throughout the

---

33. The earliest detailed description of the process comes from Yang Wanli in the Southern Song (*Cheng zhai ji* 74.2b–4a), as discussed in chap. 6. See also Katkov, "The Domestication of Concubinage," 203–7. Elvin, "Female Virtue and the State," 129–35, and T'ien Ju-k'ang, *Male Anxiety and Female Chastity*, 5–7, discuss in detail the bureaucratic procedures employed in the Ming and Qing.

34. The category of "righteous household" was first adopted during the Five Dynasties (e.g., Xue Juzheng, *Jiu Wudai shi* 78.1030). Taizong issued at least half a dozen such awards (*SHY, li*, 61.1a–b). A surviving early Song preface for a powerful family that had been named a "righteous household" adds further credence to the notion that such awards were a means of co-opting local power-holders. See Wang Yucheng, *Xiao xu ji* 19.21a–22a.

Northern Song continued to be in this category. An ultimately more significant change was made in the reign of Zhenzong (r. 998–1022), when the government made an official policy of the sometime practice of extending tax relief to awardees: henceforth the household of any person receiving a government award would be excused from all corvée labor duties.[35] Although the households of government officials were generally exempt from such levies in any case, Zhenzong's policy represented a substantial benefit for ordinary commoner families who managed to secure an award. Still, for most of the Northern Song very few families received such privileges: after the reign of Taizong, the number of awards given to exemplars tapered off significantly. According to the surviving record, Zhenzong honored a few harmonious households, and Renzong issued awards to harmonious households, a filial son, a heroic woman (*lie nü*) who died resisting rape, and a heroically filial woman who had saved her father from a tiger.[36] No evidence exists of awards issued during Yingzong's short reign, in spite of an edict of 1066 calling for exemplars "put forward by the multitude" to be investigated and their cases submitted to the court. With the beginning of the factional conflict under Shenzong, however, the situation began to change.

As discussed in chapter 2, one of the earliest uses of exemplars to serve factional political ends involved the case of Zhu Shouchang, whom Shenzong had recognized for his exceptional filiality in searching for his long-lost birth mother.[37] Significantly, although it had been the New Policies government that honored Zhu Shouchang, the impetus for his recognition had come from the opposition, which had drawn attention to Zhu's filiality in part to highlight the failings of Wang Anshi's protégé Li Ding. The factional ploy was not entirely successful: although Shenzong restored Zhu to office, he stopped short of issuing an award, and he continued to support Li Ding. But when the opponents of the

---

35. *SHY, li*, 61.2b. The edict, here dated 1008, stipulated that the families would still be liable for the regular "two taxes," but would be excused from all other miscellaneous levies. The *Chang bian* dates this edict to the eighth month of 1009 (*Chang bian* 72.1630).

36. *SHY, li*, 61.3; *Chang bian* 101.2344, 157.3811–12, 187.1058, and 194.4710.

37. *Chang bian* 212.5143–44. The *SHY* records no awards at all given during Shenzong's reign, but given the later rewriting of the records of this period, there is reason to believe the accounts are not complete.

New Policies were brought into power after Shenzong's death in 1085, the court began to place unprecedented emphasis on the celebration of exemplars, especially through the issuance of government awards.[38]

The sources do not reveal precisely why the court under the regency of Dowager Empress Xuanren became so active in rewarding exemplars: I have found no edict calling for exemplars' names to be submitted, no memorial urging the court to honor virtuous behavior. But in the eight years of her regency, the court issued awards at an unprecedented rate, and the reports of exemplary behavior in this period took on a new cast. Compared with earlier in the dynasty, the exemplars of the Zhezong reign were disproportionately filial sons and principled women, and the reports of their exemplary behavior increasingly emphasized supernatural manifestations.[39] An award issued in 1086 went to Woman Cui, wife of Bao Yi, because the local officials reported that "her principled behavior (*jie xing*) was famous in the district": she had rescued and reared a male descendant of her father-in-law, a famed official.[40] Another award went to a widow who saw to the burial of several of her husband's relatives.[41] This was followed in 1088 by three awards to "righteous families," the second of which was particularly notable because the trees in the family compound garden had grown together. In 1092 Madame Wu, whose biography opened this chapter, was recognized for her efforts at leading corvée laborers, and later that same year the state acknowledged another righteous family. It also issued an award of silk to the official Huang Gao, who according to local reports had lived in a hut next to his father's grave for three years, causing a profusion of auspicious fungi to sprout on the grave.[42] Under the Dowager Empress, Zhezong's court

---

38. Sue Takashi has suggested that a similar escalation of awards to temple deities was also tied to factionalism. Sue sees awards proliferating first in the seventh year of the Xining period, as the court attempted to convince its subjects that the New Policies had the support of Heaven, and again during Huizong's reign ("The Shock of the Year Hsuan-ho 2": 80–125).

39. The *SHY* records that, out of a total of more than eighty awards issued during the Northern Song, only five celebrated principled women. Three of the five were issued during the reign of Zhezong, the other two during Huizong's reign.

40. *SHY, li*, 61.3a–b; *Su Shi wen ji* 38.1066. Woman Cui will reappear in later chapters.

41. *Chang bian* 385.9382.

42. *SHY, li*, 61.3a–4a.

even appropriated exemplars who had appeared in Shenzong's reign. A filial commoner named Zhi Jian had first received a government award in 1083, but in 1093 the conservative minister Fan Zuyu, in what appears to be a bid to assert the moral superiority of the conservative administration of the Yuanyou reign period, reported:

> Recently I was editing the Veritable Records of Emperor Shenzong. I respectfully observed that in the sixth year of the Yuanfeng period [1083] Zi prefecture reported that Zhi Jian, a commoner of Ziyang county, during the Xining period [1068–77] had mourned in a hut beside his mother's grave. [His actions] were attended by many auspicious phenomena, and so it was commanded that he receive grain and silk. While I was editing the Standard History I again contacted Zi prefecture to inquire about Zhi Jian. I understand that his age is now eighty-five; during the five years of the Yuanyou period [that is, during the period of conservative control of government], his white hair has again turned black, and four teeth that had fallen out have regrown.[43]

If escalation of interest in exemplars first took place under the conservatives, however, the process took on a life of its own thereafter. This was especially the case with the accession of Zhezong's brother Huizong in 1101.[44] Recent scholarship on the Huizong era has established that the emperor was above all anxious to see himself as a sage ruler whose own virtue would morally transform (*jiao hua* 教化) his realm. Although he brought back and even expanded many of the activist government policies of the reformers, he justified these policies with the lofty moral rhetoric of the conservatives. His court was obsessed with the promulgation and recording of auspicious signs from Heaven demonstrating that he had achieved his goal of sage rulership.[45] The rewarding of exem-

---

43. *SHY*, *li*, 61.4. Fan concluded by requesting that Zhi be given an official title, and the court awarded him with the title of Instructor. The *Chang bian* dates the initial award to 1083 and gives a detailed account of Zhi Jian's background, explaining that his grief-stricken mourning at his mother's grave had caused even the local fauna—a variety of strange birds and foxes—to appear in sympathy (*Chang bian* 335.15b–16b). Cf. Elvin, "Female Virtue and the State," 120.

44. With the death of his grandmother in 1093, Zhezong took the reins of power and reversed his grandmother's policies, again bringing back the reformers. During the remaining seven years of his reign, awards were issued to a faithful wife and two filial sons.

45. Several of the articles in Ebrey and Bickford, *Emperor Huizong*, touch on this phenomenon. See especially Bickford, "Huizong's Paintings," 453–513. Another important discussion of Huizong's concern for auspicious omens is Sturman, "Cranes above Kaifeng."

plary behavior, associated as it was with auspicious manifestations, was very much a part of this paradigm, and during his twenty-five years on the throne Huizong issued at least twenty exemplar rewards—a higher annual rate than any other Song emperor.⁴⁶ This attention to exemplary behavior was heightened still further by a policy Huizong established a few years after coming to the throne, calling for some official positions to be awarded on the basis of virtue alone. Like the system of government rewards, this "Eight Behaviors" (*ba xing* 八行) policy called for local administrators to identify virtuous residents of their districts and recommend them to the throne, in this case as candidates for office.⁴⁷ The court's interest in (and rewarding of) exemplars did not go unnoticed by contemporaries. In 1124, the author of a funerary inscription for a filial son observed, "In recent times, when officials have experienced Heavenly response to the filial virtue such as that [experienced by] milord, they have all been rewarded by the court and thoroughly detailed in the eyes and ears of the world."⁴⁸

Although the majority of exemplars honored in the last decades of the Northern Song were men, the enhanced political significance of virtuous behavior in this period began to have an impact on biographical writings for both men and women, and on funerary inscriptions as well as other biographical forms. I have already noted the proliferation of funerary inscriptions for filial sons who sought out their expelled birth mothers.⁴⁹

---

46. According to the records preserved in the *SHY*, Huizong's government issued ten awards to filial sons, two to women who died to preserve chastity, two to faithful wives, one for brotherliness, one for a filial daughter-in-law, and four to righteous households.

47. Chaffee, *The Thorny Gates of Learning*, 78–79. The precise date of this policy is uncertain: Chaffee, based on a document in the *Wen xian tong kao*, puts it at 1104; other sources, including the *Song History*, put it in the third month of 1107 (*SS* 20.378). The policy evidently did succeed in bringing new blood into the bureaucracy: see Davis, *Court and Family*, 42–43.

48. Ge Shengzhong, *Danyang ji* 13.17b–19b, funerary inscription for Zhou Bang, who was led to his birth mother's grave by a mysterious dream. The author complains that because Zhou held only modest appointments and was often in retirement, his circumstances have not received sufficient attention.

49. On filial children, in addition to the examples cited in chap. 2, see Liu Yan, *Longyun ji* 31.13b–16b, funerary text for "Xiao, the Filial and Honest" (note that although the subject of this text died in 1071, the text was not composed until 1093), and the materials on Xu Ji described below.

Likewise, we see in this period heightened focus on exemplary loyalty in the funerary inscriptions of upper-class widows.

Several of the funerary texts for filial sons were composed by the conservative minister Fan Zuyu, and Fan also turns out to have been a prolific writer of inscriptions valorizing faithful widows. In 1094, for example, he composed a funerary inscription for a Madame Yang, the wife of an imperial clansman. In conventional terms Fan notes that Yang was amiable, quiet, and filial to her in-laws. Then he explains that she was only twenty *sui* when her husband died. When her mother suggested she remarry, "she cried and would not permit it. Her mother was sympathetic to her principles and did not force her." Fan then gives us a biography of a standard virtuous widow: she discarded her ornaments, dressed simply, and insisted on educating her sons in spite of the fact that, as members of the imperial clan, they would be wealthy and noble in any case. Particularly striking is the *ming* 銘 or epitaph with which Fan concludes his account:

> The mother of Wei had seven sons but was not content in her chamber; her neighbors disdained her, and thus the "Air of Kai" was composed. The Song [dynasty] had a clanswoman who was widowed at twenty and until her death did not take another [spouse], following her husband in righteousness. She began as a faithful widow and ended as a virtuous mother; for a thousand generations her grave should be taken as a model.[50]

Fan's opening reference is to a poem in the *Book of Odes* that refers to the licentious Kingdom of Wei, in which even a mother with seven sons "could not be content in her chamber." The point of the "Air of Kai" ("Kai feng" 凱風) poem is to depict a son who, by being exceptionally filial, is able to comfort his mother (and presumably keep her at home!). In this epitaph, Fan's allusion is surely meant in part to flatter the filiality of Yang's son, who probably commissioned the epitaph; it likewise clearly asserts the virtue of the dynasty, which (unlike the Kingdom of Wei) had produced such a faithful woman. In the process, however, it also has the effect of highlighting her status as an exemplary faithful widow.

---

50. Fan Zuyu, *Fan Taishi ji* 51.15b–17. The "Air of Kai" poem appears in the chapter of the "Airs of Bei" ("Bei feng" 邶風) in the *Book of Odes*. See Karlgren, *The Book of Odes*, 20.

We see a similar rhetorical move in a funerary inscription, composed about 1095 by a different author, for a woman surnamed Zhou. This inscription reveals its agenda early on, claiming that the subject was so remarkable that even when she was a child, "The wise among her relatives all commented, 'Someday she will certainly be able to uphold the principled and righteous conduct of the ancients.'" The author describes Zhou's early widowhood, her refusal to remarry, and then her abstemious conduct as a widow: serving her in-laws, educating her sons, never crossing the threshold except when visiting her parents. Like Fan Zuyu, this author drives home his message by citing famous allusions to faithful wives in the *Book of Odes*, once again suggesting that his subject should be regarded as an exemplar. He concludes, rather defensively, "This is something that everyone knows, not something I've privately [concocted]."⁵¹

Funerary inscriptions like these differ from those written earlier in the dynasty in their emphasis on widows' determination to remain faithful to their deceased husbands. Still, even as they put increased stress on the women's loyalty, late Northern Song authors continued to praise their subjects more for their *actions* as widows than for their fidelity per se. In 1113, Bi Zhongyou praised a widow not only for "upholding righteousness" (*shou yi* 守義) and refusing to remarry, but for her assiduous and indefatigable service to her widowed mother-in-law over a period of forty-two years. He stressed that all of the people of Luo, whether they knew her or not, acclaimed her filiality.⁵² Similarly, when people encouraged the twenty-seven-year-old Madame Mu (d. 1096) to remarry, she wept and insisted that she could not abandon her widowed mother: her faithfulness was less to her husband than to her natal family.⁵³ Another young widow is praised for managing to accompany her husband's body from his posting in the south back to the capital, despite the fact that she was traveling with an infant son and incompetent help. Her eulogist exclaims admiringly, "With that, everyone knew her talents were not limited to regular women's work."⁵⁴ As in the biography of Madame Wu, although

---

51. Li Fu, *Yushui ji* 8.14b–16b.
52. Bi Zhongyou, *Xi tai ji* 14.226–27.
53. Chao Buzhi, *Ji le ji* 65.2b–4b.
54. Zhang Lei, *Ke shan ji* 50.568–69; Wong Yu-Hsuan, "Tō Sō boshi," 51.

these inscriptions make it a point to characterize their subjects as "faithful wives," the women's fidelity to their husbands is not the central theme.⁵⁵ Indeed, when one author describes a Northern Song widow as "*jie yi* 節義" (a term that in later eras almost exclusively referred to the "fidelity and righteousness" of widows), it turns out that he is referring to the fact that she was frugal and refused to accept gifts from the court!⁵⁶

These funerary biographies of upper-class widows reveal a new interest in female fidelity in the late Northern Song. They also reveal a subtle shift in generic characteristics. For although these texts are funerary inscriptions for upper-class women, in casting their subjects as exemplary figures to be publicized and emulated (and perhaps ultimately rewarded), they begin to partake of characteristics more often associated with *zhuan* biographies. On its own, the rhetorical shift in these texts might seem too subtle to bespeak historical change; but in the same period we see the theme of faithful wife emerging in a small set of very different texts that likewise begin to blur boundaries in genres of writing about women.

## *Hybrid Texts*

One of these texts is a *zhuan* biography composed by the court official Zhao Dingchen, written to praise the strikingly unusual fidelity of Zhao's own cousin. In conspicuously colloquial language, Zhao's biography describes how his cousin's parents were tricked by a go-between into marrying her to an unworthy husband, a gambler and drunkard who ended up in trouble with the law. When her horrified natal family wanted the couple to divorce, she adamantly refused, choosing to remain in poverty and shame rather than abandon her relationship with her husband. Zhao admits that public opinion regarded her as unfilial and even stupid, but he defends her as faithful, more faithful even than the exemplars of the classics, for although the classical exemplars demonstrated their fidelity by dying, she maintained hers in spite of an unrighteous husband, against parental directive, and in the face of continuing misery.⁵⁷

---

55. Wong Yu-Hsuan suggests that funerary inscriptions by Wang Anshi particularly stress women's fidelity ("Tō Sō boshi," 47–48).
56. Wang Gui, *Huayang ji* 40.562–63.
57. Zhao Dingchen, *Zhu yin ji shi ji* 14.1a–4b.

It is possible that Zhao Dingchen intended this biography of his cousin as a political allegory (the fact that the cousin's surname is "Wu" ["military"] lends credence to this possibility). But however it was meant to be read, Zhao's text is significant for blending elements of traditional funerary biography with both the exemplar and entertainment aspects of the *zhuan* genre. In its message of female fidelity, Zhao's text echoed the funerary inscriptions that his contemporaries wrote for faithful widows; but in its use of the *zhuan* form, its informal diction, its frank discussion of family scandal, and the unconventional nature of the cousin's fidelity, it reads like an entertainment text.[58] The text is also notable in tethering the biography of a female relative (however vaguely identified[59]) to a polemical moral agenda directed at men: echoing Ouyang Xiu, Zhao's conclusion explicitly compares the resoluteness of his cousin with the moral vacillations of men—even scholars supposedly versed in righteousness and principle—when confronted with benefit or danger.

Zhao's text is idiosyncratic, but a similar blurring of exemplary female fidelity and entertainment elements can be found in an even more extraordinary set of texts from the late Northern Song, preserved in the collected writings of the minor official named Xu Ji 徐積 [1028–1103]. The conspicuously entertaining nature of Xu's work suggests that political forces may not have been the only impetus behind the new popularity of the faithful-wife theme.

## Xu Ji and *The Principled and Filial Collection*

Xu Ji's collected works are entitled *The Principled and Filial Collection* (*Jie xiao ji* 節孝集).[60] We will see that Xu's collection does indeed contain many biographies of principled and filial persons, but the title refers not to the contents, but to Xu Ji himself: he was a court-recognized moral exemplar. In the early months of Zhezong's reign, Xu had been acclaimed

---

58. As noted above, the *zhuan* form was not generally used for biographies of upper-class women, especially by their relatives.
59. Zhao never gives the names of his cousin, her father, or her husband. He does describe her father and indicates that she was married uxorilocally.
60. Xu Ji, *Jie xiao ji* 3.5b–7, 3.7b–8, 13.8b–11. An earlier version of this discussion of Xu Ji and his works appears in Bossler, "Fantasies of Fidelity," 167–70.

as a filial son; two decades later, under Huizong, he was honored with the posthumous title "Principled and Filial."⁶¹

Xu Ji is an interesting and unusual character. According to a biography composed more than a decade after his death, he was the son of a low-ranking official, but had lost his father at the tender age of two (three *sui*).⁶² His mother apparently returned home (though, significantly, no fuss is made about her widowhood), for Ji was reared in the household of her natal family. As a young man he went to study with the renowned scholar Hu Yuan 胡瑗 (993–1059), passed the examinations, and eventually held low-level offices, although some sort of hearing problem kept him from pursuing a regular bureaucratic career. To this basic information Xu's biographer adds a litany of examples showing his exceptionally filial behavior. We are told that even at age two, Ji crawled around inconsolably, seeking his deceased father; and since his father had been named "Rock" (*shi* 石), he not only refused to use stone tools but for his whole life avoided stepping on stones. When his uncles proposed to divide the family property, Ji cried bitterly; when he couldn't stop them he took only what they left behind, books and a broken-down shack. Later, he carried out their funerals and took care of a surviving aunt. He was devoted to his mother, leading the family in children's games to amuse her, taking her with him when he went to the examinations because he couldn't bear to leave her behind, and putting off marriage for fear that the wrong daughter-in-law would upset her. When she died he mourned so sincerely that supernatural manifestations routinely appeared at her grave.

As a result of his spectacular austerities, Xu Ji became a moral authority in the community. He revived the "community compact" ceremony and adjudicated lawsuits. Some sources even hint that he became a figure of religious veneration. Eventually, his reputation as an exemplar made him a minor celebrity. In 1093 (when the conservatives held sway at court), he

---

61. *Chang bian* 357.8530; Xu Ji, *Jie xiao ji* 32.10b–17b. The fragmentary surviving record hints that in the early twelfth century reformist and conservative factions competed to claim Xu Ji as their own. Li Tao, the author of the *Chang bian*, comments that the Veritable Records of Huizong's reign claimed that Xu Ji was first awarded office in 1100, a claim that Li dismisses as "extremely erroneous (*wu shen yi* 誤甚矣)." The posthumous title was awarded in 1116.

62. The biography was composed by one Wang Zishen 王資深, who calls himself an affinal relative—perhaps a son-in-law or distaff nephew? See Xu Ji, *Jie xiao ji* 32.10b–17b.

6. The filial son Xu Ji 徐積, shown worshipping at the tomb of his parents. From Siwujushi 四勿居士, *Lun tu bian lan* 倫圖便覽 (Ban cang Pei ying shu ju, 1886), 1.47a. Courtesy of the C. V. Starr East Asian Library, University of California, Berkeley.

was recommended to the throne as a great moral model who, if employed in the imperial university, could contribute to the moral transformation of the realm.[63] He exchanged poetry with some of the most eminent writers of the day, including Su Shi and Qin Guan. In Huizong's reign, the court showered him with several posthumous honors.[64]

But our interest in Xu Ji here is due less to his own reputation as an exemplar than to the extraordinary oeuvre that he left behind.[65] Xu's contemporary Su Shi noted the contradiction between Xu's exemplary persona and his "strange and uninhibited" (*guai er fang* 怪而放) writings.[66] And indeed, his writings are not at all what one finds in the typical collected works of Northern Song literati.

Consider, for example, Xu Ji's "Song of Ai'ai" (愛愛歌). The work opens with a long preface. Here Xu explains that he is reworking an earlier "Ai'ai ge" that had been written by "Zimei" (almost certainly the Northern Song writer Su Shunqin 蘇舜欽 [1008–48]). Xu indicates that Su's version did not survive in his own day, but at any rate, he complains, the original song had been licentious, "did not get at Ai'ai's true nature and contained nothing that could be shown to later students."[67] His new version, Xu explains, is designed to "relieve the confusion of scholars." Xu then tells the story of Ai'ai. An orphan from Wu, Ai'ai was reared in a courtesan's household, but she was unwilling to live as a courtesan herself.

---

63. Zeng Zhao, *Qufu ji* 2.34b.

64. Ge Shengzhong, in a biography for Ge Shusi, mentions that in 1124 a group of officials memorialized the court that Ge be given a posthumous title on the precedent of Xu Ji, so Xu had already received posthumous honors by that point (*Danyang ji* 15.17b).

65. Xu Ji's collected works as they currently exist appear to have been collated in the early Southern Song, and were published in 1169 (see Zhu Shangshu, *Song ren bie ji xu lu*, 369). However, at least some of Xu's writings would seem to have circulated in the Northern Song, as Su Shi is said to have commented on them.

66. Su Shi, *Dongpo zhi lin* 2.2b. Su also points out (satirically?) the contradiction that, although Xu Ji was so deaf he could communicate only by writing with a stick on the ground and spent his days meditating in solitude, he was somehow known to everyone. In their bibliographic note on Xu Ji's collection, the editors of the *Si ku quan shu* collectanea concur that Xu's writings are "wild, abandoned, self-assured, unrestrained by rules and models," and "mix the elegant and the vulgar" (though they insist that overall they "do not stray from the words of a Confucian").

67. In fact, a version of an "Ai'ai ge" attributed to Su Shunqin survives in Zhang Bangji's 張邦畿 (or sometimes 張邦基) *Shi' er xiao ming lu shi yi* 3.8–8b. For more on Zhang's collection, see chap. 5, n. 4.

She fled the courtesan quarters with a wealthy patron who brought her to the capital. After several years, the patron returned to Jiangnan and died there. Ai'ai remained in the capital, styling herself "one who hasn't died" (*wei wang ren* 未亡人, the traditional self-description of a faithful widow). She was impervious to the entreaties of wealthy and noble men who sought to become her patrons, remaining faithful until her death. Xu Ji extols Ai'ai's fidelity, comparing her to the righteous and heroic women of the past, and condemns her patron as unworthy. The preface is then followed by a long ballad in simple seven-character lines, describing the beautiful Ai'ai: "Dancing and singing, number one in Wu; just fifteen years old, paired chignons black-blue." In extremely trite language, it highlights her vow of fidelity: "the mountains can disintegrate, ah, the oceans dry up; in life there is only one, ah, in death not two." And finally, taking on her persona, it describes her feelings after her lover's death: "this year, this day, all has come to an end; fine gauzes and precious jade I regard as mud."[68]

We have seen this type of literature before, of course, in the *chuan qi* biographies of Wen Wan and her sister courtesans.[69] Even the form of the biography is reminiscent of *chuan qi* stories, for Ai'ai's biography is presented as a lengthy prose preface to a poem that comments on her

---

68. Xu Ji, *Jie xiao ji* 13.8b–11.

69. Nor are these the only unusual pieces in Xu Ji's collection. Xu has poetry devoted to decrying the decadent lifestyles of the rich and famous, in which he is forced to describe those lifestyles in exquisite detail: a pair of beauties helping people onto ivory beds, lovely maidens urging guests to drain their glasses, and so forth (*Jie xiao ji* 4.11b–13 ["On wealth and nobility, in answer to Magistrate Li"] [*Fu gui pian, da Li ling*]). He has a number of poems on the well-established "Concubines are ill-fated" (*Qie bo ming*) theme: in a preface to the lengthiest of these, he explains that it was inspired by a "wall poem," written by a miserable concubine, that had attracted the sympathy of other literati. Xu's own version of the poem is written in the concubine's voice and laments her miserable fate, but only after describing her lustrous skin, green-black hair, and talent at poetry (*Jie xiao ji* 11.7–8, 21.1–2). He also has a set of ten short poems meant to be written on fans, one each describing a Confucian, a Daoist, and Buddhist, and the rest devoted to images of women: the chaste girl, the chaste wife, the woman at her toilette, a poor girl, a sleeping woman, an abandoned woman, a widow. Many images in these poems are frankly erotic (for example, the "abandoned woman" poem opens, "For several years now I have not blown on the purple flute" and concludes, "Ever since that traveler crossed over into Liao, only the cool breeze ruffles my clothes") (*Jie xiao ji* 22.3–4).

actions.[70] But unlike stories of courtesans, this tale of Ai'ai appears in the collected works of an upright Confucian gentleman. And although his account does not shy away from evoking Ai'ai's erotic appeal, it reconfigures the courtesan romance into an account of a faithful wife, making her fidelity both the central theme of the story and the defining feature of Ai'ai's life. A courtesan's fidelity—which appears in other entertainment texts as based in romantic attachment—is here recast as moral imperative.

Xu employs the same preface/poem format for biographies of other exemplary women. In the preface to a "Poem for the Righteous Wife of Huaiyin" (淮陰義婦詩), Xu Ji describes the beautiful wife, née Li, of a wealthy merchant. Li's beauty attracted the attention of her husband's colleague, who murdered her husband by drowning him. Pretending to befriend the widow, the murderer went to great lengths to bring the dead man's body home, turned his earnings over to Li, and waited patiently as she completed the mourning for her husband. Then, taking advantage of her sense of gratitude, he proposed marriage. Li accepted and had begun to raise a family with her new husband, when

> one day there was a great flood, and bubbles formed in the water. Her [new] husband laughed, and the righteous wife asked why. When at first he didn't answer, she persisted. Relying on the fact that she had already borne him two sons, he expected that she would bear him no enmity, so he told her the truth, saying, "Your husband's drowning was my doing. After he was already under water, he reemerged, as if he were going to save himself. I stabbed him with the boat pole, and he went back under. The place where I stabbed him bubbled up just like what we saw today." The righteous wife was silent, suddenly understanding his plot, and enmity was born in her heart.

---

70. Glen Dudbridge has observed that the format of a prose preface to a narrative poem was central to the development of early *chuan qi* (*The Tale of Li Wa*, 25–26). I have unearthed only one other poetry preface of Song date written in honor of a woman: significantly, it was written to cap a collection of poetry in honor of a courtesan. See "Zhang Wenrou *shi xu*" in Liu Yan, *Longyun ji* 24.17–19b. For a detailed discussion of this preface, see Bossler, "Fantasies of Fidelity," 165–66. Poetry prefaces were occasionally used in the Northern Song to honor exemplary men. Sima Guang composed a poem intended for a poetry collection honoring one Chen Yong, whose harmonious family had hoped to receive a government award but had been unsuccessful (Sima Guang, *Sima wen zheng gong chuan jia ji* 2.8). See also the discussion of Zhu Shouchang in chap. 2.

Xu relates that Li immediately turned her new husband in to the authorities. Then, distraught that her own beauty had caused her husband's death, and that her children had been sired by her husband's enemy, she bound the two boys and threw them in the river, throwing herself in after them.

Before turning to the poem, Xu defends his designation of his subject as a "righteous wife," arguing that although she had remarried, she had done so out of obligation. He points out that once she learned the truth, "the intimacy of the marital bed did not weigh in her heart in the slightest," and thus she was able to kill her own sons.[71] Like the poem for Ai'ai, the poem for the "righteous wife" slips in and out of the subject's voice, employing simple language and clichéd images: "The woman of Huaiyin, how determined and heroic! Her face like a flower, her heart like iron."[72]

Here we have a biography of a respectable (albeit still not upper-class) woman that highlights her beauty and celebrates her virtue in poetry, in a form reminiscent of the biographies of courtesans. Xu Ji quite explicitly intends this work as moral proselytization, as indicated in his commentary on the righteous wife's story:

> Hearing of her spirit, strong men and heroic gentlemen become somber on her behalf, to the point that they kneel down and cry. And evil ministers and traitorous factions may also be somewhat shamed.... Since the Wei and Jin there have been many high ministers who have instructed people to raise armies and kill their lords. If the righteous woman saw them, what sort of things would she think they were? What a pity that her affair has not reached the court, and her loyalty and righteousness have not been rewarded (*jing*) in the village. How tragic!

This language, like that in Zhao Dingchen's biography of his cousin, is reminiscent of that employed in Ouyang Xiu's biography of Wang

---

71. This story, and Xu Ji's commentary on it, are also discussed in Elvin, "Female Virtue and the State," 140.

72. Xu Ji, *Jie xiao ji* 3.5b–7. In the Southern Song, Hong Mai's *Yijian zhi* featured a story with many similar elements (including bubbles on water exposing a murder). But in Hong Mai's version, far from being a faithful wife, the victim's wife had been having an illicit affair with the murderer. See Hong Mai, *Yijian zhi* (hereafter *YJZ*), *zhi bu*, 5.1590. Although Hong recorded the story long after Xu Ji did, the alternative version raises the possibility that Xu Ji was here rewriting an existing story, as he had done with "Ai'ai ge."

Ning's wife. It reminds us that Ouyang's biography was also based on a "story" (*xiao shuo*) that had an entertainment pedigree. Xu's reference to a government award and his condemnation of "traitorous factions" likewise suggests his awareness of the political dimensions of his heroine's virtue. Finally, his text suggests again that the boundaries between genres meant to entertain—in this case, the poem with biographical preface—and those designed to exhort were beginning to blur.[73]

Neither Zhao Dingchen's nor Xu Ji's texts can be considered representative of literati writings at the end of the Northern Song: on the contrary, they stand out as exceptional in that period. But they presage several important developments that were to emerge more clearly in the Southern Song and Yuan. Most notable among these is new attention to female fidelity, expressed not in funerary inscriptions but in more public and circulating (and entertaining) genres, such as poetry prefaces and *zhuan* biographies.

## Conclusion

Although the figure of the "principled woman" had a long and venerable history in China, throughout most of the Northern Song the category of "faithful wife" that was to become so dominant in writings on women in later imperial China had little political or cultural salience. By the end of the Northern Song, however, court politics led to ostentatious celebration of exemplary behavior, and writers of funerary inscriptions began emphasizing not only the filial sentiments of concubines' sons but also the fidelity of upper-class widows such as Madame Wu, whose biography opened this chapter. All of these writings focused new attention on family relations and proper roles within the family (as did, from the opposite angle, indictments of men for inappropriate relationships with courtesans or concubines). In this, they both reflected and contributed to a convergence of private or personal life with public and political discourse.

The new interest in female fidelity was connected in complex and subtle ways with social concerns about courtesans and concubines.

---

73. Chap. 9 will show that in the Yuan, poetry prefaces became the standard format for writing about faithful wives.

Although writers at the time posited no explicit connections between the filiality of concubines' sons and the loyalty of wives, the filial crises of men like Zhu Shouchang and Li Ding exposed the reality that concubines routinely moved in and out of families, highlighting the ideal that *wives* not do so. Meanwhile, authors of entertainment literature fantasized about the romantic loyalty of courtesans, casting them very much in the model of loyal literati wives.[74] Finally, both entertainment literature focusing on dramatic acts of romantic fidelity and the political demand for stories of exemplars helped legitimize the use of new genres—such as *zhuan* biography and poetry with biographical prefaces—for writing about exemplary women, including women of the upper class.

In the early twelfth century, the discourse on female fidelity was still a very minor element in literati writings. Surviving biographies of Northern Song exemplars focus more or less equally on men and women, and discussion of female fidelity in elite women (with the singular exception of Zhao Dingchen's cousin) was limited to the relatively private genre of funerary inscriptions. That state of affairs was to change drastically after 1126, as the traumatic fall of the dynasty radically altered the social and political context in which literati writings were produced.

---

74. For further development of this point, see Bossler, "Fantasies of Fidelity," 162–65.

PART TWO

*Markets, Mayhem, and
Morality in the Southern Song*

# 4

## *Performance Anxiety*

### Yan Rui 嚴蕊

The Taizhou government slave Yan Rui was exceptionally talented and thoughtful; she was broadly read and thoroughly understood both ancient and contemporary events. Tang Zhongyou was the prefect, and was quite taken with her. Zhu Xi served as supervisor in Eastern Zhe; he led his subordinates in uncovering the affair, and had Rui put in prison. In thrashing her, they regarded 500 strokes as a light beating. They then took her under escort to Kuaiji where the case was tried again. Rui was cruelly punished and consigned to the music registers as before. Yue Lin was a judicial supervisor who due to his sagacious judgments was sent to Tai prefecture. Rui submitted a petition asking to be released. Yue ordered her to compose a poem, and she responded immediately, reciting, "It is not that I love the wind and dust; it seems I've been wronged by a previous incarnation. Flowers fall and flowers bloom each in its own time, it is all under the control of the Eastern Lord. Leave, in the end I must leave; stay, how can I stay? If you are able to cover your head with wildflowers, don't ask where this slave has gone." Yue therefore ordered that she be released to commoner status.[1]

In this manner, the famous Southern Song collector of anecdotes Hong Mai 洪邁 (1123–1202) retold the story of one of the most fascinating legal cases of the era. As we shall see further below, Zhu Xi's 朱熹 (1130–1200) attack on Yan Rui was emblematic of growing Southern Song concerns about the deleterious influence of courtesans in local

---

1. *YJZ, zhi geng*, 10.1216–17. The story of Yan Rui has fascinated observers ever since the Southern Song: it was developed into a vernacular version by the late Ming writer Ling Mengchu 凌濛初 (1580–1644), in the twelfth chapter of his *Er ke pai an jing qi* 二刻拍案驚奇 (I am grateful to Wilt Idema for pointing me to Ling's collection), and continues to fascinate readers today. See the Chinese Wikipedia site devoted to her: http://zh.wikipedia.org/wiki/嚴蕊 (accessed July 18, 2011).

government. But here she appears as a heroine, a lovely and talented young woman unfairly and pathetically abused, clever enough to win her release from service by impressing an appreciative official with a brilliant poetic composition. In this, Hong Mai's anecdote clearly owes a debt to earlier romantic fiction, which frequently depicted courtesans as talented romantic heroines. Yet Hong's anecdote, with its naturalistic retelling of a putatively "true" story, and its focus on regional rather than court officials, is also emblematic of a shift in the nature of discourses about courtesans in the Southern Song. In part the shift was the result of population growth and other broad social change. The continuing expansion of the literate sector of the population in the Southern Song meant that increasing numbers of men began to record and consume gossipy anecdotes such as this one.[2] As cities proliferated, so too did the courtesan entertainments associated with them, along with urban guidebooks that described such entertainments to an avid public.[3] The commercialization of printing meant that many of these works circulated widely, and this expanding entertainment literature helped to define the emerging culture of the local elite in the Southern Song.[4] Rather than focusing on the court and its denizens, such works took as their subjects clerks and minor bureaucrats, aspiring scholars, prosperous householders, and petty merchants.

Whereas in the Northern Song courtesans were emblems of refined official culture, in the Southern Song they figure conspicuously as prominent participants in an increasingly commodified society, and also as extremely evocative symbols of that commodification. As entertainments proliferated, courtesans were subject to the blurring of social

---

2. As Ronald Egan has pointed out, the anecdotally driven "Remarks on Poetry" genre, with its concern for aesthetics and the circumstances of poetry production, had itself become newly respectable in the Northern Song. See Egan, *The Problem of Beauty*, chap. 2.

3. On the development of urban literature in the Song, see West, "Huang hou," 197–218.

4. For example, the first part of Hu Zi's miscellany, *Tiaoxi yu yin cong hua*, compiled by 1148, had found its way into print by 1194 (*Tiaoxi yu yin cong hua, xu*, 1). Wider circulation also meant that such texts were more likely to survive down to modern times. On the expansion of printing in the Song, see Chia, *Printing for Profit*. On the limits of that expansion, see McDermott, *A Social History*, 43–78.

boundaries that characterized the Southern Song more generally: boundaries between court and urban entertainments dissolved, and distinctions between registered and unregistered performers broke down. Courtesans' increased presence also gave them new opportunities to serve as *vehicles* of cultural, class, and political blurring. Finally, the expanded presence of entertainers in Southern Song society precipitated new concerns about the dangers of entertainment to good government, especially at the local level, as well as intensified anxiety about courtesans' pernicious influence on social mores. By the thirteenth century, a few lone moralists even began to call for an end to the system of government-courtesans.

## *Courtesans in the Cataclysm*

The collapse of the Northern Song in 1127 had a traumatic effect on virtually all of Song society, entertainers no less than others. The court and capital were most directly affected, for the actual capture of Kaifeng was preceded by more than a year of intermittent siege and ruthless pillaging of the capital's wealth. The populace saw their glittering city reduced to ruins, their officials humiliated, and eventually the entire court taken captive.[5] Refugees streamed into the south, vulnerable to the terrors and uncertainties faced by refugees everywhere—loss of loved ones in the panic and confusion, extortion and robbery by soldiers and profiteers on both sides, the struggles of trying to rebuild one's life in a new place. Nor was the south itself safe: for more than a decade after the new emperor Gaozong 高宗 (r. 1127–62) announced the reconstitution of the dynasty in 1127, the nascent Southern Song regime was beleaguered by external attacks and internal treachery, and managed to settle into a temporary capital in Hangzhou (renamed Lin'an, "Temporary Peace") only in 1138.

Courtesans were among the lowest-status members of society, but at the same time they had desirable attributes: this combination left them particularly vulnerable in such times of chaos. When the Jin captured the Song imperial family, they also seized skilled palace servitors of all types. Doctors, artisans, and palace entertainers (*ji* 妓) were among the

---

5. For a riveting if horrifying account of the sieges and their aftermath, see Ebrey, "Introduction," in Ebrey and Bickford, *Emperor Huizong*, 1–4.

thousands of people carried off to the north.⁶ The musical paraphernalia of the court—props, dance charts, famous antique zithers, the musical instruments belonging to the Entertainment Bureau, music books, ritual objects, and so forth—were entirely lost.⁷ Meanwhile, in the prefectures, courtesans sometimes found themselves treated as bargaining chips when officials in besieged towns negotiated with marauding troops. In the summer of 1127, for example, a rebel leader attacked the northern city of Yizhou 沂州. The prefect closed the city gates and sent out ten government-courtesans to the rebels. They responded by moving on to the next town, leaving Yizhou unmolested.⁸ A few years later, the rebel commander Li Heng promised to abandon his ten-week siege of De'an prefecture if the city's defender Chen Ju would turn over to him a certain renowned government entertainer. Chen's generals begged him to comply, arguing that the sacrifice of one woman to save the entire city was surely an acceptable trade-off. Chen, however, refused, saying, "If doing so causes Heng to retreat, then I would be using a woman to bargain for peace. Not to mention that he might take her and still not retreat!" The retelling of this incident is obviously designed to demonstrate Chen's virtue and sagacity (especially since he went on to save his city by military means), but it reveals the widespread understanding that courtesans were both valuable and expendable.⁹

Like other objects of desire, courtesans also tended to be regarded as the fair spoils of war. When Changzhou was attacked in 1129, the ill-prepared prefect attempted to buy off bandits with gold and silk, but his efforts were to no avail. The brigands entered the city and immediately called the local courtesans to drink with them; they subsequently went on a looting rampage that lasted several days.¹⁰ When the city of Hezhou fell to the Jin in 1134, the prefect's courtesans were taken away along with his gold and silk.¹¹ Although certainly all kinds of women were vulnerable to the predations of invading soldiers, courtesans were treated as war

---

6. Li Xinchuan, *Jianyan yi lai xi nian yao lu* 1.46a. Cf. Idema and West, *Chinese Theater*, 84.
7. *SS* 129.3027.
8. Li Xinchuan, *Jianyan yi lai xi nian yao lu* 7.2b.
9. Ibid., 57.12b–13a.
10. Ibid., 9.21a.
11. Ibid., 82.14a–b.

booty even by the Song defenders. When the generals Zhang Jun 張俊 and Wang Yuan 王淵 defeated the bandit Chen Tong 陳通, Zhang Jun took the top Hangzhou courtesan Zhang Nong 張穠 back home as his concubine.[12]

Stories like these show that even as the Northern Song was collapsing, entertainers continued to be regarded as symbols of power and privilege. As peace was gradually restored and prosperity returned to the southern regions, the fashion for courtesan entertainments continued to spread. As entertainments proliferated, the social roles of entertainers—and their image in the literati imagination—alike were transformed.

## *Entertainers Between Court and Populace*

One important contributor to that transformation was the Southern Song court's decision to dissolve the Court Entertainment Bureau. As early as 1125, under severe threat from the Jin, Emperor Huizong had ordered that all the music bureaus be disbanded and all supernumerary entertainment personnel dismissed.[13] When the court was reconstituted around Gaozong, some sort of Entertainment Bureau was reestablished under eunuch supervision, but by 1128, with the new court's very existence still threatened, Gaozong complained that he was hardly in the mood for entertainments and ordered that it again be abolished.[14] Still, once peace was established entertainments were apparently reintroduced: the birthday of Grand Councilor Qin Gui in 1143 was celebrated with a court banquet featuring musical performances and variety shows, and in 1144 the Court Entertainment Bureau was formally reestablished, with 460 performers placed under the direction of palace eunuchs.[15] This state of affairs lasted nearly twenty years, until in mid-1161, near the end of his reign, Gaozong once again dissolved the Entertainment Bureau,

---

12. Li Xinchuan, *Jianyan yi lai xi nian yao lu* 11.3. Later, Zhang even made her into his legal wife. In so doing, he not only broke laws about marriage between classes, but also ignored the powerful taboo against same-surname marriage. Later the concubine's surname was changed in order to disguise the irregularity. Cf. Bossler, "Shifting Identities," 25.
13. *SS* 129.3027.
14. Li Xinchuan, *Jianyan yi lai xi nian yao lu* 13.12b.
15. Ibid., 150.18b; 151.6a; *SS* 142.3359.

specifically stipulating that the performers were free to do as they pleased (其樂工許自便).¹⁶ Why Gaozong dissolved the Bureau at this point is not entirely clear: one observer suggested that the emperor's action was inspired by the fact that enemies were making military preparations, and especially by reports that the Jin were particularly seeking female musicians from the emperor's court.¹⁷ This interpretation is given some credence by the emperor's strenuous efforts, in an edict issued ten days later, to quash rumors that he had acted for any reason other than concern to reduce expenses for the good of the realm.¹⁸ Yet Gaozong had indeed been systematically attempting to reduce palace expenses for several years, often by reducing the number of palace entertainment personnel. Several hundred musicians had been let go in early 1160, in response to a memorial by Minister of Personnel Zhang Tao 張燾.¹⁹

Whatever the circumstances leading to Gaozong's final elimination of the Entertainment Bureau, his decision was soon reiterated by his successor Xiaozong 孝宗 (r. 1163–89). When in preparation for a birthday banquet in 1164 the question of musical entertainment arose,

---

16. Ibid., 190.26a. See also Idema and West, *Chinese Theater*, 103–4.
17. Xu Mengxin, *San chao bei meng hui bian* 229.4b.
18. Li Xinchuan, *Jianyan yi lai xi nian yao lu* 191.2a; Xu Mengxin, *San chao bei meng hui bian* 229.7a. On the basis of the emperor's disclaimer, Li Xinchuan rejects the suggestion that the emperor was responding to rumors about the Jin (*Jianyan yi lai xi nian yao lu* 190.23a). Still, the Jin were in fact making preparations to attack the Song, though their expedition did not begin until October of 1161. The Jin ruler had also reportedly written Chinese poetry that expressed his desire to take possession of the Song emperor's palace women (see Mote, *Imperial China*, 233–35). So it seems plausible that such rumors did circulate, whether or not Gaozong based his decision on them.
19. Li Xinchuan, *Jianyan yi lai xi nian yao lu* 184.6b. See also *SS* 142.3361. Zhao Sheng's *Chao ye lei yao* 1.30 (preface dated 1236), attributes the dissolution of the Bureau to a memorial by the censor Wang Shipeng (1112–71). Wang did complain about the extravagance of palace entertainments in his examination essay of 1157, to which the emperor responded by ordering that gold and jade not be used in the clothing and ornaments of palace denizens (*Wang Shipeng quan ji, wen ji* 1.573–90; Li Xinchuan, *Jianyan yi lai xi nian yao lu* 176.17b). Wang also later wrote a memorial asking that inner-court expenses be reduced (*Wang Shipeng quan ji, wen ji* 3.623), but this latter memorial did not specifically raise the issue of entertainments, and moreover seems to have been after Gaozong's retirement, since it refers to the Deshou palace that was built to house Gaozong in his retirement (see Gong Yanming, *Song dai guan zhi ci dian* 611–12). In short, I have been unable to locate any evidence that Gaozong was specifically responding to Wang in eliminating the Entertainment Bureau.

Xiaozong pointed out that the performers were only needed twice a year, to celebrate the imperial birthdays. His advisors suggested that, rather than establishing an Entertainment Bureau, musicians could simply be hired on a temporary basis. The emperor agreed, and from that point on, when envoys from the Jin came to pay their twice-yearly birthday visits, the court simply ordered the Palace Maintenance Office (*xiu nei si* 修內司) to gather musicians and hold rehearsals for a fortnight or so prior to the performance.[20]

As Wilt Idema and Stephen West have pointed out, however, the dissolution of the Court Entertainment Bureau did not mean that court entertainments were abrogated or even much reduced. Many of the best musicians were employed in other court offices—particularly in the Deshou palace, the residence of the retired emperor Gaozong and eventually of his empress as well—and still others joined the ranks of musicians attached to Lin'an prefecture (the court's efforts to reduce expenses by limiting entertainments were decidedly not imitated by lower-level government offices, which continued to maintain government-courtesans as before). All of these musicians, as well as other performers in the city, were eligible to be called to perform at court banquets as occasion demanded.[21] The court also continued to maintain a Music Instruction Office (*jiao yue suo* 教樂所) that was responsible for hiring and rehearsing the temporary companies of entertainers who were gathered to put on performances.

"Privatizing" entertainments, as it were, may indeed have saved the court some of the expenses of supporting and training the court entertainers, but a more significant result, as Idema and West also note, was the increased movement of entertainers and entertainment forms between the court and the urban populace.[22] This movement was important precisely because entertainment continued to be such a prominent feature of both court and urban life in the Southern Song—so much so that many observers continued to use the term "Entertainment

---

20. *SS* 142.3359; Li Xinchuan, *Jianyan yi lai chao ye za ji*, *jia ji* 3.101; *yi ji* 4.577. See also Idema and West, *Chinese Theater*, 102.
21. Zhao Sheng, *Chao ye lei yao* 1.30; Wu Zimu, *Meng liang lu* 20.308; Idema and West, *Chinese Theater*, 102–3.
22. Idema and West, *Chinese Theater*, 103–4.

Bureau" long after the institution itself had been abolished. Thus when Guangzong 光宗 (r. 1190–94) came to the throne, an official reminded him that upon the death of Gaozong in 1187, Xiaozong had sent away all the "Entertainment Bureau musicians and all of the entertainers and entertainment officials" (教坊樂人及一應俳優伶官等). The official urged Guangzong to follow Xiaozong's precedent and order all the entertainers to withdraw temporarily until the mourning period was over.[23] Whether Guangzong heeded this suggestion is unknown, but in any case entertainers were back at court in force by 1191. In the spring of that year, an inauspicious spring snowstorm led a chastened Guangzong to appeal to his ministers for advice. In response, the official Wei Jing submitted a memorial outlining nine flaws in Guangzong's administration. The third of these concerned court entertainments:

> I have heard that rulers take diligence and frugality as a virtue and must not regard their position as pleasurable. If they use music and beauty to delight their ears and eyes, making [the entertainments] constantly more novel and elaborate, there will be no leisure to devote to other affairs. . . . I have personally heard that, when you have leisure from the myriad duties of governance, the banquets and drinking parties in the palace are incessant, and musicians compete to present themselves. The services of the six palaces cannot be called insufficient, yet pretty-faced performers and comical actors of the marketplace are commanded to array themselves indiscriminately before you. The word on the street is not always worthy of belief, but when the criticism reaches this level there must be something to it.[24]

Thus nearly thirty years after the Entertainment Bureau was dissolved, officials were still complaining about the frequency with which the emperor indulged himself with entertainment, and especially about the unregulated intercourse between the palace and marketplace entertainers. That intercourse reached a logical (and literal) extreme in the reign of Guangzong's successor Ningzong 寧宗 (r. 1195–1224) when a young entertainer, the daughter of a singer, entered the palace as a child actress and ended up as the leading lady of the land. Empress Yang (1162–1232), as she was known to later history, attracted the attention

---

23. Yuan Shuoyou, *Dong tang ji* 13.3b–4.
24. Wei Jing, *Hou le ji* 10.16b–17a. For a fuller discussion of this memorial and its implications in the context of the Southern Song court, see Bossler, "Gender and Entertainment," 269–70.

of the future emperor Ningzong when he was still heir apparent. His interest in her lasted over the years, and when he became emperor in 1195 she was given consort titles. Five years later, Ningzong's first empress (a descendant of an early Song grand councilor) died, and despite the objections of the outer court the erstwhile entertainer became the new empress.[25] Court entertainments and entertainers continued to prosper through the succeeding reign of Emperor Lizong 理宗 (r. 1225–64), whom one author has called "one of the infamous lechers of Chinese imperial history."[26] According to one contemporary account, the court in this period continued to hire private entertainers to supplement those attached to the government. The author complained, "Most are those fellows from the cities and lanes. If you demand that they know pitch and understand music, I'm afraid it will not necessarily be the case."[27] Others noted that the entertainers and ne'er-do-wells who frequented Lizong's palace were able to make a comfortable living off the extravagant rewards they received for their performances.[28]

## *The Elaboration of Urban Entertainments*

Throughout most of the Southern Song, then, the court continued to be a center of music and popular entertainment, providing employment for hundreds of musicians, actors, and entertainers, and insuring its own primacy as the center of culture and fashion.[29] At the same time, the boundaries between the court and urban spaces outside it had almost

---

25. *SS* 243.8656. Like her Northern Song predecessor Empress Liu, Yang went on to play powerful roles in court politics, most notably helping to engineer the death of Han Tuozhou and (with some reluctance) the succession of Lizong. When Lizong took the throne she shared power with him, and she remained a force in court politics until her death in 1232. See *SS* 243.8657–58; Davis, *Court and Family*, 96–101. For more on Empress Yang's entertainer background, see Bossler, "Gender and Entertainment," 273–76. For her activities as empress, see Hui-shu Lee, *Empresses, Art, and Agency*, chap. 4.
26. Mote, *Imperial China*, 310.
27. Zhao Sheng, *Chao ye lei yao* 1.30.
28. Liu Yiqing, *Qiantang yi shi* 5.8–9.
29. In this context, the dissolution of the Entertainment Bureau must be understood as a face-saving gesture designed to appease critics of imperial extravagance in a time of fiscal difficulty. For more detailed information about the institutional structures of the Southern Song *jiao fang*, see Kishibe, "Sōdai kyōbō," 324–59.

completely broken down. As in the late Tang, the influx of court entertainers into the streets and lanes of the capital contributed to the proliferation of performance venues and varieties of entertainment.[30] Late Song accounts reveal that during the Southern Song the best government-courtesans in the capital could be hired for banquets not only by officials but even by students in the various residential colleges or dormitories (*zhai* 齋) within the court's "Three Institutes" (*san xue* 三學: the Imperial Clan School 宗學, the Imperial University 太學, and the Military Academy 武學).[31] Indeed, the mid-thirteenth century observer Zhou Mi remarked that the residential colleges always had courtesans at their banquets, each formally issuing an invitation under the seal of the college, saying, "We respectfully request the presence of Disciple (*di zi* 弟子) so-and-so at such-and-such a place to attend the banquet of our college."[32] Demand for some of the top courtesans was such that it occasionally led to brawls.[33] Zhou also complained that other people who wanted to obtain the services of courtesans had to have connections with some member of a college, and only by going through such a connection could they issue an invitation.[34] Government-courtesans could also be

---

30. For a detailed discussion of the evolution of theater arts in the Southern Song, see Idema and West, *Chinese Theater*, 102–41.

31. See Gong Yanming, *Song dai guan zhi ci dian*, 358; Wu Zimu, *Meng liang lu* 20.309. Within the Three Institutes, students were grouped into *zhai*: an edict of 1079 had stipulated that the Imperial University be expanded to include 2,400 students organized into 80 *zhai* of 30 students each (*SS* 157.3660). The passage indicates that *zhai* were in effect "residential colleges": each *zhai* of 30 students was supposed to be 5 "pillars" in size. Chaffee, *Branches of Heaven*, 169, indicates that the Southern Song clan school was established only in 1214.

32. As we saw in chap. 1, the term *di zi* (lit., "disciples") was an allusion to the entertainers in the palace of Emperor Xuanzong of the Tang, who were called "Disciples of the Pear Garden." By the mid Song it had become a common way of referring to courtesans: cf. Zhu Xi's use of the term below.

33. Zhou Mi, *Gui xin za shi, bie ji, shang*, 229, on Lin Qiao. Elsewhere Zhou describes the courtesan being fought over here as one of several known for their beauty and skills (*Gui xin za shi, xu ji, xia*, 167–68).

34. Zhou Mi, *Gui xin za shi, hou ji*, 66. Zhou notes that he does not know when this custom began, and declares it extremely unreasonable and the cause of many untoward incidents. On the disruptiveness of students in the late Song capital, see Smith, "Impressions," 87. On the phenomenon of better courtesans being more difficult to obtain because they were often reserved, see also the poem "Xi Sun Jifan" (戲孫季蕃) in Liu Kezhuang, *Hou cun ji* 2.6b–7.

found in attendance at semiofficial occasions such as the banquets of "same-year societies" (*tong nian hui* 同年會, groups of officials who had passed the examinations in the same year) and "native place associations" (*xiang hui* 鄉會, associations of scholars and officials who hailed from the same native place).[35]

In this period, entertainers registered to the government were typically dispatched not directly from government offices but from the various government-owned wine storehouses (*jiu ku* 酒庫). According to Southern Song observers, this custom (known as *she fa mai jiu* 設法賣酒) had first been introduced in the 1070s and 1080s, in conjunction with Wang Anshi's Green Sprouts policy. That policy sought to enhance the state's revenues by loaning seed money to farmers in the spring, to be paid back at interest during the harvest period. But entrepreneurial officials soon found ways to separate the farmers from their newly acquired loans:

> The authorities distributed the Green Sprouts money at the yamen, and set up wine shops at the watchtower gates. When people went out carrying their money, they were enticed to come and drink, typically spending 20 or 30 percent of their funds. The [authorities] also worried that [the farmers] would ignore them [the wine shops], so they ordered courtesans (*chang nü* 娼女) to sit in the wine shops and make music to lure and beguile them.[36]

Whether or not this was precisely how the custom began, in the Southern Song providing courtesan entertainment at the government wine storehouses was clearly common practice. By the thirteenth century many of

---

35. Wu Zimu, *Meng liang lu* 20.309. The passages on which I have based this acount are translated in Idema and West, *Chinese Theater*, 73–74; however, these authors understand *san xue* as the "Three Learnings" (Buddhism, Daoism, and Confucianism). On same-year societes and native place associations, see Zhao Sheng, *Chao ye lei yao*, 5.9–9b; Zhao says that native place associations could include students of the Three Institutes as well as court offcials.
36. Wang Yong, *Yan yi yi mou lu* 3.3–3b. I have found no direct Northern Song reference to this practice. A passage in Yang Shi's "Collected Conversations" (*yu lu*), putatively dating to 1114 or 1115, is nominally the earliest critique of this practice, but the passage (which also blames Wang Anshi's New Policies) does not appear in all versions of Yang's conversations, and, given the factional rewriting of history that took place in the Southern Song, may be a later interpolation (it is featured in Zhu Xi's *Yi luo yuan yuan lu*). See the discussion of Yang Shi later in this chapter. Wang Yong's text makes it clear that the system was in place at the time he was writing, about 1227.

these government storehouses had become full-fledged winehouses (*jiu lou* 酒樓), providing food and entertainment as well as wine (though Zhou Mi complained that the winehouses, too, tended to be monopolized by members of the colleges, and that it was difficult for outsiders to enter).[37]

Even as government-courtesans found themselves entertaining outside of government offices, the number and variety of entertainments available on the open market—as well as the independent performers who provided them—proliferated. Both commoners without official connections and officials who wanted to hold a private party could hire unregistered itinerant performers (*san yue* 散樂) from the various city entertainment districts, or seek out the narrow back lanes and hire courtesans who could sing.[38] For men who did not wish to entertain at home, privately owned winehouses, like the government storehouses, provided elegant accoutrements as well as courtesan entertainment. These private winehouses typically encompassed a dozen or so private chambers (*ge* 閣) luxuriously appointed with serving vessels of gold and silver. Each house held a complement of several dozen courtesans, all fashionably made up and gorgeously dressed, as well as "little chignon" (*xiao huan*) apprentices who would present themselves without invitation, singing noisily in hopes of a tip. Musicians played various types of music, and old ladies proffered braziers of burning incense. In both government and private winehouses, vendors provided snacks or meals in great profusion and variety to accompany the wine.[39] The entertainment at such houses was primarily limited to drinking and music; but other establishments, known as "straw-hut wine shops" (*an jiu dian* 菴酒店) and recognizable by the red gardenia lamps hanging at their doors, had sleeping platforms discreetly hidden in the wine chambers. At the larger winehouses, the courtesans merely kept customers company while they drank, and if one wanted further pleasures, it was customary to go to the courtesans' residences (*wang qi ju* 往其居).[40]

---

37. Zhou Mi, *Wulin jiu shi*, 442.
38. Wu Zimu, *Meng liang lu* 20.309. Cf. Idema and West, *Chinese Theater*, 70. Naideweng, *Du cheng ji sheng*, also repeatedly describes different levels of entertainment at different prices and degrees of elegance; see esp. 92–98. On the status of itinerant musicians in the Song, see Liang Gengyao, "Song dai ji yi ren de she hui di wei," 100–116.
39. Zhou Mi, *Wulin jiu shi*, 442–43.
40. Naideweng, *Du cheng ji sheng*, 92–93.

Both government and private winehouses were distinct from what Zhou Mi identifies as "singing houses" (*ge guan* 歌館), where, in Zhou's delicate euphemism, "the fresh flowers gathered." Most of these "singing houses" called themselves "tea shops" (*cha fang* 茶坊) and they were ruinously expensive:

> When you first enter the door, there is someone who holds a bottle and offers you a drink—even a cup of tea will set you back several thousand: it is called "selecting flower tea." If you go inside and just drink a glass, you must first give them several strings: this is called "defraying the wine." Afterward they call out and offer things to buy, and you can set up a banquet to your liking. All kinds of people rush around serving and selling things; the expense can be considerable. Some like to invite other courtesans, and even if they are coming from across the street, they will call for a sedan chair and arrive ensconced therein, calling it a "Street-crossing palanquin."[41]

Throughout the entertainment districts, Zhou Mi observed, "the sounds of amusement and laughter go on every night until dawn, frequently greeting the carts and horses of [those going to] the morning court audience. No matter if it is windy, rainy, hot, or snowy, it is not in the slightest diminished."[42]

Admittedly, most of the evidence just discussed dates from after the fall of the Southern Song and focuses on the capital of Lin'an. But evidence for the proliferation of entertainment in the Southern Song can be found in the countryside as well, where the institution of government-courtesans spread from prefectures to lower-level government offices, and where distinctions between registered and unregistered performers were increasingly blurred.

## *The Proliferation of Entertainers in the Southern Song Countryside*

As in the Northern Song, courtesan entertainments continued to be a central feature of official life in the countryside. This is visible, for example, in the daily diaries recorded by the court official Zhou Bida 周必大 (1126–1204) during trips he made when he was temporarily out of office.

---

41. Zhou Mi, *Wulin jiu shi*, 442–43. Hong Mai likewise depicts courtesans as traveling in sedan chairs, attended by servants (*YJZ, zhi jia*, 4.741).
42. Zhou Mi, *Wulin jiu shi*, 442–43.

Zhou's accounts detail the weather and travel conditions, the famous sites he visited, and the numerous people he encountered. Despite the fact that he was not traveling on official business, at most prefectures through which he traveled Zhou paid formal visits to the local officials, and usually he was treated in return to "prefectural banquets" (*zhou hui* 州會 or *fu hui* 府會). Sometimes these banquets began early and lasted all day, and they seem always to have included wine and entertainment. Describing a party he attended on the ninth day of the ninth month of 1167, Zhou relates:

> In the morning there was a prefectural banquet: we climbed up to Nanhua terrace. With Han, Ye, Zhang, Hou, and I, there were some forty guests in all. While we were still drinking the moon came out near the terrace. Military music was played, and we ordered the courtesan Li Su 李素 to do a western-style dance. All the guests drained their glasses. I came back and vomited copiously.[43]

A few days later, having arrived at another prefecture, Zhou once again found himself at a prefectural banquet. This time he noted names of the local wines that were served ("Clear Hall" and "Gushu Spring"), and complained that the assembled courtesans were "common and crude, lacking the romantic spirit of [the Northern Song poets] Ou[yang Xiu] and Mei [Yaochen]."[44] On the twenty-fifth of the same month, there was another banquet at another prefecture: here Zhou presented to the company a song (*xiao ci* 小詞) he had written (and which he recorded in his diary). He also took notice of one of the entertainers:

> The government-courtesan Cao Mian 曹眄 was rather pure and reserved. Some took it ill that she was slow of speech and not statuesque. They teased her and she became all the more shy.[45]

The frequency of banquets with courtesans in the lives of local

---

43. Zhou Bida, *Wenzhong ji* 168.26b. Western-style dance (lit. "barbarian dance" *hu wu* 胡舞) refers to a dance in what we would call Middle Eastern style. Such dances became very popular in China in the late Tang and remained part of the standard courtesan repertoire.

44. Zhou Bida, *Wenzhong ji* 168.29a. Gushu was the name of one of the counties in Taizhou prefecture, where the banquet took place.

45. Zhou Bida, *Wenzhong ji* 168.35b. This episode was later picked up and retold by Zhou Mi in the latter's *Qi dong ye yu* 15.282–83. In Zhou Mi's version, the courtesan is called Cao Pin 曹聘. Zhou Mi also asserts explicitly what is only hinted at in Bida's original, that is, that the song was written in response to the courtesan's situation.

administrators is likewise evident in Southern Song anecdotal literature. The stories in Hong Mai's *Yijian zhi*, for example, are primarily concerned with recounting strange or supernatural occurrences, but they treat the presence of female entertainers in government offices—and more generally in the lives of officials—as standard practice. One story describes a prefectural instructor traveling to another prefecture to take an examination, after which he immediately repairs to a banquet at the prefectural yamen.[46] In another, a promising student dreams that he is taken to a banquet where beauties with elaborate coiffures and wide red robes were dancing and singing, "like the government-courtesans of the prefectures" (*ru zhou jun guan ji* 如州郡官妓).[47] An official who wants to murder a bureaucratic rival does so by having a government-courtesan put poison in the wine cup that she serves to the victim while toasting his longevity.[48] And the wife of the magistrate Wei Changxian, on hearing that a beautiful young woman had been seen with her husband in his court chambers, immediately assumes that her rival is Wang Daonu, a government-courtesan whose beauty was much admired in the district.[49]

This last anecdote is particularly notable in that the wayward husband was not a prefectural official, but a mere county magistrate. Various sources attest that by the mid-twelfth century, courtesans had become standard features at county as well as prefectural yamens and were available to a wide variety of patrons. Regulations from as early as the 1140s show the Song government fighting an apparently fruitless battle against unauthorized persons seeking to hire government-courtesans. An 1143 edict warned that unless there was an official banquet or a holiday, it was prohibited for anyone other than the two top prefectural officials to use courtesans and musicians and to gather for a banquet.[50] In 1150 a prefect returning from Sichuan requested that a strict law be enacted to prohibit prefects and magistrates from using courtesans and musicians and from holding banquets during the annual "exhorting agriculture"

---

46. *YJZ, zhi yi*, 6.840–41.
47. *YJZ, zhi jia*, 7.765.
48. *YJZ, yi zhi*, 19.344. Hong Mai here and throughout his work often uses the term "government slave" (*guan nu* 官奴) to refer to government-courtesans. See the anecdote *yi zhi*, 20.358, where he uses the terms *ji* and *guan nu* interchangeably.
49. *YJZ, zhi ding*, 6.1016.
50. Li Xinchuan, *Jianyan yi lai xi nian yao lu* 148.16b.

ritual, in which officials were supposed to travel around the countryside to encourage villagers to be diligent in their farming. Emperor Gaozong, although observing that Sichuan's distance from the capital meant that many affairs there were handled carelessly, agreed.[51] By 1156 another official was complaining that lower-level prefectural and county officials were having all-night parties with courtesans, often misappropriating government funds in the process. When circuit inspectors and prefects tried to restrain them, slander arose. The court responded by ruling—again—that only prefects had the right to have courtesan entertainment at public banquets on their days off, intoning sternly, "others are certainly not allowed to presume on their authority and 'borrow' them."[52]

An administrative collection compiled in the late 1190s elaborated on these regulations, reiterating that it was illegal for prefectural or county officials to attend courtesan banquets except on the emperor's birthday or when they were invited to a public banquet at the prefecture. Certain higher-level officials such as supply commissioners and other circuit supervisors (*fa yun jian si* 發運監司), as well as officials in charge of state granaries, were forbidden to attend courtesan banquets at all, on pain of two years' exile.[53] Prefectural instructors (*jiao shou* 教授), too, were barred from courtesan banquets, except on the emperor's birthday, or when the instructor held other offices concurrently.[54] Regulations against any use of courtesan entertainments in the context of "exhorting agriculture" were reiterated, and any official found to have obstructed public affairs in the context of banqueting was to be beaten with one hundred strokes.[55]

The very repetition of such regulations, however, reveals their ineffectiveness, while other sources suggest that the use of courtesans in official banqueting was not only continuing but expanding. A funerary

---

51. Ibid., 161.13–13b; *SHY, xing fa*, 2.152.
52. Ibid., 172.3b; *SHY, xing fa*, 2.153b. Such laws were apparently not very effective, as the mid-ranked official Chen Zao (1133–1203) showed no hesitation in admitting in 1182 that he had "borrowed" some of the prefectural courtesans to entertain his guests (予借郡妓飲客) (Chen Zao, *Jianghuchangweng ji* 22.15b).
53. *Qingyuan tiao fa shi lei* 9.5b–6b.
54. Ibid. The punishment for instructors attending courtesan banquets was a beating of eighty strokes.
55. *Qingyuan tiao fa shi lei* 9.5b–6b.

biography of a man who died in 1166 praises as a singular virtue the fact that although "in exhorting the plowing in spring, the precedent was to take along courtesans and musicians" (*chun geng quan nong, li xie ji yue* 春勸耕例攜妓樂), the subject did not do so.[56] Several Southern Song handbooks for local administration attest to the ubiquity of courtesans at county-level offices in the late twelfth and thirteenth centuries.[57]

In this context, and in parallel with the dissolution of the Court Entertainment Bureau, the distinctions between government and independent (or registered and unregistered) courtesans continued to erode. Hong Mai describes an official banquet he attended where the entertainment was provided not only by government-courtesans but by itinerant actors and musicians (he refers both to *lu qi ling nü* 路岐伶女 and *san yue* 散樂) hired for the occasion.[58] By 1260 or so, even the government storehouses had come to feature both government and independent courtesans.[59] We shall see below that, juridically, the categories of courtesans officially registered to the government and those who were independent continued to have some salience, but the performing venues and practices of the two types of courtesans increasingly overlapped.

In sum, elite men in the Southern Song had at their disposal a wide range of courtesan entertainments, suitable for nearly every taste and budget. What in the Northern Song had been standard practice for the nobility and the higher ranks of officialdom by the Southern Song had filtered down to a much broader elite that included petty officials, local landowners, and moderately wealthy merchants. The spread of

---

56. Zhang Gang, *Huayang ji* 40.19b.
57. Anon., *Zhou xian ti gang* 1.8; Hu Taichu, *Zhou lian xu lun*, section 2.4b; section 15.38.b–39a. Cf. Bossler, "Shifting Identities," 26.
58. *YJZ, zhi yi*, 6.841. For a partial translation of this anecdote, emphasizing the types of songs performed, see Idema and West, *Chinese Theater*, 27. On the use of *san yue* performers at government banquets, see also the discussion of Zhu Xi and Tang Zhongyou below.
59. Wu Zimu, *Meng liang lu* 20.309–10. Idema and West (*Chinese Theater*) translate this passage to suggest that the "*she fa mai jiu*" system was in place only since the Jingding period (1260–64), but both Wang Yong and Yang Shi indicate that the system had carried over from the Northern Song into the early Southern Song. It is possible that this system was outlawed at some point in the interim, but I think it more likely that the distinction Wu Zimu is making here is that only after 1260 did government storehouses begin employing independent as well as government-courtesans.

commercialized entertainment, and of commercialized sex as one facet thereof, affected all levels of Southern Song society: the elites who purchased courtesan entertainments (and whose daughters sometimes declined into courtesan status); the underclass of brokers who bought and sold girls into the trade; the men and women who managed courtesan houses and other entertainment venues; and the families of farmers and petty townsmen who knew that, if necessary, they could sell a clever and attractive daughter for a tempting sum. In response, the image of entertainers in literati writings shifted as well.

## Southern Song Images of Courtesans

To a certain extent, the new representations of entertainers that appear in Southern Song sources reflect broader historiographical changes, especially the general shift of focus from capital to countryside. Yet the changes also point to new attitudes about courtesans and their place in literati life. The collected works of Southern Song literati, for example, contain fewer poems depicting the delights of courtesan banquets or the talents of the performers, and more suggesting that such banquets were unrefined and undesirable. Thus when a friend expressed resentment that Yu Chou (1163 *jin shi*) had not joined them on an outing to drink with courtesans, Chou set out his excuses in a series of five matching poems. As in the following excerpt, Chou suggested that such entertainments were too rich for his blood, and that in any case he preferred the quietude of the study hall:

| | |
|---|---|
| 廣文官舍自蕭然 | The Hall of Broad Learning is naturally calm and peaceful; |
| 好事何人與酒錢 | Who among you good fellows would give me money for wine? |
| 慣伴諸生甘寂寞 | I am accustomed to the company of students and take pleasure in solitude; |
| 倦從獧子醉妖妍 | I'm weary of accompanying wastrels to get drunk with bewitching beauties.[60] |

---

60. Yu Chou, *Zun bai tang ji* 3.11b. The Hall of Broad Learning (*Guang wen guan* 廣文館) was the name of a division of the Imperial University in the Tang. Huang Tingjian in the Northern Song seems to have been the first to refer to it as the "*Guang wen guan she*" (as Yu Chou does here), but thereafter many poets used that phrase. In poetic references The Hall of Broad Learning is typically associated with cold and quiet.

In similar fashion, Yu's slightly later contemporary Liu Guo (1154–1206) admitted that customers came from far and wide to spend lavishly at courtesan houses, but subtly associated such extravagance with political irresponsibility:

| | |
|---|---|
| 夜上青樓去 | At night, we head out to the emerald pavilions,[61] |
| 如迷洞府深 | Deep and dark like mysterious caves. |
| 妓歌千調曲 | The courtesans sing a thousand tunes. |
| 客雜五方音 | The guests mingle the sounds of the five directions. |
| 藕白玲瓏玉 | Lotus-white, the jade pendants tinkle; |
| 柑黃磊落金 | Yellow-orange, the gold piles up; |
| 酣歌恣蕭散 | Tipsy songs are free and abandoned |
| 無復越中吟 | And are no longer the "songs of Yue."[62] |

A somewhat parallel shift can be observed in Southern Song anecdotal literature. Although the distinctions are not absolute, Southern Song anecdotes featuring courtesans fall into two main categories. Anecdotes in the first category are highly nostalgic and focus especially on luminaries of the Northern Song court. Anecdotes in the second category, by contrast, are primarily concerned with contemporary life: they focus on denizens of county towns and prefectures, and evince a significantly less sanguine view of courtesans and their entertainments.

## Nostalgia for the North

Northern Song anecdotalists had written about the high and mighty among their contemporaries or among the generation immediately preceding them, and many Southern Song anecdotalists repeated, embellished, and created new stories about these famous figures. This tendency is especially evident in the numerous "Remarks on Poetry" texts, which highlight Northern Song literary giants like Mei Yaochen,

---

61. An "emerald pavilion" (*qing lou* 青樓) refers to an elaborately painted and decorated building. From at least the period of the Southern Dynasties, such buildings were associated with beautiful entertainers (perhaps because wealthy families kept many such women), and by the mid-eighth century the term was used to designate brothels.

62. Liu Guo, *Longzhou ji* 7.7. The phrase "songs of Yue" originates in a story from the *Shi ji*, and was used proverbially to mean the songs of one's homeland. Here Liu suggests that the drunken revelers are no longer thinking about their "homeland," that is, the territory that the Song had lost to the Jin.

Ouyang Xiu, Su Shi, Huang Tingjian, and Qin Guan. But the same fascination with eminent Northern Song officials is also visible in more generalized anecdotal collections. Some writers explicitly anthologized existing anecdotes or even whole collections, meticulously citing the Northern Song provenance of the items they included.[63] Others recorded anecdotes about Northern Song figures side by side with stories about individuals of their own day.

A favored pretext for such anecdotes was to supply the context for a particular line of poetry. The gossipy Zhang Bangji, for example, claimed to have come across three wall poems in the hand of Liao Minglue. The meaning of the poems was obscure until local relatives explained that Liao had been infatuated with two government-courtesans, one of whom ended up marrying a wealthy merchant. Liao's poem suggests that one of the courtesans had "sought out a seaside husband" which, Zhang explains, was a jesting allusion to a famous proverb referring to people of peculiar tastes.[64] Such explications were no doubt amusing to read, but even contemporaries recognized that they were frequently unreliable.[65]

Certain popular anecdotes were repeated in collection after collection. In the mid-twelfth century, Wu Zeng described how the eminent Northern Song Grand Councilor Fan Zhongyan had once served as prefect in Poyang, where he had become enamored of a very young government-courtesan. According to Wu, when Fan was transferred he wrote a poem to his successor Wei Jie, saying:

| | |
|---|---|
| 慶朔堂前花自栽 | In front of Qingshuo Hall is a flower I planted myself; |
| 便移官去未曾開 | When I left to transfer office it had not yet bloomed. |
| 年年長有別離恨 | Year after year I feel regret at leaving it; |
| 已託東風幹當來 | I leave it to the Eastern Wind to come and care for it. |

---

63. Examples include Zeng Zao's *Lei shuo*; Jiang Shaoyu's *Song chao shi shi lei yuan*; and Hu Zi's *Tiaoxi yu yin cong hua*.

64. Zhang Bangji, *Mo zhuang man lu* 5.149–50. The proverb, literally meaning "At the seaside there are those who follow smelly men," might loosely be rendered as "There is no accounting for taste." The proverb derived from a story from the *Spring and Autumn Annals*, about a man so smelly no one could live with him. He took up residence at the seaside, and there some began to follow him (see *Han yu da ci dian* 10.890, entry for *zhu chou* 逐臭). Liao's poem is suggesting that the courtesan has peculiar taste in marrying a merchant.

65. See, for example, Wu Zeng's scathing critique of a poetry explication by Liu Fu (*Neng gai zhai man lu* 4.81).

According to Wu Zeng, Wei Jie then purchased the girl to bestow upon Fan.[66]

At about the same time, a different version of the anecdote appeared in the work of Yao Kuan. Yao provided a slightly variant wording of Fan's poem and said nothing of Wei Jie. Rather, he indicated that on returning to the capital Fan had sent the girl a container of rouge with another poem:

| 江南有美人 | South of the river there is a beauty; |
| 別後長相憶 | On parting we think of each other across the distance. |
| 何以慰相思 | How can I assuage our mutual longing? |
| 贈汝好顏色 | I send you lovely color for your face. |

According to Yao, the letter with Fan's calligraphy still survived in the household of a Poyang official.[67] The story was repeated, with further variations, in the works of several other writers and collectors.[68]

The popularity of such anecdotes reflects Southern Song nostalgia for the remembered (and imagined) glories of the Northern Song bureaucratic elite. Here courtesans signified the glamour and elegance of Northern Song gatherings, the casual brilliance and romantic élan of Northern Song poet-officials. Thus Zhang Bangji also wrote of the beautiful and talented Ma Pan, a courtesan of Xuzhou admired by Su Shi who was talented at imitating Su's calligraphy. According to Zhang, she was so skilled that when she wrote four characters in a text Su Shi was writing, he laughed and left them as they were, so that the characters preserved on the stele were hers.[69] The association of courtesans with nostalgia for a brilliant and romantic past had already been established in the late Tang, with the *Beili zhi* accounts of the courtesan quarters of Chang'an, and was to remain a feature of writing about courtesans throughout the imperial era and beyond.[70]

---

66. Wu further claimed that there was a stele still at the prefectural offices commemorating the event (Wu Zeng, *Neng gai zhai man lu* 11.307).

67. Yao Kuan, *Xixi cong yu, xia*, 93.

68. See Xu Du, *Que sao bian, xia*, 156; Yu Wenbao, *Chui jian lu wai ji* 30a–b; Zhu Mu, *Gu jin shi wen lei ju, hou ji* 17.9a.

69. Zhang Bangji, *Mo zhuang man lu* 3.92.

70. Cf. Sun Qi, *Beili zhi*. On nostalgia about courtesans in later eras, see Ropp, "Ambiguous Images"; Waiyee Li, "The Late Ming Courtesan"; Mann, *Precious Records*, 128–35; Hershatter, *Dangerous Pleasures*, 67–177.

By similar logic, the disaster of the Northern Song collapse was represented in stories of the sad decline of individual courtesans. Wang Mingqing recounted how, after the fall of the North, his friend found Qin Miaoguan, one of the most famous courtesans of the Xuanhe period (1119–25), as a filthy old woman begging in a Lin'an market. Wang also described a courtesan who had once served Su Shi in Hangzhou but had ended up as an old servant in the household of a Hangzhou prefect, where she regaled her master with stories of the magnificent spring banquets Su once held. Her master sighed in admiration, saying "truly those were glorious events of the era."[71] In this nostalgic literature, Southern Song literati relived their glorious heritage, while tacitly acknowledging the failure of the present generation to measure up to the past.[72]

In keeping with their nostalgic tone, these anecdotes tend to portray courtesans and their patrons in a highly positive light. Men like Su Shi casually toss off brilliant poetry in response to the requests of government-courtesans; a "Righteous Courtesan" (*yi chang* 義倡), known for singing the *ci* lyrics of the famous poet Qin Guan, on hearing of Qin's death travels a great distance to attend to his funeral then throws herself on his coffin and expires.[73] In this nostalgic context, even a man who was officially reprimanded for an inappropriate relationship with a courtesan could appear as a hero, as in Wang Mingqing's brief biography of the official Li Zhiyi. In 1113, Li Zhiyi was removed from office and demoted to commoner status for "debauched behavior" with the courtesan Beauty Yang (Yang Shu 楊姝) and for requesting *yin* privilege for the courtesan's son, whom he believed to be his own.[74] The judgment in the case ordered that the son "follow his mother" (and so be relegated to *za hu* status) and that the certificate awarding him an official title be confiscated and destroyed.[75] Writing about this incident in the late twelfth century,

---

71. Wang Mingqing, *Yu zhao xin zhi* 3.1a, and *Hui zhu lu, hou lu*, 6.161.

72. I am grateful to Mark Halperin for the suggestion that Southern Song literati were painfully aware of their inadequacy with respect to the brilliance of their Northern Song predecessors.

73. *YJZ, zhi bu*, 2.1559–62. Hong Mai originally presented this anecdote as true but later disavowed it. See Zhou Hui, *Qing bo za shi* 9.396–97, n. 1.

74. The system of *yin* privilege allowed officials of certain ranks to obtain official titles for their sons and other relatives.

75. Two local officials were punished along with Li for failing to uncover his crime. The case is recorded in the *SHY, zhiguan*, 68.29.

Wang Mingqing first comments extensively on Li's literary talent, then describes the vicissitudes of his career.⁷⁶ Wang mentions that Beauty Yang was a "prefectural courtesan" whose beauty and talent had been praised in the poetry of Huang Tingjian, and he openly acknowledges that Li "kept (*xu* 蓄) Yang at home," where she gave birth to a son. But he excuses their relationship by pointing out that Li's wife had died and he had no heir. Wang blames the lawsuit on the enmity of a literary rival, though he does not refrain from repeating a scurrilous ditty composed by the rival to humiliate Li:

| | |
|---|---|
| 七十餘歲老朝郎 | The old court gentleman, past seventy years |
| 曾向元祐説文章 | Once gave lectures for his Yuanyou peers. |
| 如今白首歸田後 | Now, white-headed, he's back in the sticks, |
| 却與楊姝洗杖瘡 | Where he and Beauty Yang are cleaning their licks!⁷⁷ |

To be sure, both the case against Li and Wang Mingqing's apologia have to be understood in the context of the factionalist politics (and rewriting of history) in the late eleventh and twelfth centuries. Nonetheless, Wang's willingness to excuse Li's unseemly and strictly illegal involvement with a government-courtesan is striking.⁷⁸

## Debauchery, Disappointment, and Danger in the South

The indulgence with which Southern Song men wrote about the interactions of Northern Song men with courtesans contrasts sharply with the way they wrote about such behavior among court officials of their own day—to the extent that they wrote about such men at all. Although the association of courtesans with excess and debauchery was already

---

76. This section of Wang's *Hui zhu lu* was completed in the 1190s, though there is some evidence that parts of it had been drafted before 1177. See the editors' introduction ("*Chu ban shuo ming*"), 1 and 6–7, n. 2.

77. Wang Mingqing, *Hui zhu lu, hou lu*, 159–61. The Chinese text makes clear that the wounds were caused by the beatings Li and Yang received.

78. Wang even claims that later, when men favorable to Li Zhiyi became powerful, the case was reopened and Li received a total exoneration, with his son returned to office. Unfortunately, the men said to have vindicated Li were in power in 1107–9, *before* Li's dismissal, which the *SHY* dates to 1113. All other contemporary sources, including Li's own collected works, suggest he ended his life living quietly in the countryside, officially disgraced (cf. Wang Cheng, *Dong du shi lue* 116.5b). Thus Wang Mingqing's account appears to be an after-the-fact attempt to redeem a Yuanyou partisan.

a common motif in the Northern Song, Southern Song writers seldom spoke of Northern Song officials in those terms; but they did so characterize court officials of their own day.[79] Thus Lu You contemptuously recounted how Qin Xi (d. 1161), son of the despised Southern Song Grand Councilor Qin Gui (1090–1155), had arranged for his traveling entourage to be extravagantly entertained with decorated pavilions filled with government-courtesans providing music and dance.[80] Zhou Mi described how the retired Vice Grand Councilor Li Zongmian (d. 1239) threw his weight around in local affairs, including attempting to pressure the local magistrate to release a government-courtesan he happened to favor.[81]

The majority of Southern Song anecdotes involving courtesans, however, focus not on the court but on local society. In contrast to nostalgic images of courtesans at the capital exchanging elegant poetry with accomplished scholars and officials, we see courtesans who have become wives of mountain villagers, of city dwellers, of fortune tellers, and of clerks, or who have ended up as servants in the households of the wealthy.[82] And here, too, more often than not, courtesans are

---

79. A few officials of the very late Northern Song are similarly castigated. For example, Zeng Zao described how court officials in 1125 "competed to take courtesans, red-wheeled vehicles, and precious horses" on excursions to a park outside the city, where they then gambled all night. Zeng Zao's anecdote concludes with someone remarking, "It is not that the high officials are all gamblers, it is that gamblers are serving as high officials" (*Gao zhai man lu* 15b). Similarly, Zhang Duanyi (1179–ca. 1250) described Huizong's alleged encounter with poet Zhou Bangyan at the residence of the famed courtesan Li Shishi, concluding, "When lord and ministers meet at the houses of performers and degraded types, one can easily imagine the state of the country's security or danger and administration or chaos." (Zhang Duanyi, *Gui er ji, xia*, 6a).
80. Lu You, *Lao xue an bi ji*, 623.
81. Zhou Mi, *Gui xin za shi, hou ji*, 78. The magistrate in this case happened to be Zhou Mi's father.
82. *YJZ, zhi jia*, 4.739, *yi zhi*. 19.350, *bing zhi*, 3.386–89, *jia zhi*, 15.130; Wang Mingqing, *Hui zhu lu, hou lu*, 6.161. The image conveyed in these anecdotes is borne out in the legal sources. See *QMJ* 2.40, where a tax supervisor appears to be married to an entertainer; *QMJ* 14.525, where a government-courtesan is the concubine of a local bully, and Zhang Zi, *Shi xue gui fan* 30.10, where the wife of a prison official is an ex-courtesan. *QMJ* 10.410–11 also describes two courtesan houses as run by women who were presumably former courtesans themselves. I have benefited greatly from being able to consult the meticulous Japanese translations of the *Ming gong shu pan qing ming ji* by Takahashi Yoshirō and by Osawa Masaaki in conjunction with members of the

associated not with elegance and panache, but with disappointment and danger.

Even the most romantic Southern Song stories tend to involve protagonists of fairly modest status. There is the story of the young student Zhang who pledges to return to his courtesan lover in half a year. His return is delayed by parental demands, and he finally arrives only to find that his beloved was forcibly married off to a rich merchant just days earlier.[83] There is the story of Chen Gong, a magistrate who falls in love with a government-courtesan who is also an accomplished poet. When their plans for a dramatic double suicide are foiled by a sharp-eyed retainer, their romance falls apart; he is dismissed, and she declines into a lonely old age.[84] A happier tale tells of the poor tradesman Pan Jinyun, who seeks shelter from a storm at a roadside residence, not realizing it is the home of a courtesan. That night the lady of the house dreams of a black dragon curled up next to her door; on arising she finds Pan huddled under the eves. Marveling, she invites him in. Although, pleading poverty, he initially refuses her advances, a drunken interlude undermines his resistance. They fall in love and at first she acts as his financial support, but subsequently his business prospers, he marries her, and their son later passes the examinations and becomes an official.[85] The trajectory of Pan's life is reversed in the story of the scholar Yao, a talented young man who took top honors in the prefectural examinations only to fail repeatedly at the capital. Discouraged, he took to drinking and fell in with a courtesan; twenty years and several children later he threw himself on the mercy of a local official, begging the official to release his wife from the courtesan registers so that his family could have a future.[86]

The topoi of these stories are all well known in later imperial Chinese vernacular fiction and drama: both the story of the righteous courtesan

---

Seimeishū kenkyūkai (*Qing ming ji* research group) under Professor Osawa's direction. I am indebted to Professors Takahashi and Osawa for sharing their work with me.

83. Wang Mingqing, *Yu zhao xin zhi* 1.13b–14a. The conflict between literati and merchants over the affections of courtesans was also to become a popular theme in Yuan drama.

84. *YJZ, jia zhi*, 6.51–52.

85. *YJZ, jia zhi*, 11.98. Cf. the similar anecdote in Zhang Duanyi, *Gui er ji, zhong*, 35a–35b.

86. Zhou Hui, *Qing bo za zhi* 8.361–62.

and the story of the scholar fallen into dissolution were taken up more or less directly as the plots of Yuan plays.[87] Their appearance in the classical-language literature of the Song reminds us again how the interpenetration of elite and vernacular culture was facilitated by courtesans, whose lives constantly transgressed and disrupted the boundaries between lower and upper classes. These stories emphasize changes in social position, the power of money, and the importance of personal integrity; their popularity suggests new anxieties about social status, and about the dangers posed by commodified sexuality to norms of personal and family morality. Such anxieties were even more clearly reflected in anecdotes presenting courtesans as money-grubbing, cruel, and dangerous. The Tangzhou courtesan Ma Wang'er, unhappy with the fee proffered by one of her clients, responded by stealing all of the youth's clothing.[88] The wife of the clerk Zhang San had originally been a courtesan; she was unspeakably cruel to the servants and even murdered several concubines. Her comeuppance came after she murdered her daughter-in-law and the corpse was found under a bed. Because of her courtesan background, the authorities determined that she could not be treated as a legal wife. Her case was treated as "murder among people of the same status," with the result that she was executed and her corpse displayed in the marketplace.[89] Courtesans were also portrayed as vengeful to those who abandoned them. When a friend was startled to find Hu Shijiang sick in bed, Hu tearfully reported that he had been visited by the ghost of a courtesan he once knew, who reprimanded him:

> You once made a vow with me; how could you say in the beginning that you would not deceive me, and then turn your back on me? When I was ill, you never even came to see me; is there anyone in the world so heartless as you? Today it is over—I'll say no more. But you are also going to become ill, and your illness will be just like mine. Even though I am here, I will certainly not come to see you—see if you can stand it!

---

87. For the composition of a Yuan play (by Bao Jifu 鮑吉甫) about a loyal courtesan, see the annotator's remarks in Zhou Hui, *Qing bo za zhi* 9.396–97, n. 1. For a Yuan play on the theme of a wayward scholar, see Idema and West, *Chinese Theater*, 205–35.

88. *YJZ, yi zhi*, 19.350. Ma Wang'er's avarice during her life is presented as the explanation for the mysterious disappearance of her clothing from her body after her death. The greediness of courtesans was to become a standard theme in Yuan and Ming drama.

89. *YJZ, jia zhi*, 15.130. This implies that distinctions of *liang* and *jian* still had salience in legal matters.

Sure enough, Hu died a week later, and his associates confirmed that his illness had been just as the ghost had warned.[90]

Vengeful or not, courtesans often turn out to have been dangerous ghosts; or, to put it another way, the long-popular Chinese fox spirit—the beautiful maiden who seduces and then sucks the life out of unsuspecting young men—in Southern Song anecdotes often takes the form of a courtesan.[91] Numerous stories depict young men risking their very lives by falling in love with demonic entertainers.[92] The image of courtesans as dangerous and evil was not new in the Southern Song—the courtesan as fox spirit had already appeared in a few Northern Song anecdotes—but it was more common. This shift in the anecdotal literature was matched by (and perhaps reflected) the rhetoric of government documents, which in the Southern Song evince dramatically increased concern about the dangers of courtesans to local government and social order.

## *Greed, Graft, and Local Corruption*

We have seen that the Southern Song government was hard-pressed to control the use of courtesans by county officials and other unauthorized persons. It was also forced to issue a steady stream of indictments against prefectural officials for misuse of courtesan entertainments, such as "being immersed in women and song, and not paying attention to the people's affairs," or "intimacy with courtesans, waste of public funds, and bad legal judgments."[93] Similar indictments had of course also been issued in the Northern Song, particularly during the years of factional conflict. Yet the Southern Song saw far greater numbers of men indicted, and the men themselves tended to be less centrally involved in factional

---

90. *YJZ, bing zhi*, 6.412.

91. Stories of fox spirits, with their clear message about the dangers of female sexuality, long predate the Song. Courtesans occasionally appear as fox spirits in the Northern Song, and courtesan-concubines appear commonly in this guise in the Southern Song (see chap. 5).

92. For examples, see *YJZ, jia zhi*, 18.159, *yi zhi*, 8.377, *yi zhi*, 9.257; Wang Mingqing, *Tou xia lu* 4b–5, 25. For Northern Song examples, see Liu Fu, *Qing suo gao yi, qian ji*, 5.54–56.

93. *SHY, zhiguan*, 70.46; *SHY, zhiguan*, 72.7.

court politics.[94] More important, the more locally focused sources of the Southern Song reveal that the debauched behavior of officials was only the beginning of the problems that courtesans could cause in government administration. These problems are particularly visible in legal sources, such as the records of the controversial case fomented by the famed moral philosopher Zhu Xi, and the sole surviving Southern Song legal casebook, the *Enlightened Judgments* (*Ming gong shu pan qing ming ji* 名公書判清明集).

### Zhu Xi, Yan Rui, and Tang Zhongyou

In 1182, Zhu Xi composed a series of indictments directed against his colleague Tang Zhongyou, then prefect of Taizhou in Zhejiang.[95] At the time, Zhu was emerging as a leader in the Confucian revivalist movement, based on the ideas of the Northern Song Cheng brothers, that was coming to be known as Learning of the Way (*dao xue* 道學).[96] The case,

---

94. The disparities between the survival of Northern and Southern material sources make direct comparisons dangerous, but I think it is significant that the *zhiguan* section of the *SHY* contains only five indictments for Northern Song men involved with courtesans, but sixteen such indictments for Southern Song men—especially since the *SHY* contains virtually no records for the last several decades of the dynasty. For other Southern Song cases, see *SHY, zhiguan*, 70.11, 71.23, 72.21, 73.46, 73.61, 74.33, 74.42, 75.31.

95. I have discussed the case of Zhu Xi and Tang Zhongyou in Bossler, "Teisei Chūgoku." I would like to express my gratitude to Professor Hirata Shigeki for giving me the opportunity to present my research in Japan. The case has also been the subject of a recent study by Toda Yuji, which uses Zhu's indictments to discuss corruption in local administration (Toda Yuji, "Tō Chūyū"). I am grateful to Professor Toda for kindly sending me a copy of his article.

96. I am here adopting the useful distinction introduced by Hilde De Weerdt in her *Competition over Content*. De Weerdt distinguishes between a broad group of scholars interested in the teachings of the Cheng brothers and its concomitant commitment to moral cultivation ("Cheng Learning"), and the more narrow interpretation of Cheng Learning developed by Zhu Xi in the late twelfth century, known as *Daoxue* or Learning of the Way. This episode took place during one of Zhu Xi's few interludes of active office-holding, and at a time when he seems to have seen himself as newly responsible for the leadership of the Cheng Learning movement. As Hoyt Tillman points out, two other leading figures of the movement, Zhang Shi and Lü Zuqian, had recently died (Zhang in 1180, Lü in 1181), and Zhu Xi seems to have seen himself as destined to carry on in their place. (Tillman, *Confucian Discourse*, 133–36; see also Schirokauer, "Chu Hsi's Political Career").

briefly summarized in the biography of Yan Rui with which this chapter opened, was controversial in part because the object of the attack, Tang Zhongyou, was also a widely respected scholar who had his own connections to Cheng Learning scholarly circles. The episode became particularly notorious in part because Zhu's virulent attacks on Tang—or the political assertiveness those attacks represented—purportedly caused a backlash of sentiment against the Learning of the Way movement, a backlash that later commentators saw as the origin of the eventual government proscription of Learning of the Way as "False Learning" in 1196.[97]

The episode began when Zhu Xi, who had been appointed Supervisor for Tea, Salt, and Ever-Normal Granaries in eastern Zhejiang (*ti ju cha yan chang ping deng gong shi* 提舉茶鹽常平等公事), was charged with investigating the impact of a severe drought in the normally prosperous Zhedong area.[98] According to Zhu's own account, he had been traveling toward Taizhou from Shaoxing prefecture when he began to see refugees on the road. Upon inquiry, he learned that the refugees were fleeing the ravages of drought combined with pitiless pressure for taxes from the Taizhou prefectural government. Alarmed, he began to investigate, and in the process uncovered (or so he claimed) that the prefect Tang Zhongyou, abetted by his relatives, was engaged in all manner of nefarious behavior. In language we have seen elsewhere, Zhu complains that Tang Zhongyou left clerks in charge of prefectural business, dispensed justice arbitrarily, misused public funds, and expropriated public property for private use. More interesting for our purposes here, however, is the detail Zhu provides about Tang's interaction with the government-courtesans (Zhu calls them "disciples" or "disciple-courtesans" *di zi* 弟子 or *di ji* 弟妓) in the prefectural offices.

According to Zhu, Tang Zhongyou was constantly banqueting with courtesans and moreover had had a love affair with the head courtesan Yan Rui 嚴蕊. Zhu reports with disgust that Tang made no attempt to disguise his affection for Yan Rui, even at public banquets. Eventually,

---

97. See Tillman, *Confucian Discourse*, 134–36, as well as the scholarship he cites on p. 280, nn. 1–2.
98. Zhu's appointment was based in part on his success in administering relief efforts elsewhere. See Schirokauer, "Chu Hsi's Political Career," 172–73. Schirokauer notes that Zhu had indicted a number of other officials in the region before he began his condemnation of Tang Zhongyou.

7. The Courtesan Yan Rui of Tiantai (Tiantai Yan Rui 天台嚴蕊). In this illustration from a Late Imperial collection of *Biographies of Exemplary Women,* Yan Rui is portrayed as the noble and wronged heroine, refusing even under torture to incriminate the upright official who has been accused of having an affair with her. From Liu Xiang 劉向, *Hui tu Lie nü zhuan* 繪圖列女傳 [Illustrated biographies of exemplary women], edited by (Qing) Wang Geng 汪庚, illustrations by (Ming) Qiu Ying 仇英). Reprint of *Zhi bu zu zhai cang ban* (Taipei: Zheng zhong shu ju, 1971), 12.21b–22a.

he blatantly (and illegally) released her from registered service at the prefecture, on the false pretext that she was old and had fulfilled her term of duty. Tang then handsomely rewarded Yan Rui's mother and brother and had her sent—in a government sedan chair—to a relative's home in his native Wuzhou (presumably so that she could join him later as a concubine). Sending her off in style, Tang ordered an extravagant banquet at public expense, in spite of the fact that it was the death-anniversary of Tang's own grandmother, a day when all festivities should have been tabooed. Zhu also reported that Tang released three other courtesans from the prefectural registers, without submitting the proper bureaucratic paperwork for any of them.[99]

---

99. *Zhu Xi ji* 18.730, 19.739. Here and elsewhere in these indictments Zhu provides a rare glimpse into the bureaucratic management of courtesan-musicians. His accounts mention more than half a dozen entertainers by name and take for granted that such women were necessary participants in the banquets and ceremonies held at the prefecture. Zhu indicates that both registered government-courtesans and unregistered

Even after Yan Rui's departure, Tang continued to be involved with courtesans. Zhu reports that "recently the courtesans Shen Fang 沈芳, Wang Jing 王靜, Shen Yu 沈玉, Zhang Chan 張嬋, Zhu Miao 朱妙, and others have stayed overnight at the residence hall and attended Zhongyou at his bath."[100] Zhu accuses Tang of abusing his authority to satisfy his desires, describing how Tang once sent a local boy to neighboring Ninghai county to bring back the itinerant courtesans (*san yue di zi* 散樂弟子) Wang Chounu 王醜奴 and Zhang Bai'er 張百二 to attend at the prefecture. When Zhang Bai'er did not appear, Tang had the boy put into a cangue and sent to the prefectural court to be investigated and punished.[101] Zhu also criticizes Tang for lavishing government money on courtesans, pointing out that he bought extravagant clothing for the more than forty courtesans and musicians who entertained at his son's wedding. Zhu adds, "the entire prefecture was appalled: never before had a prefect had clothing made for courtesans!"[102] Finally, Zhu points out that it was only to be expected that Tang's bad example would be imitated by his sons, and he duly recounts that the boys were accustomed to riding sedan chairs to and from courtesan houses in broad daylight, sometimes going so far as to cause fights and public disturbances.[103]

In Zhu's eyes, Tang's debauchery had cosmic implications, and he directly connects Tang's behavior to the disastrous drought that was afflicting the area. Zhu points out that as the presiding official Tang

---

itinerant musicians could be pressed into service for prefectural functions, again demonstrating both that the state recognized two distinct categories of entertainer and that their roles were frequently identical. His reference to the process of releasing courtesans from the registers reveals the existence of a prefectural level "Bureau of Courtesan Music" (*ji yue si* 妓樂司) to which Tang had failed to submit paperwork. The existence of a *ji yue si* is mentioned in only one other source in the entire electronic *Si ku quan shu*, in Fang Hui's 方回 (1227–1307) *Gu jin kao xu* 古今考續 (also called *Xu gu jin kao* 續古今考). Fang describes the Bureau as a "recent" institution no longer in operation at the time of writing (after 1267). It is possible that *ji yue si* is an informal term (or perhaps a Southern Song neologism) for an office that oversaw the prefectural musicians and entertainers known as *ya qian yue* 衙前樂. On the *ya qian yue*, see Gong Yanming, *Song dai guan zhi ci dian*, 281.

100. *Zhu Xi ji* 18.739.
101. *Zhu Xi ji* 19.747.
102. *Zhu Xi ji* 18.733–34.
103. *Zhu Xi ji* 18.730.

should have been purifying himself and praying for rain; instead he "sought out ten or more courtesans from neighboring counties, as well as twenty or thirty itinerant musicians. For several days these entertainers went in and out of the residence hall, on the excuse of playing chess and strumming the lute, openly coming back and forth in front of the ceremonial grounds."[104] During this period Tang's eldest son, returning from a party drunk and with several courtesans in tow, had had the temerity to make fun of local people who were preparing a solemn sacrifice to pray for rain. Zhu observes that the local people were furious, adding, "[When] the prefect is like this, and his sons are also like this, how could there possibly be a favorable response of rain from Heaven?"[105]

Even more problematic in Zhu Xi's eyes was the fact that the courtesans in Taizhou routinely interfered in government affairs. His outrage at Tang's love affair with Yan Rui was especially inflamed by the fact that she had presumed on the relationship to broker legal cases and otherwise subvert justice. Yan Rui had persuaded Tang to release her brother, one Zhou Zhao, from corvée duties, and had received a bribe of forty-two strings of cash to persuade Tang to excuse several clerks from wine-selling duties. She and another courtesan had also received bribes of money and cloth to convince Tang to dismiss a case of a man hiding his "companion courtesan" (*kang di zi* 伉弟子).[106]

Zhu further documented the influence-brokering activities of another government-courtesan, Wang Jing 王靜, whom he claimed had been intimate with Tang Zhongyou's eldest son, Tang Shijun 唐士俊.[107] Zhu asserted that Shijun had persuaded his father to appoint Wang as head courtesan after Yan Rui had departed, and thereupon lavished her with presents and began regularly spending the night at her residence. Outsiders thus realized that she had influence, and those who wanted to subvert

---

104. *Zhu Xi ji* 18.739.
105. *Zhu Xi ji* 18.739.
106. *Zhu Xi ji* 18.730, 19.746–47.
107. Curiously, throughout his discussion of Wang Jing's involvement with Tang Shijun, Zhu refers to Tang as "Eighteenth Gentleman for Instruction" (*shi ba xuan jiao* 十八宣教), although in earlier indictments he had called him by name (e.g., *Zhu Xi ji* 18.738). This usage seems to be idiosyncratic to Zhu Xi—I have found no other usage of this title with a number except in Zhu's indictments of Tang—though it is reminiscent of the numbering system used to identify individuals in Song and later genealogies.

justice began to approach her with bribes.¹⁰⁸ According to Zhu, Wang brokered the case of the young boy apprehended for not bringing back the itinerant courtesans, and got his punishment reduced; she also helped a couple accused of adultery get their punishment of a beating commuted to a fine. She received five strings of cash in return for asking Tang Shijun to appoint the soldier Xie Rong as a servant in the prefectural academy, and was promised government notes in the amount of eleven strings to help Wang Fifty-Seven's brother-in-law get out of trouble. Zhu even claimed to have found an incriminating letter from Tang Shijun to Wang Jing in the former's own hand, outlining their plans to intervene in a case.¹⁰⁹ In a similar vein, Zhu reported that the courtesan Shen Yu received bribes on several occasions, using her relationship with Tang Zhongyou's nephew in order to influence the uncle.¹¹⁰

Zhu Xi's indictments reveal that by the Southern Song the danger of courtesans to local administration was less debauchery than their potential to broker prefectural judicial affairs. Even more than the notorious "clerks and runners" of the yamen staff, courtesans were in the unique position of having access—often very intimate access—to the men who made judicial decisions, at the same time that they were also publicly visible and easily approachable by people at virtually any level of society. Zhu's account suggests that courtesans were quite willing to use their privileged position to improve their income, accepting both the presents bestowed (often at government expense) by their powerful lovers and the bribes offered by anxious petitioners.¹¹¹ Nor was it necessary that a courtesan capture the heart of the prefect himself: Zhu Xi—and evidently most of the populace—took it for granted that courtesans who became the lovers of Tang's sons and nephews would have sufficient influence to

---

108. *Zhu Xi ji* 19.747.
109. *Zhu Xi ji* 19.748.
110. *Zhu Xi ji* 19.749. Zhu identifies the nephew only as "Thirty-Sixth Gentleman for Instruction" (*san liu xuan xiao* 三六宣教).
111. Not all courtesans enjoyed such privileged positions, and Zhu shows that courtesans could be petitioners as well as brokers. He describes how the courtesan He Hui 何蕙 paid ten strings' worth of official notes to a friend of Tang, in hopes that he could arrange the return of her sister (*Zhu Xi ji* 19.750). The text does not explain why the sister was sent away).

alter the course of prefectural affairs.[112] Zhu's evidence also suggests that courtesans may have played a special role in brokering lawsuits on behalf of women. He describes how a Li Sixth Miss (李六娘), under investigation for having illicit relations with the Daoist Wang Yongchang, went with the courtesans Wang Jing and Bao Shuang 鮑雙 to pay a visit to Tang's eldest son. Li was rewarded for her efforts by having the investigation closed.[113] Similarly, one of those who approached the courtesan Shen Yu was the wife of one Bao Bu 鮑卜, who sought a favor from Tang Zhongyou through his nephew.[114] Although in the absence of other evidence we can only speculate, it seems plausible that women like these found it easier to approach other women for help than to seek aid from the notoriously rapacious yamen underlings. Here the courtesan's ability to traverse social boundaries gave her substantial—and in some eyes dangerous—political influence.

## THE *ENLIGHTENED JUDGMENTS*

The Tang Zhongyou case reveals the havoc that courtesans could wreak on prefectural administration; likewise, a rare source on late Song local government affords us a detailed look at the realities behind government indictments of "debauched" county officials.[115] The *Enlightened Judgments*, a collection of decisions on local court cases from the late twelfth to the mid-thirteenth centuries, provides a frequently shocking picture of government breakdown associated with the interaction of county officials and sub-officials with government and independent

---

112. That this was a reasonable assumption is borne out in other indictments of men for tolerating improprieties with courtesans by sons or government underlings. See *SHY, zhiguan*, 72.30; 75.5. See also the memorial (1208) in which one Wu Yong defends himself against accusations that his sons were involved with courtesans (Wu Yong, *Helin ji* 23.7a).

113. *Zhu Xi ji* 18.729, 19.748.

114. *Zhu Xi ji* 19.749. Bao Bu reportedly wanted Tang Zhongyou to *ci jun* 刺軍, a phrase that usually refers to the tattooing of soldiers. Perhaps her husband wanted to become a soldier?

115. See also *SHY, xing fa*, 6.34, for the case of a county wine-tax supervisor and a county magistrate, both of whom had misappropriated funds and engaged in debauchery with courtesans. On the office of tax supervisor, see McKnight and Liu, *Enlightened Judgements*, 509, n. 42.

entertainers.[116] In one of the most revealing cases, the investigating official Chen Zeng 陳增 (1200–1266) was horrified to discover that an unnamed magistrate of an unnamed county in Jianning 建寧 prefecture (near present-day Jian'ou 建甌 in Fujian) was known throughout the area for his debauched behavior and corrupt administration.[117] Chen's inquiries among the local clerks and courtesans elicited universal reports that the magistrate was in the habit of holding nightly drinking parties, often lasting until dawn, at which he "ordered the courtesans to be licentious and intimate, stopping at nothing." Chen reports that the magistrate completely abrogated his administrative responsibilities, seldom seeing his clerks or the people of his district. Whenever there was a lawsuit in his county, the clerks made recommendations according to the bribes they received: the magistrate's judgments simply followed their suggestions. When drunk, the magistrate imposed cruel punishments as if it were a game, committing all kinds of illegal and immoral acts.

In spite of these crimes, some of which Chen Zeng found "difficult to commit to pen and paper," the corrupt magistrate's punishment was merely to exchange positions with the county registrar.[118] As for the courtesans on whom the magistrate had forced his attentions, Chen, too, focused on their role as intermediaries, castigating them as accessories to or at least facilitators of the magistrate's crimes: "All of these courtesans were associates [lit., "go-betweens"] in the magistrates' muddled thinking and corrupt government." Still, in the end, Chen did not punish the women. Instead, he argued that "if we do not hide [the courtesans] in other districts, the objects of desire will be right before [the magistrate's] eyes, and it will be difficult for him to reform." He then simply had the women temporarily registered in neighboring counties—a move that

---

116. My understanding of these cases has been enhanced by the research of the Song dai guan jian yan du hui (Song dynasty official handbook reading group) in Taiwan, and especially their publication, *Song dai she hui yu fa lü*.

117. *QMJ* 2.42–43. Judging from the four neighboring counties mentioned in the account, the miscreant was the magistrate of either Jianyang 建陽 or Jian'an 建安 prefecture.

118. This extraordinarily mild reprimand, in conjunction with Chen's painstaking discretion about the magistrate's name and location, suggest that the offender was powerfully connected and that Chen did not dare to treat him harshly: in contrast, several of the clerks involved were sentenced to severe beatings.

may have been as much for their own protection as for the magistrate's benefit. Even more striking here, however, is the number of women involved: Chen lists fourteen courtesans by name, apportioning them out to four neighboring counties.

This account reveals that sizable numbers of government-courtesans could be maintained at county-level yamens and shows that they were highly vulnerable to the predations of local officials. There seems little reason to think that the situation depicted here was unusual, except perhaps in the level of corruption and cruelty displayed by this particular magistrate. Indeed, in his opening remarks to another of the *Judgments*, the thirteenth-century official Cai Hang 蔡杭 observed that in Yiyang 弋陽 county, the only county officials who were *not* intimate with courtesans were the magistrate and the sheriff.[119] Elsewhere, the *Judgments* show that not only officials but clerks in both county and prefectural yamens were susceptible to involvement with entertainers. A corrupt county clerk was punished for, among other crimes, getting drunk at nunneries and courtesan houses, and thereby failing in his duty to go out and greet a visiting prefectural official.[120] In addition to other nefarious activities, a prefectural clerk not only liked to get drunk and enjoy himself singing at local courtesan establishments, but took it on himself to "appropriate" and maintain (*zhan yang* 占養) two courtesans.[121] Still another county clerk was caught taking bribes, managing courtesans, appropriating land, and otherwise disturbing the people.[122]

## Courtesans and Social Decline

Even more importantly, the concerns of Southern Song critics were not limited to courtesans' influence on local administration; rather, they increasingly associated courtesans with problems in the wider society.

---

119. *QMJ* 1.24. The author is given in the text as Cai Jiuxuan, Jiuxuan being a sobriquet of Cai Hang (see *QMJ, fu lu* 1). The judgment unfortunately gives no further details about the case, merely calling for various individuals to be brought to the yamen under escort.

120. *QMJ* 11.416.

121. *QMJ* 11.410–11. It is unclear to me whether this implies that the clerk was the exclusive customer of the two women or whether it suggests that he acted as their pimp.

122. *QMJ* 11.427.

Early in the Southern Song, censors had complained that many refugee women in the temporary capital, separated from their families in the chaos, were taken in by strangers only to find themselves sold as serving maids or forced to become courtesans. The censors urged the court to take strong action against such exploitation.¹²³ Law cases reveal that, like the clerks we have seen above, local bullies and gangsters often "managed" courtesans as part of their various illegal activities.¹²⁴ Descriptions of social disruption caused by courtesans also begin to appear in the funerary biographies of erstwhile local officials. We learn from one such biography that the soldier Wu Shun kicked the commoner Chen Sheseng to death in a courtesan house; another details a case concerning a man falsely accused of murdering his courtesan lover.¹²⁵

Equally disturbing were the threats courtesans posed to normative family relations. The Jiaxing commoner Zhang Jin, having brought home a government-courtesan from Lin'an, wanted to expel his wife and children. His elder brother, unable to reason with him, brought suit at the prefecture. Only the intervention of an upright official saved the situation: the prefect sent the courtesan back to Lin'an, and "with great righteousness" instructed Zhang until the latter was enlightened and restored to proper relations with his family.¹²⁶ Nor were officials themselves exempt from such family disruptions: an assistant fiscal commissioner of Tongchuan 潼川 prefecture was dismissed for keeping courtesans and expelling his wife, and the imperial clansman Zhao Buchuo 趙不拙 found himself cashiered from his position as Chief Supervisor of Sichuan Horse Trading for having been so "undisciplined" as to take a courtesan as a wife.¹²⁷ Even more common was the illegal appropriation of courtesans as concubines.¹²⁸ The

---

123. *SHY, xing fa*, 2.148.
124. *QMJ* 11.398–99; McKnight and Liu, *Enlightened Judgments*, 386–88.
125. See the biography of Luo Yuan (entitled "Yingzhou tai shou mu zhi" 郢州太守墓誌) appended to his *[Luo] Ezhou xiao ji* (separately paginated, following *juan* 6), and Li Liuqian, *Dan zhai ji* 17.7a, funerary inscription for Sun Guan'guo. The description of the first case centers on the subject's efforts to bring Wu Shun to justice but does not explain the motive for the murder; in the second case, the perspicacious official discovers that what looked like murder was a failed double suicide.
126. Lu You, *Weinan wen ji* 38.234.
127. *SHY, zhiguan*, 70.24, 71.23b.
128. For indictments of men who took courtesans as concubines, see *Wang Shipeng quan ji* 3.625; Xu Jingsun, *Jushan cun gao* 1.16b; and Xu Yuanjie, *Mei ye ji* 4.13b. Xu

difficulty of preventing this sort of situation is evident in the vehemence of this writer in the *Enlightened Judgments*:

> Those who are recognized as literati but marry government-courtesans, are they not criminals against propriety? Are they not a disgrace to their literati friends? It is not permissible! It is not permissible! It is absolutely not permissible!" (*bu ke, bu ke, da bu ke!* 不可, 不可, 大不可)."[129]

One senses that the magistrate knew he was fighting a losing battle.

Strikingly, despite all these problems, most men continued to see the presence of female entertainers at banquets as essential to the proper conduct of festivities. Even Chen Zeng, in sending the fourteen courtesans away to other counties, stipulated that they be brought back when it was time for the imperial birthday celebrations.[130] And well into the thirteenth century, prefectural ceremonies on imperial birthdays still included "several tens of groups" of courtesans, dancing in formation to create the words "All-under-Heaven at peace" (*tian xian tai ping* 天下太平).[131] Only very late in the Southern Song did a small number of men begin to call for an end to the entire system of government-courtesans.

## *Courtesans and Cheng Learning*

Perhaps not surprisingly, the few Southern Song voices calling for an end to the system of government-courtesans tended to be those of men associated with Cheng Learning and its successor, the Learning of the Way movement. But this is not at all to say that the proponents of Cheng Learning as a group opposed the use of courtesans. On the contrary, most men associated with the movement did not see the presence of courtesans at government offices as a serious moral problem. We

---

Jingsun also accused a number of other officials of being intimate with courtesans (*Jushan cun gao* 1.19b).

129. *QMJ* 9.344. Yuan Cai also warned his peers against setting up exclusive relationships with courtesans, but his concern was infidelity on the courtesan's part, not fear of government disapproval (*Yuan shi shi fan, xia,* 6a; cf. Yuan Cai in Ebrey, *Family and Property,* 287). See also *QMJ* 14.525–26.

130. *QMJ* 2.42–43.

131. Zhou Mi, *Qi dong ye yu,* 10.189. It is not clear whether Zhou is describing ceremonies he saw before the fall of the Song or after.

have seen that the founders of the movement, the Cheng brothers, did not even bother to discuss courtesans.[132] In fact, the earliest complaint about courtesans by a man associated with Cheng Learning was reportedly made by Yang Shi 楊時 (1053–1135), their student, in about 1114. According to the "Record of Discourses" (*yu lu* 語錄) published by Yang's disciples, Yang virulently objected to the use of courtesans at government winehouses:

> The court's policy of selling wine by "*she fa*" is in the hands of the officials and clerks; thus they set out music and gather courtesans to get the people to come. This is the worst detriment to moral teaching and must be avoided. [Mencius] said, "Share one's pleasure with the people": is this not a complete misunderstanding? To entice the ignorant people [so as] to seize their wealth, even if ordinary people were doing it, in principle it ought to be forbidden; but clerks and officials do it, and no one above or below thinks it strange. They do not know that they have transgressed the method of governing. Now, when the people have wealth, it is necessary that those above cherish it for them; not to cherish it for them and instead to craftily and secretly seek to acquire it, even though there is no whip forcing them, it is worse than using a whip. When I was in Liuyang county in Tanzhou, whenever the officials distributed the [money for] green sprouts [loans], I closed down all the winehouses, restaurants, and theaters that ensnared the wealth of the people. When the distribution [of loan money] was complete, only then did I order a return to normal.[133]

Yang's comments were meant as a strident critique of the reformist New Policies: notably, his objection was not to the use of government-courtesans per se, and certainly not to their use as entertainment for officials, but only to their use in enticing simple farmers to spend their precious seed money. More importantly, for nearly a century after Yang's diatribe, no other leader of the Cheng Learning movement took up the issue.[134] The scholar Zhang Shi (1133–80) once complained, "Today, because of their interest in sex, people lose their innate tendency to respect the virtuous, and thus we see why the Dao does not prevail." But beyond this he had nothing to say about the dangers of courtesans.[135] Lü Zuqian (1127–81), in his family rules, instructed his sons not

---

132. See chap. 1.
133. Yang Shi, *Guishan ji* 10.26a–b.
134. In identifying the major thinkers of the movement, I am relying on Tillman, *Confucian Discourse*.
135. Zhang Shi, *Gui si Lun yu jie* 9.15b.

to attend courtesan banquets unless it was the weekend, but he did not otherwise forbid such entertainments.¹³⁶ Chen Liang (1143–94), always something of a maverick, far from disapproving of courtesan banquets was widely known to enjoy them. He nearly got himself executed for lèse-majesté after one drunken revel, at which he acted out a court scene with a courtesan taking the part of an imperial concubine.¹³⁷ Chen was also reported to have sought—from none other than Tang Zhongyou— the release of a prefectural courtesan with whom he had become intimate.¹³⁸ Chen's more restrained contemporary Lu Jiuyuan (1139–93) once expressed disappointment in a colleague who was besotted with "green wine cups and pink courtesans," and he admonished a disciple that dalliance with courtesans was simply incompatible with the pursuit of Confucian learning; but he expressed no objection to the presence of courtesans at government offices.¹³⁹

Significantly, even Zhu Xi, despite his virulent attacks on Tang Zhongyou's involvement with courtesans, did not seem to oppose the institution itself.¹⁴⁰ Later chapters will detail Zhu's profound concern with the regulation of the family and his interest in many types of social reforms. But although he included Yang Shi's complaint in his compendium of Learning of the Way teachings, the *Yi luo yuan yuan lu* 伊洛淵源錄, he did not himself call for the reform or abolition of courtesan entertainments.¹⁴¹ Zhu did praise a man who, at considerable cost, redeemed and married off a girl of literati family who had fallen into courtesan status.¹⁴² And he warned of a general who used his resources to throw a courtesan banquet and provide handsome rewards to the entertainers, only to have his disaffected soldiers refuse to fight. But when a

---

136. Lü Zuqian, *Donglai ji, bie ji* 6.1, *jia fan* 6 (*guan jian*), 2a. The term I am translating as "weekend" (*xun xiu* 旬休) more literally means "the day off in the ten-day period."

137. Ye Shaoweng, *Si chao wen jian lu, jia*, 24–25.

138. Zhou Mi, *Qi dong ye yu* 17.323–24. Zhou claimed that this was the proximate cause of Zhu Xi's attack on Tang.

139. Lu Jiuyuan, *Lu Jiuyuan ji* 9.122; Tang Guizhang, *Song ci ji shi*, 329 (section on Xie Zhi 謝直 [Ximeng 希孟]).

140. It is also notable here that Zhu Xi's Cheng Learning colleagues did not seem to share his outrage at Tang Zhongyou. See Bossler, "Teisei Chūgoku," 178, 182, n. 46.

141. Zhu Xi, *Yi luo yuan yuan lu* 10.19b–20b.

142. *Zhu Xi ji* 94.4779–81, in funerary inscription for Teng Zhu.

student asked Zhu whether it was acceptable to have courtesans entertain at banquets, he reportedly replied, "Today the prefectures and counties all use them, why should one not use them?"[143]

Only in the thirteenth century, perhaps responding to the spread of entertainments and the concomitant breaking down of social boundaries, did a few Learning of the Way adherents begin to suggest that courtesans were a problem that the government should address. In a book of advice on proper governing, Zhu Xi's follower Zhen Dexiu 眞德秀 (1178–1235) explained that when in local office he had restricted the bestowal of banquets celebrating the emperor's birthday. Zhen listed a number of crimes to which such banquets could give rise, including the selling of goods at inflated prices and the forcing of commoners' wives and daughters onto the courtesan registers; he recommended that these crimes should be punished severely.[144] But although Zhen Dexiu thus identified courtesan banquets as potentially troublesome, even he did not condemn the system of government-courtesans per se. A somewhat harder line was taken by Zhen's contemporary Yang Jian 楊簡 (1141–1226), a disciple of Lu Jiuyuan. Like Yang Shi before him, Jian wanted to abolish the *she fa* system of selling wine, which he referred to as "establishing the law to lead people into licentiousness" (*she fa dao yin* 設法導淫).[145] But Jian went even further, advocating the abolition of courtesan registers and the return of all courtesans to respectable commoner status. Arguing that "there is nothing worse than this for disordering the hearts of the people," he explained,

> Elaborate makeup and lovely looks draw all eyes to them; when young men's blood and *qi* are still unsettled, and when customs have long been bad, how many are able to be aloof and unmoved? It is to the point that even famous ministers and talented scholars sink down among them, knowing no shame, constantly promoting them in songs and poems, and no one in the whole world thinks it strange. How far will the corruption, perversity, and recalcitrance of people's hearts go? The disaster of chaos and collapse in previous eras was based on the absence of morality in people's hearts. The Zhou lineage developed the custom of virtuous action and skills of the Dao, and good fortune lasted for 800 generations. How can the lords and ministers be without fear? But the bureaucrats and scholars embrace "great desire" and follow the common custom,

---

143. Zhu Xi, *Zhuzi yu lei* 92.2349.
144. Zhen Dexiu, *Xishan zheng xun*, 9–10.
145. Yang Jian, *Cihu yi shu* 16.5b.

valuing it rather than getting rid of it, until the country experiences irretrievable disaster. Alas! How painful!¹⁴⁶

Although Yang was unable to persuade the emperor to act on his suggestions, on taking up a position as prefect of Wenzhou in the early thirteenth century he immediately abolished the courtesan registers and decreed that the courtesans there return to respectable commoner status.¹⁴⁷ But the impact of his reforms was both localized and short-lived. No other Learning of the Way scholar took up his cause, and government-registered courtesans continued to be a ubiquitous feature of government and social life for centuries to come.

## *Conclusion*

The Southern Song was marked by a proliferation and elaboration of courtesan entertainments. In the capital, the dissolution of the Court Entertainment Bureau meant that entertainers trained for the court took their knowledge and skills to the streets, while marketplace performers gained unprecedented access to the precincts of the palace. In the countryside, the institution of government-courtesans spread from the prefectures down to county government offices, and courtesans became intermediaries not only between social classes but between local officials and the populace they sought to govern. Attitudes toward courtesans shifted accordingly: although one strain of discourse nostalgically celebrated the role that female entertainers had played in the Northern Song capital, another strain acknowledged, with far greater ambivalence, their presence in the lives of students, low-level officials, and moderately well-to-do commoners. By late in the Song, courtesans were routinely associated with decline in local governance and society, though few seemed able to imagine life without them.

Against this generally negative view of courtesans as a group, however, in the final decades of the dynasty we also see the first inklings of an alternative discourse highlighting the humanity of specific entertainers as individuals, depicting them as objects of sympathy and even

---

146. Yang Jian, *Cihu yi shu* 16.8b–9a. "Great desire" (*da yu* 大欲) refers to the human desire for food and sex.

147. Yang Jian, *Cihu yi shu, fu lu*, 18a.

admiration. Even in the Northern Song, anecdotal and romance literature had sometimes shown appreciation for courtesans as individuals, evoking sympathy for their feelings and appreciation for their talents and moral potential. The generally more pedestrian anecdotal literature of the Southern Song continued this trend. One story describes a courtesan of such powerful passion (*qing* 情) that the spirit of a temple guardian is moved to abandon his post and visit her.[148] Numerous anecdotes describe the wit and verbal dexterity of particular courtesans in banquet settings, admiring their ability to provide a snappy comeback or compose a moving extemporaneous poem.[149] As in the tale of the righteous courtesan who loved Qin Guan, occasionally a courtesan was extolled for her loyalty to a particular lover, her fidelity all the more remarkable and appealing because so at odds with her profession.[150] And the anecdotalist Luo Dajing (1226 *jin shi*), relating how the ex-courtesan wife of the general Han Shizhong reported her husband to the court for losing an opportunity to capture an enemy, concluded, "This is how wise and brave she was!"[151]

More significantly, in the late Southern Song we begin to see occasional evidence of sympathy and respect for courtesans not just in anecdotes but in the more formal writings preserved in literati collected works. Cao Yuanyue (1157–1228) wrote a poem praising the Hunan courtesan Xiuying not for her voice or looks but for her skill at ink painting, which he compared to that of the Tang calligraphy master Zhang Dian. In a poem simply titled "Old Courtesan, a Verse" (老妓一首), Liu Kezhuang (1187–1269) sensitively evoked the melancholy of an aging entertainer, lying awake alone in her bed and envying the boisterous commotion at

---

148. *YJZ*, *jia zhi*, 17.146.
149. *YJZ*, *zhi jia*, 4.741; *zhi yi*, 6.840–41; *zhi yi*, 6.841.
150. Glen Dudbridge has noted the dramatic power of stories in which a woman of low status, from whom no moral expectations are due, holds up the standard of morality to those who should be her moral superiors (see Dudbridge, *The Tale of Li Wa*, 73). Dudbridge sees such stories as still a creative experiment in the fiction of the late Tang, but we have seen the same idea reiterated in Northern Song texts, from Ouyang Xiu's story of Wang Ning's wife to Xu Ji's biography of the courtesan Ai'ai. This was to become a standard trope in biographies of heroic martyrs in the Southern Song, as seen in chap. 6.
151. Luo Dajing, *Helin yu lu*, *bing bian*, 2.266.

the gates of a young competitor. The official Li Maoying (1201–57), faced with the case of an itinerant entertainer (here called a *lu ji san yue* 路妓散樂) who had gotten in trouble when a clerk stole government funds to visit her house, refused to take responsibility for consigning her to the government-courtesan registers. "To put an entertainer on the registers so that she can never again be a respectable commoner," he remarked, "is not a very virtuous affair." He pointed out that an itinerant entertainer was able to travel all over in pursuit of her occupation, but once registered she would have to stay in one place until she died, never able to be free: "It would be like a bird being put into a cage, or a fish in a bowl, watching other fish and fowl fly and swim in the vast heavens and wide oceans, desperately envious but unable to obtain [freedom]. Benevolent men and superior gentlemen on seeing this would certainly feel sympathy." Rather than make a decision himself, Li sent the courtesan back to the district for judgment, where presumably his eloquent disquisition helped to plead her case.[152] Yao Mian (1216–62) showed similar appreciation for a courtesan's feelings in a poem he composed for a woman whose winehouse his brother had often frequented. Yao's preface to the poem bitterly recalls that when his brother died, some of his closest friends did not mourn him. But "the courtesan Zheng Yunying of Cloud Tower alone loved him and could not forget him. Grief-stricken, she mourned him; regularly she sacrificed to him. She can be called a Righteous Courtesan." Yao Mian indicated that he presented his poem, entitled "Lament of the Righteous Courtesan" (義娼吟), to the bereaved woman, and in rhetoric that recalled the exemplar literature of the late Northern Song, he expressed the hope that his poem would "shame those under heaven who are people's friends but turn their backs on them in death."[153]

In short, even as courtesans in general were an increasing cause for concern, we see in the very late Song hints of a growing willingness on the part of some literati to acknowledge individual entertainers as human beings with hopes and desires—and the potential for ethical and even exemplary behavior. This attitude was of a piece with the philosophy of

---

152. Cao Yuanyue, *Chang gu ji* 1.11b; Liu Kezhuang, *Hou cun ji* 2.2b; Li Maoying, *Wen xi ji* 11.3b–4a. See also Yang Wanli's praise of an erstwhile courtesan for remaining loyal to her deceased husband, discussed in chap. 6.

153. Yao Mian, *Xue po ji* 21.7b–8a.

Cheng Learning and its proposal that all human beings shared a "heart" that was fundamentally good—but, significantly, in the Southern Song it was not adherents of Learning of the Way who expressed admiration for courtesans. Rather, such attitudes were most conspicuously articulated in entertainment literature. In anecdotes like Hong Mai's tale of Yan Rui, the depraved, calculating creature of Zhu Xi's lawsuit becomes the sympathetic heroine, buffeted by fate but triumphing through talent and upright perseverance. Such sympathetic depictions were, I think, an important factor in humanizing the figure of the courtesan in the minds of male literati, and thereby further eroding the boundaries between respectable and degraded persons. But equally if not more salient to that erosion was the continued proliferation in literati families of concubines who were not only entertainers, but mothers as well.

# 5

# *Entertainers to Ancestors*

## Zhang Zhihe 張致和

My maternal grandmother Zhang was named Zhihe. She was a person of Deqing in Huzhou. She was born in the seventh month of the sixth year of the Jiading period (1213). Her father so-and-so had served Prince Chong and his son over two generations as a musician-entertainer [*yue ji* 樂伎].[1] At the age of six years, Zhang fully understood the pitches and modes. [Zhang's mother-in-law,] my maternal great-grandmother the Princess Xin'an, [was a daughter of Prince Chong]. Once when she had returned to the prince's household for a visit, she had seen [Zhang] and liked her. The Princess took Zhang home as a servant for [her son], my maternal grandfather Master Shi [Binzhi, 1190–1251]. When Zhang was a bit older, she became his attendant-charmer. The family was complex and complicated; she thoroughly comprehended and conformed to the rules. My grandfather by nature was strict and forceful. Zhang augmented his strengths and concealed his shortcomings, serving him without contravening his wishes. In ordering the content of his containers and cases, in accord with his directions and instructions she would set things out before him. It was like this for more than thirty years. She gave birth to two daughters. The elder, Lady Hezheng, married the Military Commissioner Xie Ye 謝埜. The second was my late mother, Lady Kuaiji. She married my late father [Yuan] Hong [袁]洪 (1245–98), Associate Area Commander of Chuzhou circuit. Both daughters married into grand councilor families. At the time, the Xie family were ennobled and renowned as the relatives of the empress. When my father was an official in [the capital] Lin'an, he always humbly kept his distance. Although my maternal grandmother had long lived in the households of great officials, when she saw that her Xie son-in-law was extravagant and unrestrained, she was unhappy and stayed often at the home of my father, content with peace and quiet.

In the sixth month of 1266, my lady mother gave birth to me. Seven days later, she was struck with dysentery and died. Shortly thereafter, my father became extremely ill; he had a high fever and was in danger of dying. Everyone said the misfortune I had brought to my mother was now affecting my father. Milord Xie wanted to take me to rear himself. My father from his sickbed waved his hand in

---

1. Prince Chong's personal name was Zhao Bogui 趙伯圭. He was the elder brother of Emperor Xiaozong.

disapproval, and my grandmother rejected the idea with loud invective, putting a stop to it. Thereafter she daily instructed and corrected me, vowing, "This child will become someone his grandfather Shi would be proud of." In 1272, Milord Xie died. She said tearfully, "I always knew it would be like this. I will exhaust my energies rearing my Yuan grandchild; where else can I go?" Eventually she saw me take a wife and father a daughter. She died in the second month of 1287, at the age of 74. She was buried some distance to the left of my mother's tomb.[2]

In this manner, Yuan Jue 袁桷 (1266–1327) recorded the biography of his maternal grandmother, a clearly remarkable woman who was reared as a household entertainer, became an entertainer-concubine, and, though she bore only daughters, ended up as the fondly remembered, nobly titled, and formally commemorated grandmother of a prominent official.[3] Although Zhang Zhihe was unusual in marrying into an extremely high-ranking family, her life is emblematic of an important shift in the roles of concubines over the course of the Southern Song, as women taken in for their entertainment skills became the mothers and grandmothers of literati men. The social impact of this phenomenon was all the more profound in that, during the twelfth and early thirteenth centuries, the craze for concubines, and especially entertainer-concubines, that had marked the office-holding elite of the Northern Song spread to ever-lower levels of society. Like the proliferation of courtesans outside the home, the spread of concubinage in the Southern Song was accompanied by increased attention to the problems that the commodification of women's bodies caused to government and social order; but the impact of widespread concubinage was felt even more strongly in families. Writers and moralists responded by attempting to redefine the proper place of concubines and their children in the family context, de-emphasizing concubines' function as erotic paramours and highlighting their role as mothers of descendants.

---

2. Yuan Jue, *Qing rong ju shi ji* 33.578; *Quan Yuan wen* 23: 730.535–37.
3. Yuan Jue indicates that he has composed this text in part to be sure that his descendants will understand the important role that Zhang played in his life, and not think that his commemoration of her was inappropriately ostentatious for a concubine.

## The "Serving Babe" Fad

The increasing popularity of concubines in general, and of entertainer-concubines in particular, is evident in a variety of twelfth- and thirteenth-century sources. One early harbinger was the sudden emergence of literary works specifically devoted to recounting the poetic or evocative names bestowed on entertainer-concubines by their masters. The earliest of these texts, titled *Record of the Pet Names of Serving Maids* (*Shi'er xiao ming lu* 侍兒小名錄), appears to have been compiled shortly before the fall of the Northern Song. Over the course of the following century, it was followed by a *Supplement to the Record of the Pet Names of Serving Maids* (*Bu shi'er xiao ming lu* 補⋯); a *Continued Supplement to the Record of the Pet Names of Serving Maids* (*Xu bu shi'er xiao ming lu* 續⋯); and an *Addendum to the Record of the Pet Names of Serving Maids* (*Shi'er xiao ming lu shi yi* ⋯拾遺).[4] The Song *Pet Names* collections were nominally modeled on a late Tang text, the *Record of Pet Names* (*Xiao ming lu*) by Lu Guimeng 陸龜蒙 (fl. 850s). But in content they were quite different. The Tang *Record of Pet Names*, as its title implies, was concerned with identifying childhood or other nicknames of some hundred or so historical personages—men as well as women—of the Han and Six Dynasties. In contrast, the Song texts focused specifically on the nicknames of entertainer-concubines. Like their Tang model, most of them focused on the pre-Song period, recounting romantic anecdotes from the histories of the Han, Six Dynasties, and Tang. The

---

4. The textual history of these works is murky, to say the least. The *Shi'er xiao ming lu* is variously attributed in Song and Yuan sources to Hong Chu 洪芻 (1094 *jin shi*), his brother Hong Yan 洪炎 (ca. 1090 *jin shi*), Hong Sui 洪遂 (n.d.), or Hong Kuo 洪适 (see Yong Rong, *Qin ding Si ku quan shu zong mu* 137.8b–9a, entry for *Bu shi'er xiao ming lu*; Tao Zongyi, *Shuo fu*, 77 *shang*, 45; and *SS* 126.5229). In any case, a text of this name was clearly in circulation by 1151, when it was cited in Chao Gongwu's *Jun zhai du shu zhi* and was said to have been composed in 1110. The *Shi'er xiao ming lu shi yi* is generally attributed to Zhang Bangji (sometimes given as 張邦畿), but the *Si ku* editors note that even in the Southern Song other attributions were suggested (*Si ku quan shu zong mu* 137.12b). The author of the [*Xu bu*] *shi'er xiao ming lu* is one Wen Yu 溫豫, but nothing further is known of this individual. Only the [*Bu*] *shi'er xiao ming lu* is definitively attributed to a well-known figure, Wang Zhi (王銍, fl. ca. 1130). All of these texts are contained in Tao Zongyi, *Shuo fu*, 77 *shang*, 33–59, where they are given the identical title *Shi'er xiao ming lu*.

*Addendum*, however, also featured famous couples of the Northern Song period, borrowing freely from other anecdotal collections that circulated at the time.⁵ In that regard, the *Addendum* can be seen as belonging to the literature of nostalgia discussed in chapter 4: it recounted the romances of Northern Song luminaries, albeit with their household entertainers rather than with public courtesans. But the *Pet Names* texts had a more specific social function, as noted by that astute observer of mores, Zhou Hui 周煇 (1127–after 1193):

> Hong Jufu [Yan] collected the *Pet Names of Serving Maids* in three chapters; Wang Xingzhi [Zhi] continued it with one chapter, and busybodies again filled in what was incomplete. Although it can be said that the selection was not very apropos, and what was included is not comprehensive, it still suffices to aid in joking around at banquets. Gentlemen and officials fancy the pleasures of skirt-chasing, and they regard acquiring personal maids [lit., those who serve with towel and comb] as extraordinarily difficult. When a man manages to obtain one—never mind her looks and skills, and even if she is of the most common and lowly sort—he will call her something extravagantly beautiful. The name far exceeds the reality; mostly it is just ridiculous. I suppose the reason they boast is to compensate for their long-held fantasies—[the reality] is inadequate so they exaggerate. Someone said, "West Lake can be compared to a beautiful woman; bare-faced and heavy makeup are both becoming."⁶ The name "Both-becoming" would be excellent, but I'm very much afraid there is no one who "dares to assume it."⁷

Zhou Hui tells us, first of all, that the *Pet Names* texts were grist for the gossip and clever wordplay that, along with poetry, were the measure and currency of literati social interaction. He then notes that taking a concubine who could be construed as a talented and lovely romantic partner had become a fad among the "gentlemen and officials" of his

---

5. Another text very similar in content if not in title is the *Gan zhu ji* 紺珠集 [*Memory Pearl Collection*] attributed to Zhu Shengfei (1137 preface).

6. The line is from a poem by Su Shi, in which he contemplates the vista of West Lake in both cloudy and clear conditions (飲湖上初晴後雨: 水光瀲灩晴方好, 山色空濛雨亦奇. 若把西湖比西子, 淡粧濃抹總相宜).

7. Zhou Hui, *Qing bo za zhi* 9.390–91. I have cited part of this passage in Bossler, "Shifting Identities," 30. I have added the final set of quotation marks because I believe Zhou is making a subtle and humorous display of his erudition here, quoting a comment Su Shi is said to have made about apricots and plums (*li*) "not daring to assume" (*bu gan cheng dang* 不敢承當) the place of plum-blossoms (*mei hua*) in a poem. See the entry for *cheng dang* in Luo Zhufeng, *Han yu da ci dian*.

day, and he ridicules those who, unable to find (or afford?) a woman of true skill and beauty, think they can compensate by giving elegant names to the concubines they *are* able to acquire. He concludes by offering a suggestion for just such a name, drawn from a well-known poem by Su Shi. In making his suggestion, Zhou employs a complex double allusion, and the purpose of his comments was undoubtedly to demonstrate his own skill at literati wordplay. But he reveals as well that by the late twelfth century taking an entertainer-concubine had become a status symbol, common not just among the nobility and high-ranking court officials (who often kept dozens of women), but among men of more modest means, for whom acquiring even a single such woman was a challenge.[8] The circulation of the *Pet Names* texts simultaneously reflected the spreading interest in elegantly named serving maids and helped promote that interest, publicizing and providing venerable historical precedents for the idea that men of means should keep lovely and talented serving maids. Few Song men seem to have noticed the slippage between anecdotes describing the Six Dynasties and the early Tang, when aristocratic households kept troupes of musician-slaves who were sometimes "favored" by their masters, and the circumstances of their own day, when men of a much broader elite class sought romance in the form of entertainer-concubines acquired from the flourishing market in women and girls.

To be sure, not all women who were designated as concubines in the Southern Song were necessarily entertainers: the term *qie* could still encompass roles ranging from servant to quasi-wife. But by the mid Southern Song most people seem to have taken for granted that entertainment was one of the common functions a concubine would provide. Thus Yuan Cai's 袁采 (1163 *jin shi*) famous advice book, *Precepts for Social Life*, advises householders that when they "establish maids and concubines (*bi qie*) and teach them to dance and sing, or have them 'urge the wine cups' to entertain guests," they should not keep those who are especially pretty or clever. Yuan's concern is that such women are likely

---

8. Note the difference between Zhou Hui's observation that gentlemen and officials (*shi dai fu* 士大夫) liked to buy concubines, and the observation (cited in chap. 2) made by Zhu Yu in the late Northern Song that the nobility (*gui ren* 貴人) sought to purchase them.

to attract the illicit desires of guests who may resort to all sorts of nefarious schemes to obtain the women, but the important point here is that he takes for granted that men will expect their concubines to entertain their guests.[9] Somewhat later, the author of an early thirteenth-century handbook for local officials found it necessary to warn his peers against inviting professional courtesans into their homes to teach their charmer-concubines to sing and dance.[10]

As in the Northern Song, men at the top of the Southern Song political elite enjoyed the company of household-courtesans, and sometimes wrote poetry teasing friends and associates about their own handmaids. The Vice Grand Councilor Fan Chengda 范成大 (1126–93) wrote poems on the fans of two household-charmers of an associate, cleverly working the names of the women into his poem.[11] Later anecdotalists reported that Fan himself kept two household-courtesans, one of whom he bestowed as a present on the poet Jiang Kui 姜夔 (1155–1235).[12] Fan's contemporary and friend, the Grand Councilor Zhou Bida, likewise wrote poetry for his associates' entertainer-concubines, including a poem that he titled: "Bangheng set out wine and brought out a 'little chignon' (*xiao huan*). I named her 'Government Willow' [*guan liu* 官柳, a reference to trees that lined government highways]. I had heard that recently Bangheng had bought a maid named 'Wild Plum' (*ye mei* 野梅), so I wrote this poem pairing them."[13] Zhou's travel accounts also describe a number of other parties at which he was entertained by the hosts' concubines: in one case, he remarks on the fact that although the host was seventy-three years old, he still kept ten charmers (*ji* 姬).[14] Zhou was particularly pleased to be at a banquet at which Zhao Yanbo, an imperial kinsman and high-ranking official, treated his guests to a dance performance by a household-courtesan named Little Jade (Xiaoqiong 小瓊). Zhou remarks:

---

9. Yuan Cai, *Yuan shi shi fan*, xia, 7a; cf. Ebrey, *Family and Property*, 288.
10. Hu Taichu, *Zhou lian xu lun*, section 15, 38b–39.
11. Fan Chengda, *Shihu shi ji* 11.10b.
12. See Lu Youren, *Yan bei za zhi*, xia, 38b.
13. Bangheng is the courtesy name of Hu Quan 胡銓 (1102–80), an eminent official who hailed from Zhou Bida's hometown.
14. Zhou Bida singles out one entertainer in particular for her skill at drinking games (*jiu xi* 酒戲): Zhou Bida, *Wenzhong ji* 168.27a–28a.

> Formerly, I heard Fan [Chengda] say, "Among the beauties (*shu li* 姝麗) of the court officials, there are three outstanding ones: that of Han [Yuanji], that of Chao Boru, and the household-courtesan [Little] Jade. Even the court has heard of her."

Zhou proceeded to write several poems in Little Jade's honor, explaining that he was also teasing his host because the latter had recently taken a second concubine, and the competition between the two women had forced him to set up his couch outside.[15] But Zhou's comments also reveal that household-courtesans had become emblems of status, the subject of admiring gossip and envy.

Like Su Shi in the Northern Song, Zhou Bida also wrote a short funerary record (*zang ji* 葬記) for his own attendant-concubine (*shi qie*). The record relates that the woman, to whom Zhou had given the poetic name Yunxiang (芸香, "Rue"), came from Qiantang and was the daughter of a man surnamed De. Zhou describes her as "pure and quiet, careful and cautious, clever at needlework, and somewhat able to make the new music" (*po neng wei xin sheng* 頗能爲新聲). He explains that Yunxiang first served him when he was living at the capital, when she was sixteen (and he was forty-four). When he left office two years later, she returned with him to his home town of Luling, and she died there of illness less than a year thereafter.[16]

Zhou's collected works say little else about Yunxiang: in contrast to Su Shi, Zhou seems to have written no poetry directed to her or about her (or at least none that survives). But his casual reference to the "new music" reveals her entertainer status in a manner much more open than any of Su Shi's writings for Zhaoyun, and shows again the extent to which entertainment had become not only an acceptable function for a concubine, but one taken for granted. That Zhou composed a funerary inscription for Yunxiang also attests to his emotional attachment to her. Two letters that Zhou wrote to Fan Chengda confirm these points. In the first, Zhou remarks that "It has already been half a year since the maid (*bi* 婢) Yun died; thinking of this I have not been able to work on the books; since you asked, I am mentioning it." In the second letter, he explains further:

---

15. Zhou Bida, *Wenzhong ji* 168.35b–36a. The incident was later remarked on by Zhou Mi, *Qi dong ye yu* 15.282–83.
16. *QSW* 232: 5177.313.

Formerly when I was in Zhe I obtained [the maid] Eastern Wall; on returning I also added a courtesan (*ji* 妓) who was rather able to sing and dance. Originally I only wanted to entertain my guests, but within two years I lost both of them, and since then I no longer have such thoughts. I presume on your friendship to touch on these trifling matters.[17]

It is hardly surprising that Zhou Bida, a high-ranking court official, should take in entertainer-concubines. But in the Southern Song men of much lesser political standing were also doing so. The collator of the poetry of the mid-ranked official Huang Gongdu 黃公度 (1109–56), for example, prefaced a nostalgic song-lyric about a dancing girl by noting that it related to Huang's experience with his two serving maids (*shi'er*): Huang's poem echoed themes in other poems written in honor of the girls by Huang's friends and relatives.[18] When the local official Chen Zhaodu 陳昭度 (1111–67) "took in a charmer" (*na ji* 納姬), his friend Zhao Gongyu 趙公豫 (1130s *jin shi*) wrote a teasing poem, likening the couple to fish playing in water and complaining that her (presumably post-coital) languor prevented her from coming out to the study to serve drinks.[19] The failed tutor and poet Chen Zao 陳造 (1133–1203) wrote a poem on a fan belonging to the *shi'er* of his friend Pan Cheng 潘檉 (n.d.), teasing her for having left Pan and then having returned.[20] Likewise, the famed lyricist Jiang Kui described outings with household-courtesans (*jia ji*), and also teased the serving maid of the prefect Chen Ye 陳曄 (fl. 1190s) for reading books:

| | |
|---|---|
| 繹句尋章久未休 | Sentences and paragraphs hours without end |
| 花房日晏不梳頭， | It's nearing sundown and the flower hasn't combed her hair. |
| 誰教郎主能多事 | Who told the master to be so demanding, |
| 乞與冥冥千古愁 | Causing her confusion and no end of grief![21] |

---

17. *QSW* 229: 5103.324–26. The name "Eastern Wall" suggests that the concubine may have had book-collating skills. I am grateful to Professors Bao Weimin and Liu Ching-cheng and Dr. Wu Yating for their assistance with this issue.
18. Huang Gongdu, *Zhi jia weng ji*, xia, 69a–b.
19. Zhao Gongyu, *Yan tang shi gao* 2a.
20. Chen Zao, *Jianghuchangweng ji* 19.24.
21. Jiang Kui, *Baishidaoren ge qu* 2.2a–b; *Baishidaoren shi ji*, xia, 18a. In a less flattering interpretation, the phrase "ming ming" which I have translated as "confusion" could also be rendered as "the benighted one," thereby suggesting that the girl's attempts at literacy were futile.

Although many men seem to have contented themselves with one or two serving maids, the biographer of the versifier and bon vivant Fang Yinglong 方應龍 (1173–1239) notes that at one point in his life he purchased several tens of charmer-concubines who played music, sang, and danced for the amusement of his guests.[22] And the would-be recluse Liu Zai 劉宰 (1166–1234), while praising a man who abjured such pleasures, observed that in the early thirteenth century literati (*shi dai fu*) competed to outdo one another with musical entertainments.[23]

Finally, anecdotes in Hong Mai's *Yijian zhi* suggest that even families of quite modest means might be interested in keeping a woman trained to entertain:

> Duan Zai lived in the Pujiang county temple in Wuzhou. His wife was once watching at the gate when a grown woman walked by begging for alms. When Duan's wife inquired after her name and circumstances, she replied that she had no husband and no affinal relatives. Duan's wife then asked, "In that case, rather than begging for food, why don't you become someone's concubine (*qie*)? Would you be willing to attend me?" The woman replied, "It isn't that I don't want to, but people see that I am poor and lowly (*pin jian* 貧賤) and are unwilling to take me in. If I could get a job doing kitchen labor, it would truly be a blessing from Heaven!" Duan's wife bade her come in, had her bathe and gave her a change of clothes, and sent the cook to teach her to make food and drink. In a week she was able to do it. Then they instructed her in poetic songs; in less than a month the songs were all completely perfect. After she had been trained for some time, her appearance and demeanor became quite attractive. Duan gave her the name "Oriole" and made her into his "side chamber" [*ce shi* 側室]. For five or six years, their only fear was that she would leave.[24]

The subtle differences between this account and the tale of "Director Li" recounted in chapter 2 are telling. The protagonist of the Northern Song story was an official from a powerful family, who purchased a girl from a broker for the express purpose of training her to entertain; here we see the wife of a commoner who lives in the local temple taking in a beggar woman for the same purpose. The shift reveals how deeply the fad for entertainer-concubines had penetrated Southern Song society.

---

22. Wang Mai, *Qu xuan ji* 11.3a.
23. Liu Zai, *Man tang ji* 34.9a–b, in funerary inscription for Madame Wu, wife of Liang Jibi.
24. *YJZ*, *Jia zhi*, 3.22. I have discussed this anecdote in a different context in "Song dai de jia ji he qie," 213–14.

The spread of the *shi'er* fad, however, also meant the proliferation in Southern Song society of problems occasioned by the widespread exchange of women as commodities. Those problems are quite explicitly on view in government documents, law cases, and anecdotal accounts, where (like the courtesans we saw in chapter 4), concubines were increasingly portrayed as a cause of political malfeasance and social disorder.

## *Concubines and Disorder*

As in the Northern Song, administrative documents of the Southern Song reveal that the state was frequently obliged to censure men who abused their authority to obtain concubines illicitly. But whereas the Northern Song saw major legal cases mostly involving pandering to high-ranking officials in the capital, the Southern Song was marked instead by a steady stream of reports detailing abuses by local officials. A few examples will suffice. In 1177, an erstwhile Supervisor of Fujian was cashiered for having his subordinates buy concubines and deliver them to his house, in exchange for which he had recommended them for promotions.[25] In 1181, an enterprising prefect found himself out of a job when the inspecting officials caught him bringing false charges against local commoners in the hopes of forcing their daughters to become concubines, apparently planning to have them entertain at a wine garden he opened.[26] In 1198 the Jiyang prefect was accused of being so "besotted with wine and sex" that he forced two daughters of a local headman to serve as his concubines, and in 1215 the prefect of Xinzhou lost his position in part for appropriating the young concubine of a military official.[27]

Southern Song sources also show that the desire for concubines caused problems for the state even when officials were not directly involved. One of the *Enlightened Judgments* records the activities of a local bully, Wang Yuanji, who among other crimes coerced a daughter of good commoner family into becoming his "minor wife" (*xiao qi* 小妻), causing her father to commit suicide.[28] Wang's crony Yang

---

25. *SHY, zhiguan,* 72.17b.
26. *SHY, zhiguan,* 72.31a.
27. *SHY, zhiguan,* 74.3a and 75.8a.
28. *QMJ* 12.466; cf. McKnight and Liu, *Enlightened Judgments,* 432–34.

Zigao forced no fewer than seven girls of good family into becoming his minor wives and favored maids (*chong bi* 寵婢); not one of them dared bring her plaint to the court.²⁹ Another locally powerful family, which reportedly tyrannized their district for some thirty years, was known for kidnapping the daughters and wives of their neighbors and making them into servant girls or remarrying them off to their henchmen, to the point that "parents could not keep their children as children and husbands could not keep their wives as wives."³⁰ Sometimes conflicts over concubines led to lawsuits that could ruin the reputations and careers not of the accused, but of those attempting to serve justice. Zhou Bida described two cases of such collateral damage. In the first, a court official brought suit against the notorious late Northern Song Grand Councilor Wang Fu 王黼 (1079–1126), claiming that Wang had forcibly taken his concubine and spent the night with her. Although the investigating censor first ruled for the plaintiff, Wang succeeded in securing a change of venue. As a result the plaintiff was beaten and convicted of false accusation, and the censor demoted.³¹ In a second case, Zhou Bida's friend Gao Kui 高夔 (1138–98) was serving as prefect when a local official brought suit against a circuit intendant for stealing a beloved concubine (*ai qie*). Gao attempted to investigate, but the circuit intendant was protected by his superior and Gao himself ended up demoted for his efforts.³²

Lawsuits involving concubines could also put local officials in very sensitive positions, as seen in an anecdote praising the then-local official Luo Dian 羅點 (1150–94) for his handling of a delicate case. A landlord had brought suit charging that an expelled tenant owed him money. Investigation bore out the landlord's claim, but the case became more complicated when the tenant volunteered that he had had an illicit relationship with the master's "kitchen charmer" (*kui zhi ji* 饋之姬). Luo's

---

29. *QMJ* 12.467.
30. *QMJ* 12.471–73; McKnight and Liu, *Enlightened Judgments*, 435–39 (translation slightly emended).
31. Zhou Bida, *Wenzhong ji* 165.15b–16b.
32. Zhou Bida, *Wenzhong ji* 65.9, 76.5. The latter text is a funerary inscription for Gao's mother: Zhou praises her for urging her son to do the right thing even if his career will suffer. Yuan Cai remarked that he knew of "many" such cases (Yuan Cai, *Yuan shi shi fan, xia,* 7a; cf. Ebrey, *Family and Property,* 288).

8. Exiling a crafty tenant (*Duan pei xia pu* 斷配黠僕). Angry at his master, the crafty tenant sought to exact revenge by claiming an illicit relationship with the master's favorite concubine. His schemes were foiled by a clever judge, and he is shown here on his way into exile to do forced labor. The anecdote hints at the complicated social effects of the spread of concubinage. From Kangxi 康熙, Emperor of China, *Sheng yu xiang jie* 聖諭像解, edited by Liang Yannian 梁延 (Bei yang guan bao ju, 1903), 12.23a. Qing dynasty. Courtesy of the C. V. Starr East Asian Library, University of California, Berkeley.

resolution of the case demonstrated the finesse that was ultimately to propel him into high office: he had the tenant provide a detailed confession and then punished him in accordance therewith, both for owing money and for illicit sex. But he prudently chose to defer questioning the serving girl (*nü shi*) "until the day the master brings suit." The author of the anecdote assures us that the "crafty" tenant sought only to smear the landlord's good name, and that there was no truth to his claim. Whether or not that was the case, we can see why "everyone who heard of [the verdict] was delighted."[33]

Finally, the Southern Song also saw the appearance of new kinds of accusations leveled at local officials who let their own concubines subvert justice. Echoing indictments of officials who allowed government-courtesans to disrupt local administration, in 1175 censors accused the official Li Anguo of crimes in several of his prior postings, including a claim that during his term as prefect of Changzhou he had let a favored concubine get involved in government affairs.[34] In 1198, both the Wuzhou prefect Mu Daiwen and his successor Wang Ji were reduced to temple sinecures because Mu's son's concubine had taken bribes: things had gotten so bad, the prosecuting officials complained, that no prefectural business could be done without a payoff.[35] In the early thirteenth century, Zhao Chonggui, erstwhile prefect of Huzhou, was demoted twice because in that position he had let his concubine monopolize power and control access to him.[36] Such cases suggest that some concubines (like government-courtesans) occupied a position between the inner and outer quarters: while enjoying intimate access to their master, they also had a public presence.

Nor was it only government that could be adversely affected by the desire for concubines: in the Southern Song, such desire also began to be depicted as the cause of other kinds of social disruption, from abrogation of ritual norms to outright violence. The anecdotalist Zhou Hui remarked with disdain on the willingness of men of his class to violate even death taboos in order to obtain beautiful women:

---

33. Zhou Mi, *Qi dong ye yu* 8.133.
34. *SHY*, *zhiguan*, 72.2a.
35. *SHY*, *zhiguan*, 74.5a.
36. *SHY*, *zhiguan*, 74.45b, 75.16a.

Gentlemen and officials want to preserve their wealth and position forever; they have taboos on certain movements, and especially interdict talking about death. [But] when they lose themselves [lit., drown] in beautiful women, there is nothing they will not do. When they hear that among someone's charmer-attendants there is one who is graceful and lovely, at the moment the master stops breathing they have already made plans, paying off a go-between to wait until she is released and then buy her. Even though by custom those in mourning are inauspicious, they disregard it.[37]

Hong Mai's anecdotal collection recounts just such a case, while also suggesting that men who violated death taboos could find themselves victims of supernatural retribution. Hong described how Yu Mengwen 虞孟文 doted on a skilled and beautiful concubine whom he had purchased for a high price. When Mengwen died, his callous younger cousin, Zhongwen 仲文, forced the widow to sell him the concubine. Only a few months later, the concubine dreamt that her late husband came and scolded her. The cousin dismissed her fears, saying "He's already dead, how can he frighten me?" But when the next morning Zhongwen rose to relieve himself, he discovered the dead husband sitting in his reception hall, armed with a club. The husband chased and beat him, and although Zhongwen survived the encounter, he shortly thereafter sickened and died.[38] Zhou Mi later recounted a similar case, in which the concubine's new owner likewise ended up dead.[39]

Still, unseemly haste in the purchase of a dead man's concubine was a mild offense in comparison with the appalling transgressions reported in Southern Song legal cases. One case recounts a fight between two upper-class men, Wang Mu and Chen Xian, over a woman known as A-lian (Lotus). When an initial conflict between them ended up in court,

---

37. Zhou Hui, *Qing bo za zhi* 3.101–2. Cf. Bossler, "Shifting Identities," 30. In the same entry, Zhou discusses a parallel phenomenon of connoisseurs being fond of jade that has been "permeated by the corpse" (that is, jade that has absorbed oils used to anoint a corpse), so that such jade fetches several times the price of ordinary jade and grave goods end up becoming playthings that people value. He concludes that neither of these things can be restrained by principle.

38. *YJZ, bing zhi*, 15.491.

39. Zhou Mi, *Qi dong ye yu* 20.372. The story relates how a magistrate surnamed Liang purchased the concubine of his deceased friend, surnamed Ma. Later, a banquet guest declaimed a joking poem that punned on the names of the two masters, to the effect that the concubine had mourned Ma and should not "pass [away]" Although his guests laughed uproariously, Liang was not amused, and shortly thereafter he died.

Wang and Chen, as sons of literati families, escaped punishment; Lotus, however, was convicted of adultery with them and relegated to "miscellaneous household" (*za hu*) status. Unchastened, Wang Mu proceeded to take Lotus into his household. When Chen responded by spreading jokes and insults about her and blocking her way in the street, Wang recruited Lotus's son; the two of them kidnapped Chen, beat him, and doused him with foul matter.[40]

The judge in this case (a Magistrate Zhao) is outraged not only that Wang attacked Chen, but that Wang attempted to justify taking Lotus into his household by putting it about that she had been a maid (*bi shi* 婢使) of his father: he is shocked that Wang is unaware that having relations with a maid who belonged to one's father is illegal.[41] The judge is also irate that Wang's relationship with Lotus has led him to put off marriage, noting that "treating a concubine as a wife was proscribed by the ancients." Bewailing the fact that Wang's sexual impulses have led him astray, the judge orders him to meditate on Confucian and Buddhist discipline, expel Lotus, and establish a proper wife. Lotus is to be handed over to her uncle to be remarried to someone else, with the warning that should she ever return to the Wang household, she will be dealt with severely.

If desire led Wang and Chen into inappropriate behavior, the actions of Wu Zihui and his wife's uncle Chen Jiyuan—both descendants of official families—were even more egregious. In the outraged and circuitous judgment on this case, we learn that Ms. Chen, a sixth-generation descendant of a Northern Song grand councilor, was married to Wu Zihui, "who was also the descendant of an official family." Her husband proved unable to support her, so they went to live with her uncle, Chen

---

40. *QMJ* 12.442–44.

41. The threat that young concubines were often close in age to (and might be attracted to) the adult sons of their master had long been recognized, and strict rules prohibited men from having relationships with their fathers' or grandfathers' maids. In theory, a man was to regard his father's concubine as a stepmother, and thus sexual relations with such a woman were tantamount to incest, one of the most serious crimes on the books. The problem was common enough that Yuan Cai warned men with concubines of the need for particular vigilance with regard to "sons and younger brothers" (*zi di*) as well as household servants, and noted that this could especially be a problem if the master were old (Yuan Cai, *Yuan shi shi fan*, xia, 6b; Ebrey, *Family and Property*, 287).

Jiyuan, where Ms. Chen contributed to the household income with her needlework. The judge acknowledges that such decline was not uncommon:

> Among the descendants of gentleman-officials, there are those who are virtuous and those who are dissolute, and therefore there is no guarantee that they will always have wealth and prosperity and live up to the family heritage.

But, he observes, although a sympathetic man would have sought to help someone in Chen's circumstances, instead her uncle colluded with her husband to sell her as a serving maid to a minor official, Revenue Manager Lei. The judge is clearly disgusted at what has happened to Chen. He rails against the uncle for taking advantage of Chen's poverty and "tempt[ing] her to become a maid," wailing "if one can bear to do this, what couldn't he bear to do?!" He scolds Lei for his intemperateness:

> Revenue Manager Lei is the descendant of a famous family and has prospects for position and reputation. What advantage did he see in one woman that he went against propriety and subjected himself to blame and scorn?

Yet for all his outrage the judge admits he is pursuing the case only because Chen is the descendant of a high-ranking official:

> Ms. Chen's mother née Liu brought a plaint, and seeing that she is a descendant of Chen [Shengzhi], the court cannot bear to ignore the fact that she has lost her chastity, eternally disgracing her forebears. This case must be prosecuted.

The judge's concern for status prerogatives likewise shapes both his investigation and the final disposition of the miscreants. After discovering that Lei had first persuaded Wu to leave Chen with him overnight, the judge refrains from questioning Chen herself, for fear of revealing "extreme improprieties." Then, although by law Wu and Chen should have been divorced (on the grounds that in selling her he had "extinguished sentiment" [*jin qing* 盡情] between them), instead the judge temporarily sends Chen home with her mother and decrees that if Wu can find a way to support her, she can return to him. (Otherwise, her mother is permitted to arrange another marriage for her.) The judge castigates Chen Jiyuan's heartlessness in taking a bribe from Lei to sell off his own niece, but merely remands him to his family elders for punishment, stipulating only that he should be denied his allotment of rice from the family's charitable estate. Finally, and most remarkably, beyond ordering that the contract of Chen's sale be destroyed, the magistrate decrees no punishment whatever for Lei.

He does, however, exhort Lei in a rhetorical style we have seen before:

> In previous eras there was an official whose convoy of transport boats was sunk, and who was about to sell his wife and daughters to make restitution; a famous worthy saw this and emptied his own purse to give to the official, and then arranged dowries and married the women off, ensuring that they had a [proper] place to go.[42] This has been recorded in biographical records, to the point that it has become a common parable. When Revenue Manager Lei hears of this, can he fail to be mortified?[43]

These cases are striking not only in showing the ways that the spread of concubinage—and the increasing commodification of women that it occasioned—was disrupting the social order, but also in revealing how little the state could do about it. The state simply had few weapons with which to combat the fluid markets in women and the breakdown of status hierarchies that those markets helped engender. Wang Mu was clearly undeterred by Lotus's original conviction as an adulteress and concomitant status of "miscellaneous household" (both of which technically barred her from becoming a legitimate concubine), and indeed even the judge does not make an issue of their status disparity. Wang was also either ignorant of or chose to disregard other norms and laws intended to preserve social and familial hierarchies, such as those barring a man from taking over the concubine of a senior family member or from treating a concubine as a wife. Similarly, the men surrounding the unfortunate Ms. Chen put profit before considerations of status and family reputation. Although the legal judgments in these cases conspicuously sought to reestablish social hierarchies, in the highly commercialized economy of the late Southern Song, the forces of money and sexual desire left women of even the most illustrious family heritage vulnerable to the vagaries of fortune and the market for female flesh.[44]

In this context, accounts praising literati men for saving girls of their class from concubinage, already popular in the Northern Song, became increasingly numerous and elaborate. Examples are legion, for in Southern

---

42. The judge here seems to be referring to the anecdote involving Wang Anshi marrying off a concubine (see chap. 2).

43. *QMJ* 10.382–83.

44. Even imperial clanswomen could end up sold as concubines: see the case of Ye Fen (1076–1147), who was indicted for buying an imperial clanswoman as a concubine, but exonerated when the purchaser turned out to be a different official of the same surname. Li Mixun, *Yunxi ji* 24.1–2.

Song biographical writings, rescuing upper-class girls from servitude was no longer portrayed as an exceptional act of virtue by extraordinary men, but as a conventionally honorable act that might be undertaken by—even expected of—any ethical individual.[45] One new development that suggests just how broad the market in women had become is the emergence of accounts of upper-class men, and even women, rescuing *courtesans* of genteel background.[46] These accounts bespeak widespread anxiety about downward social mobility and especially the vulnerability of women to it. Conversely, we also see attempts to make sense of this alarming social instability, in assertions that women who declined from genteel upbringing into concubine or courtesan status were suffering karmic retribution for the sins of their ancestors.[47]

---

45. For example, one account tells of how Li Hong 李宏 not only married off orphans of his own lineage and, on learning that a concubine he had purchased was from a literati family, immediately married her off; he also sought out a young woman of his hamlet who had declined and wandered to another district, redeemed her, and returned her to her family (Han Yuanji, *Nan jian jia yi gao* 20.392). In service in the deep south, Zhou Ziqiang 周自強 (1120–81) was aghast to discover that when poor officials there died suddenly, their wives and daughters often had no means of support, to the point that they were led to sell themselves as maids and concubines. Zhou memorialized to establish a law forbidding this practice, and then provided official funds to aid or marry the women off (ibid., 22.446). Among other good deeds he performed as a local official, Peng Hanlao 彭漢老 (1134–1200) apportioned off part of his own emolument to marry off the gently bred concubine of a colleague. Later in Peng's career he also encountered a distant descendant of an early Northern Song grand councilor, living as an impoverished widow with her two daughters; he arranged both daughters' marriages, providing all of their dowry expenses from his savings (*QSW* 233: 5189.87–89).

46. When a daughter of a literati (*shi*) family "declined into" a courtesan house as a small child, Teng Zhu wished to redeem her; but the courtesan broker, knowing Teng's funds were limited, forged a contract in which the child's value was greatly exaggerated. Teng's plans were thwarted until his son Lin went to participate in the examinations, at which point the prefecture presented him with a generous "encouragement" gift. Teng gave the entire amount to the broker, retrieved the girl and married her off without questioning the price (*Zhu Xi ji* 94.4779–81). Huang Zhen 黃震 (1213–80), a follower of Zhu Xi's teachings, later credited Teng Lin for saving girls who declined into courtesan houses (*Huang shi ri chao* 36.32). At a banquet attended by Woman Cai, one of the government-courtesans confessed that she was the daughter of an official family; Cai gathered money for a dowry and married her off as the wife of a literatus (Liu Zai, *Man tang ji* 34.17b).

47. Chen Zao 陳造 (1133–1203) described a banquet he attended in 1182, at which the guests learned that one of the government-courtesans was the daughter of a general.

Even as some stories portrayed concubines as innocent victims of social circumstance or karmic debt, the turmoil that concubinage was creating in Southern Song society also found expression in anecdotes depicting concubines as sources of death and destruction. The ending of the story of Duan Zai and the woman he named Oriole, introduced above, is typical:

> One night, late, the Duan family had all gone to bed. From outside the door someone hailed the gatekeeper, saying "I'm Oriole's husband." The servant answered, "I've never heard that Oriole had a husband. Even if it is as you say, it won't be too late if you wait for morning, why does it have to be in the middle of the night?" The person angrily responded, "If you don't open the door, I'll get in through a crack." The servant was furious, and knocking on the entryway to the hall, informed Duan of the conversation. Oriole overheard. Seemingly pleased, she said, "He's come!" and hurriedly went out. Duan feared she was running away: grabbing a torch, he pursued her to the corridor. Suddenly there was a loud noise, and the torch went out. His wife sent a servant girl out to look; Duan was already dead, bleeding from all seven orifices. The outer-door bolt was fastened as usual, and in the end they never discovered what weird thing it was.[48]

Although other stories differ in detail, the general pattern is the same: a chance encounter leads a man to take in a concubine; over time he becomes infatuated with her, but eventually a supernatural force intervenes and the master usually ends up dead.[49] As with the courtesans discussed in chapter 4, the women in these stories can be seen as examples of that age-old Chinese representation of the dangers of female sexuality, the fox spirit. But it is precisely this new incarnation of the fox spirit that is significant. In the Tang, vulnerable young men tended to meet fox spirits in secluded farmhouses in the course of their travels, and the courtesan fox spirits described in chapter 4 were likewise women encountered in the always-threatening public world, outside the safety of the family circle. But here the dangerous paramours are women that

---

Although some of the guests wanted to put money together for her dowry, the courtesan's madam refused on the grounds that the girl was also supporting her two brothers. Chen ruminates on the vicissitudes of fame and fortune, and concludes that the courtesan's poor fate was karmic retribution for the fact that her father had once stolen another man's wife (Chen Zao, *Jianghuchangweng ji* 22.15b–17).

48. *YJZ, jia zhi*, 3.22.

49. See, e.g., *YJZ, jia zhi*, 8.65–66; *jia zhi*, 18.163; *jia zhi*, 13.115–16; *yi zhi*, 2.195; *yi zhi*, 5.226. Similar stories are told of men's affairs with courtesans, e.g., *YJZ, jia zhi*, 8.70.

men have brought into their own homes as concubines. These stories thus hint at the new emotional tensions and interpersonal conflicts that concubinage was creating in Song families.

## Emotional Complexities and Family Conflicts

The complexity of the new emotional landscape created by the widespread presence of concubines in Southern Song families is reflected, first of all, in the appearance of poetry written on the occasion of men marrying off their concubines to other men. Like the poems that Northern Song men wrote teasing one another about their serving maids, these poems are usually playful; but notably these Southern Song poems focus less on romance than on the contradictions and complications that concubine relationships could occasion. Xu Lun (d. 1209), for example, wrote a verse to match one his father-in-law had written when the latter married off two of his serving maids (*shi'er*). Xu's poem remarked on the ambiguous sexual status of concubines by proposing (satirically?) that removal of the girls' makeup helped restore their virginal state:

| | |
|---|---|
| 出水芙蓉寧受汙? | Who says the lotus taken from the water is polluted? |
| 鉛華洗盡見眞清 | When the white powder is washed away they appear pure and fresh.[50] |

In a more solemn vein, Sun Di in the 1130s wrote a whole series of poems for his friend He Jiahui (n.d.) when He married off his concubine. Several of Sun's poems emphasize He's melancholy, occasioned both by the concubine's departure and by his awareness that she is joining a younger man. The final poem in the series, titled "Jiahui Had a Farewell Banquet for His Beloved Charmer; in Great Grief They Parted" (嘉會飲餞愛姬, 大慟而別), portrays He as the unhappiest person at the banquet, his face covered in tears.[51]

A different but equally fraught set of emotions is evoked in a poem that Cai Kan (1166 *jin shi*) wrote for his friend and drinking companion, the prefect Zhu Jiang (1117–98), when Zhu married off a serving maid. The title of the poem reads: "Zhu [Jiang] sacrificed his love (*ge ai* 割愛) and married off his serving maid. Casting off emotion (*wang qing* 忘情)

---

50. Xu Lun [Xu Jizhi], *She zhai ji* 15.17a.
51. Sun Di, *Hong qing ju shi ji* 2.16b–18b.

like this is truly admirable. Accordingly I have written a 'Casting Off Emotion Lament' to convey [her] feelings of pain and resentment." The somewhat self-contradictory (even sarcastic) tone of the title is carried through the song, which praises Zhu's moral vigor in being able to free himself from worldly emotional ties, but simultaneously castigates his heartlessness. The verses open with a description of an attractive fourteen- or fifteen-year-old girl, one among several in the inner quarters of a passionate young man. The narrator of the song is in fact this young girl, who compares herself to a dazzlingly beautiful flower and bewails that her master's heart is like iron and stone. She recalls their former intimacy and laments its destruction. Observing that the famed Tang erudites Han Yu and Bo Juyi also had concubines who did not want to leave them, the poet remarks, "Although the two gentlemen are regarded as knowing the Dao, they did not avoid having emotions of love and desire roiling in their breasts. Therefore, for being able to discard someone like an old shoe, from ancient times there has never been one virtuous as you." (二公爲號知道者,未免愛慾纏胸中；果能脫去如敝屣,自古未有賢於公). The last stanza returns to the voice of Cai Kan, who indicates that he is expressing resentment on the girl's behalf because "the phoenix taking leave of the crane has difficulty making a sound." And finally, the last couplet raises suspicions that Zhu's motives may not be what they seem:

| 憐新棄舊似淺薄 | Loving the new and discarding the old seems to be rather shallow; |
| 如君未必眞忘情 | Your concubine/Someone like you has not necessarily truly cast off emotions.[52] |

Cai suggests that rather than truly ridding himself of emotion, Zhu has merely tired of one woman and moved on to the next.

Poems like these began to take note of the emotional costs of the frequent movement of women in and out of Southern Song households. Cai Kan's poem, in particular, is interested in asking the reader to imagine the feelings of the women who found themselves in this situation. Here (as in Xu Ji's "My Fate Is Poor" poems in the late Northern Song), the longstanding poetic trope of "boudoir lament" is reconfigured: rather than portraying a neglected palace woman (who was in any case

---

52. Cai Kan, *Ding zhai ji* 16.17a–18a. The phrase *ru jun* is a standard polite term for someone's concubine, but it can also be read as "someone like you."

often meant as a stand-in for the unappreciated poet), the poet endeavors to express the feelings of a lower-class serving maid, tacitly asking the reader to sympathize with her situation. Even if we accept that such poems were meant playfully, they highlight the new—or more broadly experienced—tensions within Song families.

Those tensions are equally evident in other types of sources. The aged official Hu Quan (1102–80), warning that infatuation with women could distract young men from their duties in maintaining the family heritage, invoked the dangers of both courtesans and concubines. In a set of rhymed family instructions composed after the Emperor Xiaozong had praised his family's long-term success in office, Hu painted a garish picture of the coddled descendants of successful families, with soft, oiled skin like that of women, devoting themselves to "embracing lovely women in the rear apartments," "piling up gold to select 'moth eyebrows,'" "in the morning drinking with their gambling friends and in the evening heading to the courtesan houses," until in short order the patrimony was ruined.[53]

Relationships with concubines were also becoming the source of domestic lawsuits, even among commoner families, arising from conflicts between concubines and wives. The commoner Yu Wenzi brought suit against his son-in-law Huang Ding, claiming that Ding had attacked him; but the proximate cause of the conflict was that Ding favored his concubine (she had recently produced a son) and Wenzi had sought to protect his daughter's interests.[54] The woman Li, whose husband had divorced her and then subsequently taken her to court for adultery, justified her behavior by claiming that well before her own transgression, her husband had taken a serving maid (*nü shi*) and then abandoned Li in distressed circumstances.[55] We saw in chapter 4 a case in which a commoner brought home a courtesan to be his concubine, and attempted to drive out his wife and children.[56] As concubinage

---

53. Hu Quan, *Dan'an wen ji* 3.5–7b. We have seen above that Hu Quan (who was the friend Zhou Bida called "Bangheng") was himself was not above enjoying the pleasures of female company.
54. *QMJ* 10.381–82.
55. *QMJ* 12.446–47; cf. McKnight and Liu, *Enlightened Judgments*, 422–24. The judge declined to investigate Li's claims.
56. Lu You, *Weinan wen ji* 38.234 (funerary inscription for Zhang Guan).

spread to less well-to-do families, a wife's very survival could be threatened by a concubine's presence.

Concubines' children, too, frequently became the focus of lawsuits. Some concubines found it necessary to go to court to protect their children's interests from the aggrandizing of their deceased husbands' kinsmen.[57] On other occasions, concubine mothers themselves attempted to appropriate their children's inheritances for their own purposes, forcing the state to step in to protect the children's patrimony.[58] As in the Northern Song, the children of expelled concubines were a particular locus of legal and social concern, though in the humbler families we see in Southern Song sources, the issue was less proper mourning relations than property rights. Sun Hua, a man of some wealth, was disconcerted to find that a tenant on his property was putting it about that he was Hua's son, and had gone so far as to change his surname to Sun. Sun Hua sued the youth in court. Ten years after Rao Cao's death, the twenty-year-old son of one of Rao's servants brought suit claiming that he was actually Rao's son. In both cases, the court's investigations confirmed that the claimants' mothers had in fact been maids in the masters' households, though in the end the court rejected the paternity claims. But this type of lawsuit was common enough that Yuan Cai warned:

> If you have illicit relations with some promiscuous person, or if you have a maid or concubine who is expelled for some reason, you must clarify the situation while you are still alive. Otherwise I fear that after you die there may be children who seek to return to the descent line, and the facts of the case will be murky. Your sons and grandsons will be the ones to suffer.[59]

---

57. *QMJ* 7.232–33 (cf. McKnight and Liu, *Enlightened Judgments*, 259–62; on this case see also Birge, *Women, Property, and Confucian Reaction*, 96; *QMJ* 7.238–39 (cf. McKnight and Liu, 265–67). We saw in chap. 2 that in the Northern Song, Li Gou had already described a case in which a man contrived to "treat his half-brother as a person of another surname" (*yi shu di wei yi xing zhe* 以庶弟爲異姓者, thus depriving him of inheritance rights), until a lecture by an upright official caused him to change his ways. Patricia Ebrey has also noted the vulnerability of concubines' children (*Inner Quarters*, 230).

58. *QMJ* 7.230–32; McKnight and Liu, *Enlightened Judgments*, 255–58. See also Birge, *Women, Property, and Confucian Reaction*, 97.

59. Yuan Cai, *Yuan shi shi fan, shang*, 21 (translation slightly altered from Ebrey, *Family and Property*, 216). For specific examples of dubious paternity resulting from the movement of concubines in and out of literati households, see Wang Mingqing, *Hui zhu lu, hou lu*, 6.162–3, and an example in Zhou Bida's family (*QSW* 231: 5155.323).

Increased anxiety about concubines' presence within the household was also expressed in anecdotes depicting fraught relationships between concubines and wives. The wife of a prefect (whose name Hong Mai says he doesn't want to record) was cruel and jealous, and she dealt with a defiant attendant-concubine by beating her and cutting out her tongue; the girl eventually died of her injuries. Jealous of her husband's affection for his concubine, the woman Zhang took advantage of her husband's absence to beat the girl to death. The wife of Qian Lingwang was cruel by nature and beat maids and concubines for even the slightest transgressions; several died under her blows. Hong Mai's point in all of these stories is to show that the cruel wives received grim supernatural retribution for their crimes: all were haunted by the ghosts of those they killed, and died of illness brought on by those ghosts in spite of their families' efforts to exorcise the spirits or mollify them with religious offerings.[60] One might be tempted to read these stories simply as warnings to jealous wives, but the emergence of jealous violence as a literary theme suggests broader social concerns. If fox spirit stories intimated the dangers of courtesan or concubine sexuality, stories of wives supernaturally punished for torturing and murdering concubines highlighted the dangers to family stability of conflicts among a household's women.[61]

## *Concubines and Cheng Learning*

Given the problems that the fad for entertainer-concubines seems to have caused in Southern Song social life, we should not be surprised that moral philosophers, with their avowed interest in the Confucian family order, became concerned about the proper role of concubines in

---

60. *YJZ, zhi jia,* 4.742; *yi zhi,* 15.311; *bing zhi,* 7.423.

61. On the most literal level, we might also read these stories as evidence that violence toward maids and concubines was commonplace (and that upper-class families were seldom held to account for such violence, at least in this world). Cf. Ebrey, "Concubines in Song China," 13. Another hint that literati wives were finding it necessary to compete with concubines in new ways is found in a comment by a twelfth-century anecdotalist who observed, "in earlier generations, the way of managing the family was that the so-called principal mother (*zhu mu* 主母) always maintained a plain and simple [appearance], while the charmer-attendants were elaborately made up and beautifully dressed." The implication seems to be that in his own day, wives are no longer dressing simply (Li Heng, *Le an yu lu* 2.4a).

the family. Yet although a number of Cheng Learning adherents did write about concubinage, they did so in ways rather different from what we might expect.⁶² Most strikingly, in spite of Cheng Learning's identification of human desire (*ren yu* 人欲) as a threat to moral self-cultivation, Cheng Learning adherents rarely took on the issue of concubines as objects of desire. Instead, they accepted and even upheld the validity of the institution of concubinage, creating a new model of the virtuous marital couple's relationship to concubines and highlighting the concubine's function as producer of descendants.

A few writers did acknowledge that desire was behind some men's interest in keeping concubines. Lü Zuqian (1127–81), in a brief passage on family management, admonished his descendants to be pure and frugal, prevent their womenfolk from getting involved in affairs external to the household, educate their sons, distribute charity appropriately, and refrain from keeping "rare objects and precious baubles, beautiful concubines or boy servants."⁶³ But he did not elaborate beyond this. Zhu Xi, the great twelfth-century synthesizer of Cheng Learning, formally addressed the problem of desire for concubines only once, in an 1189 memorial warning the emperor of the need for rectification of his person and his palace.⁶⁴ Here Zhu first reminded the emperor that proper governance of the realm had to begin with the governance of his household, and then offered instructions on how this was to be accomplished:

---

62. On the growing popularity of Cheng learning in the Southern Song, see James Liu, "A Neo-Confucian School"; Ebrey, "Women, Money, and Class." Hilde De Weerdt has shown that at least some of the appeal of Cheng Learning in the twelfth century stemmed from the success of its teachers in producing examination graduates (*Competition over Content*).

63. Lü Zuqian, *Shao yi wai zhuan, xia*, 1a–b.

64. According to the anecdotalist Luo Dajing, Zhu Xi also once wrote a poem entitled "A Warning to Myself" ("Zi Jing" 自警), which remarked on the failure of the earlier Confucian master Hu Yuan to rid himself of desire for his household concubine and included the line, "In the world there is nothing more dangerous than human desires; how many have had their lives ruined by this?!" (世上無如人欲險, 幾人到此誤平生) (Luo Dajing, *Helin yu lu, yi bian*, 6.229–30). This suggests that Zhu recognized that desire for concubines could present a moral challenge, but he never expounded on this issue. The editors of the *Si ku quan shu* observe that the poem is not be found in Zhu Xi's collected works, and surmise that someone expunged it after seeing Luo's comment (Yong Rong, *Qin ding Si ku quan shu zong mu*, 158.8b).

I have heard that the basis of All-under-Heaven is in the kingdom, and the basis of the kingdom is in the family. If the family of the ruler is regulated, there is nothing under Heaven that will be ungoverned; if the family of the ruler is unregulated, there is none who will be able to govern All-under-Heaven. This is why the flourishing of the Three Ages, the ability of sage and virtuous rulers to cultivate their government, all originated in regulating the family. Now, men's proper position is outside, and women's proper position is inside; when distinctions between male and female are strict, the family will be regulated. When the wife shares her husband's position above and concubines serve them below, and the distinctions between principal (*di*) and lesser (*shu*) are established, the family will be regulated.

Thus far, Zhu Xi sounds much like Cheng Yi. But he goes on:

Select the virtuous, restrict music and sex, stay close to the serious and respectful, distance yourself from the clever, and the family will be regulated. When inner words do not go out and outer words do not enter, when presents of food are not extended and requests for favors are not solicited, the family is regulated. Now, within the inner quarters, favor frequently overcomes righteousness; this is because even men with the talents of heroes are often stymied by liquor and sex, drown in emotions and love, and cannot control themselves. If one does not correct his heart and cultivate his body, originate his actions in ritual and righteousness, and make sure that others accord with his righteousness and fear his majesty, then how can the back palace be regulated, the requests be blocked, the imperial relatives controlled, and the sprouts of disaster be prevented?[65]

Zhu Xi follows Cheng Yi in insisting on the importance of proper maintenance of hierarchy in the family. Yet where Cheng Yi had argued that (at least with respect to concubines) the maintenance of hierarchy was women's responsibility (and dependent on their moral behavior), Zhu Xi here acknowledges that men are vulnerable to sexual desires, and that their affection for the objects of their desire can undermine proper household hierarchies. His solution is that men must "correct [their] hearts and cultivate [their] bodies."[66] Still, Zhu Xi was addressing the emperor, not his peers, and neither he nor other scholars associated with Cheng Learning portray concubines as a major source of danger to Song families.

---

65. *Zhu Xi ji* 12.489–500 (quoted passage, 491–92).

66. Zhu Xi's oeuvre does contain other remarks on the power of sexual desire to undermine men's moral will, e.g., *Zhuzi yu lei* 72.1815, where in a discussion of "stimulus-response" (*gan ying* 感應) he reiterates a Northern Song anecdote about the Grand Councilor Wang Dan, who became more extravagant after the emperor presented him with two charmer-concubines (*ji qie* 姬妾).

Indeed, the only indication that Cheng Learning adherents harbored concerns about desire for concubines (and then only indirectly) was in their reiteration of the idea that truly moral men would not keep concubines, or would be oblivious to those they had. This idea was an old one, and in the Northern Song it had not been particularly associated with the Cheng brothers' teachings. But in the Southern Song it appears frequently, though not exclusively, in the work of men associated with the Cheng Learning movement. Yang Shi (1053–1135), writing in the early twelfth century, observed of the literatus Zhang Fu (1045–1106): "Throughout his life, milord had no fondness for female entertainers or precious and rare objects; he only read books by the thousands, annotating and collating until they were covered with his markings."[67] Zhu Xi praised the general Zhang Jun 張浚 for not setting up a concubine in his entire life, and the official Fu Zide for refusing to accept a concubine from a well-meaning admirer.[68] Liu Zai praised the "old-style virtue" of Lu Jun (1155–1216), who told his friend that "'ritual begins with care in the relationship between husband and wife,'" and who throughout his life didn't approach even his own concubines. Liu Kezhuang marveled that Ao Taosun and his wife cooked their own meals rather than keep concubines.[69]

Still, however much they admired men who did not keep concubines, neither Zhu Xi nor any of his compatriots went so far as to suggest that concubinage as an institution should be done away with. On the contrary, the Confucian imperative for the production of descendants provided an unquestionable (and unquestioned) moral legitimacy to the practice. Zhu Xi, in fact, went so far as to proffer a new, cosmological justification for the right of a man to marry more than one woman, while reiterating that a woman could have only one husband. A student had queried this point, citing the Northern Song thinker Zhang Zai 張載 (1020–77), who (like Cheng Yi) had argued that according to [Heavenly] Principle men should take only one wife, and that second (successor) wives were

---

67. Yang Shi, *Guishan ji* 35.4b. Internal evidence shows this text was composed no earlier than 1128.
68. *Zhu Xi ji*, 95 xia, 4900, 98.5011. Zhu Xi also praised Hu Anguo for refusing to buy a concubine (*Yi luo yuan yuan lu* 13.12).
69. Liu Zai, *Man tang ji* 28.25b; Liu Kezhuang, *Hou cun ji* 37.15b. Other Southern Song references praising men for not keeping concubines include Liu Yizhi, *Tiaoxi ji* 49.22b; Wei Liaoweng, *Heshan ji* 73.25b; and Wu Yong, *Helin ji* 35.20.

permitted only as a matter of practical necessity. (Zhang had argued that, accordingly, only the first principal wife should receive sacrifices.) Zhu responded that Zhang Zai had gone too far, and argued that "the righteousness between husband and wife is like the greatness of [the hexagram] *Qian* and the completeness of [the hexagram] *Kun*; of itself it is hierarchical. Thus while they are alive, the husband is allowed to have wives *and concubines*, but as [her husband is] the wife's Heaven, there cannot be two [husbands]" (emphasis added). This passage is notable not only as an explicit justification of concubinage as well as male remarriage, but also because in the process Zhu conflates the status of wives and concubines—a point I shall return to below.[70]

By the thirteenth century, the rather self-contradictory position that a man had every right to take a concubine, but that eschewing concubinage was morally admirable, had given rise to a new model of the virtuous married couple. In this new model, the virtuous wife's lack of jealousy was matched by her husband's lack of desire for other women. Yuan Xie 袁燮 (1144–1224), an official and disciple of the Cheng Learning scholar Lu Jiuyuan, related in 1219 that he was shocked to find his friend Jiang Ruhui serving in office with only his son to attend him, and no one to manage the cooking or clothing. Since Jiang had been reared in an eminent family and was certainly not used to living like a poor scholar, Yuan was perplexed. In response to his queries, Jiang explained,

> My wife did not come [with me] because she was afraid of the distance. Accordingly, she once selected a serving maid (*bi*) to attend me in her stead. But my understanding is that anciently, when the wife was not present, concubines (*qie yu* 妾御) did not dare to spend the night. This is written in the ritual classics. For this reason I did not bring the concubine with me.

Yuan comments:

> For a woman to be without jealousy, for a man to be without desire: since ancient times this has been difficult. Now milord's wife has chosen a concubine (*qie ying* 妾媵) to serve him—clearly she is without jealousy. Milord himself is calm and self-composed, untroubled by desire, austere like an ascetic of the wilderness. They can be called a true husband and wife: how far beyond vulgar custom they are![71]

---

70. *Zhu Xi ji* 62.3253–54.
71. Yuan Xie 袁燮, *Jie zhai ji* 絜齋集 21.347. Yuan Xie represented his grandparents as a similarly virtuous couple, with the grandmother wanting to set up a concubine and the grandfather refusing (*Jie zhai ji* 17.279–81).

In similar terms, Lou Yue later described Heaven's recompense for such virtue: after the childless Shi Jun (1129–1203) refused his wife's suggestion that he set up a concubine, the couple was blessed with a son.[72]

Southern Song philosophers tended to be oblique in addressing the issue of desire for concubines, but they were in contrast quite vociferous in expressing concerns about the ritual recognition of concubines in the family context. In the work of Zhu Xi, in particular, support for the superior hierarchical position of the principal wife—so adamantly asserted by Northern Song moralists—began to be undercut by new insistence on the ritual recognition of concubine mothers.

Here again, Zhu Xi's position seems to have reflected, rather than instigated, broader social trends. General sentiment favoring the recognition of concubine mothers had increased even in the Northern Song, as evident in the court's willingness to grant them titles of enfeoffment. This trend expanded in the Southern Song. In 1153, for example, Emperor Gaozong approved a number of honors for family members of the deceased Zhao Shiniao, who had once helped save him from a coup. Among these honors (requested by Shiniao's son) were enfeoffments for the concubine mothers of five of Shiniao's daughters.[73] The demand for enfeoffment of concubines was sufficiently persistent that by 1175 the court began to worry that the practice had gotten out of hand. In the eleventh month of that year, Emperor Xiaozong had consented to bestow a title of nobility on the birth mother of the imperial clansman Zhao Buqu; but a month later, when asked to approve a stipend for her as an "imperial clan wife of fifth mourning grade, level three," the emperor demurred. Exclaiming, "The stipend is not worth worrying about, but how can status distinctions be confused?" he ordered the attending officials to make a note of his decision to stand as a precedent for later cases.[74]

The widespread desire to enfeoff concubines—and not just concubine mothers—was observed with disdain by Zhou Hui, who first related a story of an upright Tang official who refused the emperor's

---

72. Lou Yue, *Gong kui ji* 105.1485.
73. *SHY, di xi*, 6.22a. On the attempted coup against Gaozong and Shiniao's role therein, see Chaffee, *Branches of Heaven*, 132–33.
74. *SHY, di xi*, 2.49a.

offer to enfeoff his concubine. Zhou then remarked sarcastically, "Today gentlemen and officials indulge in emotion and love intimately, hating the fact that they don't have the ability to raise [their concubines] to the level of their superiors: would they be willing to refuse an imperial command?"[75] Like Xiaozong, Zhou recognized that awarding ranks to concubines undercut the hierarchies that distinguished concubines from wives. The same concern also seems to have informed the court's rejection of a proposal by the minister Zhang Xiaoxiang (1132–70) that the court could easily increase its revenues by selling noble titles to wives, daughters, and concubines in the families of the nobility and officials.[76] The court dismissed Zhang's proposal on the grounds that selling titles would unnecessarily tempt women and undermine sumptuary regulations.[77] Still, although the state's refusal to implement Zhang's proposal reveals its awareness of the conflicts between recognizing concubines and preserving the status of wives, the proposal itself bespeaks a remarkable shift from the early Northern Song, when Yin Zhu had proposed that the court could earn money by selling the right to purchase concubines themselves.[78] The shift dramatically illustrates the increasingly legitimized position of concubines, both as mothers and as consorts.

Zhu Xi, too, struggled with a desire to preserve the ritual superiority of the principal wife, on the one hand, and his own conviction that concubines who were mothers of descendants should also be honored, on the other. Zhu seems to have acquiesced in Cheng Yi's insistence that only a man's first legal wife could receive sacrifices in the family temple, but he was also at pains to identify proper rituals for the recognition of ancestresses who were not first legal wives (in other words, both successor

---

75. Zhou Hui, *Qing bo za zhi* 5.212.

76. Zhang Xiaoxiang in *QSW* 253: 5693.345. In the same proposal, Zhang advocated that enfeoffments also be sold to mothers, wives, and daughters in commoner families.

77. Zhang's initiative was inspired by an effort to reduce the sale of monks' certificates to earn revenue, and he pointed out that unlike selling ordination certificates, sales of titles for concubines would not harm population growth. On the rejection of Zhang's proposal, see Zhou Hui, *Qing bo za zhi* 7.312–13. Zhou Hui implies that the proposal was tendered in the Chunxi period (1174–89), but it must have been earlier, as Zhang Xiaoxiang died in 1170.

78. See chap. 2.

wives and concubines).⁷⁹ He fretted over inconsistencies in the classical texts with respect to sacrifices for concubine ancestresses.⁸⁰ When asked how a concubine's grandson offering a sacrifice should refer to her, he hedged, saying that he didn't know if such sacrifices were appropriate; but he then contradicted his uncertainty by concluding that if one were to offer a sacrifice one should "without a doubt" refer to the ancestress as "grandmother," and oneself as "grandson."⁸¹

Where mothers (as opposed to more distant ancestresses) were concerned, Zhu was far more definitive, and here his pronouncements uniformly upheld the full recognition of concubines. He insisted that a concubine's son should address his mother simply as "mother," and not as "concubine mother" (*shu mu* 庶母). He instructs a student that the latter term should be used only for a father's concubine who has borne sons other than oneself, and he allows that for such a woman one wears only the lowest grade of mourning. But where one's own birth mother is concerned, "one doesn't ask whether she is father's wife or father's concubine; in either case she takes the name of 'mother.'" Even in the case of titles and enfeoffments, one refers to her as birth mother (*suo sheng mu* 所生母), not as concubine mother.⁸² Similarly, and significantly, Zhu also wished to clarify the distinction between an "expelled" (*chu* 出) birth mother, to whom a son did not owe mourning, and a mother who had simply been "married out" (*jia* 嫁), to whom a son did owe mourning. Zhu seems to limit the term "expelled" to apply only to

---

79. *Zhu Xi ji* 30.1285–86, 43.2009, 62.3253–54. For further discussion of the ritual status of concubines and Zhu Xi's interest therein, see Ebrey, "Concubines in Song China," 3–5, and her *Confucianism and Family Rituals*, 125–35.

80. *Zhu Xi ji* 51.2546–47, 59.3029. The ritual texts at one point stated that worship of a concubine did not extend past her sons' generation, but elsewhere indicated that a concubine's tablet should be placed with that of concubine grandmothers, implicitly suggesting that concubine grandmothers should be worshipped.

81. *Zhu Xi ji* 59.3029. Ebrey, "Concubines in Song China," 3–4.

82. *Zhu Xi ji* 55.2773, "Da Li Shou-yue" 答李守約. The implication of this passage is that a concubine's son should mourn his birth mother for the full three years due a parent, though this is not explicitly stated. (Elsewhere Zhu suggests that "mourning in the heart" is appropriate for a birth mother; see Li Guangdi 李光地, *Zhuzi li zuan* 朱子禮纂, 3.6a). At the end of the passage, Zhu tells his interlocutor that it would probably not be appropriate for a family heir to worship his *father's* concubine birth mother, but he says he needs to do further research on the issue.

those women whose departure from the family was occasioned by one of the "seven grounds" for divorce, ensuring that most concubines who left a household would fall into the category of "married out" rather than "expelled."[83]

Despite all his efforts, however, Zhu Xi was unable to establish with canonical certainty rules for all of the practical questions his students brought to him.[84] More to the point, the frequency with which students asked their questions reveals that in the late twelfth century there was still considerable disagreement about how much honor and sustenance a son owed to his father's concubines, in life as well as death.[85] Still, as others have pointed out, the general tenor of Zhu Xi's pronouncements on concubine mothers was to strengthen their place as members of the ritual family.[86] Other sources of the late Southern Song suggest that in this, too, Zhu Xi was in sync with broader social trends.

## *Normative Shifts in the Late Southern Song*

That concubines were beginning to have a new place in families in the late Southern Song is most clearly evident in funerary inscriptions, the genre in which Song men wrote in greatest detail—and in most idealized terms—about family life. Precisely because funerary inscriptions present an idealized view of their subjects, the increased attention they give to

---

83. *Zhu Xi ji* 84.4356–57. The "seven [grounds for] expulsion" were failure to produce a male heir, adultery, disrespect to parents-in-law, quarrelsomeness, stealing, jealousy, and vile disease. In this passage Zhu does suggest that the son of a married-out mother should not take her back into his household, though if she has no other family to go to he can set her up and support her in a separate residence. Zhu's position here is succinctly summarized by his follower Huang Zhen: "A married-out mother is not an expelled mother; you cannot not mourn her. To support her, set up a small building outside" (Huang Zhen, *Huang shi ri chao*, 36.20a).

84. *Zhu Xi ji* 63.3310.

85. Patricia Ebrey notes that a late Song encyclopedia says a man should mourn a concubine mother only at grade 5, while a late twelfth century law code allowed a man to order his sons to mourn any of his concubines as a legal mother ("Concubines in Song China," 4–5). Legal cases likewise reveal that both families and courts were unsure about their obligations to support concubines of a deceased family head. See *QMJ* 4.115, 7.232.

86. Katkov, "The Domestication of Concubinage," 102; Ebrey, "Concubines in Song China," 5.

concubines bespeaks the development of new social norms, norms that worked to ameliorate the disruption that concubines could cause in families by highlighting their role as family members.[87] This development was gradual, and did not reach its full flowering until the Yuan dynasty, but from at least the thirteenth century funerary inscriptions began to emphasize the respect due to concubines by other family members and increasingly insisted that concubines' children should be treated equally with those of wives. The shift in the rhetoric of funerary inscriptions was consonant with Southern Song legal judgments concerning the familial rights of concubines and their children, and both fed into the increasingly patrilineal orientation of Southern Song households.

We have seen that Northern Song writers of funerary inscriptions sometimes praised their subjects for filiality to concubine mothers, but in the Southern Song treating a concubine mother well came to be a standard element in accounts of virtuous male behavior.[88] Early on, Sun Di praised Zhu Zong (d. 1140) for never leaving the side of his birth mother throughout his career and retirement, noting that she was utterly bereft when he predeceased her.[89] Zhang Shi described how his cousin led his wife and children to serve his birth mother, fully meeting all her expectations; he also highlighted Xiang Shen's (1108–71) efforts to get a posthumous title for his birth mother Li, noting that onlookers found it particularly heartbreaking that Xiang died before achieving his goal.[90] As the Southern Song progressed, references to men serving their concubine birth mothers with "utmost respect" (*jin jing* 盡敬) or "filial care" (*xiao jin* 孝謹) or "particular care" (*wei jin* 惟謹) became nearly conventional.[91] Inscription writers also paid more attention to how men

---

87. An earlier version of the following discussion, in Chinese, appears in Bossler, "Song-Yuan mu zhi."

88. As noted in chap. 2, apart from exemplar texts for men who sought out expelled mothers, I have found only one Northern Song reference praising a man for serving his concubine mother (though there are many late Northern Song references to men *mourning* their birth mothers).

89. Sun Di, *Hong qing ju shi ji* 33.5.

90. Zhang Shi, *Nanxuan ji* 39.5b, 39.14b. Note that while enfoeffing concubine mothers was admired as an act of filial piety, enfeoffing a concubine-consort was regarded as unseemly at best. See Zhou Hui, *Qing bo za zhi* 5.212.

91. Zhou Bida, *Wenzhong ji* 32.15a; Lu You, *Weinan wen ji* 36.225; Wei Liaoweng, *Heshan ji* 84.11b.

mourned their birth mothers. Cheng Ju (1078–1144) commended the imperial kinsman Zhao Zizhou (1089–1142) for performing three years of mourning "in his heart" (*xin sang* 心喪) for his birth mother. A few decades later, Zhou Bida praised Song Ying for interrupting his career to mourn "in his heart" his birth mother, whom Zhou designated by name and title. Liu Kezhuang likewise highlighted the fact that Chen Su refused an official appointment because he was "mourning in his heart" for his birth mother, Respected Lady (*gong ren* 恭人) Wu. Liu recalled that, after the death of Chen's principal mother, he had served Wu as if she were his principal mother.[92] Finally, particularly in late Song texts, we also see increasing references to women serving the concubine mothers of their husbands. Liu Kezhuang tells us that since her husband's legal parents had died, Madame Zhao served her husband's birth mother with great care; Wen Tianxiang describes how at age seventy-six Madame Luo was still serving her husband's birth mother, who in 1273 was one hundred *sui*.[93]

These references to filial treatment of concubine mothers echo late Northern Song political concerns about proper mourning of birth mothers, and, as in the late Northern Song, stories about men who sought out and located birth mothers who had left the family also continued to be featured in funerary inscriptions and other writings. Several authors recounted how Li Zongzhi's (d. 1184) father died when he was only eight *sui*, and his birth mother née Zhan shortly thereafter left the family. In the chaos of the fall of the Northern Song, the family had been scattered, and Zongzhi ended up in Sichuan reared by a lineage aunt. Eventually, he was able to reunite with a married elder sister in the capital, and there he miraculously encountered his mother. Lou Yue, in his funerary inscription for Zongzhi, says that people saw their reunion after more than ten years' separation as a Heavenly response to Zongzhi's filiality (*xiao gan* 孝感). Yang Wanli, in a biography (*zhuan* 傳) he wrote for Li, elaborated the story greatly, recounting that Li had searched high and low, shouting "Mother Zhan, Mother Zhan" from the mountaintops in his efforts

---

92. Cheng Ju, *Beishan ji* 北山集, 33.21b; Zhou Bida, *Wenzhong ji* 31.5b; Liu Kezhuang, *Hou cun ji* 39.6b–7. Zhang Shi also mentioned that his cousin interrupted his career to mourn his birth mother (*Nanxuan ji* 39.2).

93. Liu Kezhuang, *Hou cun ji* 39.21b; Wen Tianxiang, *Wenshan ji* 16.21b–23.

to locate her.⁹⁴ In a funerary text for Li Qishou (d. 1230, no relation to Zongzhi) Wei Liaoweng described how Qishou had been reared by his principal mother, and was only told upon her death that in fact he had been born of a concubine. When, after ten years of searching, Qishou located his birth mother, he brought her home in a special carriage, her relatives following behind: passersby were moved to tears. Wei remarks that scholars and officials celebrated the event in poetry, filling an entire volume.⁹⁵ Although among funerary inscriptions in general such stories were hardly common, seeking out a birth mother clearly continued to be a dramatic and admirable expression of filial piety. At the same time these stories reveal that the expulsion of concubines, even those who had borne sons, continued to be common in the Southern Song.

Attention to the treatment of concubines by family members other than their sons also seems to have increased in the mid- to late Southern Song. I have already described how short stories posited supernatural retribution to people who treated concubines badly; it was perhaps just such concerns that led Li Shi 李石 (1108–after 1176) to compose a contrite sacrificial ode to a woman he says served his family for more than twenty-four years, sharing his joys and sorrows from the time he was still a commoner. Li makes excuses to the concubine's spirit for not having found a spouse for her, assures her that they have set up an heir, and promises that she will receive sacrifices in perpetuity in recognition of her righteousness.⁹⁶ Eulogists also began to praise men for taking care of other families' concubines. Liu Zai stressed that Sun Su (1169–1234) not only took in the seventy-year-old birth mother of his cousin, he also had her eat with the rest of the family, without distinction. Liu

---

94. Lou Yue, in *QSW* 266: 5995.30–33; Yang Wanli, *Cheng zhai ji* 117.10a–12a.

95. Wei Liaoweng, *Heshan ji* 79.20b ff. Note that Lou Yue also suggests that, although Li Zongzhi was born to a prosperous family, his life was adversely affected by the fact that he was an "orphan" (that is, his father had died) and the son of a concubine (*gu bi* 孤孼). The Ming author Huang Zongxi reported that the late Song figure Zou Jinren in middle age located his birth mother after an extensive search, only to have her refuse to return home with him. Zou reportedly remembered his mother from the time she left when he was three until his principal mother's death some thirty-five years later. Nonplussed when she wouldn't return home with him, he asked his teacher Yang Jian what to do; Yang's advice was that it would be sufficient to visit her at seasonal festivals (Huang Zongxi, *Song Yuan xue an* 74.2494).

96. Li Shi, *Fang zhou ji* 18.33a–b.

characterizes this as an extraordinary act of charity, noting that contemporaries considered Sun's action "extremely difficult."[97]

New attention to the position of concubines in families extended to their children as well. Southern Song funerary inscriptions not only highlight wives who were loving to their concubine-born stepsons, they stress how men were generous to their half-brothers. The idea that women should treat their stepchildren well certainly long predated the Song, but in the majority of Northern Song funerary inscriptions, the stepchild is described as the child of a prior principal wife.[98] In the Southern Song, explicit and detailed references to women's relationships with *concubines'* children multiply. In a "mourning record" Hu Yin composed at his wife's death in 1137, he noted that she early on foretold that she herself would bear him only one son, and urged him to treat his concubines' children well. He recalled that when later a concubine's son became dangerously ill, she watched over the child tearfully, employing every possible method to save him; when the boy finally recovered, she was beside herself with joy.[99] Sun Di relates that an empress on a visit home was impressed by her sister-in-law (d. 1139), who embraced the children of concubines in the same manner as she embraced her own. Lü Zuqian reverses the phrase, praising the woman Guo (d. 1170) for treating her own children just as she treated the children of concubines (*qie ying suo chu*).[100] Yao Mian waxed rhapsodic about the extraordinary virtue of Mother Ge (Ge *mu* 葛母), who reared one son who was adopted from an elder sister, and another who was the child of a concubine. Yao observes, "There are many tenderhearted mothers, but only when one is tenderhearted toward children

---

97. Liu Zai, *Man tang ji* 31.32b.
98. I have found only two Northern Song funerary inscriptions that refer explicitly to a woman rearing the children of concubines: Huang Tingjian tells us that the woman Jin (d. 1095) treated her husband's concubines (*ji qie*) like sisters-in-law, and reared the various sons (*zhu zi* 諸子) as if they were her own (*Huang Tingjian quan ji, wai ji*, 22.1395). Ouyang Xiu mentions that the woman Murong reared her sons "without regard to *di* and *shu*" (*Ouyang Xiu quan ji* 37.549–50). Wong Yu-Hsuan cites an early ninth-century example of similar rhetoric ("Tōdai," 132).
99. Hu Yin, *Fei ran ji* 20.412–13.
100. Sun Di, *Hong qing ju shi ji* 40.2b; Lü Zuqian, *Donglai ji* 10.12b.

she has not borne herself is tenderheartedness truly manifest."[101] Many other examples could be cited.[102]

More strikingly, in the Southern Song we begin to see for the first time references to men treating their lesser or half-brothers (*shu di* 庶弟) well. An early such reference appears in an inscription composed in 1170 by Zhou Bida. Here we are told simply that even though the subject's father died, his lesser younger brothers and his various younger sisters were all married at the proper time.[103] Without dwelling on the issue, Zhou wishes us to understand that the subject endowed his half-brothers and sisters with sufficient resources that they could make proper marriages. Ye Shi similarly mentions that his subject reared his half-brothers with friendliness and love.[104]

Even as funerary inscriptions began to emphasize generous treatment of concubines' children, however, they also frequently reveal that such children did not receive the same treatment as children of wives. For example, we learn from a funerary inscription for Zhou Bizheng (1125–1205) that some time in the mid- to late twelfth century a concubine of Bizheng's elder brother was dismissed, and the child she had borne drifted into the neighboring prefecture. Bizheng is praised for retrieving the lad and providing him with property, but the house he built for his nephew was not in the Zhous' home county of Luling but in a neighboring county. Not only was the concubine's son not treated as descendant of the household during his youth, even as an adult he does not seem to have been considered a full-fledged member of the family. In a similar vein, Chen Liang recounts his own efforts to retrieve a lost half-brother (d. 1187) who had been born to his father's maid and adopted out to another family when barely four months old.[105] Other inscriptions reinforce the impression that

---

101. Yao Mian, *Xue po ji* 50.14a–b. Yao Mian also emphasizes the extraordinary filiality of the two sons, who were able to be filial to a woman who had not borne them.

102. For similar references, see Liu Yizhi, *Tiaoxi ji* 51.13; Huang Gan, *Mian zhai ji* 38.48b; Yao Mian, *Xue po ji* 50.8a. See also Lin Guangchao, *Ai xuan ji* 9.21b–22a for a description of a woman nurturing a blind daughter born to a concubine.

103. Zhou Bida, *Wenzhong ji* 32.3a. The only earlier Song inscription reference to *shu di* concerns a legal case adjudicated by the subject of the inscription, as described below.

104. *Ye Shi ji* 23.449.

105. Lu You, *Weinan wen ji* 38.238; *Chen Liang ji* 28.414–15. In a similar vein, Lou Yue recounts how one Shi Wen (the husband of Yue's distant cousin) was reared by his

sons of concubines were far more likely than the sons of the principal wife to be adopted out of their natal descent lines. Guo Shuyi (1155–1233) was his father's second son, born to a concubine; he was selected to be the heir of his father's younger brother, who had no sons of his own.[106]

Funerary inscriptions also reveal that concubines' children were especially vulnerable because they were often a full generation or more younger than their half-siblings, and frequently still in infancy when their fathers died.[107] Given the importance to Chinese families of established heirs to the descent line, concubines' sons who were the sole heirs of their fathers were almost certainly welcomed and recognized as heirs. Thus Yao Mian explains that when, after the death of his first wife and her child, his concubine gave birth to a son, he reported the birth in the family temple and thereby formally legitimized the boy (*li er di zhi* 立而嫡之). But in families with many sons, and especially in families where the patrimony was not extensive, the position of a concubine's children could be precarious, to say the least—all the more so when their mother's place in the family was temporary. Yao Mian himself found it extraordinary that his second wife was willing to give up her firstborn son to be heir to Yao Mian's childless older brother and rear the concubine's son as her own instead.[108] More typical, it seems, was the attitude of four Wang family brothers, who, when their father took a concubine late in life, worried that she would become pregnant and their already small patrimony have to be split still further.[109]

Still, even as funerary inscriptions show that the children of concubines were often not treated as the equals of their principal-wife siblings,

---

concubine mother after losing his father when less than a year old. Yue stresses that the two lived in poverty and distress, despite the fact that the Shi descent group as a whole was "exceedingly prosperous" (*zui sheng* 最盛) (*Gong kui ji* 105.1489–90).

106. Wei Liaoweng, *Heshan ji* 83.9b. By the same logic, it seems plausible that concubine daughters were more likely than their half-sisters to be married off as concubines themselves, but specific evidence is lacking.

107. For example, Lu You was sixty-one when his infant daughter died (*Weinan wen ji* 33.207); Lou Yue's maternal uncle Wang Dading (d. 1198) was born in his father's sixtieth year: though they were uncle and nephew he and Lou Yue were born the same year and grew up together in their maternal grandfather's house (Lou Yue, *Gong kui ji* 103.1457–61).

108. Yao Mian, *Xue po ji* 50.9b–11b.

109. Wang Yishan, *Jia cun lei gao* 29.13b.

other sources suggest that the moral message of equality was being asserted with greater insistence as the Song wore on. More importantly, this shift was associated with new ideas about the relative importance of maternity and paternity. This is especially evident in legal cases. In the cases preserved in the *Enlightened Judgments,* judges routinely upheld the rights of concubines' children as heirs in their fathers' estates.[110] Accordingly, when one man died sonless, the state set up a new heir, but also allotted a share of property to the man's daughter by a maid (*bi*). The birth mother was ordered to rear the daughter until marriage, when she would receive cash, paper currency, and silver that the court held in escrow for her.[111] In a case where a concubine mother sued her deceased husband's kinsman, the judge first made a point of explicitly rejecting the kinsman's argument that the mother's status as concubine disqualified her suit. The judge did make a modest allotment of property for the kinsman, but he also continued a small stipend that the concubine's father had been receiving from her master, and he put the concubine herself in charge of handling the rents and income from the husband's estate (to be used to rear her children). Finally, he also put the estate's movable property into escrow for her children to inherit when they reached their majority.[112] In a third case, even when a servant (*bi*) remarried and took her daughter away with her after her master's death, the daughter was awarded a share of her natural father's estate.[113] Finally, a much-disputed case recorded by the activist Learning of the Way judge

---

110. In addition to the examples cited below, see *QMJ* 8.251–57.

111. *QMJ* 7.230–32; McKnight and Liu, *Enlightened Judgments,* 256–58.

112. *QMJ* 7.232–33; McKnight and Liu, *Enlightened Judgments,* 259–62; see also Birge, *Women, Property, and Confucian Reaction,* 96, n. 2. McKnight and Liu stress the fact that the movable property is to be held in trust for the two "daughters" when they come of age, not when they are married, but in fact the text nowhere specifies the sex of the children, consistently referring to them as "young ones" (*yu* 幼). It seems to me just as likely that the children were boys, especially as no mention is made of the need to establish an heir.

113. *QMJ* 7.238–39 (McKnight and Liu, *Enlightened Judgments,* 265–67). In this case, the property was split between the daughter and a posthumously appointed heir. McKnight and Liu note that the daughter did not receive as large a share as the law would generally have awarded her; they speculate that this was because her mother was merely a maid, but they also cite the possibility that it was because she was no longer living "at home" with her father's kinsmen (*Enlightened Judgments,* 532, n. 146).

Huang Gan articulated the principle that not only a father's estate but even the personal property of the principal mother should be divided equally among all sons, regardless of maternity.[114] In short, especially where the father's estate was concerned, judges unequivocally supported the rights of concubine's children to property shares equal to those of their principal siblings.[115]

At the same time, however, judges' compassion for concubines' children was conspicuously restricted to those children whose paternity was explicitly acknowledged during their fathers' lifetimes. We saw above that in two cases where men claimed to be natural sons, the judges rejected the claims even while conceding that the plaintiffs' mothers had been concubines in the households of the putative fathers. One of those judges even claimed that a statute forbade courts to rule on cases where a son was reared outside his father's home and could supply no proof of paternity after the father's death; he also stressed that a father could not be forced to recognize a natural son if he chose not to.[116] Further insight into contemporary thinking on this issue is found in a

---

114. *QMJ, fu lu*, 2.606–8. For an extended discussion of this case, see Birge, *Women, Property, and Confucian Reaction*, 194–96. The son of the principal mother had originally divided his father's property equally with his two half-brothers, but kept his mother's (considerable) property for himself. A series of lawsuits had led to a variety of judgments, some upholding the principal son's right to monopolize his mother's property, some holding that the concubine's sons should receive a lesser share of that property, and still others holding that the principal mother's property should be divided equally. Huang Gan argues emphatically that all the sons were equally sons of the principal mother (though in the end he upholds the previous judgment in the case, which was to give one half of the mother's property to the heirs of the son she bore, and the other half to be split between the two "lesser" sons). On p. 198 Birge points out that Huang Gan sees the wife's property as belonging to her husband's children (that is, it is no longer her own), and ties this attitude to his views on the unacceptability of widow remarriage.

115. For another example, see the case described by Zhen Dexiu, in which a landlord sued his tenant for nonpayment of rent. When the two men appeared in court, the judge noticed a resemblance between them, and ultimately determined that the tenant was actually the landlord's half-brother. The judge ordered that the tenant return to his original occupation and that the family property be split evenly between the two men (Zhen Dexiu, *Xishan wen ji* 42.26). Inheritance rights did, however, differ by sex; that is, daughters inherited less than sons. For a thorough discussion of women's property rights in the Song, see Birge, *Women, Property, and Confucian Reaction*, passim.

116. *QMJ* 8.292–94 (McKnight and Liu, *Enlightened Judgments*, 303–5).

third case involving similar circumstances. This judge, too, acknowledged that the mother of the plaintiff, Dong Three-Eight, had been a maidservant in the household of Assistant Magistrate Han before being married off to Dong Two-Three. But the judge ruled against Dong's paternity claim on the grounds that, as an educated man who "understood ritual and righteousness," Han would certainly have known that "the son of a favored concubine would be a 'dragon born in a snake's belly.' How could he bear to cast him off in a vegetable-seller's family, letting the years pass without taking him in? Why would he neglect his own posterity in this way?" He adds that if indeed Dong's mother had been pregnant when she had left Han's household and had borne a child within a few months thereafter, she should have gone back to Han's household; if Han's wife had not permitted that, she should have gone to the authorities to establish proof. The judge concluded that since twenty-seven years had passed without a lawsuit and since during that time Han himself had made no move to acknowledge an outside son, the claim was undoubtedly false. He ordered that Dong Two-Three and his mother each be beaten eighty strokes.[117]

The insistence of late Song judges on explicit demonstration of paternity stands in striking contrast to their willingness to accept as legitimate mothers women of *any* status. For although Song judges clearly acknowledged the important status distinctions between principal wives, concubines, and serving maids, they treated all of them as legitimate mothers. In one judgment, Liu Kezhuang even rebukes a concubine (*ce shi*) for thinking that her child had greater rights to family property than the children of a serving maid (*shi nü*).[118]

In other words, by the late Southern Song, in law and increasingly in custom, maternity (that is, whether a son was born to the principal mother, a concubine, or a maid) was irrelevant to legitimacy, but paternal recognition was increasingly essential. By helping to make all children equal as descendants of the father, this attitude presumably helped reduce some of the conflicts engendered by the widespread presence of concubines in Southern Song households. At the same time, it

---

117. *QMJ* 7.239–41.
118. *QMJ* 8.251–57; see also the discussions of this case in Birge, *Women, Property, and Confucian Reaction*, 224; and Lau Napyin, "Songdai nü'er," 189–90.

contributed to the increasingly patrilineal orientation of those households, by rendering the mother and her relatives less relevant to a child's place in the patriline.

## *Conclusion*

Over the course of the Southern Song, the increasing presence of concubines, especially entertainer-concubines, in the families of the expanded elite gave rise to new types of family and societal conflicts. The widespread presence of non-upper class women as consorts and mothers in literati households further eroded the already crumbling status differences between masters and servitors, respectable persons and dishonorable persons. The flourishing markets in women were a constant threat to upper-class women who, through a father's early death or a political calamity, could find themselves reduced to servitude themselves. Wives, meanwhile, found it more difficult to maintain their authority in the household over women whose social inferiority was increasingly understood to be mostly a matter of luck.

By late in the Southern Song, these problems were beginning to be addressed in new efforts to legitimize the roles of concubines and their children in the family. Drawing on a wider social consensus, moral philosophers acknowledged the full personhood of maids and concubines by insisting that they receive ritual recognition as mothers of sons. Writers of funerary inscriptions gave increasing acknowledgment to concubines as mothers and praised men for treating their concubine-born siblings well. Judges repeatedly upheld the principle that concubines' sons were full coparceners in their fathers' estates. Treating concubines as mothers in this way served as something of an antidote to the rampant commodification of women that the spread of concubinage had engendered in Song society; for insisting that a concubine's role was that of family member served to deny, or at least obscure, that she was subject to being bought and sold. Still, even as distinctions between wives and concubines were dissolving inside the home, the fraught political context of the Southern Song was also creating new concerns about men's loyalty and women's virtue. Together, these forces helped to intensify a discourse that highlighted the particular loyalty of literati wives.

# 6

## Loss, Loyalty, and Local Leverage

### Madame He 何夫人

Since the end of the Xuanhe period (ca. 1125), the northern kingdom had its eye on the central plains; in the year 1129, their soldiers came from east of the river into the eastern Zhe area. In the second month of the following year, they marched through the southeast prefectures of Ming, Yue, Hang, and Xiu to Suzhou, and then returned. The officials said they would defend the city resolutely, and the people were calm. But when the enemy approached the city the officials all left in the night; more than 500,000 people died. At that time the Suzhou resident Wu Yongnian took his mother and fled; his widowed elder sister and his wife, née He, followed. The next day, their pursuers caught up with them. The mother was aged and could walk only with support. They looked around and saw that there was no means of escape. The wife and sister were taken by the bandits. As they were captured, they dissembled: "You gentlemen certainly are brave! Wherever you want to go, we will obey." The enemy believed them. As they walked along the bank of the river, [the wife] said to her husband, "I will not turn my back on you." When her words ended she sank into the river; his sister followed her.

Alas! It is the responsibility of the generals and prime ministers to preserve All-under-Heaven; it is the responsibility of the prefects and magistrates to preserve a district; it is the responsibility of women and girls to preserve one body. [But] since the ancient teachings have become obscure, the high and low all contravene principle; they regard what they ought to do as irrelevant and immaterial.[1] In the midst of such benighted customs, [this] one woman was able to die to fulfill her responsibility: this should make those who reside in the ranks of gentlemen and officials hold the city walls and preserve the territory! She was as valiant as the autumn frost, unwavering.[2] As for those in the world who hold their positions but abandon their responsibilities, what should they make of this!

---

1. Lit., "regard them as [the people of Yue regard] the fatness or thinness of the people of Qin" (*Yue ren shi Qin ren* 越人視秦人), that is, to regard them as something unimportant or irrelevant. The locus classicus of this expression is (Tang) Han Yu's *Zheng chen lun*. See Luo Zhufeng, *Han yu da ci dian* (entry for Qin-Yue 秦越).

2. Lit., "If you beckon, it does not come, if you dismiss it, it does not go."

Confucius composed the *Spring and Autumn* [*Annals*]. Describing a period of 242 years, he wrote only, "The Song was extinguished, and Boji died."[3] This was because she died appropriately. Now, in the long period of 242 years, there must have been some [virtuous] lords and officials, superiors and inferiors. That the sage promoted a single woman, is it not because the sage was also moved by [her actions]? In 1132 I heard [the story of Madame He] from a son of the Huang family. Huang was a friend of the husband; what he said is certainly reliable. I regret the fact that [these two women] could stand with Boji without shame, but my own virtue and righteousness are insignificant, and I am unable to make them stand with the ancients. Moved by this, I sigh repeatedly, and write the "Biography of Two Heroic Women." My intent is like that of the *Spring and Autumn*.[4]

In this poignant account, the minor official Chen Changfang (1108–48) deployed a dramatic story of valiant women in order to shame men of less resolve. Although Chen here echoes the rhetoric of Ouyang Xiu, he was not passing judgment on men of earlier dynasties but rather exhorting his contemporaries. And unlike Ouyang Xiu, Chen described not a quasi-fictional heroine of commoner origins, but women of his own class, who traveled in circles that overlapped with his. In these respects, Chen Changfang's account is representative of—and helped contribute to—an emerging discourse on women's loyalty in the Southern Song.

This chapter traces the multifaceted origins of this discourse. It shows that the new attention to women's loyalty was inspired in part by widespread social and political anxiety about male loyalty, occasioned by the fall of the Northern Song. It was also a direct response to the stark reality that many women died defending themselves from rape by the invaders, and to the tragedy, poignance, and cultural resonance of their sacrifices. But this chapter reveals that the Southern Song concern with female loyalty was also a response to societal interest in exemplars more generally, for reasons that were only tangentially related to women: the

---

3. Boji 伯姬 was the heroine of a story in the *Biographies of Exemplary Women*. She was the wife of Song Gong gong 宋共公. When her husband died, she remained faithful to him by not remarrying. Later there was a fire in the palace and everyone urged her to flee, but she refused and died in the fire. See Liu Xiang, *Lie nü zhuan* 4.133–34.

4. Chen Changfang, *Wei shi ji* 2.8–9. Chen says he heard of this incident in 1132.

efforts of Cheng Learning scholars to proselytize their teachings, the usefulness of exemplars to social and literary aggrandizing, and the ease with which stories of exemplars could serve as entertainment or inspiration. The larger social context of the commodification of women also played a significant if indirect role. The confluence of these factors led to more writing about exemplary women and the spread of that writing to new literary genres. And by the end of the period, that writing increasingly focused on faithful widows. These developments were gradual, and overall the topic of female fidelity remained a relatively minor theme in Southern Song social and moral discourse. But the changes of the Southern Song set the stage for the emergence of a full-blown fidelity discourse in the Yuan.

## Dynastic Debacle and Government Awards

We saw in earlier chapters that the fall of the Northern Song was a tremendous shock to the Song elite. Even those who never directly encountered the violence or disruptions of warfare were traumatized by the sudden collapse of the long-standing political order and grave uncertainties about the future. The experience of dynastic collapse was also highly gendered. Whereas men might die in battle or be taken into humiliating captivity, women were raped and treated as war booty. Even before Kaifeng fell, women found themselves used in lieu of cash in an attempt to ransom the city: the Chinese court turned some 11,000 women over to the Jurchen invaders for this purpose. In a calculation that brutally highlighted their status as human commodities, each woman's "value" was assessed according to her court rank (princesses worth more than imperial clanswomen, titled ladies more than entertainers, and so forth).[5] When, somewhat later, the entire court was captured and taken north, shocking tales of the degradation visited on Song court women, even members of the imperial family, filtered back to horrified Southern Song survivors.[6]

The sexual humiliation of Song women at the hands of the Jurchen only compounded the devastating sense of shame that Southern Song

---

5. Ebrey, "Introduction," in Ebrey and Bickford, *Emperor Huizong*, 2.
6. James Liu, *China Turning Inward*, 56–58. See also West, "Crossing Over," 565–608. West examines a Southern Song text that graphically (if probably spuriously) details the humiliations suffered by the Song imperial family in captivity.

literati felt at the loss of the Chinese heartland. The military had been exposed as hopelessly weak; Emperor Huizong and his hapless successor Qinzong 欽宗 (r. 1126) had allowed themselves to be taken captive; and scores of officials and scholars, the supposed upholders of Confucian principles of loyalty and righteousness, had abruptly abandoned their moral pretensions to scramble cravenly for survival or political advantage. Even after the government was reestablished, confidence in the superiority of Confucian culture over that of the "barbarians" was deeply shaken.[7] One desperately important task facing the early Southern Song court, then, was to reaffirm the values and social efficacy of Confucian ethical culture, and thereby to shore up the legitimacy of the regime.

As part of this process, the court turned to a practice that was both time-honored and in recent vogue: it called for the identification and celebration of Confucian exemplars. In his first year on the throne, Gaozong issued the standard call for righteous men, women of integrity, filial sons, and obedient grandsons to have their names submitted to the court, and he reissued such calls with some regularity during his reign.[8] But in the precarious political context of the early Southern Song, the new emperor was especially anxious to foster the value of loyalty and its presumed foundation, filiality.[9] In the fourth month

---

7. On the numerous traitorous acts of disloyal officials and the outrage they engendered in loyal men, see James T. C. Liu, *China Turning Inward*, 55–63. Tillman sees the sense of shame of early Southern Song literati as an important motivating factor in new directions in Confucian thought in the Southern Song period (*Confucian Discourse*, 19).

8. The call in the first year of Gaozong's reign is recorded in Li Gang, *Liangxi ji* 179.11b. This call does not appear in the *SHY*, but the latter source shows similar calls in 1129, 1140, and 1142. Part of the discussion below is drawn from Bossler, "Maidens."

9. Confucian doctrine held that a man who had been brought up to be a filial son to his father would naturally also be a faithful minister to his lord. The cultural obsession with loyalty in the Southern Song has been observed by scholars writing on a variety of topics. Jennifer Jay's study of loyalism at the end of the Southern Song argues that "the vulnerability of the Song state to border incursions" had led to a narrower definition of political loyalty even in the Northern Song, as evident in the writings of Ouyang Xiu and Sima Guang (Jay, *A Change in Dynasties*, 94–95), and Naomi Standen has stressed that Song ideas about loyalty represented a radical departure from Five Dynasties norms (*Unbounded Loyalty*, passim). Charles Hartman has noted the anxiety of early Southern Song men whose record with respect to loyalty was less than pristine to "fix the historical record, to bring historical clarity to ambiguous events, and to demonstrate personal loyalty and integrity" (Hartman, "The Making of a Villain," 87–88). Mark

of 1129, he issued a special edict designed to foreground those values: the edict called for local authorities to identify surviving graves of loyal ministers and filial sons, secure further enfeoffments for them, and protect them as models and inspiration for others.[10] Over the next two decades, Gaozong's court issued awards at a rate that surpassed even that of the Huizong era.[11] Between 1130 and 1148, a total of thirteen awards for filiality (including one to a grandson and one to a daughter-in-law) were issued. More significantly, for the first time the court also began to bestow awards honoring officials specifically for their loyalty (*zhong*) or integrity (*jie*).[12] Although, at least in the surviving court records, the rate of awards slackened somewhat under later Southern Song emperors, during Xiaozong's reign no fewer than four court edicts called for the submission of exemplars.[13]

As in the Northern Song, literati responded to the court's appeals by composing texts in honor of exemplars, but they now focused especially on political loyalty rather than on filial piety. In the 1130s, Ye Mengde composed an inscription to commemorate the building of a temple honoring a loyal minister of the Six Dynasties period. Ye pointed out that rebuilding the temple had made people more aware of the loyalty of the man honored there, enabling them to "know the righteousness of sacrificing one's body for the country."[14] Others wrote about heroes of the recent conflict: Fan Jun celebrated Xu Huiyan, a low-ranking

---

Halperin has also noted the "intense concern about the loyalty and morale of Song subjects" as evident in temple commemorations from the Southern Song (Halperin, "Buddhist Temples," 89). Richard Davis's monograph on the last years of the Song describes men of that period as obsessed with demonstrations of political loyalty (*Wind Against the Mountain*).

10. *SHY*, *li*, 61.8 (1677/2).

11. This effort seems part and parcel of Gaozong's effort to portray himself as both sage emperor and culture hero. See Li Cho-ying and Hartman, "A Newly Discovered Inscription," 397–98.

12. *SHY*, *li*, 61.8–10 (1677/2–1678/4). In all, eight officials were honored, in 1131, 1135, 1139 (four), and 1140 (two). During Gaozong's reign the court also issued two awards to harmonious households.

13. Surviving records in the *SHY* show eleven awards issued during Xiaozong's twenty-six years on the throne, none during Guangzong's four years, and three during Ningzong's twenty-nine years. (The *SHY* has no evidence for later reigns.) The awards were overwhelmingly in honor of filial children.

14. Ye Mengde, *Jiankang ji* 8.13b–16b.

military official who had valiantly defended his district and died defiantly affirming his loyalty to the Song.[15] Wang Zao commemorated the county magistrate Guo Yong, who had died with his entire family rather than submit to the Jin.[16]

But literati writers did not limit themselves to writing about men: rather, the court's call inspired a number of authors who, like Chen Changfang, composed texts praising the sacrifices of women who had died while refusing to submit to invading soldiers. The official and poet Zhou Zizhi (1082–1155), for example, wrote a biography of a Maiden of Huyin (Huyin *nü zi* 湖陰女子), describing the tragic demise of a young woman surnamed Zhan. Zhou explains that Zhan was the lovely sixteen-year-old daughter of a poor scholar. Her father, a widower, tutored young children but had difficulty making ends meet; Zhan sold her handiwork in order to help support him and her brother. She was literate, for Zhou tells us she copied out the biographies of heroic women of old, and was in the habit of reciting them four times each evening before she slept. Then, amid the chaos attending the fall of the Northern Song, bandits came to Huyin. Zhou continues:

> In tears, the maiden's father approached her saying, "I am already old; if I die there will be no regrets. But what about you?" The maiden replied, "Father, you needn't worry. I have already devised a plan. At times like these, is it possible both father and child can survive?" Shortly, the bandits arrived. Grasping swords, they prepared to kill her father and brother. As the blade was about to fall, the maiden came forward and said to the bandits, "My father is poor and old. You can't be after gold and silks, but must want me. If I may be so fortunate as to hold the towel and comb and serve your lordship, please release my father's bonds. Otherwise, father and child will both die, and you will get no benefit." The bandit ordered that they be released. The maiden waved her father away, urging him to leave quickly and not worry. "If I can become his lordship's wife, I can die without regret." The bandit took the maiden with him for several *li*. When they crossed the East Market Bridge, she jumped into the water and died.

---

15. Fan Jun, *Xiangxi ji* 21.197–200. Fan Jun also wrote a biography of a filial son who committed suicide to save his father from prison. Here filiality is understood as the ultimate loyalty to parents (*Xiangxi ji* 21.202–3).

16. Wang Zao, *Fuxi ji* 20.227–30. The biography seems to have been composed to help celebrate the fact that Guo received posthumous titles and his sons were awarded office. For other examples of Southern Song biographies of loyal men, see Bossler, "Maidens," 756–58.

256  *Markets, Mayhem, and Morality in the Southern Song*

9. The Maiden of Huyin (Huyin *nü zi* 湖陰女子) pleads with bandits (here in the guise of foreign soldiers) to take her in exchange for her father's freedom. From Liu Xiang 劉向, *Hui tu Lie nü zhuan* 繪圖列女傳 [Illustrated biographies of exemplary women], edited by (Qing) Wang Geng汪庚, illustrations by (Ming) Qiu Ying 仇英). Reprint of Zhi bu zu zhai cang ban (Taipei: Zheng zhong shu ju, 1971), 12.3b–4a.

Zhou concludes the story by relating how, several days after these events, Zhan's cousin and his wife both had dreams in which she came to them and told them of her death; the very next day, someone came with news of her demise. Zhou then comments,

> Alas, the maiden with her pliant and quiet demeanor, though faced with a hundred blades in a moment of extreme chaos and uncertainty, was able to speak calmly to the bandits and persuade them to let her father and brother live. Then she was able to die to keep her own body pure. This can be called complete integrity. Someone from her district said to me that it was because she always liked to read the biographies of past heroines, and deep in her heart [understood] past and present, that she was able to do this heroic thing (*da zhang fu shi* 大丈夫事). I humbly disagree. It must have been her Heaven-given nature; this is not something that can be learned. Recently the virtuous gentlemen and officials chanted the words of the ancients, but those who gave themselves over to the bandits, seeking survival at all costs, are too many to count. In the end they are not equal to a single girl! Thus I have recorded this to fill the lacuna in the National History.[17]

---

17. Zhou Zizhi, *Tai cang ti mi ji* 49.4b–6a.

Like Chen Changfang (and Ouyang Xiu before him), Zhou tells the story of a heroic woman, but in the process he contrasts the integrity of his heroine with the cowardly disloyalty of officials. The same sort of rhetoric suffuses a number of texts from the period. The court official Cheng Ju (1078–1144), for example, composed an "appreciation" (*zan* 贊) for a biography of a Principled Woman Rong, who had been captured and killed by bandits because she refused to abandon her aged mother-in-law. Cheng commented:

> As across the realm soldiers arose and chaos gave way to unthinkable change, gentlemen who were able to keep their bodies pure and maintain their integrity were not more than one in a thousand: how many fewer were those able to maintain their will in the face of death! Yet a woman was able to die to complete her integrity. Her purity is like jade and as hard as rock or iron: she can be shattered or broken, but cannot be bent or stained. This woman: she can be called heroic![18]

The biography of Woman Rong apparently circulated fairly widely, for it was also the subject of a postface by the official Wang Zhiwang (1103–70). Wang compared Rong favorably to the classical exemplar Boji and insisted that she was equally deserving of being recorded by historians.[19] Wang also composed a "Biography of Maiden Gui" (*Gui nü zhuan* 桂女傳), which, like Zhou Zizhi's account of Maiden Zhan, described a filial daughter who saved her father from bandits at the cost of her own life. Wang, too, concluded his biography by comparing his heroine to men:

> Today those who are ministers receive emoluments from their lord and enjoy lofty positions; [still, they] do not speak of virtue but plan evil, watch with equanimity as their lord falls, and even take employment from the enemy and exacerbate the disaster. The reason they are content in their shame and are unable to commit suicide is not necessarily because they are evil; it is only that they fear death. Of all the disasters under Heaven, there is none greater than fearing death. If one fears death, then there is nothing he will not do in order to live, though it is not necessarily the case that he will not die. Such people are really no better than animals, though they present a human face to the world and think themselves clever at avoiding disaster. When they hear of the spirit of Maiden Gui, will they not be somewhat ashamed?![20]

---

18. Cheng Ju, *Beishan ji* 17.3b.
19. Wang Zhiwang, *Han bin ji* 15.5a–5b.
20. Ibid., 15.6a–8a.

Several points can be made about the emergence of such texts in the early Southern Song. At the most basic level, this type of writing was clearly a response to the violence attendant on the fall of the Northern Song: the extraordinary circumstances of dynastic transition—and the government's efforts to honor loyalty—provided both the subject matter and the inspiration for literati men to write about heroic women (both Madame He and Principled Woman Rong were later included in the "Exemplary Women" section of the *Song History*).[21] But it should be emphasized that the public circulation of biographies of upper-class women like these was something of a new phenomenon. As discussed in chapter 3, most earlier exemplars were women of the lower class, and accounts of upper-class women were primarily limited to the genre of funerary inscriptions. There were obvious precursors to the circulating exemplary biographies of the Southern Song, of course: most notably those of late Northern Song filial sons, and perhaps also the (fictive?) biographies of courtesans like Wen Wan, which likewise were passed around, and gathered prefaces and postscripts.[22] In their moral framing, the Southern Song biographies are also reminiscent of Xu Ji's stories of the loyal courtesan Ai'ai and the Righteous Wife of Huaiyin. But the Southern Song circulation of biographies of upper-class heroic martyrs brought the lives (and deaths) of literati women into the public eye in an unprecedented way, and thereby helped legitimize the idea that upper-class women could or should be the subjects of public discourse. Moreover, by generating new prefaces and postfaces, the circulation of texts contributed to the expansion of that discourse. Finally, we should note that despite their focus on female heroism, these biographies were clearly not directed at a female audience. These texts were nominally about women, but they were not intended to inspire further martyrdom among women; rather, they were directed at men.

As the Southern Song progressed, writing about exemplars, both male and female, became more common. In part this was because the political

---

21. *SS* 460.13481, 13482.

22. For further discussion of the influence of courtesan biographies on texts for faithful women, see Bossler, "Fantasies of Fidelity." As in the case of the filial sons, the publicizing of upper-class heroines' biographies may well have been designed to elicit government recognition.

situation of the Southern Song remained precarious and loyalty a serious concern. But a number of other social and cultural forces contributed to a gradual increase in the production of exemplar texts (for both men and women) in the Southern Song, and these deserve to be considered in turn.

## Shrine-Building and Learning of the Way

One important factor in the propagation of exemplar texts in the Southern Song was the drive to rebuild or refurbish shrines to exemplary figures. In some cases, these figures were historical individuals who had long been revered or had even become local deities. As part of its effort to restore faith in its government, the early Southern Song court had called for the refurbishment of such popular shrines, and local officials responded by petitioning for recognition of deities in their jurisdictions. The great majority of these petitions concerned male figures, but I have found one petition requesting honors for a female deity. In 1133, one Chen Gongfeng composed an inscription requesting government recognition for a Pure and Heroic Shrine (*zhen lie ci* 貞烈祠) honoring a Tang dynasty woman surnamed Wen. According to Chen's account, Wen's betrothed had been killed by a tiger: she mourned him for three years and thereafter served her in-laws filially. One day she disappeared into the mountains, whence she was seen ascending to Heaven as an immortal. From that point on, prayers at the shrine were always answered. Chen describes how, shortly after he took office, his district was stricken with drought. He and the local magistrate went to pray at the shrine, and the local people requested that a stele be erected in the deity's honor. The magistrate agreed, and the next day it rained profusely. Chen admits that "previous generations seldom spoke of the affairs of spirits and immortals, regarding what was transmitted as fantasy and close to shamanism," but he insists that Wen's pure and virtuous behavior, as well as her continued spiritual efficaciousness, deserve recognition.[23]

---

23. Hao Yulin, *Guangdong tong zhi* 59.63a–64a. This example suggests that the distinction Carlitz has noted for the fifteenth century, between literati-approved shrines to Confucian exemplars and those to efficacious deities, was less salient at this point in the Song. See Carlitz, "Shrines," 634. I have not been able further to identify Chen Gongfeng.

Chen's celebration of Wen reminds us that ideas about the spiritual power of female virtue (perhaps especially when paired with virginity) ran deep in Chinese tradition; it also reveals how the Southern Song political context could reanimate those ideas. Still, Chen's account is exceptional, if not unique, and celebrations of female deities were not a major contributor to the discourse on female exemplars. Rather, a more important impetus for shrine-building, and for the text production associated therewith, was the development of the Cheng Learning movement.

Like the Song state, adherents of the Cheng brothers were interested in the moral transformation （*jiao hua* 教化) of the populace, and they saw the celebration of exemplars as an effective means to such transformation. Moreover, while taking advantage of the state's interest in recognizing exemplars, members of the movement sought to shape moral transformation according to their own particular moral vision, especially by creating or rebuilding shrines to "former worthies" (*xian xian* 先賢).[24]

As Ellen Neskar has shown, the great majority of shrines built by Cheng Learning adherents in the Southern Song were "transmission shrines," dedicated to commemorating the Cheng brothers and other Northern Song originators of Cheng Learning ideology. By celebrating Northern Song men whose ideology they shared, the founders of such shrines promoted both the movement's political agendas and its moral ones.[25] But Cheng Learning adherents also participated in the creation and refurbishing of shrines to other figures. Zhu Xi was active in several efforts to establish shrines to loyal officials who had died fighting various internal and external enemies, and Lou Yue commemorated the 1196 restoration of a shrine to a filial son from the Han dynasty.[26] A few decades later Zhen Dexiu commemorated a sacrifice at a Loyalty and Filiality Shrine (*zhong xiao ci*), honoring a filial son from the Tang and a loyal official of the Northern Song.[27]

---

24. See Neskar, *Politics and Prayer*, passim. I am grateful to Prof. Neskar for making the proofs of her important forthcoming book available to me.
25. Ellen Neskar, *Politics and Prayer*, 153–61.
26. *Zhu Xi ji* 19.797–98, 89.4568–70; Lou Yue, *Gong kui ji* 55.763–64.
27. Zhen Dexiu, *Xishan wen ji* 24.11b–13b. Note that this text is virtually identical to one attributed to Liu Yue (*Yun zhuang ji* 4.43a–45a).

As Neskar has also noted, almost all of the subjects of Cheng Learning shrines were men.[28] But in two cases, Cheng Learning adherents wrote shrine inscriptions that valorized the actions of women. Since these help reveal Cheng Learning attitudes toward female virtue, they are worth considering in detail. In the first case, we learn about an exemplary woman in the context of a shrine inscription composed to honor her father-in-law. In this 1183 commemoration, the court official Han Yuanji first explained that the Northern Song judicial official Bao Zheng had been known for his filiality and later for his principled service in office. Although Bao died (in 1062) less than a year after the local people had raised a "living" shrine in his honor, "down to today the people of his district continue to worship him beneath the Principled Woman Terrace." Han then describes the origins of the Principled Woman Terrace. It turns out that the principled woman was Bao Zheng's daughter-in-law, née Cui, the wife of his son Bao Yi. When Yi died in office, Han explains, Cui "maintained her will" (*shou zhi* 守志), devoting herself to serving her in-laws. We saw in chapter 3 that Cui had been recognized as an exemplar early in the Yuanyou period, receiving a government award for her "principled behavior." But Han Yuanji explains in greater detail precisely what her contribution was:

> Bao [Cheng] himself was heartbroken at the loss of his only son, until Cui said to him, "Milord has a young son; can you still cast him off?" Stunned, Bao asked what she meant. Cui replied, "Milord formerly had a concubine who was expelled; she gave birth to a son at her parents' home. He looks much like milord, and is able to recite the Classics. He is now six years old." Bao looked at his wife in delight; they retrieved the child and brought him home. Patting him fondly, Bao remarked, "If it hadn't been for Cui, you would not have been able to become my son." After Bao's death, Cui's own son also died. Her mother came from Xingzhou, wanting to steal her away and marry her off. Cui vowed [fidelity] and would not agree. She personally escorted her mother home, and then returned. She also threatened, "If you force me to stay [home], I will die at the end of a sash. I would be grateful if you would return my corpse to the Bao family." Ultimately, the local people reported the affair to the court, and she received enfeoffments and an insignia for her doorway. Later the old Bao residence was destroyed in the fighting, and the award terrace alone was left proudly standing. It was known as the Principled Woman Terrace. So they also fashioned an image of milord to make a shrine, and in times of rain, drought, or plague, they would always pray there.[29]

---

28. Neskar, *Politics and Prayer*, 317, n. 20. Ebrey also notes that Zhu Xi put relatively little emphasis on female exemplars ("Women, Money, and Class," 662).

29. Han Yuanji, *Nan jian jia yi gao* 15.298–300.

10. Principled Woman Cui, daughter-in-law of Bao Zheng (Cui *jie fu* 崔節婦, Bao Xiaosu *xi* 包孝肅媳) presents her in-laws with Bao's young son, who had been born to an expelled concubine. In showing the child reaching back to his birth mother, the artist subtly invokes the emotional complexities that concubine motherhood engendered in Chinese families. From Liu Xiang 劉向, *Hui tu Lie nü zhuan* 繪圖列女傳 (Illustrated biographies of exemplary women), edited by (Qing) Wang Geng 汪庚, illustrations by (Ming) Qiu Ying 仇英). Reprint of Zhi bu zu zhai cang ban (Taipei: Zheng zhong shu ju, 1971), 11.5b–6a.

Han Yuanji complains that the shrine was "cramped and shoddy"—a standard Cheng Learning reference to shrines that were the focus of popular worship—and not the sort of place for people of the prefecture to observe sacrifices to former worthies.[30] He relates with satisfaction that the shrine has now been rebuilt with Judge Bao's image in the center, and images of his wife, son, and daughter-in-law in the back room, "just like a family."

Han Yuanji's inscription reveals that the Cheng Learning creation of exemplar shrines sometimes overlapped with, or sought to rechannel, popular impulses to honor exemplary figures perceived to be

---

30. Neskar shows that one way Cheng Learning disciples distinguished their own shrines from those used for popular worship was in architecture, and that they frequently dismissed popular shrines as "cramped" and "dusty," or "lowly" (*bi lou* 庳陋) (Neskar, *Politics and Prayer*, 4, 123).

*Loss, Loyalty, and Local Leverage* 263

supernaturally powerful. Indeed, Han Yuanji here may well have been recasting a popular shrine dedicated to Cui into one honoring Judge Bao. But most important for our current purpose is the fact that Han is not interested in establishing Cui as a model of fidelity. Although he does indeed extol Cui for her dramatic vow of faithfulness to her deceased husband, when he describes what he sees as the shrine's didactic function, he refers only to Judge Bao and Ma Liang, another official enshrined there: "When young and old line up to view them, gathering round to worship in respect, seeing again the two gentlemen fully robed and solemn in the golden chamber, this can be called 'teaching without speaking.'"[31] Moreover, Han devotes the majority of his discussion of Cui to recounting her role in uniting Bao with the son of his expelled concubine: rather than widow fidelity per se, the central lesson of Cui's story seems to be the value of retaining concubines' sons in the interest of maintaining the patriline.

Another important theme in Han's inscription for Judge Bao is that of local pride: Han emphasizes that both Bao Zheng and Ma Liang were born in the district where the shrine was being established, and he makes a point that Bao is known not only throughout the country but also among the "barbarians."[32] Such local pride is also the central point of the only identifiable Cheng Learning shrine inscription focused exclusively on a woman. Dedicated to a heroine surnamed Zhang, the shrine was restored by the Ezhou prefect (and sometime local historian) Luo Yuan in 1184.[33] As Luo tells her story, Woman Zhang was the wife of a local commoner. She had first received enfeoffments and honors from the court in 1058, after she died defending herself from rape by a village

---

31. Han Yuanji, *Nan jian jia yi gao* 15.298–300. Han's text indicates that the image of another worthy, Ma Liang, was added at the behest of a local official, but the great majority of his text is devoted to Bao.

32. Neskar argues that Cheng Learning shrines were frequently deployed to claim significance for the local community (*Politics and Prayer*, chap. 2). Carlitz likewise notes that celebrating heroic women was a means of asserting local authority in the early Ming ("Shrines," 633–37), and Mann finds the same phenomenon in the Qing ("Widows," 43).

33. Luo Yuan, *[Luo] Ezhou xiao ji* 4.40–42. This shrine anticipates the Ming dynasty Confucian shrines to female exemplars that Carlitz has described, and shares many of the same features, such as concern for local standing and a broad effort to promote Confucian ideals. See Carlitz, "Shrines," 624–36.

youth. Luo notes that the original Northern Song memorial to Zhang had been destroyed by war and chaos, so he himself chose a spot just outside of town and erected a shrine to her "in order to manifest the abiding intention of the enlightened edict." But Luo holds up Zhang as a model of admirable behavior primarily to claim her as a sign of the excellence of the local customs of her native Ezhou. He suggests that the virtue of the local people reflects the prefecture's place on convenient communication networks, which facilitated the early spread of the civilizing influence of the Zhou dynasty (ca. 1050–256 BCE).[34] At the same time, Luo asserts the relevance of this local exemplar of virtue to national issues. He stresses that preserving the distinction between men and women is not only what "distinguishes human beings from animals," but is also what makes "China more noble than the northeastern barbarians (*Zhongguo zhi suo yi gui yu yidi* 中國之所以貴於夷狄)."[35] In Luo Yuan's rhetoric, Woman Zhang is not only a sign of the enlightened customs of Ezhou, but an emblem of Chinese cultural superiority. In that regard, and in contrast to texts honoring martyrs to the invasion, Luo does hold up his heroine as a model for both men and women: he suggests that men who see that Zhang was able to end her life for ritual will be unable to bear throwing themselves away in unrighteousness, and women and girls will be transformed, realizing that in crisis she was able to "do what was difficult."

In addition to the texts they created for shrines, the scholars and officials who sought to spread the values of Cheng Learning occasionally composed other kinds of texts celebrating the actions of exemplary figures, again with an eye to proselytizing Cheng Learning values. We

---

34. Luo takes as his proof a poem from the "Zhou nan" (south of the Zhou) section of the *Book of Odes*. In distinct contradiction to Luo Yuan's account, a *SS* description of the refurbishing of the Ezhou shrine casts it as an attempt to improve the scandalously benighted local customs, wherein the people routinely worshipped demons and consulted shamans, cremated the dead, and engaged in uxorilocal marriages. See *SS* 437.12954, in the biography of Liu Qingzhi 劉清之. The *SS* account again suggests that the refurbishment of shrines was an excuse and a means to convert the populace to elite values.

35. Luo Yuan, [*Luo*] *Ezhou xiao ji* 4.41. Significantly, in the version of this text preserved in a Qing epigraphy collection, this line of the text is omitted. See Yang Shoujing, *Hubei jin shi zhi*, 12.13a–14b.

see the proselytizing impulse in Chen Liang's moving *zhuan* biography of Zhao Jiuling, a stalwart youth whose loyal efforts to contribute to the defense of the Northern Song court had been thwarted by distrustful officials. We see the impulse also in a funerary inscription composed by the late Southern Song teacher Yang Jian, for a filial son who cut out his liver to make porridge for his dying mother.[36] A few such texts also celebrated the virtues of women. We shall see below that Chen Liang wrote biographies commemorating two female martyrs, and Zhen Dexiu, in his office as prefect, bestowed the title Virtuous Filiality Hamlet on the village of a young woman who had prayed to take her dying father's place in the underworld and also cut flesh from her thigh to make soup for him.[37]

Taken together, these examples demonstrate that the proselytizing efforts of Cheng Learning adherents, while certainly intended to improve social morality in general, were not intended to promote female fidelity per se. Rather, like the writers anxious to exhort political loyalty in men, believers in Cheng Learning found that a variety of behaviors in women—from resistance to rape to service to in-laws—could be described as expressions of integrity (*jie*) and thus be promoted as models of moral conduct. This flexibility in the concept of *jie* was an important factor in the growing popularity of writings on female exemplars in particular, as we shall see further below. But the increase in writings for exemplars more generally was also fueled by the fact that such writings fulfilled social functions that went well beyond the inculcation of moral behavior.

## Social Aggrandizing

Cheng Learning advocates used exemplar texts to assert the significance of their localities in the empire. But such texts could also function on a more personal level, to make a statement about the status of a family in

---

36. *Chen Liang ji* 13.158–60; Yang Jian, *Cihu yi shu* 18.30a–31b. Chen's biography of Zhao takes the form of a preface to a collection of classified biographies of remarkable men from the fall of the Northern Song that Chen Liang apparently intended to compile; it appears that only this preface survives.

37. Zhen Dexiu, *Xishan ji* 24.11a–12b. The father's recovery was marked by numerous supernatural manifestations; *Chen Liang ji* 13.160–62. I discuss these biographies in detail below.

its home locality. This kind of social aggrandizing was another powerful impetus for the production of exemplar texts in the Southern Song. In 1132, for example, the scholar Yang Shi was approached by Xu Ji's son with a request for a postface to grace a collection of poetry that famous men had written for Xu Ji. The son's plan was to have the work carved in stone so it could be saved for posterity. Yang acceded to the request, but in his postface he demurs that Xu Ji's integrity and righteousness are like a ritual object made of jade: "not engraved, its beauty is already manifest; it isn't something that carving or painting can embellish." Yang ultimately justifies his participation in the project by pointing out that the poets with whom Xu Ji corresponded were all famous men and their words worthy of credence, so that carving their words on stone to inspire future generations could be of substantial benefit.[38] In like manner, by the late Southern Song not a few descendants of exemplars were actively capitalizing on their ancestors' fame by soliciting celebratory texts, as well as more tangible memorials, in their honor.

This dynamic is evident, for example, in a number of texts that the eminent official Zhou Bida was asked to write in the latter decades of the twelfth century. In 1140, one Li Jing had died a martyr in battle with the Jin; in 1172, his son Sizhong 思忠, ("Thinking of loyalty") paid a visit to Zhou Bida to request a biography. Sizhong explained that at the time of his death his father had been low in rank, and Sizhou himself too young to take advantage of the imperial grace extended to the sons of martyrs. He begged Zhou to compose a biography of his father "to spread the word to the four quarters and to [my father in] the Nine Springs, and to save from obscurity the imperial grace of rewarding martyrs and pitying their orphans."[39] Li Sizhong's entrepreneurial efforts were far exceeded by the descendants of another early Song martyr, Zhao Xunzhi 趙訓之. In 1199, Zhao's grandsons brought Zhou a collated volume (*juan* 卷) entitled *Record of Loyalty and Integrity* (*Zhong jie lu* 忠節錄) that contained their ancestor's funerary biography, the text of the edict honoring his martyrdom, his biography for the standard history, and additional

---

38. Yang Shi, *Guishan ji* 26.11b–12a.
39. *QSW* 232: 5170.203–4. Zhou questioned why, if the goal was merely to publicize the father, the son had not approached him while he had been a court historian, but he was ultimately persuaded to write the text.

"remembrances and colophons by various notables." In the preface he wrote at the grandsons' behest, Zhou points out several discrepancies between the biographies of Zhao collected in the volume and existing records in the local history, explaining that he does not want men of later ages to have doubts. Whether Zhou was seriously trying to set the record straight, or subtly hinting that the descendants had embellished the record, his preface reveals the increasingly elaborate ways that exemplary behavior was being packaged and promulgated. Ultimately, the Zhao descendants proved even more enterprising, for at about the same time they secured Zhou's preface, they also arranged to have a new shrine built at Zhao Xunzhi's grave, containing images of Zhao and his wife; they then sought imperial recognition of the shrine. In the shrine record he composed for them in 1203, Zhou observes that the court dispatched officials to investigate the case, and all confirmed that the spirit's "fidelity and righteousness were manifest, prayers were regularly answered, and [Zhao] was truly of benefit to the people." In addition to giving permission for a shrine plaque and a ceremonial stele to be erected, the court issued a set of ceremonial songs to be used in welcoming and sending off the spirit. The songs reveal that Zhao by this time had become a guardian of the local populace, a deity to whom regular sacrifices were offered in return for timely weather and deliverance from evil influences. We cannot know precisely what local advantages accrued to the Zhao family in establishing their ancestor as the focus of this sort of community cult, but those advantages were presumably considerable. And outside of their locality, the process of securing government imprimatur for the cult assured that the Zhao sons' names became known to senior officials at various levels of the bureaucracy.

Other Southern Song families similarly found it worthwhile to publicize the exemplary behavior of their ancestors.[40] Occasionally, they even

---

40. For example, the seventh-generation descendants of a filial son Guo, who had originally been honored as an exemplar in 997, paid for the reconstruction of a shrine to their ancestor and commissioned several local notables to compose formal records of their efforts (Du Fan, *Qing xian ji* 16.8b–10a; Wu Ziliang, "Record of the shrine to Filial Son Guo," in Lin Biaomin, *Chicheng ji* 9.1a–2b. A record of the original award to Guo also appears in *SHY, li*, 61.2). One of these inscriptions takes the local officials to task for not restoring the shrine themselves, thus forcing the descendants to take responsibility for it. In other cases, local officials found it worthwhile to construct

turned to exemplary ancestresses. One such case was also documented by Zhou Bida, who described a Principled Woman Liao who had died in 1133 while protecting her mother-in-law from bandits. Zhou explains that the local prefect had attempted to get the central government to issue an award honoring Liao, but that the central authorities acknowledged his petition without responding to it. Repeated requests by Liao's son also went unheeded. Zhou then complains that the regulations for issuing government awards discriminated against women like Liao. He observes that the state regulations on the one hand called for local officials to succor and extol "righteous men, faithful women, filial sons, and obedient grandsons," and on the other called for local officials to embellish the graves of "loyal officials and filial sons." He adds:

> Now, the first statement concerns only the living. Thus it does not extend to someone like Liao, who has died for integrity. Although the latter statement concerns the dead, it speaks only of loyal officials and filial sons. Thus once again the principled woman is left out. This is something that the officials, who when writing the laws [merely] continue past precedent, have not considered. If someday her case can be set forth in detail, Liao will certainly be rewarded; then will [her son's] hopes perhaps be fulfilled?[41]

Zhou does not explain how he came to write this particular text, but the title indicates that it is a postface to a stele for Faithful Woman Liao of Linjiang (*Ba Linjiang jun Liao jiefu bei* 跋臨江軍廖節婦碑). In other words, even in the absence of a government award, Liao's son had taken the initiative to erect a monument in her honor. Texts like these demonstrate that although state recognition continued to be valuable and sought after, literati families had begun to take the celebration of exemplars into their own hands.[42]

---

shrines of their own volition, assiduously reporting their efforts to the court. Thus Yuan Fu's inscription for the Promoting Filiality Shrine (*xing xiao* 興孝祠) erected by Lin Jiahui, the magistrate of Dongyang county, portrays the establishment of the shrine as evidence of Lin's good government (Yuan Fu, *Meng zhai ji* 13.189–90).

41. Zhou Bida, *Wenzhong ji* 18.8b–9a. Quite possibly due to Zhou Bida's efforts, Liao was ultimately commemorated in a biography in the *SS* (460.13485). This material appears in Bossler, "Martyrs," 516–17, but I have slightly emended the translation here.

42. A stele record preserved in a Qing gazetteer similarly records the establishment in 1196 of a stele in honor of a principled woman who first received a government award in 1113 (at the height of the Huizong exemplar hysteria). The text is falsely attributed to Wang Zao (汪藻), who died in 1154, long before the text was written, and is notable

# Loss, Loyalty, and Local Leverage    269

11. Principled Woman Liao (Liao *jie fu* 廖節婦, Ou Xiwen *qi* 歐希文妻). The success of woman Liao's descendants in publicizing her heroism is demonstrated by her appearance in a Qing collection of biographies of exemplary women. She is shown here with her husband, Ou Xiwen, and her mother-in-law as they flee Jin soldiers. From Liu Xiang 劉向, *Hui tu Lie nü zhuan* 繪圖列女傳 [Illustrated biographies of exemplary women], edited by (Qing) Wang Geng 汪庚, illustrations by (Ming) Qiu Ying 仇英). Reprint of Zhi bu zu zhai cang ban (Taipei: Zheng zhong shu ju, 1971), 11.13b–14a.

Yet social aggrandizing through the promulgation of exemplar texts was not limited to the families of the exemplars. If the commissioning of new texts and monuments allowed descendants to participate in the prestige associated with their ancestors' exemplary behavior, the creation and circulation of texts about exemplars also became a way for *authors*

---

because the husband's family were traders, not literati. But the principled woman is praised for insisting on educating her son, and the stele carefully details the names of more than fifteen officials among her grandsons, great-grandsons, and great-great-grandsons. Here again, the stele clearly served both to celebrate the descent group's success and to glorify it to the larger community. See "Shi shi jie xing bei" 施氏節行碑 in Shen Yiji, *Zhejiang tong zhi*, 266.6a–9b. Public celebration of ancestors here seems to be of a piece with the new interest in genealogies in the Southern Song and Yuan, as discussed in Bol, "Local History," 307–48. I address this similarity in greater detail in the conclusion to this book. See Jay for accounts of similar aggrandizing by Ming and Qing descendants of late Song loyalists ("Memoirs and Official Accounts," 605–8).

to participate vicariously in that prestige.[43] The colophons and prefaces appended to exemplar biographies circulated with those biographies, spreading the fame of the commentators along with that of the exemplars. This fact was well recognized by contemporaries, as seen in the remarks of several writers who contributed to the accumulation of encomia for Xu Ji. In a preface to the same collection of letters and poems to which Yang Shi had contributed, the eminent official Hong Kuo likewise suggested, "The name of a gentleman of complete virtue will last as long as Heaven and Earth; the poems and letters of the five notables are unnecessary." But Hong conceded that perpetuating Xu Ji's fame was a way of making up for the fact that fate had not fairly rewarded his descendants: "Still, the gentleman stepped loftily in the hills and gardens, content to tend his illness in poverty; today his grandsons eat only vegetables and still go hungry. The phrase, '[Good fortune will be manifest] not in his life, [but] in [that of] his sons and grandsons' is truly difficult to fathom!"[44] The famous patriot and poet Lu You was far less sympathetic: in his postface to Xu Ji's "Collected Sayings," he remarked acerbically: "[Xu Ji]'s name is everywhere: who doesn't know to look up to and respect him? Even if we didn't have what Master Su [Shi] said, it would be all right; how much less the others! What is recorded before and after this collection ought to be completely expunged!"[45] Lu You clearly objected to the attempts of latter-day writers to attach themselves to Xu Ji's coattails, though he did not eschew the opportunity to record his own point of view.

Some authors openly admitted that the production of biographies of exemplars provided occasions to deploy one's literary artistry. Zhou Bida, asked to contribute "a word" in honor of a filial son, devoted over half his text to discussing a funerary inscription that Ouyang Xiu had composed for a different filial son. After describing in detail his own painstaking efforts to identify the subject of Ouyang's work (whose name had been lost over time), Zhou remarks:

---

43. The correlation of virtue and social prestige, and the attempt to capitalize on virtue for social ends, had a long history in China. See, for example, Knapp, *Selfless Offspring*; Holcombe, "The Exemplar State," 93–139.
44. Hong Kuo, *Panzhou wen ji* 63.9b.
45. Lu You, *Weinan wen ji* 31.196. Lu refers to Xu by his sobriquet, "Zhongju."

Milord [Ouyang] once said that he liked to transmit the affairs of people, and he especially admired Sima Qian's ability to transmit the extraordinary and imposing, which led people to enjoy reading and want to emulate Qian's works. Later, he composed the *History of the Five Dynasties*: his style lacks nothing compared to that of Qian. As for me, I admire his writing the way he admired that of Qian; it is just that I have been unable to emulate his writing the way he was able to emulate Qian.⁴⁶

Here Zhou Bida, like Ouyang Xiu before him, expressed aspirations to create biographies that could move and inspire readers in the manner of Sima Qian's riveting *Historical Records*. His modest disclaimers of inadequacy do not fully disguise the fact that he regarded such biographical writing as a means to establishing literary reputation. But Zhou's comment alerts us to another important element underlying the production of exemplar texts in the Southern Song: in acknowledging the importance of readers' enjoyment, Zhou reminds us that these texts could also function as entertainment.

## *Exemplary Entertainment*

In the Northern Song work of Xu Ji, we saw stories of exemplary virtue cloaked in dramatic narratives of violence and tragedy. Similarly vivid rhetoric found its way into many Southern Song exemplar biographies, and—significantly—was especially prominent in biographies of female martyrs.⁴⁷ We have already seen intimations of this in the stories of Wu Yongnian's wife and of Zhan, the Maiden of Huyin. But it is even clearer in the appearance, in the mid- and late Southern Song, of heroic martyrs in poetry and in prose genres meant primarily for entertainment.

In some instances, the figure of the heroic martyr could serve as a more or less abstract inspiration for poetic meditations on virtue, tragedy,

---

46. Zhou Bida, *Wenzhong ji* 75.23b–25b. Zhou returns to the putative subject of his piece by noting that since Ouyang Xiu had selected a filial son from a distant place and publicized him, he himself could hardly refuse to write about a filial son who hailed from nearby. The Ouyang Xiu passage to which Zhou refers appears in *Ouyang Xiu quan ji* 66.969–72 (at the end of "Biography of Sang Yi" [*Sang Yi zhuan* 桑懌傳]).

47. Katharine Carlitz has noted that biographies of female martyrs were often at least as dramatic as they were didactic. She shows that by Ming times the mixing of didactic stories with erotic images was de rigueur in didactic texts for women. See Carlitz, "Desire, Danger, and the Body" and "Social Uses."

and loss. This is the case in a series of poems written by Southern Song literati to celebrate a Virtuous Maiden Shrine (*xian nü ci* 賢女祠). The shrine had first received imperial recognition in the late tenth century, and was renovated during Huizong's reign. It may have been around that time that the official Liao Gang (1071–1143) composed a poem to honor the shrine's subject. In his preface Liao explained:

> Of old, at the border of Nan'an commandery, there was a Pure Maiden Niche (*Zhen nü pu* 貞女鋪). It was said that there was once a girl who had been betrothed, but not married, when her fiancé died. Her family then betrothed her to the fiancé's brother. The girl felt that in righteousness she could neither refuse nor go through with [the marriage], so she threw herself into the water and drowned. The niche was above the pond, and so it got this name. Later, to avoid a taboo, it was changed to the current name.[48]

The poem that follows is everything we might expect of a verse on this topic: it begins by imagining the girl's thoughts as she determines that death is preferable to a lifetime of shame, then shifts to images of the bright moon on the pure blue water, the melancholy of a lone cloud in the setting sun, and the sympathetic grief of the visitor. Like the pathetic courtesans of earlier chapters, here the Virtuous Maiden and her shrine provide the occasion for Liao to express both his emotional sensitivity and his literary skill.

There is no evidence that the Virtuous Maiden Shrine received state recognition in the Southern Song, though its very existence shows that suicide was popularly seen as a powerful—even magical—force. In any case, the shrine remained active through the Southern Song and beyond as a tourist (and sacred?) site and as an inspiration for literati writings. Luo Yuan, who wrote the shrine record to the Ezhou heroine Zhang, discussed above, also composed a "Preface for the Virtuous Maiden Niche" (題賢女鋪) in verse form, playing on several of the images in Liao's poem.[49] Somewhat later, the poet Dai Fugu (b. 1167) not only wrote a poem in the Virtuous Maiden's honor, but added interest to her story by providing a preface that elaborated significantly on Liao's account:

> Twenty *li* outside of Nankang county there is a Maiden Shrine. Formerly there was a girl surnamed Liu, young and intelligent. Her parents initially betrothed

---

48. Liao Gang, *Gao feng wen ji* 10.3b.
49. Luo Yuan, [*Luo*] *Ezhou xiao ji* 1.6. See also Zeng Feng, *Yuan du ji* 2.13a–b.

her to Cai; then without reason they broke it off and betrothed her to Wu. When Wu died they again betrothed her to Cai. The girl said, "Your daughter's body was first betrothed to Cai; it has already been two years since it was wrested away and betrothed to Wu. Now Wu is gone and again you betroth me to Cai. Can one girl betrothed to two people still have the face to enter someone's household?" She threw her body into a pond and died.

Dai's poem, in a somewhat less elevated register than Liao's, compares her integrity with men's shameful lack thereof, stressing her ability to take death lightly and insisting that her good name will flourish for 1,000 years.[50] Dai's efforts in turn attracted the attention of later authors: the late Song poet and anecdotalist Chen Yu (d. 1275) included both Dai's preface and his poem in an anecdotal collection. Chen then added his own commentary, comparing the Virtuous Maiden to two notoriously disloyal ministers of the past and exclaiming: "How shameful that they were not as principled and honorable as this girl!" A poem by the late Song Minister Liu Fu (1262 *jin shi*), prefaced by a truncated version of Dai's account, obliquely told the Virtuous Maiden's story and concluded by claiming kinship with her: "When our lineage has a girl like that, what about those called boys?" (吾宗女猶爾,況復號男兒).[51]

These poems, celebrating an almost mythic figure of the distant past, differ in significant ways from the biographies of upper-class martyrs we have seen thus far. They are understandably less personal (though Dai's elaboration suggests a desire to make the Virtuous Maiden's story more immediately compelling), and as literary rather than moral texts they are less didactic (though Dai, Chen, and Liu all make a point of comparing the Virtuous Maiden favorably with men). These texts are important, however, first for reminding us of the ease with which female martyrdom—and especially that of young nubile women—lent itself to poetic treatment. More importantly, they demonstrate the tendency for one literary effort to inspire others, leading not only to the production of new texts but also to intertextual influence and generic innovation. Thus in the late Southern Song, we find the court historian Zhang Ruyu 章如愚 (1196 *jin shi*) incorporating Dai Fugu's story of the Virtuous Maiden

---

50. Dai Fugu, *Shi ping shi ji* 2.4b.
51. Chen Yu, *Cang yi hua yu* 5b–6a; Liu Fu, *Meng chuan yi gao* 2.15b–16a. Cf. also Xie Min, *Jiangxi tong zhi* 109.46a. The latter source indicates that the shrine was again renovated in the Ming.

wholesale into the formal biography of an upper-class woman who had been issued an award for deciding not to marry after her fiancé died.[52]

By the same token, we find other Song writers taking up as poetic subjects heroic women of their own day. Zhou Zizhi (1082–1155), in addition to his commemoration of the Maiden of Huyin, composed a set of two poems with a preface inspired by a friend's account of a heroic suicide among his relatives. Zhou's preface explains that the wife of one Jiao Wei, a daughter of the official Hong Yu, one day encountered bandits near the river. Refusing to be "polluted" by them, she threw herself into the river. But—perhaps out of discretion?—in the rest of the preface and the verses which follow Zhou focuses not on Hong but on her serving maids (*shi'er*), who had thrown themselves into the river after their mistress: Zhou names them individually, notes they were sisters, and indicates that they were lovely and skilled at playing the pipa. His poem stresses the maids' "jade countenances" and the dancing of their red sleeves in the water:

| | |
|---|---|
| 就死由來不自疑 | Facing death, there was never a moment's self-doubt: |
| 玉顏那爲賊鋒低 | How could the jade countenance be ruined by the bandit's sword? |
| 了知今日投淵婦 | Certainly you know that the women who today threw themselves into the deep |
| 猶勝當年斷臂妻 | Even outdo the wife who once cut off her arm. |
| 殺氣駸駸戰艦驕 | The air of death was pressing, the warships fierce; |
| 春江漫漫濕金翹 | The spring river flowed, moistening the golden headdresses. |
| 但將紅袖供歌舞 | But toward the red sleeves offering song and dance, |
| 却爲周郎笑二喬 | Master Zhou can't help but smile for the two sisters.[53] |

The subtle eroticism of Zhou's poem is found as well in a poem by Li Lü 李呂 (1122–98), dedicated to the Pure Wife (*zhen fu* 貞婦) of a lazy farmer. The poem describes how the subject, a woman of "pale complexion and ebony sidelocks" (臉白兩鬢青), committed suicide in

---

52. Zhang Ruyu, "Ru ren Ye shi jie yi zhuan" 孺人葉氏節義傳, in Cheng Minzheng, *Xin'an wenxian zhi* 98.17b–19a. This text is discussed in detail below.

53. Zhou Zizhi, *Tai cang ti mi ji* 10.13. Elsewhere in his collected works, Zhou reveals that the author of the account that inspired this poem was his patron. The last line of the poem plays on a Three Kingdoms Period (220–280) story about two beautiful sisters, the younger of whom married the hero Zhou Yu ("Master Zhou"), and Zhou Zizhi's own surname.

order to fend off the attentions of a stranger who wanted to seduce her.⁵⁴ Significantly, these poems, with their emphasis on the women's appearance, still focus on lower-class women. Yet in his collection of 1192, the anecdotalist Fei Gun not only repeated the story of Hong Yu's daughter and her maids (including Zhou Zizhi's poems), he also added brief biographies of several other young upper-class women who had died resisting bandits. Fei's biographies were straightforward and, beyond noting their young ages and determination to remain pure, did not emphasize his subjects' physical attributes. But by appending their stories to Zhou's account of Hong's maids, Fei helped to blur the distinctions between texts meant to exhort and those meant to entertain, and to naturalize the presence of upper-class women in the latter.⁵⁵

An even clearer example of this phenomenon is found in the story of the "Principled Death of the Daughter of Cheng Shuqing" (*Cheng Shuqing nü si jie shi*).⁵⁶ The original account of Ms. Cheng's death seems to have been composed in the mid-twelfth century by a relative of Luo Yuan.⁵⁷ The text begins by explaining that in the early days of the Fang La rebellion (1120–21), the family of Cheng Shuqing of She county took refuge south of the city. Once there, the parents took stock of the situation. They acknowledged that they might not escape death themselves, but their main concern was their attractive seventeen-year-old daughter: "If by chance she is polluted by the bandits, how will we be able to face our friends and relatives?" They called the daughter to them, saying:

> "It is the custom of our prefecture that licentiousness is particularly unthinkable. You are the daughter of a good family, your feet never leaving the women's quarters. If the bandits threaten you with weapons, what ought you to do?" The daughter replied, "How could I go with the bandits? It is certainly not permitted! I should die fighting them off!" Other relatives also questioned her in like

---

54. Li Lü, *Dan xuan ji* 1.11b.
55. Fei Gun, *Liangxi man zhi* 8.98.
56. The following discussion of Cheng Shuqing's daughter has been revised from Bossler, "Maidens," 774–76.
57. Entitled "Record of the Loyal Death of the Daughter of Cheng Shuqing" (*Ji Cheng Shuqing nü si jie shi* 記程叔清女死節事), the text is variously attributed to Luo Yuan's older brother Luo Song 頌 (d. 1191) (in Luo Yuan's *Xin'an zhi* 新安志, 10.37b–38b, as well as in *YJZ, zhi bu*, 1.1557) or to his brother or cousin Luo Qi 頎 (in the version appended to the end of Luo Yuan's collected works, [*Luo*] *Ezhou xiao ji*, "Yingzhou zhou tai shou mu zhi" 郢州太守墓誌, 2).

manner. The girl consequently took the clothing satchel she was carrying and threw it over her shoulder [as if] fleeing. She pretended to be captured and curse the bandits. Her parents said happily, "If you can behave like this, you are truly our daughter! We have heard that when someone dies at the hands of bandits, by having the Daoists recite the Ritual of the Nine Dark Regions the soul will be raised up and delivered.[58] Don't you fear!" The daughter smiled and assented.

The following day the worst transpired, and the girl was captured by a bandit. He first attempted to sweet-talk her: "If I take you back to His Highness, you needn't worry about not being wealthy and noble." She replied angrily, "You ruffians deceive Heaven and harm people, worse than dogs and pigs—what 'Highness' could you possibly have?" The bandit resorted to further threats and blandishments, even cutting off her chignon with his knife. But the girl continued to shout and curse at him until finally, "Realizing that she would not submit, he slashed furiously at her, scattered her corpse, and departed." The account concludes by relating, "Two children who were hidden behind a great boulder nearby saw the whole thing, and reported it to the family. Gratified even in the midst of its grief, the family buried her in the mountains of the Eastern Embankment."

Here we have an exciting, even titillating drama of sex and violence, replete with lively dialogue, suspenseful action, and a poignant denouement. The story stands on its own: the moralizing comments that frame many other accounts of female heroic fidelity are strikingly absent here, and the author does not even explain his motivation in recording the event. Probably the account was not composed specifically as entertainment, but it was read that way, for it was taken up by Hong Mai for inclusion in his anecdotal collection the *Yijian zhi*.[59] Hong's collection

---

58. Daoist rites that function to release souls from the Nine Dark Regions date back to at least the fifth century. See, for example, Bokenkamp, "Purification Ritual," 268–77.

59. Hong does appear to have made minor changes to the story. Overall, his version is more elegant: the original's "Now that we're in this [mess]" (*Wo deng chu ci* 我等處此) in Hong Mai becomes "[Now that] our family has encountered this" (*Wu jia ju ci* 吾家居此); "[I] should resist them unto death" (*dang yi si ju zhi* 當以死拒之) becomes "There is nothing for it but to die" (*Wei si er yi* 唯死而以). Hong Mai truncates the death scene somewhat, and (in the interest of seemliness?) omits the references to other relatives questioning the daughter, to the parents' gratification at the end of the story, and to the promised salvation via Daoist ceremonies. In short, Hong Mai seems to present a somewhat cleaned up version of the story, while retaining the tension and pathos of the original.

contains several other examples of the exemplar text genre, many of which seem to originate, like the story just described, in the writings of literati.[60] By the mid- Southern Song, then, the blurring of didacticism and entertainment we first saw in Xu Ji was increasingly a feature of exemplar texts, especially those whose subjects were women.

That entertaining stories could also be useful in conveying moral messages was not lost on proponents of Cheng Learning. Chen Liang argued that in order to effect change in the world it was necessary to move people, and he cited the example of Confucius using the ancient songs to teach people about ritual.[61] Chen evidently took his own advice seriously, as evident in a "Biography of Two Heroic Girls" that he composed.[62] Chen begins by introducing his beautiful heroine:

> The virtuous girl was surnamed Du; she was the daughter of an important family in Yongkang. From her birth, she was well mannered and lovely. In the winter of 1120, the fiendish [rebel leader Fang] La arose; wherever he went he gathered men to plunder and kill. In the village a fierce band of bandits approached the Du household. In loud voices they demanded, "Hand over your daughter; if you don't, today you will all become ancestors!" The family members cried out in alarm: they could not bear to give her to them, but if they did not, they faced

---

60. Examples include "The Fidelity of Ms. Tan" (*Tan shi jie cao* 譚氏節操) (*YJZ, jia zhi*, 10.84); "A Righteous Man and Principled Wife" (*Yi fu jie fu* 義夫節婦) (*YJZ, jia zhi*, 20.182–83); "The Filial Woman Wu of Duchang" (*Duchang Wu xiao fu* 都昌吳孝婦) (*YJZ, zhi bu*, 1.1555); "Biography of the Righteous Courtesan" (*Yi chang zhuan* 義倡傳) (*YJZ, zhi bu*, 2.1559). Hong Mai also repeated Zhou Zizhi's story of the Maiden of Huyin, under the title "The Filial Daughter of Wuhu" (*Wuhu xiao nü* 蕪湖孝女) (*YJZ, zhi bu*, 1.1553). It may be significant that several of these stories appear in the first supplementary section of the modern text, which represents items lost from most later imperial editions of the text but preserved in a classified edition (arranged by subject) and published as a supplement in the *Han fen lou* edition (see *YJZ, zhu jia xu ba*, 1841–42). It seems at least possible that some of these texts were not part of Hong Mai''s original collection. The same section also includes several stories of individuals who were conspicuously *lacking* in virtue, who tend to come to appropriately dreadful ends. Christian de Pee has examined anecdotes in the *YJZ* that focus on widow fidelity, in which women tend to be supernaturally punished for not remaining faithful to their deceased husbands. De Pee notes that these are treated as cases of personal betrayal, and "the fidelity of the widow is *not* compared to the loyalty of a man to the state" (Christian de Pee, "Women in the *Yi Jian Zhi*," 75; emphasis added).

61. *Chen Liang ji* 20.277; cf. Tillman, *Confucian Discourse*, 165.

62. *Chen Liang ji* 13.160. The discussion that follows is slightly emended from Bossler, "Maidens," 771–72.

disaster. They spoke to their daughter, who replied, "Have no fear. To give one daughter in exchange for the whole family, what is wrong with that? Wait for me to bathe, and I will go." She then set about preparing hot water. The family informed the bandits, who shouted and joked as they waited. When she had bathed, she took a mirror and dusted herself with pearl powder. She put on her clothes and completed her toilette. Suddenly she climbed on a stool, threaded her sash over a beam and formed the end into a ring. Realizing that the loop would not fit over her headdress, she took the headdress off. She then slipped her head into the noose, adjusted her hair, and replaced the headdress. And so she died.

The final line of the story reveals that the family put up such a hue and cry on discovering her body that the bandits were frightened off.

In his commentary on this story, Chen Liang employs the by now familiar trope, observing that it is rare to find even high-ranking lords and ministers who refuse to submit in times of disaster, and exclaiming at the fact that a girl was able to do so. He expresses special admiration for Du's serenity and self-control in the face of death.

For our purposes, equally admirable is the rhetorical sleight of hand employed in Chen Liang's account. Chen readily acknowledges that he did not see Du's death with his own eyes: "My family has lived in Yongkang for generations, and we live no more than about ten *li* from the Dus. Even though I did not see this event myself, my grandparents frequently told me it was like this." But of course no one—not Chen Liang's grandparents, not even her own family—could have known what transpired in Du's boudoir. Chen Liang's description is a fantasy, based, at best, on reconstruction after the fact. But by taking the reader into the boudoir of a nubile young woman as she bathes and adorns herself for (the reader expects) a violent sexual encounter, Chen turns his didactic tale into titillating entertainment.

Still, Chen Liang's didactic intent is clear from the remainder of his account. After comparing Du to virtuous exemplars of classical times, he continues:

> I wanted to publicize this story, and I showed it to my friend Ying Zhongshi. Zhongshi then told me, "In 1121, government soldiers were dispatched to capture the bandits. Wherever they went, they took advantage of their power to pillage and plunder. On the way to Yongkang, they went through Jinyun. Near the border, two daughters of a wealthy Chen family were captured. The soldier stuck his sword in the ground and addressed them, 'If you go with me, I'll make you my wives; otherwise you die.' The elder daughter was undaunted: she grasped her hair and extended her neck, asking to receive the blade. The soldier cut her throat. The second daughter in the end was despoiled. Later,

someone remonstrated with her, saying 'Why couldn't you behave like your older sister?' The younger daughter could only repeat in mortification, 'So difficult, so difficult.'"

Chen continues:

> Those who like to censure people always say they are behaving like girls. But wasn't the behavior of Chen and Du also that of girls? People encounter disaster and behave like girls, then when the incident is over they make up all sorts of wild excuses for themselves, brazen and smug. When they see the remorse of the second Chen daughter, what will they have to say? Zhongshi got this story from Mr. Hu Jingzhong. Both men are gentlemen of careful speech. I have thus recorded it here.[63]

Like the authors of most other Southern Song accounts of heroic women, Chen Liang aims his moral lessons at men, in this case castigating not only their weakness in the face of physical threat but their failure even to feel remorse about their moral failings. But Chen's artful construction of his account helps us to see *why* Southern Song men so consistently used female martyrs to address the problem of male loyalty. Like Ouyang Xiu and Xu Ji before him, Chen Liang understood that women's assumed weakness, and their very real sexual vulnerability, automatically invested their stories with tension and poignance.[64]

## *From Heroic Martyrs to Faithful Widows*

Perhaps partly for this reason, throughout the twelfth century texts featuring exemplary women focused almost exclusively on martyrs who died rather than submit to rape. In the thirteenth century, however, a few authors began assimilating the rhetoric of heroic exemplar texts into descriptions of faithful widows.

I have found four late Song texts that present faithful widows, rather than heroines, as models of exemplary behavior. Three were composed at the turn of the thirteenth century; the fourth some decades later. Three

---

63. *Chen Liang ji* 160–61.
64. The poignant suffering of women seems to have a universal resonance, as seen in depictions of saints' lives in Europe. Filial children made similarly compelling subjects, especially when they were quite young and when dramatic or violently filial acts were involved. E.g., see Zhang Zhihan, *Xi yan ji* 13.19a –20b.

of the four are explicitly titled as exemplar texts, referring to their upper-class subjects as principled women (*jie fu*), though two of these are in the form of funerary inscriptions. Another focuses on a woman somewhat further down the social scale and describes her in the context of the biography of her husband. All four texts can be seen as early precursors of a style of text that was to become extremely popular in the Yuan, and so are worthy of careful attention here.

Two of the texts in the group were composed by the famed late twelfth-century scholar-official and poet Yang Wanli. The first is not strictly speaking an exemplar text: it is nominally the biography of a man named Liu Hu (Guoli), a minor military official with whom Yang had become friendly and for whom he had written occasional recommendations.[65] Yang praises Liu for his sincerity and righteousness in friendship—a sincerity unmatched, Yang observes, by his many so-called "companions in the Dao and Righteousness" (*dao yi zhi jiao zhe* 道義之交者). After Liu's unexpected death, Yang was surprised to learn not only that Liu's wife had not remarried, but that his six concubines had not remarried either. He observes:

> I knew something of [Liu's] family circumstances. His wife Jiang was originally a courtesan (倡). The boy Yongge [Liu's son] was actually the son of someone surnamed Yong. Guoli and his wife reared him as their own child. And as for the six concubines, Jiang controlled them with extreme cruelty. Now Guoli is dead, and his wife, child, and concubines ought to have dispersed and never have stayed together; but instead they have united and will not be dispersed. Is this not virtuous? Generally, human feelings are such that when people hear the name of "courtesan," they hold their noses. When they hear a son is not one's own, they treat him differently [lit., their hearts are changed]. When they hear a mistress controls the concubines without human principle, they get so angry their hair stands on end. Having these three types of people living together without a master to order them, it would be difficult to hope that they would not immediately separate! Now Guoli is dead, but his wife, son, and concubines are able to be more mutually considerate and protective than when he was alive. Is this not admirable! These days, gentlemen and scholars frequently die in the morning and their wives leave in the evening. Is there one who is not shamed by Guoli's wife? Not only are they shamed by Guoli's wife, is there one who is not shamed by Guoli's concubines? Nor is it only the wives of gentlemen and

---

65. "Liu Guoli zhuan" (劉國禮傳), in *QSW* 240: 5358.38–40. Yang explicitly describes Liu as uneducated (*wei chang xue* 未嘗學). This text cannot be precisely dated, though Liu appears to have died in the late 1170s, when Yang was serving in Changzhou 常州.

scholars. The gentlemen and scholars establish someone's dynasty and enjoy someone's emolument. The dynastic officials say "I will die for the dynasty;" the border officials say, "I will die [to maintain] the border." But as soon as there is a crisis, is there one who is not shamed by Guoli's wife? Not only are they shamed by Guoli's wife, is there one who is not shamed by Guoli's concubines?

This text includes many of the tropes of exemplar writing we have seen above. Although he does not explicitly dignify them with the term "principled" (*jie*), Yang asserts that despite their despised status and (in the wife's case) cruel nature, Liu's wife, adopted son, and concubines nonetheless were able to uphold fidelity and thereby shame the inconstancy of the dynasty's officials. But in this case upholding fidelity did not consist of martyrdom to avoid rape, but simply of keeping the family together and not remarrying. Moreover, Yang holds up this faithful behavior as a model not only for officials, but for other widowed women who too often rushed to remarry after their husbands' deaths.

The same stress on widow fidelity is found in a funerary inscription that Yang composed in 1200 for another woman surnamed Liu, in response to a request by Liu's son.[66] Yang begins by describing a virtuous gentleman of his acquaintance, one Mr. Western Spring, who once received state awards for his virtue.[67] Yang waxes eloquent on the transformative influence of this man's virtue on those around him, as evinced especially in the exemplary behavior of his daughter.

Yang Wanli then tells us the young woman's story. Married at twenty-three *sui*, she was widowed three years later, with her in-laws still alive and a young son to rear. Neighborhood opinion assumed that she would remarry but, citing classical precedents, she vowed fidelity to her deceased husband. She sold her jewelry to pay for the funeral, sold her hair to pay for her son's studies, prepared pure food for her in-laws, and was diligent and frugal. Yang continues the litany of her virtues: she bought books and invited teachers for her son, so that he became well known; she helped others and distributed charity so that the whole family depended on her; she bore all these burdens for forty years without complaint. He

---

66. Yang Wanli, *Cheng zhai ji* 131.3b–6a. The discussion of this text and that of Liu Kezhuang below is revised from Bossler, "Maidens," 765–69.

67. In fact, in 1176 Yang had composed a record commemorating the state's award for filiality and other virtues to Woman Liu's father. See Yang Wanli, *Cheng zhai ji* 74.2b–4.

concludes: "If this is not what is called a principled woman, what else would you call her?" (*zi bu wei jie fu er wei zhi he zai* 茲不為節婦而為之何哉). He describes how inspired he was by her story, and then returns to his opening theme: "Someone who didn't know about Western Spring's virtue need not look at him, but could look at his sons; need not look at his sons, but could look at his daughter. She can be called a contemporary 'Song Boji' or 'Filial Daughter-in-Law Chen.'"[68]

Strikingly, in this text, Yang does not hold Liu up as a model for the behavior of others: he does not compare her to cowardly officials or to inconstant widows. Rather, he employs all the conventional rhetoric we are accustomed to seeing in funerary biographies of widows who did not remarry. But far more than even Fan Zuyu's late Northern Song inscriptions for such widows, this inscription puts exceptional emphasis on Liu's widowed state. It not only makes a dramatic moment of her decision to remain a widow and compares her to classical exemplars, it defines her virtue—and indeed her very existence—in terms of her actions as a widow. In the process, Yang explicitly defines the term "principled woman" in terms of widow fidelity. Moreover, Yang signals his intent to identify Liu as an exemplar in the title of the inscription: "Funerary Inscription of the Principled Woman Liu" (*Jie fu Liu shi mu ming* 節婦劉氏墓銘). Rather than identifying Liu simply by her natal or marital surnames, as was conventional up to this time, the title takes the unprecedented step of explicitly proclaiming Liu a *jie fu*.[69] Finally, he does so in spite of the fact that this assertion of her exemplar status is based simply on his own personal opinion: Liu was not the recipient of a state award or other formal honors.

---

68. These are references to classical models of virtuous women from Liu Xiang's *Biographies of Exemplary Women*. On Boji, see n. 3 above. Filial daughter-in-law Chen heeded her husband's instructions to take care of his mother, and after his death served her mother-in-law with great care, threatening suicide when her parents tried to get her to remarry. She was eventually recognized by the state for her filiality. See Liu Xiang, *Lie nü zhuan* 4.162–63.

69. To my knowledge, this and Liu Kezhuang's inscription (discussed below) are the only two Southern Song funerary inscriptions for women that signal the subject's exemplar status in the title, though this was to become common practice in the Yuan and Ming. Yang Wanli was a prolific producer of exemplar texts, composing biographies and other texts celebrating loyal officials and filial sons, including one who sought out a concubine mother.

Here Yang Wanli blends genres, making a funerary inscription for an ordinary widow into an exemplar text. The same sort of blending—and the same exemplar title—is found in one other late Song funerary inscription, composed by Liu Kezhuang in about 1232 for Principled Woman Li (Li *jie fu*).[70] In contrast to most funerary inscriptions, Liu here says virtually nothing about his subject's background, and instead focuses almost exclusively on her fidelity to her husband. He begins the inscription by explaining that Li was widowed a few months after marriage. Local villagers admired her beauty and virtue, and many sought her hand; her brothers, pitying her youth, were also anxious that she be remarried. But Li adamantly refused, saying it would be unrighteous to turn her back on her dead husband and unfilial to abandon her aged mother-in-law. When people pointed out that she would be poor and sonless, she was unfazed. Her neighbors admired her resolution, but suspected that she would regret her decision. Over the course of the next twenty years, however, they were proven wrong and moved to admiration, as Li served her mother-in-law, reared two adopted sons, and ultimately became a grandmother. Liu praises Li for raising her household out of poverty into middling wealth, so that she was able to marry the living and bury the dead without borrowing. He observes that when she died after twenty-eight years of widowhood, everyone mourned.

Here again we have rhetoric quite different even from the exemplar-style funerary inscriptions written at the end of the Northern Song. The specific details of Li's life and personality are almost erased, for she has become simply a model. Moreover, Liu goes even further than Yang Wanli in assimilating Li's biography to the rhetoric of exemplar texts, for he concludes:

> Formerly, Master Ou[yang Xiu] wrote of the severed-armed woman in order to shame the ministers of the Five Dynasties. [Now] I am recording the circumstances of Ms. Li: her vicissitudes can serve not only as a model for the inner [quarters]; they are also sufficient to serve as a warning to gentlemen and ministers. Here someone mild and amiable from the inner quarters, encountering [disastrous] change, was able to establish herself so admirably. This should certainly make men who encounter change in the world [i.e., a change in dynasty] able to establish their wills like [Bo] Yi and [Shu] Qi, and make men

---

70. Liu Kezhuang, *Hou cun ji* 38.12a–14a.

who accept a commission from someone able to carry it out like [Cheng] Ying and [Gongsun Chu] Jiu.⁷¹ Alas, how awe-inspiring! How awe-inspiring!

Rather than a private account meant to preserve the memory, however idealized, of a real woman for posterity, this funerary inscription has become an exemplar text, designed to present its subject as a model to inspire other women and men. Liu's inscription represents a further softening of the social code—and generic conventions—by which the lives of upper-class women had been shielded from public scrutiny. And here again, we see the assertion that simple widowhood, marked indeed by patient devotion but not by radical sacrifice, constituted not just admirable but exemplary behavior.⁷²

The final of the four late Song texts for faithful widows is the only one composed for an officially recognized exemplar. It was written by Zhang Ruyu about 1205, when Zhang was serving as an editorial assistant in the history office.⁷³ Entitled "Account of the Integrity and Righteousness of the Gentlewoman Ye" (*Ru ren Ye shi jie yi zhuan* 孺人葉氏節義傳), the text was written at imperial command to honor a woman who had received a court award. Zhang opens the inscription by telling the story of the same Virtuous Maiden Shrine we saw earlier, and then by describing another historical figure known for insisting that "Not to step into two courtyards is a constant principle for women." Zhang comments, "Ah, if people were able to understand this principle and make it constant, then human relations would be ordered and All-under-Heaven would be governed. Would that not be deeply fortunate for the Dao of the world?"

Zhang then describes his subject: the daughter of a Ye family in his county, she was betrothed to a man named Cheng. Before the marriage

---

71. Bo Yi and Shu Qi were sons of the last king of Yin, who were celebrated by Sima Qian for starving to death rather than eating the grain of the succeeding dynasty (cf. chap. 3, n. 6). Cheng Ying and Gongsun Chu Jiu were men of the Chunqiu period who went to great lengths to preserve the young heir of the Zhao line.

72. It is possible that in fact Yang and Liu's funerary inscriptions were meant to help to gain government recognition for their subjects.

73. Zhang Ruyu, in Cheng Minzheng, *Xin'an wenxian zhi* 98.17b–19a. Zhang is a rather obscure figure who once served as a prefect, was briefly called to court, but was then cashiered for attacking the powerful minister Han Tuozhou. He spent the rest of his life as a teacher. His surviving works suggest that he was interested in Learning of the Way ideas. See Chang Bide, *Song ren zhuan ji* 3.2091.

took place, Cheng died. Ye requested that her father allow her to go to the Cheng family to mourn her betrothed and rear his heir. Her parents agreed, the matter was submitted to the court, and a government award was duly issued to Ye, along with a noble title.[74]

Notably, however, Zhang Ruyu is unenthusiastic about this turn of events. He quotes from Confucius to demonstrate that what Ye has done is completely uncanonical: for an unmarried woman to remain faithful to her betrothed goes beyond and thus contravenes ritual propriety. Still, at the end of his inscription Zhang grudgingly acknowledges that, "Today the Dao has declined, and spouses who treat each other as enemies are common. At the moment of death, they immediately turn their backs on the affection of former days. When they see Ye's lofty behavior, can they fail to be ashamed?!" He concludes that the court's bestowal of honors "truly helps improve customs."

This text is noteworthy, first of all, in showing how easily the rhetoric of heroic martyrdom could be appropriated to the discussion of faithful widows. Zhang invokes the Virtuous Maiden, thereby quietly implying that Lady Ye (although she did not commit suicide) is equally heroic. But this text is also important in revealing Zhang's ambivalence about the case he is celebrating. On the one hand, he strongly supports the principle of widow fidelity, and claims it as a key to the ordering of human relations; on the other hand, he is deeply troubled by the fact that Ye was merely a fiancée, from whom lifelong fidelity was not expected or sanctioned by classical authorities.

Taken together, these four inscriptions demonstrate a number of subtle but important shifts in late Song rhetoric about female fidelity. Like earlier writers, both Yang Wanli and Liu Kuzhuang express continued concern for male loyalty, but they also suggest that their subjects can serve as models for women. Like Zhang Ruyu, Yang Wanli frets that widows of his day are rushing to remarry, and both he and Zhang assert that proper family relations, especially as upheld by women, are

---

74. We might also note here that, although Ye is clearly what would later be called a "chaste maiden" (*zhen nü* 貞女), Zhang does not employ that term, suggesting that her behavior did not yet belong to a recognized category. Instead, he refers to her as "Principled and Righteous" (*jie yi* 節義). On the chaste maiden phenomenon in Qing times, see Weijing Lu, *True to Her Word*.

important for ordering the world more broadly. Zhang, while asserting the value of exemplars to "transform customs," expresses ambivalence about exemplary behavior that is not in accord with classical principles. All of these were to become important themes in exemplar discourse in the Yuan. Finally, it is notable here that, while all three authors express ideas associated with the Learning of the Way philosophy, none of them was a leader or major figure in the movement. In other words, although Learning of the Way ideas were gaining in influence during this period, and were certainly consonant with the model of female fidelity being expressed in these texts, the impetus for exemplar discourse was elsewhere.[75]

The remaining decades of the Song saw continued cultural fascination with exemplars. This was evident in the appearance of collections of didactic exemplar stories, designed to be easy to read and recite, as well as in the continued production of individual exemplar texts.[76] Most of the latter were devoted to men, but the few for women celebrated faithful widows. Chen Zhu (1214–97) wrote a poem honoring his sister, commemorating the fact that she had received a government award as a faithful widow. Jia Xuanweng (1213–after 1295) composed a record for a hall that the family of a faithful widow had named "Faithful and Filial" in her honor.[77] Here again, the interest in female exemplars shifts to faithful widows, and upper-class faithful widows appear in a widening range of genres.

---

75. On the proliferation of Learning of the Way ideology in examination writings in the thirteenth century see De Weerdt, *Competition over Content*, chap. 7.

76. See Lin Tong's *Poems on Filiality* (*Xiao shi* 孝詩), which sums up stories of historical filial exemplars in short, easy-to-recite poems. James T.C. Liu, in *China Turning Inward*, 140, notes that proponents of Learning of the Way printed "rhymed quotations" as moralistic propaganda to the uneducated, and Lin's text seems to fit that description. It contains stories of filial women, but not faithful widows. Lin Tong's collection was preceded by a text, no longer extant, called *History of Filiality* (*Xiao shi* 孝史), by the court official and teacher Xie E 謝諤 (1121–94).

77. Chen Zhu, *Ben tang ji* 23.3; Jia Xuanweng, *Ze tang ji* 2.22a–23b. Like Liu Kezhuang, Jia cites Ouyang Xiu's biography of the severed-armed wife of Wang Ning as precedent for his text. Neither of these texts can be precisely dated; it is possible they were not composed until after the Yuan conquest.

## Conclusion

Over the course of the Southern Song, we see the very beginnings of the development of a discourse of female fidelity, in the form of a gradual increase in texts celebrating exemplars of female virtue.[78] Driven in part by the government's desire to demonstrate its Confucian legitimacy and by Cheng Learning efforts to proselytize the faith, writing about exemplars also flourished because it served a variety of functions useful to the burgeoning local elite of the Southern Song. Within this broader discourse, texts for men slightly outnumbered those for women; in addition, even when authors celebrated female exemplars, they did so overwhelmingly in the interests of encouraging male morality, and especially male political loyalty.[79] In other words, at this early stage, the discourse of female virtue was generally not directed at shaping or improving the conduct of women.

Still, within the expanding discourse on exemplary behavior we do see two significant changes in the way that women, in particular, were written about. First, from fairly early in the Southern Song we see an unprecedented appearance of upper-class women, and especially upper-class wives, in publicly circulating genres such as biographies, prefaces, and postfaces (that is, outside of the more conventional—because putatively more private—genre of funerary inscriptions). Moreover, these upper-class women tended to belong to the author's own social circles. Rather than representing relatively abstract symbols of extraordinary virtue, exemplars could now be found among one's personal acquaintances.

A second subtle but very important shift took place in the thirteenth century, as writers began to write about not just heroic martyrs but faithful widows, and not just as models for male loyalty but as models for other women, or for ethical behavior in society more generally. This shift

---

78. We shall see in chap. 9 that, in comparison with later eras, the total number of exemplar texts produced in the Song was still quite small. I have identified roughly ninety exemplar texts from the Song period, of which about eighteen date from the Northern Song. These numbers cannot be absolute, as many texts cannot be precisely dated and many authors transcend the Northern Song–Southern Song divide; but there are clearly significantly more texts from the Southern Song than from the Northern Song.

79. Texts for women represent about forty percent of the total number of Song exemplar texts; this proportion remains essentially constant across both halves of the dynasty.

bears close scrutiny, and like the use of women as models for men, it was possible largely due to the fertile polysemy of Chinese notions of female integrity (*jie*).

Earlier chapters have noted that in Confucian theory, the bond of loyalty between wife and husband was analogous to that between minister and ruler. Note, however, that the Southern Song women held up as models for male political loyalty included a daughter who died to save her father and brother, a woman who died protecting her mother-in-law, and several unmarried women who died simply to preserve their physical purity. Indeed, the majority of the women celebrated as principled women by Southern Song authors were distinguished not by loyalty to a spouse but by refusal to submit to rape by bandits or invaders.

The symbolic resonance of such refusal transcends culture: the fundamental hierarchies of gender worldwide have meant that, in virtually all times and places, the invasion of women's bodies has served as a powerful and all-too-literal analogy for the invasion of political territories.[80] Conversely, women's refusal of rape by invaders is readily seen as analogous to the political loyalty of men (recall Chen Changfang: "It is the responsibility of women and girls to preserve one body"). Accordingly, in the Song context, a woman's refusal to submit to bodily invasion was understood as both a stinging indictment of men who had *not* refused to let the country be invaded, and an inspiration to the political loyalty of other men. But we should be conscious of the rhetorical slippage that was also occurring here: women's integrity as expressed in these suicides was simultaneously construed as loyalty or filiality to other persons, and loyalty to cultural (Confucian) ideals.[81]

---

80. Cf. the systematic use of rape as a tactic of warfare in the twentieth century and down to today, from the Rape of Nanjing to recent conflicts in Bosnia and Somalia.

81. For further exploration of this point, see Bossler, "Gender and Empire," 202–4, 215–16. Jay argues that most women who committed suicide rather than submit to invaders did not act out of loyalty to the state (though she acknowledges a few exceptions; see *A Change in Dynasties*, 129–31); Davis suggests that late Song men rejected the idea that women could have "civic consciousness," because they were threatened by the active presence of women in Song political and cultural life (*Wind Against the Mountain*, 184–88). I would argue, rather, that where women's loyalty was concerned the distinction is moot: from classical times in China, women's loyal martyrdom was always understood as having simultaneously personal and broader cultural/political implications.

The multiple meanings attached to female bodily integrity helped make possible the seamless shift in late Song from upholding female martyrs as models for male political loyalty and the preservation of Confucian culture, to upholding faithful widows for the same purposes. Again, in one respect, this was not an innovation: the idea that a faithful widow could be a model for male political loyalty was enshrined in the classical husband/wife, ruler/minister analogy, and Ouyang Xiu had deployed the severed-armed wife of Wang Ning in exactly that way. But for all that, the thirteenth-century claims that ordinary faithful widows (as opposed to those who cut off their arms) should be taken as models of male loyalty were *new* (such rhetoric does not appear in the late Northern Song funerary inscriptions for faithful widows). Here we see the critical role played by public circulation of texts for martyrs: only after a discourse in which female martyrs served as models for male loyalty was well established (and had proven advantageous to literati families) did literati authors begin asserting that the fidelity of ordinary widows should also be construed as an act of extraordinary political and cultural loyalty.

Finally, we should also remember that the gradually increasing attention to female—and especially widow—loyalty in the Southern Song was taking place in an environment marked by the increasing commodification of women. Earlier chapters have outlined the threat that this commodification represented to Chinese families and society. Although Song writings for exemplars do not explicitly address that threat, a woman's refusal to be treated as war booty, and a widow's refusal to be sold into another household after her husband's death, took on additional significance as a rejection of such commodification.

With the fall of the Southern Song, the social and political world of Chinese literati was radically reconfgured. The Yuan conquest was to create extraordinarily fertile conditions for the discourse on female fidelity to expand, not only by providing a new set of female martyrs to be commemorated, but by blurring even further the boundaries between courtesans, concubines, and wives.

PART THREE

*Conquerors and Culture in the Yuan*

# 7

# *Exemplary Entertainers*

### Zhu Lianxiu 珠帘秀

If one concentrates his effort in study, over time he will have ability; [but] growing old in an art, no one can ever become perfect. [Yet] there is a woman in whom all the arts are arrayed. In a tall cap she becomes a Daoist; with a round pate she is a Buddhist monk; in flowing robes she is a scholar; in a military helmet she is a soldier. In a short coat she is a galloping horse; with a fish-shaped tally she becomes a noble minister. As a fortune-teller she predicts disaster and blessings; as a doctor she decides life and death. When she is a mother, she is kind and tender; as a wife she is filial and chaste; when she is a go-between she is self-assured and smooth-talking; as a cloistered maiden she is graceful and charming. [She enacts] the eastern and southern barbarians, the hundred spirits and myriad apparitions, the customs of the five directions, the accents of the various thoroughfares, the events of the ancient past, the statutes and punishments of the historical eras. [She portrays] lowly clerks, corrupt and greedy; and senior officials, equitable and pure of conduct. Speaking of the hundred commodities she is a traveling merchant or local vendor; doing manual labor she is a woman weaving or a man plowing. At home the father is kind and the son filial; at court the lord is sage and the minister perspicacious. At parting banquets and elegant gatherings, in side halls and secluded pavilions, she strikes the spring-breeze harp and plays the bright-moon lute. If poor, then her hairpins are thorn and her skirt of coarse cloth; if rich and voluptuous, then the rooms are of gold and the screens of silver. The nine schools and the hundred skills, the various beauties and gathered brilliances: externally she entirely realizes their demeanor; internally she thoroughly comprehends their emotions. Her heart achieves [the spiritual state of] samadhi, and [the characters] naturally come into being. She manifests the cultivation of the age, and takes pleasure in a century of great peace.[1]

---

1. Hu Zhiyu, *Zi shan da quan ji* 8.9a–10a.

In this effusive prose, the scholar and eminent official Hu Zhiyu described the actress Zhu Lianxiu, whose consummate skill and thorough understanding of her craft allowed her to transform herself into all manner of convincing characters. Hu's text—one of several poetry prefaces that he wrote for entertainers—is unusual first of all simply in being written by an prominent official in honor of an actress.[2] More significant, however, is the *way* Hu describes his subject. Hu not only credits Zhu with almost supernatural talent, he suggests that her skill is grounded in self-cultivation, a self-cultivation no less authentic—indeed more difficult—than that of the scholar. Hu Zhiyu's preface, I will argue, is symptomatic of a new attitude toward entertainers that, though hinted at in the late Song, fully emerges only in the Yuan.

The new attitudes evident in the Yuan may have originated in trends already established in the Song, but they were also facilitated by the particular circumstances of the Yuan conquest. The painfully slow fall of the Southern Song to the Mongols, in combination with the new dynasty's rapacious approach to governance and the "compressed Yuan dynastic cycle,"[3] meant that during the century and a half from the mid-thirteenth century to the turn of the fifteenth century, life in China was marked by frequent disorder, violence, and disruption. Against that chaos, the Mongol government attempted to order society through a rigid and hereditary organizational structure. That structure, along with the enthusiastic patronage of the Mongol court, contributed to the continued development and growing social influence of the theater arts. Although under Yuan policies performers were theoretically constituted as a distinct, hereditary occupational group, in practice the boundaries between performers and other social classes remained fluid. Moreover, the dynasty's harsh treatment of Chinese literati, especially in the south, encouraged the literati to turn to the production and appreciation of

---

2. As noted in chap. 3, one poetry preface in honor of a courtesan survives from the Northern Song (I know of none from the Southern Song). However, that preface, although admiring of the courtesan's looks and dancing, does not dwell on her talent and is not addressed to her. Rather, it emphasizes the literary efforts of the contributors to the volume.

3. This felicitous phrase was coined by Paul Smith in "Fear of Gynarchy," 3. Smith notes that the Yuan was hardest on southern Chinese elite not in its conquest, but in its failure to rule well.

dramatic performance. The result was a new valorization of entertainers' talents and a growing recognition of their shared humanity, expressed (as in Hu Zhiyu's preface) through the presentation of entertainers as exemplars of Confucian values. The acknowledgment of shared humanity in turn contributed to further breakdown in the social boundaries separating courtesans from other kinds of women, especially concubines and wives.

## Entertainment Institutions Under the Yuan

The Yuan emperors loved entertainment. During his second year on the Chinese throne, Qubilai (r. 1260–94) reestablished a Court Entertainment Bureau (*jiao fang si* 教坊司) to oversee more than 500 households of entertainers, some in full-time, permanent troupes of actors and acrobats, and some "on call" (*cheng ying* 承應). In this manner, Qubilai incorporated aspects of both the Northern and Southern Song court music institutions.[4] As in the Northern Song, the court maintained a discrete bureaucracy charged with managing the entertainers required for court banquets and celebrations.[5] But as in most of the Southern Song period, at least some of the entertainers involved did not strictly speaking "belong" to the court, but were simply called in when occasion demanded. When not in service to the court, the entertainer households of the Yuan *jiao fang* were apparently free to ply their trade in the public markets of the capital, ensuring

---

4. Song Lian, *Yuan shi* (hereafter *YS*), 85.2139; Farquhar, *Government of China*, 195–96. Note that the two offices subordinate to the Court Entertainment Bureau—one for female entertainers and actors (妓女雜扮隊戲) and one for male and female acrobats (雜把戲男女)—each managed 150 performers, but the Bureau as a whole was in charge of 500 households of entertainers.

5. For ranks and titles, see Farquhar, *Government of China*, 195–96. In addition to the Court Entertainment Bureau, the court established an Office of Ceremonial Music (*Yi feng si* 儀鳳司), which was focused on ritual music and sacrifices. Idema and West suggest that the Office of Ceremonial Music controlled musicians whereas the Entertainment Bureau managed "actors and other entertainers of non-musical skills" (*Chinese Theater*, 104). However, the Entertainment Bureau also had jurisdiction over certain types of musicians (*YS* 85.2138), and there was considerable bureaucratic overlap and movement between the two offices over the course of the Yuan (see Farquhar, *Government of China*, 194), suggesting that the distinctions between "ritual and "entertainment" and between "musicians" and "entertainers" were often blurred.

continued interchange between elite and popular entertainment forms and dramatic themes.

By 1274 Qubilai had more than doubled the size of the *jiao fang*, ordering that an additional 800 musicians be brought under its jurisdiction.[6] His successors shared his theatrical interests, as reflected in the unprecedented favor they granted to entertainment officials. The position of head of the *jiao fang*, initially ranked 5a, by 1304 had been raised as high as 3a, before being scaled back to 4a in 1320.[7] During some reigns individual *jiao fang* officials received even more extravagant honors. Within months of his accession to the throne in 1307, for example, Khaishan (Emperor Wuzong [r. 1307–11]) bestowed the exalted honorary rank of Manager of Governmental Affairs (*ping zhang zheng shi* 平章政事) on the heads of both the ritual music (*yi feng si* 儀鳳司) and popular music (*jiao fang si* 教坊司) offices.[8] Although Khaishan's action can be seen as part of a broader pattern of prolific, even promiscuous distribution of honors during his reign,[9] in 1315 Ayurbarwada Khaghan (Emperor Renzong [r. 1312–20]), ostensibly the most Confucian of the Yuan emperors, attempted to promote the head of his *jiao fang* to the position of Minister of Rites (*li bu shang shu* 禮部尚書).[10] Other emperors contented themselves with rewarding musicians and their official overseers with silver and other tangible expressions of their appreciation, as when in 1329 Tugh Temür (Emperor Wenzong [r. 1328–29]) gave the head of the Entertainment Bureau some 300 ingots' worth of paper money that had been collected in fines by the censorate.[11] At various points during the dynasty, other court officials complained about the privileges given to the *jiao fang*

---

6. *YS* 8.158.

7. *YS* 85.2139.

8. *YS* 22.484. See also Zhang Yanghao's memorial of 1310, in which he complains bitterly about the high offices bestowed on performers (*Gui tian lei gao* 2.1a ff., esp. 10a–b).

9. Hsiao Ch'i-ch'ing, "Mid-Yuan Politics," 508.

10. *YS* 175.4073, in the biography of Zhang Gui 張珪. The *YS* reports that Zhang Gui vehemently objected to the promotion, but does not record whether his objections were heeded.

11. *YS* 33.729. Smith describes Kong Qi as complaining that official appointments, too, were granted to entertainers and degraded people ("Impressions," 93). See also Kong Qi, *Zhizheng zhi ji* 4.153–54.

officials (in particular there was extended wrangling about whether such officials should be allowed to stand with regular officials during ceremonies), but overall the Entertainment Bureau received unprecedented favor during the Yuan.[12]

Courtesan entertainments remained popular with officials outside the court as well. Although evidence is sparse, the court model of maintaining a registry of on-call musicians appears to have been replicated in the provincial capitals.[13] In other words, the Song institution of government-courtesans (*guan ji* 官妓) attached to prefectural and county yamens gave way in the Yuan to a system in which courtesans were merely on call, rather than permanently attached to the yamen as they had been in the Song.[14] The late Song/early Yuan literatus and official Fang Hui (1227–1307) remarked on the Song system and its demise:

> In recent eras evil aspects of the law [were] that eunuchs could promote sons, leading to the castration of innocent people, and that respectable girls who committed illicit sex with more than three people were reduced to "miscellaneous households" (*za hu* 雜戶) status [thus juridically lower in status than commoners], beaten severely, and sent to be under the jurisdiction of the courtesan-music office. These became the disorderly strumpets [*wu hang di zi* 無行弟子] of the prefectures. Generation after generation they reared girls to serve at the banquets of officials. When in service they wore topknots, red cloaks, hats, and girdle ornaments, sending off and greeting [the officials] on the first and the

---

12. On arguments about where music officials should be allowed to stand during ceremonies, see *YS* 139.3356–57, 172.4027, 184.4237. Waley suggests that in about 1341 the Entertainment Bureau officials lost status as regular officials (see Waley, *Secret History*, 98), but I have been unable to confirm this.

13. *YS* 16.340 contains a 1289 order that the Jiang-huai Branch Secretariat investigate the tax and corvée obligations of Jiangnan musicians under the management of the Provincial Entertainment Bureau (*xing jiao fang si* 行教坊司). This is the only reference to such a provincial institution that I have discovered; however, Farquhar indicates that, in general, central government institutions were replicated at the provincial level (*Government of China*, 5–6). Cf. Idema and West, *Chinese Theater*, 104–8.

14. We have seen that this process was already underway in the Song, when entertainers at government banquets could include both registered government-courtesans and unregistered itinerant musicians. The few Yuan sources that refer to contemporary *guan ji* seem to apply the term to any women who performed at government banquets. Similarly, the term "Entertainment Bureau" seems to have been applied to all entertainers, not just those associated with the court. Conversely, the Song category of yamen musicians (*ya qian yue* 衙前樂) apparently no longer existed in the Yuan.

fifteenth [of the month], following the crowds and clearing the way like men. *Today they no longer have them* (今日遂無之) (emphasis added).[15]

Fang's observations provide us with new insight into the duties of government-courtesans under the Song (although they also reveal a strikingly limited understanding of how most Song government-courtesans were recruited). The new relationship between courtesans and the government was also remarked by the anecdotalist Tao Zongyi (ca. 1320–ca. 1403), who reported, "Today they use courtesans (*ji* 妓) to serve as 'official slaves' (*guan nu* 官奴), that is to say, 'government maidservants' (*guan bi* 官婢)."[16] In other words, rather than women who were already government slaves being pressed into service as entertainers, as seems to have happened in the early Song, here we have the reverse: in Tao's understanding, women who were first and foremost entertainers were being pressed into service at the yamen. The Yuan government acknowledged "entertainer" as a professional identity, rather than seeing it as a sometime duty of female slaves.

The Yuan system also put an end to the distinction, already blurring in the Southern Song, between government- and independent courtesans. All entertainers were liable for government service as a form of corvée, but they were also free to entertain private clients.[17] In this respect, the Yuan government treated entertainer households in essentially the same manner as they treated military or artisan households, that is, as groups of hereditary service providers. And just as they found it necessary to make laws prohibiting officials from overextracting supplies and services of other types, in 1284 the court was forced to issue regulations limiting

---

15. Fang Hui, *Gu jin kao xu* 36.10a–11a. I translate "disciple" (*di zi*) as "strumpet" here to reflect the generally more negative valence of the term in the Yuan. On the Song law requiring women convicted of illicit sex with three or more people to serve as government-courtesans, see chap. 1, n. 23.

16. Tao Zongyi, *Nancun chuo geng lu* 7.87. Tao goes on to quote the *Rites of Zhou* and the Han commentator Zheng Xuan on Zhou and Han precedents for maidservants in government offices.

17. To put it another way, at least officially, unregistered entertainers or *san yue* no longer existed during the Yuan. On these entertainers and their prevalence in the Song, cf. Idema and West, *Chinese Theater*, 118–27; Liang, "Song dai ji yi ren." On the Yuan government's attempts to fix the structure of society, see Franke and Twitchett, *Cambridge History*, 648–56. We saw in earlier chapters that in the Southern Song, even unregistered entertainers could sometimes be called to serve at official banquets.

the ability of officials to demand sexual services from courtesans under their jurisdictions.[18]

In attempting to establish entertainers as a closed and self-perpetuating occupational category, the Yuan government found itself fighting an uphill battle against the dominant social forces of the day. To be sure, even under Song law entertainer status was (at least in theory) hereditary, and, according to the letter of the law, individuals of entertainer status were forbidden to marry respectable commoners. But those laws were seldom enforced in the Song, and moving into respectable status through marriage with a commoner, or even an official, was imagined as the ideal denouement of the courtesan's professional life. By contrast, the Yuan government actively undertook legislation designed to keep entertainers separate from the rest of society.[19] For example, the Yuan government insisted that all entertainer families (*chang ji zhi jia* 倡妓之家) regularly report the birth of children, male and female, and forbade such families to practice abortion or infanticide.[20] It also attempted to put an end to the constant recruitment of women of respectable (*liang*) background into the profession, threatening entertainer families who purchased respectable women, as well as officials who colluded in such fraud, with "severe punishment" (*tong sheng* 痛繩).[21] The laws stipulated that both buyers and sellers in such transactions would be punished, and the purchase price would be split evenly between the government and the whistle-blower.[22] Making female prisoners of war into entertainers (*chang* 娼) was forbidden, and the court also found it necessary explicitly to prohibit forcing a wife or concubine to sell her services as an entertainer, adopting a girl of good family to become an entertainer,

---

18. *Da Yuan sheng zheng guo chao dian zhang* (hereafter *YDZ*) 36.12a–13a.

19. The fact that contemporaries could point to several families that produced famous entertainers over several generations suggests that the notion of entertainment as a hereditary occupation held at least some sway during the Yuan. See Xia Tingzhi, *Qing lou ji jian zhu* (hereafter *QLJJZ*), 132–33.

20. *YS* 105.2687; see also the law against an outsider forcing a courtesan to abort, *YS* 103.1644. These and other Yuan laws regarding the control of entertainers are described in Sommer, *Sex, Law, and Society*, 219–30.

21. *YS* 105.2687. The prohibitions on making respectable women into entertainers were repeatedly "clarified" (*YS* 9.185).

22. *YS* 103.2644–45.

or coercing one's slaves to serve as entertainers (*chang* 倡). Conversely, although the Yuan abandoned the Song practice of penalizing adulterous women by forcing them to serve as government-courtesans, it did permit a respectable woman who had committed adultery and was no longer wanted by her husband to become a courtesan of her own volition.[23]

At the same time as they attempted to prevent respectable women from becoming entertainers, the Yuan government also attempted to stem the constant outflow of entertainers into the inner quarters of wealthy and powerful men. Any official who attempted to marry a courtesan was subject to a beating of fifty-seven strokes, loss of office, and compulsory divorce.[24] The specificity of this regulation already represents a major departure from at least the early Song, when the authors of the statutes seem to have considered taking a courtesan as a wife so unlikely that they did not even bother to address the possibility, and even taking a courtesan as a concubine was grounds for impeachment.[25] In contrast, by Yuan times the penchant of officials for taking courtesans into their households had become a major source of concern. In 1278 the Palace Provisions Commission (*Xuan hui yuan* 宣徽院), the court office then in charge of entertainer households, complained that because officials and wealthy power-holders were purchasing the most beautiful and talented of its performers as wives and concubines, the office was in danger of not being able to provide the necessary quota of performers to the court. In response to the Commission's petition, the court reiterated the principle that musicians should only marry other musicians, and explicitly forbade "officials and wealthy households" (*guan ren fu hu* 官人富戶) from "forcibly taking them in marriage" (*qiang qu* 強娶).[26] This injunction was apparently not very effective, as it was reiterated in 1293 and 1311.[27]

---

23. *YS* 4.73; *YS* 103.2644. See also *YDZ* 45.9a.
24. *YS* 103.2643.
25. This crime was apparently sufficiently rare that no specific penalty for it ever seems to have been established. When Song men were prosecuted for attempting to make courtesans into wives, their cases were treated on an ad hoc basis (cf. the case of Li Zhiyi discussed in chap. 4). On Yuan marriage law, see de Pee, *The Writing of Weddings*, 203–20.
26. *YDZ* 18.46a.
27. *YDZ* 18.46a–b.

It is particularly telling here that, although the regulations also forbade ordinary commoners to intermarry with courtesans, they were primarily directed at officials. Equally significant is that mere debauchery with courtesans no longer seems to have been grounds for the impeachment of officials. In the Song, as we have seen, charges of intimacy with courtesans were common, and could threaten a man's career; in contrast, surviving Yuan records contain not a single indictment of officials for intimacy or debauchery with courtesans—in spite of the fact that (as we will see in chapter 8) taking professional entertainers as concubines became something of a fad among high-ranking Yuan bureaucrats.[28]

As the regulations forbidding the marriage of entertainers with commoners or officials indicate, performers in the Yuan continued in theory to belong to a despised status that distinguished them from *liang* or respectable individuals. Yet by this point confusion about the categories of "respectable" and "base" (*jian*) had become so endemic that the author of an introductory handbook for those aspiring to become clerks in local government offices (a common path to office in the Yuan) found it necessary to explicate the terms in some detail. This author, the southerner Xu Yuanrui 徐元瑞 (fl. 1300), carefully elucidated the distinctions between the categories of respectable (*liang*), base (*jian*), slave (*zi* 孳), and chattel (*chan* 產). Xu first introduces the dyad *gui jian* 貴賤 (noble and humble), noting that in opposition to noble, *jian* simply means of low status and without office. Quoting an earlier legal commentary, he notes that in this context, even a gentleman may sometimes hold the status of *jian*. He then contrasts *gui jian* with the dyad *liang jian* (respectable and base), noting that the latter pair of terms refers to household registration status: ordinary people are *liang*; but innkeepers (*dian hu* 店戶), "courtesans and players" (*chang you* 倡優), and official and private slaves (*guan si nu bi* 官私奴婢) are all referred to (*wei zhi* 謂之) as *jian*. Again

---

28. Early in the dynasty, Wang Yun impeached a county magistrate for, among other crimes, attempting to take a courtesan as a wife (Wang Yun, *Qiujian ji* 88.23a–25a). I have found no other evidence of officials indicted for relationships with courtesans, in spite of the fact that both government documents and descriptions of legal cases show that courtesans continued to be a ubiquitous and often disruptive presence in local government offices. See Wang Yun, *Qiujian ji* 88.18a–19a, 88.22a; Yu Ji, *Dao yuan xue gu lu* 19.324–25.

quoting the earlier legal commentary, he points out that in this context even a petty person is ashamed to be *jian*. Xu also finds it necessary to explicate further what he means by "entertainer" and "innkeeper," explaining that skilled performers (acrobats, magicians, and the like) and musicians (*ji yue* 伎樂) are *chang*, whereas those who jest and do skits (*xie xi* 諧戲) are *you*, and in general the phrase *chang you* refers to the households of entertainers, singers, and dancers. Innkeeper households, he says, are those who personally manage hostels or places where performers (*chang ji* 倡伎) stay.[29]

Xu Yuanrui's handbook reveals that highly specialized performers had become common in the countryside and suggests that there was widespread uncertainty about their status.[30] Confusion about the types and statuses of performers is also evident in other Yuan regulations, which seem to recognize varying social "levels" of entertainers. Some Yuan sumptuary regulations, for example, distinguish between "musician-artists" (*yue yi ren* 樂藝人) who are allowed to wear the same clothing and use the same implements as respectable commoners, and members of courtesan households (*chang jia* 娼家), who are officially required to wear black vests and are forbidden to ride on horses or in carts.[31] How the court determined which performers were musician-artists and which were courtesans is not clear: it may have been attempting to distinguish between musicians who played ritual music and popular entertainers, or (more likely) it may have been attempting to separate those who merely provided dramatic entertainment from those who sold sexual services.[32] However these distinctions

---

29. Xu Yuanrui, *Li xue zhi nan*, 103–4.

30. Xu's discussion shows that ambiguity and slippage between the legal and moral understandings of the terms *liang* and *jian* was endemic long before the Late Imperial period. This fact somewhat complicates Matthew Sommer's arguments about the evolving use of these terms in the Qing (Sommer, *Sex, Law, and Society*, 312–19). I discuss Sommer's work further in the conclusion of this book.

31. These regulations appear in identical form in *YDZ* 29.4a; in the compendium of legal statutes *Da yuan tong zhi tiao ge* 9.4 (345); and in *YS* 78.1943. Christian de Pee also notes the unprecedentedly detailed sumptuary regulations established by the Yuan. He suggests that this was an effort to stem litigation, though he also notes the court's concern with proper class boundaries. See de Pee, *The Writing of Weddings*, 191, 201–2, 206.

32. The distinction is also implicit in the 1333 examination success of a man from a ritual music household (*li yue hu* 禮樂戶) at a time when those who were "related to

were defined, in practice the regulations were mostly moot in any case. Sumptuary regulations in general seem to have been routinely flouted: a lawsuit of 1301 reports that the harlot-courtesan (*chang ji* 娼妓) Zhang Derong 張德榮 had not only failed to wear the prescribed clothing of her profession, but had secretly moved out of the entertainment district where courtesans were supposed to live to settle near the marketplace, where she was inappropriately "mixing with gentlemen and commoners and defiling the steps and thoroughfares." More to the point, the lawsuit addressed Zhang's illegal clothing and residence only in passing: the real reason she was prosecuted was that she had had the temerity to bid up the price of a piece of property in competition with a foreigner (Mongol?) who also wanted to buy it.[33] Evidently Zhang was a woman of considerable means and economic savvy. Moreover, although this lawsuit exposed Zhang's breech of the sumptuary regulations, two years later the official Zheng Jiefu 鄭介夫 was still complaining that "base people of the lanes" were wearing pearls and ornaments more appropriate to empresses.[34] A poem by Zhang Zhu likewise describes courtesans obediently traveling back and forth from the courtesan district on the backs of donkeys, as per the regulations, but he describes them as wearing precisely the sort of bamboo hat (*li* 笠) that the regulations explicitly prohibited them from wearing:[35]

| 長川妓子早晨來 | One after another, each morning the courtesans come, |
| 戴笠騎驢帕擁腮 | Wearing bamboo hats, riding donkeys, their faces hidden by veils. |

---

singing-girls or actors" (*chang you zhi jia* 倡優之家) were not eligible to participate in the examinations (Farquhar, *Government of China*, 48; *YS* 81.2022). Wang Ning suggests that the *yue ren* of the Yuan were basically the *san yue* (itinerant performers) of the Song (*Song Yuan yue ji yu xi ju*, 90–91), but we have seen that such a distinction was not acknowledged in other Yuan laws, and at least some Yuan plays treat itinerant performers as identical to courtesans. Thus in *Wind and Moon in the Courtyard of Purple Clouds* (*Feng yue zi yun ting* 風月紫雲庭), the heroine is a member of a band of itinerant players, but she is also clearly under pressure from her madam to entice customers (see Idema and West, *Chinese Theater*, 242–78. Idema and West note that the characterization of the heroine varies between "courtesan" and "actress" in different versions of the story).

33. *YDZ* 19.31a; the passage identifies her competitor Hami (哈迷) only by his name, but he was clearly non-Han.

34. Yang Shiqi, *Li dai ming chen zou yi* 67.40.

35. Zhang Zhu, *Tui an ji* 5.25. For the prohibition on this type of headgear, see *YDZ* 29.8b.

| 總在狹斜坊裏住 | They live together in the district's narrow winding lanes |
| 敎坊日日聽差回 | And daily return from their labor at the Entertainment Bureau. |

The extraordinary attention paid to entertainers in Yuan government regulations reflects in part the Yuan obsession with maintaining fixed social hierarchies; but the court's unprecedented attempt to make distinctions between different types of performers, its elaboration of specific sumptuary regulations dictating what entertainers would wear, and its inability consistently to enforce those regulations can all be seen as a reflection of the prominent—and often problematic—presence of entertainers in the population at large.[36] This prominence of entertainers in social life was also reflected in the development, particularly visible in the Yuan, of ever more complex and sophisticated forms of entertainment, most notably full-length narrative performances.

## *Courtesans and Yuan Drama*

Scholars agree that the development of full-length narrative dramas through the late Song, Jin, and Yuan was closely associated with the courtesan quarters.[37] By the Yuan, courtesans were central to the increasingly complex dramatic performances of the day: contemporary accounts show that courtesans played all of the various role-types, performing as both male and female characters in plays encompassing a wide variety of themes.[38] Perhaps the best evidence of the close association between

---

36. Here it is worth noting that, although the Song court occasionally complained that "base people like entertainers" dressed above their station, and forbade them to wear certain luxury items, they never established specific clothing for courtesans to wear. See *SS* 153.3577.

37. The literature on Yuan drama is vast, and I do not pretend to be other than a novice in the field. The following discussion is heavily indebted to the pioneering work of Idema and West (see especially *Chinese Theater*), and to the more recent scholarship on the influence of courtesans in Chinese drama by Wang Ning (*Song Yuan yue ji*).

38. By this period Chinese drama (often called "opera," because it typically involved songs interspersed with speech) had developed the classic role "types" that remained characteristic throughout its history (see Idema and West, *Chinese Theater*, 134–41). William Dolby notes that women dominated Yuan performances, and speculates that female performers were of greater interest to the foreign emissaries for whose enjoyment many court dramas were performed (Dolby, "Some Mysteries and Mootings" 86–87). Cf. Wang Ning, *Song Yuan yue ji*, 39.

drama and courtesans, however, was the popularity of dramas *about* courtesans. In plays like *Zhao Pan'er's Flirtation Saves a Courtesan* (*Zhao Pan'er feng yue jiu feng chen* 趙盼兒風月救風塵), *Du Ruiniang Wisely Appreciates Gold Thread Pond* (*Du Ruiniang zhi shang Jin xian chi* 杜蕊娘智賞金線池), *Governor Qian Wisely Dotes on Xie Tianxiang* (*Qian Da yin zhi chong Xie Tianxiang* 錢大尹智寵謝天香), and many others, audiences could vicariously experience both the glamour and the miseries of life in the entertainment quarters.[39] More importantly for our purposes here, the texts of these plays reveal something of contemporary understandings of and attitudes toward entertainers as a group.

Both the themes and the personae of Song anecdotal literature are amplified in Yuan dramas, and the ambivalent attitudes evident in anecdotes and *chuan qi* stories from the late Tang and the Song become exaggerated for the stage. Thus on one hand, Yuan dramas portray the entertainment profession as venal and duplicitous, and suggest that the denizens of courtesan houses live only to part men from their money by false displays of affection. As the courtesan Du Ruiniang remarks, "We have no capital, but entirely rely on five words to get gold and silver. Which five words? None other than 'Corruption, perversity, malice, treachery, and cruelty.'"[40] The madams of such houses come in for particular vilification: they are almost universally portrayed as calculating and cruel, interested in squeezing everything they can out of both the hapless male clients and the girls who attract them.[41] But some of their charges are not much better. For example, Song Yinzhang in *Zhao Pan'er's Flirtation Saves a Courtesan* is fickle, fond of luxury, and innocent of the most basic housewifely skills.[42] Yet, on the other hand, these

---

39. On the numerous plays that appear to have been about courtesans but are no longer extant, see Wang Ning, *Song Yuan yue ji*, 120 ff. See also Johnson, *Gold Thread Pond*, 113–14. Wang Ning has argued that courtesans were acting in plays that featured stories about courtesan life as early as the Jin. See *Song Yuan yue ji*, 77–79. The entry on the actress Fan Shizhen in the *Emerald Pavilion Collection* says that "busybodies" made a play based on her life: see *QLJJZ*, 138–39.

40. *Gold Thread Pond*, Act 1. Translation emended from Johnson, "Guan Hanqing's Music Dramas," 131.

41. The mothers in *Gold Thread Pond* and in *Wind and Moon in the Courtyard of Purple Clouds* are typical here. See respectively Johnson, "Guan Hanqing's Music Dramas," and Idema and West, *Chinese Theater*, 236–78.

42. A more striking example is the title character of the early Ming drama *Liu Jin'er*

negative images paradoxically serve to underscore the virtue of the courtesan-heroines of these dramas.[43] Significantly, the contrast here is not between evil courtesans and virtuous commoner girls (as it was in some didactic literati poetry; see below), but between ordinary courtesans and those whose intelligence and nobility of character distinguish them from their peers. The courtesan-heroines Xie Tianxiang and Du Ruiniang are clever and talented at poetry; Zhao Pan'er is wise and generous; Han Chulan, Wang Jinbang, and Li Yaxian endure separation and hardship but remain steadfastly faithful to their literati lovers.

It is particularly notable here that virtuous courtesans are always the heroines of the dramas in which they figure. In this respect, Yuan drama continued the trend of Song courtesan stories, which frequently portrayed their protagonists as virtuous and faithful. But in Yuan plays, audiences were exposed at length and in much more detail to the mental universe of the courtesan-heroine. As other scholars have pointed out, the conventions of Yuan *za ju* 雜劇 drama assigned all the arias in a play to a single role: the action of the play develops through the eyes of a single protagonist, providing "psychological interest" and "an expansion of the 'inner world'" of that character.[44] This is especially the case because the arias sung are, after all, poetry—the medium through which, in Chinese culture, the deepest emotions of the individual could be expressed.[45] Thus in Yuan plays audiences were called on to sympathize with the courtesan-heroine's dreams and despair. They listened as virtuous courtesans themselves condemned the evils of their profession and the cruelty of their "mothers," and wept when they sang poignantly of the pain of being separated from their beloveds.[46] In short, Yuan drama allowed audiences,

---

*from Xuanping Ward Becomes a Sing-Song Girl Again*, who is a shameless hussy who marries numerous times, abuses her in-laws, and even falsely accuses one husband of murder. See Idema and West, *Chinese Theater*, 351–54, 358–87.

43. Idema and West (*Chinese Theater*, 143) note that courtesans in Yuan drama tend to be stereotyped as either "a money-loving succubus" or "the whore with the pure heart."

44. Idema and West, *Chinese Theater*, 243. Note that even in *Liu Jin'er from Xuanping Ward Becomes a Sing-Song Girl Again*, the main arias are given not to the title character, the disreputable Liu, but to four different characters (all sung by the same lead actress), all of whom serve as virtuous foils to her. See Idema and West, *Chinese Theater*, 352.

45. Chen Jingsong, "To Make People Happy," 40–41.

46. For example, in *Courtyard of the Purple Clouds*, Act 2, Han Chulan sings, "As we part, remember our first meeting/ Your feelings knew, my heart understood./You know

commoners and literati alike, to experience the humanity, and even the nobility of sentiment, of nominally "base" performers.

The expansion of drama as a performing art, and the prominence of courtesans as both performers and protagonists in those dramas, contributed to subtle changes in the ways courtesans were written about in gossipy sources detailing their interactions with literati men. The well-known late Yuan record of performers, Xia Tingzhi's *Emerald Pavilion Collection* (*Qing lou ji*), is illuminating here.[47] Composed in the mid-fourteenth century by a man known for frequenting the courtesan quarters, the *Emerald Pavilion Collection* obeys well-worn conventions of the genre. Like its late Tang predecessor, the *Record of the Northern Wards* (*Beili zhi*), and the Song "serving maid" (*shi'er*) collections, the *Emerald Pavilion Collection* lists the names of famous entertainers and describes their interactions with their clients. Like other anecdotal collections featuring courtesans, it often relates stories as a pretext for conveying a particularly clever line of poetry. But innovations in the *Emerald Pavilion Collection* expose the radically new social and cultural context in which it was written.

To begin with, the *Emerald Pavilion Collection* pays far more attention than earlier texts to specific dramatic skills. In the *Record of the Northern Wards* and similar texts, most of the courtesans named are described as being good at witty conversation. Sometimes their intelligence is mentioned, and a few are credited with being able to sing or do calligraphy, but there is no particular emphasis on their performing skills. In contrast, in the *Collection* every courtesan listed is associated with a performing specialty, and this information is included in even the briefest entries: "Nie Tanxiang: Her appearance was charming, her songs and rhymes pure and

---

me, I know you./There were no bad times, remember the good./Never think I'll carry on with another/ This heart of mine is as if pierced by a dagger!" Translation based on Idema and West, *Chinese Theater*, p. 267–68, following the emended original in Xu Qinjun, *Xin jiao Yuan kan za ju san shi zhong*, 1:338–39.

47. QLJJZ. The *Emerald Pavilion Collection* has attracted the interest of a number of scholars. For an early translation, see Waley (he called the text the *Green Bower Collection*), *Secret History*, 89–107. More scholarly translations appear in Idema and West, *Chinese Theater*, 147–49 and 157–67, and West provides updated translations of a few sections in "Yuan Entertainers," 115–26. A number of the anecdotes found in the *Emerald Pavilion Collection* are reiterated in Tao Zongyi's *Nancun chuo geng lu*, suggesting that the text was circulating in literati circles during the Yuan.

round; Prince Yan of Dongping deeply loved her"; or "Nanchunyan: Her carriage and countenance were extraordinarily beautiful; she was good at palace plays and was one of the best performers in the capital."[48]

Even more striking is the *Collection*'s unprecedented concern with performance lineages. We not only learn that Yanshanxiu was a disciple of Zhu Lianxiu, and that Wang Ben'er and Zhao Pianxi had careers as teachers of their arts; we are also told that Zhang Yumei's son and daughter-in-law were both admired performers, and her granddaughter Guanguan had established a reputation by the time she was seven or eight years old.[49] Tongtong, the daughter of Shixiaotong, was, like her mother, a performer of *xiao shuo*; the actress Xiaoyumei's daughter Bianbian was known for being able to master a play after a mere glance at the script, and *her* daughter, Xiaoyumei's granddaughter, took up the tradition in turn.[50] The text contains many similar examples, revealing that acting was often the hereditary occupation that the Yuan government intended it to be;[51] but the larger point here is that in itemizing the performers' specialties and the details of their lineage Xia Tingzhi is not merely providing grist for romantic poetry or gossip about famous officials, or even making a claim for the author's—and reader's—status as cognoscenti. Rather, Xia's record of the names and family connections of these performers seems to be motivated, as his preface insists that it is, by a genuine esteem for their talent.[52]

That performing ability, rather than simple erotic appeal, was more centrally at issue by Yuan times is also reflected in the *Collection*'s unhesitating reference to the actor-husbands of the courtesans. The *Record* had stressed that even the "mothers" in courtesan houses of the late Tang had

---

48. *QLJJZ*, 116–17. Palace plays (*jia tou za ju* 駕頭雜劇) were plays about the emperor and the palace.

49. *QLJJZ*, 222, 150, 156, 132. Cf. also Idema and West, *Chinese Theater*, 148.

50. *QLJJZ*, 151, 170.

51. Other scholars of this text have commented on the importance of hereditary lineages to the development of Yuan drama. See *QLJJZ*, 132–33, and Idema and West, *Chinese Theater*, 147–48.

52. *QLJJZ*, 43–44. Xia's preface emphasizes that few among the myriad courtesans of the realm were sufficiently talented and beautiful to be regarded as extraordinary. He suggests that his record will help make it possible for later ages to know that "even among female performers there were such people." See the slightly different rendering in Idema and West, *Chinese Theater*, 158.

no husbands: "Those who have not deteriorated too badly are all kept by local functionaries; others privately keep men to sleep with them, but they don't treat them with the ritual befitting a husband."[53] The "girls" in the houses run by these mothers are never described as married, except when they leave the profession to marry wealthy and powerful men as concubines. In contrast, the *Emerald Pavilion Collection* not only openly acknowledges the presence of performer-husbands, it often celebrates their accomplishments.[54] Thus the husband of the multitalented Liangyuanxiu is said to have had unexcelled musicianship; the husband of Sixth Sister-in-law Song accompanied his wife's singing by playing on the *bi li* 觱篥 (a recorder-like instrument), and "their brilliance entered celestial ranks"; Zhujinxiu's dramatic performances were matched by those of her husband, Houshuaqiao, leading the author to compare them to another famous performing couple of an earlier generation.[55] To be sure, having a husband did not necessarily preclude romantic relationships with others: Li Jiao'er, wife of one Wang Deming, was nonetheless "favored" by a prominent official, and Sai Tianxiang, wife of "Fishhead" Li, managed to attract the obsessively fastidious Ni Zan. Liu Poxi, wife of the musician Li the Fourth, first tried to run away with a paramour and later became a concubine (*ce shi*) of the high-ranking official Quan Buyan Sari.[56] Still, Yuan courtesans seem to have been more likely than their predecessors to be integrated into traditional family structures within the entertainment community—or at least their literati admirers more readily acknowledged the existence of such family structures.

---

53. Sun Qi, *Beili zhi*, 25; Sun Ch'i and des Rotours, *Courtisanes Chinoises*, 67–68.

54. Interestingly, the *Jiao fang ji* (a guidebook, dating from the mid-eighth century and describing the early eighth-century Court Entertainment Bureau), suggests that the professional court entertainers of that era were sometimes married to one another. See Cui Lingqin, *Jiao fang ji jian ding*, 49.

55. QLJJZ, 61, 119, 167.

56. QLJJZ, 179, 183, 213. In Liu Poxi's case, the text suggests that she and her paramour ran away in part because they "resented that her husband obstructed them" (*ku qi fu jian zu* 苦其夫間阻), suggesting that husbands might indeed interfere in courtesans' liaisons with other men. Note that Stephen West's most recent translation of this line renders it as "Fearful his wife would come between them" ("Yuan Entertainers," 124). However, West himself has elsewhere translated the line as "she suffered some hindrance from her husband" (Idema and West, *Chinese Theater*, 164), and "husband" seems to me the more natural understanding of *fu* 夫 here.

12. The Yuan courtesan Liu Poxi 劉婆惜 bows to her new husband/master, the official Quan Buyan Sari. Despite regulations against intermarriage of entertainers and other classes, high-ranking Yuan officials frequently took famous entertainers as concubines. From Mei Yujin (Dingzuo) 梅禹金(鼎祚), comp., *Hui tu Qing ni lian hua ji* 繪圖青泥蓮花記 (Beijing, Zi qiang shu ju), 1910, *li*.4a. Ming dynasty. Courtesy of Hathi Trust. (http://hdl.handle.net/2027/mdp.39015070911931?urlappend=%3Bseq=176 Google-digitized, image of page n175)

In sum, the author of the *Emerald Pavilion Collection* not only records information about an unprecedented number of entertainers, he writes about those entertainers in a new way, celebrating their talents and acknowledging that they have families. Certainly, there is much that is ambiguous or dubious in these biographies, and they by no means depict fully realized human beings.[57] The *Collection* also occasionally delights in showing how literati made fun of entertainers, as when Zhong Jixian described the stocky Wang Youmei as having "a voice full like a chime, a body like a chime mallet," or when Guan Yunshi slyly described the actress Yang Mainu's skirt as trailing a "white sash," suggesting that she carried a sexually transmitted disease.[58] Yet overall, the social and psychological gulf between entertainers and their patrons seems narrower here than in earlier depictions. As people of recognized talent and members of families, performers in this account seem less like commodities and more like human beings.

## *Literati Images of Courtesans*

A similar shift is even more strongly evident in the formal writings of Yuan literati, despite the fact that much Yuan writing about courtesans follow a pattern well-established in the Song.[59] Thus, on the one hand, high-ranking officials and others continued to write appreciatively of courtesan performances they had seen. Yelü Chucai (1190–1244), in a series of poems written for the general Fucha, describes a "white-sleeved

---

57. On the uncertainties in the text, see West, "Yuan Entertainers," 115. West also observes, "One will look in vain for any hint of personalized character. [The women] are treated as literary playthings...objects to be fetishized as poets fetishized other exotic, beautiful creations." Still, although this is undoubtedly true in some cases, the great majority of the biographies in the *Emerald Pavilion Collection* do not contain poetry at all, but simply describe the performer's dramatic specialties, her relationships with other performers, and so forth. Thus I see the *Emerald Pavilion Collection* as far less concerned with fetishizing its subjects than, for example, texts in the Song *shi hua* genre.

58. *QLJJZ*, 164, 172. "White sash" (*bai dai* 白帶) is the common name for leukorrhea. Cf. Idema and West, *Chinese Theater*, 161.

59. The reader should be aware that there is a clear historiographical bias in the surviving sources from the Yuan, in that they are overwhelmingly the work of southerners. This is especially true of authors born after the turn of the fourteenth century.

beauty learning the Han dances" while a "raven-locked government-courtesan strums the foreign lute" (素袖佳人學漢舞/碧髩官妓撥胡琴). His son, Yelü Zhu (1221–85), dedicated a poem to a "serving maid" (*shi'er*) on the music registers of the palace's Court of Immortal Voices (贈仙音院樂籍侍兒), in which he invoked voluptuous if hackneyed images of rainbow clothing, fragrant incense, and drunken flutes. Somewhat later, the Daoist master Ma Zhen (1254–ca. 1318) composed three poems commemorating the imperial favor he received at a court audience. One likens the Entertainment Bureau musicians to a gathering of immortals; another indicates that Ma was invited to view the dancers up close, and describes their bodies as "moist with a heavenly fragrance" (特旨向前觀妓樂,滿身雨露浥天香).[60] Outside the court, both officials and men without rank enjoyed outings at which courtesans entertained, and wrote poetry to commemorate those occasions.[61] Liu Chenweng (1232–97), living in retirement in his native Jiangxi, wrote a cycle of three poems on a New Year's Day festival. In the first, he describes the colorful procession and the spectacle of luxuriously adorned courtesans whose "songs of Yan and dances of Zhao move the man of the south"(釵頭燕,勝金釧,燕歌趙舞動南人). The third poem in the cycle, subtitled "presented to a courtesan" (*zeng ji* 贈妓), imagines the sound of her song following the clouds as late-season snowflakes drift into the wine cups. Liu concludes with the suggestive line, "Hold up the candle so it penetrates the flowered scarf; only then can you see the flush on the beauty's jade countenance" (直須把燭穿花幛,方見佳人玉面紅).[62]

On the other hand, a number of Yuan literati (especially though not exclusively those affiliated with the Learning of the Way movement)

---

60. Ma Zhen, *Xia wai shi ji* 3.15b–16a. Here Ma puns on the dual meanings of both *yu lu* 雨露 (rain, dew, but also imperial favor) and *tian xiang* 天香 (fragrant incense used at the court, but also a beautiful woman).

61. Zhang Hongfan, *Huaiyang ji*, 2; Yao Sui, *Mu an ji* 33.421; Wang Yun, *Qiujian ji* 7.13, 12.3b, 15.3b; Fang Hui, *Tongjiang xu ji* 3.5b, 10.7, 11.19, 21.17b–18b. See also references to Yao Sui and Wang Yun in the *Emerald Pavilion Collection*. Fang's contemporary Zhou Mi wrote scathingly of Fang's involvement with and fawning attitude toward courtesans. See Zhou Mi, *Gui xin za shi*, 249. Ankeny Weitz characterizes Fang as "Zhou Mi's archrival." See her *Record of Clouds*, 83.

62. Liu Chenweng, *Xu xi ji* 8.35–35b. See also the poetry of Wei Zongwu (*Qiu sheng ji* 3.34a, 3.36a); Wang Yuanliang (*Hu shan lei gao* 4.6a, 5.5b–6a); and Dong Sigao (*Lushan ji* 5.16a).

reiterated negative views of entertainers. The eminent official Yu Ji (1272–1348) composed a colophon describing how he had encountered, in a friend's art collection, a piece of calligraphy by Su Shi. The calligraphy commemorated an incident in which the Hangzhou entertainer Zhou Shao had secured her release from the courtesan registers by impressing a well-known prefect with an extemporaneous poem.[63] Yu Ji, though admitting that this scroll was among the very few Song scrolls his friend had bothered to keep in his collection, was scandalized. In his view, the "three poems about Prefect Chen releasing the government-courtesan... disgrace the old gentleman's [i.e., Su Shi's] calligraphy."

The Learning of the Way scholar Wu Cheng (1249–1333) expressed a similarly jaundiced view of entertainers, depicting them as emblematic of venal, self-interested behavior. In an admonitory preface to a colleague, he excoriated officials who did not act as proper Confucians, comparing them both to "ravenous wolves in power, who injure people and harm things to fatten themselves, and are never satisfied," and to "beauties who lean in doorways, flirting with their eyes and inviting with their hearts in order to obtain benefit, and are without shame." He added, "Their faces are those of human beings, but their hearts are those of animals; their bodies are those of officials, but their actions are those of entertainers."[64] Wu Cheng's younger contemporary Li Cun (1281–1354) likewise scorned entertainers as fawning sycophants. Defending himself against charges that he was haughty and severe, Li countered, "How could one go so far as to behave like performers and slaves, compliant and submissive, in order to ingratiate oneself with women and children?"[65] In a direct echo of Song themes, other Yuan writers treated the presence of courtesans as an emblem of decadence and decline. In a poem entitled "Lament on Facing the Landscape" (對景吟), the southern scholar Wang Mian (1287–1359) juxtaposed

---

63. Yu Ji, *Dao yuan xue gu lu* 4.73. Su Shi had recorded her poem, as well as those written by two of her peers to celebrate her release, in his own hand, commenting, "From this we know that people of Hangzhou are often intelligent." The content of Su's text had been transmitted by Zhao Lingzhi in the early Southern Song (*Hou qing lu* 7.180–81), and the original calligraphy was among that viewed and appreciated by Zhou Mi in the early Yuan (*Yun yan guo yan lu* 2.1–1b).
64. Wu Cheng, *Wu wen zheng ji* 33.1a–2a.
65. Li Cun, *Si an ji* 12.4b–6a.

images of "pink peach trees and jade willows" of the past with images of current devastation.[66] The poem concludes:

| | |
|---|---|
| 淮南千里無烟火 | South of the Huai for a thousand *li* there are no cooking fires; |
| 淮東近日多軍馬 | To the east of the Huai in recent days are many troops and horses. |
| 寸薪粒粟不論錢 | An inch of firewood, a kernel of rice, don't talk about the cost; |
| 行客相看淚盈把 | Refugees look at each other, tears filling their hands. |
| 如何五陵年少郎 | How is it that the wealthy young man of the capital |
| 賣田去買青樓娼 | Sells land to go and buy courtesans of the emerald pavilions? |
| 吳歌楚舞不知夜 | The songs of Wu, the dances of Chu, the night passes unnoticed. |
| 歸來也學山翁狂 | Returning, he resembles the drunk old man of the mountain. |
| 明朝酒醒入官府 | The next morning, sobered up, he enters the government offices, |
| 方知不是城南杜 | Only then realizing that he is not like the Dus of Chengnan.[67] |
| 落花風急雨蕭蕭 | The flowers drop, the wind rages, the rain soughs. |
| 索寞無言面如土 | Despondent, he is wordless and ashamed. |

Yuan writings like these—both poetry praising courtesan performances and poetry associating courtesans with decadence—reflect the perpetuation of well-established literary tropes and reveal little about shifts in social attitudes. Against this background, however, we also see the expression of new literary themes associated with courtesans, and these are of greater historical interest.

One new theme in Yuan writings about courtesans is the notion that poor but honest women are better off than women who make their living as entertainers. The Learning of the Way teacher Jin Lüxiang (1232–1303) wrote an early poem on this topic, apparently inspired by an actual experience.[68]

---

66. Wang Mian, *Zhu zhai ji*, *xia*, 41b. Along the same lines, see Zheng Yu's (1298–1358) comments on the inferiority of literary and artistic works in his own day: "Alas, the poetic lines of recent gentlemen are like those on the banners of wine shops; their calligraphy and painting is like that of singing girls in courtesan houses, even further from that of the ancients." Zheng Yu, *Shishan ji*, *yi wen*, 3.16b–17b.
67  The Dus of Chengnan were a prestigious "great family" of the Tang period.
68. Jin Lüxiang, *Renshan ji* 4.75a. The poem is entitled "Ji shi" 即事, a generic title for poems inspired by situations the poet directly experienced.

Jin's poem celebrates the good fortune of a courtesan who has managed to marry a commoner and thereby become respectable (*cong liang* 從良):

| | |
|---|---|
| 佳人早幸已從良 | The beauty was fortunate early, and has already "become respectable." |
| 好治絲麻理素粧 | She likes to manage the silk and hemp and to use plain makeup; |
| 休向人前售歌舞 | No longer selling songs and dances in front of others. |
| 春風寧得幾時香 | After all, how long can the spring wind remain fragrant? |

A few decades later, Ma Zuchang (1279–1338) made this case more powerfully in his "Song for the Wheat-Gathering Girl" (拾麥女歌), which describes a hardworking widow in tattered clothing, laboring all morning to fill her basket with grain as her hungry child cries. Ma continues: "How could she not have seen the concubine of the noble family, how could she not know about the women of courtesan houses, with their embroidered silk jackets and their swaying lotus steps? With silver knives they mince fish and assist with wine cups; crowding together, tipsily singing, they worry about the setting sun." Ma's final lines then address the wheat-gatherer directly:

| | |
|---|---|
| 拾麥女, 拾麥女, 爾莫嗟, 爾莫憂 | Wheat-gathering girl, wheat-gathering girl, don't you sigh, don't you worry. |
| 人生賦命各有由 | The fortunes of human lives each have their reasons. |
| 前年貴家妾, 籍入爲官婢 | The concubine who in former years [served] a noble house has been registered as a government slave. |
| 今日娼家婦, 年老爲人棄 | Today's women of the courtesan houses in old age will be discarded. |
| 貧賤艱難且莫辭 | Don't speak anymore of poverty, degradation, and hardship |
| 畢竟榮華成底事 | In the end what do glory and splendor amount to?[69] |

Although Ma's poem might be read as a general commentary on the fickleness of fate, Zhang Xian's (fl. 1341) "Lament of the Quiet Girl" (靜女吟) even more explicitly contrasts the fortunes of an "alluring girl" (*yan nü* 艷女) with those of a "quiet girl" (*jing nü*). The alluring girl dresses in silks whereas the quiet girl wears coarse garments. The alluring girl marries

---

69. Ma Zuchang, *Shi tian wen ji* 5.2b–3a.

a great general, whereas the quiet girl marries into a farming household. But when the general dies at the border, the alluring girl is distressed by her empty boudoir; meanwhile the farming family prepares its fields and the quiet girl works diligently. Ultimately, the alluring girl marries three times and ends up as a courtesan, whereas the quiet girl brings up her sons into adulthood and is showered with blessings in her stately hall.[70]

This sort of poetry—exhorting young women not to be enticed by the apparent luxury of entertainers' lives—is not found in the Song, and it is difficult to know what inspired it and for whom it was intended. The poems may have been meant as proselytization, intended to discourage commoner women from joining the entertainment profession. The fact that they are framed as songs and laments suggests that these poems were intended for performance, as poetry meant for proselytizing would have been. But the poems may simply represent the poets' wistful (and wishful) ruminations on the various paths open to women. In either case, they suggest a heightened awareness that the profession of entertainer had become an ever-present alternative to the traditionally valorized role of farmer's wife. More importantly, although these poems portrayed the lives of entertainers in a negative light, the more striking and dominant development in Yuan literati writing was a growing acknowledgment of entertainers as individuals worthy of respect and even admiration.

The new empathy of literati for entertainers was undoubtedly related to the more general upending of traditional Chinese hierarchies of status and power attendant on the Mongol reign. In stark contrast to the Chinese, the Mongols had no particular appreciation for scholarship. They placed scholars among the lowest of the hereditary occupational categories they created, and did not adopt an examination system for official recruitment until 1315, preferring to award office on the basis of recommendation. Chinese literati, especially those in the south, were frequently forced to turn to occupations that in earlier dynasties would have been considered beneath them, employing their literacy in the capacity of "clerks, teachers,

---

70. Zhang Xian, *Yu si ji* 3.16a–16b. The didactic purpose of Zhang Xian's poem is strikingly highlighted when it is compared with its obvious precursor, an eponymous poem by Meng Jiao of the Tang. Meng's poem simply contrasts the alluring girl's jealousy and obsession with appearance with the quiet girl's restrained behavior and interest in virtue. It makes no reference to their status differences or ultimate fates.

medical practitioners, fortune-tellers, or lesser callings."[71] Among those lesser callings were various forms of entertainment. And as some literati joined entertainment circles, entertainers began to appear as friends and associates in the writings of other literati. Jia Xuanweng, for example, wrote a poem entitled "Presented to the Storyteller Gao Pengju" (贈談故人高鵬舉), in which he noted the performer's scholarly background and expressed the hope that he would one day return to his studies:[72]

| | |
|---|---|
| 東鄰歌呼鬧如市, | In the eastern neighborhood the songs and shouting are as raucous as a marketplace; |
| 西鄰笙簫正鼎沸. | In the western neighborhood the sounds of stringed instruments are like a boiling cauldron. |
| 高生擇術頗可人 | Master Gao selected a skill in which he is rather talented; |
| 夜闌挑燈説書史. | As night deepens he lifts a lamp and speaks of the histories. |
| 説出忠臣烈士報國心 | He tells of patriotic hearts of loyal ministers and heroic gentlemen, |
| 四座聞者爲墮淚. | On four sides his listeners shed tears. |
| 聞君年少曾讀書, | I've heard that when you were young you once read books; |
| 壯大無成乃與優伶俱. | When you grew up you were unsuccessful and so gathered with the entertainers. |
| 左手執簻右秉翟, | "The left hand carries a flute, the right...holds feathers,"[73] |
| 念到簡兮應嗟吁. | When you think of Jian Xi you must heave a sigh. |
| 他年了却官中呼 | Some other year when you finish shouting among the officials, |
| 仍作書生挾冊歸里閭. | You can still be a student, clutching your books as you return to your hometown. |

---

71. Franke and Twitchett, *Cambridge History*, 634–35. Hsiao Ch'i-ch'ing has noted that the status of the scholar class was not as low in the Yuan as is sometimes claimed; see Hsiao Ch'i-ch'ing, *Yuan dai shi xin tan*, 4. On the proliferation of literati medical practitioners under the Yuan, see Hymes, "Not Quite Gentlemen," 9–76.

72. Jia Xuanweng, *Ze tang ji* 5.14b–15. Jia's lifetime spanned the late Song and early Yuan; this text could conceivably date from before the fall of the Song. The topos of a son of a literati household becoming a performer was dramatized in the famous Yuan play, *A Playboy from a Noble House Opts for the Wrong Career* (*Huan men di zi cuo li shen* 宦門弟子錯立身). See Idema and West, *Chinese Theater*, 205–35.

73. The quoted line is drawn from the poem "Jian Xi" 簡兮 in the *Bei feng* 邶風 section of the *Book of Odes*. The poem describes a dancer performing and being rewarded by his lord. See Karlgren, *The Book of Odes*, 24–25.

Nothing is known of Gao Pengju outside of Jia's poem, and it is certainly possible that the description of his scholarly background is a polite fiction. But even if it is mere literary posturing, Jia's attribution of scholarly credentials not only dignifies the entertainer, it subtly elides the social distinctions between entertainers and scholars in general. Jia still clearly sees a scholarly career as preferable to that of entertainer, but he depicts "entertainer" as a career choice, not an irreversible social position. Most importantly, the moral stigma that was attached to performing in earlier writings (and still upheld in Yuan regulations) is completely absent here.

Hu Zhiyu, whose preface in honor of the actress Zhu Lianxiu opened this chapter, was another noted aficionado of the theater. As we have seen, Hu's preface for Zhu suggests that artistic accomplishment is actually more difficult to achieve than scholarly attainment, and he makes a similar claim in a lengthy poetry preface for another actor, the male comedian Zhao Wenyi.[74] Hu begins his preface for Zhao by asserting the importance of innovation and creativity in acting:

> Vinegar, salt, ginger, and cinnamon, when combined by someone clever, create a taste that goes beyond sour, salty, spicy, or sweet. When every day it is new and does not just perpetuate the conventional, those who eat do not tire of it. Comedy is also like this. The inept repeat and follow the old and cannot change it into something new; they cause the audience to detest listening and tire of viewing.

Hu then explains that recently audiences have become very sophisticated, making the job of the entertainer extremely difficult. Still, there are some who are able to surpass their peers:

> The Zhao family has several brothers; there is one called Wenyi who rather likes to read and know about past and present and to study with scholars and gentlemen. Thus in his profession he is ashamed to follow the crude and hackneyed; he uses novel cleverness and transforms the clumsy, surpassing what the crowds expect and [offering] what people have neither seen nor heard. Everyone of the age loves and delights in him. When he encounters a famous scholar, he always seeks poetry or prose, calligraphy or painting. It is as if he takes some pride in what he studies, already accomplished but seeking to be further accomplished, in the end never daring to be satisfied or to disdain his comrades. Ah! Someone like this, although an actor, is still able to progress without end!

---

74. Hu Zhiyu, *Zi shan da quan ji* 8.13b–15a.

Wilt Idema and Stephen West have argued that Hu Zhiyu, like other Yuan literati with a passion for the theater, sought to establish drama as a legitimate literary form.[75] I would stress further that Hu was interested in legitimating the *performers* of drama. Yet Hu's claims for the legitimacy of drama and its performers were not without ambivalence: as Idema and West have also observed, Yuan theater aficionados knew that their interactions with entertainers would be suspect in the eyes of many.[76] Hu himself acknowledges this awareness in many of his writings for performers. Toward the end of his preface for Zhu Lianxiu, for example, Hu concedes that, unlike other types of cultivation, drama does not help sustain the individual:

> What a pity! Spitting out reverberating rhymes of "forest oriole" and "bedewed orchid," offering the utmost of your talents, even if you are able to give a deeply meaningful performance, I'm afraid it is not a way to take care of youth and preserve longevity.[77]

Moreover, he suggests that in writing about Zhu he is imitating the eminent Northern Song historian Ouyang Xiu, who "grasped his historian's brush and transmitted the biographies of the music officials." This is a curious precedent to claim, for (as Hu and the majority of his readers surely knew) in general Ouyang Xiu held a very low opinion of performers; he included their biographies in his discussion of Emperor Zhuangzong (r. 923–26) of the Latter Tang dynasty (923–36) explicitly to highlight the danger to the state of imperial interest in drama.[78] By invoking Ouyang here, Hu paradoxically reminds his readers of the

---

75. Idema and West, *Chinese Theater*, 155–60. Describing another text that Hu wrote for a performer, Idema and West suggest that Hu was attempting "to grant to Comedy the moral and literary legitimacy normally bestowed only on polite literature."

76. Idema and West, *Chinese Theater*, 157.

77. Here Hu employs an allusion to the *Book of Rites*: the phrase "yi chang er san tan" 一唱而三嘆 (lit., one song and three sighs, which I have rendered as "a deeply meaningful performance") indicates music that is simple but moving.

78. See Ouyang Xiu, *Xin Wudai shi* 37.397–402. Admittedly, not all of Ouyang's portrayals of performers were unsympathetic: he provides several amusing examples of the cleverness of the comedian Jingxinmo, and even credits Jing with using his art to admonish the emperor (*Xin Wudai shi*, 37.399). So in that respect at least Ouyang did provide a precedent for Hu's positive assessments of performers. See also Ouyang Xiu, *Historical Records*, 311–12.

drama's dubious reputation, even as he praises the performer as a cultivated person.[79]

Still, in the end Hu was able to turn Ouyang Xiu's examples to his own purposes, as we see at the end of his preface for Zhao Wenyi. Here Hu explicitly invokes Zhuangzong:

> I am moved by the fact that in the Five Dynasties reign of (Latter) Tang Zhuangzong, [there were those who] enjoyed great names without having true learning, who occupied important offices without true talent. Their reputations were excessive, but they did not feel ashamed. Even down to the nine schools and hundred crafts, there were none who were not like this. What the sage called "a cornered vessel without corners"[80] were too many to enumerate. Yet there was no one who criticized their failures and irresponsibility, none who ridiculed them for having reputation without reality. As people became accustomed to hearing and seeing it, they took it for granted.
>
> Acting is a base art. If but once the jokes are not to the point, the entire audience claps and ridicules [the performer]; if the jokes repeatedly miss, then the audience won't go to see him. Everyone is a critic [lit., every person has a judgmental heart]. To chastise entertainers but not chastise the [supposedly] virtuous, isn't it laughable? Isn't it lamentable?[81]

Hu here acknowledges that acting is a base art (*jian yi* 賤藝), but he defends the integrity of the performer, complaining that people are quick to criticize performers without applying the same standards to others. In other words, Hu implies that people are people and should all be judged by a single standard of behavior. Zhao Wenyi's efforts to improve himself stand as a reproach to those who would consider themselves superior by dint of profession rather than conduct. Particularly notable here is that Hu's rhetoric echoes that of exemplar texts, which reprimanded literati men by comparing them unfavorably with weak women or children. Now entertainers, too, could serve as models for literati behavior.

The sympathetic view of entertainers expressed by Hu Zhiyu was clearly related to his own familiarity with and enjoyment of the theater, but he was not alone among Yuan literati in seeing performers as sometimes worthy of admiration.[82] Interestingly, a number of similarly

---

79. Hu may also intend his comparison as a subtle critique of the poor governance of the Yuan regime.
80. A reference from the *Analects*, implying that the name is not matched by reality.
81. Hu Zhiyu, *Zi shan da quan ji* 8.14b–15a.
82. A passage in Hu Zhiyu's "recorded sayings" (*yu lü* 語錄) portrays a much harsher

sympathetic accounts were penned by men who most emphatically did not share Hu's appreciation of the performing arts. Hu's slightly younger contemporary, the southerner Dai Biaoyuan (1244–1310), provides a case in point.

In contrast to Hu, a northerner who attained office early in the Yuan and later attained high-ranking posts, Dai was a southerner who had had the misfortune to pass the examinations under the Song, just as the dynasty was on the verge of collapse. He held office briefly, but within a few years he had returned home, and he spent the majority of his adult life as an itinerant tutor.[83] Dai moved in social circles quite different from those of Hu Zhiyu, and his collected works contain no references to courtesan banquets or theater performances. Nonetheless, Dai transmitted the story of two unnamed performers (he refers to them simply as "singers" [*ge zhe* 歌者]). Rather than focusing on their skills and arts, Dai's story is about their moral behavior.

Dai recounts that in Hangzhou in the early 1270s there were two excellent singers, famous for their talent and good looks.[84] During the chaos of the fall of the Song they lost track of each other. One ended up as the favored concubine of an important general, wealthy and powerful. The other became a wife of a commoner under the general's jurisdiction. Although their paths did not cross, they got news of each other, and the fortunate one decided to invite her friend to share her good fortune. She built a guesthouse and invited the other to stay. At first the commoner's

---

attitude toward the theater (*Zi shan da quan ji* 26.32a–33a). Here Hu asserts that an individual's personality and interests are fixed and cannot be changed, and that by observing a man's interests one can predict his success or failure. He portrays men who "delight in drinking and in music with actors and courtesans" as incapable of devoting themselves to administration, and he castigates Emperor Zhuangzong for his intimacies with actors, arguing that this shows that the emperor's nature was "lowly and common." These statements are rather strikingly at odds both with Hu's other writings and with his own predilection for the company of actors and musicians, and suggest that he (or his disciples) may have included this tirade to defend his reputation.

83. See Yuan Jue, *Qing rong ju shi ji* 28.487–89. In 1304, when he was already sixty, Dai was offered a local educational office; he declined it due to illness and died six years later.

84. Dai Biaoyuan, *Yan yuan ji* 24.366–67. The *Cong shu ji cheng xin bian* edition of the text says there were ten singers, but since the rest of the text is about two singers, I here follow the *Si ku quan shu* version, which says two singers.

wife demurred, even turning down the invitation three times. But the fortunate one would not take no for an answer, and in the end the two were reunited. Fearing that if she simply had her stay, the commoner's wife would not be at peace, the fortunate one produced several young girl slaves and beseeched the commoner's wife to teach her songs to them, paying her a regular salary with which she could compensate her husband's family. The commoner's wife had already begun to decline, and although she had been a good singer, she had no other way to use her skills. So she began to teach the slave girls rigorously. Thereafter, when the fortunate one would come from the general's house, she would no sooner arrive than she would examine the songs taught. If there was progress she was happy, if not she would gently scold, as if she feared that the teaching was not wholehearted. The commoner's wife was so regretful she could hardly bear it, but she was conscious of the benevolence she had received and of the effort that had already been made, so in the end she dared not complain, and the two were able to live in harmony.

Dai's postface explains his purpose in telling this story:

> When I was in Hang[zhou], I often saw scholars and officials interacting on the basis of literature and moral virtue. As soon as the disasters hit, they turned their faces away as if they didn't recognize one another. Now, the two singers belonged to the realm of entertainers and artisans (*chang you ji yi*) 倡優技藝, the kind of people on whom in times of peace one would not dare to bestow effusive praise. When their behavior is like this, is there anything to be ashamed of? Yet those who discuss these things still maintain that even if the noble and fortunate one maintained her old [friend] with righteousness, she should not have criticized her failings. Even if the lowly and poor one refused the favors with ritual, she should not have fawningly accorded with her friend's wishes. This is going a bit too far in seeking perfection! A gentlemen would not reproach them for this.

Dai Biaoyuan's attitude toward the performers he describes is clearly quite different from that of Hu Zhiyu. He is not impressed by their artistic skills or the cultivation such skills require; rather, he suggests that performers as a group are appropriately disdained. He transmits (or invents?) the story of these two singers to make a point about human relations in times of crisis, and in particular to contrast their unexpectedly virtuous behavior with that of men of his own class. In its pointed reproach to literati men, Dai's story operates rhetorically very much like the biographies of faithful wives. But in this case it is not merely women, but women of dishonorable status, who are held up as exemplars. Dai's parable may well have been based on his own experience—as an itinerant tutor, he certainly knew what it was to be the recipient of barely disguised charity. But like Hu Zhiyu's prefaces, his story presents entertainers as individuals with a certain amount of personal and moral autonomy, as individuals who can be compared with—even favorably compared with—literati men.

Accounts like these, which acknowledged the potential for moral integrity in entertainers, became increasingly prevalent in later Yuan texts. We see another, albeit grudging, example in a poetry preface by the fourteenth-century Learning of the Way adherent Dai Liang (no relation to Dai Biaoyuan):

> The musician Ni Changnian of Yuyao in serving his mother was able to exhaust filiality. One day his mother was very ill; Changnian prayed for her to the spirits, and received a response. Thereupon he made by hand a viburnum-flower lantern (*qiong hua deng* 瓊花燈) and offered it at the shrine, to proclaim and requite the spirit's favor. The lantern was most ingenious and took several months to complete. Those who saw it, from near and far, all sighed in praise over it. At that, the county elders Master Yingning Hua and Master Yongan Song both wrote poetry and prose to praise him, and asked me to write a preface.
>
> Ah! Musicians are degraded entertainers; viburnum-flower lanterns are a decadent craft; both are things that gentlemen (*shi jun zi* 士君子) do not discuss. Yingning and Yongan are model gentlemen, but having seen Changnian are happy to discuss him like this. Is it not because of his filiality? Now, filiality is the foundation of all behavior, the regulator of the myriad virtues. If a person is able to be filial, even if he is very insignificant and common, he is still worthy of mention. When the Tang history recorded incidents of filiality and brotherliness, such as that of Wan Nian, Wang Shigui, and others, they were mostly commoners of the villages and lanes. Moreover, the *Book of Ritual* says "minor filiality requires effort" (*xiao xiao yong li* 小孝用力), that is to say, [in great filiality] "thinking of [a parent's] tender love, one forgets effort." Looking at this from the perspective of Changnian today, the skills of a musician are truly base; [but] with regard to those commoners of the villages and lanes, is there really a distinction? The craft of making a lamp is certainly decadent; [but] to compare it to the "filiality that forgets effort," is it really so perverse? The fact that Yingning and Yongan are happy to discuss this without stopping is probably because they have obtained the transmitted intent of those who wrote histories and ritual. I do not know Changnian, but I believe the words of the two gentlemen are worthy of belief, so I have explicated their intent and written this at the end.[85]

---

85. Dai Liang, *Jiu ling shan fang ji* 19.285–87.

Like Dai Biaoyuan, Dai Liang expresses some disdain for the entertainment professions, yet he too acknowledges the possibility that even people in such occupations can embody Confucian virtue.[86] The anecdotalist Tao Zongyi made the case even more explicitly. In his collection of anecdotes and social commentary, the *Nancun chuo geng lu*, Tao tells of a concubine purportedly obtained by Jia Xuanweng when he was serving in high office in the late Song. The concubine's only skill was her ability to warm wine to the perfect drinking temperature every time, but Jia kept her for his entire life; at his death she inherited his property, becoming a wealthy woman. Tao observes:

> Ah! This woman was no more than a base slavey (*jian li* 賤隸). [But] by doing one thing exceptionally well she was able to move people. This was also because she concentrated her mind and extended her will to the utmost (*zhuan xin zhi zhi* 專心致志). Those gentlemen who study the Dao of exhausting principle, rectifying the mind, cultivating the self, and governing the people, but are unable to extend it as far as they ought—they are unable to match her.[87]

Here again, Tao favorably contrasts the behavior of a "base slavey" with that of Confucian scholar-officials. But more important is the specific rhetoric he employs. He credits the concubine with being able to "concentrate her mind" and "extend her will to the utmost"—stock phrases employed by Learning of the Way adherents to refer to Confucian moral self-cultivation. In other words, Tao assumes that the Learning of the Way premise—that all human beings share the "mind" of the Dao and the propensity for moral behavior—indeed applies to *all* people, including those of base status. To be sure, Jia's concubine was not strictly speaking an entertainer. But in acknowledging that someone of base standing could nonetheless possess a moral mind, the Learning of the Way rhetoric that Tao employs here was further evidence of the growing acceptance of entertainers' shared humanity.[88]

---

86. A similar paean to Ni Changnian is found in the collected works of the late Yuan/early Ming scholar Zhao Huiqian. See Zhao Huiqian, *Zhao kao gu wen ji* 趙考古文集 2.11a–12a.

87. Tao Zongyi, *Nancun chuo geng lu* 7.86.

88. Elsewhere Tao does indeed discuss virtuous entertainers: see chap. 9.

## Conclusion

The Yuan period saw the continuing flourishing and even expansion of courtesan entertainments, as teahouse song cycles developed into full-fledged narrative drama. The Yuan court attempted to relegate entertainers to a hereditary, endogamous, and juridically disadvantaged class, but paradoxically, the interaction of literati and performers seems only to have increased in this period.[89] Disenfranchised literati entered the entertainment profession and wrote plays highlighting the noble behavior of courtesan-heroines. Eminent officials became enamored of the theater and wrote encomia for their favorite performers. Literati wrote essays recording the stories of entertainers whose virtue shamed that of ordinary—and even elite—men and women.

The historian Lynn Hunt has demonstrated how, in eighteenth-century Europe, popular fiction contributed to the development of new ideas about equality and human rights.[90] More specifically, Hunt argues that epistolary novels presenting, or at least purporting to present, the trials and tribulations of lower-class women through their own eyes allowed upper-class men (and women) to experience a "psychological identification" with those outside their own class, and ultimately to recognize "others as their equals, as like them in some fundamental fashion."[91] Obviously, differences between the societies of China in the fourteenth century and Europe in the eighteenth were vast, and I am by no means trying to assert that changes in one were precisely parallel to

---

89. Even Yu Ji, who claimed to be scandalized by Su Shi's calligraphy about a courtesan, reportedly admired the cleverness of an entertainer he encountered at a banquet. See Tao Zongyi, *Nancun chuo geng lu* 4.52–53.

90. Hunt, *Inventing Human Rights*, 35–69.

91. Ibid., esp. 48–58. Particularly interesting here is Hunt's suggestion that only the novel, with its interior monologues, could have permitted readers to identify with the protagonist: "A play, in contrast, could not linger in this way on the unfolding of an inner self, which on the stage usually has to be inferred from action or speech" (ibid., 45). But, as noted above, the arias of Yuan drama were devoted to precisely the sort of "unfolding of an inner self" that served to evoke empathy in an audience. One might add that in drama, as in the epistolary novels that Hunt examined, "there is no one authorial point of view outside and above the action," and that Chinese drama, in particular, "facilitated the development of a 'character,' that is, a person with an inner self" (ibid., 42–43).

changes in the other. That said, in Yuan China we find a phenomenon rather similar to that which Hunt finds in eighteenth-century Europe: the popularity of dramas (and, to a lesser extent, fiction) that depicted the feelings and self-perceptions of entertainers contributed to changing attitudes toward them, and especially to the growing acceptance of entertainers as individuals capable of moral action. This trend was of a piece with the growing influence of Learning of the Way philosophy, with its insistence that all individuals shared a moral mind endowed by Heaven. The upshot of these trends was that by the end of the Yuan period the social distance between performers and literati was diminishing. Although the profession of courtesan continued to be disdained, individuals who participated in that profession were no longer seen as necessarily incommensurable with respectable women. This was all the more so when courtesans from the marketplace were becoming concubines in the households of the elite.

# 8

## *Performers, Paramours, and Parents*

### Li Cui'e 李翠娥, Wang Qiao'er 王巧兒, and Wang Lianlian 汪憐憐

The reason that entertainer-concubines [*ji qie* 妓妾] use their looks and talents to garner affection and covet the favor of their masters is simply because they are moved by wealth and nobility. If by chance you should encounter disaster, poverty, or illness, they will certainly coldly seek the means to leave you. How could they be willing to preserve their will and not serve another! Those like Green Pearl of the Golden Valley Garden, Panpan of the Swallow Tower, Han Xiang with respect to Ye, and Ai'ai with respect to Zhang Cheng are very few indeed![1] Since the Great Yuan unification, there have been three. Li Cui'e was a famous performer [*ming chang* 名倡] of Weiyang. The *duruhaci* Shi Jiushan took her in and set her up in a separate establishment. When Shi died, Li swore she would not disgrace herself by marrying someone else. All day long she stayed in a closed chamber reciting scriptures. She lived to be over seventy, and at the seasonal festivals the *duruhaci*'s descendants all came to pay their respects to her. On the music registers, this was passed down as a glorious affair. Wang Qiao'er was a superior beauty of the capital. Administrator Chen Yunqiao was intimate with her, and took her to Hang(zhou). When Chen died, she served his principal wife Tie and lived out her life in purity, prudence, diligence, and frugality. Wang Lianlian was a top courtesan of Huzhou. Registrar Niegubo was quite taken with her. Wang said, "If milord does not disdain my humble status, he should treat me as a secondary wife [*ce shi* 側室]. Engaging in illicit relations [lit. "pilfering like a rat and filching like a dog"] is something I absolutely will not do." Nie accordingly sent a go-between and married her with full pomp and ritual. Three years later, he died. Wang shaved her head and entered a nunnery. Periodically ministers and gentlemen would go and visit her, so she destroyed her appearance to put an end to their wild ideas. In the end she grew old as a nun. Those like this are truly able to walk in the footsteps of the principled and virtuous of former eras.[2]

---

1. The women mentioned, all heroines of romance literature, were courtesans or entertainer-concubines who remained faithful to their husbands or paramours. Green Pearl and Ai'ai appeared in earlier chapters.
2. Tao Zongyi, *Nancun chuo geng lu* 1.180–81. Tao's accounts of Li Cui'e, Wang Qiao'er, and Wang Lianlian are virtually identical to those found in the *Emerald Pavilion Collection* (although the *Collection* calls Li Cui'e "Cuihexiu," and adds further

Here the Yuan dynasty anecdotalist Tao Zongyi praises the marital fidelity of three erstwhile courtesans who became the concubines of Yuan officials. Although Tao does express cynicism about the moral integrity of most entertainer-concubines, his willingness to rank courtesans with virtuous exemplars of the past is notable. Equally striking is his utter lack of concern about the appropriateness of officials taking professional courtesans as concubines. These women were not household-courtesans reared from birth in the homes of the wealthy and noble (as Yuan Jue's grandmother, whose story opened chapter 5, had been). Nor were they even women bought on the market as young girls and brought home to serve as entertainer-concubines. Rather, these were women who had already established reputations as public performers, who moved from the courtesan registers into the homes of Yuan officials. In the Yuan as in the Song, taking such a woman as a concubine was an indictable offense. But where in the Song taking a courtesan as a concubine was also widely regarded as inappropriate and unseemly, Tao is nonchalant—an outlook that bespeaks the more accepting attitude toward entertainers discussed in chapter 7. Tao's emphasis on the marital loyalty evinced by these concubines also reflects a shift in attitudes toward concubines and their place in the family. Both of these shifts betokened a blurring of status distinctions: between nominally dishonorable performers and respectable commoners, in the first case, and between concubines and wives in the second. And both shifts were consonant with the Learning of the Way ideals that were ever more evident in Yuan society.

## Dynastic Debacle and Status Breakdown

The Yuan dynasty was marked by considerable social disruption. Large sectors of the population were displaced as elite and commoner alike fled wartime destruction and peacetime misrule. Literati families were frequently forced to rely on the charity of others for survival, and normative family relations often fell by the wayside.[3] Yet precisely for that reason, concern for family relations was intensified in both

---

detail about Wang Qiao'er). See *QLJJZ*, 190, 184, 147. Cf. also Waley, *Secret History*, 104 and 106; West, "Yuan Entertainers," 124–25; Idema and West, *Chinese Theater*, 163.

3. See Smith, "Family" and "Fear of Gynarchy."

13. The loyal courtesan-concubine Li Cui'e 李翠娥 (also known as Cuihexiu 翠荷秀) sweeps the austere chamber in which she lived alone chanting scriptures after the death of her husband/master. From Mei Yujin (Dingzuo) 梅禹金(鼎祚), comp., *Hui tu Qing ni lian hua ji* 繪圖青泥蓮花記 (Beijing, Zi qiang shu ju), 1910, *li*, 4a. Ming dynasty. Courtesy of Hathi Trust. (http://hdl.handle.net/2027/mdp.39015070911931?urlappend=%3Bseq=182 Google-digitized, image of page n181)

legal and moral rhetoric. Concubines were directly implicated in this process.

We have seen that the Yuan government's approach to controlling Chinese society was to attempt to establish fixed, hereditary social classes. This, in combination with the rapacity of the conquest itself, led to the reemergence of slavery on a widespread scale. Tao Zongyi relates that when Yuan commanders conquered new territories, they paired off their prisoners into couples and treated any children born to them as lifelong slaves. Such slaves could be legally bought and sold, and in theory their descendants were to remain slaves in perpetuity.[4] Others, having managed to escape outright capture, nonetheless acquiesced in servitude as a means of survival. We learn from one observer, for example, that during a year of dearth a prominent official took in dozens of men and women from his district. The beautiful women he made into concubines; the strong men he made into slaves; the rest he planned to present to powerful men of the day in hopes of currying favor.[5] The prevalence of this sort of servitude was reflected in the resurgence of terminology that had all but died out in the Song, designating an intricate variety of servile and semi-servile statuses. A Yuan guide to legal terminology thus offers new glosses on pre-Song terms like *guan jian hu* 官監戶 ("Descendants of those who were dependents in earlier eras, or those of this dynasty who are convict laborers or dependents in the prefectures or counties and have no fixed residence; that is, those who today have been attached to a master's household. Those who are respectable commoners are called *jian hu*; those who are slaves are called *guan hu*"); *bu qu* 部曲 ("Those who, when young and having no place to go, attach themselves to someone for food and clothing. Their masters rear them as slaves, and they don't have a separate household registration but follow that of their masters...when they reach adulthood they are permitted to marry respectable commoners"); and *ke nü* 客女 ("This refers to maids [*bi*] who have been manumitted, as well as expelled concubines. The daughters of *bu qu* also fall into this category").[6]

---

4. Tao Zongyi, *Nancun chuo geng lu* 17.208.
5. Zhang Yanghao, *San shi zhong gao* 2.7a–7b.
6. Xu Yuanrui, *Li xue zhi nan*, 103.

The government's attempt to fix categories of servile status was a central element of its policies toward concubinage. As noted above, concubinage in the Song was marked by very blurred and fluid social boundaries between various types of concubines and maidservants. This was in part because concubines in the Song participated in a broad market of temporary indentured labor, which undercut social categories by turning respectable commoners into temporary slaves or dependents. A series of judgments in the *Statutes and Precedents of the Yuan* (*Da Yuan sheng zheng guo chao dian zhang*, or *Yuan dian zhang*) reveals that the Yuan government struggled both to understand and to put an end to such indentures and the unstable social categories they occasioned. Their confusion is evident in a judgment of 1282, which characterized the indenturing of the sons and daughters of tenant households as "a harmful policy of the fallen Song," and exclaimed, "Among our subjects, how can landlord families regard tenant families as slave labor and indenture them?"[7] Fundamentally, the Yuan authorities had difficulty reconciling Chinese ideas about temporary, occupationally based slavery with their own ideas of slavery as an unalterable personal identity. In 1294, another ruling forbade the indenture of children of *se mu* families, again complaining that such indenture caused "innocent respectable commoners to sink eternally into slave labor."[8]

The authorities were particularly anxious to put an end to the indenture of respectable women. Just as the government had forbidden respectable women to be sold into base occupations like entertainment, they were anxious to prevent them from entering indenture. An early Yuan pronouncement (1278) prohibiting the indenture of a wife to another man reflects primarily these status (rather than moral) concerns, stressing that the husband should not have indentured a "respectable commoner" (*liang ren*). By 1292, however, the government began to introduce Confucian moral rhetoric in support of the ban on indenturing wives to other men:

---

7. *YDZ* 57.12b–13a.
8. *YDZ* 57.14a–b. *Se mu* were people who were neither Han Chinese nor Mongol, belonging to one of a number of other ethnicities. These ethnic categories corresponded to juridical status in Yuan law, with *se mu* people generally more privileged than Han Chinese, though not as much as Mongols. The law also distinguished northern Chinese from southerners, as discussed below.

> I have heard that husband and wife is the central relationship of all humanity: thus there is a saying that wives match the bodies of their husbands, and that when a husband dies there is no ritual for remarriage. In the central plains, extremely poor commoners, even facing great hunger, would rather throw themselves in a ditch with their wives and children; how could they indenture them to someone else? The Jiang and Huai regions have been unified for fifteen years, [but] the customs are shallow and debased; as before, people still do things one cannot bear to hear of. [When] their wives enter the homes of the indenturers, they openly become as husband and wife with them, or become maids or concubines (*bi qie*). Frequently, they are supposed to be released in three or five years. When the time is up, even though they are supposed to go back to their original master, in some cases the indenturing master covets the wife's beauty and pays money again; sometimes the woman is fond of the affluence of the indenturing master and rejects and despises her husband-and-master. After a long period, the new couple mutually love each other; in these circumstances it cannot be otherwise. In mild cases, money is added and she is indentured again; in severe cases, she abandons [her husband]. In some instances the new couple have feelings for one another and can't bear to give each other up, with the result that there have been cases of people getting killed. According to the law, if a man receives money to allow his wife to have illicit sex with someone, it is not a minor crime. The benighted people of the south openly take money to indenture their wives to others, and for several years they act like husband and wife: is this not worse than having one's wife break the law a single time?!

The judgment concluded that the indenturing of a woman who already had a husband was forbidden, unless the couple were indentured together.[9]

Despite repeated rulings, however, the Yuan authorities ultimately admitted their inability to stem the custom of indenture. The 1294 ruling on *se mu* children grudgingly acknowledged that the custom of indenturing boys and girls was thoroughly engrained in the culture of southern China, and allowed that "With respect to southerners only, when they mutually indenture each other, in the end they remain respectable commoners; it is permissible to temporarily let the poor people among them follow their customary law."[10] Less than a year later, a very lengthy ruling again acknowledged that the recent years of famine had led commoners to indenture their wives and children, and this had been impossible to prohibit. The officials pointed out that the custom had a

---

9. *YDZ* 57.13b–14a.
10. *YDZ* 57.14a–b.

long history in the Wu-Yue area, and in previous eras the practice had not been outlawed. They also admitted that given the famine conditions that had now spread to other areas, in recent years, even in the northern part of the country, starving men had sold their wives, concubines, sons, and daughters. The court reiterated that the husband-wife and father-child relationships were central to human morality and observed that all those who had been involved—as either buyers or sellers—in the indenture of wives, concubines, and children had broken the law. Yet (presumably in recognition of practical realities) the court concluded that past offenses should be granted retroactive amnesty, while insisting that henceforth all indenture of wives, concubines, sons, and daughters should be forbidden.[11]

All told, the Yuan government's repeated efforts to prohibit indenture and freeze social classes are best taken as evidence for the continued volatility and confusion of class status during the Yuan. Even the nominal reemergence of hereditary slavery did not succeed in stemming the long-term trend toward flexible and variable social statuses. On the contrary, because erstwhile upper-class people sometimes found themselves enslaved in the Yuan, the reemergence of slavery arguably helped further break down the correlation between slavery as a personal identity and slavery as an economic condition. As Tao Zongyi observed, where in earlier eras only convicts (and their descendants) had been made into slaves, in his own day most slaves had ancestors who were perfectly blameless.[12] As a result, despite the resurgence of slavery, the association between servile status and personal dishonor was not reestablished. Rather, distinctions between those of respectable status and those considered to be base continued to erode, helped along by the more general chaos in social relations.

Concomitant with its (largely futile) efforts to stem indenture, the Yuan court also attempted to establish rules for acceptable, legal forms of concubinage. Their policies were initially complicated by disparities between Chinese norms and steppe practices, which unlike Chinese

---

11. *YDZ* 57.14b–15a. Cf. *YS* 103.2642.
12. Tao Zongyi, *Nancun chuo geng lu* 17.208. Richard Davis describes how a Yuan descendant of the eminent Shi family of the Southern Song ended up sold into slavery (Davis, *Court and Family*, 166–67).

custom permitted men to take multiple wives who were higher in status than concubines.[13] Steppe practices seem to have prevailed in the territory controlled by the Jin in the twelfth and early thirteenth centuries, so in a ruling of 1273 the court attempted to resolve ambiguities and uphold the principles of Chinese custom. The ruling stipulated that a man who had a principal wife could not take a second wife, but it allowed second wives taken before 1271 to be redesignated as concubines if the parties involved so wished.[14] A case in 1276 clarified that a man could take a "second[ary] wife" (*ci qi* 次妻), but only on the grounds that she was clearly not a principal wife.[15] This ruling in effect downgraded what in steppe practice would have been a "second wife" into the equivalent of a concubine in Chinese ways of thinking.[16]

More importantly, the law of 1273 also required that any man wishing to take a concubine set up a clear marital contract.[17] Here the law reiterated principles set out in Tang and early Song statutes on concubinage, which drew a sharp distinction between concubines, who were of respectable status and formally "married," and maids of dishonorable status who were not formally recognized as consorts.[18] The Yuan went even further than Tang law in upholding the position of concubines, however, for they forbade the resale of any concubine "who was contractually married" (*yi shu bi qu* 以書幣取).[19] Taken together, Yuan laws

---

13. As early as 1162, Zhou Bida had memorialized the court about what titles could be appropriately bestowed on the womenfolk of a Jin defector to the Song. The deceased husband, of Qidan ethnicity, had a wife, a secondary wife, and a concubine. The court originally awarded one title to the wife and slightly less exalted titles to the secondary wife and the concubine. Zhou Bida intervened to explain that the term used to designate the second wife (*ci qi* 次妻) had created confusion about her status, arguing that she should be distinguished from the concubine. He recommended that she be designated a minor wife (*xiao qi* 小妻). The court appears to have complied, giving her a higher-ranking title. See Zhou Bida, *Wenzhong ji* 97.2b–6a, esp. 97.4a–6a.

14. *YDZ* 18.43a.

15. *YDZ* 18.43a.

16. We likewise see in the Yuan the first unambiguous usage of the term *ci shi* 次室, which had earlier often implied successor wife, to mean concubine. See Chen Lü, *An ya tang ji* 11.12b, in a funerary inscription for Yang Ying.

17. *YDZ* 18.43a.

18. See the discussion of the Tang statutes in chap. 2.

19. *YS* 103.2643. In accordance with this law, a surviving Yuan dynasty contract for indenturing a daughter as a concubine repeatedly stresses that she has never been

attempted to tie concubines more closely to their husbands' families and bring them into a position closer to that of wives, while simultaneously delegitimating the position of serving maids and other consorts whose relationships were not regularized by contract.

As with the laws on indenture, however, there is little evidence that the Yuan rulings on concubinage were observed in practice. Nowhere was this more clear than in the traffic of public performers in and out of the homes of high officials, as amply documented in the *Emerald Pavilion Collection*.[20] It appears to be from this collection that Tao Zongyi drew his account of the three virtuous courtesan-concubines; but the *Collection* recounts many other instances of entertainers who at one point or another in their careers became concubines (the term usually used is "side chamber" [*ce shi* 側室]) of eminent officials. In chapter 7 we encountered Liu Poxi, who left her husband to become the concubine of Vice Grand Councilor Quan Buyan Sari. In similar fashion Duan Xiqunjing was set up as a concubine by the high-ranking Zhang Jiusi (1242–1302), and Jin Shoutou was taken in (*na* 納) by the Jiangxi Privy Councilor Guan Zhige.[21] A classic romantic story is told of the courtesan Li Zhentong, who in her early teens was already famous in the Jiang and Zhe areas. When the controller of Zhe province, Da Tianshan, encountered her, he fell in love at first sight. After three years his term of office ended, and he had to return to the capital to await reappointment. In his absence, Li became a Daoist nun, closing her door to visitors and devoting herself to burning incense and reciting scripture. When Da received his new post, he returned and "married her with full ritual" (*bei li qu zhi* 備禮取之).[22] Although Li's example presents the appealing image of the faithful courtesan, other stories in the *Collection* show that such fidelity was not the norm: Gu Shanshan, born to a respectable commoner household, first married a musician,

---

married or "served" any one else. See Huang Shijian, *Yuan dai fa lü zi liao ji cun*, 246–47. Cf. Ebrey, "Concubines in Song China," 10. The law also forbade the sale of wives as slaves or bondmaids, explicitly calling for such women to be returned to respectable commoner status, and stipulated that a deceased father's concubine could not be given away to another man to privatize (*si* 私). See *YS* 103.2644.

20. The *Emerald Pavilion Collection* was introduced in chap. 7.
21. *QLJJZ* 115, 144.
22. *QLJJZ* 200.

then after his death became a concubine of a Mongol magistrate; still later she returned to the courtesan registers, as did Zhang Yulian after her own stint as the concubine of an official.[23]

We see here that in spite of laws repeatedly prohibiting "marriage" with entertainers, high-ranking officials (and undoubtedly others as well) flouted the rules with impunity.[24] This sometimes put the authorities in an awkward position, as when the authors of a 1311 ruling reiterating the prohibition against taking musicians as wives found it necessary to point out that the recent marriage of an entertainer to the son of a prominent court minister was permitted only by special favor of the emperor.[25] The lax enforcement of such prohibitions is also reflected in the fact that the *Yuan History* records only one case of an official indicted for marrying a courtesan and getting enfeoffments for her, and then only to explain that the indicting official had by this means offended a superior, with drastic consequences for his own career.[26] In the one other case I have found of a Yuan official—in this case a county magistrate—being indicted for marrying a courtesan, the indictment stresses less her courtesan status than the fact that she was under the official's jurisdiction.[27] Elsewhere, a funerary inscription praises an official for his efforts to keep another official's courtesan-turned-concubine from participating in court ceremonies—suggesting that her marriage to the official was in itself not at issue.[28]

---

23. QLJJZ 194, 173–74; cf. Idema and West, *Chinese Theater*, 147, 162; Waley, *Secret History*, 104, 101–2.

24. Waley suggests that perhaps the edict of 1278 forbidding marriage between officials and musicians applied only to women of the *jiao fang* and/or did not apply to concubines, because the children of concubines "did not count as legitimate" (*Secret History*, 92). Yet many of the women described in the *Emerald Pavilion Collection* as becoming concubines were explicitly described as being "on the registers," and as we will see below, in the Yuan as in earlier times, children of concubines were generally regarded as legitimate.

25. YDZ 18.46b.

26. YS 144.3435. Note that in this case it is not clear whether the entertainer was married as a wife or as a concubine.

27. Wang Yun, *Qiujian ji* 88.23a–25a. The indictment argues that old precedents forbade officials to marry commoners under their jurisdiction, and that marriage with a courtesan should be even less acceptable.

28. Song Jiong, *Yan shi ji* 14.5a.

To be sure, not everyone approved of taking courtesans in as concubines. The late Yuan memoirist and moralist Kong Qi decried the practice as extremely inauspicious:

> This type of person has observed many people, and has a myriad of seductive poses in her personal repertoire. If you have her enter your courtyard, she will certainly not stay long. Moreover she will beguile your sons, daughters, and the various concubines, and unbecoming incidents may well occur—I've seen it often. There are none who take courtesans as concubines who do not end up ruined. Therefore the saying goes, "At the banquet you can't do without them, in the household you can't do with them."[29]

Yet note that even Kong does not suggest that taking in a courtesan is inappropriate from the perspective of class standing: rather, for Kong, it is the sexuality of the courtesan that poses a danger to the household.

All of this bespeaks a significant change from the Song, not only in practice but in social attitudes. Mongol ideas about defined classes notwithstanding, nothing in the *Emerald Pavilion Collection* suggests that there is anything shameful or déclassé about an official bringing a public courtesan into his inner quarters.[30] Quite the contrary: the *Collection*'s breathless descriptions (and even Tao Zongyi's more measured accounts) suggest that in the higher echelons of the Yuan bureaucracy, acquiring a famous professional entertainer as a concubine was a sign of masculine power and status, just as keeping talented (albeit not professional) entertainer-concubines had been in the Song. Still, even as these anecdotal sources reveal the continued popularity of entertainer-concubines, Yuan sources more generally reveal that attitudes toward the institution were changing.

## *The End of Romance: Concubines and Family Disorder*

One sign of new attitudes toward entertainer-concubines in the Yuan is that such women are far less visible in the collected works of literati than they

---

29. Kong Qi, *Zhizheng zhi ji* 2.48.

30. The *Emerald Pavilion Collection* contains one reference to an official being demoted for his relationship with a courtesan: it reports that the Shandong Censor Jia Gu (n.d.) was demoted for writing a romantic poem to a courtesan, and "down to today this is regarded as a lovely tale in Shandong." Jia Gu cannot be identified in more formal Yuan sources.

were in earlier eras. In particular, the discourse of romance that had been so prominent a feature of Northern Song writings on concubines, and was still evident in the Southern Song, appears very muted in the Yuan.

Admittedly, we do still see occasional literati poems that acknowledge a friend's relationship with a beloved serving maid or household-courtesan. Bai Pu (1226–after 1306) was touched when a fellow northerner who had been residing temporarily in the south took leave of his *shi'er* Fragrant Sleep. Bai wrote a poem cast in the girl's voice, expressing sadness at being abandoned.[31] Zhang Yan (1248–1320) composed a lyric inspired by the singing and dancing of his friend's household-charmer, Beloved Chrysanthemum.[32] Yang Weizhen (1296–1370) described how in 1360 his friend Xie Lüzhai brought out his "old charmer" (*lao ji* 老姬) Southern Fragrance to play the flute as they drank.[33] Yet such references are rarer and generally less detailed than in the collected works of Song men. The shift away from romance is also evident in subtle differences in the funerary inscriptions men wrote for their concubines. Although in the Song men like Su Shi and Zhou Bida wrote funerary inscriptions for women they acknowledged as *shi qie,* whose elegant, courtesan-like names they revealed, in the Yuan this was no longer the case. The few surviving Yuan funerary inscriptions for concubines are notably circumspect: they provide only the women's surnames and depict them as model wives.[34] The shift is visible even in gossipy anecdotal sources. Where in the Southern Song Zhou Hui had poked fun at his contemporaries for bestowing flowery names on unattractive maidservants (and then proffered his own clever idea for a suitably poetic moniker), Kong Qi inveighed against the naming practice, calling it "most inelegant" and arguing that gentlemen should take it as taboo.[35]

---

31. Bai Pu, *Tian lai ji, xia,* 10b–11a.
32. Zhang Yan, *Shan zhong bai yun ci* 5.2a–b.
33. Yang Weizhen, *Dong wei zi ji* 29.11b–12a. Yang elsewhere refers to Xie having purchased a very young courtesan whom Yang named Little Fragrance (*Dong wei zi ji* 29.9a).
34. Lu Wengui, *Qiang dong lei gao* 13.35a–36a; Dai Liang, *Jiu ling shan fang ji* 14.14b–15b. Only in the poetic *ming* 銘 of his inscription does Lu Wengui suggest that his relationship with his concubine was romantic, expressing grief that her beauty is obscured by earth and alluding to the death of Su Shi's concubine Morning Cloud.
35. Kong Qi, *Zhizheng zhi ji* 2.48.

In short, the romantic discourse—so prevalent in earlier eras—that had highlighted the allure of household-courtesans and valorized their romantic relationships with friends and associates is almost entirely absent from the writings of Yuan literati. Instead, Yuan writing about concubines overwhelmingly focuses on them in the context of the family, where as often as not they appear as a source of danger and disorder.

In part, this focus on disorder can be related to the larger Yuan context, in which tumult was endemic and conventional Chinese norms of family relations were frequently violated.[36] A number of Yuan officials described with great specificity the deviant behavior they saw around them. In a lengthy memorial on proper governance that he submitted to the throne in 1303, for example, Zheng Jiefu devoted one section to the need for "improving customs" (*hou su* 厚俗). After observing that correct morality had to begin with proper relations between men and women, Zheng recounted:

> Now in the markets and lanes they set up stands to sell wine; they send out their wives to solicit sex, secretly acting as harlot-courtesans (*chang ji* 娼妓) and publicly taking payment: they call this "marrying a bloke" (*jia han* 嫁漢). There are also respectable commoner families who privately set up [secondary] husbands, eating and drinking with the new husbands and sleeping in the same place, completely without distinctions of host and guest or inner and outer: it is called "holding hands to survive together" (*ba shou he huo* 把手合活).[37] There are also those who indenture respectable women and support them as "adopted daughters." They gather three or four of them to entice guests, who drink with them by day and sleep with them at night. They distinguish themselves from harlot households (*chang hu* 娼戶), calling themselves "the ones who sit" (*zuo zi ren jia* 坐子人家). Around the capital, nine houses out of ten are like this, and every circuit and prefecture competes to imitate it. This trend is extremely foul.[38]

---

36. Certainly elite rules for normative behavior were often violated in the Song as well (see Zhu Xi's comments about deviant marriage customs in *Zhu Xi ji* 100.5101), but Yuan sources do seem to reflect far greater prevalence of non-normative practices even among the elite.

37. This appears to be a reference to the sorts of polyandric practices Matthew Sommer has found in the Qing. See Sommer, "Polyandry."

38. Chen Dezhi, *Yuan dai zou yi ji lu, xia*, 52–112 (the cited passage appears on 74–75). The date of the memorial is given in the version that appears in Yang Shiqi's *Li dai ming chen zou yi* 67.1a. In addition to the rampant illicit sex described in this passage, Zheng also complained about the widespread practice of levirate marriage, the incidence of lawsuits by servants and slaves suing their masters, a general lack of filiality among the populace, the prevalence of slave markets, and the extensive flouting of sumptuary regulations.

Zheng's comments were echoed a decade or so later by the author of a handbook for local clerks:

> In recent years, the ritual teachings are not practiced, customs are shallow and depraved, there is no distinction between male and female, and monks and nuns intermix. There are indeed many gentlemen who understand the rituals, whose family rules are strict and clear, and whose inner quarters are regulated and solemn. But if you listen in the streets and lanes, you find quite a few girls of respectable family chasing after people to attach themselves to, going in and out of the houses of the powerful, losing all restraint: how can there not be evils therein? There are also poor people who never received any education, who enjoy associating with polluted and degraded people, losing all sense of shame: it is too painful to detail. And again there are women who like to bring lawsuits, who never leave the government offices, content to bear whipping and beatings, totally without shame or chagrin.[39]

These sources suggest that even if a few literati families were able to maintain their upright traditions, ordinary people were too concerned with survival to worry about the niceties of Confucian morality. Other accounts suggest that even among the elite, the circumstances of the Yuan occupation put pressure on traditional mores.[40] Unconventional marriage arrangements were common, as Paul Smith has shown in his exploration of Kong Qi's memoir. Kong's own family had experienced several generations of uxorilocal marriage, and he complained bitterly about the family problems he saw as stemming from the inadequate control of women.[41] In particular, Kong traces a great many family problems to the common literati penchant for keeping entertainer-concubines and serving maids.

Kong repeatedly warns about the dangers of keeping maids and entertainers, arguing that they are impossible to control. He warns that they lead each other into lasciviousness and engender jealousy in wives.[42] He gives specific examples of men in his circle whose concubines had affairs with other servants and passed off their sons as belonging to the master, and of a man who took in entertainers (*ling nü* 伶女) late in life, only to have them seduce his sons after his death.[43] Most strikingly, we learn

---

39. Wang Jie, *Shan su yao yi*, 354.
40. See Smith, "Family," esp. 678–80.
41. Smith, "Fear of Gynarchy," passim.
42. Kong Qi, *Zhizheng zhi ji* 1.26, 1.33.
43. Kong Qi, *Zhizheng zhi ji* 2.51–52, 1.35.

that Kong's sensitivity on this issue was born of bitter personal experience. He confides that when his own aged grandfather asked a distaff grandson to help him acquire a concubine, the girl was already pregnant by the grandson when she entered the grandfather's household. Later she also had relations with slaves in the family, and the unfilial sons she bore "caused trouble in my family for more than fifty years." Kong continues that his own father also set up "three or four semi-fine maids (*ban xi bi* 半細婢)" late in life, and in spite of both parents' efforts to control them carefully, the women ultimately engaged in trickery and had relations with younger males in the family.[44]

Echoing the Yuan government, Kong also takes special exception to the continuing custom of serial indenture of concubines:

> Among the shallow customs of the Zhexi region, none is worse than the practice of indenturing a daughter to one person, and when she returns after her period of service is complete, indenturing her to someone else. Sometimes they do this several times before they finally marry her off. The customs are so bad that if one suggests they shouldn't do this, everyone reproaches him saying, "No one will want her." Apparently by being indentured frequently, the girls acquire more goods. This custom is especially popular in Suzhou and Hangzhou.

Kong's distaste for this practice is so profound that, like Yuan lawmakers, he advises a return to a style of concubinage that was closer to marriage:

> I respectfully suggest that when one buys a concubine, one also should investigate her surname and generation, or else carry out a divination before taking her in.[45] You should see that she lives out her life [in your household] and at her death bury her "in attendance." Do not let her be polluted, and do not let her marry someone else: this is what a benevolent person should do. If she behaves badly, then you should expel her: this is something she has brought on herself, and not your responsibility. With respect to maids it is the same. One who is favored and takes care to fulfill expectations without error, serving the master loyally, should be treated the same as a concubine. If there is one who serves loyally and diligently and makes the principal wife jealous, you must investigate in detail and take care not to let her blamelessly suffer abuse.[46]

---

44. Kong Qi, *Zhizheng zhi ji* 2.51–52; Smith, "Fear of Gynarchy," 39.

45. The purpose of divination was to ascertain that the concubine did not share her potential husband's surname, as same-surname marriage was taboo.

46. Kong Qi, *Zhizheng zhi ji* 2.53. Kong Qi may have had personal reasons for these attitudes: as Smith notes, Kong and his brothers were children of a concubine, and lost control of property to their principal half-sister. See Smith, "Fear of Gynarchy," 52–53.

Significantly, however, although Kong Qi shared the Yuan authorities' dislike for the custom of temporary concubines, he did not accept the government's definition of who could constitute a proper concubine. Kong insisted that not only women officially "married in" as concubines but also favored maids should be granted a recognized place in the master's household, kept on even after the master's death, and buried near him after her own. Here Kong rejects the status distinctions between concubines and maids articulated in Yuan law; instead, like Liu Kezhuang in the late Southern Song and in keeping with popular practice, he considers a maid who has been sexually involved with the master as the equivalent of a concubine.[47] Still, Kong agrees with the government that concubines should be permanent members of the family, with concomitant ritual obligations and privileges. As if to prove his point, Kong tells an inspiring story of a jealous wife who was persuaded *not* to expel a pregnant concubine after their husband died. Instead, she reared the son lovingly and was rewarded by seeing him pass the examinations.[48]

Such generous and virtuous wives were apparently rare, however. Echoing themes seen in the Southern Song, Kong and other anecdotalists told stories of jealous wives who mistreated or even murdered concubines and their children. In such accounts, family disorder is often intimately tied to karmic forces. Thus Kong related how the wife of a deceased Mongol official expelled his natural son by a concubine, ruining the family and nearly cutting off the official's descent line. Kong attributed this turn of events to Heaven's retribution for the cruel actions of the official's father during the conquest of the Song. In similar fashion, in a story he explicitly characterizes as a warning to jealous wives, Tao Zongyi tells of a strange illness experienced by a cruel wife who had driven a pregnant concubine to suicide.[49] But even when authors were not concerned with demonstrating the moral workings of Heaven, they warned that conflicts between wives and concubines could undermine families. The author of a

---

47. See chap. 5 for Liu Kezhuang's legal decision treating a maid and a concubine as equal coparceners.

48. Kong Qi, *Zhizheng zhi ji* 2.74.

49. Tao Zongyi, *Nancun chuo geng lu* 9.116; Kong Qi, *Zhizheng zhi ji* 1.9, 1.10. Kong Qi also asserts that forcing women to become concubines is one of the evil actions sure to bring down Heaven's wrath (*Zhizheng zhi ji* 2.55–56); cf. Smith, "Fear of Gynarchy," 47.

magistrate's handbook remarked on the tendency of stepmothers and late-married concubines to want to harm the children of the principal wife, and urged that property disputes be secretly and carefully investigated.[50] Tao Zongyi praised the success of a clever magistrate who unraveled a legal case in which a husband had accused his wife of trying to murder him by means of a voodoo doll. Although the wife had already confessed, the skeptical magistrate discovered that in fact the doll had been created by a jealous concubine, who had hoped thereby to frame the wife and have her executed by the authorities.[51]

## Moralist Responses

Anecdotalists' concerns about the detrimental effects of concubines on families were shared by Yuan moralists. As in the Southern Song, some authors (especially but not exclusively those associated with the increasingly influential Learning of the Way school) responded by suggesting that truly virtuous men would do without concubines. Wu Cheng related that the scholar Zheng Song (d. 1307) was indifferent to the desires of food and sex (*yin shi nan nü* 飲食男女), and from the time he was young did not keep *bi qie*.[52] Dai Liang recalls that after his wife died young, Jin Hongdao (d. 1365) screened off a small room and, keeping no charmer-attendants by his side, spent his days with his books and his evenings instructing his sons.[53] Fu Ruojin (1303–42), in a funerary biography of Zhao Sigong, stressed Zhao's efforts to recommend virtuous men, his frugality, and the fact that he kept no *shi qie*.[54] Along similar lines, in

---

50. Xu Yuanrui, *Li xue zhi nan*, 147. Xu adds that most conflicts between males in a family are due to concubines married late in life or sisters-in-law fighting over the family property.

51. Tao Zongyi, *Nancun chuo geng lu* 5.62.

52. Wu Cheng, *Wu wen zheng ji* 74.4b. With regard to the high-ranking Yuan official Zhang Honggang, Wu Cheng was reduced to making the more modest claim that he was personally frugal, so that even his beloved concubines (*ai qie*) didn't have gorgeous clothing (*Wu wen zheng ji* 69.3b).

53. Dai Liang, *Jiu ling shan fang ji* 9.125–27. Dai also praised Chen Lin 陳麟 (d. 1368) for having few desires, remarking that Chen's apartments had no *ji shi* 姬侍, his storehouses no surplus wealth (15.208–11).

54. Fu Ruojin, *Fu Yuli shi wen ji* 10.5a–5b. For similar examples, see Cheng Duanli, *Wei zhai ji* 6.15, and Yu Ji, *Dao yuan xue gu lu* 43.735.

a funerary biography for Chen Tianxiang (1240–1316), Zhang Yanghao (1269–1329) recounted that when Chen was stationed with a number of other men far away from their families, it was ordered that each take an attendant-concubine to help "settle his desires." When Chen did not do so, his compatriots arranged for a beautiful girl of respectable family to be presented to him. Chen protested, "Milords, please do not disturb yourselves. I have no need of this," and in the end he refused her.[55]

Yet even as moralists valorized men for lack of desire for concubines, they were increasingly vehement about the importance of wives' receptiveness to them. This is evident, for example, in a preface by Wu Cheng praising the "filial behavior" of a woman surnamed Xing, of Datong. Wu begins by citing an example from the fourth century, of a woman surnamed Yu who not only reared her brother's son in the same manner as her own, but also encouraged her husband to take many concubines, likewise rearing the concubines' sons as her own. Wu uses Yu's example as a foil for Xing: he stresses that Xing's behavior was equally virtuous, despite the fact that, unlike Yu, she was reared among the people and had received no education. Wu then laments that few other women of his day are able to live up to Xing's example:

> Alas! In recent eras gentlemen and officials are unable to correct themselves and control their families. They let their wives be violently jealous and unrighteous. Even if childless [the wives] are unwilling to take their brothers' children as their own; they shackle their husbands and prevent them from taking concubines, or restrict the concubines and do not allow them to have children. I have seen many who go so far as to cut off the succession and end up as ghosts who receive no sacrifices. When they hear of the spirit of Ms. Xing, how can they help but be ashamed![56]

Here Wu celebrates a woman whose "filial" behavior resides primarily in her absence of jealousy and her willingness to rear the children of concubines. The concern for perpetuation of patrilines inherent in Wu's comments were echoed by Lu Wengui (1252–1336) in a funerary inscription he composed for a woman surnamed Du (1276–1325). Lu first establishes that Du understood the principles of the Learning of the Way (here called the "Learning of Nature" *xing xue* 性學), which

---

55. Zhang Yanghao, *Gui tian lei gao* 10.7a.
56. Wu Cheng, *Wu wen zheng ji* 24.7b–8a.

she learned sitting by her father's side as he read from the *Four Books*. Later, having married the Jurchen official Wugusun Ze, she became quite concerned when her husband reached the age of fifty without a son to succeed him.[57] Accordingly, when Wugusun considered proposing to a wealthy and titled widow, Du encouraged him to do so, saying, "You are planning for your posterity, what doubt could there be?" The two women got along companionably, and Du even deferred to the slightly older second wife. Then, a year or so later, Du herself gave birth to a son. Insisting that he had taken the second wife only out of concern for the succession, and over Du's protests, her husband then returned the second wife along with her dowry of "10,000 golds" (*wan jin* 萬金). Lu tells us, "People thought both [husband and wife] virtuous" (*ren liang xian zhi* 人兩賢之).[58] Here we have another example of the ideal virtuous couple of the Learning of the Way model; although he is describing a second wife rather than a concubine per se, Lu's larger point is that a virtuous woman should welcome a second consort without hesitation.

On the one hand, then, class animus against entertainers continued to erode in the Yuan, and entertainer-concubines continued to be popular. On the other hand, the discourse of romance that once surrounded entertainer-concubines faded, replaced by a generally negative image of concubines as disruptive to family. That disruptive potential was addressed by Learning of the Way moralists, who reiterated a late Song discourse that praised both men who eschewed concubines and women who willingly accepted them. Meanwhile, the image of the concubine as romantic paramour was further undermined by the marked intensification of another late Song discourse, as funerary biographies increasingly configured concubines as mothers and their children as full-fledged family members.

## From Paramour to Parent: The Domesticated Concubine

As noted in chapter 5, beginning in the late Southern Song, authors of funerary inscriptions had devoted increased attention to the treatment of

---

57. Lu Wengui's funerary inscription for Wugusun Ze reveals that Du was a successor wife, and Ze was twenty-six years older than Du (Lu Wengui, *Qiang dong lei gao* 12.1a–12b). Ze's funerary inscription does not mention the second wife.

58. Lu Wengui, *Qiang dong lei gao* 13.29b–33a.

concubine mothers and lesser half-siblings. The rhetorical assimilation of concubines and their progeny into Chinese families continued in the Yuan. Not only did authors of funerary inscriptions increasingly valorize the proper treatment of concubines and their children, but they began to accord concubines a place in the most ritualized or standardized parts of inscriptions, those places where the most basic and regularized information about the subject's family were conveyed.

The existence of a concubine in the family could be noted almost anywhere in a funerary biography: recall that even in the Northern Song, authors sometimes pointed out that a subject had temporarily retired from office to mourn a deceased birth mother. But in the stylized genre of funerary inscriptions, there were three places where mention of a concubine endowed her with special significance and dignified her position in the family. First, funerary inscriptions in the Song and Yuan conventionally included a catalog of three generations of the subject's ancestors: it was customary for the subject's great-grandfather, grandfather, and father, as well as the wives of these men, to be mentioned in this list. The appearance of a concubine in this context meant that she was being formally acknowledged as an ancestress of the subject. Second, when the subject was male, funerary inscriptions generally listed his spouses. Here, the mention of a concubine along with the principal wife or wives recognized her status as a consort. Finally, a third place where concubines might be mentioned was in lists of descendants, distinguishing her children from those of the principal wife and highlighting her status as a mother.

Before the very late Song, the authors of funerary biographies only rarely included concubines in lists of ancestors, and most of the cases in which they did so involved high-ranking families and concubines who had received honorific titles.[59] In the Yuan, however, we not only see a

---

59. Funerary inscriptions for members of the imperial clan are most notable here, for where close imperial relatives were concerned it seems to have been accepted practice even in the Northern Song to list first the subject's official mother (and usually her title) and then his or her birth mother (*suo sheng mu*). The inclusion of titled concubines in lists of ancestors obviously redounded to the glory of husbands and sons. Only in the mid-thirteenth century do we see two Song authors listing untitled concubine mothers of politically undistinguished men (Liu Kezhuang, *Hou cun ji* 40.5b; Yao Mian, *Xue po ji* 49.1b). For more detailed discussion of other Song cases, see Bossler, "Song-Yuan mu zhi," 101–4.

relative increase in the number of inscriptions mentioning concubine ancestresses, but fewer than half involve politically prominent families, and only two involve concubines with titles.[60] For some Yuan authors, then, the mere fact of motherhood was enough to earn a concubine a place among her son's formally acknowledged forebears. Similarly, although Song inscriptions virtually never listed concubines among a man's spouses, in the Yuan we begin to see for the first time a few authors listing concubines, by name, along with wives.[61]

Most dramatic, however, is the attention that Yuan authors began to pay to the maternity of descendants. From the early Song, it had been conventional in funerary inscriptions to list the subject's sons, grandsons, and great-grandsons, but before the very late Song these lists virtually never distinguished descendants by maternity.[62] Rather, inscriptions typically listed a man's wife and, where applicable, successor wives, and then listed the descendants who, by implication, all "belonged" to the living principal wife, as per law and custom.[63] Attention to concubine maternity is first seen in the last decades of the Southern Song, with the

---

60. In each of the Southern Song and Yuan periods, I have found seven mentions of birth mothers as ancestors in funerary inscriptions. However, since there are far fewer surviving sources for the Yuan than for the Southern Song, this represents a significant increase in the percentage of mentions. The Yuan examples are: Huang Zhongyuan, *Si ru ji* 4.20a; Zhao Mengfu, *Song xue zhai ji, wai ji*, 22a; Huang Jin, *Huang Wenxian gong ji* 8a.327–28, 9a.399–400; Chen Lü, *An ya tang ji* 11.12b; Hu Han, *Hu Zhongzi ji* 9.13a; Yin Kui, *Qiang zhai ji* 4.2b.

61. Hu Zhiyu, *Zi shan da quan ji* 18.27; Cheng Jufu, *Xue lou ji* 17.15a; Xiao Ju, *Qin zhai ji* 3.22b, 3.24; Tong Shu, *Ju an ji* 8.9b.

62. I have found only one Northern Song funerary inscription that distinguishes the maternity of descendants: in a 1060 inscription for an imperial kinsman, Wang Gui noted that the subject's principal wife had no children, but that his concubine (*qi ce shi* 其側室) (whom Wang does not bother to name), bore a son and a daughter (Wang Gui, *Huayang ji* 39.535–36). Notably, this is also the earliest use of the term *ce shi* in Song funerary inscriptions preserved in the *Si ku quan shu* collection. In contrast, Wong Yu-Hsuan has found a number of inscriptions from the late Tang that distinguish children born of concubines from those born of wives ("Tōdai," passim). The difference may have to do with the fact that many of the inscriptions Wong uses were preserved in archeological collections (and thus tend to be more varied) rather than in the literary collections of famous men. The latter tend to be more conventional and circumspect, in keeping with the reputations of their authors.

63. In a very few cases, Northern Song inscription authors distinguish between the children of the first wife and later principal (i.e., successor) wives.

appearance of inscriptions like one by Liu Kezhuang, which mentions that the subject (Liu's nephew, d. 1244) had a wife who bore a daughter, a successor wife who bore a son, and also a daughter born of an (unnamed) concubine (*shu sheng* 庶生). Likewise, in an inscription he wrote for his own wife, Liu lists several children and then adds that there were also a young boy and girl who were children of concubines (*shu sheng*).[64] Another author mentions that Li Renhou, dead in 1230 at the untimely age of twenty-eight *sui*, was survived by a four-year-old son who was the child of an unnamed concubine (*pang ce shi* 旁側室).[65]

In Yuan sources, such references become exceedingly common. In an inscription for Zhao Liang (d. 1287), for example, Ren Shilin begins by listing Zhao's wife's surname and the names and titles of her three sons. He observes that the eight daughters all married into famous families, then remarks that the second was born of a concubine née Niu (*ce shi* 側室牛氏). In like manner, writing of the eminent Yuan official Gao Kegong (d. 1310), Deng Wenyuan lists Gao's first wife with her children, a second wife with hers, and concludes, "the son of the concubine . . . is still young."[66]

The pattern continues: In an inscription for a Han man who refused to serve the Mongols, Cheng Jufu notes that although the subject's wife died childless, three sons were born of a woman surnamed Hu.[67] Tong Shu tells us that Jiao Rong's (d. 1317) four sons were born of his virtuous wife Du, but that his daughter was the child of his *ce shi* Wu.[68] In describing the descendants of Zhang Zhi (d. 1307), Yu Ji distinguishes between the children born to Zhang's first wife, those borne by his successor wife (*ji shi* 繼室), and those born to his *ce shi*.[69]

---

64. Liu Kezhuang, *Hou cun ji* 40.5b, 37.12b. Although he does not mention concubines, Yang Wanli expresses similar concern about the maternity of descendants when he observes that his affine Li Gai 李檠 (d. 1200) was married three times, but that the children were all born of the first two wives (Yang Wanli, *Cheng zhai ji* 132.2b).

65. Liu Zai, *Man tang ji* 31.16.

66. Ren Shilin, *Song xiang ji* 3.15b; Deng Wenyuan, *Ba xi ji, xia*, 22a. The ellipsis represents a lacuna in the original text.

67. Cheng Jufu, *Xue lou ji* 17.15, 19.7–7b. Cheng says nothing about Hu's status, nor does he tell us who gave birth to the subject's five daughters.

68. Tong Shu, *Ju an ji* 7.15b; elsewhere Tong Shu reports that the wife of Guo Haode (d. 1321) was the daughter of Guo's maternal uncle, and his *ce shi* was a woman surnamed Liang; he then provides details on their respective children (*Ju an ji* 8.9b).

69. Yu Ji, *Dao yuan xue gu lu* 18.307–8.

Indeed, as the fourteenth century progressed, it became more or less routine to note the maternal origins of descendants. Such references appear in multiple inscriptions by numerous Yuan authors, and the practice continued as the Yuan gave way to the Ming.[70] In short, by about the mid-Yuan Chinese authors had come to find it appropriate, even "natural," that funerary inscriptions—understood to be the official record of an individual's life for all posterity—would explicitly acknowledge the role of concubine mothers in producing descendants. Their frank recognition of concubine mothers stands in striking contrast to the virtual silence regarding descendants' maternity in inscriptions from the Northern and most of the Southern Song.

Before considering what this change might tell us about shifts in the roles of concubines from the Song to the Yuan, other changes in funerary inscription rhetoric are worthy of attention. We observed in chapter 5 that Southern Song funerary inscriptions increasingly praised wives for treating concubines and their children well, and sons for their filiality to their concubine birth mothers. Such rhetoric continued to be common in the Yuan.[71] By the fourteenth century men also began to be praised for serving their fathers' concubines who were not their own birth mothers. When Sun Huishu's (d. 1303) successor mother died, he served the mother of his half-brother (*shu di* 庶弟) as if she had been his own birth

---

70. For the Yuan see Wang Xu, *Lan xuan ji* 13.16a, 16.3b–4a; Li Cun, *Si an ji* 25.6b–8a, 25.19b–20a; Su Tianjue, *Zixi wen gao* 11.7a–7b, 13.14b; Gong Shitai, *Wan zhai ji* 10.54a, 10.55a–55b; Xie Yingfang, *Gui chao gao* 13.5a; Zhao Fang, *Dong shan cun gao* 7.57a; Yang Weizhen, *Dong wei zi ji* 24.6a. Ming examples include Song Lian, *Song xue shi quan ji* 22.819; Lin Bi, *Lin Dengzhou ji* 19.12a, 19.5a; Bei Qiong, *Qingjiang wen ji* 21.10a–12a; Su Boheng, *Su Pingzhong wen ji* 12.7a, 13.10b, 13.13a, 13.37b, 14.10a; Wang Xing, *Ban xuan ji* 9.7b; Yin Kui, *Qiang zhai ji* 4.6a, 4.20a, 4.20b, 4.24; Wu Sidao, *Chun cao zhai ji* 5.8a—and others could be cited. There is every evidence that this practice continued to be common throughout the later imperial era.

71. On women treating concubines well, see Deng Wenyuan, *Ba xi ji, xia*, 42a; Liu Yin, *Jing xiu wen ji* 4.63a; Wang Yun, *Qiujian ji* 52.13a–15b for woman Ling 凌. See also Wu Cheng, *Wu wen zheng ji* 82.4b, which praises a woman for acquiring a concubine for her husband. It may be significant that no Yuan author mentions the beating of concubines: this may be another sign of the increasing status of concubines in the household. For sons being filial to concubine mothers, see Liu Yueshen, *Shen zhai ji* 9.4b; Jie Xisi, *Jie Xisi quan ji* 8.396; Su Boheng, *Su Pingzhong wen ji* 13.10b. See also Huang Jin, *Huang Wenxian gong ji* 9a.377, where a man whose concubine mother died shortly after his birth is obsessed with the idea of seeing to her reburial.

mother.⁷² Both Zhang Keyong (d. 1374) and Huang Jue (1300–1370) were praised for responding to *shu mu* who were cruel to them by redoubling their efforts to be filial.⁷³ These references suggest that by Yuan times the men who wrote funerary inscriptions were willing to acknowledge a concubine mother (particularly in the absence of a main wife) as the female household head, worthy of the full respect of all members of the household, not just that of her own sons. In similar fashion, Yuan funerary inscriptions for women continued to praise them for filial treatment of concubine mothers-in-law.⁷⁴

The greater respect for concubine mothers seen in Yuan funerary inscriptions—and perhaps even the influence of Yuan law—is reflected as well in a decline in references to such mothers leaving (or being married out of) the family. Although some Song funerary inscriptions refer to the subject's birth mother having left the family, no Yuan inscriptions do so.⁷⁵ On the contrary, where Yuan funerary inscriptions do allude to pregnant concubines being married out by jealous wives, these cases never involve the subject's own family. Rather, they show the subject, usually in the course of official duties, intervening to right this wrong in other people's families.⁷⁶ Although the evidence here is sparse, it suggests

---

72. Cheng Duanxue, *Ji zhai ji* 5.12b.
73. Ling, *Zhe xuan ji* 4.37b; Xie Su, *Mi an ji* 8.16a–19b.
74. Wu Cheng, *Wu wen zheng ji* 78.8b, 82.4b. See also Gong Shitai, *Wan zhai ji* 10.54a; Su Boheng, *Su Pingzhong wen ji* 14.27a; and Gao Qi, *Fu zao ji* 5.29a. In fact, although more references to men serving their birth mothers survive from the Southern Song than from the Yuan, the reverse is true of references to women serving their husbands' birth mothers. The numbers are admittedly small, and this apparent shift may simply reflect the idiosyncrasies of source survival, but it is of a piece with other evidence suggesting that in the Yuan responsibilities for upholding family morality were increasingly shifting onto women.
75. Four Northern Song inscriptions mention expelled concubine mothers, as do two Southern Song inscriptions. See Bossler, "Song-Yuan mu zhi," 108–9.
76. In one instance, we are told that the childless wife of a grand councilor expelled his pregnant concubine; later both the concubine and the son she bore fell into slavery. The subject of the inscription is praised for redeeming them, finding employment for the son, and sending the mother back to the grand councilor's family (Liu Yueshen, *Shen zhai ji* 8.16a). Two other Yuan inscriptions praise the sagacity of their subjects in solving lawsuits that involved the adult offspring of pregnant concubines who had been expelled decades previously (Ma Zuchang, *Shi tian wen ji* 12.3a; Su Tianjue, *Zixi wen gao* 12.4a).

that by Yuan times it had become less socially acceptable for families to marry out the concubine mothers of their children. In saying this, I do not mean to suggest that the practice was necessarily less *frequent* in the Yuan than in the Song: we have already seen Kong Qi's complaint that temporary indenturing of concubines was common, especially in the southeast. Kong's observations are also supported by an early Yuan biography of an exemplary filial son (*xiao zi* 孝子), which explains that in certain areas of the south it had become standard custom for fertile (*yi zi* 宜子) women to be hired for a period of a year or two expressly for the purpose of bearing a son, and then returned to their families to be hired out again.[77] Still, at the same time that the biography shows us that the practice continued, it also reveals that at least in some circles attitudes toward the custom were changing. The biography, which dramatically portrays the efforts of the filial son to find his long-lost birth mother, excoriates the practice and was clearly meant as propaganda against it. That funerary inscription writers seem to have become more hesitant to mention that birth mothers had been married out likewise suggests such propaganda was beginning to have an effect.

On the surface, the increased attention to concubine maternity in the late Song and Yuan might seem to be at odds with what was otherwise an increasing emphasis on paternity in this period. Closer analysis shows that this was not necessarily the case. In recognizing the concubine's role in motherhood, funerary inscription rhetoric rendered her position closer to that of the wife, and thereby undercut the status of the wife in the family: where heretofore the wife's contribution to the production of descendants had been recognized as equal to that of her husband, now she became just one of a number of women who assisted her husband in that goal. Although legally, principal wives continued to be considered the official mothers of all children in a family, they were no longer so recognized in funerary inscriptions. As with late Song legal decisions recognizing the legitimacy of concubines' children, the net effect of recognizing multiple mothers was to highlight the singular role of the father, and thus to reinforce patrilineal ideology.

---

77. Hu Changru (1249–1323), *Chen xiao zi zhuang* [Biography of Filial Son Chen], as preserved in Su Tianjue, *Yuan wen lei* 69.11a–15a.

## Concubines' Children

An interest in preserving patrilines is likewise evident in Yuan funerary inscriptions' continued attention to the treatment of concubines' children. The early Yuan Learning of the Way adherent Jin Lüxiang, writing a postface to a set of family instructions composed by his neighbor and affine Bao Yongshu, took the opportunity to retell the salutary lesson of Judge Bao and his daughter-in-law Cui. In the process of gently rejecting the local family's claim to be descended from Judge Bao, Jin reminded his readers that Judge Bao's lesser son (*shu zi*) had been discarded and not reared by the family. (He added the new detail that the son had ended up as a shepherd.) When Bao's only principal heir died sonless, the deceased heir's wife (Ms. Cui) remained faithful (and Jin Lüxiang duly notes the government award she received). Only because Ms. Cui sought out the concubine's son and begged that he be retrieved was the Bao family saved from extinction. Jin concludes solemnly: "For fathers and sons mutually to discard one another harms Heavenly nature. That someone as virtuous as Judge Bao did this should be taken as warning by those who seek to cultivate themselves and regulate their families."[78] In short, Jin used his postface to the Bao family instructions as a vehicle to proselytize for the rearing of concubines' children.

The rhetoric of treating half-siblings well, which first made an appearance in the Southern Song, likewise became a prominent feature in Yuan funerary inscriptions, especially those composed by Learning of the Way authors. Liu Yueshen not only tells us that Xiao Rui (d. 1331) married off his half-brothers and half-sisters (*shu di mei* 庶弟妹) uniformly; he adds that Xiao divided his property equally with his two half-brothers, and credits him with the fact that the two were able to live out their lives in comfort. We learn that Tang Ju (d. 1292), having married uxorilocally into the Zhang family, purchased a concubine for his sonless sixty-year-old father-in-law. The boy produced by the concubine was only eight months old when his father died; Tang reared the child (his wife's half-brother), saw to his marriage, and returned all of the Zhang property to him. Gong Shitai explains that Deng Deming (d. 1358) was originally the middle son

---

78. Jin Lüxiang, *Renshan wen ji* (Wen yuan ge edition), 4.27a–b. (This text does not appear in the *CSJCXB* version of Jin's collected works.)

of a family surnamed Xiong; his mother's sister served a childless man surnamed Deng, and Deming was adopted as their son. Evidently other children were born later, because Deming is credited with instructing his two *shu di* and, when they married, returning all the Deng family land to them. Song Lian, writing of Huang Yi (d. 1358), observes that even though Huang's *shu di* was adopted out to be the heir of a distant uncle, Huang feared that the brother would be poor, and divided his own land in half to share with him. Su Boheng notes that Xu Biyou (d. 1354) treated his lesser half-brother (*shu di*) benevolently, going so far as to arrange for a new wife when the brother's first wife died, and building him a new house because his was old and broken-down.[79] In an interesting twist on this theme, Wu Cheng described how Gong Mengkui, a principal son, maintained his virtue even in the face of mistreatment by an uncle, his father's lesser half-brother. The uncle's own son turned out to be dim-witted (*bu hui* 不慧), and when he died the uncle's line was extinguished. Mengkui set up an heir to maintain the sacrifices, and when people praised him for repaying evil with virtue, he replied, "This is simply how things should be; where is the virtue in it?"[80]

All of the examples just cited can be seen as promoting loyalty to the patriline, but Learning of the Way authors showed themselves to be even more concerned about loyalty to the larger patrilineal kin group, and to the principles of ritual and generational hierarchy that upheld it. This is evident in their new and vocal critique of the practice of making concubines' sons the heirs of their half-brothers. This practice dated back to the late Song, if not earlier: Liu Kezhuang, in dealing with a legal case that involved a man becoming the heir of someone in the same generation, observed, "In popular custom, making a younger brother into a son is indeed sometimes done; as long as the lineage does not dispute this, it is permissible."[81] But the practice was conspicuously common in the Yuan. Thus when a son and son-in-law of Huang Zhangyuan

---

79. Liu Yueshen, *Shen zhai ji* 11.19a; Hu Zhiyu, *Zi shan da quan ji* 18.16b; Gong Shitai, *Wan zhai ji* 10.37b; Song Lian, *Song xue shi quan ji* 19.720; Su Boheng, *Su Pingzhong wen ji* 13.10b.
80. Wu Cheng, *Wu wen zheng ji* 75.14a.
81. *QMJ* 8.251. The case Liu was commenting on involved a man attempting to make his own son the heir of his nephew, but the idea of appointing a same-generation heir is the same in either case.

(1261–1323) both died, two concubines' sons (*nie zi* 孽子) and Huang's second grandson were appointed to serve as their heirs.[82] Liu Keshi (d. 1287) was the son of a concubine and later became the heir of his principal older half-brother (*di xiong* 嫡兄).[83] When a posthumous child of her father-in-law was born to a concubine, the woman Zhou insisted that she would rear the child (her husband's half-*brother*) as her own, saying: "He is of the same *qi* 氣 as my husband; I will love him like my own *son*, and then the whole family will regard him as no different from my *sons*" (emphasis added).[84]

Handling the succession in this manner was undoubtedly encouraged by the simple fact that, as noted in chapter 5, concubines' sons were often the same age as the children of their principal (*di*) half-brothers. Men of middle age commonly took as concubines girls in their late teens, and when such men died their adult sons (and daughters-in-law) frequently found themselves in the position of rearing these much younger half-siblings.[85] Appointing those siblings as heirs when their elder half-brothers died provided a practical solution to a number of problems: it ensured that the deceased man would have descendants and not become a hungry ghost; it prevented the government from confiscating the property of the defunct descent line; it provided an inheritance for the concubines' sons, without having them directly compete with sons of wives; and it kept the descent-line property in the hands of natural sons of the father, obviating the need to adopt from another line. All of these were clearly useful strategies for families worried about preservation of the patriline. At the same time, however, appointing concubines' sons as their brothers' heirs masked the fact that they were not being treated as equal coparceners in their fathers' estates: they should have been dividing the property equally

---

82. Wu Cheng, *Wu wen zheng ji* 84.10a. The inscription does not explain why three children were appointed as heirs for the two men.

83. This succession was later challenged by another concubine's son (Liu Chenweng, *Xu xi ji* 7.19a–20a).

84. Wu Cheng, *Wu wen zheng ji* 80.10a.

85. For Song cases of men (and their wives) rearing their half-brothers, see Liu Kezhuang, *Hou cun ji* 38.24a; Zhou Bida, *Wenzhong ji* 33.3a; and Ye Shi, *Ye Shi ji* 23.449. In some cases, we are told that virtuous wives regarded the concubines themselves as their own children. See Liu Yizhi, *Tiaoxi ji* 50.8a; Zhao Dingchen, *Zhu yin ji shi ji* 19.13b.

with their brothers, not inheriting from them. From a Learning of the Way perspective, even more problematic was that the practical logic of making concubines' sons the heirs of their brothers directly contravened Confucian ritual (and legal strictures) about generational hierarchy. Not a few families went so far as to disguise the irregularity by manipulating generational naming patterns, assigning concubines' sons names that corresponded with those of their nephews (their fathers' grandsons).[86]

By the mid-Yuan, Learning of the Way moralists were actively agitating against this practice. Yu Ji related how the aged Huang Dongzhi (d. 1336) approached him for advice. Huang confessed that as a young man, concerned about his lack of sons, he had appointed his half-brother (*yi mu di* 異母弟) to serve as his heir. Later he had become uncomfortable with this arrangement, so when in old age he still had no sons of his own, he adopted the half-brother's youngest son to be his heir, thus reestablishing proper generational hierarchy. In response to Huang's request for his opinion of this arrangement, Yu Ji observed, "Knowing that [your actions] contravened ritual is what made you uncomfortable. But being able in that situation fearlessly to reverse yourself, was that not also the Dao of the gentleman?" (知禮之所不可, 心之所未安. 而能不憚於自返焉, 不亦君子之道乎?).[87] In telling this story, of course, Yu Ji was also in effect proselytizing against the custom. Kong Qi, who shared many Learning of the Way views, also explicitly denounced the practice:

> In recent eras genteel families (*shi zu* 士族) sometimes set up brothers by concubines as heirs. This greatly disrupts orderly human relations, and those who know ritual ought to take care to prohibit it.[88]

Despite the intensified rhetoric of patrilineal loyalty and sibling equality, however, Yuan sources show that, as in the Song, children of concubines were not always afforded equal treatment with their principal siblings. Although moralists may have insisted that the children of

---

86. The *nie zi* of Huang Zhangyuan were given names that matched the generational naming pattern not of Huang's other sons, but of his grandsons, and Li Dun's 李敦 (d. 1333) *shu di*—whom Li is given credit for rearing with great care—shared the naming pattern of Li's son. See Wu Cheng, *Wu wen zheng ji* 84.10a, and Zheng Yuanyou, *Qiao Wu ji* 12.15a.
87. Yu Ji, *Dao yuan xue gu lu* 43.736–37.
88. Kong Qi, *Zhizheng zhi ji* 2.52.

wives and concubines equally carried the essence of their fathers, even Yuan law did not totally support full equality of concubines' children. As in the Song, distribution of hereditary titles and *yin* privilege still followed a system of modified primogeniture that upheld principal-lesser distinctions. Thus men born of concubines were eligible to inherit titles or *yin* privilege only if there was no surviving principal son or grandson (that is, only if the principal line had effectively been extinguished).[89] More strikingly, even where property inheritance was concerned, Yuan judges did not necessarily follow the long-established ideal (and ample Song precedent) of equal shares for all sons. A Yuan case of 1274 overturned an earlier ruling that had given a principal son and a maid's son equal shares, instead awarding eight-tenths of the property to the principal son and only two-tenths to his half-brother. This judgment seems to accord with an "old precedent" (*jiu li* 舊例) cited in a slightly later case (1309), which again awarded a principal son the majority of the property. The statute held that "when property rights are contested, sons of wives each get four shares; sons of concubines each get three shares, and children by illicit sex with a respectable woman or by a favored bondmaid each get one share."[90] So concubines' sons in the Yuan could not always count on the court to uphold their claims to equal inheritance with their half-brothers. Nor did all families practice the ideals of equality and kind treatment of half-brothers valorized in Yuan funerary inscriptions. For example, the poet and moralist Huang Jie wrote a song celebrating one Zhang Moufu, who donated a valuable ritual vessel to his lineage to support sacrifices for two heirless kinsmen. Huang explains:

> Moufu was a lesser son (*shu nie zi* 庶孽子) of the Zhang family. His origins were humble, so he was not able to rank with his other brothers. He farmed to support himself. When the property was divided he received a single gold ritual vessel. At the time his kinsman Junfu was repairing the local school in Blue Dragon Market. One day Moufu took the vessel and said to him, "I am a farmer and have no use for this. Two gentlemen in my family died without heirs; I would like to sell this and set up a shrine next to the school hall, and buy land and collect the

---

89. Katkov discusses in detail the subtle but significant shifts in Song and Yuan law regarding succession to titles and privilege ("The Domestication of Concubinage," 133–53).

90. *YDZ* 19.15a–b, 19.16b–17a. Other Yuan cases do uphold equal shares split between a concubine's sons and an adopted heir; see *YDZ* 19.17a–18b, 19.18b–19a.

rents to carry out sacrifices to them in the spring and fall, praying to the former sages and former worthies for blessings."[91]

Certainly Huang intends us to see Moufu's dedication to the lineage—despite the fact that he was not treated as a full member thereof—as especially admirable. But he does not seem to find Moufu's disadvantaged position shocking or even surprising. And whereas Huang's song, like other Yuan writings we have seen, can be understood as propaganda designed to encourage more equal treatment of concubines' sons, it reveals that such treatment was not yet the norm.

## *Conclusion*

What, then, can we conclude about changes in concubines' roles in the Yuan? Clearly, keeping concubines (including entertainer-concubines) continued to be a widespread practice among the Yuan elite. High-ranking officials took some of the most admired professional performers of the day into their households, and ordinary literati purchased (or rented) lovely young women to keep them company, entertain their friends, and even bear children. At the same time, Yuan writers tended to downplay the elements of romance and desire that were the raison d'être of many such relationships. Rather, by emphasizing how men served their concubine mothers and took care of their half-brothers, and how women served their concubine mothers-in-law and reared the children of their husbands' concubines, Yuan authors de-emphasized the roles of concubines as servants, entertainers, or paramours and highlighted their status as family members and mothers of descendants.[92] In this respect, the evidence found in biographical writings strongly supports the hypothesis that concubines were becoming, as Neil Katkov has put it, "domesticated" over the course of the Song and Yuan.[93]

---

91. Huang Jie, *Bian shan xiao yin yin lu* 2.33a–b.
92. Wong Yu-Hsuan indicates that Tang inscriptions for concubines frequently praised their subjects for skill in dancing, playing instruments, singing, etc. ("Tō dai," 151). As shown in chap. 5, in the late twelfth century Zhou Bida was still willing to acknowledge that his concubine Yunxiang was "somewhat able to make the new music," but I have seen no Yuan funerary inscription that praises a concubine for entertainment skills.
93. Katkov, "The Domestication of Concubinage," 46. Katkov finds the domesticating trend continuing into the Ming.

This trend can be seen as a response to the social tensions—also well documented in the sources—created by the widespread presence of various types of concubines in literati families. The sources suggest that the critical period of concubines' "domestication"—the period when biographers came routinely to acknowledge concubines as mothers of descendants—was from the thirteenth to fourteenth centuries. This was, of course, precisely the period in which the influence of Learning of the Way ideology was expanding in Chinese society, and to a certain extent the domesticating rhetoric of late Song and Yuan inscriptions was undeniably associated with Learning of the Way ideals (not least because the funerary biographies in which we find that rhetoric expressed were an important medium by which Learning of the Way thinkers publicized their values).[94] The domestication of concubines dovetailed with Learning of the Way concerns in two ways. First, inscriptions stressing service to concubine mothers and fairness to half-brothers can be understood as helping to integrate concubines into the developing Learning of the Way model of family relations, with its emphasis on filial piety and devotion to preservation of patrilineal kin groups. Secondly, emphasis on the role of concubines as mothers and calls to keep them in the family can be seen as addressing the moral problem posed by the popular association of concubines with entertainment and sexual desire. For Learning of the Way thinkers, the essence of moral cultivation was control of desire. Concubinage for the Confucian imperative of producing an heir did not threaten such cultivation. But as we have seen, over the course of the Song concubinage had come overwhelmingly to be associated with the taking in of lovely young women for entertainment and amusement, and this type of concubinage was indeed problematic for, if not inimical to, Confucian spiritual and ethical pursuits. As Neil Katkov has pointed out, by recasting concubines as mothers and family members, this problematic aspect of concubinage could be downplayed, without threatening the institution (and its usefulness for the perpetuation of patrilines) as a whole.[95]

---

94. Hoyt Tillman has noted the importance of funerary inscriptions and memorial services in identifying those associated with the *"Tao-hsueh (dao xue)"* fellowship. Tillman, *Confucian Discourse*, 3–4.

95. Katkov, "The Domestication of Concubinage," 102. Katkov drew this conclusion on the basis of legal sources.

Still, however much the domestication of concubines seen in inscription rhetoric corresponded with the imperatives of Learning of the Way, such rhetoric was not limited to authors associated with Learning of the Way circles. On the contrary, the valorization of concubine mothers is evident in writings by late-Song and Yuan men from across the political and philosophical spectra. Likewise, suspicion of desire, or more accurately admiration of men who were free of desire, was widely expressed. Yuan authors not only perpetuated the well-worn theme of "man of virtue refuses to accept concubine of literati background," but in a new twist, began to relate admiring accounts of men whose concubines, after several years of service, were married off as virgins. Such accounts promoted the notion that a man could have concubines who were not objects of sexual desire, and were featured both in anecdotal sources and in guides to moral action that proliferated in the Yuan.[96]

Here again, then, rather than seeing Learning of the Way thinkers as imposing their values on society, we might more accurately see them as articulating concerns shared by the larger society, or as successfully developing an ethical or moral ideology that corresponded with the needs of the expanding and more fluid elite that had come into being over the course of the late Tang and Song. Central to this ethical ideology was the assumption of the moral potential (or, to put it another way, basic moral equality) of all human beings, and by extension the assumption that the true value of a person was to be measured by his or her moral behavior. This classical Confucian tenet had been eclipsed during much of Early Imperial China, when society was highly stratified, but in the extremely fluid society of the Five Dynasties and the Song it found new adherents. As we have seen, by the early Song the distinctions between respectable (*liang*) concubines and dishonorable (*jian*) maids was already breaking down, and the call for literati men to be filial to their birth mothers undoubtedly contributed to that trend. By the Yuan, in spite of government efforts to reassert strict class distinctions, Chinese literati were willing to see the potential for morality (and thus humanity) even in members of nominally degraded professions.

---

96. Tao Zongyi, *Nancun chuo geng lu* 5.62, 4.53, and 8.102. For examples in morality guides, see Zhang Guangzu, *Yan xing gui jian* 4.7a–b; and Hu Bingwen, *Chun zheng meng qiu, xia*, 15a–b.

At the same time, the extreme fluidity of Chinese society, exacerbated by the disruptions of the Yuan conquest, led some members of society to call for strengthened kinship bonds as a means of forestalling downward mobility. Here, too, the dignifying of concubines' roles as mothers had a contribution to make. From the perspective of elite families (and nascent lineages), keeping concubine mothers in the household was likely to enhance the successful rearing of descendants. A child who had its mother's care in its early years was more likely to thrive. And to the extent that loyalty to the descent line and lineage was built on filial piety to parents, enhancing the concubine's connection to the family could enhance her sons' loyalty to it. In other words, keeping concubines in the family and valorizing their role as mothers helped foster family solidarity among their descendants. The concomitant stress on the equal status of concubines' sons served the same function.

Emphasizing concubines' role as mothers also helped to keep them in the family setting and reduced the potential dangers associated with the movement of undomesticated women in and out of the household. We have seen the frequent warnings in Song and Yuan sources that women brought in as entertainers were an unsavory influence in the household, with the potential to undermine the moral behavior of wives and daughters. Although taking in famous professional entertainers may have added luster to the households of high-ranking bureaucrats in the capital, for the majority of disenfranchised Han literati in the countryside, carousing with entertainers did nothing to improve either a family's economic position or its social reputation. It was therefore an activity lineages were inclined to discourage. To the extent that the emphasis on concubines as mothers undermined the image of concubines as entertainers, it served the interests of lineages.

Finally, integrating concubines into the family as mothers also afforded some protection to the women who became concubines—including women who were themselves sometimes the daughters of well-to-do or even official lineages. A family crisis, especially the death of a father, was often all it took to reduce the daughters of official families to concubinage: this is what happened to the women who became the concubines of Liu Kezhuang in the Southern Song and Dai Liang in the Yuan.[97] We

---

97. Liu Kezhuang, *Hou cun xian sheng da quan ji* 161.10a–10b (cf. also Ebrey, *Inner Quarters*, 226); Dai Liang, *Jiu ling shan fang ji* 14.14b.

have seen that in both the Song and the Yuan keeping female relatives out of concubinage became a source of pride, and coming to the aid of other indigent young women of genteel background was celebrated as an act of virtue.[98] Increased respect for concubine mothers can, I think, be seen as an extension of this line of thinking: in enhancing the dignity of women whose status in the household was low, it tacitly acknowledged the precariousness of prosperity and position—all the more so in the extraordinarily perilous conditions of the Yuan.

Yet for all the social forces conducive to the increased domestication of concubines in the late Song and Yuan, that "domestication" was not and never could be more than partial. Moralist rhetoric could mask, but not eliminate, the contradictions inherent in the very concept of concubines who were like wives but still not actual wives. Appreciation of concubines as mothers not only could not eliminate the structural inequalities of the concubine's position—inequalities that other moralist rhetoric insisted upon—it paradoxically served to exacerbate tensions in the inner quarters. I have suggested above that when maternity became irrelevant to determining the status of a descendant, the distinctions between wives and concubines were elided. Women who produced sons were valorized over those who did not, and wives no longer got sole credit for sons they did not bear themselves. Concubines whose status thus became closer to that of wives were far more threatening to wives' authority than those who were clearly relegated to the position of servants and whose sons were not considered to be their own. Here we see one of the important reasons that the improvement of concubines' status in late Song and Yuan families was accompanied by increased emphasis on wives not being jealous.

Still, by far the most serious contradiction in the domestication of concubines was that from the standpoint of the descent line the value of concubinage was precisely that concubines did not have to be treated like wives. Although lineages and society more generally may have benefited from stability provided by the integration of concubines into families as mothers, at the level of individual patrilines concubinage was useful because it afforded a degree of flexibility that marriage did not. Unlike

---

98. In this regard the Song-Yuan situation seems to have differed from earlier periods. Compare Liu Kai's admission that his cousin was a concubine, as discussed in chap. 2.

wives, concubines (and their progeny) could be incorporated into the family or expelled from it, as circumstances dictated.[99] A concubine could come to be respected by all as the female head of household, or, even after thirty years of service, could be summarily dismissed.[100] Throughout later imperial China, which remained a society marked by fluidity of social status and intense competition among the elite, the flexibility provided by concubinage gave elite families an important competitive edge, even as the moralist rhetoric of domestication disguised the contradictions inherent in the system.[101]

Finally, the limits of the domestication of concubinage in the Song and Yuan can be seen particularly in the fact that, in this period, the ideal of concubines remaining with the family after their husbands' deaths was not couched in terms of female fidelity: we see praise for families who do not expel concubines whose masters have died, but, at least in formal literati writings, not paeans to concubines who remained loyal to their deceased husband's patrilines. Anecdotalists like Tao Zongyi might praise the romantic faithfulness of courtesan-concubines who declined other lovers when a paramour died; but as the next chapter describes, in a context where not only sex for pleasure but sex for procreative purposes had become highly commodified, an intensified rhetoric of *wifely* loyalty continued to distinguish women who were properly married from those who were simply bought.

---

99. Here it is telling that although Yuan inscription writers praised men who took care of their own concubine mothers and men who reared their half-siblings, they were mostly silent about what happened to a father's concubines after his death.

100. Thus Lü Zuqian praises Pan Haogu (d. 1170) for dismissing a concubine of thirty years who presumed on her favored position to become arrogant and jealous. Whether she had borne any of Pan's children is unclear. See Lü Zuqian, *Donglai ji* 10.8a.

101. In this sense, concubinage can be seen as one important strategy facilitating the perpetuation of elite families in the Late Imperial period.

# 9

## Entertaining Exemplars

### Madame Zou 鄒夫人

In the beginning, the father of Li Jingshun of Yangqiu died in the southern campaigns. Jingshun and his younger sister were still young. Their great-grandparents and grandparents were both old and extremely poor. His mother Zou cried out to Heaven, saying, "My husband is gone. I have no life. But who can these four old parents and two young children rely on? Heaven has surely commanded me." So she diligently shouldered the difficulties and accepted cold and bitterness with equanimity; she was industrious and assiduous for a full forty years, with no change from beginning to end. Accordingly, with regard to serving her mother- and father-in-law, when they were living she served and nurtured them with utmost respect; when they died she mourned and buried them in accord with the rituals. With regard to rearing the surviving orphans, the girl was married off into a good family and was able to fulfill the Dao of wifehood; the boy devoted himself to the *Odes* and *Histories* and became an admirable gentleman. He married and had three sons, and there were also two grandsons. After some time, the village respected and marveled at her, saying "This is what the edict calls a faithful woman." So together they enlightened the officials, who reported her to the court. It was ordered that her corvée labor assessment be relieved, and that her hamlet receive an insignia. The insignia contained eight characters; Master Zhao of West Gao did the calligraphy in large script and carved it. The villagers thought it glorious. At that, the gentlemen and scholars who commonly associated with Jingshun were pleased to write songs and poems in praise of her virtue, and asked me for a preface. I was also delighted to hear of it and write a word on her behalf.

The *Great Commentary* on the *Changes* says: "The Dao of *Qian* creates males, the Dao of *Kun* creates females; thereafter there are husbands and wives. When there are husbands and wives, there are fathers and sons. When there are fathers and sons, there are lords and ministers. When there are lords and ministers, there are the high and lowly. When there are high and lowly, then ritual and righteousness have a place to settle. Therefore we know that male and female are the partners of *Qian* and *Kun*, and husband and wife are the origin of human relations."

Now, *Qian* is unyielding and the master of strength; *Kun* is yielding and finds virtue in purity. Thus males manifest the hundred actions and females maintain singular integrity. This is why the *Changes* celebrates the auspiciousness of keeping with one until the end, and the *Rituals* do not have the ceremony of remarriage. When [a woman] first marries, it is called "returning home." When her husband dies, she is called "the one who has not died." Therefore, when a body is yielding and pure and partners the firm and strong, it completes the changes of Heaven, and is the beginning of correct human relations. Ah! The righteousness of husband and wife is weighty indeed! Now the Kingly benevolence was exhausted and customs degraded, to the point that a woman who had "seven sons could still not be content in her rooms," and the poetry of the "Air of Kai" down to today laments this. Alas! How long has the world declined! Those who are able not to follow what the "Air of Kai" laments are few indeed! But Jingshun's mother, from the sincerity of a single thought, was able to make the righteousness of Heaven and Earth illuminate the basis of human relations. In the end, virtuous sons and filial grandsons lined up like a forest in front of her. The Li family have unexpectedly become a great family, and her peaceful and glorious longevity completes the beauty of her sage goodness. This can be called a foundational pillar for a degenerate [age], a standard for vacillating customs. Thus with respect to the so-called promoting and dissemination of awards and poetry for her, dare we be remiss?[1]

Writing in the ninth month of 1298, the Yuan court official Liu Minzhong (1243–1318) thus celebrated the government's decision to designate the mother of Li Jingshun as a "principled woman." In some respects, this text—the earliest extant Yuan dynasty text in honor of a widow who did not remarry—looks similar to texts we have seen from the Song. Like the funerary inscriptions that Yang Wanli and Liu Kezhuang composed for faithful widows in the late Song, this text focuses almost exclusively on Zou's widowhood, and interprets the significance of her widowhood in exclusively moral terms. Yet there are important differences between this text and those of the late Song. Liu does not suggest that Zou is a model for the political loyalty of men, but rather presents her as a moral model for all society. He highlights the cosmic import of her moral action, and suggests that her longevity and the family's success are Heaven's rewards for her virtue. An equally significant change is the form that Liu's text takes: it is not a funerary

---

1. Liu Minzhong, *Zhong an ji* 9.10a–11b.

inscription, but a preface for a volume of poetry that, as Liu tells us, was composed in Zou's honor by her son's friends and acquaintances, to celebrate the government's recognition of her exemplar status. I have shown that in the late Northern Song such poetry collections (*shi juan* 詩卷) had been compiled in honor of male exemplars such as Xu Ji and Zhu Shouchang, as well as in honor of courtesans, both fictive and real. But poetry collections in honor of upper-class women seem to have been entirely new in the Yuan.[2] More importantly, such poetry collections—especially those in honor of faithful widows—became extremely widespread in the Yuan. They were part of a dramatic proliferation of many kinds of texts for exemplars, as well as a significant shift in the focus of such texts, that took place in that period.

A very rough statistical overview provides some sense of these changes.[3] Whereas the surviving collected works of Song authors contain in total about ninety texts explicitly devoted to the celebration of exemplars, the far fewer extant collected works of Yuan authors contain more than five times that number: in all, more than 460 Yuan texts are dedicated to faithful wives, heroic women, filial children, and the occasional

---

2. As noted in chap. 6, a poem for a faithful wife (the author's sister) survives in Chen Zhu's collected works. The text cannot be precisely dated (Chen lived until 1297), but in any case there is no indication that it was intended to be part of a poetry collection. The Yuan also saw the creation of other kinds of poetry collections for women, most notably those celebrating their longevity. See Nomura Ayuko, "Ming Qing nü xing shou xu kao." Poetry collections for faithful women may have served as the model for these longevity collections, for, as Nomura notes, the longevity prefaces often celebrated the subject's fidelity; see also the example of Hua Youwu's mother below.

3. These statistics obviously depend on how one defines exemplar texts. For the purposes of this discussion, I take as "exemplar texts" those texts devoted to the biographical or celebratory accounts of specific individuals, the titles of which explicitly refer to the exemplary qualities of their subjects (i.e., the titles contain references to filiality, fidelity, loyalty, righteousness, and so on), and the content of which is devoted to highlighting the subject's exemplary quality. (I have excluded a very small number of texts that have exemplary titles but on inspection prove not to focus on exemplary behavior.) The statistics presented here are based on a survey of the electronic version of the Wen yuan ge edition of the *Si ku quan shu*. They are meant here to provide only a general overview of the data: I do not see these numbers as in any way absolute. Certainly there are exemplar texts that survive in sources not included in the *Si ku quan shu*, and more importantly there were undoubtedly many texts written that do not survive today. Nonetheless, I think these statistics provide a useful overview of shifts in the quantities and types of texts composed.

righteous gentleman (*yi shi* 義士).⁴ But the difference goes beyond mere numbers. Song and Yuan authors also chose different genres for writing about exemplars. Nearly a quarter of all Song texts honoring exemplars are records (*ji* 記) commemorating the building or rebuilding of shrines to exemplars; about a third take the form of biographies (including both *zhuan* and funerary inscriptions). Another quarter of the total are poems.⁵ In the Yuan, shrine records were a very minor element in exemplar accounts, representing barely 3 percent of the extant texts. Similarly, straight narrative biography, whether in the form of *zhuan* or funerary biographies, became relatively less important, representing only about 15 percent of the total number of texts celebrating exemplars.⁶ Conversely, poetry about exemplary figures became much more important than it had been in the Song, constituting more than 40 percent of the surviving texts.⁷ Song and Yuan authors also wrote about different types of people. About half of Song exemplar texts concern individuals from earlier dynasties; in contrast, the great majority of Yuan exemplar texts extol the virtue of people contemporary or nearly contemporary with the author. Song-era poems for exemplars often take the form of set pieces, written on the theme of the principled woman or the filial son. In such cases, the figure of the exemplar represents an image or an ideal about which the poet can muse.⁸ In the Yuan, exemplar poetry was most

---

4. Note that these numbers do not include funerary inscriptions for faithful wives that do not signal their exemplar status in the title. I have discovered only a few literati exemplar texts from the Jin, and none that refer to government awards. The preface to the "Biographies of the Filial and Amicable" in the *Jin History* (*Jin shi*) says only six people were known for receiving *jing biao* awards during that period (Tuotuo, *Jin shi* 127.2745–46). Xu Bingyu, citing evidence in the *Gu jin tu shu ji cheng*, suggests that there were seven Jin faithful wives who received government awards (Xu Bingyu, "Liao, Jin, Yuan," 223–24), but in any case the number was small.

5. Prefaces and colophons make up 10 percent of the total, and the remaining 10 percent are divided between a number of miscellaneous genres including *zan*, prayers, stele texts, and so forth. Many of these latter types do include biographical material as well.

6. The writing of ordinary funerary inscriptions, which did not designate the subject as a model figure, continued unabated; those texts are not included in these numbers.

7. This number does not include prefaces to poetry volumes or prefaces and colophons to individual poems, which together constitute another 20 percent of the total number of texts. Miscellaneous genres make up the rest.

8. See the discussion of the Virtuous Maiden Shrine in chap. 6.

often devoted to the celebration of a specific individual, usually someone directly known to the author. This reflects the very different purposes to which these texts were put. Finally, and most importantly, although both Song and Yuan writers celebrated filial sons and faithful women, they did so in greatly different proportions. Fewer than 40 percent of the surviving Song texts concern women, and only 40 percent of them were faithful wives (and still fewer faithful widows). By contrast, 66 percent of Yuan texts focused on women, and 70 percent of these celebrated faithful wives.

In all, more than sixteen times as many texts honoring faithful women survive from the Yuan than from the Song, out of a much smaller total corpus.[9] Moreover, for the most part these were faithful widows, held up not as models for male loyalty as they were in the Song, but as models for other women. The reasons for this dramatic shift were varied, ranging from the enhanced practical advantages of obtaining a government award and the usefulness of faithful-widow encomia in local social aggrandizing, to concerns about preserving Chinese culture in the face of both Mongol occupation and wrenching social upheaval. But in the process of composing hundreds if not thousands of texts in honor of faithful wives, Yuan authors redefined the term *jie* (integrity) as it applied to women and profoundly altered the gender ideology of Late Imperial China.

## *The Government Effect*

As in the Song, one important impetus in the Yuan for the production of exemplar texts was the issuing of government awards for virtue; indeed, both the impetus to obtain government awards and the association of awards with text production were greatly intensified under

---

9. More specifically: out of ninety Song texts honoring exemplars, thirty-three are for women, and of these thirteen are for faithful wives, four of whom were widows. In Yuan, out of 463 texts, 307 are for women, of which 216 are for faithful wives, the great majority of whom were widows. As a crude measure of the differing amounts of material surviving from the Song and the Yuan, the Song collected works section of the Wen yuan ge edition of the *Si ku* collection comprises 104 volumes; the Yuan collected works section is contained in 31 volumes.

the Yuan.¹⁰ Surviving information about the structure of government awards in the Yuan is somewhat less systematic than that for the Song, but the basic institution seems to have continued into the Yuan without interruption. The Yuan court issued awards to filial sons as early as 1271, and even earlier court officials had debated the desirability of rewarding such extreme filial behaviors as cutting out the liver and gouging out the eyes.¹¹ In short, even before the conquest of the Song was fully complete, the Yuan government had begun to honor exemplary behavior and to reflect on the principles involved in so doing.

Following long-established custom, Yuan government edicts typically called for awards to be issued to "filial sons and obedient grandsons, righteous men and principled women."¹² Surviving evidence shows that the government did indeed issue awards to filial sons and principled women; and especially after 1330, when a new regulation made it possible essentially to purchase a government award with a contribution of relief grain, awards were also issued to "righteous gentlemen."¹³ I have seen no awards explicitly issued to "obedient grandsons," but the Yuan did occasionally honor "harmonious households" and "heroic martyrs," and sometimes less-traditional exemplars as well. Thus under the category of Filial and Principled (*xiao jie*), Yuan regulations stipulated that the household of a woman who bore triplet males could be exempted from corvée. Awards bestowed in honor of extremely advanced age were also fairly common.¹⁴

---

10. An earlier version of the discussion that follows appears in Bossler, "Martyrs."
11. *YS* 197.4442; *YDZ* 33.19a–19b. Filial children cut out their livers to make medicinal soup for sick parents. In 1266 the Board of Rites decided that these behaviors should be forbidden.
12. E.g., *YS* 92.2343–44; *YDZ* 2.27b.
13. The regulation is described in *YS* 82.2053. During a famine in 1330, it was stipulated that wealthy families who contributed grain to the state could be given official rank, with the level of rank corresponding to the amount given. The lowest award, for those who contributed 30 or more piculs (*shi* 石) of rice, earned the donor a *jing biao*. Farquhar notes that similar regulations had existed on an ad hoc basis from as early as 1288 (*Government of China*, 48–49), and there is evidence that awards for grain contributions were also issued before 1330 (e.g., Deng Wenyuan, *Ba xi ji, xia*, 53–55b). In contrast to earlier eras, in which righteous gentlemen were called *yi fu* 義夫, Yuan grain contributors were designated as *yi shi* 義士. For evolution of the term *yi fu* in later eras, see Elvin, "Female Virtue and the State," 126–27.
14. *YDZ* 33.16a; Chen Lü, *An ya tang ji* 12.22b–25a.

In one of the dynasty's most celebrated cases, the government honored a heroic wife (*lie fu* 烈婦) who had pulled her husband from the mouth of a tiger.[15] The procedure for obtaining these awards likewise seems to have followed Song precedent, with exemplars being identified by local authorities whose recommendations were transmitted up through each level of the bureaucracy until the Board of Rites itself approved the award.[16] This process gave local literati and officials considerable influence in determining who was recommended for awards, though it limited their control over who ultimately received them.

The available sources do not reveal what led the Mongol rulers to adopt the custom of honoring exemplars. Indeed, at least one Yuan official explicitly warned the court against issuing awards. In a policy proposal submitted to Qubilai, Wang Yun (1227–1304) observed that people struggling to get by had little leisure to concern themselves with ritual and righteousness. Wang insisted that attempts to improve customs by awarding honors and remitting corvée were without the slightest effect—"nothing more than spurious writings and empty names." The government would do better, he suggested, to focus on practical measures such as improving the people's livelihood, easing taxes and punishments, and making the laws more consistent.[17] Still, in the face of those alternatives it must have seemed easier for Qubilai to take the advice of other ministers, who on a regular basis assured the court that conferring honors on the households of exemplars was a time-tested way of improving customs and "transforming" the population.[18] The usefulness of such awards in helping the new government to establish legitimacy and demonstrate moral authority was no doubt also a factor. In any case, the Yuan appears to have issued a significantly greater number of awards than had been common in earlier dynasties. Moreover, much of this proliferation can be attributed to increased solicitation of awards

---

15. *YS* 200.4485, entry for Heroic Wife Hu. I discuss this case in more detail below.

16. For descriptions of the procedure in the Yuan, see Liu Guan, *Dai zhi ji* 13.19a–20a; Pu Daoyuan, *Xian ju cong gao* 25.1a–3a.

17. Wang Yun, *Qiujian ji* 35.1–16b, esp. pp. 13b–15. It is worth noting, however, that Wang Yun himself wrote at least one text in honor of a government-certified faithful widow (*Qiujian ji* 43.12–13b).

18. See, for example, the memorials by Zhao Bi 趙璧 (1250–1308) and Zhao Tianlin 趙天麟 (fl. late 13th c.) in Yang Shiqi, *Li dai ming chen zou yi* 65.24b–25 and 217.33b–35b.

on the part of local authorities. Indeed, the number of recommendations for awards apparently escalated so rapidly that over the course of the first half of the dynasty the Yuan court was on several occasions moved to issue regulations designed to curb excessive demand.

By 1270, for example, the Board of Rites had already determined that the state should no longer reward filial children who cut their thighs to make medicine for sick parents, observing that "recently" this practice had come to contradict the sage admonition that the body bequeathed by parents should not be injured. Although the Board stopped short of forbidding thigh-cutting altogether, it noted "there is no need to reward it," and the following year it did forbid the practice of expressing filiality by lying naked on ice.[19] In 1293 the Board responded quite angrily to a request that honors be given to a family who had remained together for three generations. It pointed out that families that included grandparents and grandchildren were extremely common, and warned "if this one family is honored, everyone will be pointing to this precedent." The Board determined that only households living in harmony for five generations should receive honors as "harmonious households," concluding with satisfaction that "that ought to stop the flood."[20] Finally, in response to a 1304 request to honor a principled woman, the Board complained that although government honors were meant to transform inferior customs, "now what we see in every place is always praise that 'her husband died and she maintained her will (*fu wang shou zhi* 夫亡守志, i.e., she did not remarry).' We do not see any exceptional or extraordinary conduct. Most of them are connected with wealthy and powerful families scheming to evade corvée." The Board then cited classical precedents to indicate the sorts of exemplars who, in their view, did deserve awards: filial sons like Cai Yong, who wept blood in the grave hut; righteous men like Xue Bao of the Han, who gave his wealth to his brothers; faithful widows who, like the author of the poem "Cypress Boat" ("Bo zhou"), vowed to

---

19. *YDZ* 33.19a–19b. Medicine made with flesh cut from a filial child's thigh was thought to have miraculously curative effects. Lying on ice was intended to demonstrate filial feelings in hopes of moving Heaven to restore an ill parent to health.
20. *YDZ* 33.16–16b. For another complaint that the Board was "flooded" with recommendations, see Zhang Yanghao, *Gui tian lei gao* 3.2b–4.

maintain their integrity.[21] The Board concluded by restricting awards for faithful wives to those women who were widowed before age thirty and who "maintained their will" until over age fifty, and by stipulating that all cases of exemplary behavior should be carefully investigated and perpetrators of fraud duly punished.[22] One important outcome of this edict was that it effectively narrowed the definition of "principled woman" (*jie fu*) to mean "faithful widow."

In short, the Yuan government was extremely active in awarding exemplary behavior, but in the face of excessive numbers of recommendations from local authorities, the center acted more to limit awards than to encourage them. To put it another way, in rewarding exemplars, the central government was responding to outside forces more than asserting its own agenda. The most important of those outside forces were local officials, who were responsible for forwarding petitions for exemplar rewards to the central government.

The reason for the local officials' enthusiasm is hinted at in the Board's complaint: "Most of them are connected with wealthy and powerful families scheming to evade corvée." This possibility was acknowledged even in texts that men wrote to honor exemplars. Liu Renben concludes a poem for a widow who failed to receive a government award with the line, "What a pity that those who receive awards for being extraordinary are mostly the noble and powerful."[23] Su Tianjue admitted that some people "do not understand where the transformation of customs

---

21. According to tradition, the poem "Bo zhou" 柏舟 (Mao no. 45) in the *Book of Odes* was composed by the widow Gong Jiang to express her determination not to remarry. By Yuan times the term "Cypress Boat" had become emblematic of wifely fidelity. Another poem with the same title (Mao no. 26) was apparently read in similar fashion.

22. *YDZ* 33.16b–17a. Cf. Elvin, "Female Virtue and the State," 123; Birge, *Women, Property, and Confucian Reaction*, 264–65; and Zheng Guiying, "Yuan chao fu nü," 66–69. All three authors emphasize that this was the first law to institutionalize wifely fidelity with a strict definition of age qualifications. I think the edict is more accurately seen as a bureaucratic move explicitly meant to rectify a bureaucratic problem: it was less an attempt to assert a stricter moral standard than simply to impose practical limits on the number of women recognized as exemplars. In this respect, I find untenable Birge's suggestion that the 1304 ruling represented "new legislation promoting widow chastity" (Birge, *Women, Property, and Confucian Reaction*, 264).

23. Liu Renben, *Yu ting ji* 2.1b. See also 6.38b–39a, where Liu makes similar comments in a biography of another faithful widow.

originates, saying instead that it is the powerful seeking to have their corvée levies remitted."[24] The court official Zhang Yanghao was even more blunt:

> At the time I served on the Board of Rites, we were drowning in documents from near and far concerning women renowned for their fidelity, sons put forward for their filiality, and men recommended for their righteousness. My eyes tired of perusing them, my wrists shrank from recording them. And when I inquired about them from people, [I discovered] there were some who used their power to obtain [the recommendations], and others who used bribes to get them.[25]

Here, then, is one important explanation for the proliferation of government awards and the concomitant explosion of interest in exemplars in the Yuan: elite families actively sought government awards because they released the holder's family from corvée obligations, which in the Yuan were particularly onerous. In the Song, literati families had generally been able to avoid corvée by dint of participation in office, or even by participation in the examination system. But in the Yuan, most Han literati (and especially those in the south) were shut out of office; and for most of the Yuan period, the examination system was suspended. Producing an exemplar thus became one of the very few methods by which literati families could hope to avoid corvée demands. Liu Renben's comments suggest that local officials, anxious to obtain the cooperation of the locally powerful families in their jurisdictions, were only too happy to oblige by submitting requests for awards to the central government.

The desire for government awards was thus undoubtedly an important impetus for the proliferation of exemplar writings about women in the Yuan. But although many Yuan exemplar texts were produced to celebrate those who had received government awards, a far greater number were produced for men and women who had not received such recognition.[26] So the government's recognition of exemplars cannot alone explain the proliferation of Yuan texts in honor

---

24. Su Tianjue, *Zixi wen gao* 29.21b–22a.
25. Zhang Yanghao, *Gui tian lei gao* 3.2b–4a.
26. Somewhat less than a quarter of the identified exemplar texts explicitly mention that the subject received a government award. A few texts specify that the subject did not receive an award, but the great majority of texts simply do not indicate this one way or the other.

of exemplars. Moreover, even if government awards were the major inspiration for exemplar texts, that would not explain why in the Yuan such texts increasingly took the form of poetry, or why Yuan writers increasingly focused on women. To understand the process by which poetry about women came to dominate Yuan exemplar texts, we need to look more closely at the texts themselves. For although all exemplar poetry nominally served to celebrate the morally elevated behavior of its subjects, the poems reveal that authors wrote exemplar poetry in widely varying contexts and for widely varying purposes. For many of these purposes, women—and especially faithful widows—proved to be superior subjects.

## *Heroines, Cultural Crisis, and Literary Networks*

We saw in chapter 6 that throughout most of the Song, exemplar texts about women focused primarily on heroines and held them up as models for male loyalty. In the Yuan, too, heroic action by women attracted the attention of some authors, but overall heroines represented a much smaller proportion of the exemplars celebrated in the Yuan, and the uses to which these heroines were put differed significantly from those in the Song.

The most obvious of these differences is that in the Yuan, writings for heroines are distinguished by the tendency for a single heroic figure to become the focus of repeated texts. We see this in the popular figure of Pure Wife (*zhen fu*) Wang, who became the subject of a chain of poems and biographies linking male authors across the Yuan period. Wang had been captured by Yuan soldiers during the fighting of 1276, but she seems to have attracted the attention of literati writers mostly after a shrine was erected to her in the 1320s. Wang's story, although differing in details from author to author, was indeed highly dramatic and inspirational. After her capture, Wang was handed over to a Yuan commander, who intended to add her to his harem. Cleverly, Wang postponed the inevitable by persuading him it that it would be inauspicious for her to marry until she had completed mourning for her husband. Although she was kept under close guard, as she was marched through the mountains Wang managed to bite her finger until it bled, compose a poem in blood on the side of a cliff, and then throw herself into an abyss. Local legend had it that her blood had entered the rock

14. Pure Wife Wang of Linhai (Wang *zhen fu* 王貞婦, Linhai *min qi* 臨海民妻) plunges off the cliff to her death rather than be taken by Mongol soldiers. Her death inspired a shrine, a succession of poems, and other commemorative works by literati of the Yuan and later dynasties. From Liu Xiang 劉向, *Hui tu Lie nü zhuan* 繪圖列女傳 (Illustrated biographies of exemplary women), edited by (Qing) Wang Geng 汪庚, illustrations by (Ming) Qiu Ying 仇英. Reprint of Zhi bu zu zhai cang ban (Taipei: Zheng zhong shu ju, 1971), 11.42b–43a.

permanently, so that when it rained the bloody characters reappeared just as she had written them.[27]

At least half a dozen poets were inspired not only by their own visits to Wang's shrine, but also by the example of other writers' efforts on her behalf. Thus the late Yuan poet Qian Weishan (fl. 1341–71) admitted that he was following the lead of the noted writer Zhang Zhu (1287–1368), who Qian claimed was the first to have written a poem for Wang and who had invited "interested parties" (*hao shi zhe* 好事者) to

---

27. Li Xiaoguang, *Wu feng ji* 1.19a–20b and 8.13b. Fong, "Signifying Bodies," 122, takes Wang (whose biography was also recorded in the *SS*) as an early example of women who wrote suicide poems. I find the putative circumstances extremely implausible and think it equally likely that the whole story was legendary and the poetry written by men. Nonetheless, as such stories circulated they might well have inspired later women to follow their example.

*Entertaining Exemplars* 375

do likewise.[28] Qian dedicated his poem both to Wang and to an earlier heroine who had been popularized in poetry by the Jin writer Hao Jing. Qian quotes several lines from the earlier poems, observing that "gentlemen all savored them."[29]

We saw something similar to this loose literary network in the Southern Song poems inspired by the Virtuous Maiden Shrine, but in the Yuan case the poetic borrowings and sense of shared participation in a literary community are much more explicit. This element of community was even more central in the poetry written for a heroic wife (*lie fu*) surnamed Hu, who became the subject of the earliest known Yuan poetry volume compiled in honor of an exemplary woman. In 1279, the Wenzhou scholar Yu Delin (1232–93) described how a "guest from the north" showed him a painting of this heroic wife. Hu was a poor commoner woman (one author calls her an "uncivilized woman" [*ye fu* 野婦]), who sometime in 1270 had been traveling with her young son and husband to the latter's new military posting. Along the way, they camped for the night, and after they had gone to sleep her husband was suddenly attacked by a tiger. Awakened by his shouts, Hu rushed out and attacked the tiger with her bare hands. Ultimately, her son managed to slip her a knife, and she succeeded in killing the beast. Her injured husband was taken to the next town, where the local authorities took them in and provided medical attention. Unfortunately, the best doctors the state could provide were unable to save Hu's husband from his injuries—but an account of Hu's bravery was sent up (along with the tiger skin) to the court. The government honored her as an exemplar, both awarding her money to pay for her husband's burial and granting her remission from corvée labor. Within a decade, Hu had become the subject of a painting that in turn had accumulated several songs and poems celebrating her bravery. On being shown this collection, Yu Delin was moved to compose a poetry preface (*shi xu* 詩序) in Hu's honor.[30]

---

28. A poem to Wang survives in Zhang Zhu's collected works, though without any commentary exhorting others to follow suit. See Zhang Zhu, *Tui an ji* 1.12a–12b.

29. Qian Weishan, *Jiang yue song feng ji* 1.5a–6a. Another writer likewise indicates that *his* poem for Wang matches rhymes with a poem written by an earlier author (Huang Jie, *Bian shan xiao yin yin lu* 2.38b–39a). Other poems to Wang can be found in Chen Gao, *Bu xi zhou yu ji* 3.9a–9b; and Liu Renben, *Yu ting ji* 3.29b.

30. Yu Delin, *Pei wei zhai ji* 10.13a–14a.

Yu's preface employs standard Song-style rhetoric, comparing Hu's valor in the face of the tiger to the poor performance of men who not only had failed to fight for their lord in the face of a different sort of "tiger," but had been complacent or had even sought their own advantage in the situation. But although Hu's story continued to attract the attention of many writers over the course of the Yuan—at least a dozen other texts in her honor survive today—the rhetoric of those texts varied from author to author. The northern official Hu Zhiyu (1227–95) took Hu's brave deed as evidence of the superior customs prevailing under Mongol rule. In contrast, the southern scholar Liu Jiangsun (1257–after 1305) interpreted the tiger as a symbol for those whose greediness leads to their own destruction, and cast Hu as a model of determination and competence who refused to give up in the face of a difficult situation.[31] A few authors held up Hu as a model for other women: Ren Shilin (1253–1309) stressed that "she knew only this one husband," suggesting that her devotion to him allowed her to overcome her fear of the tiger; Zhang Zhihan (1243–96) imagined the chagrin Hu's behavior would inspire in jealous women who devoted their energies to putting on makeup and trying to be beautiful.[32] A number of other authors eschewed explicit prose commentary but celebrated Hu's achievement with descriptive poetry, sometimes producing several verses in her honor.[33] Liu Minzhong (the author of Zou's poetry preface) composed a full-fledged narrative ballad that begins by describing Hu's marriage (depicting her wedding garb and glowing makeup) and continues by tracing her diligence in the face of her husband's poverty, movingly depicting the emotional attachment that led to her decision to accompany him to his post, and so forth.[34]

In the writings for Hu as well as those for Wang, we see the appropriation of exemplar heroines as the focus and raison d'être of literary and cultural communities.[35] This community function is very clear

---

31. Hu Zhiyu, *Zi shan da quan ji* 4.25b–26a; Liu Jiangsun, *Yang wu zhai ji* 26.19b–20b. Wang Yun, *Qiujian ji* 49.15a–16a, characterizes Hu as heroic.

32. Ren Shilin, *Song xiang ji* 4.5a–6a; Zhang Zhihan, *Xi yan ji* 4.9b–10a.

33. For example, see Wang Yun, *Qiujian ji* 28.7a, 34.22a–b; Wu Shidao, *Li bu ji* 4.7b, 11b–12b; Chen Lü, *An ya tang ji* 3.19b; Zhang Zhu, *Tui an ji* 1.21b–22a; Yang Weizhen, *Tie yai gu yue fu*, 7.8b. This list is not exhaustive.

34. Liu Minzhong, *Zhong an ji* 1.23a–24a.

35. Other heroic subjects likewise attracted the attentions of multiple authors, such

in Yu Delin's account of how he came to write a preface for Hu; it is equally evident in Qian Weishan's genealogy of the poetry written for Pure Wife Wang. In Hu's case the community was initially comprised of contemporaries acquainted with one another, and in this respect the phenomenon is reminiscent of the poetic chains linking Northern Song literary men commenting on each others' concubines. But in both Yuan cases, participants in the community ultimately came to include a broad and diverse group of northerners and southerners, high-ranking officials and unemployed scholars, men born in the early thirteenth century and men born nearly three-quarters of a century later. The community in which such men claimed membership was empire-wide in scope and based less on personal social interaction than on expressed commitment to Confucian values (however those were understood) and on shared literary appreciation. In other words, much more so than in the Song, in the Yuan writing about heroic women became a way to assert participation in Han literati culture.

The Yuan conquest very much intensified the need or desire for this sort of participation. Several scholars have elucidated the sense of cultural crisis that the Mongol occupation precipitated among surviving members of the Chinese literati class. Hoyt Tillman has argued that many literati experienced severe psychological trauma with the fall of the Song, trauma that led some to take refuge in literary or other cultural activities as a means to cope with their distress.[36] For some, writing about the violence of the conquest seems to have provided a means of catharsis: in the heroic actions of the women depicted in these writings, authors could find meaning in what was otherwise senseless and devastating loss. Here we might see text production by literati

---

as two filial sisters from the Tang dynasty who had thrown themselves down the shaft of a tin mine to protest the government's arrest of their father for failing to provide the government with the requisite quota of tin. Their action led the government to release their father and exempt their native county from the tin levy. Grateful for this exemption—and perhaps anxious to ensure that the government would continue to honor it—local officials erected a shrine to the sisters in 1300. When the shrine was rebuilt in 1335, the presiding official Wei Su commissioned a number of commemorative texts. See Yu Ji, *Dao yuan xue gu lu* 30.520–21; Li Cun, *Si an ji* 13.2a–3a; and Su Tianjue, *Zixi wen gao* 28.20a–b.

36. Tillman, "Disorder (*Luan*) as Trauma."

as parallel to the erection of shrines to martyrs at the popular level: just as shrines were built to dispel the inauspicious auras or propitiate the haunted and haunting spirits of women who died violently, so too did the literati texts commemorating those shrines help individuals come to terms with and find meaning in the wrenching violence of the "compressed dynastic cycle" of the Yuan.[37]

Texts for heroines served a number of other purposes as well. Production of exemplar texts allowed men who had *not* behaved heroically during the conquest to participate vicariously in the heroism of their subjects. This was true both for the writer (as seen especially in poetry written in the subject's persona) and for the reader who "savored" the text. There were also significant social reasons that participation in poetry networks was popular in the Yuan. In the Song, membership in the literati elite had been established above all by participation in the examination system. In the absence of that system, and when few other avenues to elite status were available to Han men, production of poetry and participation in poetic communities could also be a way to assert one's identity as a literatus, as a man of learning and culture.[38]

For all of these purposes, the rich and flexible symbolism of women's loyalty was inordinately useful. As we see clearly in the case of Tiger-Killer Hu, the heroic actions of women served as an almost infinitely mutable signifier onto which male authors could project their agendas, from the political to the moral to the literary. Thus, even as there was little consensus on the specific moral meaning (if any) of Hu's actions, a wide variety of authors found in her, as they had in Wang, a useful focus for their literary efforts.

In sum, Yuan writing about heroic martyrs served both social and literary purposes, as scholars responded to what others had written and thereby asserted their own participation in a cultural and literary community. As a result, and in contrast to the situation of most Song martyrs, the heroines they celebrated figured more as literary or cultural

---

37. A few other Yuan authors also wrote poems for female heroic martyrs associated with popular shrines. See Chen Gao, *Bu xi zhou yu ji* 9.6a–7a; Xie Yingfang, *Gui chao gao* 3.57b–59a. On the "compressed dynastic cycle," see chap. 7, n. 3.

38. Lao also portrays the "great outpouring of poetry" in the Yuan as a side effect of the lack of an examination system, though he sees that outpouring as driven by intellectual rather than social factors ("Southern Chinese Scholars," 108–9).

icons than as moral rallying points. Instead, the center of moral discourse shifted, to focus on the everyday constancy of faithful widows.

## *Faithful Widows and Social Aggrandizing*

Texts, and especially poetry collections, written in honor of faithful widows differed from those for heroines in both form and function. Unlike those of heroines, the stories of faithful widows seldom lent themselves to excitement and suspense and were thus less amenable to literary treatment. Occasionally we are told that a widow threatened to harm herself if she were forced to remarry, and a few widows (like the heroines of courtesan stories) dramatized their vows to remain celibate with passionate gestures like cutting off their hair or even disfiguring their faces.[39] But for the most part the biographies of faithful widows follow the standard, even clichéd, format we saw in late Song funerary inscriptions: the husband dies when the widow is young, often leaving her with small children or even an unborn child. Others (parents, siblings, or in-laws) suggest that she remarry, but she tearfully refuses. She lives frugally, often in semi-isolation, helping to support the family with her own labor; she rears her children, teaching them to be upright; she cares for the elders, sparing no effort. Not infrequently the family prospers under her management, and the biographer characterizes her longevity and multiple descendants as Heaven's reward for her virtuous diligence.

With few exceptions, women like these did not become nationally-famous figures celebrated in the works of well-known poets; on the contrary, most of the faithful widows described in extant Yuan works are represented in a single surviving text, sometimes a biography or poetry preface but most often a poem, usually by an author who had a personal connection with the subject.[40] In other words, rather than reflecting

---

39. Holmgren notes that slashing of the cheeks and forehead in mourning was a common steppe custom, and may have influenced Chinese practices ("Observations on Marriage," 184).

40. In a few cases, there is more than one extant text to the same faithful wife, for example a text written by Liu Guan (*Dai zhi ji* 13.19a–20b) and Chen Lü (*An ya tang ji* 13.24a–15b) for a non-Han woman, and one written by Gong Shitai (*Wan zhai ji* 8.36b–37a) and Liu Renben (*Yu ting ji* 6.42b–43a) for Liu's maternal aunt. Since we know that in many if not most cases poems and prefaces to faithful wives were part of

emotional or literary inspiration, most exemplar poems dedicated to faithful widows were composed in the context of social obligation. The poetry was usually solicited (or even commissioned) from the author by a member of the subject's family (and a number of authors admit that such requests could become tiresome).[41] The celebrated widows tended to be the mothers of friends or patrons, the kinswomen of acquaintances, the wives of relatives or neighbors.[42] This means, again in contrast to heroic martyrs, that the faithful widows extolled in Yuan exemplar poetry were virtually all members of the elite.

We do not know precisely when Yuan literati began producing poetry volumes in honor of upper-class faithful widows. The earliest datable evidence of such a collection is Liu Minzhong's 1298 preface for Madame Zou, with which this chapter opened.[43] Liu's preface was composed nearly twenty years after Yu Delin wrote his poetry preface for Tiger-Killer Hu (a commoner), and its matter-of-fact tone suggests that making collections of songs and poems in honor of upper-class faithful wives was already common practice by that time. That impression is furthered by a 1299 preface by Dai Biaoyuan, honoring another government-recognized principled woman: Dai's preface likewise remarks that "the gentlemen and officials (*jin shen shi dai fu* 縉紳士大夫) all wrote songs and poems."[44] By no later than the turn of the fourteenth century, then, poetry collections in honor of upper-class faithful widows appear to have become commonplace.

Government awards may indeed have provided the initial impetus for such collections: both Liu and Dai were writing for women who had been

---

larger collections dedicated to the subject, we must assume that most of the participating authors were too obscure to have their works survive.

41. E.g., Pu Daoyuan, *Xian ju cong gao* 20.1a–2b.

42. Thus Wang Yi was visited by Hu Shiyuan, who requested a preface for a volume of poetry honoring his grandmother (Wang Yi, *Yi bin ji* 14.4b–5a); Cheng Jufu wrote a preface and a poem to extol the mother of his friend Zhi Zhongqian (Cheng Jufu, *Xue lou ji* 14.12b–14a).

43. A 1243 record of a hall built for a faithful wife also has an accompanying poem, and Zhang Zhihan wrote a poetic colophon in honor of a faithful wife surnamed Zeng at some point before his death in 1296, but neither of these makes reference to a poetry volume. See Li Junmin, *Zhuang jing ji* 莊靖集 8.12b–14a; Zhang Zhihan, *Xi yan ji* 2.7b.

44. Dai Biaoyuan had at one time lived as a guest or retainer in the household of his subject's son (Dai Biaoyuan, *Yan yuan ji* 10.149–50).

designated as faithful widows by the government, and many of the extant texts seem to have been written with an eye to fulfilling the 1304 Board of Rites criteria for an award, explicitly mentioning that the woman had been widowed before age thirty and had remained a widow until the age of fifty. But before long such collections were also being created for many women who had not received awards. Yuan authors created poetry collections for faithful widows who had refused to let their sons recommend them for awards, and (more frequently) for women whose sons' efforts to secure awards had been unsuccessful. Several texts intimate that the sons of widowed women were under significant social pressure to see their mothers recognized by the state. In a poem for a faithful widow Wang, Xu Youren asserts that the way to repay a widowed mother's tender care is to see that she is commemorated by the censors and the historians.[45] Other poetry prefaces describe filial sons, heartbroken because they have failed to secure an award for their mothers, seeking poetry from their friends as a sort of consolation prize.[46] By the late Yuan, if not before, a collection of poetry to celebrate a faithful widow had also become a means to help secure a government award for her, rather than being a post-facto celebration of an award. Thus Su Tianjue describes how a son sought poetry in honor of his mother, and predicts that a virtuous official will certainly soon arrive and submit her name to the court; Xie Yingfang composed a poem explicitly titled "Poem to Faithful Widow Zhou, Submitted to the Prefectural and County Officials" (周節婦詩呈府縣官).[47]

In the Yuan as in the Song, the composition of texts celebrating exemplars served to enhance the status of authors and subjects alike, and it is not hard to see why faithful widows became a favorite subject for such social aggrandizing. To begin with, faithful widows as a category provided a large pool of potential subjects. High mortality rates assured that many women would be widowed at a young age, and for women with children and some resources, faithful widowhood might well have held greater appeal than remarriage. Obtaining an award

---

45. Xu Youren, *Zhizheng ji* 22.2b.
46. Gong Shitai, *Wan zhai ji* 8.36a–36b; Pu Daoyuan, *Xian ju cong gao* 20.1a–2b.
47. Su Tianjue, *Zixi wen gao* 5.2a–3a. See also Xu Qian, *Bai yun ji* 3.52–53; Xie Yingfang, *Gui chao gao* 16.39b–40b. It is possible that this latter text, which is not dated, was written in the early Ming.

for faithful widowhood might also have been easier than obtaining one for filial piety. State recognition of faithful widowhood required only that a woman survive long enough (and have sufficiently good political connections!) to be recognized. In contrast, state recognition of exceptional filiality seems to have required significant austerities—cutting one's flesh or even one's liver as medicine; drastic acts of self-mortification to move the spirits, or intense mourning after a parent's death. We can also begin to see why poetry became the preferred form of celebrating exemplars: whether or not a woman received state recognition, the compilation of poetry volumes permitted a large number of individuals to participate in the glory that a woman brought to her family. Authors, as much as the subject and her family, could see their names circulated and brought to the attention of the official asked to compose a preface.

As with heroines, the loyalty of faithful widows could also be made to serve a variety of rhetorical purposes. Some saw the brutality and dislocation of life under the Yuan as evidence that their peers had abandoned the moral values that were fundamental to Chinese cultural identity. Authors of this type depicted the promotion of faithful widows as a means to shore up the culture, by inspiring (or shaming) others to follow suit. Employing the standard tropes of the genre, Wu Cheng's poetry preface for Faithful Widow Xiang thus observed,

> Alas! The customs of the world have declined. Even some officials and gentlemen have lost their pure hearts (*liang xin* 良心), how much more so women! There are even some who have seven sons and still cannot be content in their chambers. For someone in the prime of life and without sons to "follow one to the end," can she not be called virtuous!

After comparing Xiang to several famous exemplars of old, Wu concludes, "Among those who love this virtue and uprightness, who knows whether there will not be one who will compose poems to glorify her, write in praise of her, and show a model to the world? I am recording her affair here, to wait for the investigations of one who will continue the *Biographies of Exemplary Women*."[48]

---

48. Wu Cheng, *Wu wen zheng ji* 24.8b–9a. For other examples of this type of rhetoric, see Liu Minzhong, *Zhong an ji* 9.10a–11b; Zhang Yanghao, *Gui tian lei gao* 7.4a–6b. This attitude is also exhibited by Kong Qi. On the woman with seven sons, see chap. 3 and the story with which this chapter begins.

But if some men sought to improve what they saw as the benighted customs around them, still others took refuge in the conviction that "[although] the world is lost, the Dao is not."[49] For the latter, examples of female fidelity served as important and reassuring evidence that Chinese culture had survived. This line of thinking harked back to Ouyang Xiu's biography of Wang Ning's severed-armed wife, and it had been used in reference to another heroine by the Jin poet Yuan Haowen.[50] But by Yuan times, this rhetoric was also frequently deployed in the context of faithful widowhood. Thus the scholar An Xi (1270–1311), in a preface to a poem for a faithful widow surnamed Gao, remarked:

> Whenever I read Master Ouyang's *History of the Five Dynasties*, and see his preface for those who died for fidelity and loyalty and what he wrote of Wang Ning's wife in his "Miscellaneous Biographies," I always set down the book and sigh. Today, seeing Gao's behavior, one can again believe that Heavenly principles and constant human [relations] truly cannot be extinguished.[51]

Similarly, like the heroines we saw in the Song, faithful widows could also be claimed by local dignitaries as evidence for the superior customs of the areas in which they lived.[52]

Whether they saw customs around them as degraded and in need of transformation, or as evidence of the survival of the Dao, the great majority of educated men under the Yuan participated in the production of texts celebrating faithful widows. Yet, although surviving prefaces demonstrate that hundreds of poetry volumes were produced in honor of such women, almost none of those volumes survive today.[53] This fact

---

49. Lao, "Southern Chinese Scholars," 132, as cited in Tillman, "Disorder (*Luan*) as Trauma," 15.

50. Yuan included the filial widow Nie among a list of ten individuals who died notable deaths at the end of the Jin, and then insisted, "As long as one branch remains, you cannot say [the river] is extinguished…as long as one individual has established her will, you cannot say that the country has collapsed" (Yuan Haowen, *Yishan xian sheng wen ji* 25.338–39).

51. An Xi, *An Mo'an xian sheng wen ji* 1.6–7. For other examples of this sort of rhetoric, see Pu Daoyuan, *Xian ju cong gao* 20.1a–2b; Ma Zuchang, *Shi tian wen ji* 9.9b–10b, 15.7b–8b; Su Tianjue, *Zi xi wen gao* 29.21b–22a.

52. See, for example, Liu Guan, *Dai zhi ji* 17.4a–5b; Chen Lü, *An ya tang ji* 4.12a–13; Su Tianjue, *Zi xi wen gao* 30.21b–22a.

53. It is possible that such volumes survive in private family collections, but I have been unable to locate any in major Chinese libraries. Faithful-wife poetry volumes (*jie fu shi juan*) do survive from the Ming and Qing.

surely bears testament to the incidental and primarily social nature (and often forgettable quality) of such poetry. But the chance survival of two exemplar poetry volumes—one in honor of a faithful widow, one in honor of her son—permits us to explore in some detail how such collections could be the pretext for both establishing and cementing social connections.[54]

## Making Connections

According to the record preserved in these two volumes (titled respectively *Pure and Faithful Folio* [*Zhen jie juan* 貞節卷] and *Spring Grass Folio* [*Chun cao juan* 春草卷]), the faithful widow Chen was the wife of a man of Wuxi named Hua Xuan 華鉉 (1287–1312).[55] While he was still very young, Hua had been recommended for office and had served as a Palace Guard under Emperor Wuzong. He became ill, returned home, and died at the age of twenty-six. At that time Chen was twenty-eight; she was left with a three-year-old son and two young daughters. Chen vowed not to remarry, and for some thirty years acted as a typical faithful widow: she eschewed self-adornment and personally carried out the sacrifices; she served her in-laws with filiality and respect, and she was cordial to her affinal relatives. We are told that she worked assiduously at managing the family and reared her children to be filial, so that her son and four grandsons all became excellent scholars. Ultimately the local elders recommended her for a government award, which she

---

54. The two sets of poetry are preserved in a Ming compendium of model writing, where they are jointly titled *The Pure and Faithful and Spring Grass Folios of the Hua Family of Wuxi* (*Wuxi Hua shi zhen jie chun cao er juan* 無錫華氏貞節春草二卷, in Zhao Qimei, *Zhao shi tie wang shan hu*, 9.47a–68b). The same two sets are also preserved in (Qing) Bian Yongyu, *Shi gu tang shu hua hui kao*, 21.21–32 and 21.32–42 respectively, under the titles *Yuan Authors' Hua Family Spring Grass Studio Folio* (*Yuan ren ti Hua shi chun cao xuan juan* 元人題華氏春草軒卷) and *Yuan Authors' Hua Family Pure and Faithful Hall Folio* (*Yuan ren ti Hua shi zhen jie tang juan* 元人題華氏貞節堂卷). Although many individual poems in honor of faithful women survive in Yuan authors' collected works, this is the only case I have found that preserves the contents of an entire volume of exemplar poetry from the Yuan. Both compendia preserve several exemplar poetry collections from the Ming.

55. Hua Xuan's eulogist Huang Jin indicates Xuan was also known by the name Yexian 野仙, which is how Huang refers to him. In Hua genealogical records, he is called Hua Xuan, and I use that name for convenience here.

received in 1342. A few years later, in recognition of his mother's contribution to preserving his father's line, Chen's son Hua Youwu built two halls, one of which he named Pure and Faithful Hall (*zhen jie tang* 貞節堂), and the other of which he named Spring Grass Studio (*chun cao xuan* 春草軒). He then commissioned writings to commemorate the new structures.

Two funerary inscriptions composed by the eminent Learning of the Way scholar and official Huang Jin, along with a rare copy of a family-sponsored genealogical volume, allow us to reconstruct the Hua family's background. They also shed light on the specific circumstances that surrounded the creation of the poetry collections for Faithful Widow Chen.[56] As we will see, Huang Jin was an important if apparently reluctant participant in the process.

In the earlier of the two funerary inscriptions, written for the reburial of Hua Youwu's grandfather Hua Pu (1265–1331) sometime after 1336, Huang Jin details the putative ancient ancestry of the family and explains

---

56. Huang Jin's funerary inscriptions for the Hua family are preserved in the *Xu Jinhua cong shu* edition of his collected works (Huang Jin, *Jinhua Huang xian sheng wen ji* 29.5a–6a, 37.14a–15b), but notably they are not included in other, more common versions of Huang's collected works, such as that contained in the *Si ku quan shu* or in the *Cong shu ji cheng* series. Evidently early editors felt that these works did not reflect particularly well on their author. The family genealogical volume, first compiled in the fifteenth century and recompiled ca. 1645 by one Hua Yuncheng 華允誠, is entitled *Hua shi chuan fang ji* 華氏傳芳集 (hereafter *Chuan fang ji*). I am grateful to the Gest and Firestone libraries at Princeton University for allowing me to view and make copies from a microfilm of this work; the original is held in the National Central Library, Taiwan. The *Chuan fang ji* contains brief biographical notices of the Hua family's founding ancestors, as well as funerary inscriptions, prefaces, and so forth related to family members. The Huang Jin inscription for Hua Pu appears, with some variations, in *Chuan fang ji* 1.23a–24a, though it is there attributed to a "Wang Jin" 王溍 rather than to Huang Jin. The original compilation of the *Chuan fang ji* is described in an inscription by Wu Kuan 吳寬 (1435–1504), written to celebrate the fact that a seventh-generation descendant of Hua Youwu had built a special room to house the collection. Wu explains that the *Chuan fang ji* text was first compiled by a fifth-generation descendant of the principled woman's son, Hua Youwu. See Wu Kuan, "Hua shi cui mo xuan ji" 華氏粹墨軒記 in his *Jia zang ji* 35.8–9b. This Hua family later became prominent patrons of the mid-Ming painter Wen Zhenming. See Clunas, *Elegant Debts*, 130–37; the connection is made explicit in the preface to Feng Daosheng 豐道生's "*Zhen Shang zhai fu*" 真賞齋賦 (Rhyme-prose on the Studio of True Connoisseurship). See Chen Yuanlong, (*Yu ding*) *Li dai fu hui* 28.16a–19b, especially 19a.

their more recent family background. Huang's account depicts the Huas as having come from very typical Song local-elite stock. At one point they lived near Kaifeng but fled south to avoid soldiers, presumably at the fall of the Northern Song. The earliest evidence of office-holding was by Hua Pu's own grandfather, Hua Quan 詮 (1205–85), who held a low-ranking prestige title (*jiang shi lang* 將仕郎).[57] Early in the Yuan, Hua Pu's father Hua Youwen 友聞 (1242–1313) had served as a superintendant of the commercial tax office in the Huas' home prefecture (*ti ling shui yu* 提領稅務), suggesting that the family's rise to prominence owed something to an early collaboration with the Yuan authorities.[58] Huang Jin portrays Hua Pu as the quintessential local gentleman, while making it clear that the Huas were extremely wealthy. Less flatteringly, Huang shows Hua Pu using his connections to obtain a high-ranking appointment in the Yuan bureaucracy, though political upheavals at court led him ultimately to refuse office.[59]

---

57. The *Chuan fang ji* contains a slightly more detailed version of the genealogy than Huang Jin reports, but is equally vague before the generation of Hua Pu's great-grandfather, for whom it provides little more than birth and death dates. The *Chuan fang ji* is explicit that the rise of the family truly began in the generation of Hua Pu's grandfather Quan (1206–85), saying "*Hua shi zhi sheng zi ci shi yan*" 華氏之盛自此始焉 (*Chuan fang ji* 1.12). It observes that Quan's wealth and property were greatest among the grand families of Chang 常 prefecture and explains that Quan received his title for contributions of grain and served as a county registrar (*Chuan fang ji* 1.12a). It also indicates that all five of Hua Quan's sons held office in the late thirteenth and early fourteenth centuries (*Chuan fang ji* 1.13a–19a).

58. Hucker indicates that the Commercial Tax Office was a Yuan institution (Hucker, *Dictionary of Official Titles*). A funerary inscription in the *Chuan fang ji* also provides detailed discussion of Hua Pu's father's role in managing local taxes, portraying him as taking on the onerous job to prevent others from going bankrupt (*Chuan fang ji* 1.15a–16b). The *Chuan fang ji* attributes this inscription to the well-known Yuan writer Jie Xisi, although extant editions of Jie's writings (including a recently published collection billed as "complete works") do not include it. See *Jie Xisi quan ji*.

59. Huang depicts Hua Pu interacting with an unnamed monk and insisting that he would not accept less than a rank three office. Through the monk's efforts Hua was ultimately offered such an office, but about that time a prominent official suddenly fell from power; Hua Pu became frightened and declined to serve. The *Chuan fang ji* version omits the references to such things as Hua Pu's moneylending, the fact that the usual reason for donating grain to the government was to receive office, and all discussion of the monk's role. The *Chuan fang ji* does not contain Huang's text for Hua Youwu's father, Hua Xuan 華鉉 (also called Yexian 野仙), but its "genealogical biography" for him quotes (without attribution) from Huang's inscription (*Chuang fang ji* 3a–b).

Huang Jin explains that he originally agreed to write the funerary inscription for Hua Pu because he was prevailed on to do so by his friend Chen Qian 陳謙 (Ziping).⁶⁰ Thereafter, Hua Youwu took the existence of the first inscription as a pretext to approach Huang for a second, in honor of his father Hua Xuan. Huang tells the reader that, old and emotional as he was, he did not want to have to write inscriptions for both a father and son; but again Chen Qian intervened until finally Huan "could not bear to refuse."

In somewhat loaded language, Huang then relates the story of Hua Xuan, the husband of Faithful Widow Chen. Huang depicts Xuan as forthright and stubborn: "when he made a decision, there was no dissuading him." Xuan had ambitions to make a name for himself, and pushed to associate with accomplished officials and nobles, "never once allowing his youth and humble position to cause him to be backward or retiring." Xuan's equally ambitious grandfather sent him to the capital, where he was soon appointed to the imperial bodyguards and as a secretary of Buddhist affairs. Not long afterward, however, he became ill, and in spite of the ministrations of court doctors, he was forced to return home to convalesce. He died at home some five months later.

Taken together, Huang's inscriptions and information in the Hua family genealogy reveal that the Huas of Wuxi rose to considerable wealth during the course of the Song-Yuan transition. They then took active advantage of the Yuan political system to enhance their power and prestige. By the time Hua Youwu reached adulthood in the late 1320s, however, Yuan central authority was beginning to break down (as Youwu's grandfather seems to have realized). Perhaps for that reason, Hua Youwu refrained from seeking office, and turned his ambitions instead to enhancing his local standing as a Confucian gentleman. He hired a family tutor with connections to Learning of the Way circles and attempted (without much success) to cultivate a reputation as a poet.⁶¹

---

60. This information appears in the inscription for Hua Xuan (Huang Jin, *Jinhua Huang xian sheng wen ji* 37.14a–15b).
61. The Hua family tutor, Chen Fang, titled the volume of Hua Youwu's collected poetry *Huang Yang ji*, in reference to the mythical figure Huang Yang, who was said to have grown slightly in ordinary years but shrunk significantly in years with intercalary (*run* 閏) months. The editors of the *Si ku quan shu* take this to suggest that Hua loved to write poetry but was too busy to make much progress (Yong Rong, *Qin ding Si ku quan shu zong mu* 174.73a).

We do not know if he was actively involved in securing the government award that established his mother as an officially recognized faithful widow in 1342, but he clearly made every effort to capitalize on that reward by building halls and soliciting prose and poetry in her honor from most of the most prominent writers of the day.

Significantly, it was again Huang Jin whom Hua Youwu first approached to solicit an inscription (*ming* 銘) for the Pure and Faithful Hall. The text that Huang produced in response to this request is perfunctory (this may be the reason that it does not appear in Huang Jin's collected works).[62] Huang duly reports the basic facts of widow Chen's background, though he connects the government award less with her outstanding virtue than with the fact that she became old and that her son Youwu had "worked hard to become a distinguished gentleman" (*ke zi li wei jia shi* 克自勵爲佳士). Even more striking is Huang's final line: after noting that Hua had asked him to write an inscription, Huang comments, "As long as it can promote the fame of his parent, there is nothing he will not do" (*gai fan ke yi xian qi qin zhe, wu bu wei ye* 蓋凡可以顯其親者無不爲也). On the surface, this line praises Youwu's filiality: he is anxious to do everything he can to see that his mother's virtue is recognized. But as most of Huang's readers were aware, the phrase "nothing he will not do" (*wu bu wei*) more commonly had a negative resonance, suggesting that one would not refrain even from immoral behavior.[63] In this context, the turn of phrase is odd, for it could be read as implying Youwu is directing his efforts less to the filial duty of pleasing his mother than to publicizing her (and his own) name. (Perhaps this is why the author of Hua Youwu's own funerary inscription borrows the concept but changes the phrase, claiming that "If his effort could please his parent, there was nothing he would not do" [*li ke yi yu qi qin zhe, wu bu wei zhi* 力可以娛其親者無不爲之].)[64]

---

62. The text is found in the collection preserved in Zhao Qimei's *Zhao shi tie wang shan hu* 9.50a–b.

63. Mencius, in particular, had argued that without a regular livelihood, ordinary people would be unable to maintain a sense of morality and there would be "nothing they would not do." See Mencius, *Mengzi yi zhu*, Liang Hui wang, *shang*, 7:17. Later moralists often remarked that if one feared death, "there is nothing one would not do," including behaving in an immoral fashion, in order to stay alive. This rhetoric is seen frequently in paeans to heroic martyrs, as shown in chap. 6.

64. *Chuan fang ji* 2.23a.

Still, whatever reservations Huang may have had about Hua Youwu's motives, he did write the inscription; and the frequent mention of that fact by others who contributed to the two poetry collections suggests that Huang's imprimatur was meaningful in their own decisions to participate. Interestingly, the *Spring Grass Folio* collection, which celebrated Hua Youwu's filiality, appears to have been compiled first, and here the figure of Chen Qian (the friend who prevailed on Huang Jin to write funerary inscriptions for Hua) was central. In the poetry preface he composed for the volume, Chen reveals that he was in fact a retainer of Hua Youwu. He stresses that, at the time he was writing, Huang Jin had already written funerary inscriptions for Hua Youwu's ancestors, and that the well-connected scholar and Hanlin official Zhang Zhu 張翥 (1287–1368) had already composed a "record" (*ji* 記) to celebrate the construction of the Spring Grass Studio.[65] Although neither says so explicitly, it is tempting to imagine that Chen Qian served as the intermediary to Zhang, just as he had to Huang: we know from other sources that Chen and Zhang associated with one another.[66] Indeed, it begins to appear that one of the functions of retainers like Chen was to deploy their social networks on behalf of their patron.

However Zhang came to write the record of the Spring Grass Studio, Chen relates that the inspiration for a poetry volume came during a banquet that Hua Youwu held there, apparently in honor of his mother's birthday.[67] Chen observes, "The literati and gentlemen (*jin shen xian sheng* 搢紳先生) all wrote poems praising the fact that the studio is called 'Spring Grass,' and Youwu insisted that he get a piece from me explicating the meaning of the name." Chen goes on to explain that the

---

65. Zhao Qimei, *Zhao shi tie wang shan hu* 9.57a–59a. Zhang Zhu's record indicates that, having obtained Huang's inscription for the Pure and Faithful Hall, Hua decided that the second hall also ought to have a commemoration, and so approached Zhang.

66. See Zhang Zhu's poem to Chen, "Chen Ziping ji suo zuo Qiong hua da xie" 陳子平寄所作瓊花答謝 (Zhang Zhu, *Tui an ji* 3.33b–34a).

67. We do not know exactly when the birthday banquet was held. Widow Chen's funerary inscription in the *Chuan fang ji* indicates she was born on the 6th day of the fourth month of 1285. She would have celebrated the important sixtieth birthday (returning to the same year in the sixty-year cycle of stems and branches) in the spring of 1345.

term Spring Grass alludes to a poem entitled "Song of the Wandering Son" (遊子吟) by the Tang dynasty author Meng Jiao. Meng's poem had described a mother's tender concern for a son who would soon be leaving home. The name Spring Grass Studio played on the final line of the poem: "Who says this heart like tender grass can repay three years of spring sunshine?"[68] Many of the poems in the collection employed images and language from Meng's poem to suggest that the filial Hua Youwu was like that tender grass, basking in the spring sunshine of his mother's loving care.

We do not know whether any of the poems that survive in the current collection were actually written at the banquet. The earliest datable item in the *Spring Grass Folio* (many are not dated) is a poem from the first day of the third month of 1347. Although the author of this poem mentions a banquet, he indicates that he was writing at the "Yanling hostel" (Yanling *yi* 延陵驛), not at the Spring Grass Studio. Another author indicates he was writing in the twelfth month of 1347, at a Daoist hermitage in Liangxi (Liangxi *dao guan shu* 梁溪道館書).[69] The dates of these poems demonstrate that the collection was compiled over a period of some time: in fact, Chen Qian himself, at Hua Youwu's request, added his own "Song of the Wandering Son" ("*You zi yin*") to the collection a full three years after his original preface.[70]

---

68. Meng Jiao's poem reads: 慈母手中線,遊子身上衣;臨行密密縫,意恐遲遲歸;誰言寸草心,報得三春暉. *Meng Dongye shi ji* 1.3b. The idea of three years of spring sunshine plays on the understanding, set out in the *Classic of Filial Piety*, that human parents nurture their helpless infants for three years. Meng Jiao's phrase "heart like tender grass" (*cun cao xin* 寸草心) thereafter became an emblem for filiality. Hua's rhetorical question of "How can I possibly repay her" clearly resonates with the poem. Several of the authors in the collection also exploited another of Meng Jiao's poems on this theme for images they used in their own poems. See "Wandering Son" *You zi* 遊子 (*Meng Dongye shi ji* 3.2b).

69. Zhao Qimei, *Zhao shi tie wang shan hu* 9.63b–64b; 9.63a–b. Yanling was a county southwest of present-day Danyang city in Jiangsu; Liangxi is a creek that connects the city of Wuxi with Taihu.

70. See Zhao Qimei, *Zhao shi tie wang shan hu* 9.64b–65a. Chen's poem is dated "three years after writing the preface, on the twentieth day of the seventh month." This is the latest datable item in the collection. There are several minor inconsistencies in the dating of the texts associated with the *Spring Grass Folio*. For example, Chen Qian's poetry preface is dated the twenty-first day of the third month of 1347. It mentions Zhang Zhu's "record" for the building, but the latter text is dated the *li xia* 立夏, which in that year should have fallen on about the twenty-fifth day of the third month.

The compilation of the *Pure and Faithful Folio* likewise seems to have taken place over a period of several years. Although various texts indicate that Huang Jin's inscription for the hall was completed before 1347, the record (*ji* 記) and later record (*hou ji* 後記) for the Pure and Faithful Hall were not composed until early in 1349, and the preface for the poetry collection not until the seventh month of 1351. Here we have further evidence that the celebration of his mother's fidelity was rather an afterthought for Hua Youwu, secondary to the celebration of his own filiality. As with the earlier volume, however, Hua was clearly interested in using his connections to secure texts and in using the pretext of gathering texts to make new connections. Gan Wenchuan 干文傳 (1266–1343), author of the record, explains that Youwu was introduced to him by his old colleague Hua Bocheng 伯成, an assistant prefect and a distant uncle of Youwu.[71] A month later, the eminent scholar Zheng Yuanyou 鄭元佑 (1292–1364) wrote with some resignation that, although what Gan Wenchuan had written in praise of Youwu's mother was already complete, Youwu had nonetheless solicited a second record from him.

Many of the authors who ultimately contributed to Hua Youwu's folios are unknown today, but several were famous writers: indeed, the tables of contents of the volumes read like rosters of eminent literary figures of the Yuan. In addition, almost all the authors can be shown to have associated—through exchange of poetry, letters, or gifts—with other participants. The title of Yang Weizhen's 楊維楨 (1296–1370) poem in the *Spring Grass Folio* even says explicitly that it was written in response to the entry by poet Hu Zhu 胡助 (1278–1355).[72]

That Hua Youwu's association with such eminent men added luster to his own reputation is attested to in later biographical texts. Hua Youwu's own funerary biography stresses that he was "especially diligent in selecting friends from among the respected and virtuous," and claims that Huang Jin, Zhang Zhu, Gan Wenchuan, and others "all disregarded seniority to affiliate with him." The biography goes on: "The gentleman [Hua Youwu] served them all strictly. Therefore they were all happy

---

71. I have been unable to otherwise identify this kinsman.
72. Zhao Qimei, *Zhao shi tie wang shan hu* 9.62a–b, "Tong Hu Tai chang fu Chun cao ci" (同胡太常賦春草辭). Note that Yang's poem does not really "match" that of Hu: it is written in seven-character lines rather than five, and in a different rhyme scheme.

to write about and sing of the virtue of his ancestors. Because of this, the gentleman's own studies improved daily, and his reputation flourished among the various officials and ministers."[73] The biographer here acknowledges both Hua Youwu's social inferiority and his assiduous efforts to cultivate useful connections. Indeed, the very survival of Hua's folios in later anthologies can be attributed to his success in obtaining the contributions of famous writers. Notably, this was true even when the connections were merely indirect: the preface to Yang Weizhen's poem as it appears in Yang's collected works indicates that Yang had merely "heard" about Hua, and did not actually know him.[74]

The case of Hua Youwu and his mother confirm that the social benefits accruing to the families of faithful widows and those who wrote about them were critical elements in encouraging the proliferation of exemplar texts in the Yuan. Yet the will to social reputation was not the only factor at work. As Huang Jin's ambivalent texts for Hua Youwu hint, the self-interested social aggrandizing of some was balanced by the sincere efforts of others, especially those who saw themselves as heirs to the Song Learning of the Way movement, to promote Confucian morality in the broader society.

## Learning of the Way, Cultural Crisis, and Family Survival

While most Yuan literati composed texts for exemplars, the scholars committed to the philosophical and moral agendas of the Learning of the Way movement were especially prolific in their composition of such texts. Now, at first blush, this is not surprising: for centuries, scholars of Chinese history were accustomed to associating the Late Imperial valorization of female fidelity, and especially faithful widowhood, with "Cheng-Zhu Learning." Still, I have shown in earlier chapters that the leaders of the Learning of the Way movement in the Song were not centrally concerned with promoting female fidelity. In fact, promotion of female exemplars

---

73. *Chuan fang ji* 2.23a, in "Qi bi chu shi Hua gong zhi ming" 栖碧處士華公誌銘. Note that the text erroneously has "Chen Mingde" for Zheng Mingde (鄭明德), that is, Zheng Yuanyou. Wu Kuan, the late fifteenth-century author of a preface in honor of a Hua descendant, likewise makes a point of naming "the best" (*you zhe* 優者) among the contributors. See Wu Kuan, *Jia zang ji* 35.8a–9b.

74. Yang Weizhen, *Tie gu yue fu* 6.10a–b.

created something of a moral quandary for Learning of the Way thinkers. We have seen that in the Northern Song, Sima Guang had suggested that even composing funerary inscriptions for women was inappropriate, and in the late Song, Zhang Ruyu had objected to a case of fiancée fidelity as noncanonical.[75] In the Yuan, too, Learning of the Way scholars wrestled with classical ritual injunctions forbidding the public discussion of women's behavior. Accordingly, after noting how famous gentlemen and eminent scholars had written in praise of the faithful widow Zhu in hopes of securing a government award for her, the Yuan scholar Xu Qian observed, "Madame Zhu was merely completing the Dao of a woman, and need not seek to be known among others. Anciently, a woman's reputation did not extend beyond the inner quarters. If you reminded Madame Zhu of this principle, would she be vexed if you did not contravene it?" In much stronger terms, the scholar Dai Liang concluded a funerary record for a faithful widow Wei with the assertion:

> Alas, of old, women did not recognize the reception room screen; their laughter and speech was not heard in the villages, their names did not extend beyond their immediate surroundings, and [knowledge of] their virtuous behavior stopped within the door of the inner quarters. Today, when the faithful widow is alive her behavior is celebrated with commendations; when she dies her story is recorded for transmission. Does this not contravene the ancient Dao? Although that is the case, the world today does not match the ancient. Since ministers and officials are not completely faithful, and this woman is able to be so, it is appropriate to commend and transmit [her story]. This, too, is the extinguishing of the Dao. Alas, how tragic![76]

In composing texts in honor of faithful widows, then, Learning of the Way adherents first had to overcome concerns about the canonical appropriateness of such writing. They also had to ignore the very real possibility that the virtues of their subjects had been exaggerated. That this was often the case is confirmed by that jaded observer of Yuan mores, Kong Qi. Kong first reports the remarks of an unnamed interlocutor:

> I see that today those who in the villages amass wealth are not those who love ritual, and their families are often not upright. Moreover their wealth is obtained in unrighteous ways, and their enfeoffments obtained by acts not in accord with ritual, [but they] constantly get famous gentlemen to write about them, saying

---

75. See chap. 3, n. 18, and chap. 6.
76. Xu Qian, *Bai yun ji* 3.52–53; Dai Liang, *Jiu ling shan fang ji* 9.131–32.

that they love goodness and delight in righteousness, do good works and establish merit. With respect to the families of faithful widows and the chaste and heroic, I am always suspicious that they make literature the tool of empty bragging, or are just pretty parables for later ages."

In response, Kong himself comments on the extremely licentious behavior of women of the capital, noting that "among them there are more 'faithful widows' than you can count: if you approach the Board of Rites it is easy to get [such a designation]." He concludes, "The empty words and phrases of literati and gentlemen of talent cannot be trusted; only if...the local villagers make a record can it be believed. What is written by the various scholars of the Hanlin is not worthy of regard: the way they inflate the value of their names only makes the villagers scorn and ridicule them."[77]

Huang Jin's understated inscription for Hua Youwu's mother revealed that he was all too aware of this problem, and his ambivalence is similarly evident in a number of other exemplar texts that he wrote. In a colophon to a poem honoring a Faithful Wife He, for example, Huang describes how "various gentlemen" secured a government award for her, then "mutually congratulated one another and wrote poems and songs about it." He adds gravely, "I do not know whether in the end this accorded with her own wishes or not. I respectfully append my name at the end of the folio, to record her discomfiture and relieve any doubts."[78] Writing of a young man surnamed Mei whose filial behavior was reportedly attended by numerous supernatural phenomena, Huang pointedly quoted the Northern Song minister Zeng Gong:

> Zeng [Gong] once said, "Today as in the past, when mighty and illustrious gentlemen discuss righteous behavior that is not recorded in the histories, they often utilize the strange in order to move customs. Sometimes the affair is lofty and hard to continue; sometimes they relate one person's virtue and deride the world for not being able to match it. Although [their writing] originates in helping to teach and awaken the world, when it is investigated against the Mean, it sometimes is too extreme."

Huang then continued:

---

77. Kong Qi, *Zhizheng zhi ji* 2.62–63. The conversation takes place in the context of a larger discussion about whether the writings of the ancients can be trusted.
78. Huang Jin, *Huang Wenxian gong ji* 4.165–66.

Based on what I have heard of the affair of the Mei son, those who discuss it truly come close to being too extreme. But, if wanting to make those of middle status or below see the extreme and know benevolence, and be ashamed that they don't themselves reach it, then recording and transmitting it is probably all right.[79]

In statements like this, Learning of the Way scholars expressed their discomfort with the process of celebrating exemplars in the very act of promulgating exemplar texts. Why, in the face of that discomfort, did these scholars continue to participate so avidly in the creation of exemplar texts?

Certainly, social pressure must sometimes have been a factor: Chen Qian's persistence had overcome Huang Jin's reluctance to write for Hua Youwu, and there must have been many occasions on which scholars found themselves "unable to refuse" requests for exemplar texts. Indeed, I think we can see texts that dwell less on the subject's virtue than on the author's qualms as a clever response to the social and moral dilemmas occasioned by such requests. Still, we must also take seriously the assertion, made by virtually all these authors, that their real reason for writing was the hope that praise for exemplars would lead others to admire and emulate their behavior. In other words, Learning of the Way scholars were convinced that the production of exemplar texts—and perhaps especially poetry and songs—was an important tool in their central project: the moral transformation of society, or *jiao hua* 教化.[80] This commitment to transforming society, and the conviction that publicizing exemplary behavior could contribute to that transformation, led even men such as Zhang Yanghao, disgusted as he was with the rampant cheating that plagued the system of government awards, to continue to participate in the process. Otherwise, Zhang explained, "I fear that

---

79. Huang Jin, *Huang Wenxian gong ji* 3.132–33. See also Wu Cheng's colophon for a poetry volume for another filial son, in which he says explicitly that he refuses to flatter the subject as other friends of the family have done, and instead calls on the subject to intensify his efforts to be filial (Wu Cheng, *Wu wen zheng ji* 56.2a–3a). See also Yu Ji, *Dao yuan xue gu lu* 11.206.

80. The assertion that exemplars can help reform customs (made by men both within and without the Learning of the Way movement) appears too often to cite exhaustively. For some examples see Hu Bingwen, *Yun feng ji* 5.7b–8b; Chen Lü, *An ya tang ji* 13.24a–25b; Zhang Zhihan, *Xi yan ji* 2.7b; Liu Guan, *Dai zhi ji* 17.4a–5b; Wang Xu, *Lan xuan ji* 3.15a–b.

those who want to do good would lose hope, stay in old habits, and not reform; I also fear that those who accumulate evil would have nothing to warn them."[81] Or, as Pu Daoyuan explained, "When I am at leisure from the History Office, each year more than a dozen people bring faithful-widow poetry collections seeking prefaces and poems. It is tiresome, but because it concerns the transformation of customs, I never fail to exert myself to respond to their requests."[82]

If Learning of the Way scholars were motivated by the desire to transform customs, they also seem to have seen faithful widows, in particular, as having an especially important role in the moral renovation they were trying to effect. We see this clearly in Liu Minzhong's text for Madame Zou, with which this chapter opens, and it was reiterated by others as well. Thus Pu Daoyuan remarked:

> Humankind has always originated in husbands and wives. Therefore the first volume of the *Book of Changes* begins with [the hexagrams] *Qian* [the male principle] and *Kun* [the female principle]; the second volume begins with *Jian* [completion] and *Heng* [constancy], and the *Book of Odes* takes "The Call of the Waterfowl" as the correct beginning. In human relations there is nothing more important than this.[83]

And Song Lian explained in more straightforward terms:

> Why is it that Ritual begins with husband and wife? It is because [only] after there are husband and wife are there father and son. [Only] after there are father and son are there lord and minister. Although these three are different, their Dao is one. Thus if a wife does not have two husbands, a son does not shame his parents, and a minister is able to be loyal to his lord, how can it be that All-under-Heaven will not be long governed? Why is it that the teaching of this age has declined? Among the gentlemen and officials who recite the laws of the former kings, there are always some who go so far as to revolt against their lords or fathers. When there is someone gentle like a girl or woman, who doesn't know much about book-learning but is able to uphold her fidelity and preserve herself, it is sufficient to augment the magnitude of the five relationships.[84]

---

81. Zhang Yanghao, *Gui tian lei gao* 3.2b–4a.
82. Pu Daoyuan, *Xian ju cong gao* 20.1a–2b.
83. *Ibid.* "The Call of the Waterfowl" ("Guan ju" 關雎) is the title of the first poem in the *Book of Odes*; the poem was generally understood to refer to fidelity between a man and woman.
84. Song Lian, *Song xue shi quan ji* 11.405–7.

In other words, since relationships between men and women give rise to human life, the actions of women are critical to the proper ordering of human relations. And since Learning of the Way adherents believed that the order of the cosmos was in turn predicated on the proper ordering of human relations, women's morality took on cosmic importance.

But of course all of this had been true in the Song as well: why was it only in the Yuan that Learning of the Way scholars began actively promoting faithful-widow exemplars? The answer appears to be that Yuan writers were considerably more concerned than Song authors about the current state of women's—and especially wives'—morality. In spite of all the faithful widows he recorded, Wu Cheng also complained of wives whose jealousy led them to threaten their husband's posterity. Liu Guan observed that few women were able to avoid the sorrow of taking a second husband, and Chen Lü argued that although there was nothing remarkable about the principle of women not remarrying, only one or two out of thousands could accomplish it. He added that even when those in charge rewarded faithful widows to exhort the people, "the bad customs did not disappear." Li Cun agreed, reiterating the cliché that "customs today are such that some have seven sons and still cannot be content in their chambers."[85] Their concern about wifely morality is particularly evident in the fact that, unlike Song authors of exemplar texts, these Yuan authors were not holding up women as models for men. Rather, alarmed that women around them were "not content in their chambers," they presented their faithful subjects specifically as models for other women.

We have no way to determine how, or even whether, women's behavior in the Yuan was different from that in Song. Still, we saw in chapter 8 ample evidence that the political chaos of the era had taken its toll on norms of family life. The disruption of social norms is also evident in the outraged accounts of female transgressions found in Kong Qi's memoir, and in biographies and funerary inscriptions showing families resorting to uxorilocal marriages and other unusual tactics much more often than in the Song.[86] More significantly, although the world of courtesans

---

85. Liu Guan, *Dai zhi ji* 17.4a–5b; Chen Lü, *An ya tang ji* 13.26b–27a; Li Cun, *Si an ji* 21.1a–1b.
86. On Kong Qi, see Smith, "Fear of Gynarchy," passim. For poetry comparing the lives of virtuous and luxury-loving women, see chap. 7. For examples of uxorilocal

and concubine entertainments is largely absent from the Yuan society presented in exemplar texts, we should not forget that this world was indeed the backdrop against which the promoters of exemplars were writing. (Indeed, they themselves were highly conscious of that setting, as evident in their explicit efforts to replace popular banquet music with their own, discussed below.)

In other words, I am suggesting that the new Learning of the Way focus on promoting widow fidelity was inspired in part by the less-stable social context of the Yuan, where courtesans and actresses were regularly taken into the households of officials, and concubines moved with impunity from household to household, even renting out their wombs to bear children for multiple families. We have seen that, against this disorder, moralists and others had begun to downplay the role of concubines as entertainers and to attempt to tie them more firmly to their masters' households. We should not be surprised, then, that these moralists also sought increased commitment by wives to their husbands' households. Refusal to remarry was after all one way that wives could be distinguished from concubines, who were routinely sold off when their husbands/masters died. And the need for wifely commitment was all the greater when, within the larger society, the spread of concubinage had increased opportunities for women to remarry.[87]

But even more than disorder, I think, the new Learning of the Way focus on fidelity reflected the fact that by Yuan times the role of wives had become central to the success and even survival of elite families.[88]

---

marriages, see Wang Yun, *Qiujian ji* 43.12–13b; Dai Biaoyuan, *Yan yuan ji* 15.227–28; Cheng Jufu, *Xue lou ji* 19.8b–11a; Wu Cheng, *Wu wen zheng ji* 75.15a–15b, 69.4–5b, 86.15–16b; Liu Yueshen, *Shen zhai ji* 10.16a–17a; 13.19a–21a; Huang Jin, *Huang Wenxian gong ji* 5.207–8; Xu Youren, *Zhizheng ji* 29.2b; Zheng Yuanyou, *Qiao Wu ji* 12.41b; Chen Gao, *Bu xi zhou yu ji* 13.1–2b. The increase in uxorilocal marriages may have been a result of Yuan property laws that did not allow daughters without brothers to inherit their fathers' property unless they brought in an uxorilocal husband. See Birge, "Women and Confucianism," 218.

87. From the perspective of the society as a whole, the fact that larger numbers of men were taking multiple consorts meant that some men would be left without wives, meaning that women who wished to remarry had greater choice.

88. Birge points out that this was one of the arguments made in Yuan legal rulings restricting women's rights to remarry (*Women, Property, and Confucian Reaction*, 265–66). See also Mann on the importance of women to the long-term stability of Chinese families ("Widows," 44).

In the highly competitive local elite society that had come into being over the course of the Song, patrilines and lineages alike benefited when wives were present to manage the family finances, educate the children, and supervise the inner quarters.[89] Although they couched their understanding in classical and cosmic terms, the Learning of the Way scholars recognized that, within the now firmly entrenched local elite, the morality of wives had indeed become central to the proper ordering of the household and by extension to the society itself.

In sum, once again Learning of the Way ideology responded to a broader social consensus. Just as Learning of the Way scholars had found ways to accept the humanity of courtesans and domesticate the practice of concubinage, they provided classical justifications for widow fidelity at a time when such fidelity had come to serve a variety of very useful social purposes.

## *Entertaining Exemplars*

If Learning of the Way scholars had become anxious to promote female fidelity, equally significant is the way they set about this project. Considerable evidence suggests that Learning of the Way proselytizers consciously responded to the destabilizing presence of the entertainment marketplace by creating didactic songs and poems meant to serve as entertainment, to compete with or replace the decadent music of courtesan banquets or even street performance.[90]

The power of poetry and songs to move people—for good or ill—was remarked by Li Qi, in his poetry preface for Hua Youwu's mother's Pure and Faithful Hall. Li argued for the importance of poetry in setting a moral tone for the age, noting that Confucius had collected poetry to

---

89. This is not a novel insight. There is now a sizable literature demonstrating the importance of wives to the success of local elite families. See, for example, Ebrey, *Inner Quarters*, 117–20; 183–87; Mann, *Precious Records*, 62–66, 101–5, 143–67; McDermott, "The Chinese Domestic Bursar," passim. Birge, *Women, Property, and Confucian Reaction*, chap. 3, shows that philosophers like Zhu Xi and his disciples valorized these roles for women, but we should note that they were not unique in this regard. These qualities were admired in women by numerous authors since at least the early Song. See Bossler, *Powerful Relations*, 19–20.

90. Here one is tempted to suggest a parallel to the production in our own day of self-consciously Christian rock music.

help preserve the morality of the ancient sages. Li passionately insisted on the appropriateness in his own day of praising such paragons of virtue as Hua Youwu's mother, and continued:

> I've often observed that people today admire music and beauty and devote themselves to banqueting and pleasure. They set up pavilions and gardens for their own enjoyment, and busybodies contrive clever and elaborate phrases full of empty praise to glorify them. How much more [should they praise] the true beauty of this hall! Although this is the case, whether poetry is composed or not is actually irrelevant to this hall. But if those who look at this [poetry] are thereby moved, then the heart of shame and of distinction between right and wrong will naturally develop, and the spirit of purity and fidelity will step by step arise. Ah, is this not what human hearts and the Dao of the world rely on? I therefore believe that the poetry for this hall is greatly significant, and so I am composing this preface for it.[91]

Here Li suggests that replacing poetry that celebrates banquet halls and pleasure gardens with that which celebrates monuments to fidelity can promote "the heart of shame" in people. In like manner, Song Lian explained:

> The writings of poets are plentiful, but are mostly paragraphs about mist and clouds and moon and dew, sentences about grass and trees and insects and fish. Such writing does no good, and if it were not written there would be no lack. Yet varied collections and huge volumes are published all the time. What will they think when they see the poetry about the virtuous mothers, and how it aids propriety (*ming jiao*)? Scholars who know the Dao will certainly choose it.[92]

Like Li Qi, Song Lian wants poetry composed for aesthetic entertainment to be replaced by poetry with a moral purpose. But while Li Qi and Song Lian speak of poetry that will be chosen by scholars, other Learning of the Way authors sought to transform customs on a broader scale, with poetry that could be chanted or sung.

Liu Renben, for example, wrote a set of four poems for a Faithful Widow Yu that in simple, rhythmical language tell the story of the faithful widow's life. The poems conclude with the line "My song is not excessive, I am trying to encourage the proper teachings" (*Wo ge fe*

---

91. Li Qi, "Zhen jie tang shi xu," in Zhao Qimei, *Zhao shi tie wang shan hu* 9.52b–54b.
92. Song Lian, *Song xue shi quan ji* 6.189–90. Still later in the Ming, Lü Kun likewise wrote songs to help improve female morality. See Carlitz, "Social Uses," 117.

*yi, shi li feng jiao* 我歌匪溢, 式勵風教).⁹³ In similar fashion, Huang Jin closed a poem for a filial son with the remark, "Although you may say my song is rustic, I hope it will move the simple-minded" (*Wo ge sui yun li, shu gan chi chi meng* 我歌雖云俚, 庶感蚩蚩氓). Huang also ended a poem for a faithful widow with the call to "Come hear the poems of the Faithful Widow of Wanzhou" (*Lai ting Wanzhou jie fu shi* 來聽完州節婦詩), suggesting that the poem would be performed for a listening audience.⁹⁴ Liu Guan's lengthy "Lament of Faithful Widow Zhang of Tiantai" (天台張節婦吟), closes with the lines:

| | |
|---|---|
| 絲聲按節指可尋 | The strings sound the rhythm, the fingers can follow; |
| 一彈彈爲節婦吟 | One strum after another tells the faithful widow's lament. |
| 雅頌自足開人心 | Elegant praises are themselves sufficient to open people's hearts; |
| 世乃有此瑤華音 | The world thus has this pure and glorious sound.⁹⁵ |

All of these examples suggest that Learning of the Way authors intended that their poetry would be performed: where, and for what audience, is more difficult to determine. We do know that such songs were performed at banquets honoring exemplars: several of the poems composed for Hua Youwu's mother refer to the banquet setting, and one even obliquely suggests the presence of female entertainers.⁹⁶ A comment by Yuan Jue (1266–1327) likewise indicates that poems and songs written in honor of exemplars could "originate in exhortation, and end up as banquet music" (*xian zhi yi you quan, zhong zhi yi yan yue* 先之以憂勸, 終之以燕樂).⁹⁷ But it is possible that these writers also imagined their works would enter the repertoire of popular entertainers: many surviving poems for faithful widows were written in a style that was clearly intended to appeal to broad audiences, in easy-to-understand language and often larded with colloquial phrases in the manner of *ci* poetry (reminiscent of the early didactic efforts of

---

93. Liu Renben, *Yu ting ji* 1.3a–3b.
94. Huang Jin, *Huang Wenxian gong ji* 1.16–17; 2.84.
95. Liu Guan, *Dai zhi ji* 3.29b–30a.
96. See poems by Wang Feng, Chen Yuan, and Duan Tianyou in Zhao Qimei, *Zhao shi tie wang shan hu* 9.65b–66a, 9.66b, and 9.63b–64a.
97. A similar statement is made by Cheng Tinggui, *Ju zhu xuan shi ji* 4.3b–4a; see also Yuan Jue, *Qing rong ju shi ji* 22.395–96.

Xu Ji).⁹⁸ Many take the form of popular song styles like ballads (*xing* 行) and laments (*yin* 吟).

In such poetry, the exemplary and entertainment functions of the faithful wife became completely intertwined. The faithful widow came to be a tragically poignant, romantic, and even quasi-erotic figure.⁹⁹ Wang Shixi depicted a lonely woman listening to the rain behind closed doors, while those outside pointed to the "glorious insignia" in her doorway; Wu Shidao described Faithful Widow Zhao as alone in the night, cold and crying.¹⁰⁰ Pu Daoyuan, in a mourning poem for Faithful Widow Liu, compared her to a "cassia flower, withering in the autumn wind," and to "a day lily, which expires with the evening rain."¹⁰¹ A number of authors wrote dramatic pieces in the voice of the faithful widow herself, in the mode of this one by Gong Shitai:

| | |
|---|---|
| 河可塞, 山可移 | Rivers can be stopped, mountains can be moved; |
| 志不可奪, 義不可虧 | My will cannot be overcome, righteousness cannot be abrogated. |
| 妾爲段家婦, 年紀方及笄 | When I became the wife of the Duan family, I had just reached hairpin age; |
| 上堂奉翁姑, 入室攜兩兒 | I ascended the hall and served my parents-in-law, I entered the chamber leading two sons. |
| 兒死夫亦死; 此生將何爲 | My sons died and my husband died also; how can I go on living? |
| 昔如雙鴛鴦; 今日爲孤雌 | In the past we were like a pair of mandarin ducks; Today I am a solitary hen. |
| 昔如三春花; 今日成枯枝 | In the past I was like a spring flower; now I have become a dried branch. |
| 寒風吹短髮; 明月照空帷 | The cold wind blows my short hair; the bright moon illuminates the empty curtains. |
| 百年在世能幾時 | One hundred years on the earth—how long can it last? |
| 父兮母兮不我知: 青天在上將誰欺? | My father, ah, my mother, ah: you do not know me: Who can deceive the blue sky above?¹⁰² |

---

98. E.g., see Fu Ruojin, *Fu Yuli shi wen ji* 3.11a–11b (replete with the colloquial "Don't you know" [*jun bu jian* 君不見]; 3.17b; any one of several "Ballad(s) of the Tiger-killer" ("Sha hu xing"), e.g., Wu Shidao, *Li bu ji* 9.24a–24b; Wu Lai, *Yuan ying ji* 4.40b–41a; or Yuan Jue, *Qing rong ju shi ji* 8.128.

99. See also Carlitz, "The Daughter," 39.

100. Wang Shixi 王士熙, in Su Tianjue, *Yuan wen lei* 7.13a–13b; Wu Shidao, *Li bu ji* 9.24a–24b.

101. Pu Daoyuan, *Xian ju cong gao* 4.11b–12a.

102. Gong Shitai, *Wan zhai ji* 2.1b. See also Wang Feng's poem written in the voice of a widow who committed suicide in *Wuxi ji* 2.46a–46b.

Just as Learning of the Way authors responded to perceived cultural and moral crisis by creating poetry meant to exhort and persuade through the vehicles of music and entertainment, they also began to employ dramatic and entertaining elements even in their formal encomia for literati widows. We start to see accounts of widows who slash their faces rather than remarry, and of widows who commit suicide.[103] Other widows are shown undertaking all manner of disgusting and self-mortifying tasks in service to their in-laws. Faithful widow Zhu licks the ulcers on her mother-in-law's skin, and the sores improve; faithful widow Yu, by licking her mother-in-law's sightless eyes, is able to restore her vision. Song Lian relates that when the mother-in-law of the filial daughter-in-law Fang lost her ability to move her bowels, Fang dug the feces out with her finger, not complaining even when her hands become chapped and cracked.[104] Similarly sensational elements had occasionally appeared in anecdotal accounts of commoner widows beginning in the late Southern Song, but Learning of the Way authors employed them in sober commemorations of upper-class women.[105]

Meanwhile, Yuan anecdotal accounts came to feature faithful widows along with heroic martyrs. While the depictions of martyrs featured increasingly appalling violence or supernatural manifestations, stories of faithful widows were also marked by gripping detail and moving denouements.[106] Tao Zongyi relates how the faithful widow Xiang, the

---

103. Liu Guan, *Dai zhi ji* 17.4–5b; Liu Renben, *Yu ting ji* 2.1b–2a; Wang Feng, *Wuxi ji* 2.46a–46b.

104. Liu Guan, *Dai zhi ji* 17.4–5b; Liu Renben, *Yu ting ji* 1.3a–b; Song Lian, *Song xue she quan ji* 24.899–900. Fang's story is retold in much of the same language in Lü Pu, *Zhu xi gao, xia*, 8b–9a. In a somewhat different mode, Song Lian provides a lively account of Virtuous Mother Liu, a faithful widow whose unwavering sternness earned her the sobriquet "Lady Ironface," and who was known to chase down flirtatious women in the village and beat them with a switch (Song Lian, *Song xue shi quan ji* 6.189–90).

105. For a late Southern Song anecdote for a faithful widow, see the oft-cited story of the filial widow Wu, who ate soiled rice that her mother-in-law had mistakenly thrown in the chamber pot, and later was favored with a self-replenishing supply of gold from Heaven (*YJZ, zhi bu*, 1.1555), translated in Ebrey, *Inner Quarters*, 197.

106. Stories of exemplars appear with striking prominence in Tao Zongyi's *Nancun chuo geng lu*. Tao has an entire section on "Loyal and Righteous Men" (*Nancun chuo geng lu* 14.166–70) and also recounts numerous instances of exemplary filiality (24.294–95; 27.343; 29.362; 6.74). For heroic female martyrs, see Tao Zongyi, *Nancun chuo geng lu* 27.332, 27.342–43, 10.127, 12.151–52, 22.270–71. Female heroism that engendered

15. Faithful Widow Yu (Yu *jie fu* 俞節婦, Yu Xin *qi* 俞新妻) licks the eyes of her aged and blind mother-in-law. Her assiduous attentions ultimately succeeded in restoring her mother-in-law's sight. From Liu Xiang 劉向, *Hui tu Lie nü zhuan* 繪圖列女傳 (Illustrated biographies of exemplary women), edited by (Qing) Wang Geng 汪庚, illustrations by (Ming) Qiu Ying 仇英. Reprint of Zhi bu zu zhai cang ban (Taipei: Zheng zhong shu ju, 1971), 13.1b.

wife of a traveling merchant, brought her husband's coffin back to his hometown only to discover that her mother-in-law had already remarried: Xiang then lived alone, keeping the sacrifices for her husband, and was celebrated in poetry. Woman Fu was so distraught at her husband's death that she delayed the burial until the corpse stank; in crazed grief she bit a hole in the coffin and later threw herself into the grave, though others pulled her out. When, before long, she heard her mother was planning her remarriage, she drowned herself in a well. The efforts of a powerful family to force Pure Wife Yang into remarriage led her to cut her hair and her throat, though she survived.[107]

In compelling biographies, poems, and stories like these, the prosaic

---

poetry, either that putatively composed by the victims themselves or that composed by eminent authors who were moved by their plights, was another favorite topic (3.38–40, 15.182, 27.342–43); see also Ye Ziqi, *Cao mu zi* 4.74–76.

107. Tao Zongi, *Nancun chuo geng lu* 22.274, 23.285, 29.362.

faithful widow was configured as a heroine in her own right. This process reached its apotheosis in the brilliant—and widely popular—drama *The Injustice Done to Dou E* (*Dou E yuan* 竇娥冤), by the Yuan playwright Guan Hanqing. The play tells the story of a faithful widow who refuses to abandon her vow to her husband and remarry, even when that refusal costs her her life. Significantly, Guan's play represented a radical recasting of a well-known story, changing it from a tale of perspicacious official judgment into a tale of female loyalty.

The original story, found in the *Han shu* biography of the upright official Yu Dingguo 于定國, tells of a mother-in-law who commits suicide rather than be a burden to her (unnamed) childless, widowed daughter-in-law.[108] The dead woman's daughter accuses the daughter-in-law of murder, and in spite of Yu's arguments for her innocence, the daughter-in-law is ultimately executed. A three-year drought then strikes the district, ending only when a new administrator arrives and is persuaded by Yu that the drought stems from the unjust execution. The new prefect holds sacrifices at the daughter-in-law's grave, and Heaven immediately responds with life-giving rains. Essentially, then, the original story is about good and bad government; over the centuries it was frequently alluded to in prayers for rain and served as a potent example with which to exhort emperors on the importance of just local administration.[109]

In the hands of Guan Hanqing, however, the story of the unjustly-accused daughter-in-law becomes the quintessential story of a faithful widow, who out of fidelity to her deceased husband resists remarriage even when her mother-in-law herself remarries, and later, still out of obligation to her husband, perjures herself to save her mother-in-law from judicial torture. In Guan's play, Dou E has become the indisputable heroine of the story, and—significantly—her heroism lies not in her filiality to her mother-in-law (who wants her to remarry) but in her unwavering fidelity to her husband.[110] Her steadfast loyalty moves Heaven and Earth

---

108. The language of the original story implies that once the mother-in-law is dead, the daughter-in-law will be free to remarry. See Ban Gu, *Han shu* 71.3041–42.

109. E.g., (Tang) Zhang Jiuling, *Qu jiang ji* 16.6a (in "Shang feng shi shu" 上封事書); Su Tianjue, *Zixi wen gao* 27.13a (in "Shandong jian yan san shi"山東建言三事). Cf. also Paul Cohen, *History in Three Keys*, 74.

110. See Wang Jisi, *Quan Yuan xi qu*, 1: 181–211. For an English translation of an

and imbues her with powerful moral authority. In Dou E, the notion that fidelity was the most profound of female virtues found a potent and persuasive avatar.

## Conclusion

By the last few decades of the Yuan dynasty, the figure of the faithful wife—now almost always understood as a faithful widow—was everywhere in literati culture. She appeared in a wide variety of texts, used variously (and sometimes simultaneously) to elicit material and social rewards, to express literary inspiration, for moral proselytizing, and for amusement or entertainment. The ubiquity of this faithful-widow discourse gradually began to change expectations for the behavior of women. The rising expectations are clearly evident in a comparison of the attitudes of Zhu Xi in the late twelfth century with those of his Yuan dynasty followers in the early fourteenth. Zhu Xi certainly believed that, ideally, women would remain faithful to their husbands, even unto death. Yet he admitted that "From the standpoint of ordinary customs, this is certainly unrealistic." Just how unrealistic it was in Zhu Xi's day is seen in his single—and singularly unsuccessful—effort to persuade an eminent contemporary that he should not arrange for his widowed daughter to remarry.[111] Nor was the promotion of widow fidelity particularly central to Zhu Xi's larger moral agenda: to the extent that Zhu Xi and his disciples focused on loyalty, they focused on male loyalty; to the extent they focused on wives, they were concerned primarily with maintenance of ritual distinctions within the home and with lack of jealousy toward concubines.

In contrast, Yuan authors associated with the Learning of the Way movement not only followed their peers in writing extensively of faithful widows, they were also quite adamant that all widows ought to be able to maintain fidelity. Wu Cheng, for example, rejected the notion that

---

early version of the play, see West and Idema, *Monks, Bandits, Lovers, and Immortals*, 8–36. For a trenchant discussion of how further revisions in the Ming changed the dominant metaphor of Guan's play from reciprocity (in which Dou E is seen as owing her husband a debt of fidelity) to Confucian righteousness, see West, "A Study in Appropriation."

111. For a fuller discussion, see Bossler, "Martyrs," 541–42.

women might need to remarry for financial support, suggesting that if widows died of hunger, "it is because they are lazy and inept at planning how to support themselves."[112] Yuan authors also upheld the priority of fidelity over other female virtues:

> I say that women of ancient times were not praised for their looks and attractiveness, talent or wisdom; they were only acclaimed for their fidelity and righteousness (節義). Thus those who could write like Cai Nü (蔡女)[a talented writer of the Eastern Han], or dispute like the wife of Wang (Wang *qi*, 王妻) [a reference to the famous Six Dynasties poet Xie Daoyun], were not always singled out by gentlemen. But the poems of Gong Jiang and Tao Ying [famous authors of poems on fidelity, found in the *Book of Odes* and the *Spring and Autumn Annals* respectively] have been seen repeatedly down through the ages. How could it be otherwise than for their fidelity and righteousness?[113]

One result of this was that by the end of the Yuan, what for centuries had been a broad notion of female integrity, variously manifested, had come to mean widow fidelity above all. The term *jie*, which in the Song could refer to the integrity of men or women, by the end of the Yuan had come to be associated almost exclusively with a woman's loyalty to her husband, expressed especially in refusal to remarry after his death. Moreover, what had been an ideal attainable only by a few had become an expectation held up for all.

As important work by Bettine Birge and others has shown, these new expectations also came to be supported by Yuan law, which over the course of the Yuan gradually made remarriage of widows more difficult by limiting their ability to take property into new marriages.[114] To summarize briefly: the Yuan government was anxious to preserve the fiscal integrity of tax-paying households, and in accord with steppe custom felt that wives and their property should be kept in the husbands' families even after the husbands died. Horrified by Chinese practices that allowed widows to take their property into new marriages, the

---

112. Wu Cheng, *Wu wen zheng ji* 81.3a–5a.
113. Wang Xu, *Lan xuan ji* 16.14b–16a. I am grateful to Susan Mann for identifying the wife of Wang.
114. Birge, *Women, Property, and Confucian Reaction*, 229–77; "Women and Confucianism," 230–35. See also Zheng Guiying, "Yuan chao fu nü." The basic outlines of these developments were sketched out decades ago in Holmgren, "Observations on Marriage."

Mongols in 1272 imposed the levirate on all widows, forcing them to marry their deceased husbands' younger kinsmen. A few years later, with the conquest of the Southern Song, they relaxed that imposition slightly, ruling in 1276 that women could avoid the levirate by remaining faithful and not remarrying. Still later, in the early fourteenth century, the Mongols ruled that control of a widow and her property should lie with her husband's parents (rather than with her natal family, as had been the Chinese custom to that point). A widow's in-laws were given the power to arrange her remarriage, and she was forbidden to take dowry or other property into a second marriage. In short, changes in Yuan law gradually deprived Chinese women of long-standing property rights that had made remarriage attractive, and gave husbands' families unprecedented control over widows and their property.

Birge argues that these laws reversed a Song trend toward greater property rights for women, and that they derived in part from the influence of Learning of the Way scholars at the Yuan court.[115] These views have been challenged in a review of the topic by Joseph McDermott. McDermott points out that we know so little about women's property in periods before the Song that any argument about long-term change in property regimes can only be tenuous, especially given the great diversity in customary practices across China. He demonstrates that laws restricting women's property rights were operating in some areas of China well before the Yuan, suggesting that the Mongol rulings were not completely novel. Finally, McDermott takes issue with Birge's argument for Learning of the Way influence on Yuan law, noting that her evidence is circumstantial.[116]

The findings of this book support McDermott's critique, especially with respect to this last point.[117] I have shown that, across the Song and

---

115. Birge, *Women, Property, and Confucian Reaction*, 229–77.
116. McDermott, "Women of Property," 208, 213–16. McDermott also suggests that Birge has overstated Huang Gan's position on in-laws' rights over a widow's property, and proposes that changes in laws involving landed property can be best understood by looking at landownership conditions and economic interests.
117. My evidence does not allow me directly to address Birge's argument that women's property rights improved in the Song relative to the Tang. My own reading of Song legal cases suggests that judgments were highly contingent on the specifics of individual cases (the judge's views of the moral standing of the participants, their social and

Yuan, and especially from the thirteenth century onward, a gradual but very broad cultural shift in China increasingly favored the interests of patrilineal kin groups, not least by promoting changes in the ways that women (both concubines and wives) related to those groups. Learning of the Way scholars supported that shift, but did not lead it: in the late Song, for example, the men who were most active in proselytizing for widow fidelity were at best on the periphery of Learning of the Way circles; conversely, from early in the Yuan elite men of all stripes, not just those associated with Learning of the Way, were actively proselytizing. Mongol law, based in long-standing steppe notions of women's property, may have conveniently converged with evolving Chinese attitudes to limit women's property rights and discourage widow remarriage, but there is little reason to believe that Learning of the Way advocates were particularly involved.[118] In contrast, Learning of the Way ideology was employed in earnest to support this convergence under the first Ming emperor, who adopted Mongol laws but justified them in explicitly Learning of the Way terms.[119]

Birge has made a major contribution in elucidating the process by which laws on women's property became stricter in the Yuan, and in showing how the new laws were consistent with the general social trend toward patriliny. But I would argue that far more important for the gender regime of later imperial China was the discourse of widow fidelity that developed over the course of the Song and Yuan. That discourse continued and even intensified from the Ming on: as fidelity came to be regarded as the signal female virtue, widow suicide became more common, as did the preservation of fidelity by women who had been

---

political status, and so forth). I thus find it difficult to argue for trends on the basis of case law, especially when so few cases are available. I also remain skeptical of the extent to which codified law reflected or directed social practice.

118. Birge herself seems to have modified her views on this issue: her 2003 article downplays the notion that Yuan law was directly influenced by Learning of the Way and asserts instead that the changes "were the product of a complex mixture of indigenous development and foreign influence" ("Women and Confucianism," 213). I am completely in sympathy with this latter formulation.

119. Birge, "Women and Confucianism," 238–39. For one example of the difference between Mongol and Ming attitudes, Yuan law let men marry their fathers' concubines, while Ming law punished such marriages with beheading (*ibid.*, 237–38).

only betrothed, but not actually married, to their "husbands."[120] The cult of widow fidelity, though arising from impulses that had little to do with female morality, came to shape the lives of millions of women well into the twentieth century.[121]

---

120. I have seen no Song accounts of widow suicide. Although early Yuan authors recount occasional *attempts* at widow suicide in the late thirteenth and early fourteenth centuries (see Liu Yin, *Jing xiu wen ji*), accounts of successful widow suicides become common in collected works only in the late Yuan/early Ming. Zheng Guiying, "Yuan chao fu nü," 69–70, notes that such "following in death" (*xun fu* 殉夫) suicides become a separate category of faithful women in the *Yuan history* (which was composed in the Ming), representing about 20 percent of the total. Note also that a later imperial version of Liu Yin's inscription for Widow Zhai changes the text so that instead of surviving her suicide attempt and living to a ripe old age, she is depicted as successfully committing suicide (see *Gu jin tu shu ji cheng*, as cited in Xu Bingyu, "Liao, Jin, Yuan," 222 and 236, n. 35). In general the cases collected in the *Gu jin tu shu ji cheng* portray much higher levels of violence and suicide than one sees in exemplar texts culled from Yuan collected works. Yuan sources likewise recount a very few cases of fidelity to fiancés (for one example, see Zhang Yanghao, *Gui tian lei gao* 7.4a–6b). By later imperial times, fidelity to fiancés had become a significant if controversial social phenomenon. See Weijing Lu, *True to Her Word*.

121. On the manifold ways that the fidelity discourse helped to shape twentieth-century views on women, see Judge, *The Precious Raft*.

# Conclusion

This book has traced men's writings about three categories of women over a period of nearly five centuries, showing that women were centrally implicated in the wide variety of social, political, and cultural transformations of the period. How, then, do these findings inform our understanding of broader patterns of Chinese history?

## Social Mobility and Family Strategies

The introduction to this book observed that one of the most important changes in China between the ninth and fourteenth centuries was the transformation of the elite from a small, fairly closed group of quasi-hereditary aristocrats to a significantly larger group of families whose status depended on local economic power, participation in the examination system, and occasional participation in office. The growth of markets that helped break down status hierarchies and broaden the elite in the late Tang and Song conspicuously included markets in women's labor, including entertainers, indentured servants, and "concubines" of many types. As markets created new roles for women both in and out of families, the mobility of women echoed the thrilling and terrifying mobility that Song society offered men. In theory at least, a man could pass the exams and move from lower echelons of society to higher; a woman could go from being the daughter of a desperately poor family to being a celebrated courtesan, or from being an indentured entertainer-concubine to being the nobly titled mother of a court official. Both men and women could also face downward mobility: the sons of officials could decline into obscurity, while their sisters could be consigned to concubinage or worse. (Resonances like these may help explain some of the male fascination with the "gentlewoman falling on hard times" stories.)

These processes of economic growth and status mobility dramatically altered the nature and internal dynamics of elite families, and with that the nature of their relationship to the Chinese state. In the Song, households became public and domestic life visible in new ways. Two important factors in this process were the spread of entertainment and the spread of concubinage. Where once entertainment had been provided by slave-dependents within aristocratic households, now men moved into public spaces to be entertained, and conversely women of the marketplace entered the domestic realm as entertainer-concubines. The Song state facilitated and even encouraged this process by providing government entertainers to its officials, by abandoning the sumptuary regulations that in earlier dynasties had correlated concubinage with official status, and by permitting the enfeoffment of concubine mothers and sometimes even concubine consorts. At the same time, the changes in the state's methods of official recruitment meant that men's private behavior with both courtesans and concubines took on a greater public significance: the way a man comported himself at banquets became an element in his social reputation, and the regulation of his household became a factor in judgments about his fitness for government service. This development was not uncontested: some argued that an official should be judged only by his actions in office. But scandals over dissolute banqueting and the procurement of women, in combination with factionalist demands for morality in government, ensured that the personal and domestic life of its officials would remain an arena of state concern.

One result of these developments was that the actions of a household's women took on increased public significance. Despite protestations that women's behavior, no matter how admirable, should not be publicized, by the early Southern Song discussion of elite women's lives had begun to move from funerary inscriptions into more public and circulating genres, and women's conduct became an increasingly important element in the reputation of elite households. Meanwhile, in the absence of state regulation, and driven by the social cachet of courtesan entertainments, the fad for entertainer-concubines spread throughout the expanding elite society of the Southern Song. In the countryside, some officials took courtesans from the yamen as their concubines, and government courtesans were excoriated for using those relationships to corrupt local administration. Even so, the presence of entertainers at state banquets continued to be deemed essential. Conversely, as widespread concubinage caused new tensions in elite families, the image of the concubine as a romantic and erotic entertainer began to be downplayed, replaced by an emphasis on her role as the mother of descendants. Concubines were no longer merely extra labor, but family members, and their children were (at least ideally) accorded equal status with their principal half-siblings. Paradoxically, even as concubine mothers received greater social recognition, in philosophical and legal discourse the relevance of maternity to children's status as members of the patriline was explicitly denied: paternal recognition became the critical factor in justifying claims of heredity or inheritance rights. All of these changes made concubines' status closer to that of wives, who found it necessary to guard their own positions more jealously. Philosophers responded by creating a new model of the ideal married couple, in which a man would take a concubine not out of desire but only to produce descendants, and his wife would respond not with jealousy but with joy at the prospect of extending the succession.

The Yuan government's desire to fix social status helped to reinforce this ideal. Yuan law reiterated that concubines should be of respectable background and insisted that their place in the family should be dignified by a marriage contract. These policies were emphatically meant to separate concubines, as good commoners, from public entertainers, who in theory were not to marry outside the entertainer class, and this distinction was maintained in the Ming, which reasserted Yuan laws relegating all entertainers to a sub-class of degraded persons. Yuan law remained ambivalent about the status of concubines' sons, especially with respect to property rights, but Ming policy explicitly and emphatically asserted the right of equal inheritance for all sons, "whether born of wife, concubine, or maid" (不問妻妾婢生).[1] Ming law also increased mourning for concubine mothers: the first Ming emperor wanted all sons to mourn a *shu mu* (a concubine of one's father) even if she hadn't borne sons and even if the father was still alive.[2]

---

1. Xu Pu, *Ming hui dian* 20.16. Cf. also Katkov, "The Domestication of Concubinage," 158. The Ming still distinguished between principal and lesser sons where *yin* privilege and enfeoffments were concerned.

2. Katkov, "The Domestication of Concubinage," 103–5; Ebrey, *Confucianism and Family Rituals*, 153. Thus the ritual code promulgated by the first Ming emperor further solidified concubines' position in the kinship system, although his demands

The slowly improving status of concubines in Chinese families (and perhaps the growing recognition of the moral potential of even lowly entertainers, discussed below) paralleled a very gradual increase in appreciation for the loyalty of literati wives and especially widows. Again, this phenomenon was inextricably related to political and economic developments and to state interventions. The earliest signs of augmented interest in widow loyalty emerged in the context of late Northern Song factional politics, when faithful widows and other types of principled women were celebrated along with filial sons and other exemplary persons. In this period, widows were much admired for their clever handling of family affairs and for their contributions to their husband's patrilines, but little attention was given to their loyalty to their husbands. The issue of loyalty per se came much more strongly to the fore in the Southern Song, when in the face of political crisis men began to hold up heroic female martyrs as models for male loyalty to the state. The state fed into this impulse by calling for the promotion of loyal exemplars and by rewarding exemplars generously. In part because of those rewards, by the mid- and late Southern Song claims to extraordinary virtue had become a useful tool of social aggrandizement.

In this regard, the promotion of exemplars was of a piece with other aspects of the new "localism" of the Southern Song. In a recent discussion of genealogy and local history writing in Jinhua prefecture (in Zhejiang province), Peter Bol argues that in the Southern Song, family status (at least at the local level) had come to be based on qualities such as moral reputation rather than on government service. He shows that, by the Yuan, family morality was heralded as serving a larger public good, and even as a key to the moral transformation of customs (*jiao hua* 教化) that would bring peace to the community and by extension to the state itself. Such rhetoric, Bol demonstrates, helped to justify the publicizing of family morality in genealogies and local histories, and in the preceding chapters I have shown that the same rhetoric was invoked to justify the public celebration of faithful women.[3]

---

for extensive mourning of concubine mothers were sometimes contested thereafter (Katkov, 109–10). Such contestation, and the fact that even Ming law continued to privilege wives over concubines in matters of enfeoffments, highlight the continued ambiguity of the concubine's position.

3. Bol, "Local History," 322, 329, 338–41. Bol suggests that genealogies became a way of preserving a family's reputation even in the face of declining status.

But even as state and social rewards for virtue encouraged families to promote exemplars in their midst, other social and economic dynamics ensured that the loyalty of widows was valuable to elite families in more concrete ways as well. In the highly competitive society of the Southern Song, wives' functions as household managers and educators of children were important contributors to the well-being and longevity of elite households. When a man died before his children were grown, his widow's willingness to stay and rear his descendants could be critical to the prosperity and even the survival of his line. This fact was recognized by authors who suggested that, even in the absence of state recognition, faithful widows deserved to be recognized as exemplary loyal heroines. At the same time, in a context where women and the sexual labor they provided had become highly commodified, and the status of concubines had become ever closer to that of wives, widow loyalty helped distinguish properly married wives from consorts who were merely concubines, who were typically sold or married off at their masters' deaths. In this respect, widow fidelity represented a refusal of commodification and an assertion of the integrity of the family system.

After the fall of the Southern Song, all of these factors continued to fuel the production of texts celebrating faithful widows, but other elements came into play as well. Incentives to aggrandizement increased under the Yuan, as Han men had few avenues to advancement and therefore elite families had few other opportunities for corvée relief. The Yuan government acted to restrict the runaway proliferation of awards by promulgating, for the first time in Chinese history, an official definition of a faithful widow, but the state's action was unable to stem the tide. In the face of foreign occupation, the composition and circulation of poetry volumes honoring faithful widows became a means for Han men to share in literary culture, to promote Confucian virtue, and to participate in the preservation of Han civilization. Their prolix efforts laid the foundation for the Late Imperial cult of fidelity.

A recent article by Bryna Goodman explores the impact of the Late Imperial fidelity cult on attitudes toward women's suicide in the early twentieth century. Summarizing recent findings on the later imperial period, Goodman observes: "Male scholars who recounted virtuous female suicides could have many motivations: the propagation of virtue, the erotic contemplation of exemplary female bodies, the companionship of male literary networks, the enhancement of their own family status, or commercial profit in the circulation of texts for entertainment or edification."[4] This book has shown that (with the exception of commercial profit, which does not yet seem to have been a factor in the Yuan), all of these motivations were central to the very creation of the discourse about exemplary women in the Song and Yuan. The fidelity cult, in other words, appears here not as a moral initiative that was hijacked to other social purposes; rather, these other purposes were integral to the existence of the cult in the first place. To put it another way, the investigation here suggests that the rise of the cult of fidelity was driven by social more than moral or ideological agendas.[5] This in turn raises new questions about the role of Neo-Confucian ideology in the changing gender and social orders of the Tang to Yuan period.

## *The Role of Neo-Confucianism*

In the face of the monumental changes in late Tang and early Song economy and society, the proponents of what is generally referred to as "Neo-Confucianism" articulated and systematized a moral framework that both defined and justified new social and familial roles for women (and men). As this study has shown, however, with respect to gender the putative formulators of these new frameworks (the Cheng brothers, Zhu Xi, and their followers) were drawing on ideas and attitudes already widely expressed by others. For example, in Northern Song literati writings, the abjuring of female entertainment was already portrayed as a sign of virtue. But this did not become a significant theme in Neo-Confucian writings until well after Zhu Xi, in the very late Southern Song. Likewise, although both Yang Shi in the early Southern Song and Zhu Xi somewhat later did condemn the deleterious influence of courtesans on local governance, neither advocated that the institution of government-courtesans be permanently abolished. Only in the late thirteenth and early fourteenth centuries do we see a few Neo-Confucian

---

4. Goodman, "The New Woman Commits Suicide," 68. Goodman cites Carlitz, Elvin, Ropp, and Theiss, among others. Joan Judge demonstrates the highly ramified ways that the image of the faithful woman continued to be salient in early twentieth-century debates about women's role in society. See Judge, *The Precious Raft*.

5. See also the conclusion to chap. 9.

adherents (though, interestingly, not disciples of Zhu Xi) attempting to abolish government-courtesans and praising men for eschewing concubines. Conversely, although among the elite in general we see evidence of new appreciation for and recognition of concubine mothers from at least the eleventh century, only with Zhu Xi does this become an important thread in Neo-Confucian morality. Zhu Xi did try (unsuccessfully) to persuade one high-ranking family not to marry off a widowed daughter, but he did not propagandize widow fidelity—although contemporaries like Yang Wanli were doing so.[6] In short, Neo-Confucian scholars were not so much leading changes in gender ideology as providing post-facto justifications for those changes. From this perspective, the ultimate long-term dominance of Neo-Confucian philosophy in later imperial culture seems to derive less from the movement's radical philosophical innovations than from its success in systematizing and providing classical validation for new social and cultural attitudes shaped by economic growth, new state policies, and changes in social relations.

These findings, in conjunction with several recent studies on aspects of Song intellectual and political history, call for a reassessment not only of the role of Neo-Confucianism in Song society, but also of the role of the Cheng brothers and Zhu Xi in the development of Neo-Confucian ideology, especially in its social aspects. Long-standing scholarly tradition has taught us to see Neo-Confucianism as a philosophical system created by the Cheng brothers and passed on by their disciples, and gradually coming to influence society through the proselytizing efforts of the latter. Scholarship over the past few decades has greatly complicated this picture, but scholars still tend to imagine the Cheng Learning (and later Learning of the Way) movements as involving relatively bounded groups of self-identified adherents, and tend to associate the promotion of Confucian values in Song society with that limited group. By contrast, we saw in chapter 1 that Cheng Learning–style rhetoric was expressed by Northern Song men like Huang Chang and Li Xin, who had no known connections with the movement. Other recent studies have also begun to suggest that the people we now associate with Cheng Learning in the Southern Song and Yuan also did not have a monopoly on ideas supposedly specific to a Neo-Confucian orientation. Li Cho-ying and Charles

---

6. See chap. 9 and chap. 6, respectively.

Hartman have shown that the early Southern Song Grand Councilor Qin Gui 秦檜 (1090–1155), generally depicted as an archenemy of Cheng Learning, employed in his own claims to power concepts we had thought were invented by Zhu Xi.[7] Hilde De Weerdt has likewise described how, in the early thirteenth century, examination encyclopedias that packaged Learning of the Way ideas for the commercial examination market were being compiled by teachers "unaffiliated with the Learning of the Way."[8] Although I can do no more than raise the issue here, the findings of this book likewise suggest that we need to stop thinking of Song Neo-Confucianism as defined by a particular intellectual lineage, or as the sole purview of those who claimed to be (or were later claimed as) disciples of the movement.[9]

## *Sex, Status, and the State*

This book has shown that, from at least the Song on, sex and entertainment became arenas of contestation between the state and society in China. By the Northern Song the state had become a major "owner" of female entertainers, both as court performers and as government-courtesans. The state also insisted on its right to regulate the interactions of its officials with those entertainers, and in the process subjected the private moral behavior of the former to new scrutiny. Gradually, however, commercialization and the expansion of the entertainment market largely outstripped the state's capacity for regulation and control. The Southern Song state gave up training its own entertainers for court festivities, finding it easier simply to hire needed entertainers on the open market. Simultaneously, however, the institution of government-courtesans spread from prefectures to counties, so the number of women nominally

---

7. Li Cho-ying and Hartman, "A Newly Discovered Inscription."
8. De Weerdt, *Competition over Content*, 271–76.
9. We might ask, for example, why we do not currently include men like Sima Guang (whose ideas on family morality Zhu Xi adopted wholesale into his *Family Rituals*) as among the foundational thinkers of Song Neo-Confucian thought. As Charles Hartman has pointed out, some Southern Song commentators did regard Sima Guang as a founder of the movement, and even Zhu Xi himself for a time included Sima Guang among the lineage of his teachers. See Hartman, "Li Hsin-ch'uan," 338–39, and "Zhu Xi and his World," 117, n. 13. See also Ebrey's introduction in Zhu Xi, *Chu Hsi's Family Rituals*, xv–xxii.

under state control increased. The state was increasingly hard-pressed to regulate entertainers' relationships with officials or control the abuses of local authority to which those relationships frequently gave rise.

The changes in the state's relationship with entertainers were associated with significant shifts in the social categories of respectable (*liang*) and base (*jian*). Until the late Tang, entertainers (*ji*) for the most part had been slaves or dependents of the government or in the households of a quasi-aristocratic elite. This situation changed in the late Tang and Song: the possibility that blameless and respectable commoner women could end up as entertainers, or that erstwhile entertainers could marry back into respectable status, was widely and officially recognized in the Song, and the categories of respectable and base came to be associated with (often temporary) occupation, rather than with hereditary moral quality.

With the fall of the Song, the Yuan government sought to stem the fluidity in society by (theoretically) registering all entertainers and reasserting class boundaries that would prevent the entertainers from having relationships with those outside the entertainer class. But in the absence of an effective bureaucracy, the Yuan government was unable to enforce its regulations: its highest officials flaunted their liaisons with famous entertainers, and commoners continued to take up entertainment professions. This was at least in part because within the broader society the reinvigoration of Confucian principles was helping to cement the notion that moral status was based in individual behavior, not ascriptive categories. Moral stigma continued to be a function of behavior as much as of ascriptive status, and a nominally dishonorable actress could be recognized for her artistic talent or moral virtue. The early Ming government reiterated Yuan regulations perpetuating a hereditary and endogamous class of musician-entertainers, and at one point it attempted to do away with the institution of government-courtesans altogether.[10] But it, too,

---

10. According to the fifteenth-century writer Wang Qi (1433–99), the first Ming emperor instituted very strict penalties for officials who spent the night with courtesans, and permitted no amnesties (Wang Qi, *Yu pu za ji* 1.7). This regulation was later followed by an outright ban on government-courtesans, apparently beginning in the Xuande reign period (1426–35). See Peterson, *Bitter Gourd*, 143, and Wai-yee Li, "The Late Ming Courtesan," p. 47. Note also the comment in the *Ming History* biography of Liu Guan 劉觀 (1385 *jin shi*) that "at the time, there was not yet a prohibition

was unable to stem a flourishing commercial market in entertainment, or to stop literati and officials from interacting with entertainers.

These findings provide new perspectives on Matthew Sommer's influential discussion of the Qing state's regulation of sex in the eighteenth century. Sommer has argued that the Yongzheng emperor's (r. 1723–35) 1723 abolition of the juridical category of dishonorable persons (*jian min*) was an attempt to create a new moral paradigm for Chinese society. He suggests that, up until the Yongzheng reforms, sexual norms in Chinese society were based in status categories of dishonorable or respectable. Before Yongzheng's action, engaging in sex work was not illegal for people of dishonorable status (including musicians, among others), whereas for respectable commoners, not to mention those of official status, the sale of sex was illegal. Yongzheng's abolition of all categories of dishonorable status suddenly made it incumbent on all people to behave as good commoners. Sex work in all forms became illegal, and all men and women were now held to sexual norms based on gender rather than on status performance.

Sommer is dealing with a much later period of Chinese history than that considered in this volume, and it may well be that ascriptive categories had more force in the Qing than in the period under study here: even Yuan and Ming laws establishing hereditary dishonorable categories and prohibiting the intermarriage of entertainers and other classes were by far more clearly and forcefully articulated than any we have from the Song. Still, the chapters above have shown that even when ascriptive categories were legally salient, in social practice they were often fluid and contingent. This remained true even in the Qing, when contracts of indenture continued to turn commoner women into temporary slaves, and when it remained possible for an entertainer to renounce her past and "follow the respectable" (*cong liang*), marrying into respectable status.[11]

---

against government-courtesans" (*shi wei you guan ji zhi jin* 時未有官妓之禁) (Zhang Tingyu, *Ming shi* 151.4185). It is unclear to me whether the state continued to register government-courtesans in the late fifteenth and sixteenth centuries: a few poems from this period continue to mention them. But in any case a private market in courtesans presumably continued through this period, for it was thriving by the late sixteenth and early seventeenth century, as much scholarship on the late Ming attests. For one example, see Ko, *Teachers of the Inner Chambers*, 251–82.

11. Mann, *Precious Records*, 37–42; Sommer, *Sex, Law, and Society*, 235–41.

In other words, there is ample evidence that throughout later imperial China, as in the Song and Yuan, norms of status and gender performance interacted with one another, and were highly contingent on situation and context. Sommer does demonstrate persuasively that, at lower levels of society, changes in the law occasioned by Yongzheng's edict had a significant impact. Still, the fact that the edict had no discernable effect on courtesan entertainments among the elite demonstrates that status and acceptable standards of gender performance continued to be intertwined even after 1723.[12] Although the law may have flattened juridical categories, it never applied equally to all. This in turn suggests that Yongzheng may have been less concerned about asserting a universal moral code than he was, as Sommer also notes, about containing growing "sexual anarchy" in the countryside, brought about by declining economic conditions and the growing population of poor, rogue males.[13]

## *Masculinity*

Over the past decade, a number of scholars have begun to explore the meanings of masculinity in Chinese culture. Scholars like Martin Huang and Kam Louie have identified two coexisting, and sometimes conflicting, styles of Chinese masculinity, one defined by scholarly attainment and moral uprightness, and one defined by martial (and often violent) heroism.[14] Huang's work, in particular, identifies a repertoire of gendered tropes that were invoked in discussions of manliness or masculinity from earliest times. The analogy between a rejected lover and a minister out of favor was elaborately established by Qu Yuan in the third century BCE; the idea that moral integrity, rather than action or political success,

---

12. Sommer at several points acknowledges that he finds no cases involving elite courtesans (*Sex, Law, and Society*, passim). On the High Qing courtesan quarters, see Mann, *Precious Records*, 125–41.

13. Sommer, *Sex, Law, and Society*, 306, 311, and 316–19. Rogue males were poor men who, partly due to a skewing of sex ratios brought on by female infanticide and concubinage, were unable to marry and thus lacked the constraints of family life. I return to this point below.

14. See Huang, *Negotiating Masculinities*; Louie, *Theorising Chinese Masculinity*; Mann, "The Male Bond"; and Rouzer, *Articulated Ladies*.

defined a hero, and further that moral strength was associated with rejection of female sexuality, was articulated by Mencius, and before him Confucius. The notion that writing, and especially historical writing, could redeem shameful or craven action (or inaction) was established no later than Sima Qian. Huang sensitively shows that all of these tropes informed later imperial ideals of what a man should or could be. But precisely because they were so ancient and so frequently deployed, these tropes are not easily associated with specific historical change in gender relations or gendered identities. I suggest that evolution in the ways that men wrote about women (and about other men's relationships with women) provides useful insights into shifts in male gender identities—changes in the ways men positioned themselves vis-à-vis women, and changes in ideas about how ideal men should behave. In short, part of the significance of the categories of courtesans, concubines, and faithful women in Song and Yuan gender discourse lies in the fact that these were the categories of women against which men were constantly defining themselves and being defined.

Playful interactions with courtesans and teasing about serving maids—and writing about these interactions—were an important part of what it meant to be an upper-class male in the Northern Song.[15] But by the late eleventh century alternatives to this romantic ideal were being posed, on the one hand, by sober moral philosophers like the Cheng brothers, and on the other by dedicated government bureaucrats like Sima Guang and Wang Anshi, and even by anxious social critics like Huang Chang and Li Xin.[16] The fall of the Northern Song following the romantic excesses of Emperor Huizong further discredited the model of literati as connoisseurs of art and romance. Even as (or perhaps because) government-courtesans were becoming available to lower levels of the bureaucracy and entertainer-concubines were becoming a fad among the bourgeoning local elite, the Mencian notion—that a real man is by definition a moral man who is impervious to sexual desire, and conversely that female sexuality is dangerous to male virtue and can undermine

---

15. This image of a romantic man was very much in tune with the Northern Song concern for aesthetic refinement discussed by Ronald Egan in *The Problem of Beauty*.
16. On the Cheng brothers, Sima Guang, and Wang Anshi, see Bol, "*This Culture of Ours*," especially chaps. 7–9. On Huang Chang and Li Xin, see chap. 1 above.

male action—was aggressively proselytized, with the result that by the late Southern Song the ideal man was increasingly portrayed as restrained and impervious to the charms of women, perhaps even repelled by the overt sexuality that courtesans and entertainer-concubines represented. Accordingly, where in the Tang and into the Northern Song the designation *feng liu* (風流 "romantic," dashing) could be a compliment, by the Southern Song and Yuan it was generally a criticism. This transition echoes reactions against aristocratic values familiar from other times and places, as luxury and excess were denounced in favor of values conducive to the ascent and perpetuation of families in a competitive market economy.

The transition was gradual and certainly never absolute: in the late twelfth century, Zhou Bida, Neo-Confucian sympathies notwithstanding, was still attending courtesan banquets and writing humorous poetry about friends' serving maids. But the Tang model of the ideal literatus as *feng liu* hero, fashionably dressed and pursuing relationships with elegant women, had begun to give way to alternative models of the serious bureaucrat or the self-cultivated scholar, uninterested in luxury or sex. Rather than competing with one another in poetic composition to earn the attention of beautiful women, or teasing one another about girlfriends, young men were exhorted to encourage each other in moral self-cultivation. Literati began building academies—far away from the temptations of urban centers—that provided spaces where this new model of male interaction could be inculcated and practiced. Along with these changes, men's writing energies, too, were channeled not into poetry about beautiful entertainers, but into celebrations of moral exemplars. In the Southern Song, the subjects of these writings were still mostly heroic martyrs and models of loyalty to the state, but by the Yuan they had predominantly become faithful widows, who represented above all restraint and abstemiousness for the good of the family.

In this and other respects, and like the new values for upper-class women, the new ideals for men can be seen in part as a response to a more open but also more competitive elite society, in which the widespread availability of commodified entertainment, especially sexual entertainment, was gradually reconciled with the demands of family survival and success. Just as the faithful widow's sexuality was renounced for the good of the family, the sexual energies of her husband—even with his concubines—were now theoretically channeled to the production of descendants rather than to pleasure: the ideal man was encouraged to have concubines, but discouraged from enjoying them.[17] In other words, the new values posited that the sexuality of both men and women would be constrained for the good of the patriline.

This model was reinforced by the Yuan conquest: courtesans might still be symbols of pleasure and power for members of the Mongol court, but the discourses of Han literati esteemed self-restraint. Now when Han literati wrote paeans to entertainers, they celebrated not the performers' beauty or erotic charms, but rather their talent and moral virtue: a courtesan's performance was now appreciated as an expression of the Confucian Dao.[18]

Significantly, in spite of the imperiled Southern Song political situation and the relative impotence of the literati class under the Yuan, we do not see in the Song or Yuan the sorts of anguished concern about scholarly versus active or military forms of masculinity that Huang and others have identified in later imperial China. Song and Yuan men writing about exemplars did frequently compare women's heroism to that of men, and found the latter wanting. They did suggest that men, by abrogating moral responsibility, were failing to act like proper men. But they did not blame men's weakness on their scholarly training and devotion to literature and culture (*wen*), or suggest that they should be more physically or militarily active, as some Ming writers were to do. Nor do Song fiction sources negatively compare scholars to lower-class, unrestrained martial heroes, as they do in the late Ming. And rather than satirize the fact that men are writing about heroism rather than living it, as Ming writers sometimes did, in the Song and Yuan authors still portrayed the act of writing as an appropriate form of moral (and masculine) action. In short, through the Song and Yuan *wen* forms of masculinity were overwhelmingly privileged over physical or military prowess.[19]

---

17. Recall that in the Northern Song, praise for men who did not keep concubines was couched in terms of praise for frugality; by the Southern Song and Yuan it was increasingly couched in terms of lack of desire.

18. We might see in this move a resolution of the Northern Song tension, noted by Ronald Egan, between discourses of aestheticism and connoisseurship and discourses emphasizing moral cultivation. See Egan, *The Problem of Beauty*, 374–75.

19. Based on his study of Wen Tianxiang, Richard Davis has argued that loyalty was

Paradoxically, the threat and reality of conquest itself seems to have been critical in this state of affairs. Highly militarized steppe societies may have proffered an alternative style of masculinity, but that type of masculinity was associated with cultural values that were inimical to (elite) Chinese ways of thinking and (elite) Chinese ways of life. Instead, with Chinese culture under threat from invasion and occupation, Chinese literati asserted that in writing about faithful women they were helping to serve the Dao and preserving cultural values that had been threatened by the Mongol conquest. They explicitly took comfort in the belief that by celebrating exemplars, they were fulfilling their own moral duty and assuring the survival of Chinese culture under an alien regime.[20] In this way, the discourse of widow fidelity came to construct participation in *wen* as an intensely masculine, even heroic activity. The fidelity discourse insisted that it was women's role to be virtuous, and men's role to write about virtuous women: the virtue of women proved that "proper human relations truly cannot be extinguished," and "scholars and gentlemen who understand the importance of human relations write poems to extol [them]."[21] In other words, the cult of female fidelity was both predicated on, and helped reinforce, the notion that the proper calling of elite men was above all to write.

---

the preeminent masculine virtue in the Song (*Wind Against the Mountain*). While I do not deny that Wen, and others like him, may have seen loyalty as a defining element of their masculinity, I believe I have shown that the dominant gender discourse in the late Song and Yuan focused on the loyalty of women. To be sure, those writings were by precisely the men who had not committed suicide.

20. Several scholars of the cult of fidelity in later imperial China have explored the psychological dimensions of literati devotion to writing about faithful women. While the evidence from the Yuan does not bear out T'ien Ju-k'ang's argument that men promulgated the cult of fidelity to relieve the intense psychological stress of the late imperial examination system (the examination system was not even functioning for much of the period), Yuan texts do suggest that men found writing about female exemplars psychologically satisfying. See T'ien, *Male Anxiety and Female Chastity*, especially chap. 5. Carlitz argues that men's writings about faithful-female suicides in the Ming allowed men to express a vicarious freedom and rebellion against power structures ("The Daughter," 45–46).

21. An Xi, *An Mo'an xian sheng wen ji* 1.6–7; Zhao Fang, *Dong shan cun gao* 2.31a–32b. I elaborate this point further in Bossler, "Gender and Empire," 214–16.

## Historical Cycles and Secular Change

As Huang's discussion shows, the untroubled confidence of Song and Yuan literati in the inherent manliness of *wen* was not shared by their successors in the Ming: although *wen* continued to be one important marker of elite masculinity through the remainder of the imperial era, new historical conditions were to alter its valence in different periods. More broadly, although the major transitions in social and gender relations outlined in this book established a basic pattern for the Late Imperial period, neither Chinese society nor gender relations were static after the Yuan. Rather, the interaction of economic growth and decline, state interests, and family priorities produced both cyclical and long-term linear social change in male-female relations.

For example, courtesan entertainments continued to be an important element of literati social life into the early twentieth century. Some features of literati discourse about courtesans appear cyclically: at almost every point of political transition after the mid Tang, mourning for the previous era was expressed through nostalgic writings about a lost world of elegant entertainments.[22] Yet courtesans' importance as cultural markers also varied over time. The celebration of romance and sentiment (*qing*) that characterized the late Tang and early Northern Song became muted in the Southern Song. By the early Ming, Neo-Confucian attitudes toward sex and desire seem to have limited the ways men were willing to write about their interactions with entertainers, and (as noted above), the government apparently sought to ban government-courtesans. Yet by the late Ming, as part of a reaction against what was then seen as Neo-Confucianism's unnatural stifling of human feeling, and amidst a widespread reassertion of the importance of *qing*, romantic relationships between literati and courtesans again became fashionable and celebrated.[23] In the early Qing, some expressed nostalgia for the élan of the late Ming courtesan quarters, while others deplored the decadence

---

22. The *Beili zhi*, the *DJM*, *Meng liang lu*, the *QLJJZ*, and the *Ban qiao za ji* of Yu Huai in the late Ming can all be seen in this light.

23. Or at least the nostalgic imaginings of later authors made this appear to be the case. See especially Wai-yee Lee, "The Late Ming Courtesan." One likewise wonders how much our current scholarly images of Chinese courtesans have been shaped by the focus of individual researchers.

and debauchery of the period. With economic recovery, the courtesan quarters experienced a renaissance in the High Qing, although demographic pressure made the presence of female entertainers an even greater luxury than it had been in earlier periods.[24]

Concubinage, too, remained central to Chinese family life throughout the imperial period but was imagined and described in changing ways over time. Between the ninth and twentieth centuries, the Chinese government effectively gave up trying to regulate which men could keep concubines or how many they could have.[25] We do see some changes in attitudes toward concubines after the Yuan, when Confucian efforts to promote the attachment of concubines to their masters' families seem to have had some effect. In the Yuan, celebration of the fidelity of concubines to their deceased husbands was limited to anecdotal sources.[26] In contrast, by the Ming and Qing, this had changed: exemplar texts honoring concubines (usually along with wives), became fairly common, often under the rubric of "double fidelity" (*shuang jie* 雙節).[27] The absence of restrictions on who could take a concubine, in combination with intensified expectations that neither concubines nor wives would remarry, helped contribute over time to the creation of an underclass of rogue males (*guang gun* 光棍, lit. "bare sticks") who could not afford to marry and raise a family.[28] We have no evidence for the existence of *guang gun* in the Song and Yuan, but we may see the earliest intimations of concern

---

24. Mann, *Precious Records*, 125–26.

25. The Ming code did stipulate that only sonless commoners over forty years of age were allowed to take concubines (Jiang Yonglin, *The Great Ming Code*, 84) and the Ming statutes restricted men of a few specified noble ranks to rather modest numbers of *yinq qie* (Xu Pu, *Ming hui dian* 54.15a–b), but these regulations seem not to have been enforced, and the Qing code seems not to have addressed the issue at all. Moreover, given the easy slippage in status between serving maids (numbers of which were not regulated) and concubines, these regulation were essentially moot in any case.

26. For example, Tao Zongyi recounts the *chuan qi*-like biography of Li Ge, a courtesan who refused to practice her profession and ultimately died loyally with her literatus husband, and tells of Wang Fuonu, a beautiful courtesan purchased by a merchant as his concubine, who entered a nunnery after her husband's death (*Nancun chuo geng lu* 27.331, 27.340–41). Here images of exemplars and entertainers intersected and overlapped, in tales that simultaneously edified and entertained.

27. See, e.g., (Ming) Xu Xiangqing, *Yun cun ji* 10.2a–3a.

28. See Sommer, 306. To be sure, high rates of female infanticide were also an important factor in this development.

for the ability of poor men to marry in Yuan laws that, in contrast to the Song, do not insist that a man divorce an unfaithful wife. Still, in spite of ideology promoting the attachment of concubines to their husbands' families, part of the institution's appeal continued to be precisely its flexibility, the fact that families were never *required* to make concubines permanent members of the household if they chose not to. Research on concubinage in the early twentieth century shows that Chinese families were still very much making use of this flexibility, treating concubines and maids (and their children) as kin when it was convenient to do so, but not hesitating to abandon them when circumstances warranted.[29]

Finally, the cult of fidelity, too, lasted until the end of imperial China. The Yuan definition of a faithful widow was adopted by all later dynasties, and through the centuries the fidelity cult continued to be perpetuated through the vehicle of male writing, especially the production of biographies celebrating faithful exemplars. Still, although the fidelity cult was already clearly in evidence in Yuan times, there is no question that its form in the Yuan was different in many significant respects from what it was to become in the Ming and Qing. Some of these changes were also clearly cyclical. Martyrdom became a relatively more dominant theme in writings on fidelity at times of political crisis, such as the periods of dynastic transition between the Song and the Yuan and between the Yuan and the Ming; in periods of relative peace, writings about faithful widows were more common. The policies of the Ming founder (who maintained Yuan property laws that made it economically difficult for women to remarry), the continued interests of patrilineal kin groups, and the literati penchant for social aggrandizement all contributed to the entrenchment of the ideal of female fidelity in the Ming. The widespread production of local gazetteers provided new venues for the publication of massive numbers of biographies of faithful women, while central and local government officials collaborated in the construction of shrines and other monuments commemorating them.[30] Meanwhile, standards for women's faithful behavior escalated in scope and intensity. I have already noted the increased expectation that concubines would remain faithful. More alarmingly, where suicide to follow a husband in

---

29. See Watson, "Wives, Concubines, and Maids."
30. See especially T'ien, *Male Anxiety and Female Chastity,* and Carlitz, "Shrines."

death (as opposed to suicide to avoid rape) was rare in the Yuan, and fidelity to deceased fiancés was likewise unusual in that period, both were widely celebrated in the late Ming and Qing. Violence that was seen only in informal anecdotal accounts in the Yuan had become by Ming and Qing times a common feature even of formal biographies of faithful women, including those who were widows rather than martyrs. In short, after the Song and Yuan, the fidelity cult gradually came to encompass more types of women and demanded more of them, and as in the Song and Yuan, these developments were often conditioned by social and political factors that had little to do with female morality per se.[31] By the Qing, our sources become good enough to let us begin to see the various ways women themselves viewed, negotiated, and manipulated the cult and understood their place in it.[32]

The persistence and recurrence of these patterns of social and family life over centuries bespeak the tremendous flexibility and resilience of the family system and gender order that came into being over the course of the Song and Yuan. They also reflect the salience of desire and affective relationships in historical change. Desire and romantic love helped to fuel the popularity of courtesans and concubines; affection for concubine mothers and grandmothers contributed to the breakdown in status boundaries; compassion for young women who died valiantly inspired early writers on female fidelity; filial sentiment inspired many a writer on faithful widows. These emotions came into play especially, though not exclusively, in the context of men's relationships with women, and have often been ignored or overlooked. Recognizing their importance in the lives of Song and Yuan literati enriches our understanding of them and their times, and can perhaps enhance our understanding of our own times as well.

---

31. See, for example, Theiss, *Disgraceful Matters*, and Sommer, *Sex, Law, and Society*.
32. Theiss, *Disgraceful Matters*; Weijing Lu, *True to Her Word*.

REFERENCE MATTER

# Bibliography

## ABBREVIATIONS

| | |
|---|---|
| *Chang bian* | Li Tao, *Xu zi zhi tong jian chang bian* |
| *Chuan fang ji* | Hua Yuncheng et al., *Hua shi chuan fang ji* |
| *CSJCCB* | *Cong shu ji cheng chu bian* |
| *CSJCXB* | *Cong shu ji cheng xin bian* |
| *DJM* | Meng Yuanlao, *Dongjing meng hua lu zhu* |
| *GXJBCS* | *Guo xue ji ben cong shu* |
| *QLJJZ* | Xia Tingzhi, *Qing lou ji jian zhu* |
| *QMJ* | *Ming gong shu pan qing ming ji* |
| *QSW* | *Quan Song wen* |
| *SHY* | Xu Song, *Song hui yao ji gao* |
| *SKQS* | *Si ku quan shu* |
| *SS* | Tuotuo et al., *Song shi* |
| *YDZ* | *Da Yuan sheng zheng guo chao dian zhang.* |
| *YJZ* | Hong Mai, *Yijian zhi* |
| *YS* | Song Lian et al., *Yuan shi* |

An Xi 安熙. *An Mo'an xian sheng wen ji* 安默庵先生文集. *CSJCXB* (q.v.), vol. 66. Shanghai: Shangwu yin shu guan, 1985.
Anon. *Zhou xian ti gang* 州縣提綱. *SKQS* (q.v.), vol. 602.

Bai Pu 白樸. *Tian lai ji* 天籟集. *SKQS* (q.v.), vol. 1488.
Ban Gu 班固. *Han shu* 漢書. Beijing: Zhonghua shu ju, 1962.
Bei Qiong 貝瓊. *Qingjiang wen ji* 清江文集. *SKQS* (q.v.), vol. 1228.
Bernhardt, Kathryn. "A Ming-Qing Transition in Chinese Women's History? The Perspective from Law." In *Remapping China: Fissures in Historical Terrain*, edited by Gail Hershatter et al., 42–58. Stanford: Stanford University Press, 1996.
———. *Women and Property in China.* Stanford: Stanford University Press, 1999.
Bi Zhongyou 畢仲游. *Xi tai ji* 西臺集. *CSJCXB* (q.v.), vol. 62.
Bian Yongyu 卞永譽. *Shi gu tang shu hua hui kao* 式古堂書畫彙考. *SKQS* (q.v.), vols. 827–29.
Bickford, Maggie. "Huizong's Paintings: Art and the Art of Emperorship." In *Emperor Huizong and Late Northern Song China: The Politics of Culture and the Culture of Politics*, edited by Patricia Buckley Ebrey and Maggie Bickford, 453–513 (q.v.).
Birch, Cyril, ed. *Anthology of Chinese Literature.* New York: Grove Press, 1965–72.
Birge, Bettine. "Women and Confucianism from Song to Ming: The Institutionalization of Patrilineality." In *The Song-Yuan-Ming Transition in Chinese History*, edited by Paul J. Smith and Richard von Glahn (q.v.), 212–40.

———. *Women, Property, and Confucian Reaction in Sung and Yüan China (960–1368)*. Cambridge: Cambridge University Press, 2002.
Bokenkamp, Stephen. "Purification Ritual of the Luminous Perfected." In *Religions of China in Practice*, edited by Donald Lopez, 268–77. Princeton: Princeton University Press, 1996.
Bol, Peter K. "Local History and Family in Past and Present." In *The New and the Multiple: Sung Senses of the Past*, edited by Thomas H. C. Lee, 307–48. Hong Kong: Chinese University Press, 2004.
———. *"This Culture of Ours": Intellectual Transition in Tang and Sung China*. Stanford: Stanford University Press, 1992.
Bossler, Beverly. "Faithful Wives and Heroic Maidens: Politics, Virtue, and Gender in Song China" 唐宋女性與社會. In *Tang Song nüxing yu shehui*, edited by Deng Xiaonan 鄧小南, 751–84. Shanghai: Shanghai ci shu chu ban she, 2003.
———. "Faithful Wives and Heroic Martyrs: State, Society and Discourse in the Song and Yuan" 中国の歴史世界、統合のシステムと多元的発展. In *Chūgoku no rekishi sekai, tōgō no shisutemu to tagenteki hatten*, edited by Chūgokushi gakkai 中国史学会, 507–56. Tokyo: Metropolitan University Press, 2002.
———. "Fantasies of Fidelity: Loyal Courtesans to Faithful Wives." In *Beyond Exemplar Tales: New Approaches to Chinese Women's Lives*, edited by Joan Judge and Hu Ying, 158–74. Berkeley: Global, Area, and International Archive, University of California Press, 2011.
———. "Gender and Empire: A View from Yuan China." *Journal of Medieval and Early Modern Studies* 34, no. 1 (2004): 197–223.
———. "Gender and Entertainment at the Song Court." In *Servants of the Dynasty*, edited by Anne Walthall, 261–79. Berkeley: University of California Press, 2008.
———. *Powerful Relations: Kinship, Status, and the State in Sung China (960–1279)*. Cambridge, MA: Council on East Asian Studies Publications, Harvard University Press, 1998.
———. "Shifting Identities: Courtesans and Literati in Song China." *Harvard Journal of Asiatic Studies* 62, no. 1 (June 2002): 5–37.
———. "Song dai de jia ji he qie" 宋代的家妓和妾 (Household Courtesans and Concubines in the Song Dynasty). In *Jiatingshi yanjiu de xinshiye* 家庭史研究的新視野, edited by Zhang Guogang 張国刚, 206–17. Beijing: Xin zhi san lian shu dian, 2004.
———(柏文莉). "Song-Yuan mu zhi zhong de 'qie' zai jia ting zhong de yi yi ji qi li shi bian hua" 宋元墓誌中的'妾'在家庭中的意義及其歷史變化. *Dongwu li shi xue bao (Soochow Journal of History)* 東吳歷史學報 12 (December 2004): 95–128.
———. "Teisei Chūgoku ni okeru Jendashi kenkyū no hōhō ron—Shu Shi no Tō Chūyū kokuhatsu jiken wo rei to shite" 帝政中国におけるジエンダ発史研究の方法論—朱熹の唐仲友告—事件を例として—. *Osaka shiritsu daigaku Toyoshi ronso [Journal of Osaka City University Asian History]* Special Issue No. 3 (December 2007): 171–85.
———. "Vocabularies of Pleasure: Categorizing Female Entertainers in the Late Tang Dynasty." *Harvard Journal of Asiatic Studies* 72.1 (2012): 71–99.
Bray, Francesca. *Technology and Gender: Fabrics of Power in Late Imperial China*. Berkeley: University of California Press, 1997.

Cai Kan 蔡戡. *Ding zhai ji* 定齋集. *SKQS* (q.v.), vol. 1157.
Cai Xiang 蔡襄. *Cai Xiang ji* 蔡襄集. Edited by Xu Bo 徐𤊹 and Wu Yining 吳以寧. Shanghai: Shanghai gu ji chu ban she, 1996.
Cai Yong 蔡邕. *Cai zhong lang ji* 蔡中郎集. *SKQS* (q.v.), vol. 1063.
Cao Yanyue 曹彥約. *Chang gu ji* 昌谷集. *SKQS* (q.v.), vol. 1167.
Carlitz, Katherine. "The Daughter, the Singing-Girl, and the Seduction of Suicide." *Nan Nü* 3, no. 1 (2001): 22–46.
——— . "Desire, Danger, and the Body: Stories of Women's Virtue in Late Ming China." In *Engendering China*, edited by Christine Gilmartin et al., 101–24. Cambridge, MA: Harvard University Press, 1994.
——— . "Shrines, Governing-Class Identity, and the Cult of Widow Fidelity in Mid-Ming Jiangnan." *Journal of Asian Studies* 56, no. 3 (August 1997): 612–40.
——— . "The Social Uses of Female Virtue in Late Ming Editions of *Lie nü zhuan*." *Late Imperial China* 12, no. 2 (December, 1991): 117–48.
Chaffee, John W. *Branches of Heaven: A History of the Imperial Clan of Sung China*. Harvard East Asian Monographs. Cambridge, MA: Harvard University Asia Center, Harvard University Press, 1999.
——— "The Rise and Regency of Empress Liu (969–1033)." *Journal of Song-Yuan Studies* 31 (2001): 1–25.
——— . *The Thorny Gates of Learning in Sung China: A Social History of the Examinations*. Cambridge: Cambridge University Press, 1985.
Chang Bide 昌彼得 et al. *Song ren zhuan ji zi liao suo yin* 宋人傳記資料索引. 6 vols. Taipei: Ding wen shu ju, 1974–76.
Chang, Kang-i Sun. *The Evolution of Chinese Tz'u poetry: From Late T'ang to Northern Sung*. Princeton: Princeton University Press, 1980.
Chang, Kang-i Sun, and Haun Saussy, eds. *Women Writers of Traditional China: An Anthology of Poetry and Criticism*. Stanford: Stanford University Press, 1999.
Chao Buzhi 晁補之. *Ji lei ji* 雞肋集. *SKQS* (q.v.), vol. 1118.
Chao Gongwu 晁公武. *Jun zhai du shu zhi* 郡齋讀書志. *SKQS* (q.v.), vol. 674.
Chen Changfang 陳長方. *Wei shi ji* 唯室集. *SKQS* (q.v.), vol. 1139.
Chen Cisheng 陳次升. *Dang lun ji* 讜論集. *SKQS* (q.v.), vol. 427.
Chen Dezhi 陳得芝, Qiu Shulin 邱樹林, and He Zhaoji 何兆吉. *Yuan dai zou yi ji lu* 元代奏議集錄. Yuan dai shi liao cong kan. Hangzhou: Zhejiang gu ji chu ban she, 1998.
Chen Gao 陳高. *Bu xi zhou yu ji* 不繫舟漁集. *SKQS* (q.v.), vol. 1216.
Chen Jingsong. "To Make People Happy, Drama Imitates Joy: The Chinese Theatrical Concept of Mo." *Asian Theatre Journal* 14, no. 1 (Spring 1997): 38–55.
Chen Liang 陳亮. *Chen Liang ji* 陳亮集. Beijing: Zhonghua shu ju, 1974.
Chen Lü 陳旅. *An ya tang ji* 安雅堂集. *SKQS* (q.v.), vol. 1213.
Chen Shidao 陳師道. *Hou shan ju shi wen ji* 後山居士文集. Shanghai: Shanghai gu ji chu ban she, 1984.
——— . *Hou shan shi hua* 後山詩話. In *Li dai shi hua* 歷代詩話, vol. 1, edited by (Qing) He Wenhuan 何文煥, 301–15. Beijing: Zhonghua shu ju, 1992.
——— . *Hou shan tan cong* 後山談叢. In *Hou shan tan cong; Ping zhou ke tan* 後山談叢; 萍洲可談, edited by Li Weiguo 李偉國, 1–92. Tang Song shi liao bi ji cong kan ed. Beijing: Zhonghua shu ju, 2007.

Chen Shunyu 陳舜俞. *Du guan ji* 都官集. *SKQS* (q.v.), vol. 1096.
Chen Xiang 陳襄. *Gu ling ji* 古靈集. *SKQS* (q.v.), vol. 1093.
Chen Yu 陳郁. *Cang yi hua yu: nei bian (shang xia juan); wai bian (shang xia juan)* 藏一話腴: 内編 (上下卷) 外編 (上下卷). *SKQS* (q.v.), vol. 865.
Chen Yuanlong 陳元龍, ed. *(Yu ding) Li dai fu hui* 御定歷代賦彙. *SKQS* (q.v.), vols. 1419–22.
Chen Zao 陳造. *Jianghuchangweng ji* 江湖長翁集. *SKQS* (q.v.), vol. 1166.
Chen Zhu 陳著. *Ben tang ji* 本堂集. *SKQS* (q.v.), vol. 1185.
Cheng Duanli 程端禮. *Wei zhai ji* 畏齋集. *SKQS* (q.v.), vol. 1199.
Cheng Duanxue 程端學. *Ji zhai ji* 積齋集. *SKQS* (q.v.), vol. 1212.
Cheng Hao 程顥 and Cheng Yi 程頤. *Er cheng ji* 二程集. Edited by Wang Xiaoyu 王孝魚. Beijing: Zhonghua shu ju, 1981.
Cheng Ju 程俱. *Beishan ji* 北山集. *SKQS* (q.v.), vol. 1130.
Cheng Jufu 程鉅夫 *Xue lou ji* 雪樓集. *SKQS* (q.v.), vol. 1202.
Cheng Minzheng 程敏政. *Xin'an wenxian zhi* 新安文獻志. *SKQS* (q.v.), vol. 1375–76.
Cheng Tinggui 成廷珪. *Ju zhu xuan shi ji* 居竹軒詩集. *SKQS* (q.v.), vol. 1216.
Chia, Lucille. *Printing for Profit: The Commercial Publishers of Jianyang, Fujian (11th–17th Centuries)*. Harvard-Yenching Monograph Series. Cambridge, MA: Harvard University Asia Center, Harvard University Press, 2002.
Clunas, Craig. *Elegant Debts: The Social Art of Wen Zhengming, 1470–1559*. Honolulu: University of Hawai'i Press, 2004.
———. *Superfluous Things: Material Culture and Social Status in Early Modern China*. Urbana: University of Illinois Press, 1991.
Cohen, Paul. *History in Three Keys: the Boxers as Event, Experience, and Myth*. New York: Columbia University Press, 1997.
*Cong shu ji cheng xin bian* 叢書集成新編. Taipei: Xin wen feng, 1985.
Cui Lingqin (唐) 催令欽. *Jiao fang ji jian ding* 教坊記箋訂. Edited by Ren Bantang 任半塘. Beijing: Zhonghua shu ju, 1962.

Dai Biaoyuan 戴表元. *Yan yuan ji* 剡源集. *CSJCXB* (q.v.), vol. 65.
Dai Fugu 戴復古. *Shi ping shi ji* 石屏詩集. *SKQS* (q.v.), vol. 1165.
Dai Jianguo 戴建國. "'Zhu pu ming fen' yu Song dai nu bi de fa lü di wei—Tang Song bian ge shi qi ji jie gou yan jiu zhi yi." '主仆名分'與宋代奴婢的法律地位—唐宋變革時期階級結構研究之一. *Li shi yan jiu* 历史研究 2004, no. 4: 55–73.
Dai Liang 戴良. *Jiu ling shan fang ji* 九靈山房集. *CSJCXB* (q.v.), vol. 66.
Dalby, Liza Crihfield. *Geisha*. Berkeley: University of California Press, 1983.
Daoqian 道潛. *Canliaozi shi ji* 參寥子詩集. *SKQS* (q.v.), vol. 1116.
Davis, Richard L. "Chaste and Filial Women in Chinese Historical Writings of the Eleventh Century." *Journal of the American Oriental Society* 121, no. 2 (2001): 204–18.
———. *Court and Family in Sung China, 960–1279: Bureaucratic Success and Kinship Fortunes for the Shih of Ming-chou*. Durham, NC: Duke University Press, 1986.
———. *Wind Against the Mountain: The Crisis of Politics and Culture in Thirteenth-Century China*. Cambridge, MA: Council on East Asian Studies Publications, Harvard University Press, 1996.
*Da Yuan sheng zheng guo chao dian zhang* 大元聖政國朝典章. 2 vols. Taipei: Guo li gu gong bo wu yuan, 1973.

*Da Yuan tong zhi tiao ge*. 大元通制條格. 2 vols. Taipei: Hua wen shu ju, 1968.
de Pee, Christian. "Purchase on Power: Imperial Space and Commercial Space in Song Dynasty Kaifeng, 960–1127." *Journal of the Economic and Social History of the Orient* 53 (2010): 149–84.
———. "Women in the *Yi Jian Zhi*: A Socio-Historical Study Based on Fiction." Master's Thesis, University of Leiden, 1991.
———. *The Writing of Weddings in Middle-Period China: Text and Ritual Practice in the Eighth through Fourteenth Centuries*. Edited by Roger T. Ames. SUNY Series in Chinese Philosophy and Culture. Albany: SUNY Press, 2007.
De Weerdt, Hilde. *Competition over Content: Negotiating Standards for the Civil Service Examinations in Imperial China, 1127–1279*. Harvard East Asian Monographs. Cambridge, MA: Harvard University Asia Center, Harvard University Press, 2007.
Deng Wenyuan 鄧文原. *Ba xi ji* 巴西集. *SKQS* (q.v.), vol. 1195.
Deng Xiaonan 鄧小南. "'Nei wai' zhi ji yu 'zhi xu' ge ju: jian tan Song dai shi dai fu dui yu *Zhou yi: Jia ren* de chan fa." "內外"之際与"秩序"格局：兼谈宋代士大夫对于《周易·家人》的闡發. In *Tang Song nü xing yu she hui* 唐宋女性与社会, edited by Deng Xiaonan 鄧小南, 97-123 (q.v.).
———. "'Zhou yi: Jia ren' de chan fa." "《周易.家人》的闡發." In *Tang Song nü xing yu she hui* 唐宋女性与社会, edited by Deng Xiaonan 鄧小南, 97–123. Shanghai: Shanghai ci shu chu ban she, 2003.
Dolby, William. "Some Mysteries and Mootings about the Yuan Variety Play." *Asian Theatre Journal* 11, no. 1 (Spring 1994): 81–89.
Dong Sigao 董嗣杲. *Lushan ji* 廬山集. *SKQS* (q.v.), vol. 1189.
Du Fan 杜範. *Qing xian ji* 清獻集. *SKQS* (q.v.), vol. 1175.
Du Mu 杜牧. *Fanchuan wen ji* 樊川文集. *SKQS* (q.v.), vol. 1081.
Dudbridge, Glen, and Xingjian Bai. *The Tale of Li Wa: Study and Critical Edition of a Chinese Story from the Ninth Century*. Published by Ithaca Press for the Board of the Faculty of Oriental Studies. London: Oxford University, 1983.

Ebrey, Patricia Buckley. "Concubines in Sung China." *Journal of Family History* 11, no. 2 (1986): 1–24.
———. *Confucianism and Family Rituals in Imperial China: A Social History of Writing about Rites*. Princeton: Princeton University Press, 1991.
———. "The Early Stages in the Development of Descent Group Organization." In *Kinship Organization in Late Imperial China, 1000–1940*, edited by Patricia Buckley Ebrey and James L. Watson, 16–61. Berkeley: University of California Press, 1986.
———. *Family and Property in Sung China: Yuan Ts'ai's Precepts for Social Life*. Translated by Patricia Buckley Ebrey. Princeton: Princeton University Press, 1984.
———. *The Inner Quarters: Marriage and the Lives of Chinese Women in the Sung Period*. Berkeley: University of California Press, 1993.
———. "Women, Money, and Class: Ssu-ma Kuang and Sung Neo-Confucian Views on Women." In *Papers on the Society and Culture of Early Modern China*, 613–69. Taipei, Taiwan Institute of History and Philology, Academica Sinica, 1992.
Ebrey, Patricia Buckley, and Maggie Bickford, eds. *Emperor Huizong and Late Northern Song China: The Politics of Culture and the Culture of Politics*. Cambridge, MA: Harvard University Asia Center, Harvard University Press, 2006.

Egan, Ronald C. *The Problem of Beauty: Aesthetic Thought and Pursuits in Northern Song Dynasty China*. Cambridge, MA: Harvard University Asia Center, Harvard University Press, 2006.

———. "Su Shih's 'Notes' as a Historical and Literary Source." *Harvard Journal of Asiatic Studies* 50, no. 2 (1990): 561–88.

———. *Word, Image, and Deed in the Life of Su Shi*. Harvard-Yenching Institute Monograph Series. Cambridge, MA: Council on East Asian Studies Publications, Harvard University Press, 1994.

Elvin, Mark. "Female Virtue and the State in China." *Past and Present* 104 (August 1984): 111–52.

Fan Chengda 范成大. *Shihu shi ji* 石湖詩集. SKQS (q.v.), vol. 1159.

Fan Gongcheng 范公偁. *Guo ting lu* 過庭錄. In *Mo zhuang man lu; Guo ting lu; Ke shu* 墨莊漫錄, 過庭錄, 可書, edited by Kong Fanli 孔凡禮, 307–83. Tang Song shi liao bi ji cong kan ed. Beijing: Zhonghua shu ju, 2002.

Fan Jun 范浚. *Xiangxi ji* 香溪集. CSJCCB ed. Shanghai: Shangwu yin shu guan, 1935.

Fan Zuyu 范祖禹. *Fan Taishi ji* 范太史集. SKQS (q.v.), vol. 1100.

Fang Hui 方回. *Gu jin kao xu* 古今考續. SKQS (q.v.), vol. 853.

———. *Tongjiang xu ji* 桐江續集. SKQS (q.v.), vol. 1193.

Fang Xuanling 房玄齡. *Jin shu* 晉書. Beijing: Zhonghua shu ju, 1974.

Farquhar, David M. *The Government of China under Mongolian Rule: A Reference Guide*. Münchener ostasiatische Studien. Stuttgart: Steiner, 1990.

Fei Gun 費袞. *Liangxi man zhi* 梁溪漫志. Edited by Fu Yuqian 傅毓鈐. Taiyuan: Shanxi ren min chu ban she, 1986.

Fei Siyan 費絲言. *You dian fan dao gui fan: cong Ming dai zhen jie lie nü de bian shi yu liu chuan kan zhen jie guan nian de yan ge hua* 由典範到規範：從明代貞節烈女的辨識與流傳看貞節觀念的嚴格化. Taipei: Taida chu ban wei yuan hui, 1998.

Fong, Grace S. "Signifying Bodies: The Cultural Significance of Suicide Writings by Women in Ming-Qing China." *Nan Nü* 3, no. 1 (2001): 105–42.

Franke, Herbert, and Denis Twitchett. *The Cambridge History of China, Vol. 6: Alien Regimes and Border States, 907–1368*. Cambridge: Cambridge University Press, 1994.

Fu Ruojin 傅若金. *Fu Yuli shi wen ji* 傅與礪詩文集. SKQS (q.v.), vol. 1213.

Fusek, Lois, and Ch'ung-tso Chao. *Among the Flowers: The Hua-chien chi*. New York: Columbia University Press, 1982.

Gao Qi 高啓. *Fu zao ji* 鳧藻集. SKQS (q.v.), vol. 1230.

Ge Lifang 葛立方. *Yun yu yang qiu* 韻語陽秋. In *Li dai shi hua*, vol. 2, edited by (Qing) He Wenhuan 何文煥, 479–651. Beijing: Zhonghua shu ju, 1981, 1992.

Ge Shengzhong 葛勝仲. *Danyang ji* 丹陽集. SKQS (q.v.), vol. 1127.

Gong Shitai 貢師泰. *Wan zhai ji* 玩齋集. SKQS (q.v.), vol. 1215.

Gong Yanming 龔延明. *Song dai guan zhi ci dian* 宋代管制辭典. Beijing: Zhonghua shu ju, 1997.

Goodman, Bryna. "The New Woman Commits Suicide: The Press, Cultural Memory, and the New Republic." *Journal of Asian Studies* 64, no. 1 (February 2005): 67–101.

Guo Dongxu 郭東旭. *Song dai fa zhi yan jiu* 宋代法制研究. Songshi yanjiu congshu ed. Baoding: Hebei da xue chu ban she, 1997.

Guo Xiangzheng 郭祥正. *Qing shan ji* 青山集. SKQS (q.v.), vol. 1116.

Halperin, Mark Robert. "Buddhist Temples, the War Dead, and the Song Imperial Cult." *Asia Major*, 3rd ser., 12, no. 2 (1999): 71–99.

Han Qi 韓琦. *Anyang ji bian nian jian zhu* 安陽集編年箋注. Edited by Li Zhiliang 李之亮 and Xu Zhengying 徐正英. Chengdu: Ba Shu shu she chu ban she, 2000.

Han Wei 韓維. *Nanyang ji* 南陽集. *SKQS* (q.v.), vol. 1101.

Han Yuanji 韓元吉. *Nan jian jia yi gao* 南澗甲乙稿. *CSJCCB* ed. Shanghai: Shang wu yin shu guan, 1936.

Hao Yulin 郝遇林, et al. *Guangdong tong zhi* 廣東通志. *SKQS* (q.v.), vols. 562–64.

Hartman, Charles. "Li Hsin-ch'uan and the Historical Image of Late Sung *Tao-hsueh*." *Harvard Journal of Asiatic Studies* 21, no. 2 (December 2001): 317–59.

———. "The Making of a Villain: Ch'in Kuei and Tao-hsueh." *Harvard Journal of Asiatic Studies* 58, no. 1 (1998): 59–149.

———. "A Textual History of Cai Jing's Biography in the Songshi." In *Emperor Huizong and Late Northern Song China: The Politics of Culture and the Culture of Politics*, edited by Patricia Buckley Ebrey and Maggie Bickford (q.v.), 517–52.

———. "Zhu Xi and His World." *Journal of Song-Yuan Studies* 36 (2006): 107–31.

Hawes, Colin S. C. *The Social Circulation of Poetry in the Mid-Northern Song*. Albany, NY: SUNY Press, 2005.

He Wei 何薳. *Chun zhu ji wen* 春渚紀聞. Edited by Zhang Minghua 張明華. Tang Song shi liao bi ji cong kan. Beijing: Zhonghua shu ju, 1983.

Hershatter, Gail. *Dangerous Pleasures: Prostitution and Modernity in Twentieth-Century Shanghai*. Berkeley: University of California Press, 1997.

Hightower, James R. "The Songwriter Liu Yung, Part 1." *Harvard Journal of Asiatic Studies* 41, no. 2 (1981): 323–76.

———. "The Songwriter Liu Yung, Part 2." *Harvard Journal of Asiatic Studies* 42, no. 1 (1982): 5–66.

Holcombe, Charles. "The Exemplar State: Ideology, Self-Cultivation and Power in Fourth-Century China." *Harvard Journal of Asiatic Studies* 49:1 (June 1989): 93–139.

Holmgren, Jennifer. "Observations on Marriage and Inheritance Practices in Early Mongol and Yuan Society, with Particular Reference to the Levirate." *Journal of Asian History* 20, no. 2 (1986): 127–92.

Hong Kuo 洪适. *Panzhou wen ji* 盤洲文集. *SKQS* (q.v.), vol. 1158.

Hong Mai 洪邁. *Yijian zhi* 夷堅志. Edited by He Zhuo 何卓. Beijing: Zhonghua shu ju, 1981.

Hong Sui 洪遂. *Shi'er xiao ming lu* 侍兒小名錄. In *Shuo fu* 說郛, edited by Tao Zongyi 陶宗儀. *SKQS* (q.v.), vols. 876–82, 77 *shang*, 45a–54b.

Hong Xiwen 洪希文. *Xu xuan qu ji* 續軒渠集. *SKQS* (q.v.), vol. 1205.

Hsiao Ch'i-ch'ing (Xiao Qiqing) 蕭啓慶. "Mid-Yuan Politics." In *The Cambridge History of China, Vol. 6: Alien Regimes and Border States, 907–1368*, edited by Herbert Franke and Denis Twitchett, 490–560. Cambridge: Cambridge University Press, 1994.

———. *Yuan dai shi xin tan* 元代史新探. Taipei: Xin wen feng chu ban gong si, 1983.

Hu Bingwen 胡炳文. *Chun zheng meng qiu* 純正蒙求. *SKQS* (q.v.), vol. 952.

———. *Yun feng ji* 雲峰集. *SKQS* (q.v.), vol. 1199.

Hu Han 胡翰. *Hu Zhongzi ji* 胡仲子集. *SKQS* (q.v.), vol. 1229.

Hu Quan 胡銓. *Dan'an wen ji* 澹菴文集. *SKQS* (q.v.), vol. 1137.

Hu Su 胡宿. *Wen gong ji* 文恭集. *CSJCXB* (q.v.), vol. 60.
Hu Taichu 胡太初. *Zhou lian xu lun* 晝簾緒論. *SKQS* (q.v.), vol. 602.
Hu Yin 胡寅. *Fei ran ji* 斐然集. In Rong Zhaozu 容肇祖, *Chong zheng bian; Fei ran ji* 崇正辯,斐然集. Beijing: Zhonghua shu ju, 1993.
Hu, Ying, and Joan Judge, eds. *Beyond Exemplar Tales: New Approaches to Chinese Women's Lives*. Berkeley: Global, Area, and International Archive, University of California Press, 2011.
Hu Zhiyu 胡祗遹. *Zi shan da quan ji* 紫山大全集. *SKQS* (q.v.), vol. 1196.
Hu Zi 胡仔. *Tiaoxi yu yin cong hua* 苕溪漁隱叢話. Edited by Liao Deming 廖德明 and Zhou Benchun 周本淳. Beijing: Ren min wen xue chu ban she, 1962; repr. 1993.
Hua Yuncheng 華允城 et al. *Hua shi chuan fang ji* 華氏傳芳集. (Nan Ming) Xishan Hua shi, 1645. Princeton University Microfilm, 9101/5565, reel #02581.
Huang Chang 黃裳. *Yan shan ji* 演山集. *SKQS* (q.v.), vol. 1120.
Huang Gan 黃榦. *Mian zhai ji* 勉齋集. *SKQS* (q.v.), vol. 1168.
Huang Gongdu 黃公度. *Zhi jia weng ji* 知稼翁集. *SKQS* (q.v.), vol. 1139.
Huang Jie 黃玠. *Bian shan xiao yin yin lu* 弁山小隱吟錄. *SKQS* (q.v.), vol. 1205.
Huang Jin 黃溍. *Huang Wenxian gong ji* 黃文獻公集. *CSJCCB* ed. Shanghai: Shanghai shang wu yin shu guan, 1936.
———. *Jinhua Huang xian sheng wen ji* 金華黃先生文集. Edited by Hu Zongmao 胡宗楙. Xu Jinhua cong shu 續金華叢書. Yongkang, Zhejiang: Hu shi meng xuan lou, 1924.
Huang, Martin W. *Negotiating Masculinities in Late Imperial China*. Honolulu: University of Hawai'i Press, 2006.
Huang Shijian 黃時鑑, ed. *Yuan dai fa lü zi liao ji cun* 元代法律資料輯存. Hangzhou: Zhejiang gu ji chu ban she, 1988.
Huang Tingjian 黃庭堅. *Huang Tingjian quan ji* 黃庭堅全集. Edited by Liu Lin 劉琳, Li Yongxian 李勇先, and Wang Ronggui 王蓉貴. Chengdu: Sichuan da xue chu ban she, 2001.
Huang Zhen 黃震. *Huang shi ri chao* 黃氏日抄. *SKQS* (q.v.), vols. 707–8.
Huang Zhongyuan 黃仲元. *Si ru ji* 四如集. *SKQS* (q.v.), vol. 1188.
Huang Zongxi 黃宗羲. *Song Yuan xue an* 宋元學案. Edited by Quan Zuwang 全祖望, Chen Jinsheng 陳金生, and Liang Yunhua 梁運華. 4 vols. Beijing: Zhonghua shu ju, 1986.
Hucker, Charles O. *A Dictionary of Official Titles in Imperial China*. Stanford: Stanford University Press, 1985.
Hunt, Lynn Avery. *Inventing Human Rights: A History*. New York: W. W. Norton & Co., 2007.
Hymes, Robert P. "Not Quite Gentlemen? Doctors in the Song and Yuan." *Chinese Science* 8 (1987): 9–76.

Idema, Wilt, and Beata Grant, eds. *The Red Brush: Writing Women of Imperial China*. Cambridge, MA: Harvard University Asia Center, Harvard University Press, 2004.
Idema, Wilt L., and Stephen H. West. *Chinese Theater 1100–1400, A Source Book*. Münchener ostasiatische Studien. Wiesbaden: Franz Steiner Verlag GMBH, 1982.

Jaschok, Maria. *Concubines and Bondservants*. London: Zed Books Ltd., 1988.
Jay, Jennifer W. *A Change in Dynasties: Loyalism in Thirteenth-Century China*. Bellingham, WA: Western Washington University, 1991.
———. "Memoirs and Official Accounts: The Historiography of the Song Loyalists." *Harvard Journal of Asiatic Studies* 50, no. 2 (1990): 589–612.
Jia Xuanweng 家鉉翁. *Ze tang ji* 則堂集. *SKQS* (q.v.), vol. 1213.
Jiang Kui 姜夔. *Baishidaoren ge qu* 白石道人歌曲. *SKQS* (q.v.), vol. 1488.
———. *Baishidaoren shi ji* 白石道人詩集. *SKQS* (q.v.), vol. 1175.
Jiang Shaoyu 江少虞. *Song chao shi shi lei yuan* 宋朝事實類苑. 2 vols. Shanghai: Shanghai gu ji chu ban she: Xin hua shu dian Shanghai fa xing suo fa xing, 1981.
Jiang Xiufu 江休復. *Jiang lin ji za zhi* 江鄰幾雜志. *Quan Song bi ji* 全宋筆記, *di 1 bian*, vol. 5, edited by Zhu Yi'an 朱易安 et al. Zhengzhou: Da xiang chu ban she, 2003.
Jiang, Yonglin, translator. *The Great Ming Code:* Da Ming lü. Seattle: University of Washington Press, 2005.
Jie Xisi 揭傒斯. *Jie Xisi quan ji* 揭傒斯全集. Edited by Li Mengsheng 李夢生. Shanghai: Shanghai gu ji chu ban she, 1985.
Jin Lüxiang 金履祥. *Renshan ji* 仁山集. *CSJCXB* (q.v.), vol. 64.
———. *Renshan wen ji* 仁山文集. *SKQS* (q.v.), vol. 1189.
Johnson, Dale R. "Courtesans, Lovers, and *Gold Thread Pond* in 'Guan Hanqing's Music Dramas (A Translation, with Introduction, of Guan Hanqing's *Gold Thread Pond*)." *Journal of Song-Yuan Studies* 33 (2003), 111–54.
Judge, Joan. *The Precious Raft of History: The Past, the West, and the Woman Question in China*. Stanford: Stanford University Press, 2008.

Karlgren, Bernhard. *The Book of Odes: Chinese Text, Transcription and Translation*. Stockholm: Museum of Far Eastern Antiquities, 1950.
Katkov, Neil Ennis. "The Domestication of Concubinage in Imperial China." PhD diss., Harvard University, 1997.
Kinney, Anne Behnke. *Representations of Childhood and Youth in Early China*. Stanford: Stanford University Press, 2004.
Kishibe Shigeo 岸邊成雄. *Jukkyō shakai no joseitachi* 儒教社會の女性たち. Tokyo: Hyōron sha, 1977.
———. "Sōdai kyōbō no hensen obyobi soshiki 宋代教坊の變遷及び組織." *Shigaku zasshi* 54 (1943): 280–308.
———. "Tōdai kyōbō no sōsetsu obyobi hensen 唐代教坊の創設及び變遷." *Tōyō gakuohō* 28 (1941–43): 280–308.
Knapp, Keith Nathaniel. *Selfless Offspring: Filial Children and Social Order in Medieval China*. Honolulu: University of Hawai'i Press, 2005.
Ko, Dorothy. *Teachers of the Inner Chambers: Women and Culture in Seventeenth-Century China*. Stanford: Stanford University Press, 1994.
Kong Pingzhong 孔平仲. *Tan yuan* 談苑. *Quan Song bi ji, di 2 bian*, vol. 5, edited by Zhu Yi'an 朱易安 et al. Zhengzhou: Da xiang chu ban she, 2006.
Kong Qi 孔齊. *Zhizheng zhi ji* 至正直記. Edited by Zhuang Min 莊敏 and Gu Xin 顧新. Song yuan bi ji cong kan ed. Shanghai: Shanghai gu ji chu ban she, 1987.

Lam, Joseph. "Reading Music and Eroticism in Late Ming Texts." *Nan Nü* 12 (2010): 215–54.

Lam, Lap. "A Reconsideration of Liu Yong and his 'Vulgar' Lyrics." *Journal of Song-Yuan Studies* 33 (2003): 1–47.

Langlois, John D., ed. *China under Mongol Rule*. Princeton: Princeton University Press, 1981.

Lao, Yan-shuan. "Southern Chinese Scholars and Educational Institution in the Early Yuan: Some Preliminary Remarks." In *China under Mongol Rule* (q.v.), 107–33.

Lau, Napyin 劉立言. "Songdai nü'er de fa lü quan li he ze ren." 宋代女儿的法律权利和责任. In *Jia ting shi yan jiu de xin shi ye* 家庭史研究的新视野, edited by Zhang Guogang 张国刚. Beijing: San lian shu dian, 2002.

Lee, Hui-shu. *Empresses, Art, and Agency in Song Dynasty China*. Seattle: University of Washington Press, 2010.

Lee, Jen-der (Li Zhende). "Gender and Medicine in Tang China." *Asia Major* 16, no. 2 (2003): 1–32.

Leung, Angela Ki Che (Liang Qizi) 梁其姿. "Medical Learning from the Song to the Ming." In *The Song-Yuan-Ming Transition in Chinese History*, edited by Paul J. Smith and Richard von Glahn (q.v.), 374–98.

———. "To Chasten Society: The Development of Widow Homes in the Qing, 1773–1911." *Late Imperial China* 14, no. 2 (1993): 1–32.

Levine, Ari. "Che-tsung's Reign (1085–1100)." In *The Cambridge History of China, Vol. 5 Part One: The Sung Dynasty and Its Precursors, 907–1279*, edited by Denis Twitchett and Paul J. Smith, 347–555. Cambridge: Cambridge University Press, 2009.

———. *Divided by a Common Language: Factional Conflict in Late Northern Song China*. Honolulu: University of Hawai'i Press, 2008.

Li Ao 李翱. *Li Wen gong ji* 李文公集. *SKQS* (q.v.), vol. 1078.

Li, Cho-ying, and Charles Hartman. "A Newly Discovered Inscription by Qin Gui and Its Implications for the History of Song Daoxue." *Harvard Journal of Asiatic Studies* 70, no. 2 (2010): 387–488.

Li Cun 李存. *Si an ji* 俟菴集. *SKQS* (q.v.), vol. 1213.

Li Fu 李復. *Yushui ji* 潏水集. *SKQS* (q.v.), vol. 1121.

Li Gang 李綱. *Liangxi ji* 梁谿集. *SKQS* (q.v.), vols. 1125–26.

Li Gou 李覯. *Li gou ji* 李覯集. Beijing: Zhonghua shu ju, 1981.

Li Guangdi 李光地. *Zhuzi li zuan* 朱子禮纂. *SKQS* (q.v.), vol. 142.

Li Heng 李衡. *Le an yu lu* 樂庵語錄. Edited by Gong Yu 龔昱. *SKQS* (q.v.), vol. 849.

*Li ji* 禮記 (Book of Ritual). Translated by James Legge. *The Chinese Text Project*. [http://chinese.dsturgeon.net/text.pl?node=9479&if=en].

Li Junmin 李俊民. *Zhuang jing ji* 莊靖集. *SKQS* (q.v.), vol. 1190.

Li Liuqian 李流謙. *Dan zhai ji* 澹齋集. *SKQS* (q.v.), vol. 1133.

Li Lü 李呂. *Dan xuan ji* 澹軒集. *SKQS* (q.v.), vol. 1152.

Li Maoying 李昴英. *Wen xi ji* 文溪集. *SKQS* (q.v.), vol. 1181.

Li Mixun 李彌遜. *Yunxi ji* 筠谿集. *SKQS* (q.v.), vol. 1130.

Li Peng 李彭. *Ri she yuan ji* 日涉園集. *SKQS* (q.v.), vol. 1122.

Li Shi 李石. *Fang zhou ji* 方舟集. *SKQS* (q.v.), vol. 1149.

Li Tao 李燾. *Xu zi zhi tong jian chang bian* 續資治通鑑長編. Beijing: Zhonghua shu ju, 1995.

Li, Waiyee. "The Late Ming Courtesan: Invention of a Cultural Ideal." In *Writing Women in Late Imperial China*, edited by Ellen Widmer and Kang-i Sun Chang (q.v.), 46–73.

Li Xiaoguang 李孝光. *Wu feng ji* 五峰集. SKQS (q.v.), vol. 1215.

Li Xin 李新. *Kua ao ji* 跨鼇集. SKQS (q.v.), vol. 1124.

Li Xinchuan 李心傳. *Jianyan yi lai chao ye za ji* 建炎以來朝野雜記. Edited by Xu Gui 徐規. Tang Song shi liao bi ji cong kan ed. Beijing: Zhonghua shu ju, 2000.

———. *Jianyan yi lai xi nian yao lu* 建炎以來繫年要錄. SKQS (q.v.), vol. 608.

Li Xiusheng 李修生, ed. *Quan Yuan wen* 全元文. Nanjing: Jiangsu gu ji chu ban she, 1997.

Li Zhaoqi 李昭玘. *Le jing ji* 樂靜玘. SKQS (q.v.), vol. 1122.

Liang Gengyao 梁庚堯. "Song dai ji yi ren de she hui di wei." 宋代伎藝人的社會地位. In *Song dai she hui jing ji shi lun ji* 宋代社會經濟史論集, Vol. 2, edited by Liang Gengyao, 100–116. Taipei: Yun chen wen hua, 1997.

Liao Gang 廖剛. *Gao feng wen ji* 高峰文集. SKQS (q.v.), vol. 1142.

Liao Meiyun 廖美雲. *Tang ji yan jiu* 唐伎研究. Taipei: Taiwan xue sheng shu ju, 1995.

Lin Bi 林弼. *Lin Dengzhou ji* 林登州集. SKQS (q.v.), vol. 1227.

Lin Biaomin 林表民, ed. *Chicheng ji* 赤城集. SKQS (q.v.), vol. 1356.

Lin Guangchao 林光朝. *Ai xuan ji* 艾軒集. SKQS (q.v.), vol. 1142.

Lin Shuen-fu. *The Transformation of the Chinese Lyrical Tradition: Chiang K'uei and Southern Song Tz'u Poetry*. Princeton: Princeton University Press, 1978.

Lin Tong 林同. *Xiao shi* 孝詩. SKQS (q.v.), vol. 1183.

Ling Yunhan 淩雲翰. *Zhe xuan ji* 柘軒集. SKQS (q.v.), vol. 1227.

Liu Bin 劉攽. *Peng cheng ji* 彭城集. CSJCXB (q.v.), vol. 61.

Liu Chenweng 劉辰翁. *Xu xi ji* 須溪集. SKQS (q.v.), vol. 1186.

Liu Ching-cheng (Liu Jingzhen) 劉靜貞. "Li shi ji shu yu li shi lun shu—Qian Hou Han shu zhong de Wang Zhaojun gu shi bian xi." 歷史記述與歷史論述——前後漢書中的王昭君故事辨析. In *Zheng Qinren jiao shou qi zhi shou qing lun wen ji* 鄭欽仁教授七秩壽慶論文集, edited by Zheng Qinren jiao shou qi zhi shou qing lun wen ji bian ji wei yuan hui, 13–28. Taipei: Dao xiang chu ban she, 2006.

———. "Song ben 'Lie nü zhuan' de bian jiao ji qi shi dai—wen ben, zhi shi, xing bie." 宋本《列女传》的编校及其时代—文本, 知識, 性别. In *Tang Song nü xing yu she hui* 唐宋女性与社会, edited by Deng Xiaonan 鄧小南, 22–45. Shanghai: Shanghai ci shu chu ban she, 2003.

———. "Xing bie yu wen ben—zai Song ren bi ji xia xun zhao nü xing." 性別與文本—在宋人筆下尋找女性. In *Zhongguo shi xin lun; xing bie shi fen ce* 中國史新論・性別史分冊, edited by Li Zhende 李貞德, 239–82. Taipei: Zhong yang yan jiu yuan, Lianjing chu ban shi ye gong si, 2009.

Liu Fu 劉敞. *Meng chuan yi gao* 蒙川遺稿. SKQS (q.v.), vol. 1183.

Liu Fu 劉斧. *Qing suo gao yi* 青瑣高議. Song Yuan bi ji cong shu ed. Shanghai: Shanghai gu ji chu ban she, 1983.

Liu Guan 柳貫. *Dai zhi ji* 待制集. SKQS (q.v.), vol. 1210.

Liu Guo 劉過. *Longzhou ji* 龍洲集. SKQS (q.v.), vol. 1172.

Liu, James T.C. *China Turning Inward: Intellectual-Political Changes in the Early Twelfth Century*. Cambridge, MA: Council on East Asian Studies, Harvard University Press, 1988.

———. "How Did a Neo-Confucian School Become the State Orthodoxy?" *Philosophy East and West* 23:4 (1973): 483–505.
Liu Jiangsun 劉將孫. *Yang wu zhai ji* 養吾齋集. SKQS (q.v.), vol. 1199.
Liu Kai 柳開. *He dong ji* 河東集. SKQS (q.v.), vol. 1085.
Liu Kezhuang 劉克莊. *Hou cun ji* 後村集. SKQS (q.v.), vol. 1180.
———. *Hou cun xian sheng da quan ji* 後村先生大全集. Si bu cong kan ed. Shanghai: Shang wu yin shu guan, 1922.
Liu Minzhong 劉敏中. *Zhong an ji* 中庵集. SKQS (q.v.), vol. 1206.
Liu Renben 劉仁本. *Yu ting ji* 羽庭集. SKQS (q.v.), vol. 1215.
Liu Xiang 劉向. *Hui tu Lienü zhuan* 繪圖列女傳 [Illustrated biographies of exemplary women]. Edited by (Qing) Wang Geng 汪庚. Illustrations by (Ming) Qiu Ying 仇英. Reprint of Zhi bu zu zhai cang ban. Taipei: Zheng zhong shu ju, 1971.
Liu Xiang 劉向. *Lie nü zhuan jin zhu jin yi* 列女傳今注今譯. Edited by Zhang Jing 張敬. Taipei: Shang wu yin shu guan, 1994.
Liu Xu 劉昫. *Jiu Tang shu* 舊唐書. Beijing: Zhonghua shu ju, 1975.
Liu Yan 劉弇. *Longyun ji* 龍雲集. SKQS (q.v.), vol. 1119.
Liu Yin 劉因. *Jing xiu wen ji* 靜修文集. CSJCXB (q.v.), vol. 66.
Liu Yiqing 劉一清. *Qiantang yi shi* 錢塘遺事. SKQS (q.v.), vol. 408.
Liu Yiqing 劉義慶, and (Liang) Liu Xiaobiao 劉孝標. *Shi shuo xin yu* 世說新語. Repr. of Shi jie shu ju zhu zi ji cheng ed. Shanghai: Shanghai shu dian, 1986.
———. *A New Account of Tales of the World = Shih-shuo Hsin-yü [Shi shuo xin yu]*. Translated by Richard B. Mather. Minneapolis: University of Minnesota Press, 1976.
Liu Yizhi 劉一止. *Tiaoxi ji* 苕溪集. SKQS (q.v.), vol. 1132.
Liu Yue 劉熷. *Yunzhuang ji* 雲莊集. SKQS (q.v.), vol. 1157.
Liu Yueshen 劉岳申. *Shen zhai ji* 申齋集. SKQS (q.v.), vol. 1204.
Liu Zai 劉宰. *Man tang ji* 漫塘集. SKQS (q.v.), vol. 1170.
Liu Zenggui 劉增貴. "Shi lun Han dai hun yin guan xi zhong de li fa guan nian." 試論漢代婚姻關係中的禮法觀念. In *Zhong guo fu nü shi lun ji xu ji* 中國婦女史論集續集, edited by Bao Jialin 鮑家麟, 1–36 Taipei: Dao xiang chu ban she, 1991.
———. "Wei, Jin, Nan bei chao shi dai de qie." 魏晉南北朝時代的妾. In *Zhong guo fu nü shi lun ji si ji* 中國婦女史論集四集, edited by Bao Jialin 鮑家麟, 61–100. Taipei: Dao xiang chu ban she, 1995.
Liu Zongyuan 柳宗元. *Liu Hedong ji* 柳河東集. SKQS (q.v.), vol. 1076.
Lou Yue 樓鑰. *Gong kui ji* 攻媿集. CSJCXB (q.v.), vol. 64.
Louie, Kam. *Theorising Chinese Masculinity: Society and Gender in China*. Cambridge: Cambridge University Press, 2002.
Lu Dian 陸佃. *Tao shan ji* 陶山集. CSJCXB (q.v.), vol. 62.
Lu Jiuyuan 陸九淵. *Lu Jiuyuan ji* 陸九淵集. Edited by Zhong Zhe 鐘哲. Beijing: Zhonghua shu ju, 1980.
Lü Nangong 呂南公. *Guanyuan ji* 灌園集. SKQS (q.v.), vol. 1123.
Lü Pu 呂溥. *Zhu xi gao* 竹溪稿. In *Xu Jinhua cong shu* 續金華叢書, Vol. 63, edited by Hu Zongmao 胡宗楙. Yongkang, Zhejiang: Hu shi meng xuan lou, 1924.
Lü Tao 呂陶. *Jing de ji* 淨德集. CSJCXB (q.v.), vol. 61.
Lu, Weijing. *True to Her Word : The Faithful Maiden Cult in Late Imperial China*. Stanford: Stanford University Press, 2008.
Lu Wengui 陸文圭. *Qiang dong lei gao* 牆東類稿 SKQS (q.v.), vol. 1194.
Lu You 陸游. *Jia shi jiu wen* 家世舊聞. In *Xixi cong yu; Jia shi jiu wen* 西溪叢語;家世

舊聞, edited by Kong Fanli 孔凡禮. Tang Song shi liao bi ji cong kan ed. Beijing: Zhonghua shu ju, 1993.

———. *Lao xue an bi ji* 老學庵筆記. Tang Song shi liao bi ji cong kan ed. Beijing: Zhonghua shu ju, 1979.

———. *Weinan wen ji* 渭南文集, *Lu Fangweng quan ji* 陸放翁全集. 3 vols. Hong Kong: Xianggang guang zhi shu ju, n.d.

Lu Youren 陸友仁. *Yan bei za zhi* 研北雜志. SKQS (q.v.), vol. 866.

Lü Zuqian 呂祖謙. *Donglai ji* 東萊集. SKQS (q.v.), vol. 1150.

———. *Shao yi wai zhuan* 少儀外傳. SKQS (q.v.), vol. 703.

Luo Dajing 羅大經. *Helin yu lu* 鶴林玉露. Edited by Wang Ruilai 王瑞來. Tang Song shi liao bi ji cong kan ed. Beijing: Zhonghua shu ju, 1983.

Luo Yuan 羅願. [*Luo*] *Ezhou xiao ji* [羅]鄂州小集. CSJCXB (q.v.), vol. 64.

———. *Xin'an zhi* 新安志. SKQS (q.v.), vol. 485.

Luo Zhufeng 罗竹风 et al., eds. *Han yu da ci dian* 漢語大詞典. 12 vols. Shanghai: Shanghai ci shu chu ban she, 1986–94.

Ma Zhen 馬臻. *Xia wai shi ji* 霞外詩集. SKQS (q.v.), vol. 1204.

Ma Zuchang 馬祖常. *Shi tian wen ji* 石田文集. SKQS (q.v.), vol. 1206.

Mann, Susan. "The Male Bond in Chinese History and Culture." *The American Historical Review* 105, no. 5 (2000): 1600–1614.

———. *Precious Records: Women in China's Long Eighteenth Century*. Stanford: Stanford University Press, 1997.

———. *The Talented Women of the Zhang Family*. Berkeley: University of California Press, 2007.

———. "Widows in the Kinship, Class, and Community Structures of Qing Dynasty China." *Journal of Asian Studies* 47, no. 1 (1987): 37–56.

McDermott, Joseph P. "The Chinese Domestic Bursar." *Ajia bunka kenku*. Special Issue, no. 2 (Nov. 1990): 15–32.

———. *A Social History of the Chinese Book: Books and Literati Culture in Late Imperial China*. Hong Kong: Hong Kong University Press, 2006.

———. "Women of Property in China, 960–1368: A Survey of the Scholarship." *International Journal of Asian Studies* 1, no. 2 (2004): 201–22.

McKnight, Brian, and James T.C. Liu. *The Enlightened Judgments: Ch'ing-ming chi, the Sung Dynasty Collection*. Albany, NY: SUNY Press, 1999.

McMullen, David. "The Real Judge Dee: Ti Jen-chieh and the Tang Restoration of 705." *Asia Major*, 3rd ser., 6, no. 1 (1993): 1–82.

Mei Yaochen 梅堯臣. *Mei Yaochen ji bian nian jiao zhu* 梅堯臣集編年校注. Edited by Zhu Dongrun 朱東潤. Shanghai: Shanghai gu ji chu ban she, 1980.

Mencius 孟子. *Mengzi yi zhu* 孟子譯注. Edited by Lanzhou da xue zhong wen xi Mengzi yi zhu xiao zu. Shanghai: Zhonghua shu ju, 1960.

Meng Jiao 孟郊. *Meng Dongye shi ji* 孟東野詩集. SKQS (q.v.), vol. 1078.

Meng Yuanlao 孟元老. *Dongjing meng hua lu zhu* 東京夢華錄注. Edited by Deng Zhicheng 鄧之誠. Beijing: Zhongguo shang ye chu ban she, 1982.

Meng Yuanlao 孟元老 et al. *Dongjing meng hua lu (wai si zhong)* 東京夢華錄 (外四種). Beijing: Zhonghua shu ju, 1962.

Meyer-Fong, Tobie. "Making a Place for Meaning in Early Qing Yangzhou." *Late Imperial China* 20, no. 1 (June 1999): 49–84.

*Ming gong shu pan qing ming ji* 名公書判清明集. Edited by Zhongguo she hui ke xue yuan li shi yan jiu suo Song Liao Jin Yuan shi yan jiu shi 中國社會科學院歷史研究所宋遼金元史研究室. Beijing: Zhonghua shu ju, 1987.

Mote, F.W. *Imperial China 900–1800*. Cambridge, MA: Harvard University Press, 1999.

Murong Yanfeng 慕容彦逢. *Chi wen tang ji* 摛文堂集. SKQS (q.v.), vol. 1123.

Naideweng 耐得翁. *Du cheng ji sheng* 都城紀勝. In Meng Yuanlao 孟元老 et al., *Dongjing meng hua lu (wai si zhong)*, 89–110 (q.v.).

Neskar, Ellen. *Politics and Prayer: Shrines to Local Former Worthies in Sung China*. Cambridge, MA: Harvard University Asia Center, Harvard University Press, forthcoming.

Nomura Ayuko 野村鮎子. "Ming Qing nü xing shou xu kao" 明清女性壽序考. In *Ming Qing wen xue yu xing bie yan jiu* 明清文學與性別研究 [Literature and Gender in Ming-Qing China], edited by Zhang Hongsheng 張宏生. Nanjing: Jiangsu gu ji chu ban she, 2002.

Ouyang Xiu 歐陽修. *Historical Records of the Five Dynasties*. Translated by Richard L. Davis. New York: Columbia University Press, 2004.

Ouyang Xiu. *Ouyang Xiu quan ji* 歐陽修全集. Edited by Li Yi'an 李逸安. Zhongguo gu dian wen xue ji ben cong shu ed. 6 vols. Beijing: Zhongguo shu dian, 2001.

———. *Shi ben yi* 詩本義. SKQS (q.v.), vol. 70.

———. *Xin Wudai shi* 新五代史. Beijing: Zhonghua shu ju, 1974.

Owen, Stephen. *The End of the Chinese "Middle Ages": Essays in Mid-Tang Literary Culture*. Stanford: Stanford University Press, 1996.

Peterson, Willard, and Fang Yizhi. *Bitter Gourd: Fang I-chih and the Impetus for Intellectual Change*. New Haven: Yale University Press, 1979.

Pi Rixiu 皮日休. [*Pizi*] *wen sou* 皮子文藪. SKQS (q.v.), vol. 1083.

Pu Daoyuan 蒲道源. *Xian ju cong gao* 閒居叢稿. SKQS (q.v.), vol. 1210.

Qian Shizhao 錢世昭. *Qian shi si zhi* 錢氏私誌. *Quan Song bi ji, di 2 bian*, vol. 7, edited by Zhu Yi'an 朱易安 et al. Zhengzhou: Da xiang chu ban she 2006.

Qian Weishan 錢惟善. *Jiang yue song feng ji* 江月松風集. SKQS (q.v.), vol. 1217.

*Qingyuan tiao fa shi lei* 慶元條法事類. Beijing: Zhongguo shu dian, 1981.

*Quan Song wen*. 全宋文. Edited by Zeng Zaozhuang 曾棗莊 and Liu Lin 劉琳. Shanghai: Shanghai gu ji chu ban she, 2006.

Raphals, Lisa. *Sharing the Light: Representations of Women and Virtue in Early China*. SUNY Series in Chinese Philosophy and Culture. Albany, NY: SUNY Press, 1998.

Ren Shilin 任士林. *Song xiang ji* 松鄉集. SKQS (q.v.), vol. 1196.

Ren Yuan 任淵. *Shan gu nei ji shi zhu* 山谷內集詩註. SKQS (q.v.), vol. 1114.

Ropp, Paul. "Ambiguous Images of Courtesan Culture in Late Imperial China." In *Writing Women in Late Imperial China*, edited by Ellen Widmer and Kang-i Sun Chang (q.v.), 17–45.

———. "Passionate Women: Female Suicide in Late Imperial China—Introduction." *Nan Nü* 3, no. 1 (2001): 3–21.

Rouzer, Paul F. *Articulated Ladies: Gender and the Male Community in Early Chinese Texts*. Cambridge, MA: Harvard University Asia Center, Harvard University Press, 2001.

Schirokauer, Conrad. "Chu Hsi's Political Career: A Study in Ambivalence." In *Confucian Personalities*, edited by Arthur Wright and Denis Twitchett, 162–88. Stanford: Stanford University Press, 1962.

Seimeishū Kenkyūkai 清明集研究会. Meikō shohan semeishū *yakuchū kō*「名公書判清明集」訳注稿 (jinpinmon 人品門; jinrinmon 人倫門; kanrimon 官吏門). Tokyo: Seimeishū Kenkyūkai, 2002–8.

Shao Bowen 邵伯溫. *Shao shi wen jian lu* 邵氏聞見錄. Edited by Li Jianxiong 李劍雄 and Liu Dequan 劉德權. Tang Song shi liao bi ji cong kan ed. Beijing: Zhonghua shu ju, 1983.

Shen Kuo 沈括. *Changxing ji* 長興集. SKQS (q.v.), vol. 1117.

———. *Meng xi bi tan* 夢溪筆談. Quan Song bi ji, di 2 bian, vol. 3, edited by Zhu Yi'an 朱易安 et al. Zhengzhou: Da xiang chu ban she, 2006.

Shen Liao 沈遼. *Yun chao bian* 雲巢編. SKQS (q.v.), vol. 1117.

Shen Yazhi 沈亞之. *Shen xia xian ji* 沈下賢集. SKQS (q.v.), vol. 1079.

Shen Yiji 沈翼機 and Ji Zengjun 嵇曾筠. *Zhejiang tong zhi* 浙江通志. SKQS (q.v.), vols. 519–26.

Shen Yue 沈約 et al. *Song shu* 宋書. Beijing: Zhonghua shu ju, 1974.

Shields, Anna M. *Crafting a Collection: The Cultural Contexts and Poetic Practice of the Huajian ji (Collection from Among the Flowers)*. Cambridge, MA: Harvard University Asia Center, Harvard University Press, 2006.

*Si ku quan shu* 四庫全書. Wen yuan ge ed. Taipei: Taiwan shang wu yin shu guan, 1983.

Sikong Tu 司空圖. *Sikong Biaosheng wen ji* 司空表聖文集. SKQS (q.v.), vol. 1083.

Sima Guang 司馬光. *Jia fan* 家範. SKQS (q.v.), vol. 696.

———. *Sima wen zheng gong chuan jia ji* 司馬文正公傳家集. Guo xue ji ben cong shu ed. 2 vols. Taipei: Taiwan shang wu yin shu guan, 1965.

———. *Su shui ji wen* 涑水紀聞. Edited by Deng Guangming 鄧廣銘 and Zhang Xiqing 張希清. Tang Song shi liao bi ji cong kan ed. Beijing: Zhonghua shu ju, 1989.

Sima Qian 司馬遷. *Shi ji*. SKQS (q.v.), vols. 243–44.

Smith, Paul J. "Family, Landsmann, and Status-Group Affinity in Refugee Mobility Strategies: The Mongol Invasions and the Diaspora of Sichuanese Elites, 1230–1330." *Harvard Journal of Asiatic Studies* 52, no. 2 (December 1992): 665–708.

———. "Fear of Gynarchy in an Age of Chaos: Kong Qi's Reflections on Life in South China Under Mongol Rule." *Journal of the Economic and Social History of the Orient* 41, no. 1 (1998): 1–95.

———. "Impressions of the Song-Yuan-Ming Transition: The Evidence from Biji Memoirs." In *The Song-Yuan-Ming Transition in Chinese History*, edited by Paul J. Smith and Richard von Glahn (q.v.), 69–110.

———. "Problematizing the Song-Yuan-Ming Transition." In *The Song-Yuan-Ming Transition in Chinese History*, edited by Paul J. Smith and Richard von Glahn (q.v.), 1–34.

———. "Shen-tsung's Reign and the New Policies of Wang An-shih, 1067–85." In *The Cambridge History of China, Volume 5, Part One: The Sung Dynasty and Its Precursors,*

907–1279, edited by Denis Twitchett and Paul J. Smith, 347–483. Cambridge: Cambridge University Press, 2009.

——— and Richard von Glahn, eds. *The Song-Yuan-Ming Transition in Chinese History*. Cambridge, MA: Harvard University Asia Center, Harvard University Press, 2003.

Sommer, Matthew H. "Polyandry Among the Poor in Qing Dynasty China: Survival Strategies Versus Judicial Constructions." In *Gender in Motion*, edited by Bryna Goodman and Wendy Larson, 29–54. Lanham, MD: Rowman & Littlefield Publishers, Inc., 2005.

———. *Sex, Law, and Society in Late Imperial China*. Stanford: Stanford University Press, 2000.

Song dai guan zhen yan du hui 宋代官箴研讀會, ed. *Song dai she hui yu fa lü—Ming gong shu pan qing ming ji tao lun* 宋代社會與法律：《名公書判清明集》討論. Taipei: Dong da tu shu gong si, 2001.

Song Dexi 宋德熹. "Tang dai de ji nü" 唐代的妓女. In *Zhongguo fu nü shi lun ji xu ji* 中國婦女史論集續集. edited by Bao Jialin 鮑家麟, 67–121. Taipei: Dao xiang chu ban she, 1991.

Song, Geng. *The Fragile Scholar: Power and Masculinity in Chinese Culture*. Hong Kong: University of Hong Kong Press, 2004.

Song Jiong 宋褧. *Yan shi ji* 燕石集. *SKQS* (q.v.), vol. 1212.

Song Lian 宋濂. *Song xue shi quan ji* 宋學士全集. *CSJCCB* ed. Shanghai: Shangwu yin shu guan, 1939.

Song Lian 宋濂 et al., eds. *Yuan shi* 元史. Beijing: Zhonghua shu ju, 1976.

*Song xing tong* 宋刑統. Taipei: Wen hai chu ban she, 1964.

Standen, Naomi. *Unbounded Loyalty: Frontier Crossings in Liao China*. Honolulu: University of Hawai'i Press, 2007.

Sturman, Peter C. "Cranes above Kaifeng: The Auspicious Image at the Court of Huizong." *Ars Orientalis* 20 (1990): 33–68.

Su Boheng 蘇伯衡. *Su Pingzhong wen ji* 蘇平仲文集. *SKQS* (q.v.), vol. 1228.

Su Che 蘇轍. *Luan cheng ji* 欒城集. Edited by Zeng Zaozhuang 曾棗莊 and Ma Defu 馬德富. Zhong guo fu dian wen xue cong shu. Shanghai: Shanghai gu ji chu ban she, 1987.

Su Shi 蘇軾. *Dongpo quan ji* 東坡全集. *SKQS* (q.v.), vols. 1107–8.

———. *Dongpo zhi lin* 東坡志林. *SKQS* (q.v.), vol. 863.

———. *Su Shi shi ji* 蘇軾詩集. Edited by (Qing) Wang Wengao 王文誥 and Kong Fanli 孔凡禮. 8 vols. Zhongguo gu dian wen xue ji ben cong shu. Beijing: Zhonghua shu ju, 1982.

———. *Su Shi wen ji* 蘇軾文集. Edited by Kong Fanli 孔凡禮. Beijing: Zhonghua shu ju, 1986.

———. *Za zuan er xu* 雜纂二續. In Qu Yanbin 曲彥斌, *Za zuan qi zhong* 雜纂七種, 81–100. Shanghai: Shanghai gu ji chu ban she, 1988.

Su Shunqin 蘇舜欽. *Su Shunqin ji* 蘇舜欽集. Edited by Shen Wenzhuo 沈文倬. Zhong guo fu dian wen xue cong shu 中國古典文學叢書. Shanghai: Shanghai gu ji chu ban she, 1981.

Su Song 蘇頌. *Su Weigong wen ji* 蘇魏公文集. Edited by Wang Tongce 王同策, Guan Chengxue 管成學 and Yan Zhongqi 顏中其. Beijing: Zhonghua shu ju, 1988.

Su Tianjue 蘇天爵. *Yuan wen lei* 元文類. *SKQS* (q.v.), vol. 1367.

———. *Zixi wen gao* 滋溪文稿. *SKQS* (q.v.), vol. 1214.
Su Xun 蘇洵. *Jiayou ji jian zhu* 嘉祐集箋注. Edited by Zeng Zaozhuang 曾棗莊 and Jin Chengli 金成禮. Zhongguo fu dian wen xue cong shu. Shanghai: Shanghai gu ji chu ban she, 1993.
Sue Takashi. "The Shock of the Year Hsuan-ho 2: The Abrupt Change in the Granting of Plaques and Titles during Hui-tsung's Reign." *Acta Asiatica* 84 (February 2003): 80–125.
Sun Ch'i [Sun Qi], and Robert des Rotours. *Courtisanes Chinoises à la fin des T'ang, entre circa 789 et le 8 janvier 881, Pei-li tche (Anecdotes du Quartier du Nord)*. Vol. 22. Bibliothèque de l'Institut des hautes études chinoises. Paris: Presses universitaires de France, 1968.
Sun Di 孫覿. *Hong qing ju shi ji* 鴻慶居士集. *SKQS* (q.v.), vol. 1135.
Sun Qi 孫棨. *Beili zhi* 北里志. In *Jiao fang ji, Beili zhi, Qing lou ji* 教坊記,北里志,青樓集, 22–43. Zhongguo wen xue can kao zi liao xiao cong shu ed. Shanghai: Gu dian wen xue chu ban she, 1957.

Takahashi Yoshirō 高橋芳郎. *Yakuchū meikō shohan seimeishū kokonmon: Nansōdai no minjiteki funsō to hanketsu* 訳注「名公書判清明集」戸婚門：南宋代の民事的紛争と判決. Tōkyō: Sōbunsha, 2006.
———. *Sō-Sei mibunhō no kenkyū* 宋—清身分法の研究. Hokkaido: Hokkaido University Publishing Group, 2001.
Tang Daijian 唐代劍. "Song dai qie de mai mai." 宋代妾的買賣. In *Nanchong shi yuan xue bao* 南充師院學報 1983, no. 4 (1983): 58–64.
Tang Guizhang 唐圭璋. *Song ci ji shi* 宋詞紀事. Shanghai: Shanghai gu ji chu ban she, 1982.
Tao Zongyi 陶宗儀. *Nancun chuo geng lu* 南村輟耕錄. Yuan ming shi liao bi ji cong kan ed. Beijing: Zhonghua shu ju, 1959.
———. *Shuo fu* 説郛. *SKQS* (q.v.), vols. 876–82.
Theiss, Janet M. *Disgraceful Matters: The Politics of Chastity in Eighteenth-Century China*. Berkeley: University of California Press, 2004.
T'ien Ju-K'ang. *Male Anxiety and Female Chastity: A Comparative Study of Chinese Ethical Values in Ming-Ch'ing Times*. Monographies du T'oung Pao. Leiden: E. J. Brill, 1988.
Tillman, Hoyt Cleveland. *Confucian Discourse and Chu Hsi's Ascendancy*. Honolulu: University of Hawai'i Press, 1992.
———. "Disorder (*Luan*) as Trauma: A Case Study of Reactions to the Mongol Conquest." Unpublished paper. 2002.
Toda Yuji 戸田裕司. "Tō Chūyū dangai jiken no shakaishi teki kōsatsu—NanSō chihōkan no oshoku to keirui" 唐仲友弾劾事件の社会史的考察—南宋地方官の汚職と係累. *Nangoya daigaku Tōyōshi kenkyū hōkoku* 31 (March, 2007): 93–108.
Tong Shu 同恕. *Ju an ji* 榘菴集. *SKQS* (q.v.), vol. 1206.
Tuotuo 脱脱 et al. *Jin shi* 金史. 8 vols. Beijing: Zhonghua shu ju, 1975.
———. *Song shi* 宋史. 40 vols. Beijing: Zhonghua shu ju, 1977.
Twitchett, Denis. "Merchants, Trade, and Government in the Late T'ang." *Asia Major* n.s., 14, no. 1 (1968): 63–95.

Volpp, Sophie. "The Literary Circulation of Actors in Seventeenth-century China." *Journal of Asian Studies* 61, no. 3 (August 2002): 949–84.
von Glahn, Richard. "Imagining Pre-Modern China." In *The Song-Yuan-Ming Transition in Chinese History*, edited by Paul J. Smith and Richard von Glahn (q.v.), 35–70.

Waley, Arthur. *The Secret History of the Mongols*. London: George Allen and Unwin, Ltd., 1963.
Wang Anshi 王安石. *Linchuan xian sheng wen ji* 臨川先生文集. Beijing: Zhonghua shu ju, 1959; repr. 1964.
———. *Wang wen gong wen ji* 王文公文集. Edited by Tang Wubiao 唐武標. Shanghai: Shanghai ren min chu ban she, 1974.
Wang Anzhong 王安仲. *Chu liao ji* 初寮集. SKQS (q.v.), vol. 1127.
Wang Cheng 王稱. *Dong du shi lue* 東都事略. SKQS (q.v.), vol. 382.
Wang Dang 王讜. *Tang yu lin jiao zheng* 唐語林校證. Edited by Zhou Xunchu 周勛初. 2 vols. Tang Song shi liao bi ji cong kan. Beijing: Zhonghua shu ju, 1987.
Wang Feng 王逢. *Wuxi ji* 梧溪集. SKQS (q.v.), vol. 1218.
Wang Gui 王珪. *Huayang ji* 華陽集. CSJCXB (q.v.), vol. 61.
———. *Huayang ji* 華陽集. SKQS (q.v.), vol. 1093.
Wang Jie 王結. *Shan su yao yi* 善俗要義. In Yang Na 楊訥, *Li xue zhi nan, wai san zhong* 吏學指南, 外三種, 339–64. Hangzhou: Zhejiang gu ji chu ban she, 1988.
Wang Jisi 王季思, ed. *Quan Yuan xi qu* 全元戲曲. 12 vols. Beijing: Ren min wen xue chu ban she, 1990.
Wang Junyu 王君玉. *Za zuan xu* 雜纂續. In *Za zuan qi zhong* 雜纂七種, edited by Qu Yanbin 曲彥斌, 47–80. Shanghai: Shanghai gu ji chu ban she, 1988.
Wang Ling 王令. *Guangling ji* 廣陵集. SKQS (q.v.), vol. 1106.
Wang Mai 王邁. *Qu xuan ji* 臞軒集. SKQS (q.v.), vol. 1178.
Wang Mian 王冕. *Zhu zhai ji* 竹齋集 SKQS (q.v.), vol. 1233.
Wang Mingqing 王明清. *Hui zhu lu* 揮麈錄. Song dai shi liao bi ji cong kan. Beijing: Zhonghua shu ju, 1961.
———. *Tou xia lu* 投轄錄. In Wang Xinsen 汪新森 and Zhu Juru 朱菊如, *Tou xia lu: Yu zhao xin zhi* 投轄錄; 玉照新志. Song Yuan bi ji cong shu ed. Shanghai: Shanghai gu ji chu ban she, 1991.
———. *Yu zhao xin zhi* 玉照新志. In Wang Xinsen 汪新森 and Zhu Juru 朱菊如, *Tou xia lu: Yu zhao xin zhi* 投轄錄; 玉照新志. Song Yuan bi ji cong shu ed. Shanghai: Shanghai gu ji chu ban she, 1991.
Wang Ning 王宁. *Song Yuan yue ji yu xi ju* 宋元乐妓与戏剧. Beijing: Zhongguo xi ju chu ban she, 2003.
Wang Pu 王溥. *Tang hui yao* 唐會要. SKQS (q.v.), vols. 606–7.
Wang Qi 王錡. *Yu pu za ji* 寓圃雜記. In Zhang Dexin 張德信, Lü Jinglin 呂景琳 and Yu Shenxing 于慎行, *Yu pu za ji: Gu shan bi zhu* 寓圃雜記; 穀山筆麈, 1–96. Yuan Ming shi liao bi ji cong kan ed. Beijing: Zhonghua shu ju, 1984.
Wang Shaoxi 王紹璽. *Xiao qie shi* 小妾史. Zhongguo she hui min su shi cong shu. Shanghai: Shanghai wen yi chu ban she, 1995.
Wang Shipeng 王十朋. *Wang Shipeng quan ji* 王十朋全集. Edited by Mei xi ji chong kan wei yuan hui 梅溪集重刊委員會. Shanghai: Shanghai gu ji chu ban she, 1998.

Wang Shuizhao 王水照. *Song ren suo zhuan san Su nian pu hui kan* 宋人所撰三蘇年譜彙刊. Shanghai: Shanghai gu ji chu ban she, 1989.
Wang Shunu 王書奴. *Zhongguo chang ji shi* 中國娼妓史. Shanghai: Shanghai san lian shu dian, 1988 [1933].
Wang Xing 王行. *Ban xuan ji* 半軒集. SKQS (q.v.), vol. 1231.
Wang Xu 王旭. *Lan xuan ji* 蘭軒集. SKQS (q.v.), vol. 1202.
Wang Yi 王沂. *Yi bin ji* 伊濱集. SKQS (q.v.), vol. 1208.
Wang Yishan 王義山. *Jia cun lei gao* 稼村類稿. SKQS (q.v.), vol. 1193.
Wang Yong 王烱. *Yan yi yi mou lu* 燕翼詒謀錄. SKQS (q.v.), vol. 407.
Wang Yuanliang 汪元量. *Hu shan lei gao* 湖山類稿. SKQS (q.v.), vol. 1188.
Wang Yucheng 王禹偁. *Xiao xu ji* 小畜集. SKQS (q.v.), vol. 1086.
Wang Yun 王惲. *Qiujian ji* 秋澗集. SKQS (q.v.), vol. 1200–1201.
Wang Zao 汪藻. *Fuxi ji* 浮溪集. CSJCCB ed. Shanghai: Shangwu yin shu guan, 1935.
Wang Zhi 王銍. [*Bu*] *shi'er xiao ming lu* [補]侍兒小名錄. In *Shuo fu* 說郛, edited by Tao Zongyi 陶宗儀. SKQS (q.v.), vols. 876–82, 77 *shang*, 33a–39b.
Wang Zhiwang 王之望. *Han bin ji* 漢濱集. 1139.
Watson, Rubie S. "Wives, Concubines, and Maids: Servitude and Kinship in the Hong Kong Region, 1900–1940." In *Marriage and Inequality in Chinese Society*, edited by Patricia Buckley Ebrey and Rubie S. Watson, 231–55. Berkeley: University of California Press, 1991.
Wei Jing 衛涇. *Hou le ji* 後樂集. SKQS (q.v.), vol. 1169.
Wei Liaoweng 魏了翁. *Heshan ji* 鶴山集. SKQS (q.v.), vols. 1172–73.
Wei Shou 魏收. *Wei shu* 魏書. Beijing: Zhonghua shu ju, 1974; 1992.
Wei Tai 魏泰. *Dong xuan bi lu* 東軒筆錄. Tang Song shi liao bi ji cong kan ed. Beijing: Zhonghua shu ju, 1997.
———. *Lin Han yin ju shi hua* 臨漢隱居詩話. In (Qing) He Wenhuan 何文煥, *Li dai shi hua* 歷代詩話, 317–36. Beijing: Zhonghua shu ju, 1981.
Wei Zongwu 衛宗武. *Qiu sheng ji* 秋聲集. SKQS (q.v.), vol. 1187.
Weitz, Ankeny. *Zhou Mi's "Record of Clouds and Mist Passing Before One's Eyes," An Annotated Translation*. Leiden: E. J. Brill, 2002.
Wen Tianxiang 文天祥. *Wenshan ji* 文山集 SKQS (q.v.), vol. 1184.
Wen Tong 文同. *Dan yuan ji* 丹淵集. SKQS (q.v.), vol. 1096.
Wenying 文瑩. *Xiangshan ye lu* 湘山野錄. In Zheng Shigang 鄭世剛 and Yang Liyang 楊立揚, *Xiangshan ye lu, xu lu: Yu hu qing hua* 湘山野錄, 續錄; 玉壺清話. Tang Song shi liao bi ji cong kan ed. Beijing: Zhonghua shu ju, 1984.
———. *Yu hu qing hua* 玉壺清話. In Zheng Shigang 鄭世剛 and Yang Liyang 楊立揚, *Xiangshan ye lu, xu lu: Yu hu qing hua* 湘山野錄, 續錄; 玉壺清話. Tang Song shi liao bi ji cong kan ed. Beijing: Zhonghua shu ju, 1984.
Wen Yu 溫豫. [*Xu bu*]*shi'er xiao ming lu* [續補]侍兒小名錄. In *Shuo fu* 說郛, edited by Tao Zongyi 陶宗儀. SKQS (q.v.), vol. 876–82, 77 *shang*, 40a–44b.
West, Stephen H. "Crossing Over, Huizong in the Afterglow, or the Deaths of a Troubling Emperor." In *Emperor Huizong and Late Northern Song China: The Politics of Culture and the Culture of Politics*, edited by Patricia Buckley Ebrey and Maggie Bickford (q.v.) 517–52.
———. "Huang hou, zang li, youbing yu zhu—Dong jing meng hua lu he du shi wen xue de xing qi 皇后，葬禮，油餅與豬–《東京夢華錄》和都市文學的興起

(Empresses and Funerals, Pancakes and Pigs: Dreaming a Dream of Splendor Past and the Origins of Urban Literature)." In *Wen xue, wen hua, yu shi bian* 文學,文化,與世變 (Literature, Culture, and World Change), 197–218. Taipei: Academia Sinica, 2002.

———. "The Interpretation of a Dream, The Sources, Evaluation, and Influence of the *Dongjing meng hua lu*." *T'oung Pao* 71 (1985): 63–108.

———. "Playing with Food: Food, Performance, and the Aesthetics of Artificiality in the Sung and Yuan." *Harvard Journal of Asiatic Studies* 57, no. 1 (1997): 67–106.

———. "A Study in Appropriation: Zang Maoxun's Injustice to Dou E." *Journal of the American Oriental Society* 111, no. 2 (April-June 1991): 283–302.

———. "Yuan Entertainers: Pear Screen Beauty, Little Bit, Swallow Song Liu, Zhenzhen, Mother's Compassion Liu." In *Women Writers of Traditional China: An Anthology of Poetry and Criticism*, edited by Kang-i Sun Chang and Haun Saussy, 115–26. Stanford: Stanford University Press, 1999.

West, Stephen H., and Wilt L. Idema, eds. and trans. *Monks, Bandits, Lovers, and Immortals: Eleven Early Chinese Plays*. Indianapolis/Cambridge: Hackett Publishing Company, Inc., 2010.

Widmer, Ellen, and and Kang-i Sun Chang, eds. *Writing Women in Late Imperial China*. Stanford: Stanford University Press, 1997.

Wolf, Margery. *Women and the Family in Rural Taiwan*. Stanford: Stanford University Press, 1972.

Wong Yu-Hsuan (Weng Yuxuan) 翁育瑄. "Tō Sō boshi kara mita josei no shusetsu to saikon ni tsuite—mibōjin no sentaku to so no seikatsu." 唐宋墓誌から見た女性の守節と再婚について—未亡人の選択とその生活—. *Tōdaishi kenkyu* 6 (August 2003): 41–58.

———. "Tōdai ni okeru kannin kaikyū no kekkon keitai—boshimei wo chūshin ni— 唐代における官人階級の婚姻形態—墓誌銘を中心に." *Tōyōgakuhō* 83, no. 2 (September, 2001): 131–59.

Wright, Arthur, and Denis Twitchett, eds. *Confucian Personalities*. Stanford: Stanford University Press, 1962.

Wu Cheng 吳澄. *Wu wen zheng ji* 吳文正集. *SKQS* (q.v.), vol. 1197.

Wu Chuhou 吳處厚. *Qing xiang za ji* 青箱雜記. Edited by Li Yumin 李裕民. Tang Song shi liao bi ji cong kan. Beijing: Zhonghua shu ju, 1997.

Wu Kuan 吳寬. *Jia zang ji* 家藏集. *SKQS* (q.v.), vol. 1255.

Wu Lai 吳萊. *Yuan ying ji* 淵穎集. *SKQS* (q.v.), vol. 1209.

Wu Shidao 吳師道. *Li bu ji* 禮部集. *SKQS* (q.v.), vol. 1212.

Wu Sidao 烏斯道. *Chun cao zhai ji* 春草齋集. *SKQS* (q.v.), vol. 1232.

Wu, Yenna. *The Lioness Roars: Shrew Stories from Late Imperial China*. Ithaca, NY: Cornell University East Asia Program, 1995.

Wu Yong 吳泳. *Helin ji* 鶴林集. *SKQS* (q.v.), vol. 1176.

Wu Zeng 吳曾. *Neng gai zhai man lu* 能改齋漫錄. Song yuan bi ji cong shu ed. Shanghai: Shanghai gu ji chu ban she, 1960; 1984.

Wu Zimu 吳自牧. *Meng liang lu* 夢梁錄. In Meng Yuanlao 孟元老, *Dongjing meng hua lu (wai si zhong)* 東京夢華錄 (外四種), 129–328. Shanghai: Gu dian wen xue chu ban she, 1956.

Xia Tingzhi 夏庭芝. *Qing lou ji jian zhu* 青楼集笺注. Edited by Sun Chongtao 孙崇涛 and Xu Hongtu 徐宏图. Beijing: Zhongguo xi ju chu ban she, 1990.
Xiao Ju 蕭𣂏. *Qin zhai ji* 勤齋集. *SKQS* (q.v.), vol. 1206.
Xie Ke 謝薖. *Zhu you ji* 竹友集. *SKQS* (q.v.), vol. 1122.
Xie Min 謝旻, ed. *Jiangxi tong zhi* 江西通志. *SKQS* (q.v.), vols. 513–18.
Xie Su 謝肅. *Mi an ji* 密菴集. *SKQS* (q.v.), vol. 1228.
Xie Yi 謝逸. *Xi tang ji* 溪堂集. *SKQS* (q.v.), vol. 1122.
Xie Yingfang 謝應芳. *Gui chao gao* 龜巢稿. *SKQS* (q.v.), vol. 1218.
Xu Bingyu 徐秉愉. "Liao, Jin, Yuan, san dai fu nü jie lie shi ji yu zhen jie guan nian zhi fa zhan." 遼金元三代婦女節烈事跡與貞節觀念之發展. In *Zhongguo fu nü shi lun ji xu ji*, edited by Bao Jialin 鮑家麟, 215–40. Taipei: Dao xiang chu ban she, 1991.
Xu Du 徐度. *Que sao bian* 卻掃編. *Quan Song bi ji, di 3 bian*, vol. 10, edited by Zhu Yi'an 朱易安 et al. Zhengzhou: Da xiang chu ban she, 2008.
Xu Ji 徐積. *Jie xiao ji* 節孝集. *SKQS* (q.v.), vol. 1101.
Xu Jingsun 徐經孫. *Jushan cun gao* 矩山存稿. *SKQS* (q.v.), vol. 1181.
Xu Lun (Xu Jizhi) 許綸 (許及之). *She zhai ji* 涉齋集. *SKQS* (q.v.), vol. 1154.
Xu Mengxin 徐夢莘. *San chao bei meng hui bian* 三朝北盟會編. *SKQS* (q.v.), vols. 350–52.
Xu Pu 徐溥. *Ming hui dian* 明會典. *SKQS* (q.v.), vols. 617–18.
Xu Qian 許謙. *Bai yun ji* 白雲集. *CSJCXB* (q.v.), vol. 66. Taipei: Taiwan shang wu yin shu guan, 1985.
Xu Qinjun 徐沁君. *Xin jiao Yuan kan za ju san shi zhong* 新校元刊雜劇三十種. 2 vols. Beijing: Zhonghua shu ju, 1980.
Xu Song 徐松. *Song hui yao ji gao* 宋會要輯稿. Taipei: Xin wen feng chu ban gong si, 1976.
Xu Xiangqing 許相卿. *Yun cun ji* 雲村集. *SKQS* (q.v.), vol. 1272.
Xu Xuan 徐鉉. *Qi sheng ji* 騎省集. *SKQS* (q.v.), vol. 1085.
Xu Youren 許有壬. *Zhizheng ji* 至正集. *SKQS* (q.v.), vol. 1211.
Xu Yuanjie 徐元杰. *Mei ye ji* 楳埜集. *SKQS* (q.v.), vol. 1181.
Xu Yuanrui 徐元瑞. *Li xue zhi nan* 吏學指南. In Yang Na 楊訥, *Li xue zhi nan, wai san zhong* 吏學指南, 外三種, 1–153. Zhejiang: Zhejiang gu ji chu ban she, 1988.
Xue Juzheng 薛居正 et al. *Jiu Wudai shi* 舊五代史. Beijing: Zhonghua shu ju, 1976.

Yan Ming 嚴明. *Zhongguo ming ji yi shu shi* 中國明妓藝術史. Taipei: Wenjin chu ban she, 1992.
Yanagida Setsuko 柳田節子. "Song dai de gu yong ren he nu bi." 宋代的雇傭人和奴婢. In *Guoji Songshi yantao hui lunwen xuanji* 國際宋史研討會論文選集, edited by Deng Guangming 鄧廣銘 and Qi Xia 漆俠. Hebei: Hebei da xue chu ban she, 1992.
Yang Jian 楊簡. *Cihu yi shu* 慈湖遺書. *SKQS* (q.v.), vol. 1156.
Yang Jie 楊傑. *Wu wei ji* 無為集. *SKQS* (q.v.), vol. 1099.
Yang Shi 楊時. *Guishan ji* 龜山集. *SKQS* (q.v.), vol. 1125.
Yang Shiqi 楊士奇 et al. *Li dai ming chen zou yi* 歷代名臣奏議. *SKQS* (q.v.), vol. 433–42.
Yang Shoujing 楊守敬. *Hubei jin shi zhi* 湖北金石志. Xu xiu Si ku quan shu ed. Vol. 913. Shanghai: Shanghai gu ji chu ban she, 1995–2002.
Yang Wanli 楊萬里. *Cheng zhai ji* 誠齋集. *SKQS* (q.v.), vol. 1160–61.
Yang Weizhen 楊維楨. *Dong wei zi ji* 東維子集. *SKQS* (q.v.), vol. 1221.

———. *Tie yai gu yue fu* 鐵崖古樂府. *SKQS* (q.v.), vol. 1222.
Yang Yi 楊億. *Wuyi xin ji* 武夷新集. *SKQS* (q.v.), vol. 1086.
Yao Kuan 姚寬. *Xixi cong yu* 西溪叢語. In *Xixi cong yu: Jia shi jiu wen* 西溪叢語;家世舊聞, edited by Kong Fanli 孔凡禮, 1–159. Tang Song bi ji shi liao cong kan ed. Beijing: Zhonghua shu ju, 1993.
Yao Mian 姚勉. *Xue po ji* 雪坡集. *SKQS* (q.v.), vol. 1184.
Yao Ping 姚平. "The Status of Pleasure: Courtesan and Literati Connections in T'ang China (618–907)." *Journal of Women's History* 14, no. 2 (July 2002): 26–53.
———. *Tang dai fu nü de sheng ming li cheng* 唐代婦女的生命歷程. Shanghai: Shanghai gu ji chu ban she, 2004.
Yao Silian 姚思廉. *Liang shu* 梁書. Beijing: Zhonghua shu ju, 1973.
Yao Sui 姚燧. *Mu an ji* 牧庵集. *CSJCXB* (q.v.), vol. 66.
Ye Mengde 葉夢得. *Jiankang ji* 建康集. *SKQS* (q.v.), vol. 1129.
Ye Shaoweng 葉紹翁. *Si chao wen jian lu* 四朝聞見錄. Edited by Shen Xilin 沈錫麟 and Feng Huimin 馮惠民. Tang Song shi liao bi ji cong kan ed. Beijing: Zhonghua shu ju, 1989.
Ye Shi 葉適. *Ye Shi ji* 葉適集. Edited by Liu Gongchun 劉公純, Wang Xiaoyu 王孝魚 and Li Zhefu 李哲夫. Beijing: Zhonghua shu ju, 1961.
Ye Ziqi 葉子奇. *Cao mu zi* 草木子. Yuan ming shi liao bi ji cong kan ed. Beijing: Zhonghua shu ju, 1959.
Yin Kui 殷奎. *Qiang zhai ji* 強齋集. *SKQS* (q.v.), vol. 1232.
Yin Zhu 尹洙. *Henan ji* 河南集. *SKQS* (q.v.), vol. 1090.
Yong Rong 永瑢 et al. *Qin ding Si ku quan shu zong mu* 欽定四庫全書總目. *SKQS* (q.v.), vols. 1–5.
Yu Chaogang 喻朝剛 and Zhou Hang 周航, eds. *Fen lei xin bian Liang Song jue miao hao ci* 分类新编兩宋絕妙好詞. Changchun: Jilin wen shi chu ban she, 1992.
Yu Chou 虞儔. *Zun bai tang ji* 尊白堂集. *SKQS* (q.v.), vol. 1154.
Yu Delin 俞德鄰. *Pei wei zhai ji* 佩韋齋集. *SKQS* (q.v.), vol. 1189.
Yu Ji 虞集. *Dao yuan xue gu lu* 道園學古錄. Guo xue ji ben cong shu ed. Vols. 303–4. Taipei: Taiwan shang wu yin shu guan, 1968.
Yu Wenbao 俞文豹. *Chui jian lu wai ji* 吹劍錄外集. *SKQS* (q.v.), vol. 865.
Yu Xin 庾信. *Yu Zishan ji* 庾子山集. *SKQS* (q.v.), vol. 1064.
Yuan Cai 袁采. *Yuan shi shi fan* 袁氏世範. *SKQS* (q.v.), vol. 698.
Yuan Fu 袁甫. *Meng zhai ji* 蒙齋集. *CSJCCB* ed. Shanghai: Shang wu yin shu guan, 1936.
Yuan Haowen 元好問. *Yishan xian sheng wen ji* 遺山先生文集. *GXJBCS* ed. Vol. 301. Taipei: Taiwan shang wu yin shu guan, 1968.
Yuan Jue 袁桷. *Qing rong ju shi ji* 清容居士集. *CSJCXB* (q.v.), vols. 65–66.
Yuan Shuoyou 袁説友. *Dong tang ji* 東塘集. *SKQS* (q.v.), vol. 1154.
Yuan Xie 袁燮. *Jie zhai ji* 絜齋集. *CSJCXB* (q.v.), vol. 64.

Zeitlin, Judith T. "'Notes of Flesh' and the Courtesan's Song in Seventeenth-Century China." In *The Courtesan's Arts: Cross-Cultural Perspectives*, edited by Martha Feldman and Bonnie Gordon, 75–99. New York: Oxford University Press, 2006.
Zeng Feng 曾丰. *Yuan du ji* 緣督集. *SKQS* (q.v.), vol. 1156.

Zeng Gong 曾鞏. *Zeng Gong ji* 曾鞏集. Edited by Chen Xingzhen 陳杏珍 and Chao Jizhou 晁繼周. Zhongguo gu dian wen xue ji ben cong shu. Beijing: Zhonghua shu ju, 1984.

Zeng Zao 曾慥. *Gao zhai man lu* 高齋漫錄. *SKQS* (q.v.), vol. 1038.

———. *Lei shuo* 類說. *SKQS* (q.v.), vol. 873.

Zeng Zhao 曾肇. *Qufu ji* 曲阜集. *SKQS* (q.v.), vol. 1101.

Zhang Bangji 張邦基. *Mo zhuang man lu* 墨莊漫錄. In *Mo zhuang man lu, Guo ting lu, Ke shu* 墨莊漫錄, 過庭錄, 可書, edited by Kong Fanli 孔凡禮, 1–301. Tang Song shi liao bi ji cong kan ed. Beijing: Zhonghua shu ju, 2002.

———. *Shi'er xiao ming lu shi yi* 侍兒小名錄拾遺. In *Chongtianzi* 蟲天子, *Xiang yan cong shu* 香艷叢書. 5 vols. Vol. 1. Beijing: Ren min wen xue chu ban she, 1992.

Zhang Duanyi 張端義. *Gui er ji* 貴耳集. *SKQS* (q.v.), vol. 565.

Zhang Fangping 張方平. *Le quan ji* 樂全集. *SKQS* (q.v.), vol. 1104.

Zhang Gang 張綱. *Hua yang ji* 華陽集. *SKQS* (q.v.), vol. 1131.

Zhang Guangzu 張光祖. *Yan xing gui jian* 言行龜鑑. *SKQS* (q.v.), vol. 875.

Zhang Hongfan 張宏範. *Huaiyang ji* 淮陽集. *SKQS* (q.v.), vol. 1191.

Zhang Jiuling 張九齡. *Qu jiang ji* 曲江集. *SKQS* (q.v.), vol. 1066.

Zhang Lei 張耒. *Ke shan ji* 柯山集. *CSJCXB* (q.v.), vol. 62.

Zhang Shi 張栻. *Gui si Lun yu jie* 癸巳論語解. *SKQS* (q.v.), vol. 199.

———. *Nanxuan ji* 南軒集. *SKQS* (q.v.), vol. 1167.

Zhang Shunmin 張舜民. *Hua man lu* 畫墁錄. *Quan Song bi ji, di 2 bian,* vol. 1, edited by Zhu Yi'an 朱易安 et al. Zhengzhou: Da xiang chu ban she, 2006.

Zhang Tingyu 張廷玉 et al. *Ming shi* 明史. Beijing: Zhonghua shu ju, 1974; repr. 1991.

Zhang Xian 張憲. *Yu si ji* 玉笥集 *SKQS* (q.v.), vol. 1217.

Zhang Yan 張炎. *Shan zhong bai yun ci* 山中白雲詞. *SKQS* (q.v.), vol. 1488.

Zhang Yanghao 張養浩. *Gui tian lei gao* 歸田類稿. *SKQS* (q.v.), vol. 1192.

———. *San shi zhong gao* 三事忠告. *SKQS* (q.v.), vol. 602.

Zhang Yong 張詠. *Guai ya ji* 乖崖集. *SKQS* (q.v.), vol. 1085.

Zhang Zhihan 張之翰. *Xi yan ji* 西巖集. *SKQS* (q.v.), vol. 1204.

Zhang Zhu 張翥. *Tui an ji* 蛻菴集. *SKQS* (q.v.), vol. 1215.

Zhang Zi 張鎡. *Shi xue gui fan* 仕學規範. *SKQS* (q.v.), vol. 875.

Zhangsun Wuji 長孫無忌, et. al. *Tang lü shu yi* 唐律疏義. *SKQS* (q.v.), vols. 672–73.

Zhao Bian 趙抃. *Qing xian ji* 清獻集. *SKQS* (q.v.), vol. 1094.

Zhao Dingchen 趙鼎臣. *Zhu yin ji shi ji* 竹隱畸士集. *SKQS* (q.v.), vol. 1124.

Zhao Fang 趙汸. *Dong shan cun gao* 東山存稿. *SKQS* (q.v.), vol. 1221.

Zhao Gongyu 趙公豫. *Yan tang shi gao* 燕堂詩稿. *SKQS* (q.v.), vol. 1142.

Zhao Huiqian 趙撝謙. *Zhao kao gu wen ji* 趙考古文集. *SKQS* (q.v.), vol. 1229.

Zhao Lingzhi 趙令畤. *Hou qing lu* 侯鯖錄. Tang Song shi liao bi ji cong kan ed. Beijing: Zhonghua shu ju, 2004.

Zhao Mengfu 趙孟頫. *Song xue zhai ji* 松雪齋集. *SKQS* (q.v.), vol. 1196.

Zhao Qimei 趙琦美. *Zhao shi tie wang shan hu* 趙氏鐵網珊瑚. *SKQS* (q.v.), vol. 815.

Zhao Sheng 趙升. *Chao ye lei yao (fu Chao ye lei yao yan jiu)* 朝野類要 (附朝野類要研究). Edited by Wang Ruilai 王瑞來. Tang Song shi liao bi ji cong kan ed. Beijing: Zhonghua shu ju, 2007.

Zhen Dexiu 真德秀. *Xishan wen ji* 西山文集. *SKQS* (q.v.), vol. 1174.

———. *Xishan zheng xun* 西山政訓. *CSJCXB* (q.v.), vol. 30.

Zheng Guiying 鄭桂瑩. "Yuan chao fu nü de shou jie yü zai jia—yi lü ling wei zhu de tao lun." 元朝婦女的守節與再嫁—以律令爲主的討論. Master's Thesis, Chinghwa University, Taipei, 1995.
Zheng Yu 鄭玉. *Shishan ji* 師山集. *SKQS* (q.v.), vol. 1217.
Zheng Yuanyou 鄭元祐. *Qiao Wu ji* 僑吳集. *SKQS* (q.v.), vol. 1216.
Zheng Zhimin 鄭志敏. *Xi shuo Tang ji* 細說唐妓. Taipei: Wenjin chu ban she 1997.
Zhou Bida 周必大. *Wenzhong ji* 文忠集. *SKQS* (q.v.), vols. 1147–49.
Zhou Hui 周煇. *Qing bo za zhi jiao zhu* 清波雜志校注. Edited by Liu Yongxiang 劉永翔. Tang Song shi liao bi ji cong kan ed. Beijing: Zhonghua shu ju, 1994.
Zhou Mi 周密. *Gui xin za shi* 癸辛雜識. Edited by Wu Qiming 吳企明. Tang Song bi ji shi liao cong kan ed. Beijing: Zhonghua shu ju, 1988.
——. *Qi dong ye yu* 齊東野語. Edited by Zhang Maopeng 張茂鵬. Tang Song shi liao bi ji cong kan ed. Beijing: Zhonghua shu ju, 1983; repr. 1997.
——. *Wulin jiu shi* 武林舊事. In *Dong jing meng hua lu (wai si zhong)* 東京夢華錄, 外四種, edited by Zhongguo shu ju Shanghai bian ji suo. Beijing: Zhonghua shu ju, 1962.
——. *Yun yan guo yan lu* 雲煙過眼錄. *SKQS* (q.v.), vol. 871.
Zhou Xibao 周錫保. *Zhongguo gu dai fu shi shi* 中國古代服飾史. Beijing: Zhongguo xi ju chu ban she, 1996.
Zhou Yinghe 周應合. *Jingding Jiankang zhi* 景定建康志. In Wang Xiaopo 王曉波 et al., *Song Yuan zhen xi di fang zhi cong kan, jia bian* 宋元珍稀地方志叢刊, 甲編. Vols. 1–3. Chengdu: Sichuan da xue chu ban she, 2007.
Zhou Zizhi 周紫芝. *Tai cang ti mi ji* 太倉稊米集. *SKQS* (q.v.), vol. 1141.
Zhu Gansheng 褚贛生. *Nubi shi* 奴婢史. Shanghai: Wen yi chu ban she, 1995.
Zhu Mu 朱穆. *Gu jin shi wen lei ju* 古今事文類聚. *SKQS* (q.v.), vols. 925–29.
Zhu Shangshu 祝尚書. *Song ren bie ji xu lu* 宋人別集敘錄. Beijing: Zhonghua shu ju, 1999.
Zhu Shengfei 朱勝非. *Gan zhu ji* 紺珠集 *SKQS* (q.v.), vol. 872.
Zhu Xi 朱熹. *Yi Luo yuan yuan lu* 伊洛淵源錄. *SKQS* (q.v.), vol. 448.
——. *Zhu Xi ji* 朱熹集. Edited by Yin Bo 尹波 and Guo Qi 郭齊. 10 vols. Chengdu: Sichuan jiao yu chu ban she, 1996.
——. *Zhuzi yu lei* 朱子語類. Edited by (Song) Li Jingde 黎靖德 and Wang Xingxian 王星賢. 8 vols. Beijing: Zhonghua shu ju, 1994.
——. *Chu Hsi's Family Rituals: a Twelfth-Century Chinese Manual for the Performance of Cappings, Weddings, Funerals, and Ancestral Rites*, Translated, with annotation and introduction by Patricia Buckley Ebrey. Princeton library of Asian translations. Princeton, NJ: Princeton University Press, 1991.
Zhu Yu 朱彧. *Pingzhou ke tan* 萍州可談. In *Hou shan tan cong; Ping zhou ke tan* 後山談叢; 萍洲可談, edited by Li Weiguo 李偉國. Li dai shi liao bi ji cong kan ed. Beijing: Zhonghua shu ju, 2007.
Zou Hao 鄒浩. *Dao xiang ji* 道鄉集. *SKQS* (q.v.), vol. 1121.

# Index

academies, 423
adoption, 245; by or as courtesans, 21, 24, 299, 339; by widows, 283; of concubines' children, 110, 244–45, 353, 353–55
aesthetics, 28, 35, 37
aggrandizing, 252, 415; exemplar texts in, 252, 265–71, 287, 367, 381–82, 384–92, 414–15, 428
attendant-concubines (*shi qie*), *see* entertainer-concubines
Ai'ai (Song dynasty courtesan), 154–56, 258, 327
"Air of Kai" poem ("Kai feng"), 148, 364
An Xi, 383
Ayurbarwada Khaghan (Emperor Renzong of Yuan), 296

Bai Juyi 白居易, 39, 62, 94
banqueting: courtesans' participation in, 14, 16, 18–20, 23, 167–73, 176–80, 200, 295–98; exemplars and, 389–90, 401–2; and literati identity, 28, 30–38, 79–81, 400–1, 412–13; restrictions on, 40–41, 43–44, 48–50, 177–79, 203
Bao Zheng 包拯 (Judge Bao), 261–63, 352
barracks courtesans (*ying ji* 營妓), *see* government-courtesans
*Beili zhi* 北里志, *see* Record of the Northern Wards
biography: circulation of, 126, 135, 158, 257–58, 269–70, 287, 289, 382, 412; and government awards, 143; as preface, 126, 134, 154–59, 272–74, 364–65, 375–76, 380–84; women's, genres of, 131–37, 150–58, 428–29. See also *zhuan*; funerary inscriptions; exemplar texts
Birge, Bettine, 2–3, 407–9
birth mother (*sheng mu*), *see* concubines
Bol, Peter, viii, 414
*Book of Odes* (*Shi jing* 詩經), 101–2, 148, 149, 396, 407

Cai Kan 蔡戡, 227–28
Cai Xiang 蔡襄, 39, 92
Cai Yong 蔡邕, 55, 370
charmer (*ji* 姬), *see* entertainer-concubines
Chen Changfang 陳長方, 251, 288

Chen, faithful widow (陳節婦, wife of Hua Xuan 華鉉), 384–85
Chen Liang 陳亮, 202, 244; as author of exemplar texts, 265, 277–79
Chen Qian 陳謙, 387, 389–90, 395
Chen Yu 陳郁, 273
Chen Zeng 陳增, 197–98, 200
Chen Zhizhong 陳執中, 119–20
Cheng brothers (Cheng Hao 程顥 and Cheng Yi 程頤), 5, 46–47, 201, 260, 416–17, 422; on concubines, 101–3, 233–34, 237; on remarriage, 102–3, 140–41. *See also* Cheng Learning, Learning of the Way, Neo-Confucianism
Cheng Hao 程顥, *see* Cheng brothers
Cheng Learning, 47, 191; and concubines 231–39, 246–48, 252, 277, 287; and courtesans 46–47, 200–02; 207; and exemplar shrines 260–65. *See also* Cheng brothers, Learning of the Way, Neo-Confucianism
Cheng Yi 程頤, *see* Cheng brothers
*chuan qi* 傳奇, 34, 134, 155–56
*ci* 詞 poetry, 35, 37–38, 98
commodification of women, 164–65, 224–25, 249, 252, 289
community compact, 152
concubines: and family life, 105–08, 115–16, 227–31, 239–49, 329–30, 339, 340–41; and the imperial family, 116–17, 128; conflicts with wives, 106–8, 229–31; 342–43; 361; and contracts, 334–35; "domestication" of, 2, 357–62; enfeoffment of, 209, 236–38, 336, 346–47, 412; as entertainers, 58, 61, 212–13; expulsion of, 108–10, 124, 238–39, 241–42, 261–62, 330, 350–51, 362; and factional politics, 121–27; as family members, 345–51; and family strategizing, 360–62, 428; and fidelity, 328, 335–36, 362, 427; filial piety toward, 113, 122–28, 240–42; elite women as, 73–75; and government malfeasance, 76–77, 117–20, 217, 220; history of, pre-Song, 54–64; laws concerning, 59–60, 76–77, 331–35; 413 legal cases concerning, 105–6, 115, 218–20, 221–24, 229–30; and *liang-jian* distinctions, 60, 64,

331–32, 359, 413; as luxury consumption, 104–5; and male status, 56, 68–71, 337; markets in, 73–79, 212; marriage of, 59–60; as mothers, 110, 127–28, 236–39, 239–42, 248–49, 347–49, 357–61, 413; mourning for, 122–23, 237–39, 241, 413; and Neo-Confucianism, 101–3, 231–39, 246–48, 252, 343–45, 352–55, 358–59, 417; and patrilineal kinship, 240, 246–49, 263, 344, 351–62 *passim*, 409; proliferation in Northern Song, 53–54, 78; registration of, 57; and social disorder, 217–24, 226–27, 229–30, 339–43; status in household, 55–61 *passim*, 100–2, 105–6, 233; 236–38; 334–35, 351, 361; status in society, 54–58, 59–64, 331–32; and sumptuary regulations, 55–56, 70, 412, 427; sympathy for, 74–75, 83–84, 224–25, 228–29; terminology for, 7, 54–55, 65–66; virginity in, 359; wives' acceptance of, 344–45; wife-like, 57, 66–67, 341. *See also* entertainer-concubines

children, of concubines: in funerary inscriptions 243–46 348–49; as heirs, 230, 246–49; legitimacy of, 60; status in family, 111–16, 243–49, 352–57, 413

*cong liang* 從良, 76, 299, 315, 419, 420

court: as cultural center, 19, 171; interaction with society, 15–16, 18–19, 169–71

Court Entertainment Bureau (*jiao fang* 教坊): in the Tang dynasty, 15; in Northern Song, 16–19; in Southern Song, 167–71; in the Yuan dynasty, 295–97

courtesans: advertising for, 32; appreciation of, 294–95, 306–8, 311–16; becoming concubines, 76, 335–37; called *di zi*, 20–21, 172, 191, 297; erotic appreciation of, 37–38, 311–12; as exemplars, 295, 327–29; and factional politics, 41–49, 173n36, 185, 201; and family relations, 199–200, 308–10; fidelity of, 155–56, 205, 206, 306, 327–29, 335–36; humanity of, 204–7, 424; and *liang-jian* distinctions, 22, 299, 301–4, 413, 419; and local government, 175–80, 189–98; and local society, 164, 186–89, 198–200; and male status, 28–33, 426–27; marriage of, 76, 199–200, 299–301, 329, 336; negative images of, 38–41, 42–43, 44–48, 180–86 *passim*, 188–200, 305–6, 311, 313–16; and Neo-Confucianism, 15, 46–47, 190–91, 200–4, 206–7, 312–16, 416–17; in Northern Song-Southern Song transition, 165–67; and nostalgia, 181–85, 426; "privatization" of 25, 76; organization of, 24, 172–75, 297–99; and poetry, 21, 31–33, 35, 306, 307, 311–12; recruitment of, 20–24, 299–300; registration of, 20, 21–24, 26–27, 179, 191–92, 197–98, 206; regulations regarding, 24–25, 40–41, 43–44, 49, 177–79, 297–99, 302–3; relationships with officials, 24–26, 300–1, 309; and romance, 34–38, 48, 187, 335; skills of, 14, 31, 68, 307–9; social status of, 22, 298–99, 301–4; sympathy for, 36–37, 204–7, 306–7; in the Tang dynasty, 15–16, 34; terminology for, 7, 16, 20, 23, 58; versus poor but respectable women, 314–16; in Yuan drama, 304–10. *See also* entertainer-concubines, government-courtesans; independent courtesans

Cui, Principled Woman (崔節婦, daughter-in-law of Bao Zheng), 145, 261–63; 352, 352

Dai Biaoyuan 戴表元, 321–23, 380
Dai Liang 戴良, 323–24, 343, 360
De Weerdt, Hilde, 418
Deshou palace, 169
desire, 37, 224, 422–23, 429; concubines and, 89, 101–4, 231–36; and Neo-Confucianism, 47–48, 101–2, 231–36
*di zi* 弟子 (term for courtesans), 20–21, 172, 191, 297
divorce, 428
drama, 304–10, 303; 318–20, 318–21
Du Mu 杜牧, 133
Du Yan 杜衍, 42, 70, 103

Egan, Ronald, 98
Ebrey, Patricia, 2, 3
*Emerald Pavilion Collection* (*Qing lou ji* 青樓集), 307–11, 335–36
emotion: in historical change, 429
Empress Yang 楊皇后 (consort of Ningzong), 170–71
*Enlightened judgments* (*Ming gong shu pan qing ming ji* 名公書判清明集), 196–98, 200, 217–20, 229–30, 246–49
entertainers: admiration for, 28–29, 35, 37, 294, 306–8, 311–12, 316–24, 317–24, 400; categories of, 302; as exemplars, 154–56, 293–94, 320, 322–26; and sumptuary regulations, 61, 302–4. *See also* courtesans, entertainer-concubines, government-courtesans, independent courtesans
entertainer-concubines: aesthetic appreciation

of, 66, 81–84; cloistering of, 71, 91–92; connoisseurship of, 81–83; cost of, 78, 212; and elite social life, 79–93; emotional relations with, 89–99 *passim*, 227–29; erotic appreciation of, 88–89, 92; fad for, 210–17, 412; and male bonding, 82–84, 84–93; and male status, 68, 211–17, 337; as mothers, 93–94, 209; naming of, 71, 210–12, 338; recruitment of, 73–79; and romance, 62, 89–93, 338–39, 345, 357; skills of, 68, 72; status of, 63, 71; in the Tang dynasty, 62–63; teasing about, 82–88, 91, 213–15, 227, 422, 423; and the imperial clan, 68–69; training of, 72; versus public courtesans, 71; writings about, 62–63, 337–38; young girls as, 72–73, 83–84, 88, 93. *See also* concubines, banqueting

exemplar texts: circulation of, 126, 257–58, 269–70, 287, 289, 382, 412; collections of, 286; as entertainment, 154–58, 271–79; eroticism in, 274–76, 277–79; fraud in, 371–72, 394–95; funerary inscriptions as, 147–51, 280, 282–84; genres of, 131–35, 150–58 *passim*, 252, 258–59, 271–77, 283–86, 366–67, 373; intertextuality in, 271–74; proliferation in Yuan, 365–66; and social class, 275, 284, 286, 287, 289, 379–80, 403

exemplars: 132, 142–50, 251–52; enshrinement of, 259–64, 267, 272–74; faithful wives as, 130–31, 145, 148–49; filial sons as, 124–28, 145, 147–48, 151–54; government recognition of, 142–47, 253–54, 367–73; literati writing for, 126–27, 132–34, 250–87 *passim*, 253–55, 258–59, 269–70, 272–75, 365–67, 423, 428–29; and local pride, 262–64, 383; of political loyalty, 253–55. *See also* faithful maidens, faithful women, heroic martyrs

factionalism, 6; and morality, 41–43, 48, 122–28, 142, 144–50
faithful maidens, 259–60, 272–74, 284–85, 410
faithful widow: official definition of, 371. *See also* faithful women
faithful women (*jie fu* 節婦): cosmic implications of, 396–97; courtesans as, 8, 155–56, 205, 206, 306, 327–29, 335–36; deification of, 259, 261–62; as entertaining subjects, 154–58, 271–79, 399–406; and household reputation, 412; as models for men, 151, 157–58, 256–58, 264–65, 273, 278–79, 280–81, 283–85, 287–89, 376, 414; as models for other

women, 264, 287–88, 397; multiple meanings of, 265, 287–89, 376–78, 382–83; poetry for, 286, 366–67, 379–82; as sign of Chinese cultural superiority, 263–64. *See also* fidelity, heroic martyrs, loyalty, widows
family life: concubines in, 105–8, 115–16, 227–31, 239–49, 329–30, 339, 340–41; disorder in Yuan, 329–30; 339–41; political salience of, 120–23, 127–29, 158, 412
Fan Chengda 范成大, 213, 214
Fan Jun 范浚, 254
Fan Zhongyan 范仲淹, 26, 36, 182–83
Fan Zuyu 范祖禹, 69, 146, 148, 282
Fang Hui 方回, 297–98
Fei Gun 費袞, 275
*feng liu* 風流, 423
Feng Shiyuan 馮士元, 118–19
fidelity: cult of, 2–3, 129, 415–16, 428–29; in Cheng learning 140–41, as preeminent female virtue, 406–8, 410; and romance, 156, 402. *See also* faithful women, loyalty
filial piety, 253–54, 270, 323; to concubine mothers, 113–15, 122–28, 240–43, 349–51, 360; of daughters 255–57, 265, 344, 382;
fox spirits: 189, 226–27
friendship, male, 84–93 *passim*
Fu Qiu 傳求, 74
funerary inscriptions, 66–68; as biographical genre, 135–37; concubines in, 127–28, 239–43, 338, 345–51; concubines' children in, 243–45, 352–57; generic conventions of, 135–37; and promotion of female loyalty, 148–50, 158, 159, 280, 281–84; and social aggrandizing, 387; of women, 136–37, 281–84

Gan Wenchuan 干文傳, 391
Gao Cong 高聰, 57
Gao Pengju 高鵬舉 (Yuan storyteller), 317–18
Gaozong 高宗 (Song emperor), 165, 167, 167–68, 253–54
generic conventions: of funerary inscriptions, 135–37; shifts in, 140–58, 158–59, 364–65, 366–67, 412; of *zhuan* biographies, 131–35
Gong Shitai 貢師泰, 352, 402
Goodman, Bryna, 415–16
government awards (*jing biao* 旌表), 130, 143–47, 153–54, 284–85, 375, 384–85, 388, 414; bureaucratic procedures for, 143, 369–71; categories of, 368–70; in early Northern Song, 143–44; and exemplar text production,

367, 372–73, 380–82; and factionalism, 144–47, 158; in Southern Song, 253–54, 267–68; and tax remission, 144, 363, 369, 370–71; in Yuan, 368–73, 415

government-courtesans (*guan ji, ying ji* 官妓, 營妓), 16, 49, 169, 172–78, 204, 297–98, 412–20 *passim*; contrasted with independent courtesans, 24–28, 179, 298; and government malfeasance, 190–98, 412, 419; recruitment of, 20–22, 300; and social disorder, 198–201

Green Pearl (Lü Zhu 綠珠), 86–87, 327

Guan Hanqing 關漢卿, 405–6

Guangzong 光宗 (Song emperor), 170

Gui, Maiden, 257

Han dynasty, 54, 55–56
Han Jiang 韓絳, 109–10
Han Qi 韓琦, 39, 48, 66–67, 73, 103, 111, 113
Han Wei 韓維, 29, 81–83, 91
Han Yu 韓愈, 62
Han Yuanji 韓元吉, 261–63
Hartman, Charles, 417–18
heroic martyrs (female, *lie nü* 烈女), 414; literati writing for 133–4; 250–52, 255–58, 373–79 *passim*; and poetry, 271–75; shrines for, 263–64
heroic martyrs (male), 254–55
*Historical Records* (*Shi ji* 史記), 131
Hong Mai 洪邁, 163–64, 177, 179, 207, 216, 221, 231, 276–77
household-courtesans, *see* entertainer-concubines
household order: and fitness for office, 119–28, 158, 412
Hu, Heroic Wife (胡烈婦, Tiger Killer Hu), 369, 375–77
Hu Yuan 胡瑗, 152
Hu Zhiyu 胡祗遹, 294, 318–21, 376
Hua 華 family of Wuxi 無錫, 384–92
Hua Youwu 華幼武, 385, 387–92, 399–400
Huang Chang 黃裳, 44–47, 417, 422
Huang Jie 黃玠, 356
Huang Jin 黃溍, 385–89, 394–95, 401
Huang, Martin, 421–22
Huang Tingjian 黃庭堅, 69, 72, 85–87, 98, 113, 185
Huizong 徽宗 (Song emperor), 154, 167, 253, 422; and promotion of exemplars, 146–47

Idema, Wilt, 169, 319
indenture, 53, 64, 71, 331–33, 341, 351; regional dimensions of, 77, 332–33

independent courtesans, 22–28, 76, 174, 179, 298
*Injustice Done to Dou E* (*Dou E yuan* 竇娥冤), 405–6
integrity, women of, *see* faithful women

jealousy, 69, 98: supernatural retribution for, 231, 341–42; Neo-Confucian discourse on, 102, 235–36, 344–45; and spread of concubinage 105–7, 361, 413
Jia Xuanweng 家鉉翁, 286, 317–18, 324
*jian* 賤 (base, degraded), *see liang-jian* distinctions
Jiang Kui 姜夔, 213, 215
*Jie xiao ji*, *see Principle and Filial Collection*
*jiao hua* 教化 (moral transformation), 286, 414; faithful widows in, 396–99; and Neo-Confucianism, 260–65; under Huizong, 146–47
Jin 金 dynasty, 168
Jin Lüxiang 金履祥, 314–15, 352
*jing biao*, *see* government awards
Joseph McDermott, 408–9
Judge Bao, *see* Bao Zheng

karma, 94, 96, 225–6, 342
Katkov, Neil, 357–58
Khaishan (Emperor Wuzong of Yuan), 296
Kinney, Anne, 55–56
kinship, patrilineal: 5, 424; concubines in 240, 246–49, 263, 344, 351–62 *passim*, 409
Kong Qi 孔齊, 337, 340–43, 355, 393–94
Kong Wuzhong 孔武仲, 86–87

lawsuits: and concubines, 105–6, 115, 217–20, 221–24, 229–30; and concubines' children, 230, 246–49; and courtesans, 184–85, 194–98 *passim*
Learning of the Way: 190–91; and courtesans, 200–4, 207, 312–14; and concubines, 232–39; 246–48; 343–45, 352–55, 358–59, 417; and female fidelity, 286, 326, 385–87; 392–406, 408–9, 417–18; and recognition of universal humanity, 323–24, 326. *See also* Cheng brothers; Cheng Learning; Neo-Confucianism
levirate marriage, 408
Li Ao 李翱, 133
Li Cho-ying, 417–18
Li Cui'e 李翠娥 (Yuan courtesan), 327–29
Li Cun 李存, 313, 397
Li Ding 李定, 121–27, 159

Li Maoying 李昴英, 206
Li Qi 李祁 (析), 399–400
Li, Righteous Wife of Huaiyin (Huaiyin *yi fu* 淮陰義婦), 156–57
Li 李, wife of Wang Ning (王凝妻), 138–40, 157–58, 383
Li Xin 李新, 30, 45–47, 49, 417, 422
Li Zhiyi 李之儀, 184–85
*liang-jian* 良賤 (respectable-base) distinctions: breakdown of, 22, 53, 224, 359, 413, 419–21; and concubines, 60, 64, 331–32, 359; and courtesans, 22, 299, 301–4, 419–21. See also *cong liang*
Liao Gang 廖剛, 272–74
*lie fu*, *see* heroic martyrs
*lie nü*, *see* heroic martyrs
*Lie nü zhuan* 列女傳 (*Biographies of Exemplary Women*), 132, 382
literary networks, 81–84, 90–92, 375–79, 389, 415
literati: and exemplar writing, 126–27, 132–34, 250–87 *passim*, 253–55, 258–59, 269–70, 272–75, 365–67, 373–79, 423, 428–29; and romance, 34–38 *passim*, 48, 50, 211–12, 337–39, 345, 422; status competition among, 28–38 *passim*, 75, 79–84, 211–12, 216, 398–401, 412–13, 426–27
Little Jade (concubine of Zhao Yanbo), 213–14
Liu Gongchuo 柳公綽, 63
Liu Guan 柳貫, 401
Liu Kai 柳開, 74
Liu Kezhuang 劉克莊, 342–43, 348, 360
Liu Minzhong 劉敏中, 364–65, 376, 380
Liu Poxi 劉婆惜 (Yuan courtesan), 309–10, 335
Liu Renben 劉仁本, 371–72, 400–401
Liu Xiang 劉向, 132
Liu Zongyuan 柳宗元, 63
Lizong 理宗, 171
Louie, Kam, 421
loyalty: female, 131, 251–52; male, 137–38; romantic, 131, 134, 154–56, 159; and Song politics, 141–42, 253–55; of widows, 414; women's as analogous to men's, 138–39. *See also* faithful women, fidelity
Lu Jiuyuan 陸九淵, 202, 203, 235
*lu qi ling nü* 路岐伶女, 179. *See also* independent courtesans, *san yue*
Lu Wengui 陸文圭, 344–45
Lu You 陸游, 186, 270
Lü Zuqian 呂祖謙, 201–2, 232, 243
Luo Dian 羅點, 218–20
Luo Yuan 羅願, 263–64, 272, 275
Lynn Hunt, 325–26

Ma Zuchang 馬祖常, 315
Madame Wu, *see* Wu, Madame
maids, *see* concubines, entertainer-concubines
Maiden Gui, *see* Gui, Maiden
Maiden of Huyin, *see* Zhan, Maiden of Huyin
markets in women: 50, 73–79, 224–25, 249, 411; regional dimensions of, 77–78
masculinity, 34–38, 48, 50, 345, 421–25. *See also* literati identity
maternity, 248–49, 347–49, 351, 413
Mei Yaochen 梅堯臣, 70, 82, 88, 90–92, 181
Mencius, 422, 422–23
Meng Jiao 孟郊, 390
Ming dynasty, 410, 413, 419, 424, 426–29
*Ming gong shu pan qing ming ji* 名公書判清明集, *see Enlightened Judgments*
Morning Cloud, *see* Wang Zhaoyun
moral transformation, *see jiao hua*
*mu zhi ming*, *see* funerary inscriptions
Music Instruction Office (*jiao yue suo* 教樂所), 169. *See also* Court Entertainment Bureau

*Nancun chuo geng lu* 南村輟耕錄, 324
Neo-Confucianism, 1, 2–3, 9, 416–18, 426. *See also* Cheng brothers; Cheng learning; Learning of the Way
Neskar, Ellen, 260–61
Ningzong 寧宗 (Song emperor), 170–71
Northern Song: fall of, 165–67, 184, 252–53, 258
nostalgia, 181–85, 211, 426

Ouyang Xiu 歐陽修, 82–83, 88, 270–71, 319–20, 383; on loyalty, 138

paternity, 246–49, 351, 413
Paul Smith, 294, n3, 340
personal life, *see* family life
pet names, 71, 210–12, 338
poetry: about concubines, 81–93 *passim*, 213–15, 227–29; about courtesans, 29, 311–12; courtesans as authors of, 14, 21, 31; for courtesans, 16, 30–38; didactic, 399–405; for exemplars, 126–27, 155–57, 242, 266, 271–75, 373–79, *passim*; for faithful widows, 365–67, 379–82; and Learning of the Way, 315–16, 395–97 399–405; and literary communities, 81–84, 373–77; as sign of literati status, 30–38, *passim*. *See also ci*; poetry collections; poetry prefaces

poetry collections (*shi juan* 詩卷): 242, 266, 364–65, 379–84, 415; of Hua family 385–92

poetry prefaces (*shi xu* 詩序): 134, 158–59, 294, 364–65; for entertainers 294, 318–19, 323–24; for exemplars, 126, 365

polygyny, 53

*Principled and Filial Collection* (*Jie xiao ji* 節孝集), 151–58

principled women, *see* faithful women

private life, *see* family life

property: rights of concubines' children, 246–49, 354–57; women's rights to, 408–10

Pu Daoyuan 蒲道源, 396, 402

*Pure and Faithful Folio* (*Zhen jie juan* 貞節卷), 384, 391

Qian Weishan 錢惟善, 374–75, 377
Qin Guan 秦觀, 154, 184, 205
Qin Gui 秦檜, 167, 286, 418
qing (情, emotion, passion), 205, 426
Qing dynasty, 426–29
*Qing lou ji*, *see* Emerald Pavilion Collection
Qinzong (欽宗, Song emperor), 253
Qubilai (Yuan emperor), 295

Radiance (concubine of Wang Shen 王詵), 85
rape, symbolic meanings of, 252–53, 288
*Record of the Northern Wards* (*Beili zhi* 北里志), 183, 307–9
*Record of the Pet Names of Serving Maids* (*Shi'er xiaoming lu* 侍兒小名錄), 210–12
"Remarks on Poetry" (*shi hua* 詩話), genre/texts, 164n2, 181–82
Ren Shilin 任士林, 348, 376
Righteous Wife of Huaiyin, *see* Li, Righteous Wife of Huaiyin
rogue males (*guang gun* 光棍), 421, 427–28
romance: as literati trait 34–38, passim, 48, 50, 211–12, 337–39; 345; 422; with concubines 89–99, 128; with courtesans 156, 183, 187; and female fidelity 159, 328 335, 402

*san yue* 散樂, 174, 179, 193. *See also* independent courtesans, *lu qi ling nü*
serving babes (*shi'er* 侍兒), 210–11, 217. *See also* entertainer-concubines
serving women, *see* concubines, entertainer-concubines
sexual relations: with concubines 60, 100–1, 106; with courtesans, 25, 76, 299, 302; with maids, 60, 342. *See also* sexuality, virgins

sexuality: of concubines, 60, 88–89, 100, 128, 226–27, 358–59; dangers of 188, 222, 224, 226, 337; of exemplars 278–79; and family success, 423–24; restraint of as moral good, 103–5, 233, 416–17, 422–24; and social status, 420–21. *See also* sexual relations

*she fa mai jiu* 設法賣酒, 173–74
Shen Kuo 沈括, 80
Shen Yazhi 沈亞之, 63
Shenzong 神宗 (Song emperor), 121, 126
*shi* 士, *see* literati
*Shi ji*, *see* Historical Records
*Shi shuo xin yu* 世說新語, 57
shrines: 2, 130, 259–65, 272–74, 284–85; family 267–68; and exemplar texts 366, 373–78, passim, 428. *See also* exemplars, exemplar texts
Sima Guang 司馬光, 82–83, 100, 121, 124, 393, 422; on loyalty, 138–39
Sima Qian 司馬遷, 131–32, 271, 422
Six Dynasties, 56–57, 58, 86, 142
slavery, 21n22, 55–57, 60, 64–65 n43, 330–35, 342, 412, 419; government, 20–21
social disorder, 339–40; in Yuan, 397–98
social status: breakdown of boundaries, 53, 164–65, 317–18, 325–26; 337, 419; concubines as signs of, 68–71, 212–17, courtesans as signs of, 19, 20–22, 28–33, laws concerning, 331–33; and legal judgments, 223–24; literati competition for, 28–34, 75, 79–84, 211–12, 216, 426–27; mobility, 222–23, 224–25, 249, 329–33, 411–12; morality as a factor in, 414; vulnerability of upper-class women, 73–75, 218, 411. *See also* aggrandizing
Sommer, Matthew, 420–21
Song Lian 宋濂, 396, 400, 403
*Spring Grass Folio* (*Chun cao juan* 春草卷), 384, 389–91
*Statues and Precedents of the Yuan* (*Yuan dian zhang* 元典章), 331
step-children, *see* children, of concubines
Su Che 蘇轍, 74
Su Shi 蘇軾, 124, 126–27, 154, 313; and *ci* poetry, 33, 98; interactions with courtesans, 30, 183, 184; relationship with Wang Zhaoyun, 52, 93–99
Su Shunqin 蘇舜欽, 154
Su Tianjue 蘇天爵, 371–72
Su Xun 蘇洵, 104
suicide, 272, 409–10, 428–29. *See also* heroic martyrs
Sun Di 孫覿, 227

# Index

Tang Code, 59–60
Tang Zhongyou 唐仲友, 190–96, 202
Tao Zongyi 陶宗儀, 324, 329, 330, 333, 335, 342, 343, 362, 403–4
tenants, 331
terminology: for concubines 54–55, 62, 64–66, 68, 105, 212, 238–39; for entertainers, 16, 20, 23, 301–2; for faithful women, 130, 150, 281–82; historical change in 7–8; 58, 62, 150, 371, 407–8; for servile groups, 330
Three Institutes (*san xue* 三學), 172
Tugh Temür (Emperor Wenzong 文宗 of Yuan), 296

virginity: appeal of 72–73; 88; in courtesans, 24; in concubines 227, 359; supernatural power of, 260
violence, in exemplar tales, 156-57, 271, 276, 377–78, 403, 429; in inner quarters, 108, 120, 188, 231, 342-43
Virtuous Maiden Shrine (*xian nü ci* 賢女祠), 272–74, 284, 375

Wang Anli 王安禮, 121
Wang Anshi 王安石, 122, 125–26, 129, 173, 422
Wang Lianlian 汪憐憐 (Yuan courtesan), 327
Wang Mian 王冕, 313–14
Wang Mingqing 王明清, 184, 184–85
Wang Ning's wife, *see* Li, wife of Wang Ning
Wang, Pure Wife (Wang *zhen fu* 王貞婦), 373–75
Wang Qiao'er 王巧兒 (Yuan courtesan), 327
Wang Shen 王詵, 85
Wang Yun 王惲, 369
Wang Zhaoyun 王朝雲 (Morning Cloud), 52, 69, 79, 84, 93–99; and Buddhism, 94–96, 97, 98–99; relationship with Su Shi, 93–99
Wang Zhiwang 王之望, 257
Wei Jing 衛涇, 170
Wei Tai 魏泰, 80–81
*wei wang ren* 未亡人 ("one who hasn't died"), 155
Wen Wan 溫琬 (Song courtesan) 13–14, 23–14, 27, 31, 155, 258
West, Stephen, 169, 319
widows, faithful: 130–31, 148–51, 279–86, 364, 373, 379–84, 403–4, 414–15; adoption by 283; and *jiao hua*, 396–99; poetry for 365–67, 379–82. *See also* faithful women; fidelity; exemplars

winehouses, 173–75
wives: in family success, 398–99; multiple, in Yuan, 333–34; responsible for family harmony, 100–3; status of, 351, 398, 415; treatment of concubines, 106–8. *See also* faithful women
writing: as masculine activity, 424–26; as moral act, 422, 424–25; taboos on, 393, 412 *See also* under entertainer-concubines; exemplars; heroic martyrs
Wu Cheng 吳澄, 313, 343, 344, 353, 382, 407
Wu, Madame 吳夫人 (wife of Wang Ling 王令), 129–30
Wu Shidao 吳師道, 402
Wu Zeng 吳曾, 182–83

Xia Tingzhi 夏庭芝, 306–7
*xiao huan* 小鬟 ("little chignon"), 88, 174
Xiaozong 孝宗 (Song emperor), 168–69, 170, 236–37
Xie An 謝安, 58, 62
*Xin Wudai shi* 新五代史 (*New History of the Five Dynasties*), 138–39
Xu Ji 徐積, 151–58, 258, 266, 270, 402
Xu Youren 許有壬, 381
Xu Yuanrui 徐元瑞, 301–2
Xuanren 宣仁 (Song Dowager Empress), 145–46
Xuanzong 玄宗 (Tang emperor), 61–62; 15–16, 61–62

*ya qian yue* 衙前樂 (Song yamen musicians), 20–21, 297n14
Yan Rui 嚴蕊 (Song courtesan), 163, 190–96, 207
Yan Shu 晏殊, 109
Yang Jian 楊簡, 203–4, 265
Yang Shi 楊時, 201, 234, 416
Yang Wanli 楊萬里, 280–83
Yang Weizhen 楊維楨, 338, 391–92
Yang Zhimei 楊之美, 81–84
Yao Mian 姚勉, 206, 243–44, 245
Ye Mengde 葉夢得, 254
*Yi jian zhi*, 177, 216, 276. *See also* Hong Mai
Yin Zhu 尹洙, 70–71, 237
*ying* 媵 (senior concubine), 53, 59
Yongzheng emperor 雍正, 420–21
Yu Chou 虞儔, 180
Yu Delin 俞德鄰, 375–76, 380
Yu Dingguo 于定國, 405
Yu, Faithful Widow (Yu *jie fu* 俞節婦), 403–4

Yu Ji 虞集, 313, 348, 355
Yuan Haowen 元好問, 383
Yuan Jue 袁桷, 209, 328–29, 401
Yuan Xie 袁燮, 235–36
Yuanyou 元佑 (reign period), 146
Yunxiang 芸香 (concubine of Zhou Bida), 214–15

za hu 雜戶 (miscellaneous households), 21, 184, 222, 297
Zeng Gong 曾鞏, 394
Zhan, Maiden of Huyin 詹氏, 湖陰女子, 255–57
Zhang Bangji 張邦基, 182, 183
Zhang Derong 張德榮 (Yuan courtesan), 303
Zhang Fangping 張方平, 104–5
Zhang Jun 張俊, 167
Zhang Lei 張耒, 134–35
Zhang Ruxian 張汝賢, 42, 121
Zhang Ruyu 章如愚, 284–85, 393; 273–74, 271–74
Zhang Shi 張栻, 201
Zhang Xian 張憲, 315–16
Zhang Yanghao 張養浩, 344, 372, 395–96
Zhang Zhihan 張之翰, 376
Zhang Zhihe 張致和 (grandmother of Yuan Jue), 208–9, 329
Zhang Zhu 張翥, 303, 374–75, 389, 391
Zhao Bian 趙抃, 119
Zhao Dingchen 趙鼎臣, 84, 109, 113–15, 150–51
Zhao Lingwan 趙令峴, 114
Zhao Wenyi 趙文益 (Yuan actor), 318, 320
Zhao Zongjing 趙宗景, 105, 117
Zhen Dexiu 真德修, 203, 260, 265
Zhenzong 真宗 (Song emperor), 77, 116, 118, 144
Zhou Bida 周必大, 175–76, 213–15, 218, 423; as author of exemplar texts, 266–68, 270–71
Zhou Hui 周煇, 211
Zhou Mi 周密, 172, 174–75, 186
Zhou Zizhi 周紫芝, 255–57, 274–75
Zhu Lianxiu 珠簾秀, 293–94, 318–19
Zhu Shouchang 朱壽昌, 124–28, 159
Zhu Xi 朱熹, 163–64, 202–3, 260, 406–7, 416–18; on concubines, 232–33, 234–39; and Tang Zhongyou, 190–96; on widow fidelity, 417
zhuan 傳 (biographical genre): of faithful wives, 150–58; generic conventions of, 131–35; as prefaces, 134
Zhuangzong 莊宗 (Emperor of Latter Tang), 319–20
Zou, Madame (Zou furen 鄒夫人, mother of Li Jingshun), 364

# HARVARD-YENCHING INSTITUTE MONOGRAPH SERIES
(titles now in print)

24. *Population, Disease, and Land in Early Japan, 645–900,* by William Wayne Farris
25. *Shikitei Sanba and the Comic Tradition in Edo Fiction,* by Robert W. Leutner
26. *Washing Silk: The Life and Selected Poetry of Wei Chuang (834?–910),* by Robin D. S. Yates
28. *Tang Transformation Texts: A Study of the Buddhist Contribution to the Rise of Vernacular Fiction and Drama in China,* by Victor H. Mair
30. *Readings in Chinese Literary Thought,* by Stephen Owen
31. *Remembering Paradise: Nativism and Nostalgia in Eighteenth-Century Japan,* by Peter Nosco
33. *Escape from the Wasteland: Romanticism and Realism in the Fiction of Mishima Yukio and Oe Kenzaburo,* by Susan Jolliffe Napier
34. *Inside a Service Trade: Studies in Contemporary Chinese Prose,* by Rudolf G. Wagner
35. *The Willow in Autumn: Ryutei Tanehiko, 1783–1842,* by Andrew Lawrence Markus
36. *The Confucian Transformation of Korea: A Study of Society and Ideology,* by Martina Deuchler
37. *The Korean Singer of Tales,* by Marshall R. Pihl
38. *Praying for Power: Buddhism and the Formation of Gentry Society in Late-Ming China,* by Timothy Brook
39. *Word, Image, and Deed in the Life of Su Shi,* by Ronald C. Egan
40. *The Chinese Virago: A Literary Theme,* by Yenna Wu
41. *Studies in the Comic Spirit in Modern Japanese Fiction,* by Joel R. Cohn
42. *Wind Against the Mountain: The Crisis of Politics and Culture in Thirteenth-Century China,* by Richard L. Davis
43. *Powerful Relations: Kinship, Status, and the State in Sung China (960–1279),* by Beverly Bossler
44. *Limited Views: Essays on Ideas and Letters,* by Qian Zhongshu; selected and translated by Ronald Egan
45. *Sugar and Society in China: Peasants, Technology, and the World Market,* by Sucheta Mazumdar
49. *Precious Volumes: An Introduction to Chinese Sectarian Scriptures from the Sixteenth and Seventeenth Centuries,* by Daniel L. Overmyer
50. *Poetry and Painting in Song China: The Subtle Art of Dissent,* by Alfreda Murck

51. *Evil and/or/as the Good: Omnicentrism, Intersubjectivity, and Value Paradox in Tiantai Buddhist Thought*, by Brook Ziporyn
52. *Chinese History: A Manual, Revised and Enlarged Edition*, by Endymion Wilkinson
53. *Articulated Ladies: Gender and the Male Community in Early Chinese Texts*, by Paul Rouzer
54. *Politics and Prayer: Shrines to Local Former Worthies in Sung China*, by Ellen Neskar
55. *Allegories of Desire: Esoteric Literary Commentaries of Medieval Japan*, by Susan Blakeley Klein
56. *Printing for Profit: The Commercial Publishers of Jianyang, Fujian (11th-17th Centuries)*, by Lucille Chia
57. *To Become a God: Cosmology, Sacrifice, and Self-Divinization in Early China*, by Michael J. Puett
58. *Writing and Materiality in China: Essays in Honor of Patrick Hanan*, edited by Judith T. Zeitlin and Lydia H. Liu
59. *Rulin waishi and Cultural Transformation in Late Imperial China*, by Shang Wei
60. *Words Well Put: Visions of Poetic Competence in the Chinese Tradition*, by Graham Sanders
61. *Householders: The Reizei Family in Japanese History*, by Steven D. Carter
62. *The Divine Nature of Power: Chinese Ritual Architecture at the Sacred Site of Jinci*, by Tracy Miller
63. *Beacon Fire and Shooting Star: The Literary Culture of the Liang (502–557)*, by Xiaofei Tian
64. *Lost Soul: "Confucianism" in Contemporary Chinese Academic Discourse*, by John Makeham
65. *The Sage Learning of Liu Zhi: Islamic Thought in Confucian Terms*, by Sachiko Murata, William C. Chittick, and Tu Weiming
66. *Through a Forest of Chancellors: Fugitive Histories in Liu Yuan's* Lingyan ge, *an Illustrated Book from Seventeenth-Century Suzhou*, by Anne Burkus-Chasson
67. *Empire of Texts in Motion: Chinese, Korean, and Taiwanese Transculturations of Japanese Literature*, by Karen Laura Thornber
68. *Empire's Twilight: Northeast Asia Under the Mongols*, by David M. Robinson
69. *Ancestors, Virgins, and Friars: Christianity as a Local Religion in Late Imperial China*, by Eugenio Menegon
70. *Manifest in Words, Written on Paper: Producing and Circulating Poetry in Tang Dynasty China*, by Christopher M. B. Nugent
71. *The Poetics of Sovereignty: On Emperor Taizong of the Tang Dynasty*, by Jack W. Chen
72. *Ancestral Memory in Early China*, by K. E. Brashier

73. *'Dividing the Realm in Order to Govern': The Spatial Organization of the Song State*, by Ruth Mostern
74. *The Dynamics of Masters Literature: Early Chinese Thought from Confucius to Han Feizi*, by Wiebke Denecke
75. *Songs of Contentment and Transgression: Discharged Officials and Literati Communities in Sixteenth-Century North China*, by Tian Yuan Tan
76. *Ten Thousand Scrolls: Reading and Writing in the Poetics of Huang Tingjian and the Late Northern Song*, by Yugen Wang
77. *A Northern Alternative: Xue Xuan (1389-1464) and the Hedong School*, by Khee Heong Koh
78. *Visionary Journeys: Travel Writings from Early Medieval and Nineteenth-Century China*, by Xiaofei Tian
79. *Making Personas: Transnational Film Stardom in Modern Japan*, by Hideaki Fujiki
80. *Strange Eventful Histories: Identity, Performance, and Xu Wei's* Four Cries of a Gibbon, by Shiamin Kwa
81. *Critics and Commentators: The* Book of Poems *as Classic and Literature*, by Bruce Rusk
82. *Home and the World: Editing the Glorious Ming in Woodblock-Printed Books of the Sixteenth and Seventeenth Centuries*, by Yuming He
83. *Courtesans, Concubines, and the Cult of Female Fidelity*, by Beverly Bossler